*William Faulkner:*

*THREE DECADES OF CRITICISM*

# William
# Faulkner

*THREE DECADES OF CRITICISM*

———

*Edited,*

*With an Introduction and Bibliography,*

*By*

FREDERICK J. HOFFMAN

*and*

OLGA W. VICKERY

———

A HARVEST/HBJ BOOK

HARCOURT BRACE JOVANOVICH
NEW YORK AND LONDON

# Preface to the First Edition

THE EDITORS of this book have arranged and selected these studies of William Faulkner with the aim of providing a collection of maximum usefulness. The arrangement of the essays has been made with the object of helping the reader to see Faulkner from four points of view: first, with respect to his regional "place"; second, in terms of his work as a whole; third, in the matter of his methods and especially of his style; and, finally, in terms of individual works. Except for the first essay, all of the contributions date from 1939. While there were many interesting notes and reviews of Faulkner before that date, it marks the beginning of serious critical examination of his work.

The introduction is designed primarily as a means of indicating both the *scope* of Faulkner's critical reception and the *kinds* of criticism. The bibliography, while necessarily selective, is the result of careful research and contains as full an accounting of the subject as space will permit. Since there have been hundreds of reviews, and these have often echoed and borrowed from each other, only a small number are listed; they were chosen when either the suggestions made in them or the importance of the reviewer seemed to warrant inclusion. Two reviews are reprinted[1]—Elizabeth Hardwick's and Andrew Lytle's on *Intruder in the Dust;* and these principally because they represent two opposing views of that novel, which has not yet received a full-length study.

The editors have collaborated closely in the selection of the contents. The introduction was written by Mr. Hoffman, the bibliography compiled by Mrs. Vickery; Miss Martine Darmon contributed the translations of the essays of Jean-Paul Sartre and "Rabi."

*William Faulkner: Two Decades of Criticism* is neither a tract nor a symposium. The essays reprinted were written at various times and under the influence of several kinds of critical persuasion. They possess the great merit of their occasions; they are more than "appreciations" or notes taken down hastily on a trip to Jefferson. They should, therefore, be read as a group of intelligent studies that settle some issues and raise others, and in

1. While Robert Penn Warren's essay is a review (of Malcolm Cowley's *Portable*), it is so extensive and goes so far and so competently beyond its subject that it can scarcely be classified as a contemporary notice.

any case should contribute significantly to the reader's understanding of an important and sometimes difficult artist.

April, 1951

F. J. H.
O. W. V.

## Preface to the 1960 Edition

THE FACT that criticism of Faulkner's work has grown appreciably, and matured, is testified to in the contents of this new edition of our book. From the first edition seven essays have been kept, and seventeen have been added from the rich assortment of new materials that have appeared since 1951. The introduction has been expanded, to include a detailed discussion of the past decade; the bibliography has been reorganized and brought up to date.

Since the Nobel Award, interest in Faulkner as a literary personality has of course much increased, as well as in his views on any and every matter. Of the many new sketches of him and talks with him that have appeared in the 1950's, the editors have chosen Robert Cantwell's record of his trip to Mississippi and Jean Stein's very good interview with him. They have decided to preserve the O'Donnell, Cowley, and Warren essays for their historical as well as their intrinsic value. Since there have been many new studies of the style and language, that division of the book has been enlarged and strengthened. The section of essays on individual works of course shows the most substantial change. There are new studies of books that up to 1951 had been ignored or were only indifferently noted; and in the case of Faulkner's better known works criticism has so appreciably increased as to afford the editors the privilege of choice.

Obviously some quite good pieces of Faulkner criticism are not here, simply because there is a limit to the length of any book of this nature, however generous the increase may have been. Many of those not included are discussed in the new introduction. Our criterion of choice has always been that of maximum usefulness both to the reader who is just beginning to acquaint himself with Faulkner's work and to the experienced student and critic. The collection as a whole has a double purpose: in its scope, to give a representative view of the history of Faulkner criticism; in its special perspectives and analyses, to assist the reader to his understanding of a man who has now become an acknowledged and established genius.

June, 1960                                                                F.J.H.
                                                                         O.W.V.

# Contents

# William Faulkner:

## *An Introduction*

## PART ONE: THE GROWTH OF A REPUTATION

### 1

IN AN ESSAY published in *Commentary* (October, 1950), Leslie Fiedler expressed an understandable exasperation over the misconceptions with which critics have obscured the "actual" Faulkner.

It has taken me ten years of wary reading to distinguish the actual writer of *The Sound and the Fury* from a synthetic Faulkner, compounded of sub-Marxian stereotypes . . . ; and I am aware that there is yet another pseudo-Faulkner, derived mostly from the potboiling *Sanctuary,* a more elaborate and chaotic Erskine Caldwell, revealing a world of barnyard sex and violence through a fog of highbrow rhetoric. The grain of regrettable truth in both these views is lost in their misleading emphases; and equally confusing are the less hysterical academic partial glimpses which make Faulkner primarily a historian of Southern culture, or a canny technician whose evocations of terror are secondary to Jamesian experiments with "point of view."[1]

Criticism has certainly been busy offering us many versions of "that writin' man of Oxford." From the start, however, much of it has been largely blocked by certain concerns with "society," "naturalism," and "the human condition." The strange genius from Mississippi seemed often to violate preconceived standards of taste, or capriciously to disregard sober warnings from his critics. That he should deliberately have announced (in the Preface to the Modern Library edition of *Sanctuary,* 1932) his intention of exploiting the horrible and the obscene confirmed these critics in their worst fears. Faulkner's announcement there that he had written his novel as "a

Part One is here reprinted, with minor revisions, from *William Faulkner: Two Decades of Criticism.*
1. See "R.W." (Reed Whittemore), "Notes on Mr. Faulkner," *Furioso,* 2 Summer, 1947, for a parody of Faulkner criticism.

cheap idea, . . . deliberately conceived to make money" was the beginning of the most persistent of all types of Faulkner criticism.

It is necessary to see this point of view in terms of its setting. The critics who first attended to Faulkner's work were largely of two persuasions: they were either in the "humanist" or in the "leftist" tradition. In either case, they sought a virtue of statement in literature and were much distressed when they failed to see it. It was not possible to ignore the call to responsibility, as Faulkner seemed to be doing, and remain unpunished. From the beginning of the 1930's, therefore, he was classified as a writer who had ignored the largest demands upon social taste and moral discretion. His work did not have "spiritual resonance"; it exploited obscenity and horror for their own sake or as a "cheap idea"; he did not wish for a "better world" but hated the present and brooded over the collapse of the past; he was abnormally fond of morons, idiots, perverts, and nymphomaniacs. He was, in short, the leading member of a "cult of cruelty" school of modern writing.

The leading spokesman in this attack upon Faulkner's work was Alan Reynolds Thompson, whose essay, "The Cult of Cruelty" (*The Bookman,* January-February, 1932), provided a statement of its terms. Faulkner and Robinson Jeffers, said Thompson, have established a new "school" of writing, a "tendency which we may call the cult of cruelty." Cruelty is, of course, "inherent in human nature," but there is a genuine difference between early American and modern exploitations of horror. The modern "cult" is motivated by "a pessimistic skepticism, to which morals and aspirations are merely customs and dreams, and the world is an inhuman mechanism." The work of these writers, it develops, is a consequence of blind and purposeless naturalism, a "dead end" to which the errors of the American naturalists have been leading us. Thompson agreed that the horrible is a legitimate means of achieving a great aesthetic effect, and he pointed to Oedipus and Lear as examples. But this is not the effect achieved by Faulkner; he failed "to transmute the raw material in such a way as to give [his readers] a purely aesthetic effect." His appeal is not to the mind, but to the viscera. "The response to beauty involves the higher powers of the mind. These cannot endure when the gross animal instincts are aroused."

This is the kind of criticism which, with many variations of tone and motive, pursued Faulkner through the 1930's and continues to be heard. It was frequently combined with an expression of irritation over his perversities of style and method. The two most obvious qualities of Faulkner's writing, said Granville Hicks (*The Bookman,* September, 1931), are "his preoccupation with unpleasant subjects and his experimental approach to the novel as form." As for the first of these, "The world of William Faulkner echoes with the hideous trampling march of lust and disease, brutality and death." Hicks was not without admiration for the achievement: *The Sound and the Fury* and *As I Lay Dying* seemed to him remarkable experiments in form. But he was obliged to ask a question which has since been echoed many times in Faulkner criticism: "Have we here some new, some sharply individual view of life creating for itself new forms, or a keen but mechanical intelligence posing for itself problems that it loves to solve?" His answer to that question met exactly the terms of many of his contemporaries. Faulkner was, he said, playing a game with his readers, "a game in which he displays tremendous ingenuity and gives pleasure to the reader by stimulating a like ingenuity on his part." It is even possible, said Hicks, that the order of some of Faulkner's novels was decided upon perversely, that he had been fond of "inventing his stories in the regular form and then recasting them in some distorted form." It is to Conrad Aiken's great credit that this notion, while not entirely refuted, was at least largely ridiculed in Aiken's *Atlantic Monthly* essay on Faulkner's style and method (November, 1939). Hicks's discussion of Faulkner's whimsical "game" continued, however, to afford reviewers an opportunity to complain about and to mock the style, as well as to excuse their own bewilderment. Reviews of the fiction throughout the decade emphasized the "unusual" complication of plot and the needless involution and redundancy of style. This form of objection was not unrelated to the major accusation contained in Thompson's essay: the style and the method were linked at best with moral uncertainty (see F. R. Leavis's review of *Light in August* in *Scrutiny,* June, 1933), at worst with a wicked preoccupation with irrational and subnormal forms of behavior.

Perhaps the most extreme example of the latter critical approach is the work of Camille J. McCole, first published in the *Catholic World* in 1936, then enlarged as a chapter of his *Lucifer at Large* (1937). McCole found nothing virtuous or honest either in Faulkner's intentions or in his work. Faulkner was a salesman of vice, the leader of those writers who "set themselves up in a rather profitable literary business with unmitigated cruelties and abnormalities as their regular stock-in-trade." McCole was merciless, uncompromising, and inaccurate[2] in his cataloguing of the "gruesome gal-

---

2. Typical inaccuracies: the setting of *Sartoris* is Jefferson, Missouri; Whitfield (*As I Lay Dying*) is the father of three of Addie Bundren's children; Snopes (any Snopes?) is a "pervert, reminiscent of one of Anderson's Winesburg degenerates. . . ."

lery" of "idiots, perverts, degenerates, and introverts." The plot sequences are largely and hopelessly confused; the style is intolerably dense and absurd; the horrors are compounded by Faulkner's insufferable interest in idiots and morons. Only *Sartoris* escaped the slaughter; it was Faulkner's "best book." But, said McCole, Faulkner had shrewdly discovered that such a book did not sell, and it was then that he "turned so deliberately to the exploitation of cruelty."

Such shouting was after all an extreme form of protest; the critics who followed the leads of Thompson and Hicks, or who in their own way came to similar conclusions, were usually neither so strident nor so careless. Their objections to Faulkner possessed a common air of regret that a great talent had not as yet found its direction or purpose, was too self-indulgent, lacked self-discipline, and seemed determined to stay in the blind alley of naturalism. Harlan Hatcher (*Creating the Modern American Novel,* 1935), commenting upon the "monstrous beings" who inhabited the novels, had regretfully to admit that Faulkner "defines the farthest limits to which the innovations and revolts that were at one time necessary to the continued well-being of our literature can be carried without final self-defeat." Philip Henderson (*The Novel Today,* 1936), after providing the usual catalogue of Faulkner's subjects, offered a not-unexpected comparison with Erskine Caldwell. The latter's *Tobacco Road,* said Henderson, is greatly superior to any of Faulkner's novels because Caldwell "shows us why his agricultural morons are as they are and indicates how their individual helplessness can be remedied by large-scale collective farming on the part of both whites and blacks." A social conscience made Caldwell genuine; lack of it made Faulkner cheap and aimlessly melodramatic.

Concessions were usually made; there were "hopeful signs," or in one or another novel Faulkner seemed free of his otherwise damaging preoccupations. Halford E. Luccock (*American Mirror,* 1940) saw in the horror, especially of *Soldiers' Pay,* "real data for a spiritual and moral estimate of war, and its effects, and for the spiritual history of a decade." Percy Boynton (*America in Contemporary Fiction,* 1940) saw a close parallel between abnormality of vision and aberration of judgment: ". . . it is not without significance that the technique is simpler and the content more lucid in the tales which have the greater normality, or that they become more intricate and elusive in the tales of abnormality; that, in short, technique becomes a compensation for content as content sinks in the scale of accepted values." Oscar Cargill (*Intellectual America,* 1941), while he thought that the Compsons of *The Sound and the Fury* "are so lacking in intrinsic worth that we do not really care what happens to them," and was satisfied to call *Absalom, Absalom!* "a dull book, dull, dull, dull," did hopefully point to the future as it was suggested by the publication of *The Hamlet;* a sequel, he hoped, might show Faulkner at his determined best to "come to grips with his protagonist. Then we shall know the wherefore of the Bilbos and the Huey Longs." Herbert Muller (*Modern Fiction: A Study of Values,* 1937) provided an intelligent statement of Faulkner's "technical mastery of his materials, . . . a remarkable ability to project highly original characters," but suggested that his promise of closer attention to "the main march of human affections" had as yet not been realized, was in fact dissipated in *Absalom, Absalom!* Muller concluded that the fiction was of a kind that "powerfully stimulates the imagination without greatly refining or enriching it, making it a more efficient instrument in controlling human experience." George Snell (*The Shapers of American Fiction: 1798-1947,* 1947) admired, among other things, the "affirmative attitude" he saw in "The Bear" of *Go Down, Moses;* perhaps, he said, "for once, we have seen an American writer emerge from the wild miasmal depths where Brown and Poe and Melville were at home, into freer attitudes where a view of humanity in its workaday aspects is possible." Snell did not deny, however, that the "demonic tragedy" of Faulkner's South was after all "the fundamental fructifying principle of his art."

Leftist criticism, when it did not ignore Faulkner, severely chastised him for writing in ignorance or defiance of the brave new world in the making. For all that, they sought in the fiction for hopeful signs of social consciousness. V. F. Calverton (*Modern Monthly,* March, 1938) defended Faulkner from his leftist critics who had accused him of lacking an interest in important modern issues, by saying that the South was "semi-feudal," "bankrupt and degenerate, living upon forgotten frontiers of experience. . . ." To speak of "the class struggle," therefore, would have been to point up something that scarcely existed. Edwin Berry Burgum (*The Novel and the World's Dilemma,* 1947) suggested that Faulkner's studies of the South are portraits of American decadence in general. Burgum even tried to invest Jason Compson of *The Sound and the Fury* with a kind of desperate tragic dignity: "Caught in the vicious circle of the family pattern, he only hastens their decline into a commonplace vulgarity. But he is struggling to maintain some command over his destiny and theirs." Burgum saw a social significance in *Sanctuary,* "a Southern variant of a social interpertation of American life long since established in our fiction." It lay, briefly, in Faulkner's remarking in that novel "not only that decadence is characteristic of the region as a whole, but that even more of it is to be found in the more respectable classes." Barbara Giles (*Masses and Mainstream,* February, 1950) was less charitable. Acknowledging Faulkner's new "concern" with the South's "burden" (seen in "The Bear"), she nevertheless showed profound irritation over the attitude of Gavin Stevens in *Intruder in the Dust;* what right had he to ignore "all genuine movements rooted in history (both North and South) for the true liberation of the Negro." And she concluded by classifying Faulkner as a member of a "dying class" who "cling to their self-loving myths of the past, glorifying themselves with the gaudy legends of their ancestors until the sound of their own names becomes to them like 'silver pennons downrushing at sunset.' "

These judgments, however varied and original they may individually have been, demonstrate a common preconception with respect to what Faulkner's work should have been, a standard, or a variety of standards, to which it largely did not succeed in conforming. In the course of these deliberations, some attention was necessarily paid to Faulkner as a Southerner and to his region, either by way of extenuation or of an additionally severe stricture. In large part, the faults lay with the author, and these faults were partly a consequence of the literary "creed" he had been trapped into accepting, partly of his own overbearing hatred of "modernism" which had blinded him to the virtues of progress. Two essays (chapters of books) demonstrate these two forms of explanation especially well. The first, by Harry Hartwick (*The Foreground of American Fiction,* 1934), accused Faulkner of having followed the "wrong naturalism," or rather, of having wandered into "a kind of blind alley" from which there is no escape.

The vital tradition of naturalism, which is at heart broad in its sympathies and warm in its "passionate recognition" of life, cannot rest upon such a specialized, reptilian art as that of Faulkner's; it requires thought to justify its style and meaning to adorn its emotion. It should be a "mansion of philosophy," invigorating as well as vigorous, and a source of inspiration for all those who draw their values from Nature rather than Man, not a haunted house, dark and cold, inhabited only by spiders and morons.

In this extreme view, Faulkner is discovered exploiting atrocities for his morbid pleasure in them, and without any "moral concern," which is the only excuse for an attention to the ugly and the cruel: "his books lack what might be termed 'spiritual resonance.' "

The second essay, by Maxwell Geismar (*Writers in Crisis,* 1942), at least possessed the virtue of a sincere and often intelligent effort to understand the work. Geismar's major contention did not fully appear until near the end of his long chapter, during which he had diligently attended to what he thought were Faulkner's thematic concerns. His hatred of "modern woman" and of the Negro, the "twin furies" of the novels, was, in Geismar's estimation, a form of scapegoat device, "a dangerous quirk of the psyche, . . . a trick which may end by deceiving the trickster."

For it is in the larger tradition of reversionary, neo-pagan, and neurotic discontent (from which Fascism stems) that much of Faulkner's writing must be placed—the anti-civilizational revolt rising out of modern social evils, nourished by ignorance of their true nature, and which succumbs to malice as their solution.

Geismar discovered the evidence for this rejection of "a developing American maturity" in Faulkner's obvious dislike for the Female and his hatred of the Negro. Joanna Burden is the primary scapegoat victim, as Joe Christmas becomes the malicious and corrupt instrument of destruction. The murder and the lynching are, said Geismar, the crucial expression of "his contempt for modern maturity which displays itself so eloquently in the variety of perversions which the writer contrives for his characters." This is a part of a thesis-ridden interpretation of Faulkner which at best might claim the merits of originality and a strenuous effort to provide proof. It did, however, lose sight of many facts in the fiction, ignored the all-too-obvious exceptions to it, and led to misinterpretations of various and interesting kinds. The conclusions are not unlike Hartwick's, but the procedures followed in the course of arriving at them are quite different; Geismar attempted to answer the question *why* with something more than a cliché of literary history or a prevailing expression of discontent with horrors. He was also alive to the problem of literary merit, though his occasionally shrewd observations concerning style and method were soon enough overwhelmed by the insistent plodding of a search for evidence.

This, then, was the first critical view of Faulkner's work. Many others took up the refrain and echoed the objections. The reviews were quite often duplications of the points raised in the longer studies. Critics like Pelham Edgar, H. S. Canby, and Bernard Fäy rang few changes upon the general indictment (*The Art of the Novel from 1700 to the Present Time*, 1933; *Seven Years' Harvest*, 1936; "L'École de l'infortune," in *Revue de Paris*, August 1, 1937). Only occasionally was there recognition either of the sources of Faulkner's preoccupation or of his genuine talent as an artist, his genius for formal and rhetorical expression. Faulkner could himself have learned nothing from these warnings and expressions of distress; they could only fortify him in his determination to write as he needed, and to remain aloof from all criticism but his own.

2

Favorable criticism of Faulkner, said Robert Daniel (*Perspective,* Autumn, 1950), began in 1939. Except for isolated observations (such as Robert Penn Warren's, in an essay otherwise devoted to T. S. Stribling), studies of his work were largely devoted to expressions of disgust, horror, and distress over what Faulkner was doing or failing to do. An important element of criticism was lacking—a sympathetic effort to understand Faulkner on his own terms, a willing suspension of distress. Certain matters had scarcely been touched. One of these was the region to which Faulkner had early decided to devote himself. Another was his fictional strategy—the reasons, if any were to be found, for the strangely original methods he was using with almost every publication. In 1939, Conrad Aiken published his essay on Faulkner's style in the *Atlantic Monthly.* It was followed in the spring of 1941 by a longer and more perceptive study by Warren Beck (*American Prefaces*).³ Since then, few serious considerations of Faulkner's work have neglected the place in his fiction of the specially functional language and syntax, or have failed to acknowledge the way in which, as Aiken put it, the sentences "parallel in a curious and perhaps inevitable way, and not without justification, the whole elaborate method of *deliberately withheld* meaning, of progressive and partial and delayed disclosure, which so often gives the characteristic shape to the novels themselves."

The year 1939 was the date of another important essay, George Marion O'Donnell's "Faulkner's Mythology" (*Kenyon Review,* Summer, 1939),³ an essay which established the pattern of a very distinguished form of interpretation. Its main lines of consideration were taken up subsequently by several other critics, and it has in general been acknowledged as one serious way of seeing Faulkner's work as a whole. An important contribution of O'Donnell's essay was its insistence that Faulkner "is really a traditional moralist, in the best sense." This, in the face of what had been the majority conviction concerning Faulkner's "immorality" and "nihilism," was a most necessary assertion.

O'Donnell based his interpretation upon the belief that Faulkner was "a traditional man in a modern world." The fiction had therefore followed the line of such a man, who observed, in his region of the South, "the con-

3. These essays are included in this collection.

flict between traditionalism and the anti-traditional modern world in which it is immersed." The points of view are represented by the Sartorises and the Snopeses. These two groups become in O'Donnell's interpretation not so much persons as polar antitheses in a conflict of moral codes. The Sartorises (not only as a family, but as a type of person) act "traditionally"; that is, they act always with an "ethically responsible will." The Snopeses "acknowledge no ethical duty." In such terms ("a struggle between humanism and naturalism") the works are examined. In each case the Sartorises and the Snopeses figure, but not always in simple conflict. Often the opposition leads to important insights: Quentin Compson, for example, is the sole representative (in *The Sound and the Fury*) of the Sartoris tradition. The rest of the Compsons have either gone over to the Snopes world or have found one or another means of withdrawing from it. The two poles of act and view are sometimes uncomfortably narrowing, and O'Donnell's essay must take the consequences of a too inflexible ordering of the fiction. Quentin's view of the tradition, for example, has become "formalized"; that is, he has lost an accurate sense of the tradition and substitutes a romantic version of it. The crucial issue is, of course, Candace's act, which O'Donnell calls her "yielding to the amorality of the Snopes world." Quentin's tragic effort, futile as it proves to be, is to "transform meaningless degeneracy into significant doom." The two classes of society are not economic but moral divisions; the Bundrens belong to the Sartoris tradition, and the progress described in *As I Lay Dying* is "not unlike that of the medieval soul toward redemption." The Bundrens are therefore able to "carry a genuine act of traditional morality through to its end." This is to push the novel to an extreme—the opposite of that view which called it a grim farce. As other critics have pointed out, it is scarcely either an ignoble comedy or a formal morality. O'Donnell's considerations of the other novels reveal the stresses and strains of his view: *Sanctuary* is a failure because in it Faulkner suffers the defects of Quentin Compson; he has become a formal rather than a vital traditionalist. *Light in August* presents to O'Donnell an "allegory," in which Gail Hightower stands for the "Formalized Tradition," impotent before the "Snopes," Joe Christmas. Faulkner has here given in to the fascination of the "antagonist"; the "Snopes" character dominates the reader's attention and enlists his sympathy. Such a view, carried with a grim and inflexible persistence through all of the work, can lead occasionally to strange commentaries: as in the case of O'Donnell's description of *Mosquitoes* as a "Snopes-world Bohemia." But the essay proved to be of considerable service to Faulkner criticism:

first, in suggesting a means of viewing the work as a continuous whole; second, in insisting on Faulkner as a serious, a "moral" writer in the face of scores of assertions to the contrary; third, in raising Faulkner's characters from the level to which other critics had consigned them; and, finally, in providing illumination for the problem of his use of history. It was natural enough that, when *The Hamlet* appeared, two years after O'Donnell's essay, it should be claimed not only as a part of the canon but also as an additional proof of O'Donnell's judgment. Robert Penn Warren, reviewing that novel (*Kenyon Review,* Spring, 1941), fitted it into the pattern: the contrast in this case was "between the non-aristocratic Frenchman's Bend world, unconscious of its past, and the Snopes world, which Ratliff, the characteristic Faulknerian commentator, recognizes as the enemy."

The fullest and in many respects the most ingenious adaptation of O'Donnell's construction of Faulkner came in 1946, when Malcolm Cowley published the Viking *Portable Faulkner.* Except for short stories and such longer works as "The Bear" and "Old Man" ("half" of *The Wild Palms*), the necessities of Cowley's form of order did not permit publication of Faulkner's works as a whole. The work of editing the *Portable* was undertaken at a time when Faulkner's books were almost entirely out of print; since then, they have returned, been reissued, and their author has once more become a familiar and much-discussed figure. In his introduction, Cowley attended with devotion and care to the geographical and historical revival of Yoknapatawpha County. The selections themselves recall that history, from 1820 to 1940; Faulkner's additional remarks on the Compsons push the dates back as far as 1745 and forward to 1945, a full two centuries accounted for. The "legend" which dominates Cowley's selection is explained in some detail in his introduction:

The Deep South was settled partly by aristocrats like the Sartoris clan and partly by new men like Colonel Sutpen. Both types of planters were determined to establish a lasting social order on the land they had seized from the Indians (that is, to leave sons behind them). They had the virtue of living single-mindedly by a fixed code; but there was also an inherent guilt in their "design," their way of life; it was slavery that put a curse on the land and brought about the Civil War. After the War was lost, partly as a result of their own mad heroism (for who else but men as brave as Jackson and Stuart could have frightened the Yankees into standing together and fighting back?) they tried to restore "the design" by other methods. But they no longer had the strength to achieve more than a partial success, even after they had freed their land from the carpetbaggers who followed the

Northern armies. As time passed, moreover, the men of the old order found that they had Southern enemies too: they had to fight against a new exploiting class descended from the landless whites of slavery days. In this struggle between the clan of Sartoris and the unscrupulous tribes of Snopes, the Sartorises were defeated in advance by a traditional code that kept them from using the weapons of the enemy. As a price of victory, however, the Snopeses had to serve the mechanized civilization of the North, which was morally impotent in itself, but which, with the aid of its Southern retainers, ended by corrupting the Southern nation.

Included in this variant of O'Donnell's interpretation is the crucial struggle between Sartorises and Snopeses; but the "burden" of conscience which Cowley gave the former is an additional insight into the history of Faulkner's people. The editing in this case was necessarily that of paraphrase and crucial quotation. As in the selections made, so in the introduction, too little attention was paid the separate "integrities" and unities of the works themselves. This is not to say that Cowley did not possess most excellent insights into Faulkner's art; his discussion of that art as well as of its weaknesses was one of the most perceptive and acute so far published. Cowley, however, had little respect for Faulkner as a novelist; he was considered best as a writer of *novelle,* such as "The Bear." It seemed unnecessary, therefore (as well as impossible, given the strategy of the *Portable's* organization), to consider Faulkner a novelist. The novels are thus shabbily treated, and none of them comes through with even an adequate sense of their original structure and method. What *is* accomplished in the *Portable* is a vivid evocation of imaginative reality; it is both fuller in its documentation than is O'Donnell's essay and less handicapped by the limited perspective which a too narrowly conceived thesis caused in O'Donnell's case. In consequence of Cowley's work, the influence of Thompson, Canby, and Hicks had considerably subsided; and Cowley, with O'Donnell and others, encouraged and insisted upon a serious attention to what Faulkner was saying. A major weakness in both O'Donnell and Cowley was that they did not sufficiently emphasize the importance of Faulkner's *way* of saying it.

Warren's long review of the *Portable Faulkner* (*The New Republic,* August 12 and 26, 1946)[4] marked a further step in the consideration of Faulkner's subject as it offered valuable suggestions for another kind of

---

4. Reprinted in this collection. See also Caroline Gordon's review, in the *New York Times,* April 5, 1946, in which she thoroughly approved of O'Donnell and Cowley as having seen Faulkner correctly and "as he wants to be seen."

critical study. Warren gratefully acknowledged Cowley's introduction as
"one of the few things ever written on Faulkner which is not hagridden by
prejudice or preconception and which really sheds some light on the subject." He then proceeded, after reviewing Cowley's statement of "the
legend," to examine crucial matters related to Faulkner's treatment of the
legend and its region. Warren's discussion of nature as a means of formulating judgments of Faulkner's people was an admirable extension and cor-
rection of O'Donnell's rather more abstract view of "tradition." Two
important issues concerning Faulkner's people gave Warren an opportunity
to correct certain misconceptions: those pertinent to the "poor white" and
the Negro. In each case the thesis contained in Geismar's *Writers in Crisis*
was taken to task, as was his inaccurate view of the role of humor in
Faulkner's work. The review concluded with a number of acute observations
on technique, the principal value of which was that they were suggestive
beginnings for a further range of Faulkner studies—studies that Cowley
had scarcely indicated in either his introduction or his selection. "To what
extent," Warren asked, "does Faulkner work in terms of polarities, oppositions, paradoxes, inversions of roles? How much does he employ a line
of concealed (or open) dialectic progression as a principle for his fiction?"
These questions, together with his query concerning Faulkner's development of "symbolic motifs," were perhaps the most fruitful brief challenges
thus far offered in the history of Faulkner criticism. They also pointed up a
division in that criticism which still exists. O'Donnell had, after all, suggested what Warren called "the main symbolic outline of Faulkner's fiction,"
but he had only incidental attention for technique, symbol, and form, and
then only by way of implementing a thesis or explaining it. The major question was unanswered: had Faulkner written novels, short stories, and
*novelle* which independently stood, or had he written a "history" or made a
"moral" examination of the South's past tradition and present "burden"?

Delmore Schwartz's "The Fiction of William Faulkner" (*The Southern
Review,* Summer, 1941) did not answer that question, but raised many
others. It belonged to the beginnings of the newer Faulkner criticism, but
was made less useful than contemporary pieces because of its failure to
achieve sharp definition and classification. Schwartz found a total of nine
"themes," and these proved, on closer examination, to be only subdivisions
of major concerns. They were, furthermore, not always rewarding or acute
statements (the poor white and the peasant; the primitive, the abnormal,
and the virtually insane; the city slicker and the village slicker; etc.). Some
suggestion of what were Faulkner's larger concerns did, however, come

through: "The conflict between the idea of the Old South and the progressive actuality of the New South has brought Faulkner to the extreme
where he can only seize his values, which are those of the idea of the Old
South, by imagining them being violated by the most hideous crimes."
Other important insights into Faulkner's work and worth, some of
them found in brief reviews, marked the growing maturity of Faulkner's
critical reception. Kay Boyle (*The New Republic*, March 9, 1938) had
early recognized Faulkner's genius and had insisted that it be seen in terms
of the entire work; it "resides in that entire determined collection of volumes
which reveal him to be the most absorbing writer of our time." Three of
Warren Beck's essays demonstrated his sharp intelligence with respect both
to Faulkner's views and his technique. The first ("Faulkner and the
South," *Antioch Review*, Spring, 1941) showed Beck's recognition of Faulkner as a "Mississippian who has transcended provincialism without losing
artistic devotion to a locale." The essay put much emphasis on what Beck
called a needed expiation for the "sin of human slavery" and stressed Faulkner's "moral sense," his "humane point of view" as a necessary critical
means of acquiring perspective upon Faulkner's concern with violence. The
most important question Beck asked here (important by way of challenging
contemporary protests against the violence) was this: "Is he really riding
on a momentum of a waning, vitiated romance that lends his narratives a
scandalous interest, or do the evils pictured conform fundamentally to
observable and characteristic acts of men, and do these evils pictured stand
proportionately silhouetted against an implied background of enduring
ideals?" The second of the essays (*College English*, May, 1941) posed the
question of Faulkner's point of view, as this is seen modifying and "tight-
ening" the sensibilities of his characters. The simplicity of some of his
persons is in the direct line of an honest recognition of the tensions existing
in his world. That world is not merely governed by "nihilism," though
Faulkner's protagonists are frequently (usually) defeated. That they are
defeated is not a proof of "a denial of values" but an acknowledgment of
the very real presence of evil and of "the precariousness and difficulty of
rationality."

The thematic interpretation of Faulkner, proceeding largely from
O'Donnell, was once more taken up by Russell Roth ("William Faulkner:
The Pattern of Pilgrimage") in the best of a series of essays published in
*Perspective*, Summer, 1949. The prevailing order that Roth saw in Faulk-
ner's work is discovered largely in his point-of-view characters: beginning
with the "young aesthete" of the novels of the 1920's, and moving from

there to what Roth calls the "middle-aged ethicist," Horace Benbow, whose task is "to make the humanistic Sartoris values prevail in a particular case in the naturalistic Snopes world." In *Light in August,* Roth noted "a major shift." Faulkner, no longer satisfied with the "Sartoris ethic" (rendered almost wholly ineffectual in the figure of Hightower), seeks a new "vantage point." The redeeming figure Faulkner has finally discovered is Isaac Mc-Caslin of *Go Down, Moses,* whose character "would appear as an attempt to work back to this fountainhead of intuitive strength and humility from the ruin of the Old Southern aristocracy." McCaslin is Sartoris revived and strengthened, and in him are both "the humanistic motivation and, most important, the ability to act. . . ."

The service performed by these essays, from O'Donnell to Roth, was largely the necessary one of redressing the balance of view, of forcing the reader away from incrimination and empty protest to a serious and sympathetic reading of Faulkner's larger intention.[5] The criticism had its own risks. A great improvement over the captious and impatient dismissal of Faulkner by the "cult of cruelty" reviewers and critics, it did nevertheless involve a need to force novels and stories into a pattern, or to slight them when they did not quite yield to thematic pressure. Certain errors of interpretation, largely the result of a narrowness of view, persisted through most of the criticism. *As I Lay Dying* continued to be a novel of heroic denial and obligation; the character of Vardaman continued to puzzle the critics; and novels of great subtlety of form (such as *Absalom, Absalom!*) were too often merely summarized, a procedure that almost invariably distorted them.

5. Other sympathetic studies, not considered here, include Dayton Kohler's "William Faulkner and the Social Conscience" (*College English,* December, 1949), which relies largely upon Cowley's definition of "the legend" and continues it in the light of Faulkner publications that had appeared since the *Portable* (1946). Of especial interest is Vincent F. Hopper's "Faulkner's Paradise Lost" (*Virginia Quarterly Review,* 1947), which remarks, of Faulkner's world, that it is "indisputably infernal" and deliberately so; that there is and can be no compensating "Paradise Regained"; and, finally, that Faulkner has remained "pure romanticist, with most of the romanticist's traditional reactions. He wallows in gloom and despair." A strange variant upon the thematic study is James T. Jackson's "Delta Cycle: A Study of William Faulkner" (*Chimera,* Autumn, 1946), which considers Faulkner's work in terms of seasonal analogies, with much stress upon an historical reading of the actual South as it bears upon Yoknapatawpha County. Thematic readings of Faulkner's work began also to be seen in the reviews of the 1940's, the O'Donnell and, especially, the Cowley interpretations having eventually reached the reviewers. A marked increase of this type of criticism is noticeable, beginning with the appearance of the *Portable,* which demanded a full view of the work.

## 3

For many years after the publication of an author's first book, his reputation must rely upon the reviews and notices his work receives. In many respects, Faulkner's career has depended more than most upon such treatment. Hundreds of reviews have been published, ranging from brief notes to longer "studies."[6] As in any other case, the history of these reviews provides a footnote to the career of popular and semipopular taste. That history has its definable stages: in the 1920's, Faulkner was scarcely known and indifferently reviewed; in the period from 1929 to 1932, when a large share of his best novels appeared, he was given much attention, but it was hesitant and puzzled when not downright indignant; after 1946, the date of the *Portable,* each new Faulkner publication was recognized widely and some effort made to consider it in the light of past achievement; finally, since 1948 and the controversial *Intruder in the Dust,* reviews have been disturbed over the "polemical Faulkner," the "preacher," and the garrulous Gavin Stevens.

In the case of *Soldiers' Pay,* Faulkner's first novel, the reviews were concerned chiefly to "place" it in the tradition of post-war fiction, to which it, to all appearances, belonged. As such, the novel seemed to promise nothing more than an addition to that literature. Even here, however, lines were drawn. Thomas Boyd called the novel "Honest but Slap-dash" (*Saturday Review of Literature,* April 24, 1926), and described its characters as "vague, abnormally behaving characters who waver uncertainly and fantastically. . . ." The English reviews were largely patronizing: Mr. Faulkner has talent, is fortunately young and may outgrow the faults so obvious in this tale. One English reviewer went to the opposite extreme (*The New Statesman,* June 28, 1930) and considered Faulkner superior to both Lawrence and Hemingway: "I can remember no first novel of such magnificent achievement in the last thirty years." In the reviews both of this and of the next novel (*Mosquitoes*) there are several discerning references to Faulkner's imitativeness of style, to the "echoes" from late-nineteenth-century poetry. *Mosquitoes* deservedly received severe criticism and short shrift. A *New Republic* review (July 20, 1927) pointed out its second-rate satiric "cleverness" and its "labored sophistication."

6. I am indebted to Mrs. Vickery for many of the references used in part three of the introduction. This survey of reviews has, of course, had to be reduced in length, and reactions to certain of the works have been ignored. The most regrettable omission is the reviewing of *Pylon,* interesting because English and French attention to it greatly exceeded the American. (F.J.H.)

The reviews of the second "period" are both more numerous and more varied. In *Sartoris* the reviewers sensed the beginning of a larger and perhaps more enduring preoccupation than those found in the first two novels. "In *Sartoris*," said an unsigned review in the *New Statesman and Nation* (April 2, 1932), "we are given a picture of the South, of four generations and two wars, tossed at us apparently haphazard, yet more complete, because more stimulating to our imaginations, than in many volumes of detailed family chronicles." The sense of family tradition, new to his fiction, was recognized elsewhere as well, though reviewers were for the most part unfavorably disposed. Willard Thorp, writing in *Scrutiny* (September, 1932), called the novel a product of the influence of *Beau Geste* and *Death of a Hero,* complained of its repetitions and bad literary "echoes," and went on to say: "Faulkner, if he goes on at this rate, can easily lead the pack that helps the *Saturday Evening Post* sell mouthwash to 50 million Americans." L. A. G. Strong, however, spoke in the *Spectator* (February 27, 1932) of Faulkner's genius, in fact, suggested that he was one of a very few to whom the term *genius* could be applied. In general, the English reviews, which adopted a "watch-and-wait" attitude, were kinder than the American. The most penetrating review of *Satoris* was written, some eight years or so after its publication, by Jean-Paul Sartre (*Nouvelle Revue Française,* 1938) and was, of course, aided by Sartre's knowledge of the fiction published by Faulkner since 1929.[7]

*The Sound and the Fury* challenged critical skill as no other modern American novel had thus far done. Reviewers were quick to see the exceptional uses to which Faulkner had put the stream-of-consciousness technique, and not unwilling to suspect that the novel was a work of extraordinary talent. L.A.G. Strong, from the beginning an ardent Faulkner supporter, said of this novel (*Spectator,* April 25, 1931) that its difficulty is worth mastering, since the method is indispensable to the effect needed. Henry Nash Smith (*Southwest Review,* Autumn, 1929) agreed, and added that Faulkner had been able to combine a study of

7. The French have, of all Europeans, been the most enthusiastic and the most critical. For information about French reactions, see the interesting (though sketchy) essay, "What French Readers Find in William Faulkner's Fiction," *New York Times,* December 17, 1950, and also Sartre's "American Novelists in French Eyes," *Atlantic Monthly,* August, 1946. The most diligent of French sponsors of Faulkner have been Maurice E. Coindreau, Maurice le Breton, and Sartre. In *L'Age du Roman Américain* (Paris, 1948), Claude-Edmonde Magny has provided (pp. 196-243) one of the best studies of Faulkner's work as a whole available in French criticism. For an up-to-date summary of French criticism, see Stanley D. Woodworth, *William Faulkner en France (1931-1952)* (Paris, 1959)

provincial life with certain important universal overtones. The refrain of reviewers seemed generally to applaud the method both in spite of and because of its difficulty.[8] But there were several exceptions: Francis L. Robbins, for example (*Outlook and Independent,* October 16, 1929), who complained that the novel betrayed a regrettable distrust of "familiar values" and that the "subjective analysis" weakened a potentially great theme. The London *Times Literary Supplement* (May 14, 1931) saw little but "skill" overcome by a concern with "pathological delinquency." *The Sound and the Fury* can be credited with beginning the serious general concern over Faulkner as an artist. Even those reviewers, like Thompson and Hicks, who had scarcely been willing to grant him distinction, admitted to admiration for the formal experiment. Evelyn Scott's pamphlet study of the novel, published in the same year as the novel (1929), was the first extended analysis of the form and point of view of a Faulkner work and was in that sense a landmark in Faulkner criticism.

Annoyance over *As I Lay Dying* seems to have been motivated in two ways—the obscurity of the method and the unpleasantness of the content. A grudging admission of Faulkner's "talent" usually accompanied these complaints, but the remark in the *New York Times* (October 19, 1930) was characteristic of the general reaction: "Content compels us to put this book in a high place in an inferior category." In short, the novel was called an "uncommonly forceful book, though not a pleasant one" (*The New Republic,* November 19, 1930). Admiration of Faulkner's talent was combined with horror over his "pageant of degeneracy." Clifton Fadiman (beginning a series of "clever" disparagements) found it difficult to acknowledge Faulkner as an important writer. He is clever, said Fadiman, but tedious and morbid; he does have an interesting mind, "untouched by the major intellectual platitudes of our day." Only Maurice le Breton found the novel "relatively simple" (*Revue Anglo-Américaine,* June, 1936), the writing "precise and vivid."

The objections to Faulkner had to this time been fairly confined to qualifications of earnest or puzzled admiration. With the publication of *Sanctuary,* they became more overt and bold. Each page of the book "is a calculated assault on one's sense of the normal," said Fadiman; and, though he considered it an improvement over *As I Lay Dying,* he thought it overcharged with the faults of "excessive eagerness." Faulkner evokes

8. The strongest of American endorsements appeared in the *Sewanee Review* of January, 1930, written by Abbott Martin, who claimed for Faulkner a greater artistry than Joyce's.

only fear, said John Chamberlain (*New York Times,* February 15, 1931), "whereas Dostoevsky evokes both fear and exaltation." The great share of the novel's reviews complained of that lack of "exaltation," of the grimness of the horror, the "sadistic cruelty," and the lack of "warmth." Literary talent is wasted on a "morbid theme"; the characters are of no interest save to the neurologist or criminologist.[9] When the novel was praised, it was often because the reviewer (like Herschel Brickell, *North American Review,* April, 1932) thought Faulkner courageous in telling "the truth" about the South, and in refusing to "kneel in the romantic temple." In the *Saturday Review of Literature* for October 20, 1934, Lawrence S. Kubie subjected the novel and its author to psychoanalysis. This view and the letters written in answer to it provide an interesting commentary on Faulkner's fate among the reviewers. *Sanctuary,* said Doctor Kubie, was that type of literature which "represents the working out in phantasy of the problems of impotence in men, meaning by impotence a fraility in all spheres of instinctual striving." Horace Benbow's struggle in Lee Goodwin's behalf is actually a struggle against his own "impotence and powerlessness [*sic*]." The only persons of the novel "who take life in the body with simple, earthy realism" are Lee and Ruby Goodwin. At least one of the correspondents thought Kubie had not gone far enough; J. R. Oliver felt that "Along these lines of overcompensation lie all the attempted rapes, all the cruelty and bullying that are so vividly described in Mr. Faulkner's book."[10]

Faulkner's first collection of short stories, *These Thirteen,* provoked a number of interesting reviews, perhaps really a tribute to the succession of important novels produced in the years 1929–1932. The book proved an occasion for several "total" estimates. Grenville Vernon (*The Commonweal,* January 20, 1932) rather definitively underscored the "regret" so often seen in the reviews: that a man of so much talent should be so

9. Henry Seidel Canby (*Saturday Review of Literature,* March 21, 1931) added his voice to those who accused the novel of indulging in a depraved and morbid subject; he added that such an indulgence distorted the American scene, which is infinitely varied and many-shaded; the novel therefore "exaggerates a potentiality of human nature at the expense of human truth."

10. In *Saturday Review of Literature,* November 10, 1934. One of the most discerning reviews of *Sanctuary* appeared in the *Nouvelle Revue Française* (1933): André Malraux's "Préface à 'Sanctuaire' de W. Faulkner." Its approval of the novel was explained in this way: certain great novels derive their strength from the fact that their authors are capable and are able to "submerge" them in a single dominating preoccupation: as D. H. Lawrence "s'enveloppe dans la sexualité," Faulkner buries himself "dans l'irrémédiable."

entirely concerned with "the malevolent and disgusting." A perverse genius, a Baudelairian romanticist, his appearance in literature is a sad indication of what is possible in an age deprived of faith. Lionel Trilling (*Nation,* November 4, 1931) objected to Faulkner's lack of "largeness of reference." "A Rose for Emily," for example, is "pure event without implication." "Dry September" and "Victory" escape the impeachment "because they are aerated by the writer's acceptance of the common, an acceptance which by no means limits the originality, even idiosyncrasy of their vision and style. Beside them the rest of the stories, for all their success in their own terms, have a subtle kind of stuffiness, shut off as they are in their interesting but hermetically sealed universe." Robert Penn Warren, however, in one of his first statements (*Virginia Quarterly Review,* January, 1932) found the opposite values in Faulkner's work. The narrow identification of theme and locale gives the stories their strength; the "feeling for place" strengthens the sense of reality which is always profound in Faulkner's characters. Far from being "trivial" or isolated and strange, "A Rose for Emily" is his best achievement. The publication of *These Thirteen* served, in these and other reviews, to mark off clearly as at no time hitherto the lines of critical reaction. The wide disparity between Trilling's and Warren's views was indicative of the sharpness of division: Trilling temperately stating a need for "social reference," Warren recognizing the strength that is given by a preoccupation with place and limitation.

*Light in August* caused a sharper division of opinion than had previously been seen. The period of puzzled admiration was over. Faulkner had now produced a number of books; and the novel itself was not "experimental" in any obvious sense. The expression of outrage was vehement and outspoken. Faulkner provides intense depictions of horror together with vague hints of meaning, said Geoffrey Stone (*The Bookman,* November, 1932); in his preoccupation with horrors he flees reality. Other objections were to Faulkner's refusal directly to give information, his "roundaboutness" in developing his narrative; this often as a result of bad planning, a needless and reckless luxuriance of style.[11] Such reviewers as J. Donald Adams saw in *Light in August* a "turn toward the better" (*New York Times,* October 9, 1932): the work of a man who has been "desperately hurt, a man whom life had at some point badly cheated," but who gives signs of recovering his balance. Sponsors of Faulkner found the novel equally stimulating as proof of a maturing genius: the pre-

11. Strangely, Maurice Coindreau (*Nouvelle Revue Française,* 1933) hailed *Light in August*'s clarity, comparable, he said, with that of a novel by Willa Cather.

occupation with evil seemed to them more clearly justified and more exactly defined, the intricacy of form as significant as that of *The Sound and the Fury* and more profoundly relevant.

A similar division of views was seen in the reactions to *Absalom, Absalom!* The parade of objections was of course led by Clifton Fadiman's *New Yorker* review (October 31, 1936): "every person in *Absalom, Absalom!* comes to no good end, and they all take a hell of a time coming even that far." Fadiman discoursed on what he called the "Non-Stop or Life Sentence" of the novel, citing statistics, and discussed the method of "Anti-Narrative, a set of complex devices used to keep the story from being told . . . as if a child were to go to work on it with a pair of shears. . . ." Perhaps significant of the reviewer's tastes, Fadiman concluded with a qualified approval of James T. Farrell's *A World I Never Made*: at least "what [Farrell] knows is important, what he says is clear. . . ." There was widespread agreement with Fadiman concerning the "Anti-Narrative" of *Absalom, Absalom!*, and not a little exasperation over what seemed a perversity of method carried too far. Such figures as these were employed to describe the obscurity: a man dealing cards and secretly hiding the joker; reading the novel at times little easier than trying to knit with barbed wire; an extravagant puzzle; a mixture of fog and dreams. Bernard De Voto complained (*Saturday Review of Literature*, October 31, 1936) that "When a narrative sentence has to have as many as three parentheses identifying the reference of pronouns, it signifies mere bad writing and can be justified by no psychological or esthetic principle whatever." Life is short and *Absalom, Absalom!* is very long! Faulkner's friends among the critics acknowledged the "density" of style and the complication of method, but while admitting the former explained and sometimes defended the latter with suggestions of Conrad and James. The method of "multiple narrators" provoked references not only to these but also to Ford Madox Ford.[12] William Troy suffered from the same need to defend what he was not certain of understanding (*Nation*, October 31, 1936): Faulkner is best understood as a lyric poet, said Troy; and his fiction provides no "norm" to which the reader can have access. "His imagination posits isolated people, actions, gestures, even speeches, broods upon them until they take the full shape of his vision, and then attempts to relate them in some sort of pattern." In short, *Absalom, Absalom!* proved a crucial test for Faulkner's admirers

12. See Graham Greene, "The Furies in Mississippi," *The London Mercury,* March, 1937.

as it seemed definitive proof of the long-standing objections of his de-
tractors. Not even Troy (who disapproved of the scheme of "multiple
narration") saw clearly the relevance to Quentin Compson of the Sutpen
story or came clearly to recognize its speculative nature. The complexities
of style were almost universally called an extreme case of Faulkner's
suffering from a lack of the advantage, as Mary Colum put it, "of thresh-
ing out his technical ideas around a café table."[13]

Except for Malcolm Cowley and Stephen Vincent Benét, *The Hamlet*
was received with disfavor, on the usual counts of its unintelligibility,
obscenity, and lack of purposeful direction. The Snopeses are all bad;
there is an unnecessarily long documentation of this fact. "It's a nice
bucolic idyl of insanity, avarice, cruelty, rape and murder, centering
around the meanest passel of white folks this side of a nineteenth-century
novel."[14] The principal objection was to the "spectacular" accumulation
of evil, large and small, with no relieving contrast. Ratliff seemed to most
reviewers scarcely to have existed. Benét, however, saw his importance
as a specially designated Faulkner personality (*Saturday Review of Literature,* April 6, 1940): "He doesn't, it is true, get anywhere in particular,
but his disillusioned comment represents the defeated virtues of civilization—at least by comparison with the Snopeses."

The abundance of reviews of *Intruder in the Dust* testified both to
the "arrival" of its author as a literary celebrity and to the controversial
nature of the work itself. The long direct statements made by Ike McCaslin
in *Go Down, Moses* had prepared the discerning reviewer somewhat for
the "shock" of Gavin Stevens in this novel. As a consequence of its directness, the novel became the subject of sharply drawn lines of interpretation.
Everyone admitted the greater "explicitness" of Faulkner's text, most
reviewers with regret. Edmund Wilson's *New Yorker* review (October
23, 1948) stated most sharply the two objections to the book: those to
its too false directness of polemical statement and to its defeating and
finally needless involutions of style. Of the latter Wilson said that they
are too often "the casualties of an indolent taste and a negligent workmanship" not seen so abundantly in his earlier prose. As for the "tract,"
the novel contains "a kind of counterblast to the anti-lynching bill and
to the civilrights plank in the Democratic platform." One inference drawn

13. "Faulkner's Struggle with Technique," *Forum and Century,* January, 1937.
14. *Newsweek,* April 1, 1940. *Time,* on the same day, was as extravagant in its praise
as *Newsweek* was generous with its abuse. A reviewer for the *Spectator* (September
27, 1940) was apparently so bored by the book that she misplaced its events in a
"Kentucky village."

from this novel by Faulkner's apologists was stated by Malcolm Cowley (*The New Republic,* October 18, 1948): "Now one can clearly see what so many readers formerly overlooked: that these are Faulkner's people and that he loves them in a fashion fierce and proprietary." But the major question (except for critics like Barbara Giles of *Masses and Mainstream*) was not so much Faulkner's right to "love" these people, but rather the the propriety of Gavin Stevens' "lectures": had not the "point" of them been most brilliantly and dramatically made in the first seven chapters, and especially in the very fine narrative of the Lucas-Chick Mallison tensions? Some reviewers (like Harvey Breit, *New York Times,* September 26, 1948) were willing to maintain that Stevens' arguments had been more than satisfactorily "particularized." Irving Howe (*American Mercury,* October, 1948) spoke of Faulkner's extreme use of the "official" Southern rhetoric, but found that use "significant" and exciting. On aesthetic grounds it may have to be rejected, but the sincerity of its anger is profound and meaningful. Dan S. Norton (*Virginia Quarterly Review,* Winter, 1949) thought otherwise: Gavin's role is to intervene, to violate the experiential pattern from which Chick Mallison should come to his special realizations. This was the primary objection—to a "special pleading" which, whatever its independent virtues, violated the context and caused an imbalance of narrative and recourse to blunt persuasion. In the end, the reviews of *Intruder in the Dust* provided a remarkable cross section of a considerable body of criticism, of an artist firmly established and widely read. The bulk of the reviewing was now addressed to the question which Faulkner answered (or, at least, to which he gave his own answer) in the long speeches and not to the particular experience dramatized on the courthouse square and in the graveyard. The extremes of rejection and acceptance of the novel were seen in the condescending and somewhat wrongheaded review of Elizabeth Hardwick (*Partisan Review,* October, 1948) and the sober and total endorsement of Andrew Lytle (*Sewanee Review,* Winter, 1949).

Perhaps no novelist of our century has suffered so persistent an attack in his lifetime of writing, as no author has been more valiantly defended. The reviews demonstrate a progress from obscurity to a falsely motivated popularity (in connection with the notoriety of *Sanctuary*) to what was almost a unanimous bewilderment (over the complexities of *Absalom, Absalom!*), and finally to a *succès d'estime,* originally the result of Cowley's work and then immensely enhanced by the Nobel Prize Awards in 1950. Faulkner was subjected to the abuse now conventionally expected in the case of most modern writers; but he suffered additional abuse, on the grounds of his own "regional" peculiarities and his apparent "lack of interest" in the "larger implications and responsibilities" of his work. The reviews provided abundant repetition of the "cult of cruelty" thesis first set down at the beginning of the 1930's; they revealed critics trying to define and describe Faulkner's "South" and to see a thematic discipline governing the work; they also demonstrated a concern over form, diction, language, and artistry, by way of meeting the successive challenges offered by the novels. In many of them were to be found germinal suggestions for the longer and more careful studies of Faulkner's novels which have appeared in the last few years. These are, after all, the beginnings of a substantial criticism, to which reviewing is always and properly subordinate.

4

Almost every critic and reviewer who has had anything to say about Faulkner has made some comment on his style. One of the principal complaints registered against him from the beginning had to do with his "perverse" maneuvering of syntax, his reckless disregard of grammatical "decency," and the exorbitant demands he has made upon the reader's attention. Joseph Warren Beach (*American Fiction: 1920–1940,* 1941) stated well the reader's genuine distress:

Half the time we are swimming under water, holding our breath and straining our eyes to read off the meaning of submarine phenomena, unable to tell fact from figure, to fix the reference of pronouns, or distinguish between guess and certainty. From time to time we come to the surface, gasping, to breathe the air of concrete fact and recorded truth, only to go floundering again the next moment through crashing waves of doubt and speculation.

Not only the reader, but every character is "lost in the spool of his rhetoric," said Alfred Kazin (*On Native Grounds,* 1942), a rhetoric that is "perhaps the most elaborate, intermittently incoherent and ungrammatical, thunderous, polyphonic rhetoric in all American writing. . . ." Faulkner's love of this rhetoric was explained at times on the grounds of his "Southern romantic" inheritance, at other times as a consequence of his constant "uncertainty" and attempts to evade discipline. Wyndham Lewis, writing in 1934 (*Men Without Art*), thought it merely "second-rate," cheap poetry masquerading as prose, and proceeded to document, by reference to three of Faulkner's novels, the working of his "slipshod and redundant artistic machine."

It was largely through the effort of Conrad Aiken, an American critic whose importance for modern literature has been underrated, that the "style" was seen as something more than the product of mere undisciplined whimsy. Admitting, perhaps too eagerly, that the style was "all too frequently downright bad," Aiken went on to point out what he thought was the reason (even the *necessity*) for it. The manner is an effort on Faulkner's part to make the reader "go to work," his reward being "that there *is* a situation to be given shape, a meaning to be extracted." Especially in the case of *Absalom, Absalom!*, Aiken demonstrated the advantages gained: there is no "*logical* point of entrance" in that novel; "we must first submit, and follow the circling of the author's interest, which turns a light inward toward the centre, but every moment from a new angle, a new point of view." There was no denying Faulkner's "exuberance," and especially in the earlier novels (through *Satoris*) the rhetoric was rightly seen as scarcely identified with the needs of its subject. But critics had been so fond of pointing out the obvious excesses that they often substituted a listing of them for honest criticism. In the last ten years, the emphasis has been less on these "infelicities," more frequently on the close and significant relationship of language with structure—more than that, on the advantage gained from a richness of language. Warren Beck pointed out convincingly the effectiveness of Faulkner's "intervention" in his narrative; and in comparing two passages (from the early and the late version of "Spotted Horses") he showed how much the stylistic "voice" of the author added to the narration.

If technique and structure were interdependent in Faulkner's work, then it might be proved that the style had a significant purpose; but this conclusion awaited serious and careful examinations of text. The next step in criticism involved the reading of separate novels or short stories, with the aim of attending to technique in the spirit of Mark Schorer's "Technique as Discovery":

Technique is the means by which the writer's experience, which is his subject matter, compels him to attend to it; technique is the only means he has of discovering, exploring, developing his subject, of conveying its meaning and finally of evaluating it.

The problem of defining the narratives in terms of what the text reveals has scarcely yet been solved in Faulkner's case. Unlike Hemingway's (which has perhaps been too exhaustively and too tediously examined), Faulkner's work has just begun to yield its technical evidence. In the 1940's however, important beginnings were made. The two Faulkner issues of *Perspective* (Summer, 1949, and Autumn, 1950), and the Autumn, 1948, issue of the *Kenyon Review* were largely responsible for these beginnings. Much of this work is still speculative and therefore scarcely definitive. But such essays as the following are a fine earnest: Sumner Powell's on *The Sound and the Fury,* Phyllis Hirshleifer's on *Light in August,* Ray West's on "A Rose for Emily" (*Perspective,* Summer, 1949); Olga Vickery's on *As I Lay Dying* (*Perspective,* Autumn, 1950); Lawrence Bowling's on *The Sound and the Fury* (*Kenyon Review,* 1948); and William Poirier's on *Absalom, Absalom!* Irving Howe's re-examination of *The Wild Palms* (*Tomorrow,* December, 1949) was the first serious attempt to examine that work. Other investigations are under way, in the universities and elsewhere. They are long overdue, delayed by two decades of easy dismissal or cautious reserve, and perhaps also by Faulkner's own attitude toward the criticism of his work.

That attitude has been notoriously indifferent—perhaps rightly so, for Faulkner found little to learn from his early critics and does not seem to have suffered (at least not disastrously) from his isolation. Cowley, Mrs. Colum, and others have regretted his failure to seek out advice, to join some group of fellow writers around a café table for frequent discussion and exchanges of criticism. He has occasionally announced his indifference to criticism, has spoken of the speed with which he finished manuscripts; but there is evidence that these public expressions of scorn do not accurately describe his own concerns over his writing.[15] It is absurd to suggest that that writing is a "public concern," that Faulkner needs to submit to formal training. The isolation from schools and cafés has carried its own risks of absurdity (there are many suggestions, ideas, and images in his work which seem to have been lost or discarded before their full use has been developed); but one may hazard the suggestion that it was indispensable to Faulkner's way of writing and that the "treatment" (whatever it might have been) might well have caused more damage than good. Faulkner has achieved distinction, if not in spite of, then independently of, his critics.

15. See Russell Roth, "The Brennan Papers: Faulkner in Manuscript," *Perspective,* Summer, 1949. See also *Faulkner in the University* (Charlottesville, 1959) in which Frederick L. Gwynn and Joseph L. Blotner have very usefully compiled and edited Faulkner's comments on his work, made in class conferences at the University of Virginia, 1957-1958.

## PART TWO: THE NOBEL PRIZE AND
## THE ACHIEVEMENT OF STATUS

### 1

IN NOVEMBER of 1950 Faulkner was informed that he had been granted the 1949 Nobel Prize for literature. He traveled to Stockholm in the next month, to deliver the now famous address of acceptance. It was the fourth time an American writer had gained the distinction; but perhaps Faulkner came nearest to earning a unanimous approval from his critics. Cecil B. Williams, after examining much of the press reaction to the event (*Faulkner Studies,* Summer, 1952), concluded that

perhaps it is fair to say that he is the first American author to receive the prize solely on the basis of his contributions to literature as such. The only negative article I found on the Faulkner award, by H. E. Luccock of The Yale Divinity School, did not name a worthier claimant; Luccock based his criticism solely on the ground that Faulkner belonged to a group of modern authors overly-addicted to featuring profanity in their writings.

It is of course incorrect to say that the prize changed Faulkner overnight from an unknown to a celebrity; the task of bringing him to a position of deserved reputation began in 1939 and was greatly aided by Cowley's editing of the *Portable* Faulkner, in 1946. From that date forward Faulkner criticism grew in quantity and in seriousness. The effect of the prize was to bring him "up front," to make a "public man" of him, and to exert such pressure upon the general run of critics and journalists that they could not thereafter dismiss him out of hand so casually as in the past. While the adverse reactions to Faulkner which I have labeled "The Cult of Cruelty" school of criticism did not entirely vanish, the prize discouraged some critics and frightened others into confessions of their past errors.

The difference is an amusing footnote to the history of popular criticism. Typical of the public admissions is that made by Clifton Fadiman, whose record of consistent disparagement and left-handed praise should certainly qualify him for the unofficial championship in the field. Mr. Fadi-

The following pages sum up the major critical concerns of the 1950's. An excerpt from them was read to The Modern Language Association (American Literature Division) in December, 1959, and is published in *Renascence,* October 1960 (F.J.H.)

man did not retract; instead, he asked that the history of his dissents be allowed to serve as a consolation to those who "recognize his talent but are unable to connect personally with its wave length." (*Party of One,* 1955) Without necessarily insisting upon the critics' invariable sensitivity to the pressure of public acclaim, I should note that much criticism published after the award hesitated and qualified where earlier it might have condemned with little or no equivocation. A few examples will suffice: "Mr. Faulkner's novels are interesting because of his great and undisciplined talent. But they are hamstrung by their faults. That Mr. Faulkner is a serious artist is to his credit; but it does not atone for his impenetrable prose." (Orville Prescott, *In My Opinion,* 1952); "It is impossible not to regret that Mr. Faulkner seems disposed to surrender the problem of communication quite so easily. One can only hope that, under the stimulus and encouragement of the Nobel Prize, his best work lies yet before him." (Edward Wagenknecht, *Cavalcade of the American Novel,* 1952)[1]; Faulkner is still "a major writer: and one whose peculiar limitations are almost as illuminating to the cultural historian as are his grand flashes of genius." (Maxwell Geismar, *Saturday Review,* July 12, 1952).

It was not so much fame that caused many popular critics to squirm uneasily, but the glaring light of publicity that now illuminated Faulkner's status. The obscure and isolated genius who had preferred a Mississippi town of 4,000 unsophisticated inhabitants to New York and Paris[2] was now at the center of the literary world and had become a public personality. He was called upon to speak his mind on several occasions, following upon the phenomenal success of his Stockholm address.[3] Interviewers now hopefully approached him for comment and reminiscence; he was featured in long and generously illustrated essays in the popular magazines;[4] he

1 Wagenknecht calls *Requiem for a Nun* "a hopeful book" in this connection.
2. John Maclachlan maintained that Faulkner's County (and its equivalent in reality) was responsible for the success of his work because "There is nothing between its folk and the elemental forces of the universe, no canopies, walls, clinics, ranks of professionals and bureaucrats to stand between them and life and death." (*Southern Renascence,* 1953) It is interesting to note that since the Prize Faulkner has been away from Oxford more than in it.
3. James B. Meriwether's Check List acknowledges eight published speeches, beginning with the Stockholm speech, all of them in the 1950's. Whatever Faulkner had publicly to say before the Award was apparently not of sufficient importance to record in print (See *The Princeton University Library Chronicle,* Spring, 1957).
4. Only *Time* of the important popular magazines had thought Faulkner interesting copy before 1950; the issue of January, 1939, ran a "cover story" and a review of *The Wild Palms.* See Robert Cantwell's essay (*New World Writing,* No. 2) for an interesting set of recollections of a journalist's trip to Oxford (the essay is reprinted in this collection).

was invited to visit universities, as a writer in residence or a guest speaker. More important than the surprise of public interest in his *succès d'estime* was his willingness to appear, to perform, to speak; he was apparently seriously moved by his eminence, and he endeavored to match the quality of his speech to the unaccustomed virtue of the occasion. No public event, among those succeeding the Stockholm affair, matched in impressive tone the ceremony in the Salle Gaveau, Paris, in May, 1952. As reported by Thelma Smith and Ward Miner (*Transatlantic Migration,* 1955), the event testified to the almost unbelievable prestige Faulkner had achieved in a very brief time; the approval was apparently as unequivocal as the period of waiting had been long.

The program went along about as one would expect with sometimes per-functory or sometimes hearty applause. The one variation from this pattern occurred when Faulkner was introduced by [Denis de] Rougement. Faulk-ner stood up; and he had to stand there for several minutes while the audi-ence bravoed, cheered, and gave vent to their enthusiasm in true French fashion. As one French paper described the scene, "The ovation enveloped Faulkner like a tornado—the applause of the single-minded crowd offered him a memorable greeting." And it was this single mindedness that attracted our attention. That audience had come there to see and hear William Faulkner. They had come to the Salle Gaveau that afternoon as an ex-pression of their adulation and almost worship of the writer William Faulkner.[5]

The affair of the Salle Gaveau, as well as others of its kind, was an event of great critical importance, not because of its glamor but because of its rhetoric. The truth was that Faulkner had come into a position that demanded of him an unceasing iteration of certain chosen syllables and phrases, which were to echo through the post-Stockholm years in his own writings and in critical appraisals of them. In a sense that has not yet ade-quately been appreciated, Faulkner himself took the initiative in the criticism of his own work. He was asked to explain to himself and to his admirers the meaning of what he had been saying in the past twenty-five years; and he obliged by providing catch phrases of a very high quality and a guaranteed somberness of effect. The wonder grew that this man who had described so powerfully and so frequently the ugly, chaotic, miserable, obscene, irrational world of man should have meant all along that he was upholding the

5. He had earlier, in April of 1951, been awarded the Ordre National de la Légion d'Honneur, presented to him by the French consul in New Orleans.

"eternal verities" and therefore had been without qualification on the side of the angels.

Quite aside from the notoriety of Faulkner's post-Nobel career, let us consider the rhetoric of it, as that is featured in the Stockholm Address, in the foreword to the *Faulkner Reader* (1954), in the several interviews with him that have become a critical staple since 1950,[6] in the other speeches he has given, at crucial points in the novels, and conspicuously in the book *Faulkner at Nagano* (Edited by Robert A. Jelliffe, Tokyo, 1956), which faithfully records his answers to the many questions put to him during his 1955 visit to Japan. The language is an almost incredibly neat succession of devices for accomplishing two ostensible objectives: to explain (perhaps, to explain away) what many critics had called an "unmitigated naturalism" in the description of human affairs; to affirm, in the light of what seems to have been a declared necessity to act affirmatively in the glare of public acclaim. Faulkner begins the Stockholm address[7] with an attempt to achieve the first: the phrase "life's work in the agony and sweat of the human spirit" describes both the experience of writing and the experience which is the subject of the writing. He insists that the intensity of the creative effort must equal the seriousness of the artist's role: the "problems of the human heart in conflict with itself" have been crucially intensified in the atmosphere of World War II. The artist must learn not to be afraid— I assume he means, not to yield to deterministic pressures upon his spirit, not to despair. The key phrases follow: there should be room in the writer's consciousness for nothing but "the old verities and truths of the heart, the old universal truths lacking which any story is ephemeral and doomed— love and honor and pity and pride and compassion and sacrifice." Faulkner has always used these words in his own writing; as early as *Soldiers' Pay* they appear, and they are given both a symbolic and a dramatic setting in Part IV of the famous story "The Bear." But he had never, before 1950, spoken them entirely in his own "voice," except in so far as it is possible to distinguish that voice from those of his characters. There is much in these "verities" so nakedly displayed that may suggest a justification of the "agony and sweat" of past writings: whether to bring to the light of explicit statement what had earlier "not been clear" or to reassure himself that this is what he had been saying all of the time.

6. See especially Jean Stein's interview, published in the *Paris Review* of Spring 1956, and reprinted in this volume. See bibliography, below, for checklist of printed interviews.
7. It is reprinted in this collection.

The rest of the speech is affirmation; that is, it is not merely a catalogue of phrases identifying human experience but a rhetorical exercise in
assertion and prediction.

I believe that man will not merely endure: he will prevail. He is immortal,
not because he alone among creatures has an inexhaustible voice but because he has a soul, a spirit capable of compassion and sacrifice and endurance. . . . It is [the poet's] privilege to help man endure by lifting his
heart, by reminding him of the courage and honor and pride and compassion and pity and sacrifice which have been the glory of his past. . . .

Several characteristics of these words demand scrutiny. They are a
thoroughly secular assertion; that is, they do not appeal either to religious
support or to theological sanction, nor do they quote religious documents.
Faulkner makes an important distinction between the heart and the glands,
as between an organ of life and the means of excitation to pleasure and
indulgence. It is a basic humanist distinction, to which are added the
necessary sentimentalities of whatever "the heart" has come to mean in
normal unthinking discourse. The point is that Faulkner is trying here to
find a way out of the "naturalist impasse," to which such earlier critics
as Harry Hartwick and Alan Reynolds Thompson had consigned him. Further, the rhetoric of his address reveals an overpowering desire to articulate
directly the hundreds of complex truths of "the human heart" which remain
in a tenuous and ambiguous state of suspension in his novels. To bring
them into the light of ceremonial day is to clear them of all circumstance
of doubt and obscurity. The rhetoric is overt, forcefully direct, entirely
unclear (as an instrument of understanding literature, at least), and powerfully effective. It gave the impression of changing him as if overnight from
"naturalistic monster" to "moral hero," in the position of popular contemporary reviews.[8]

## 2

In short, Faulkner has since 1950 taken a hand in the evaluation of his
own work. This is not to say that he began to direct or to command the
direction of Faulkner criticism. Rather, he has asserted himself as a moral-

8. If any proof were needed of the consistency of Faulkner's public statements, his
remarks in Japan *(Faulkner at Nagano)* are more than adequate; here he says that the
belief that man will prevail "is like the belief that one has in God, Buddha . . ." Man
is immortal because he has survived, "in spite of all the anguishes and griefs which he
himself has invented and seems to continue to invent." These are thoroughly secular
assertions; they require no dependence upon religious assumption, but merely demonstrate a humanist confidence.

ist, as a writer preoccupied by moral essentials, as a man with "moral vision." While the *effect* of the Stockholm remarks may have seemed sudden, the intent was assuredly not to strike an entirely new note, but merely to affirm the presence of an old one by reducing it to minimum essentials. It is as though he were saying to critics that they should give up fastidiously attending to the minutiae of "what he meant" and turn at least temporarily to the genera of it. As early as the summer of 1952 Russell Roth, in a letter to *Faulkner Studies,* took issue with Faulkner criticism for its having been too formalist and rhetorical, too *academic* as he put it.

I have the feeling that many critics—most of them, in fact—would prefer *not* to see what he has been driving at. . . . The reason for this reluctance is beginning to become clear: what Faulkner says—is saying—cuts the feet out from under us; it flatly denies, or contradicts, or takes issue with most of our fundamental and most dearly-cherished assumptions regarding our relation as individuals, to the world.

Whatever value this remark may have in the history of Faulkner criticism, it can quite clearly be maintained not only that in the last decade critics have explored what Faulkner "has been driving at," but that they (or many of them) have been investigating his "moral vision" and the manner and degree of his resemblance to and departure from Christian thought. This appears almost to be an about-face in criticism, both because of the harshly damning early criticism and by reason of Faulkner's own change from implicit meaning to an overt display, almost a syllabic count, of moral meanings. Much criticism of the 1940's was concerned with the developmental strategies of Faulkner's writings, but (and conspicuously in the case of George M. O'Donnell and Malcolm Cowley) was primarily historical and only incidentally moralistic. The themes, the patterns, the system of recurrences from novel to novel, were suggestive of moral concerns, but these remained largely outside of the Christian moral and diagnostic tradition; or, critics were misled (as in *Soldiers' Pay* and *Light in August*) into assuming that Faulkner was a typical modern satirist and skeptic, attacking the depravities of Christian convention.

The tenor of recent criticism is very different; it is concerned to measure Faulkner's fiction against his public statements, or to explore his analysis of contemporary moral practice, or to make remarkable inferences from the coincidences in it with the Christ story. An example of the critical survey of Faulkner's entire work is the attempt of Walton Litz to sum up the themes which elaborate Faulkner's "Moral Vision" (*South-*

*west Quarterly,* Summer, 1952). Here the conventional pattern is stressed, Faulkner's review of the American continent as somehow containing a new version of the Genesis story; the crucial event is "The Fall," when man "of his own free will" violated the conditions of God's confidence in him. The defeat of the South in the Civil War becomes "God's just retribution . . ." almost as if Rosa Coldfield's bitter denunciation of Sutpen *(Absalom, Absalom!)* were to be taken literally. Nathan A. Scott, Jr. *(Christian Century,* Sept. 18, 1957) followed closely Faulkner's own line when he called his work "a dramatization of the issues of our perplexity." Whether he portrays a Hell or a Purgatory, Faulkner gives us a magnificent "embodiment in his art to those old verities and truths of the human condition." One of the worst of the "philosophical dissertations" upon Faulkner's work was Carl Galharn's study of *The Wild Palms (Twentieth Century Literature,* October, 1955), which presented an almost inexhaustible variety of anthropological, religious, and metaphysical observations, obviously with the aim of producing a "thinking Faulkner." For example, the convict's adventure strikes him as follows: "To the convict the seemingly intransigent afflicting of his fate reeks largely of *predestined* dooming!" Galharn seems to want to say, and to be prevented by his own encumbering rhetoric from saying, that man's immortality is testified, in the convict's demonstration, in his enduring and surviving the terrors of nature. This is an extreme case of the critic's taking full advantage of the semantic obscurity caused by Faulkner's apparently "clear" generalities.

One of the major questions raised in the 1950's had to do with the degree and nature of Faulkner's commitment to Christian morality. He had not himself specified an association with any doctrinal reading of the human condition, but had been satisfied to say that his belief in man's endurance is *like* a belief in God. And surely the elaborate parallels of *A Fable* suggested at the most a secularized Christ story, a Christ reduced to the level of humanist suffering and parable. Edward Penick suggested *(Christian Scholar,* June, 1955) that Faulkner's portrayal of an infinite variety of human evil nevertheless argued the saving grace of "a high destiny," and insisted that his criticism of the falsity of much Christian practice was motivated by a genuinely Christian disturbance. There is throughout Faulkner's work a recognition of "something in man that he speaks of as an immortal spirit"; and in *A Fable* especially, "Christian symbolism is on all sides." Perhaps the most thorough analysis of this problem was undertaken by Hyatt H. Waggoner, of Brown University (in *The Tragic Vision and the Christian Faith,* 1957, and in *William Faulkner:*

*From Jefferson to the World,* 1959). Waggoner warned against the temptation to accept Faulkner as entirely within the Christian fold; but he ends by almost making an Anglican cleric of him. He is correct in pointing out the presence of moral concerns from the beginning in Faulkner's work; if there is a Christ in that work, he is the "sweet, idealistic, inspiring young man who, unfortunately, was crucified before he could complete his work of bringing an end to war and human strife." Faulkner belongs to the "conservative" party in American literature—Hawthorne, Melville, and Eliot—in his emphasis upon the consequences of human evil, as opposed to the denial of it in Emerson. In spite of much good sense in this essay, Waggoner does fall into a trap of his own devising. He is anxious to make such persons as Dilsey and Ike McCaslin out to be proto-Christians, even though they may not be doctrinally acceptable. There is much truth in his warning that for Faulkner "the Crucifixion is central and paradigmatic and the Resurrection might never have occurred,"[9] and in his further observation that without the Resurrection the story of man is "pure tragedy"—that is, that naturalistic suffering without divine grace is against the basic Christian picture of human experience. Nevertheless, Waggoner seems to be denying the distinctions so carefully made, when he concludes upon this altogether misleading, "hopeful" note:

So let us say, then, that the earlier works hover between present despair and the memory of a lost faith, and that the later works seem to be bidding us to repent and believe in God and man, as we wish, or can, or must.

### 3

It is a pardonable mistake to make, an error really of emphasis, since Faulkner had all but challenged his critics to make it. For while he had stressed so heavily the moral intention of his work, he had also placed its implications of doctrine within reach of a Christian interpretation. Faulkner's approach to Christianity was akin to that of a purist who hates and despises the forms that vitiate the spirit. Two aspects of recent Faulkner criticism draw from this feature of his meditation: discussions of his attack upon Southern (as well as imported Northern) Calvinism, and critical at-

9. Alfred Kazin put it more cogently, in his essay on *Light in August* (*Partisan Review,* Fall, 1957): "Faulkner's world is grim—a world in which the Past exerts an irresistible force, but against which there is no supernatural sanction, no redeeming belief. He believes in original sin, but not in divine love, and he is endlessly bemused by the human effort to read fate or to avoid it." Kazin's essay is reprinted in this collection.

tempts to make whole sense of his apparent flirtations with the Christ symbol.

As for the first of these, Harold J. Douglas and Robert Daniel, after having pointed out the shock of the daily headlines (concerned to point up violence and the extremes of moral deviation) of a Southern newspaper, maintained that "Faulkner's plots tend to emphasize the same kind of incident. . . ; his bootlegging and maniacal drivers, his Snopeses and Temple Drakes, furnish the proof of man's fallen condition. And by man's fallen condition Faulkner is appalled." (*Tennessee Studies in English,* 1957) His work is "steeped in Calvinism," which is not to say that it is Calvinist, but intensely outraged by the tendency of man to honor the form of observance and neglect the spirit. Hence the forms of Christian observance hedge his heroes, and its permissive treachery drives them to violent assertions of moral identity. The first critical attempt to investigate this aspect of Faulkner's moral view was William Van O'Connor's "Protestantism in Yoknapatawpha County" (*Hopkins Review,* Spring, 1952);[10] it was a most influential essay, and may be said to have had much to do with setting criticism on the track of the proper consideration of Faulkner's relationship to the Christian tradition. In line with this approach, and as a natural enough consequence of it, some attempts have been made to consider Faulkner and Hawthorne as in one tradition. Randall Stewart (*College English,* February, 1956) saw a close parallel of Dimmesdale and Joe Christmas. Douglas and Daniel claimed that *As I Lay Dying* "resembles *The Scarlet Letter* in ways that virtually establish a direct influence." And O'Connor pointed out other apparent resemblances (*Virginia Quarterly Review,* Winter, 1957).

Ilse Dusoir Lind, however, seems to have treated the problem intelligently in itself, without access to the matter of parallels, in one of her two first-rate essays on Faulkner ("The Calvinistic Burden of *Light in August,*" *New England Quarterly,* September, 1957). The question of Joe Christmas's struggle for moral identity (which makes him, in Alfred Kazin's notion, so intensely an inward character that he rarely if ever comes through as an actual person) involves him, both superficially and in unwitting blasphemy, with Christian practices. So that, because of his own intense willing of a "purity" of line and Joanna Burden's intense pressuring of him to behave as *her* principles would demand, Christmas becomes a violent, shocking, and disastrous symbolic devaluation of the formal Christian

10. Subsequently reprinted with some changes, as Chapter 6 of *The Tangled Fire of William Faulkner,* 1954.

proprieties. Mrs Lind remarks upon "the irony that Christmas, martyred by the austerity of a faith rooted in the Old Testament, becomes a symbol of the suffering endured by Christ in the New."

With respect to the story of Christ's Passion, which Faulkner is frequently on the edge of adapting to his work, he said to Jean Stein (*Paris Review*, Spring, 1956) that Christianity is "every individual's individual code of behavior by means of which he makes himself a better human being than his nature wants to be, if he followed his nature only. . . ." The Christ story is an archetype of man's will to be divine or to perfect in himself both the passive and the active virtues. The variety of suggestive notations in Faulkner's work of the Christ parallel (at times both whimsical and obsessive) has set his critics to elaborate searches and extravagant claims. It appears on occasion as though Faulkner had been playing a game of identification with them. The results of this kind of digging and matching have often exceeded the bounds of good sense. John C. Sherwood was provoked (*Faulkner Studies*, Summer, 1953) to this bit of satirical doggerel:

> When Faulkner writes a novel,
> He crowds the symbols in;
> There is a hidden meaning
> In every glass of gin,
>
> In every maiden ravished,
> In every colt that's foaled,
> And specially in characters
> That are thirty-three years old.[11]

Several of Faulkner's novels have endured this kind of parallel searching. Carvel Collins maintained (*Princeton University Library Chronicle,* Spring, 1957), among other things, that since Benjy's monologue was dated Holy Saturday, 1928, and Christ "spent Holy Saturday in Hell redeeming such pre-Christian worthies as Adam," Benjy is symbolically spending the day there with Luster, who "is certainly an agent of Hell."[12] The most

11. Sean O'Faolain (*The Vanishing Hero,* 1957), comments as follows upon this kind of symbol hunting in Faulkner criticism: "The common reader will not be unwise to remember Jowett of Balliol's remark about a certain learned German's critical methods: that such methods obscure rather than illuminate and pile up mountains of chaff when there is no more wheat—and skip lightly over Faulkner's actual or alleged symbolism."

12. *As I Lay Dying,* says Mr. Collins, exists in parallel with aspects of *The Golden Bough,* but in this case there is much of what he calls "inverse comparison"; Dewey Dell exists in "inverse comparison" with Persephone, since she is trying to have her seed destroyed.

elaborate and probably the most naive of the Christ-ings occurs in Beekman
Cottrell's study of *Light in August* (*Modern Fiction Studies,* Winter,
1956/57), which comes up with these findings: Lena Grove symbolizes
Mary, as she gives birth in a manger; she is attended by Byron Bunch, as
Joseph, and his ubiquitous mule; the name of Gail Hightower is linked to
that of Pontius Pilate (it is associated "with a whole group of Latin words
centering on *pila,* a pillar, *pons,* a bridge or the floor of a tower, and *pilatus,*
bald or close-shaved."); of course, the story of Joe Christmas follows the
life of Jesus. Cottrell concludes that "it is a testament to [Faulkner's] equally
major place in fiction that he can use symbols so subtly, both overtly and
covertly, to enrich his story. . . ."[13] Other critics have attempted to link
*Pylon's* Shumann with the Christ story. John R. Marvin remarks that
Shumann, in his death, is "re-enacting through his combined freedom and
necessity the ceremony of Christ on the Cross." (*Faulkner Studies,* Summer, 1952) Donald Torchiana (*Modern Fiction Studies,* Winter, 1957/58)
elaborates upon this claim:

> Shumann, specifically, is the exemplar of the freely-chosen sacrifice that
> counters the virulence of finance capitalism and lends such provoking
> ambiguity to the otherwise death-dealing pylon. . . . One feels that the
> ferro-concrete world of city and airport has trembled and is momentarily
> calmed and emptied of its terror.

It is natural enough that Faulkner's "clues" should have been so
eagerly seized. There is a grain of truth in his parallels or near-parallels.
But the essential problem is not that of discovering identities (through
research into etymology or calendars); nor is it merely a matter of Faulkner's wish to show a modern hero sacrificed to the gods of plunder and
progress. The two basic principles of his exploration of the symbology
available to a contemporory moral vision are his belief in a form of human
immortality (which he calls survival or endurance), and his wish to
secularize the Christian testaments, to give them a wholly human context. In this light there is much to be said for Lawrence Bowling's discussion of *The Sound and the Fury* (*Kenyon Review,* Summer, 1958),
in which he claims that that novel "is an exploration of the idea of innocence, and this exploration is carried on largely through the dramatization of two traditional views of innocence which are in conflict with

13. But see the results of William H. F. Lamont's researches, which conclude that
Christmas was not 33 but 36 at the time of his death: he "was *not* born in December
(Christmas) but September; . . . *not* crucified on a Friday . . . but on a Monday; he
was not 33 when he died, but 36." (*Modern Fiction Studies,* Winter, 1957/58)

each other." In the one tradition (which he designates as "puritan") innocence is defined as "freedom from sin, guilt, or moral wrong in general; . . ." the other (the "humanist") defines the innocent as a "guileless, simple, or unsuspecting person; . . ." "The puritans emphasize the idea that knowledge of evil must be shunned; the humanists insist that the end of man is to know." While these distinctions carry their own distracting burdens, they do enable one to perceive, without the distractions of elusive parallels, the problem of Faulkner's moral examination of humanity. Bowling's conclusions are worth attention in the light of Faulkner's own observations concerning allied matters:

Like the older humanists, Faulkner views man as bound by certain irrevocable limitations, which constitute his doom, but within this framework, man is free to choose, free to encourage either the positive or the negative elements in his situation and in his own nature.

Like O'Donnell's earlier (1939) working dichotomies, Bowling's are too neatly circumscribed and make too many demands upon the fiction to justify them. It is better to say that Faulkner is exploring both the ultimate opportunities of a secularized salvation and the persistent and discouraging evidences of his failure and weakness. When Joe Christmas appears in the Negro church during "the chase," he seems to the terrified congregation a *devil;* and the apparition, as well as its implications, has as important a meaning for Christianity and its perversions as Ahab's act of baptizing his harpoon in the name of the devil.

## 4

It is a mistake, of course, to assume that Faulkner is crystal-clear about all of this. Bowling makes him appear much too much the rational moral diagnostician, worthy of a philosopher's chair in a sub-Benthamite institution of learning. He is anything but precise in these matters. His obscurity is of two kinds: that which reveals the tensions and contradictions of the situation itself (a matter I shall discuss later); and that which comes from his forcing his language into high-sounding but basically unclear generalities and his fiction into allegory.

This second problem of cummunication is obviously at the center of the critical wrangle over *A Fable.* Several critics, confronted by this work, spoke of the "new Faulkner," as though he had changed both his convictions and his manner of representing them. The ideas are the same, unless we may say that the radical change in representation has in itself effected a qualitative change. Lately Faulkner has been giving us more "positive" works, Geoffrey Wagner said in his review of *A Fable* (*Twentieth Century,* December, 1954); and it may simply be "that his gift is not suited to this new 'positive' approach." In any case, "The negative books are, in fact, coming to mean more and more to us each year we draw nearer our thermonuclear doom. . . ." This reaction suggests both that Faulkner was "negative" in his earlier work (which is, of course, what he was repeatedly called then) and that literature has the sentimental value of confirming pessimism in the very act of accelerating its attendant gestures and moods. Indeed, several critics have admired certain of the novels (noticeably *Pylon* and the title story of *The Wild Palms*) for their having presumably subscribed to a form of Waste Land mood.[14]

The real quarrel with *A Fable*—its basis of critical contention—lies not with its being more "positive" than "negative," but with the degree of its intellectual maturity. Philip Blair Rice, late professor of philosophy at Kenyon college, accused the novel of an intellectual failure (*Kenyon Review,* Autumn, 1954).[15] He is obviously much concerned with the "message". of the Nobel speech:

That he has failed to find adequate incidents, agonists and symbols to realize it dramatically and poetically is a conviction that grows steadily and painfully upon the reader; that he has failed to dominate the intellectual problems with which he has been struggling—for the book cannot be taken as other than an effort at something like a social, a theological, a philosophical novel—is quite as evident.

If it is to be taken as such a novel, it invites and demands comparison "with such awesomely mentionable names as Melville, Tolstoy, Dostoevsky, and Mann," and it cannot long stand the glare of such comparison.

The most devastating criticism of the novel came from Norman Podhoretz (*Commentary,* September, 1954). Here the reviewer and the novelist are both intellectually and temperamentally at poles apart. For all that Faulkner knows, he says, "the Enlightenment might just as well have never been." He has no real sense of history, but "has always taken refuge from historical changes in a vague sense of doom." The failure, Podhoretz concludes, is a failure of ideas.

14. *Mosquitoes* is the subject of another search for parallels, this time with Eliot's "Prufrock." See Frederick L. Gwynn, *Journal of English and Germanic Philology,* January, 1953.
15. Reprinted in this collection.

I do not believe that Faulkner ever had ideas. Convictions, yes, and a terrifying energy behind them, but not ideas, not the wish to understand the world, only the wish to feel deeply and to transcribe what he felt and saw.[16]

Very few reviews failed to being up the matter of intellectual failure, or of the failure to match conception with presentation. A Catholic critic, Ernest Sandeen (*Review of Politics,* January, 1956), pointed up the very real theological difficulties (also suggested by Hyatt Waggoner) attendant upon the reduction of Christ to secular levels.

The source of these difficulties lies in the associations made between Christ and the character, the corporal. Because of the many superficial resemblances drawn between the two, the corporal by implication becomes an interpretation of Christ. . . . [The parallel] perversely attributes a gnostic or manichean outlook to Christ and at the same time an incarnational outlook to the Church. . . .

Two other critics called attention to the "medieval" formality of the novel's intellectual design. Roma A. King called it "a modern morality closer in concept to the medieval *Everyman* than to the modern realistic novel." These critics were disturbed not over Faulkner's right to the morality as a form but over its suitability as a means of communicating the substance. Andrew Lytle (*Sewanee Review,* Winter, 1955) stated the problem in this way:

[In medieval times] A man witnessing a morality would in the action dealing with the drama of the soul, automatically specify whatever was unique and personal in himself. But today where we have conventions empty of belief and institutions being reduced to organizations and forms which have lost the natural object, a morality lacks authority. It is why fiction as a literary form appears now and not in the fourteenth century. Everyman now must first become unique man.

The matter becomes one of credibility. To return to Christ after having strayed from virtue is an act acceptable to both God and man in a time when Christ is invested both with divinity and humanity. If it is not possible to accept such a fusion of powers, the center of moral conflict becomes man, a hero, in whom good and evil create manichaean tensions that

16. In the *Partisan Review* for Fall of 1954, V. S. Pritchett offered this shrewd comment: "He has been a writer divided between idiosyncrasies of regional genius and a nostalgia for a contemporary means of dealing with a universal subject. The division is still apparent in the rather laden majesty of this allegory where a universal subject has been treated as the compendium of a word-drunk mind."

are not easily resolved by an act of the will. The obscurity of the Nobel Prize address once more afflicts the reader and critic. That man will endure and prevail because he has survived his self-imposed agonies is an affirmation difficult to maintain and to dramatize. One is left simply with the strong conviction of one man, who has elsewhere abundantly proved himself aware of the moral contradictions in man and asserts that he will nevertheless endure and prevail over their disastrous results. Whatever the consequences of our having thus been cut adrift from Christian essentials, the attempt has been made in *A Fable* to write a Christian allegory that lacks at least one of its Christian co-ordinates. It may be that, as Dayton Kohler suggests (*College English,* May, 1955), "Faulkner's treatment of Hebraic-Christian myth is like Joyce's use of the Homeric story in *Ulysses* and Mann's adaptation of Faustian legend in *Doctor Faustus.*" But there is some doubt that the literary responsibilities of the older to the modern text in these other two cases are nearly so exacting; nor is the hero of either so necessitously linked to doctrinal demands.

*A Fable* did not lack for whole-hearted critical endorsement. The immensity of the problematic and polemical circumstance seemed in these cases to overcome any indisposition to accept its rhetorical quality. Delmore Schwartz (*Perspectives, USA,* 1955) called the novel "a masterpiece, a unique fulfillment of Faulkner's genius which gives a luminous new meaning to his work as a whole." Schwartz took Faulkner's word for it, in every respect, and was furthermore proud that Faulkner should have persisted in the Nobel affirmations in a time dominated by the terrifying question, "when will I be blown up?" This, then, is the literary equivalent of Faulkner's public rhetoric. Consulting *The Brothers Karamazov* for comparison's sake, Schwartz affirmed the moral superiority of the Corporal over Ivan:

Faulkner's intention—and his triumph—is utterly unlike Dostoevski's because he attempts to cut below the question of God's existence to a question which for many modern human beings, is prior, the root conception of Man. . . . Faulkner's very different intention is to establish man as worthy of devotion, belief, and love, whatever his misdeeds and failings, and whether or not he is God's creature.

There is, of course, some truth in this. It is as much as to say that Faulkner's purposes are far less complex than Dostoevsky's, and that they are not involved in local nineteenth century politics or doctrinal dispute. This is true, but it poses once more the question raised in

Dostoevsky's novel. If God does not exist, then what if anything is permitted; and in what ways are man's capacities to survive, endure, and prevail extra- or supra-naturalistic? Heinrich Straumann (*Anglia,* 1955),[17] wholly committed to admiration of *A Fable,* did not trouble himself with the outcome but rather measured the quality of the conflict itself. *A Fable* is "a milepost in the history of American literature," a classic Anglo-Saxon equivalent of *War and Peace.*

What makes Faulkner's work superior to that of his American contemporaries is the complexity of his subject-matter, the suspension of his intellectual magnetic field between Manichaeism, Stoicism, and Christianity . . . .

Straumann is not disturbed over the question of whether the problem can or cannot be solved, but rests his case entirely on the fact that it exists in a full and interesting variety of tensions and contradictions.

   *A Fable* received one other kind of reading. The very earliest attacks upon Faulkner had been on the grounds of permissive obscurity and obscenity. Even perceptive critics of the 1930's were uneasily suspicious that the imbalances of style and violence argued moral instability. Some variant of that reaction reappeared in the criticism following upon the release of *A Fable.* Walter Fuller Taylor (*American Scholar,* Autumn, 1957), who inherited the position from his predecessors of the early 1930's, attacked *A Fable* on the old grounds that Faulkner represents the end-result of a blind and miserable naturalism, according to which all men are "subhuman and repulsively bestial. . . ." The novel offers "the consistent grossness of the gospel according to William Faulkner." This is truly a crucial matter; Taylor warned that we are being misled into thinking that Faulkner is a "great Christian thinker," while he is in fact committed to violence and filth.

   One new variant of the "Cult of Cruelty" criticism is noticeable here: the danger to us as readers comes from the critics' naive enthusiasm over Faulkner's verbal magic:

[Out of the special, formal interests of Faulkner's critics there comes] the personal portrait of a genius astonishing in his technical virtuosity, magical in his command of myth and symbol, idealistic, and committed even in his agonies to the side of the angels—a concept which in its totality is the more insidiously false because every separate part of it is true.

17. Reprinted in this collection.

This criticism testifies, in its role of isolated exception, to the fact that Faulkner criticism has indeed matured, if only in its attention to the relationships of particulars to thematic wholes. Faulkner has himself compelled attention to the larger issues to which he alleges to have attended in all his years. That attention has not been without its penetration of the wobbly intellectual surface he offered in *A Fable* and its immediate predecessors.

## 5

The impression of Nobel publicity and *Fable* rhetoric is, however, only one phase of Faulkner criticism in the last decade. As a quite new emphasis, it testified to an all but universal desire to "see Faulkner whole," a desire shared by Faulkner himself. The line of thematic statement begun by O'Donnell and Cowley in 1939 and 1946 was pursued diligently and with many variations. Even the studies of separate novels were now more likely than not to have much recourse to literary and intellectual allusion. Robert Penn Warren's advice (1946) to young critics, concerning the areas and themes worthy of investigation, was perhaps the single most important influence on them.[18]

Faulkner's style had of course always been a matter of dispute; in the 1930's such dissidents as Bernard De Voto and Clifton Fadiman used it as a primary scapegoat. Scarcely a dissenting estimate was without protest against its involutions, its three-to-fifty-page sentences, its luxuriance of adjectives, and its use of strange locutions. In the last decade the pattern changed somewhat. Apologists for the style nevertheless occasionally saw it as excessive; but there was a serious effort, among the younger critics especially, to explain the complexity as essential to Faulkner's purposes.

Herbert Foster (*American Mercury,* December, 1951) remarked that "There is a kind of sullen Puritanic strain in Faulkner which compels him to view clarity, charm and easy persuasiveness with suspicion and hostility." Sean O'Faolain (*The Vanishing Hero,* 1957), who called Faulkner "an ingenuous man, of strong feelings, a dedicated sincerity and poor equipment: a maimed genius," went on to say that his worst fault is that "he cannot write plain English; not because he is untutored but because his psyche is completely out of control."[19] In much of the reviewing, one

18. Reprinted in this collection.
19. The lack of "plain English" seems to have bothered O'Faolain to the extent of his making several errors in fact: Caddy's daughter may have been the child of Gerald Bland; Lena Grove has come to Jefferson from "further north"; there are characters like Lucas Birch and "the Hyneses."

of the several problems raised by the critic is that of the style outrunning the substance; each successive novel seems to have been the one in which the manner—up to now explicable with effort—has finally raced far ahead both matter and reason.[20]

For the most part, however, critics exerted themselves, not only to adjust their sights to each new verbal display, but to discover a rationale of the manner applicable to the work as a whole. Robert M. Adams (*Virginia Quarterly Review,* Summer, 1953) spoke of Faulkner's "esemplastic imagination" and analyzed the text along the lines of Coleridge's theory; and R. W. Flint called the style more often poetry than prose: "Faulkner's vision can rise to poetry because it is both aware of the principal modern ideologies and able to make good use of them for what they are worth." (*Hudson Review,* Summer, 1954) Fascinated by what must have been a strangely interesting world—Faulkner in French translation[21] J. J. Mayoux spoke of his "vision fiévreuse et barbare" in this fashion: "On sent aussi que chez Faulkner nous sommes devant le rêve d'une réalité et chez Kafka devant la réalité d'un rêve. . . ." (*Études Anglaises,* February, 1952)[22] Appreciations of the complexity were not lacking, especially among fellow practitioners; Wright Morris (*The Territory Ahead,* 1959), in a chapter significantly called "The Function of Rage," had this absorbing comment:

Rage—such a rage as Faulkner's—generates the high voltage of his art, but this rage does not free him from the delusions of nostalgia. It is the very impotence of the rage that determines the style. His medium is rhetoric, handled with such power that language spreads on the canvas like paint. In his hands it is a way of painting with words.

Alfred Kazin spoke similarly, in one of two first-rate essays on Faulkner, about the relation of the rhetoric to outrage. The style is a means of communicating the violence, the sense of outrage, "astonished and furious and outraged, outraged freshly over again every day and every hour, yet still

20. See F. J. Hoffman, Preface to the 1956 edition of *The Modern Novel in America:* "It is difficult to distinguish rhetoric from pretense in [*A Fable*]; one is tempted to say that Faulkner's rhetoric has finally overcome him. The more statements rescued from its intricacies are here trite and unconvincing; they seem not at all to have emerged from any human exigency."

21. See Maurice Edgar Coindreau, "On Translating Faulkner," *Princeton University Library Chronicle,* Spring, 1957. The scope of Faulkner's reputation in France may be studied in two accounts: Thelma Smith and Ward Miner, *Transatlantic Migration* (1955); Stanley D. Woodworth *William Faulkner en France,* 1931-1952 (Paris, 1959).

22. This essay is reprinted in this collection.

trying to be impervious, to believe ourselves implacable, and by claiming our own intactness, showing that we seek to endure." (*The Inmost Leaf,* 1955)

Much of the analysis of Faulkner's style seems to have taken off from Conrad Aiken's 1939 study,[23] and especially from his suggestion that the involutions were a means of withholding meaning from the reader until it should be fully appropriate that he have it:

It is a persistent offering of obstacles, a calculated system of screens and obtrusions, of confusions and ambiguous interpolations and delays, with one express purpose; and that purpose is simply to keep the form—and the idea—fluid and unfinished, still in motion, as it were, and unknown, until the dropping into place of the very last syllable.

As did Warren's essay in the matter of Faulkner's themes, so this essay on the style, quoted from almost invariably in each fresh examination, influenced and encouraged analysis. Seen from this triple perspective—as a device to direct the manner of reading, as a means of communicating the inner "violence" of the characters, as a continuing representation of the multiplicity of experience—the rhetoric took on a new significance. At Nagano, Faulkner had said in answer to a question about the length of his sentences that the difficulty came from his "compulsion to say everything in one sentence because you may not live long enough to have two sentences." (*Faulkner at Nagano*) This compulsion forced the sentence patterns into rich, ambiguous innovations of "delayed syntax" and suggested quite new departures in the matter of balancing syntactic forms against each other. It was, as Russell Roth said (*Western Review,* Spring, 1952), a way of holding polarities in balance. It was certainly the very antithesis of Hemingway's neatly circumspect economy; and Faulkner's own underrating of Hemingway, repeated in several interviews, suggested that he believed Hemingway's "simplicity" a sign of a lack of daring, as contrasted to Wolfe and himself, who had "risked much."[24] As Kazin had said (*The Inmost Leaf*), it is useless to think of Faulkner's "benefiting" from the kind of exposure that Hemingway's writing had undergone: "I do not think Faulkner would have been any different if he had gone to school to Ezra Pound, had learned to trim his style, to be more sparing of those 'overblown' words. I think he needs those words."

23. Reprinted in this collection.
24. See also *Paris Review,* Spring, 1956: "All of us failed to match our dream of perfection. So I rate us on the basis of our splendid failure to do the impossible."

The major contributions to an understanding of Faulkner's style have consisted of analyses of passages, to show the technique and skill of balancing complex meanings, the manner of "withholding meaning," of setting up obstacles to superficiality. Other studies have contributed classifications of types of words and word-compounds, and forms of syntactic complication, symbol and image. Karl Zink (*South Atlantic Quarterly*, July, 1954) spoke of a "pervasive syntactical continuousness, a quality of intense suspension, which can be found in almost every novel." He went so far as to suggest that Faulkner does not write in sentences but in "prose patterns," and proposed therefore that he not be analyzed "in terms of the logical premises of formal grammar." F. C. Riedel (*South Atlantic Quarterly*, Autumn, 1957) described the surface chaos of the Faulkner sentence: "A sentence may rush the reader along willy-nilly, forcing upon him seemingly chaotic masses of fact and detail, thought and idea, subtle impression and vivid image, which must sort themselves out to form some semblance of order in the mind as best they may." A most interesting analysis, by Walter J. Slatoff, of the prevailing trope in Faulkner's work, the oxymoron, not only discovered an abundance of examples but suggested that it is especially appropriate as a reflection of Faulkner's quality of mind: ". . . he would consider full coherence a sign of weakness and something to be avoided. . . . His works show, in part, I believe, a quest for 'failure.' " (*Twentieth Century Literature*, October, 1927)[25]

Whether disparagingly or not, the general conviction about the style was that Faulkner had more to say than conventional forms of syntax and grammar would allow him to say. His view of character compelled him to show the inner self in uneasy tension with external event. Further, the question of time, Faulkner's major concern to show dramatically the pressure of the past upon the present moment, also required a compressed language and an elaborate syntax; the character often thought in terms of a complex of "was" and "is," and the burden of memory not infrequently made progress in time almost impossible, with the result that the style revealed a new kind of temporal suspension. This made new demands upon the language and forced sentences to proceed at length but actually in a state of energetic and tense simultaneity. It was not merely

25. Reprinted in this collection. Other useful studies of style and language are Karl Zink's "The Imagery of Stasis" (*PMLA*, June, 1956); Robert Zoellner's analysis of *Absalom, Absalom!* (*American Literature*, January, 1959); and Florence Leaver's excellent examination of word practices (*South Atlantic Quarterly*, Autumn, 1958). Mrs. Leaver's essay is also reprinted here.

a matter of "stream of consciousness."[26] Indeed, the Faulkner character was rarely entirely free of some kind of auctorial pressure. What Warren had called "the voice" forced him to achieve kinds of rhetorical urgency quite beyond his independent capacity for articulation. The relationship of the "voice" to Faulkner's characterization is a fascinating but as yet a scarcely touched matter for investigation.[27]

## 6

The principal contributions to Faulkner criticism in the last decade have been made to an elaboration of themes, all of which were suggested earlier and a few of them discussed at moderate length. Undoubtedly the major concern was to associate Faulkner with modern literature and intellectual history. At times one gets the impression of a writer alive to every cross-current of modern thought; but, while he has several times talked to interviewers about his literary interests he can scarcely be counted among the artists who were steadily in touch with the intellectual world at large.[28] More important were the attempts to establish the Faulkner hero within the canon of modern literature as a whole, and the best of these were studies of *Light in August* and Joe Christmas. There is much to be said for suggesting Christmas as a modern version of the tragic hero, quite aside from the suggestions of parallels with the Christ story. There is an intensity in the characterization, a penetration within the person that, while it made the external figure of Christmas almost unreal at times, challenged comparisons with other major heroes of isolation.[29] V. S. Pritchett (*Books in General,* 1953) thought the French enthusiasm for Faulkner

26. There are analyses of Faulkner's use of stream-of-consciousness techniques in Melvin Friedman's *Stream of Consciousness* (1955), Robert Humphrey's *Stream of Consciousness in the Modern Novel* (1954), and Leon Edel's *The Psychological Novel* (1955).
27. The problem becomes more difficult as Faulkner in his later work vacillates between leaving his characters alone and forcing them to speak out in the "Stockholm manner." For an interesting though brief discussion of the problem of Gavin Stevens, see Olga Vickery's essay in *Faulkner Studies,* Spring, 1953.
28. Both Carvel Collins (*English Institute Essays,* 1952, and *Literature and Psychology,* November, 1953) and the co-authors, Harry Campbell and Reuel Foster (*William Faulkner,* 1951) have tried to make a case for Faulkner's relationship to psychoanalysis. The Campbell and Foster study is extremely useful; Collins's suggestions are excessive and frequently naive.
29. Frederick L. Gwynn (*Modern Fiction Studies,* Summer, 1958) also suggested a parallel of Dostoevsky's Raskolnikov and the Quentin Compson of *The Sound and the Fury.* Gwynn believes that Faulkner read *Crime and Punishment* "at a time to affect the writing of *The Sound and the Fury.*"

natural enough, because his novels "exploit 'the absurd,' the cruel mean-inglessness of existence, and they hope, by making every instant of any character's consciousness a life and death matter, to collect at the end a small alluvial deposit of humanism." Most recent criticism has stressed the strange isolation of Joe Christmas, and of other characters in *Light in August,* as especially relevant to existentialist and other world pictures. The tragic significance of the novel, according to Carl Benson (*South Atlantic Quarterly,* October, 1954), comes from the conflict "between rigid patterns of self-involvement on the one hand and commitment to a solid-arity that transcends self on the other. . . ." The best consideration of this problem appeared in John L. Longley's study of Joe Christmas as a modern tragic figure (*Virginia Quarterly Review,* Spring, 1957), which brings Faulkner's novel within range of the intent and scope of Greek tragedy, in the respect that "In some highly symbolic fashion, the modern hero must typify the major myths and problems of our century." Joe Christmas is quite unlike Greek tragic figures, but he resembles them in reflecting and acting out the peculiar dilemmas and tensions of his time; and his failure, "to define himself in relation to [the modern cosmos]," is a failure not unlike the classic tragic experience.[30]

The question of Joe Christmas as modern hero raises other critical issues. Not the least of these is that concerning the range of "larger mean-ing" of Yoknapatawpha, of what Faulkner called "that little postage stamp of native soil" that he had begun in 1929 to recreate in his imagination. One of the strongest temptations was to suggest that Faulkner had all along intended to pose the wilderness and civilization as mutually exclusive ways of life and to prefer an extraordinary simplicity of social manner to all "progress." Campbell and Foster (*William Faulkner,* 1951) specified Faulkner as a "primitivist," and explained:

It becomes increasingly evident in his later books that Faulkner is implicitly setting up a scale of values in which people who follow the simple, primal drive of primitive societal life are more likely to survive than those people who have been corrupted by the false and debilitating stimuli of modern society.[31]

Not only did this thesis involve references to Dilsey and Lena Grove but it called upon idiots as well for evidence; Campbell and Foster pointed

30. The essay is reprinted in this collection.
31. Cleanth Brooks (*English Institute Essays,* 1952) took these critics to task, es-pecially for their association of primitivism with Stoicism.

to Faulkner's use of childhood, of the Indian, and of various styles and techniques, to represent the "primitive" state of mind. The most elaborate thematic discussion of this matter was Melvin Backman's "Sickness and Primitivism" (*Accent,* Winter, 1954). The "sick" characters are forever set against the primitives, as two alternative forms of life, and the primitives are invariably chosen:

It is almost exclusively to the primitives that Faulkner assigns the capacity to love and pity, the Rousseau *pitié.*

Most frequently, "The Bear" was chosen as convincing evidence of Faulkner's "primitivist" attachments. His having referred there to the wilderness and to the "puny little humans [who] swarmed and hacked at [it] in a fury of abhorrence and fear like pygmies about the ankles of a drowsing elephant" would seem conclusive. Kenneth La Budde called "The Bear" an "affirmation of primitivism" (*American Quarterly,* Winter 1950) and went so far as to maintain that Faulkner here advocated that "the only means of salvation is to sweep all this man-made structure away so that man will hold 'the earth mutual and intact in the communal anonymity of brotherhood.' " W. R. Moses, in a more perceptive essay (*Accent,* Winter, 1953), nevertheless read a part of the action with a defeating literalness: Lion stands for "the mechanization, the applied science which finally caught the wilderness fatally by the throat." Surely the most elaborate and the most intelligent of essays on "The Bear" was R. W. B. Lewis's "The Hero in the New World" (*Kenyon Review,* Autumn, 1951), which, in the spirit of his *The American Adam* (1955), described it as an admirable example of an American image of the frontier as "a new, unspoiled area in which a genuine and radical moral freedom could once again be exercised—as once, long ago, it had been, in the garden of Eden. . . ." Yet in his anxiety to prove "The Bear" a reworking of the Christ story ("we get moreover *an* incarnation, if not *the* Incarnation. . . ."), Lewis quite misrepresents the figure of Ike McCaslin, and especially ignores the marriage scene, perhaps because it does not support his argument.

"The Bear" also affords an opportunity to discuss Faulkner's attitude toward the land, containing as it does the remarkably provoking remarks in Part IV, that God had not created the earth for man to own and sell, or "repudiate," but that man was to "hold the earth mutual and intact in the communal anonymity of brotherhood, and all the fee He asked was pity and humility and sufferance and endurance and the sweat of his face for bread." With a full panoply of learned associations, Dale

Breaden brought this and other passages to bear upon his argument that Faulkner's was an "agrarian reality," that his was not far from the position taken by John Locke on natural rights and Henry George on land uses. There was a grain of truth in all of these presentations of the "wilderness theme." Faulkner did seem often to suggest two radical extremes of life, character, and cultural disposition. But while he seemed at times to propose a return to absolute simplicities, this was no more a total denial of the present than his apparent occasional nostalgia for Sartorises and Compsons meant that he was a "traditionalist," as O'Donnell had said in 1939. The sanest word on this question was said by Ursula Brumm (*Partisan Review,* Summer, 1955),[32] who, while she freely acknowledged the oppositions seen in Faulkner's work and pointed out their resemblance to other American portrayals of the hostility to civilization and progress, firmly denied that his rejection of civilization argued any savagery or paganism; instead it points to "a form of humanism, since it is marked by a reliance on the purely human qualities under exclusion of all the mechanical inventions with which civilization has armed mankind." To this view Faulkner would himself have subscribed, as indeed he did, in the interviews in Japan. Asked if he had proposed a "return to Eden" in these writings, he said that we can't go back to "an idyllic condition, in which the dream [made us think] we were happy, we were free of trouble and of sin. We must take the trouble and sin as we go. We can't go back to a condition in which there were no wars. . . ."

## 7

What distinguishes the criticism of the 1950's from that of earlier decades is the variety and scope of it, to which one might add its maturity. As we have seen, the complexity of Faulkner's style elicited new approaches to its strategies. Thematic investigations, following along the lines of Warren's suggestions in his 1946 review of Cowley's *Portable Faulkner,* extended beyond both the local peculiarities of Faulkner's county and the implications of what Cowley called the "Legend of the South," into speculations concerning the role of Faulkner's characterization in modern literature generally and conceptions of modern tragedy. Perhaps most surprising was the fact that a man who had in a majority of cases at the beginning been called an "immoral" or an "irresponsible" writer should now be soberly—even profoundly—proclaimed as a man of "moral

32. Reprinted in this collection.

vision." This was a result in part of a natural development away from the triviality of spot reviews toward substantial appraisals of a novelist who had obviously survived and transcended the uncertainties of his early career. Some eleven books on Faulkner have already appeared; four or five others are shortly to appear.[33] Those so far published are chiefly "expositions for the beginner," containing rather brief statements about the work or, as in Campbell and Foster's applying as many modern critical suggestions as possible to it.[34]

If one is to consider the criticism which comes closest to using both a maximum intelligence and the critical materials most readily and profitably available, it is the separate studies of individual Faulkner novels that remain the most satisfactory. The best of these strike a balance in the matters of style and meaning; they explain, but go beyond explaining, to plot structure in several ways, with the aim of enriching the sense of the novels. In short, these studies are both analytic and speculative; they comprehend sources without necessarily becoming exclusively indebted to them; they nicely balance the necessities of exposition with the desire for fullness of communication. There are a surprising number of these; among them are Alfred Kazin on *Light in August,* T. Y. Greet on *The Hamlet,* Ilse Dusoir Lind on *Absalom, Absalom!* and Olga W. Vickery on *As I Lay Dying.*[35] Their general excellence and usefulness augurs well for the future of Faulkner criticism. It has advanced impressively in the last decade. It promises not only to improve correspondingly in the future, but to lead to the substantial book or books which will bring all of Faulkner's work within the range of intelligent comprehenson.

F. J. H.

Madison, Wisconsin
February, 1960

---

33. See below, Bibliography. This does not include books in languages other than English.
34. Irving Howe's *William Faulkner* (1952) and Olga Vickery's *The Novels of William Faulkner* (1959) are perhaps the best so far published; perhaps the least useful or reliable are Irving Malin's *William Faulkner* (1957) and Mary Cooper Robb's *William Faulkner* (1957).
35. These are included in this collection.

# I. The Region and the Family

## THE FAULKNERS: RECOLLECTIONS OF A GIFTED FAMILY

### ROBERT CANTWELL

1

IN THE EARLY winter of 1938 I was assigned the task of writing an article about William Faulkner for *Time* magazine. The article had originally been planned for the preceding year, at the time *The Unvanquished* was published, but at the last minute a different cover was scheduled, and the managing editor decided to wait until Faulkner's next book appeared. This was *The Wild Palms,* and while I felt uneasy about introducing the deepening involutions of Faulkner's style to the magazine's readers, the fact that his writing was growing steadily more obscure suggested that the difficulty might be greater in the future, and that unless the story were done quickly it might not be possible to do it at all. I arranged to meet Faulkner at the Hotel Peabody in Memphis, and took the Southern Railway from New York.

My preparations for the journey consisted only in re-reading Faulkner's novels and in going over the available biographical material on him. In this only one new item appeared, which I was turning over in my mind as the train swayed across Tennessee. *The Mississippi Guide of the Works Progress Administration* devoted some space, in its account of the town of Ripley, Mississippi, to the career of Colonel W. C. Falkner, identified as the grandfather of the famous Mississippi novelist, and referred to as Ripley's most colorful personality.

*The Guide* went on to say that as a barefoot boy of ten Colonel Falkner walked the several hundred miles from Middleton, Tennessee, to Ripley, to make his home with an uncle, and that on arriving at dusk he found the uncle in jail, charged with murder; he sat down on the courthouse steps and swore that he would some day build a railroad over the route he had walked. *The Guide* further stated that Colonel Falkner was the

Reprinted with permission from *New World Writing*, 1952, pp. 300-15.

51

author of a novel, *The White Rose of Memphis,* that after the Civil War
he built the Ripley, Ship Island and Kentucky from Middleton to Ripley, and that in 1899, after his second election to the legislature, he was
shot down and killed on the main street of Ripley by Colonel R. J. Thurmond. In another note, describing the Hindman house, which still stands
near Ripley, *The Guide* said that it was built by Thomas Hindman, who was
killed in a duel with Colonel W. C. Falkner and buried "20 yds. w. of the
house."

It subsequently developed that most of this was wrong. Colonel
Falkner was William Faulkner's great-grandfather, not his grandfather.
Middleton is only thirty miles from Ripley, not several hundred miles.
Colonel Falkner was killed on November 5, 1889, after his first election
to the legislature, not in 1899. Colonel Falkner never fought a duel with
Thomas Hindman, nor any duels at all. He was not a typical Southerner
of his time, but had worked for years in the Ripley jail, employed by the
sheriff, while he went to school. Thomas Hindman was not killed by
Colonel Falkner, but lived to become a celebrated Arkansas politician,
a Congressman and a Confederate major-general. But despite its many errors, the Mississippi *Guide's* brief biography was valuable, for it directed
attention to the factual background for his Sartoris novels, and for the
character of Colonel Sartoris which he based on his great-grandfather.

When I entered the lobby of the Peabody, I was struck by a terrific
tumult, shouts, laughter and the blowing of horns. I made my way to the
desk and asked what was going on, and learned that it was the day of
the Tennessee-Mississippi football game. As soon as possible I retired to
my room to wait for Faulkner. He arrived at exactly five o'clock. He was
dressed in a gray suit coat, and trousers that did not match it, and wore
brown leather gloves. My notes on the meeting read: "Walks with quick
short steps, very erect, head slightly thrown back. Gives an impression
of slightly military self-conscious bearing. Also, quite short. Extremely
thin lips concealed by his mustache. Very sharp eyes, dark. Wavy hair,
now graying, gray in back. Pleasant, but not easy in his manner." He sat
down on the bed, apologized for the delay, and asked, "Are you all packed
up?" It took me a moment to realize that he wanted to start for Oxford
immediately. "I'm sorry about your waiting here," he said. "My wife sent
the telegram and she didn't know I was going to be busy today."

It was necessary for me to call the *Commercial Appeal* to arrange
for a photographer to come to Oxford and take pictures of him—something I could not arrange until I had his permission. "I've got a Leica you
can use," he said, a little impatiently. But he gave the necessary permission.

Outside, the tumult in the halls increased. There were outcries from the other rooms, the shouts of the returning football crowd, and the shrill cheerful screams of drunken women. While waiting for the arrangements to be concluded with the photographers, we spoke briefly of *The Wild Palms*. I said I thought the convict in "The Old Man" section was wonderful. He smiled briefly and replied: "I kind of liked him myself."

Conversation flagged again. There were more shouts from the hall. "This would be a hell of a place to sleep tonight," Faulkner said.

The phone rang, the arrangements were completed, and we left the room. There were a number of drunks waiting at the elevator, which was a long time coming. Faulkner said, "They must have rented the elevator space too."

At last, we managed to get into a car, in which there were more drunks, some aged couples, and two college girls talking about a psychology examination next Wednesday. "I didn't know it was next Wednesday!" said one. "Yes, honey," said the other. "Six weeks!" "Yes, I did too hear something about it!" said the first.

I thought they were singularly attractive, and their fresh Southern voices and rattling inconsequential talk gave me the same feeling I had had earlier in the day, when I entered the lobby and found it filled with football revelers—namely, the genius of the South for being always out of date, for turning on a 1929-boom-year football atmosphere in the midst of the New Deal's grim sociological determinisms, or for evoking the days of the village band concert at a time when the mood of the rest of the country was that of a court-packing plan and the end of the Spanish Civil War. I suppose it comes from the Southern consciousness of always being before an audience, or from the value placed on quickness of response, and the form of Southern politeness that consists in pretending to be (with ingenious variations) what the rest of the country believes Southerners are. This particular Southern revival of the pattern of the twenties seemed a kind of conscious re-enactment, no less deliberate than the abrupt breaks in chronological sequence in Faulkner's novels—a device that might seem artificial in fiction dealing with a different society. The tricks that Faulkner plays with time, jumping from 1928 to 1910 or scrambling the intervening years, as in *The Sound and the Fury,* have a parallel in a part of Southern life; and you can sometimes find in a Southern gathering a layer of 1912 thought, then a layer of 1890 culture, a fragment of reconstruction pottery, a broken piece of a pre-Civil War belief, as archeologists find the bronze above the Stone Age in their excavations.

We pushed through the dense crowd in the lobby and went out to

Faulkner's car. It was a Ford touring, tan, with one broken side curtain. Two boys were sitting in the front seat. They climbed into the back. Faulkner introduced them as Malcolm and Johnny, his stepson and his nephew. We got away into traffic.

"Sleeping in that hotel tonight," said Faulkner, "would be like sleeping in a fraternity house."

We drove cautiously through a traffic jam.

"This is Beale Street," Faulkner said.

The boys looked cautiously out through the side curtains. One of them said it was unsafe for a white man to be there at night. Or even in daylight, added the other.

"You sure can get some bargains in Beale Street pawn shops," Malcolm observed.

There was no further conversation for a long time. We drove grimly out of Memphis on the highway to Oxford, seventy-five miles away. I settled myself for a long and tiresome drive. Faulkner drove carefully, the car swaying and pulling to the right. One of the front tires was soft. It was discovered the next morning. Faulkner's hands seemed to bother him as he drove. He took off his gloves at intervals and clenched and unclenched his fists. The boys in the back seat said nothing at all. The road went through a series of low hills beside a railroad. The hills grew higher, the road going through a cut at the top of each hill, bright white under the new moon. There were few cars on the road. Now and then we passed a Negro couple walking along. The fields were desolate with stalks of corn or cotton and deep gullies washed out in the hills. There were a few scrubby, scattered pine trees. Now and then there was a Negro settlement, a few wan, tumbledown cabins, a patch of cleared ground, dim lights inside. They looked cold.

"Forty to nothing," said one of the boys in the back seat.

"Tennessee has a great team," said Faulkner, with something like a sigh. "When they'd come around the end I never saw so many yellow sweaters at one time."

"The first touchdown on the fourth play," said one of the boys. We drove on.

"Well, Malcolm," said Faulkner at last. "You lost your bet."

"I sure did," said Malcolm, in a high, grieved, twanging voice. "I didn't think Ole Miss'd get beat like that. After that L.S.U. game. . . ."

"I reckon Tennessee must have just about the best team in the country."

"I reckon so."

"I reckon Tennessee must have just wanted to prove they should have been picked for the Rose Bowl."

"I reckon."

A fortunate reference to Colonel Falkner ended the long silence between Faulkner and myself. Somewhat to my surprise, he was glad to talk about his great-grandfather. His principal interest seemed to be in Colonel Falkner and the Civil War, and he spoke about the independence of Civil War soldiers, their resistance to the regimentation of modern warfare—the war itself to him represented resistance to the regimentation of modern life. Outside Colonel Falkner's military career there seemed to be little in his life that interested him. He thought that *The White Rose of Memphis* was pure escapism—"The men all brave and the women all pure"—and that the Colonel had no humor and probably no sensibility.

I asked how it came about that a military man and a railroad builder turned to writing fiction.

Faulkner said he thought Colonel Falkner was probably an overbearing man. He had to be big dog. He built the railroad after the Civil War because he wanted to make a pile of money. He made it. He built the railroad by will power, raising money during the week to pay the men on Saturday night, and raising the capital from among the neighbors. There were originally three partners, but one got scared and dropped out, and Falkner and Thurmond kept on. Building a railroad in those days was like starting an air line in 1928. A train would start out and they wouldn't hear of it again for a week. They'd be out chopping down trees, clearing obstructions, the engine would go off the track and be put back by hand and then the engine would blow up entirely. But as soon as Colonel Falkner had the railroad running and had made a lot of money he lost interest in it. He wanted to go into politics, so he did that, got himself elected to the legislature, but didn't like that, at least he didn't try to go on. He wrote the novel *The White Rose of Memphis* because he wanted to be the best in that. But then he never wanted to write another. Sir Walter Scott was apparently the only writer he ever liked or read, and he named the stations on his railway after characters in Scott's novels. "The people could call the towns whatever they wanted," Faulkner said, "but, by God, he would name the depots."

Faulkner had grown animated as he spoke. He talked carefully, with characteristic pungent phrases, and grew eloquent, his words so composed and telling they could have gone down on paper without the change of a sentence. He described the Colonel's energy and arrogance, the attitude of the people toward him, the failure of his enterprises, the violent end of his life. He was overbearing, he said, hard to get along with, and he and Thurmond quarreled. "I don't believe Thurmond was a coward," Faulkner said. "But the old man probably drove him to desperation—insulted him, spread stories about him, laughed at him.

"Besides," Faulkner said thoughtfully, "he had killed two or three men. And I suppose when you've killed men something happens inside you—something happens to your character. He said he was tired of killing people. And he wasn't armed the day Thurmond shot him, although he always carried a pistol."

I asked what happened to Thurmond. "He left the country, went out West," Faulkner said. It was obvious that he was not really interested in Thurmond. "The feeling in Ripley did not die out with Colonel Falkner's death and Thurmond's leaving. I can remember myself, when I was a boy in Ripley, there were some people who would pass on the other side of the street to avoid speaking—that sort of thing."

The road went straight through the winter night, past the same cold Negro cabins, along the railroad where Colonel Falkner had fought his cavalry battles, through country that seemed to me to be increasingly cold and depressing. "One of my kinsmen is buried on that hill," Faulkner said at one point, indicating a gloomy patch of deeper darkness.

He described that country around Ripley where Colonel Falkner had lived and worked, and where his legend persisted. "People at Ripley talk of him as if he were still alive, up in the hills some place, and might come in at any time. It's a strange thing; there are lots of people who knew him well, and yet no two of them remember him alike or describe him the same way. One will say he was like me and another will swear he was six feet tall. . . . There's nothing left in the old place, the house is gone and the plantation boundaries, nothing left of his work but a statue. But he rode through that country like a living force. I like it better that way."

Faulkner had been writing about Colonel Falkner, in the character of Colonel Sartoris, when the concept of his great cycle of novels took hold of his imagination. He was halfway through *Sartoris,* after writing his first two novels, when "suddenly I discovered that writing was a mighty fine thing—you could made people stand on their hind legs and cast a shadow. I felt that I had all these people, and as soon as I discovered it I wanted to bring them all back."

We had come to Holly Springs. We drove past the big buildings of the Negro college and the new courthouse and into the crowded main street. "This was just a country lane when Van Dorn rode down and burned Grant's stores," Faulkner said.

The boys wanted to stop at a service station. We stopped. "There was a quality about these people you don't seem to find anywhere else," Faulkner said as we waited for them. "The war didn't seem to change their private lives. My great-grandfather raised his own regiment. It was attached to Longstreet's corps in Lee's army. As you probably know, the men elected their officers once a year. They elected somebody else colonel. So he just packed up and came home. If he couldn't be colonel he wouldn't have anything to do with the war. But after awhile he raised a bunch of men, mostly from his own place and around, and fought when it suited him. . . ."

"Van Dorn burned Grant's stores and kept Grant from getting into Vicksburg from the rear," he said again after a moment. "That was a pretty gallant thing to do. But about a week later some fellow caught him in bed with his wife and killed him. He might have been good for a dozen more victories. But honor meant a lot to them."

I asked him about the sources of his history.

"I never read any history," he said. "I talked to people. If I got it straight it's because I didn't worry with other people's ideas about it. When I was a boy there were a lot of people around who had lived through it, and I would pick it up—I was just saturated with it, but never read about it," He said that he had grown up with a Negro boy like the boy in *The Unvanquished*. "There were no toys in this part of the country when I was a boy," he said. "We used to play Civil War games—we would fight over the battles and the old men would tell us what it was like."

Presently we came to Oxford. It was pleasant, tree-shaded and peaceful. There was a big Saturday night crowd in town. At the base of a long hill leading into town there was the square and the tall courthouse, gray and lighted at night. Floodlights were playing on it. "There were no American flags here when I was a boy," Faulkner said. "You never saw one except on the Federal building. But they came in during the war and now every store has a socket for a flag."

Oxford is a town of no less interest than Jefferson in Faulkner's novels. It is not an old town by Southern standards, having been founded in 1836 by a physician, Thomas Isom, and it is a college town, dominated as it has always been by the University of Mississippi. The University was projected about the time the town was founded, and was established in 1848 on a level plot of oak-shaded ground a mile from the courthouse square.

Jacob Thompson, the organizer of the Confederate secret service in the Middle West, was a pioneer Oxford resident and a trustee of the college from the start. There was a good deal of Unionist sentiment in the college before the Civil War, the flag of Mississippi flying over one dormitory and the Stars and Stripes over the other. One of the early presidents was a friend of Lincoln, and one of the first professors a friend of Grant's family. But the college was closed during the war, and the students, organized as the University Grays, reached the highest point of the Confederacy, forty-seven yards beyond the farthest point reached by Pickett's men at Gettysburg. They never held a reunion.

The college buildings were converted into a Confederate hospital, the friend of the Grants remaining as caretaker. Of the 1,800 wounded cared for, beginning with those from Shiloh not far away, 700 died, and the records of their graves beside the campus were hopelessly scrambled. When Grant burned Oxford he spared the college buildings, supposedly after a plea by the friend of his family. In 1889, the year of Colonel Falkner's death, this venerable professor was abruptly discharged. He walked across the campus to his home and killed himself. The Negroes said that the building he lived in was haunted, and claimed they could tell because of the peculiar sweetish odor, like that of rattlesnakes, attributed to ghosts.

No trace of these grim events now remains over the grounds of the school. They have the shaded loveliness one often finds in these old Southern colleges, red brick buildings and white Jeffersonian pillars emerging through the foliage and beyond the expanse of grass like tangible portions of the past surviving independently of the more practical edifices around them.

Even if the college did not bulk so large in the community about which Faulkner writes, another factor would relate it closely to his fiction. The Faulkners moved to Oxford about 1900, at the beginning of the fight of the great demagogues, James Vardaman and Theodore Bilbo, against the old Bourbon aristocracy that had controlled Mississippi since Reconstruction days. The target of their attack was the traditional code and the standards of taste and intelligence that held the governing class together, and consequently they centered their fire on the institution that tried to sustain these standards, the University, of which Faulkner's father became treasurer.

For example, one of the planks of the Vardaman-Bilbo platform was the abolition of college fraternities. It was charged that non-fraternity men were ostracized by Oxford society (pop. 2,890). The student leader of the movement to abolish fraternities was an Oxford resident, who became Bilbo's right-hand man, eventually governor, and finally Bilbo's rival. During his second administration, Bilbo decided to put the university out of business altogether by combining it with the agricultural and mechanical college and moving both to his capital at Jackson. In the course of the dispute he discharged 169 faculty members and administrative officers. His Senate floor leader became dean of men.

The tactics of the Vardaman-Bilbo small fry, stalwart enemies of big business, radical-regionalists, whatever they were, were such as to make one believe that their primary target was human reason. Their anti-Negro, anti-aristocratic demagoguery was doubly provocative in a region where there were relatively few Negroes, and where the aristocracy consisted of a small professional class in moderate or straitened circumstances and a few farmers, often living in unpainted houses. Both the power and the unreality of their politics are reflected in Faulkner's novels. They are not a fictional documentation of the Vardaman-Bilbo movement, but their account of the monstrous Snopes family, gradually infiltrating the town of Jefferson, multiplying by the tens, and then apparently by the hundreds, certainly becomes more meaningful in the light of the careers of Vardaman, Bilbo and such lesser figures as Russell, of whom the country never heard.

When we drove past the square at Oxford Faulkner said that in the old days there were balconies out over the street, with doors from the second floor offices opening on them, and that in the evening the doctors and lawyers would sit in chairs on the balconies and talk. "For years the mayor was old man Stevens, with a beard that reached to here," he said. "Elections were just a formality because nobody ever thought of running against him. But now it's all changed and the people have learned political corruption all the way down."

In entering Faulkner's driveway we turned past the home of Jacob Thompson. His house was burned when Grant took Oxford and only the kitchen remained. This had recently been rebuilt into a low, modern cottage. Malcolm said that during the rebuilding a great stack of Jacob Thompson's papers were found in the attic and dumped in an unused cistern to help fill it.

The driveway of Faulkner's place was a wide curve, lined with

cedars. The lights were lit on the front porch and in the big rooms, illuminating the cheerful exterior and the tall white columns. A little girl, blonde,
pale and very pretty, came running from the house when Faulkner approached, but stopped suddenly to let him come up to her.

This was his daughter, Jill, who was then five. She was self-possessed
and met me gravely, talked with the boys about the game—she won a nickel
—and told me she had learned to ride a bicycle. I told her that my daughter
had learned to ride a bicycle. A look of displeasure flashed across her
features at learning that her accomplishment was not unique. I hastily asked
when she was going to school. "That's for Mother and Daddy to settle,"
she said coolly.

She stretched out on the floor. "I certainly like to lie on the floor,"
she observed.

Mrs. Faulkner, a charming, hospitable, young-looking woman, had
an air of having been surprised about something. We settled down and
went into the Southern Conversation. This is a semi-formalized ritual that
inaugurates a Southern visit, like the prologue of an Elizabethan play. It
is almost identical in content from one household to another, and even
from one part of the South to another. Mrs. Faulkner was expert at it,
and with great charm told us of Jill's mammy, who had been taken by the
Faulkners to California, but she had gotten sick, and had to go to the
hospital, which cost Billy $400, and in the hospital she and her husband
were addressed as Mr. and Mrs. with the result that they remained in
California and no power on earth could ever get them back to Mississippi.
Sometimes these pleasant inconsequential Southern conversations are edged.
That is, someone may have died, or some terrible catastrophe may have
taken place, but the conversation goes on just the same. I think it began
during the Civil War, when the hostesses of Vicksburg pretended that
nothing was happening when a shell came through the window.

For some reason the conversation turned to fishing. "Billy buys all
sorts of tackle but never uses it," Mrs. Faulkner said. "So Jill and I do
the fishing."

"Billy fishes," said Johnny, "but he throws them all back. He says
they're too small."

"You fish like a nigger," Malcolm said to his mother. "You keep
everything, no matter how little."

"Would you have gone to that game, Mac," Faulkner interrupted
him, "if you had known how it was going to turn out?"

"Yes," said Malcolm thoughtfully. "I wouldn't have believed it."

The next day Faulkner took me to interview his Negro mammy, Aunt Caroline Barr, then 77, who lived in the old slave quarters behind the house. She was a bright-eyed, small, high-voiced old lady, and I got an impression of her as shrewd and humorous, but we did not have much to say to each other. Aunt Caroline is said to be the original of the magnificent portrait of Dilsey in *The Sound and the Fury*. She was physically unlike Dilsey, for Dilsey is pictured as having been "a big woman once" and the massive kindly slowness of her ministry of the dying Compsons was not summoned up by the trim figure of the old colored woman in the flesh. Until three years before, Aunt Caroline had called Faulkner by a childish mispronunciation of William. One of his younger brothers as a child was unable to say William, calling it something like Meme, and Aunt Caroline called him that. About 1935, to his bewilderment, she started calling him Mr. Faulkner.

Standing in the thin sunlight outside the old slave quarters, Faulkner began talking about horses. His earliest recollection was of getting a pony at the age of three and waiting for the saddle to be made. He could not remember the name of the man who had made the saddle, and after thinking about it for some time decided to drive out to his farm to find out. An old Negro there, Uncle Ned, had been Colonel Falkner's servant, and had cared for three generations of Faulkners. "He is a cantankerous old man," said Faulkner, "who approves of nothing I do."

We drove twenty or thirty miles into the pine woods and came to a cluster of cabins under the trees in a converging fold of the hills. They formed a little settlement. John Faulkner, the novelist's younger brother, appeared from a frame house some distance apart from the Negro cabins, dressed in riding breeches and boots. Two years later John Faulkner published *Men Working,* the first of a series of wildly comic books of his own, followed by *Cabin Road* and *Uncle Good's Girls,* satirizing bureaucracy and the exaggerated political passions of Mississippi as these subjects have never been satirized in American literature. But he then expressed no literary or political interests, and the two brothers talked about the farm.

Presently John Faulkner went on and William Faulkner and I walked up a slope to Uncle Ned's cabin. It had grown quite cold. The cabin was sealed tight. There was a dish of some savory stew cooking in the fireplace. "In the wintertime they just go to bed and stay there," William Faulkner said. "They keep something cooking and when they get hungry they get up and eat, even if it's the middle of the night."

Uncle Ned greeted Faulkner almost ceremoniously. He seemed incredibly aged. Faulkner explained that I was interested in Colonel Falkner.

The thought seemed to make Ned older. We did not get very far with our conversation about him, and presently Faulkner asked, "What was the name of that man who made a saddle for me? Had a shop down by the depot?"

Ned thought a long time. He could not remember. Then he exclaimed, "Cheek!"

The recollection pleased them both enormously. It was Mr. Cheek, that's right, a very fancy saddle, made with a special thread and a tree whittled out in the shop.

Presently we returned to the subject of Colonel Falkner. Faulkner tried to draw Uncle Ned out on some personal characteristics, but the recollections seemed troubling. A silence settled on the room. We sat there for awhile. It was nearly dark. I know now that the tragedy of Colonel Falkner's life brooded almost oppressively over that cabin in the woods, but then I felt that I had intruded enough; I sensed its reality, not so much to Faulkner as to the old man, and after some further polite conversation we went on our way.

## 2

I went back to New York and wrote my story, which was eventually published without seeming to make much difference to anybody except a few readers of the magazine who bought copies of *The Wild Palms* on the strength of it, or wrote angry letters to the editor as a result. But the missing element in the story of Colonel Falkner continued to interest me.

It seemed out of the pattern of the history of the time. There were two opposed forces in the culture of the South before the Civil War, one florid and oratorical, violent and reckless, dominated by the romanticism of Scott, favoring the individual exploit and the gallant charge in warfare, the masked ball and Mardi Gras in social life, the duel in personal and political disputes and the castle in architecture. The other side of Southern culture was practical and enterprising. Southern fiction has dealt with the first and not at all with the second. Colonel Sartoris in Faulkner's novels, based on Colonel Falkner, is a symbol of the first, but Colonel Falkner himself belonged in the other category, a businessman who tried to carry into industry the code of the landed aristocracy, a plantation-owner who combined with Southern traditions the spirit of enterprise, too entangled with the Old South to detach himself intellectually from it, and too intelligent to accept it completely, too much of a Southern colonel to represent the new practical spirit, but representative enough to arouse the hostility of the supporters of the old order.

A number of years later, while working on a book of criticism dealing in part with Faulkner, I made an effort to get the facts about Colonel Falkner straight. At the very outset I found that the authorities differed as to where he had been born. He was not from Mississippi, but had spent his boyhood in Saint Genevieve, Missouri, the old French Catholic and Royalist stronghold, where his father died. The story I eventually pieced together from official and semi-official records is full of such complexities, which I can only outline here.

Colonel Falkner was the hero of some obscure conspiracy in which he may be said to have represented human intelligence against murderous forces acting according to the traditional code of the time. While he was still working in the jail at Ripley he took part in the capture of a murderer named McCannon, who had been guilty of an atrocious crime, wiping out an entire family of emigrants camped for the night near Ripley. Young Falkner rescued McCannon from a mob attempting to lynch him, and after McCannon's trial sat in his cell and took down the story of his life, which he published. It brought him the first money he had ever earned.

McCannon's narrative mentioned several prominent men in nearby communities with whom he had been friendly in his earlier days, and these accused Falkner of insulting them by associating their names with the murderer. Before anything could come of this, however, the Mexican War began, and Falkner, still in his teens, or barely out of them, was elected first lieutenant of the local company of volunteers. In the company were his two close friends, Robert and Thomas Hindman, strong and powerful men, the sons of a local celebrity who was himself famous for his courage. Thomas Hindman was second lieutenant in the company, and Robert Hindman was a private. Falkner was wounded in Mexico, and after the war returned to Ripley, married, and began to practice law.

On May 8, 1849, Falkner was suddenly attacked by Robert Hindman. He knew no reason for Hindman's fury, and his account of his bewilderment is completely convincing. The men were standing beside a house, apparently the Hindman house, and Robert Hindman drew a pistol from his right-hand pants pocket and attempted to shoot. Falkner grabbed Hindman's wrist with both hands and tried to take the pistol away from him. Hindman was stronger, and threw Falkner back against the house, placed the gun two feet from Falkner's breast and pulled the trigger. The gun failed to fire. Falkner drew his knife. Hindman cocked his pistol and pulled the trigger. It failed to fire again.

In his old age, when Falkner wrote of a comparable incident, he described "some awful mystery, some deep-laid scheme of villainy" mixed up in the entire affair. The bullets in Hindman's gun did not fit exactly. The hammer did not quite strike the cap. There was never any good reason given for the sudden change in Hindman's feeling about Falkner. It was said that he had been lied to. His name had been proposed for membership in "a secret temperance order" to which Falkner belonged. Falkner spoke in favor of his admission. The speech was reported to Hindman as having been opposed to him. At any rate, at this delicate cross-hatching of plots, Hindman had been whipped into a murderous fury, and simultaneously, with diabolical cunning, been armed with a weapon that did not work.

When Hindman fired the third time, Falkner stabbed him. Hindman died at once. Falkner was arrested and charged with his murder.

The conflict split the town in the way that the provocations before the Civil War split the North and the South. The trial was not held until the next regular session of the court, which was in February, 1851. In the meantime Falkner's wife died, after bearing him a son.

Thomas Hindman made his maiden speech as a lawyer for the prosecution at Falkner's trial. But the evidence made out a clear case of self-defense; and Falkner was acquitted.

As he stepped from the courtroom into the street, Thomas Hindman attacked him. Again only defending himself, Falkner killed a man named Morris, a friend of Hindman who had joined the fight on Hindman's side.

He was again arrested, tried for the murder of Morris, and acquitted.

The conflict had now lasted almost two years. At least two deaths, and four attempted murders, are a part of the public record, and it is probable, from the nature of the times and the community, that there were many more. The number of dead bodies lying about, the appalling ferocity of the attacks, the intimations of diabolic plotting, the obstinate refusal of Falkner to let himself be killed, and his curious manner, almost of embarrassment, that he had suddenly become so unpopular, the growing awe of the community as the signs multiplied that he bore a charmed life— all these contribute an element of exaggeration, almost of comedy, to the somber sequence of happenings. For two years Falkner had steadily refused to give way to hysteria over the violence that had focused upon him; he insisted that he had done the Hindmans no wrong and knew of no reason to fight; and he maintained his sanity under the almost intolerable pressure of a social code he refused to follow.

After his second trial, as Falkner entered the dining room of the Ripley Hotel, Thomas Hindman tried to shoot him across the table. But

Hindman dropped his gun, which fired as it struck the floor, the bullet entering the ceiling over Falkner's head. Colonel Falkner drew his own gun. He did not shoot, but "merely required Hindman to let his pistol remain where it was, telling him he did not want to shed any more blood, and he was determined not to do it when he could avoid it without giving up his own life."

Hindman challenged him to a duel, and Falkner accepted, but set terms that revealed his disgust and revulsion, stipulating that there should be no seconds or surgeons, and only one witness, who was to do nothing except keep out of the way; each man was to be armed with two pistols at fifty paces, and at the word they were to advance on each other, firing as often as they wished or were able to continue. The witness chosen was Colonel Gallaway, an editor of the *Memphis Appeal*. He became convinced that Falkner knew of no cause for the duel, and succeeded in preventing it, Hindman leaving Mississippi and settling in Arkansas.

Thereafter, Colonel Falkner's life was roughly like that of Colonel Sartoris in William Faulkner's novels, save that throughout it he stood as an exponent of common sense against the extravagant and artificial conventions of the Old South.

Nor was his death comparable to that of Colonel Sartoris in the Faulkner cycle of novels. The Jackson, Mississippi, *Clarion-Ledger* of November 14, 1889, carried this account of it:

### DEATH OF COL. W. C. FALKNER

A terrible tragedy was enacted at Ripley on Tuesday afternoon of last week—the widely and well-known Col. W. C. Falkner being the victim. Various and conflicting accounts have been published. A dispatch to the *Appeal* says:

At the time of the occurrence Col. Falkner was standing on the public square in Ripley, talking to his friend Thomas Rucker, about sawing some timber. Mr. J. H. Thurmond approached Falkner and without exchanging a word pulled out a pistol and pointed it at Col. Falkner who exclaimed, "What do you mean, Dick? Don't shoot!" but Thurmond fired and Falkner fell.

After Dr. Carter, his son-in-law, wiped the blood from his face while he was still sitting on the pavement, he (Falkner) turned to Thurmond, who was near him, and said: "Dick, what did you do it for?" J. L. Walker, Elisha Bryant, Tom Rucker and John Smith were all present and saw what occurred. Mr. Rucker was so close to Col. Falkner that his face was powder burned by Thurmond's pistol. Col. Falkner had no weapon on his person, not even a pocket knife. The ball, .44-calibre, entered the mouth, ranged from the tongue, breaking the jaw bone, and lodged in the right side of the neck under the ear. Col. Falkner died at 11 o'clock.

Thurmond was tried for murder and acquitted in one of the most sensational cases in the history of Northern Mississippi. He left the state, and established another fortune in the textile industry in North Carolina. The Falkners also left Ripley, selling the railroad, and beginning the series of moves that eventually led them to Oxford.

If we are to criticize fiction, as Faulkner's is criticized, in terms of its mythology, we are faced with the problem of evaluating the myth, which in this case is the myth of the Old South. Colonel Falkner—who as Colonel Sartoris in Faulkner's novels is made to embody that myth, of the traditional Southern aristocrat—lived in almost direct opposition to the old patterns of Southern life.

The aristocracy was utterly unable to comprehend the moral complexities of Colonel Falkner's position as opposed to its own black-and-white simplicities. Indeed, it seems to me the conventional-heroic emphasis of Southern literature and history—of the Southern myth—is inadequate when confronted with the confused human mixtures of tragedy and comedy in a story like that of Colonel Falkner's two-year ordeal in Ripley. In his story one sees the code of the aristocrats, the landowners, the military heroes—Faulkner's Sartorises—breaking down when set over against the ethical standards of the businessmen and industrialists, the enterprising and peaceful element in the Old South to which the real Colonel Falkner belonged.

# II. The Work:

## Studies of the Work as a Whole

### A. Faulkner on Himself

## WILLIAM FAULKNER: AN INTERVIEW

### JEAN STEIN

INTERVIEWER: Mr. Faulkner, you were saying a while ago that you don't like interviews.

FAULKNER: The reason I don't like interviews is that I seem to react violently to personal questions. If the questions are about the work, I try to answer them. When they are about me, I may answer or I may not, but even if I do, if the same question is asked tomorrow, the answer may be different.

INTERVIEWER: How about yourself as a writer?

FAULKNER: If I had not existed, someone else would have written me, Hemingway, Dostoevsky, all of us. Proof of that is that there are about three candidates for the authorship of Shakespeare's plays. But what is important is *Hamlet* and *Midsummer Night's Dream,* not who wrote them, but that somebody did. The artist is of no importance. Only what he creates is important, since there is nothing new to be said. Shakespeare, Balzac, Homer have all written about the same things, and if they had lived one thousand or two thousand years longer, the publishers wouldn't have needed anyone since.

INTERVIEWER: But even if there seems nothing more to be said, isn't perhaps the individuality of the writer important?

FAULKNER: Very important to himself. Everybody else should be too busy with the work to care about the individuality.

INTERVIEWER: And your contemporaries?

FAULKNER: All of us failed to match our dream of perfection. So

This conversation took place in New York City, *mid-winter,* early 1956. Reprinted with permission from the *Paris Review,* Spring, 1956, pp. 28-52.

I rate us on the basis of our splendid failure to do the impossible. In my opinion, if I could write all my work again, I am convinced that I would do it better, which is the healthiest condition for an artist. That's why he keeps on working, trying again; he believes each time that this time he will do it, bring it off. Of course he won't, which is why this condition is healthy. Once he did it, once he matched the work to the image, the dream, nothing would remain but to cut his throat, jump off the other side of that pinnacle of perfection into suicide. I'm a failed poet. Maybe every novelist wants to write poetry first, finds he can't, and then tries the short story, which is the most demanding form after poetry. And, failing at that, only then does he take up novel writing.

INTERVIEWER: Is there any possible formula to follow in order to be a good novelist?

FAULKNER: Ninety-nine per cent talent . . . 99 per cent discipline . . . 99 per cent work. He must never be satisfied with what he does. It never is as good as it can be done. Always dream and shoot higher than you know you can do. Don't bother just to be better than your contemporaries or predecessors. Try to be better than yourself. An artist is a creature driven by demons. He don't know why they choose him and he's usually too busy to wonder why. He is completely amoral in that he will rob, borrow, beg, or steal from anybody and everybody to get the work done.

INTERVIEWER: Do you mean the writer should be completely ruthless?

FAULKNER: The writer's only responsibility is to his art. He will be completely ruthless if he is a good one. He has a dream. It anguishes him so much he must get rid of it. He has no peace until then. Everything goes by the board: honor, pride, decency, security, happiness, all, to get the book written. If a writer has to rob his mother, he will not hesitate; the "Ode on a Grecian Urn" is worth any number of old ladies.

INTERVIEWER: Then could the *lack* of security, happiness, honor, be an important factor in the artist's creativity?

FAULKNER: No. They are important only to his peace and contentment, and art has no concern with peace and contentment.

INTERVIEWER: Then what would be the best environment for a writer?

FAULKNER: Art is not concerned with environment either; it doesn't care where it is. If you mean me, the best job that was ever offered to me was to become a landlord in a brothel. In my opinion it's the perfect milieu for an artist to work in. It gives him perfect economic freedom; he's free of fear and hunger; he has a roof over his head and nothing whatever to do except keep a few simple accounts and to go once every month and pay off the local police. The place is quiet during the morning hours, which is the best time of the day to work. There's enough social life in the evening, if he wishes to participate, to keep him from being bored; it gives him a certain standing in his society; he has nothing to do because the madam keeps the books; all the inmates of the house are females and would defer to him and call him "sir." All the bootleggers in the neighborhood would call him "sir." And he could call the police by their first names.

So the only environment the artist needs is whatever peace, whatever solitude, and whatever pleasure he can get at not too high a cost. All the wrong environment will do is run his blood pressure up; he will spend more time being frustrated or outraged. My own experience has been that the tools I need for my trade are paper, tobacco, food, and a little whisky.

INTERVIEWER: Bourbon, you mean?

FAULKNER: No, I ain't that particular. Between scotch and nothing, I'll take scotch.

INTERVIEWER: You mentioned economic freedom. Does the writer need it?

FAULKNER: No. The writer doesn't need economic freedom. All he needs is a pencil and some paper. I've never known anything good in writing to come from having accepted any free gift of money. The good writer never applies to a foundation. He's too busy writing something. If he isn't first rate he fools himself by saying he hasn't got time or economic freedom. Good art can come out of thieves, bootleggers, or horse swipes. People really are afraid to find out just how much hardship and poverty they can stand. They are afraid to find out how tough they are. Nothing can destroy the good writer. The only thing that can alter the good writer is death. Good ones don't have time to bother with success or getting rich. Success is feminine and like a woman; if you cringe before her, she will override you. So the way to treat her is to show her the back of your hand. Then maybe she will do the crawling.

INTERVIEWER: Can working for the movies hurt your own writing?

FAULKNER: Nothing can injure a man's writing if he's a first-rate writer. If a man is not a first-rate writer, there's not anything can help it much. The problem does not apply if he is not first rate, because he has already sold his soul for a swimming pool.

INTERVIEWER: Does a writer compromise in writing for the movies?

FAULKNER: Always, because a moving picture is by its nature a collaboration, and any collaboration is compromise because that is what the word means—to give and to take.

INTERVIEWER: Which actors do you like to work with most?

FAULKNER: Humphrey Bogart is the one I've worked with best. He and I worked together in *To Have and Have Not* and *The Big Sleep*.

INTERVIEWER: Would you like to make another movie?

FAULKNER: Yes, I would like to make one of George Orwell's *1984*. I have an idea for an ending which would prove the thesis I'm always hammering at: that man is indestructible because of his simple will to freedom.

INTERVIEWER: How do you get the best results in working for the movies?

FAULKNER: The moving-picture work of my own which seemed best to me was done by the actors and the writer throwing the script away and inventing the scene in actual rehearsal just before the camera turned. If I didn't take, or feel I was capable of taking, motion-picture work seriously, out of simple honesty to motion pictures and myself too, I would not have tried. But I know now that I will never be a good motion-picture writer; so that work will never have the urgency for me which my own medium has.

INTERVIEWER: Would you comment on that legendary Hollywood experience you were involved in?

FAULKNER: I had just completed a contract at MGM and was about to return home. The director I had worked with said, "If you would like another job here, just let me know and I will speak to the studio about a new contract." I thanked him and came home. About six months later I wired my director friend that I would like another job. Shortly after that I received a letter from my Hollywood agent enclosing my first week's paycheck. I was surprised because I had expected first to get an official notice or recall and a contract from the studio. I thought to myself the contract is delayed and will arrive in the next mail. Instead, a week later I got another letter from the agent, enclosing my second week's paycheck. That began in November 1932 and continued until May 1933. Then I received a telegram from the studio. It said: *William Faulkner, Oxford, Miss. Where are you? MGM Studio.*

I wrote out a telegram: *MGM Studio, Culver City, California. William Faulkner.*

The young lady operator said, "Where is the message, Mr. Faulkner?" I said, "That's it." She said, "The rule book says that I can't send it without a message, you have to say something." So we went through her samples and selected I forgot which one—one of the canned anniversary greeting messages. I sent that. Next was a long-distance telephone call from the studio directing me to get on the first airplane, go to New Orleans, and report to Director Browning. I could have got on a train in Oxford and been in New Orleans eight hours later. But I obeyed the studio and went to Memphis, where an airplane did occasionally go to New Orleans. Three days later one did.

I arrived at Mr. Browning's hotel about six p.m. and reported to him. A party was going on. He told me to get a good night's sleep and be ready for an early start in the morning. I asked him about the story. He said, "Oh, yes. Go to room so and so. That's the continuity writer. He'll tell you what the story is."

I went to the room as directed. The continuity writer was sitting in there alone. I told him who I was and asked him about the story. He said, "When you have written the dialogue I'll let you see the story." I went back to Browning's room and told him what had happened. "Go back," he said, "and tell that so-and-so—never mind, you get a good night's sleep so we can get an early start in the morning."

So the next morning in a very smart rented launch all of us except the continuity writer sailed down to Grand Isle, about a hundred miles away, where the picture was to be shot, reaching there just in time to eat lunch and have time to run the hundred miles back to New Orleans before dark.

That went on for three weeks. Now and then I would worry a little about the story, but Browning always said, "Stop worrying. Get a good night's sleep so we can get an early start tomorrow morning."

One evening on our return I had barely entered my room when the telephone rang. It was Browning. He told me to come to his room at once. I did so. He had a telegram. It said: *Faulkner is fired. MGM Studio.* "Don't worry," Browning said. "I'll call that so-and-so up this minute and not only make him put you back on the payroll but send you a written apology." There was a knock on the door. It was a page with another telegram. This one said: *Browning is fired. MGM Studio.* So I came back home. I presume Browning went somewhere too. I imagine that continuity writer is still sitting in a room somewhere with his weekly salary check clutched tightly in his hand. They never did finish the film. But they did build a shrimp village—a long platform on piles in the water with sheds built on it something like a wharf. The studio could have bought dozens of them for forty or fifty dollars apiece. Instead, they built one of their own, a false one. That is, a platform with a single wall on it, so that when you opened the door and stepped through it, you stepped right on off to the ocean itself. As they built it, on the first day, the Cajun fisherman paddled up in his narrow tricky pirogue made out of a hollow log. He would sit in it all day long in the broiling sun watching the strange white folks building this strange imitation platform. The next day he was back in the pirogue with his whole family, his wife nursing the baby, the other children, and the mother-in-law, all to sit all that day in the broiling sun to watch this foolish and incomprehensible activity. I was in New Orleans two or three years later and heard that the Cajun people were still coming in for miles to look at that imitation shrimp platform which a lot of white people had rushed in and built and then abandoned.

INTERVIEWER: You say that the writer must compromise in working for the motion pictures. How about his writing? Is he under any obligation to his reader?

FAULKNER: His obligation is to get the work done the best he can do it; whatever obligation he has left over after that he can spend any way he likes. I myself am too busy to care about the public. I have no time to wonder who is reading me. I don't care about John Doe's opinion on my or anyone else's work. Mine is the standard which has to be met, which is when the work makes me feel the way I do when I read *La Tentation de Saint Antoine,* or the Old Testament. They make me feel good. So does watching a bird make me feel good. You know that if I were reincarnated, I'd want to come back a buzzard. Nothing hates him or envies him or wants him or needs him. He is never bothered or in danger, and he can eat anything.

INTERVIEWER: What technique do you use to arrive at your standard?

FAULKNER: Let the writer take up surgery or bricklaying if he is interested in technique. There is no mechanical way to get the writing done, no short cut. The young writer would be a fool to follow a theory. Teach yourself by your own mistakes; people learn only by error. The good artist believes that nobody is good enough to give him advice. He has supreme vanity. No matter how much he admires the old writer, he wants to beat him.

INTERVIEWER: Then would you deny the validity of technique?

FAULKNER: By no means. Sometimes technique charges in and takes command of the dream before the writer himself can get his hands on it. That is *tour de force* and the finished work is simply a matter of fitting bricks neatly together, since the writer knows probably every single word right to the end before he puts the first one down. This happened with *As I Lay Dying.* It was not easy. No honest work is. It was simple in that all the material was already at hand. It took me just about six weeks in the spare time from a twelve-hour-a-day job at manual labor. I simply imagined a group of people and subjected them to the simple universal natural catastrophes, which are flood and fire, with a simple natural motive to give direction to their progress. But then, when technique does not intervene, in another sense writing is easier too. Because with me there is always a point in the book where the characters themselves rise up and take charge and finish the job—say somewhere about page 275. Of course I don't know what would happen if I finished the book on page 274. The quality an artist must have is objectivity in judging his work, plus the honesty and courage not to kid himself about it. Since none of my work has met my own standards, I must judge it on the basis of that one which caused me the most grief and anguish, as the mother loves the child who became the thief or murderer more than the one who became the priest.

  INTERVIEWER: What work is that?

  FAULKNER: *The Sound and the Fury.* I wrote it five separate times, trying to tell the story, to rid myself of the dream which would continue to anguish me until I did. It's a tragedy of two lost women: Caddy and her daughter. Dilsey is one of my own favorite characters, because she is brave, courageous, generous, gentle, and honest. She's much more brave and honest and generous than me.

  INTERVIEWER: How did *The Sound and the Fury* begin?

  FAULKNER: It began with a mental picture. I didn't realize at the time it was symbolical. The picture was of the muddy seat of a little girl's drawers in a pear tree, where she could see through a window where her grandmother's funeral was taking place and report what was happening to her brothers on the ground below. By the time I explained who they were and what they were doing and how her pants got muddy, I realized it would be impossible to get all of it into a short story and that it would have to be a book. And then I realized the symbolism of the soiled pants, and that image was replaced by the one of the fatherless and motherless girl climbing down the rainpipe to escape from the only home she had, where she had never been offered love or affection or understanding.

  I had already begun to tell the story through the eyes of the idiot child, since I felt that it would be more effective as told by someone capable only of knowing what happened, but not why. I saw that I had not told the story that time. I tried to tell it again, the same story through the eyes of another brother. That was still not it. I told it for the third time through the eyes of the third brother. That was still not it. I tried to gather the pieces together and fill in the gaps by making myself the spokesman. It was still not complete, not until fifteen years after the book was published, when I wrote as an appendix to another book the final effort to get the story told and off my mind, so that I myself could have some peace from it. It's the book I feel tenderest towards. I couldn't leave it alone, and I never could tell it right, though I tried hard and would like to try again, though I'd probably fail again.

INTERVIEWER: What emotion does Benjy arouse in you?

FAULKNER: The only emotion I can have for Benjy is grief and pity for all mankind. You can't feel anything for Benjy because he doesn't feel anything. The only thing I can feel about him personally is concern as to whether he is believable as I created him. He was a prologue, like the grave-digger in the Elizabethan dramas. He serves his purpose and is gone. Benjy is incapable of good and evil because he had no knowledge of good and evil.

INTERVIEWER: Could Benjy feel love?

FAULKNER: Benjy wasn't rational enough even to be selfish. He was an animal. He recognized tenderness and love though he could not have named them, and it was the threat to tenderness and love that caused him to bellow when he felt the change in Caddy. He no longer had Caddy; being an idiot he was not even aware that Caddy was missing. He knew only that something was wrong, which left a vacuum in which he grieved. He tried to fill that vacuum. The only thing he had was one of Caddy's discarded slippers. The slipper was his tenderness and love which he could not have named, but he knew only that it was missing. He was dirty because he couldn't coordinate and because dirt meant nothing to him. He could no more distinguish between dirt and cleanliness than between good and evil. The slipper gave him comfort even though he no longer remembered the person to whom it had once belonged, any more than he could remember why he grieved. If Caddy had reappeared he probably would not have known her.

INTERVIEWER: Does the narcissus given to Benjy have some significance?

FAULKNER: The narcissus was given to Benjy to distract his attention. It was simply a flower which happened to be handy that fifth of April. It was not deliberate.

INTERVIEWER: Are there any artistic advantages in casting the novel in the form of an allegory, as the Christian allegory you used in *A Fable?*

FAULKNER: Same advantage the carpenter finds in building square corners in order to build a square house. In *A Fable* the Christian allegory was the right allegory to use in that particular story, like an oblong square corner is the right corner with which to build on oblong rectangular house.

INTERVIEWER: Does that mean an artist can use Christianity simply as just another tool, as a carpenter would borrow a hammer?

FAULKNER: The carpenter we are speaking of never lacks that hammer. No one is without Christianity, if we agree on what we mean by the word. It is every individual's individual code of behavior by means of which he makes himself a better human being than his nature wants to be, if he followed his nature only. Whatever its symbol—cross or crescent or whatever—that symbol is man's reminder of his duty inside the human race. Its various allegories are the charts against which he measures himself and learns to know what he is. It cannot teach man to be good as the textbook teaches him mathematics. It shows him how to discover himself, evolve for himself a moral code and standard within his capacities and aspirations, by giving him a matchless example of suffering and sacrifice and the promise of hope. Writers have always drawn, and always will draw, upon the allegories of moral consciousness, for the reason that the allegories are matchless—the three men in *Moby Dick,* who represent the trinity of conscience: knowing nothing, knowing but not caring, knowing and caring. The same trinity is represented in *A Fable* by the young Jewish pilot officer, who said, "This is terrible. I refuse to accept it, even if I must refuse life to do so"; the old French Quartermaster General, who said, "This is terrible, but we can weep and bear it"; and the English battalion runner, who said, "This is terrible, I'm going to do something about it."

INTERVIEWER: Are the two unrelated themes in *The Wild Palms* brought together in one book for any symbolic purpose? Is it as certain critics intimate a kind of esthetic counterpoint, or is it merely haphazard?

FAULKNER: No, no. That was one story—the story of Charlotte Rittenmeyer and Harry Wilbourne, who sacrificed everything for love, and then lost that. I did not know it would be two separate stories until after I had started the book. When I reached the end of what is now the first section of *The Wild Palms,* I realized suddenly that something was missing, it needed emphasis, something to lift it like counterpoint in music. So I wrote on the "Old Man" story until "The Wild Palms" story rose back to pitch. Then I stopped the "Old Man" story at what is now its first section, and took up "The Wild Palms" story until it began again to sag. Then I raised it to pitch again with another section of its antithesis, which is the story of a man who got his love and spent the rest of the book fleeing from it, even to the extent of voluntarily going back to jail where he would be safe. They are only two stories by chance, perhaps necessity. The story is that of Charlotte and Wilbourne.

INTERVIEWER: How much of your writing is based on personal experience?

FAULKNER: I can't say. I never counted up. Because "how much" is not important. A writer needs three things, experience, observation, and imagination, any two of which, at times any one of which, can supply the lack of the others. With me, a story usually begins with a single idea or memory or mental picture. The writing of the story is simply a matter of working up to that moment, to explain why it happened or what it caused to follow. A writer is trying to create believable people in credible moving situations in the most moving way he can. Obviously he must use as one of his tools the environment which he knows. I would say that music is the easiest means in which to express, since it came first in man's experience and history. But since words are my talent, I must try to express clumsily in words what the pure music would have done better. That is, music would express better and simpler, but I prefer to use words, as I prefer to read rather than listen. I prefer silence to sound, and the image produced by words occurs in silence. That is, the thunder and the music of the prose take place in silence.

INTERVIEWER: Some people say they can't understand your writing, even after they read it two or three times. What approach would you suggest for them?

FAULKNER: Read it four times.

INTERVIEWER: You mentioned experience, observation, and imagination as being important for the writer. Would you include inspiration?

FAULKNER: I don't know anything about inspiration, because I don't know what inspiration is—I've heard about it, but I never saw it.

INTERVIEWER: As a writer you are said to be obsessed with violence.

FAULKNER: That's like saying the carpenter is obsessed with his hammer. Violence is simply one of the carpenter's tools. The writer can no more build with one tool than the carpenter can.

INTERVIEWER: Can you say how you started as a writer?

FAULKNER: I was living in New Orleans, doing whatever kind of work was necessary to earn a little money now and then. I met Sherwood Anderson. We would walk about the city in the afternoon and talk to people. In the evenings we would meet again and sit over a bottle or two while he talked and I listened. In the forenoon I would never see him. He was secluded, working. The next day we would repeat. I decided that if that was the life of a writer, then becoming a writer was the thing for me. So I began to write my first book. At once I found that writing was fun. I even forgot that I hadn't seen Mr. Anderson for three weeks until he walked in my door, the first time he ever came to see me, and said, "What's wrong? Are you mad at me?" I told him I was writing a book. He said, "My God," and walked out. When I finished the book—it was *Soldiers' Pay*—I met Mrs. Anderson on the street. She asked how the book was going, and I said I'd finished it. She said, "Sherwood says that he will make a trade with you. If he doesn't have to read your manuscript he will tell his publisher to accept it." I said, "Done," and that's how I became a writer.

INTERVIEWER: What were the kinds of work you were doing to earn that "little money now and then"?

FAULKNER: Whatever came up. I could do a little of almost anything —run boats, paint houses, fly airplanes. I never needed much money because living was cheap in New Orleans then, and all I wanted was a place to sleep, a little food, tobacco, and whisky. There were many things I could do for two or three days and earn enough money to live on for the rest of the month. By temperament I'm a vagabond and a tramp. I don't want money badly enough to work for it. In my opinion it's a shame that there is so much work in the world. One of the saddest things is that the only thing a man can do for eight hours a day, day after day, is work. You can't eat eight hours a day nor drink for eight hours a day nor make love for eight hours—all you can do for eight hours is work. Which is the reason why man makes himself and everybody else so miserable and unhappy.

INTERVIEWER: You must feel indebted to Sherwood Anderson, but how do you regard him as a writer?

FAULKNER: He was the father of my generation of American writers and the tradition of American writing which our successors will carry on. He has never received his proper evaluation. Dreiser is his older brother and Mark Twain the father of them both.

INTERVIEWER:* What about the European writers of that period?

FAULKNER: The two great men in my time were Mann and Joyce. You should approach Joyce's *Ulysses* as the illiterate Baptist preacher approaches the Old Testament: with faith.

INTERVIEWER: How did you get your background in the Bible?

* This exchange was not in the *Paris Review* interview, but was added to the version printed in *Writers at Work* (New York, 1958).

FAULKNER: My Great-Grandfather Murry was a kind and gentle man, to us children anyway. That is, although he was a Scot, he was (to us) neither especially pious nor stern either: he was simply a man of inflexible principles. One of them was, everybody, children on up through all adults present, had to have a verse from the Bible ready and glib at tongue-tip when we gathered at the table for breakfast each morning; if you didn't have your scripture verse ready, you didn't have any breakfast; you would be excused long enough to leave the room and swot one up (there was a maiden aunt, a kind of sergeant-major for this duty, who retired with the culprit and gave him a brisk breezing which carried him over the jump next time).

It had to be an authentic, correct verse. While we were little, it could be the same one, once you had it down good, morning after morning, until you got a little older and bigger, when one morning (by this time you would be pretty glib at it, galloping through without even listening to yourself since you were already five or ten minutes ahead, already among the ham and steak and fried chicken and grits and sweet potatoes and two or three kinds of hot bread) you would suddenly find his eyes on you—very blue, very kind and gentle, and even now not stern so much as inflexible; and next morning you had a new verse. In a way, that was when you discovered that your childhood was over; you had outgrown it and entered the world.*

INTERVIEWER: Do you read your contemporaries?

FAULKNER: No, the books I read are the ones I knew and loved when I was a young man and to which I return as you do to old friends: the Old Testament, Dickens, Conrad, Cervantes—*Don Quixote.* I read that every year, as some do the Bible. Flaubert, Balzac—he created an intact world of his own, a bloodstream running through twenty books—Dostoevsky, Tolstoi, Shakespeare. I read Melville occasionally, and of the poets Marlowe, Campion, Jonson, Herrick, Donne, Keats, and Shelley. I still read Housman. I've read these books so often that I don't always begin at page one and read on to the end. I just read one scene, or about one character, just as you'd meet and talk to a friend for a few minutes.

INTERVIEWER: And Freud?

FAULKNER: Everybody talked about Freud when I lived in New Orleans, but I have never read him. Neither did Shakespeare. I doubt if Melville did either, and I'm sure Moby Dick didn't.

INTERVIEWER: Do you ever read mystery stories?

FAULKNER: I read Simenon because he reminds me something of Chekhov.

INTERVIEWER: What about your favorite characters?

FAULKNER: My favorite characters are Sarah Gamp—a cruel, ruthless woman, a drunkard, opportunist, unreliable, most of her character was bad, but at least it was character; Mrs. Harris, Falstaff, Prince Hal, Don Quixote, and Sancho of course. Lady Macbeth I always admire. And Bottom, Ophelia, and Mercutio—both he and Mrs. Gamp coped with life, didn't ask any favors, never whined. Huck Finn, of course, and Jim. Tom Sawyer I never liked much—an awful prig. And then I like Sut Lovingood, from a book written by George Harris about 1840 or '50 in the Tennessee mountains. He had no illusions about himself, did the best he could; at certain times he was a coward and knew it and wasn't ashamed; he never blamed his misfortunes on anyone and never cursed God for them.

INTERVIEWER: Would you comment on the future of the novel?

FAULKNER: I imagine as long as people will continue to read novels, people will continue to write them, or vice versa; unless of course the pictorial magazines and comic strips finally atrophy man's capacity to read, and literature really is on its way back to the picture writing in the Neanderthal cave.

INTERVIEWER: And how about the function of the critics?

FAULKNER: The artist doesn't have time to listen to the critics. The ones who want to be writers read the reviews, the ones who want to write don't have the time to read reviews. The critic too is trying to say "Kilroy was here." His function is not directed toward the artist himself. The artist is a cut above the critic, for the artist is writing something which will move the critic. The critic is writing something which will move everybody but the artist.

INTERVIEWER: So you never feel the need to discuss your work with anyone?

FAULKNER: No, I am too busy writing it. It has got to please me and if it does I don't need to talk about it. If it doesn't please me, talking about it won't improve it, since the only thing to improve it is to work on it some more. I am not a literary man but only a writer. I don't get any pleasure from talking shop.

INTERVIEWER: Critics claim that blood relationships are central in your novels.

FAULKNER: That is an opinion and, as I have said, I don't read critics. I doubt that a man trying to write about people is any more interested in blood relationships than in the shape of their noses, unless they are necessary to help the story move. If the writer concentrates on what he does need to be interested in, which is the truth and the human heart, he won't have much time left for anything else, such as ideas and facts like the shape of noses or blood relationships, since in my opinion ideas and facts have very little connection with truth.

INTERVIEWER: Critics also suggest that your characters never consciously choose between good and evil.

FAULKNER: Life is not interested in good and evil. Don Quixote was constantly choosing between good and evil, but then he was choosing in his dream state. He was mad. He entered reality only when he was so busy trying to cope with people that he had no time to distinguish between good and evil. Since people exist only in life, they must devote their time simply to being alive. Life is motion, and motion is concerned with what makes man move—which is ambition, power, pleasure. What time a man can devote to morality, he must take by force from the motion of which he is a part. He is compelled to make choices between good and evil sooner or later, because moral conscience demands that from him in order that he can live with himself tomorrow. His moral conscience is the curse he had to accept from the gods in order to gain from them the right to dream.

INTERVIEWER: Could you explain more what you mean by motion in relation to the artist?

FAULKNER: The aim of every artist is to arrest motion, which is life, by artificial means and hold it fixed so that a hundred years later, when a stranger looks at it, it moves again since it is life. Since man is mortal, the only immortality possible for him is to leave something behind him that is immortal since it will always move. This is the artist's way of scribbling "Kilroy was here" on the wall of the final and irrevocable oblivion through which he must someday pass.

INTERVIEWER: It has been said by Malcolm Cowley that your characters carry a sense of submission to their fate.

FAULKNER: That is his opinion. I would say that some of them do and some of them don't, like everybody else's characters. I would say that Lena Grove in *Light in August* coped pretty well with hers. It didn't really matter to her in her destiny whether her man was Lucas Birch or not. It was her destiny to have a husband and children and she knew it, and so she went out and attended to it without asking help from anyone. She was the captain of her soul. One of the calmest, sanest speeches I ever heard was when she said to Byron Bunch at the very instant of repulsing his final desperate and despairing attempt at rape, "Ain't you ashamed? You might have woke the baby." She was never for one moment confused, frightened, alarmed. She did not even know that she didn't need pity. Her last speech for example: "Here I ain't been traveling but a month, and I'm already in Tennessee. My, my, a body does get around."

The Bundren family in *As I Lay Dying* pretty well coped with theirs. The father having lost his wife would naturally need another one, so he got one. At one blow he not only replaced the family cook, he acquired a gramophone to give them all pleasure while they were resting. The pregnant daughter failed this time to undo her condition, but she was not discouraged. She intended to try again, and even if they all failed right up to the last, it wasn't anything but just another baby.

INTERVIEWER: And Mr. Cowley says you find it hard to create characters between the ages of twenty and forty who are sympathetic.

FAULKNER: People between twenty and forty are not sympathetic. The child has the capacity to do but it can't know. It only knows when it is no longer able to do—after forty. Between twenty and forty the will of the child to do gets stronger, more dangerous, but it has not begun to learn to know yet. Since his capacity to do is forced into channels of evil through environment and pressures, man is strong before he is moral. The world's anguish is caused by people between twenty and forty. The people around my home who have caused all the interracial tension—the Milams and the Bryants (in the Emmet Till murder) and the gangs of Negroes who grab a white woman and rape her in revenge, the Hitlers, Napoleons, Lenins—all these people are symbols of human suffering and anguish, all of them between twenty and forty.

INTERVIEWER: You gave a statement to the papers at the time of the Emmet Till killing. Have you anything to add to it here?

FAULKNER: No, only to repeat what I said before: that if we Americans are to survive it will have to be because we choose and elect and defend to be first of all Americans; to present to the world one homogeneous and unbroken front, whether of white Americans or black ones or purple or blue or green. Maybe the purpose of this sorry and tragic error committed in my native Mississippi by two white adults on an afflicted Negro child is to prove to us whether or not we deserve to survive. Because if we in America have reached that point in our desperate culture when we must murder children, no matter for what reason or what color, we don't deserve to survive, and probably won't.

INTERVIEWER: What happened to you between *Soldiers' Pay* and *Sartoris*—that is, what caused you to begin the Yoknapatawpha saga?

FAULKNER: With *Soldiers' Pay* I found out writing was fun. But I found out afterward that not only each book had to have a design but the whole output or sum of an artist's work had to have a design. With *Soldiers' Pay* and *Mosquitoes* I wrote for the sake of writing because it was fun. Beginning with *Sartoris* I discovered that my own little postage stamp of native soil was worth writing about and that I would never live long enough to exhaust it, and that by sublimating the actual into the apocryphal I would have complete liberty to use whatever talent I might have to its absolute top. It opened up a gold mine of other people, so I created a cosmos of my own. I can move these people around like God, not only in space but in time too. The fact that I have moved my characters around in time successfully, at least in my own estimation, proves to me my own theory that time is a fluid condition which has no existence except in the momentary avatars of individual people. There is no such thing as *was*—only *is*. If *was* existed, there would be no grief or sorrow. I like to think of the world I created as being a kind of keystone in the universe; that, small as that keystone is, if it were ever taken away the universe itself would collapse. My last book will be the Doomsday Book, the Golden Book, of Yoknapatawpha County. Then I shall break the pencil and I'll have to stop.

## B. The Growth of Faulkner Criticism

## FAULKNER'S MYTHOLOGY

### GEORGE MARION O'DONNELL

i

WILLIAM FAULKNER is really a traditional moralist, in the best sense. One principle holds together his thirteen books of prose—including his new novel, *The Wild Palms*—giving his work unity and giving it, at times, the significance that belongs to great myth. That principle is the Southern social-economic-ethical tradition which Mr. Faulkner possesses naturally, as a part of his sensibility.

Reprinted with permission from *The Kenyon Review*, Summer, 1939, pp. 285-99.

However, Mr. Faulkner is a traditional man in a modern South. All around him the antitraditional forces are at work; and he lives among evidences of their past activity. He could not fail to be aware of them. It is not strange, then, that his novels are, primarily, a series of related myths (or aspects of a single myth) built around the conflict between traditionalism and the antitraditional modern world in which it is immersed.

In a rearrangement of the novels, say for a collected edition, *The Unvanquished* might well stand first; for the action occurs earlier, historically, than in any other of the books, and it objectifies, in the essential terms of Mr. Faulkner's mythology, the central dramatic tension of his work. On one side of the conflict there are the Sartorises, recognizable human beings who act traditionally. Against them the invading Northern armies, and their diversified allies in the reconstruction era, wage open war, aiming to make the traditional actions of the Sartorises impossible.

The invaders are unable to cope with the Sartorises; but their invasion provides another antagonist with an occasion within which his special anti-Sartoris talent makes him singularly powerful. This antagonist is the landless poor-white horse trader, Ab Snopes; his special talent is his low cunning as an *entrepreneur*. He acts without regard for the legitimacy of his means; he has no ethical code. In the crisis brought about by the war, he is enabled to use a member of the Sartoris family for his own advantage because, for the first time, he can be useful to the Sartorises. Moreover, he is enabled to make this Sartoris (Mrs. Rosa Millard) betray herself into an act of self-interest such as his, and to cause her death while using her as his tool.

The characters and the conflict are particular and credible. But they are also mythological. In Mr. Faulkner's mythology there are two kinds of characters; they are Sartorises or Snopeses, whatever the family names may be. And in the spiritual geography of Mr. Faulkner's work there are two worlds: the Sartoris world and the Snopes world. In all of his successful books, he is exploring the two worlds in detail, dramatizing the inevitable conflict between them.

It is a universal conflict. The Sartorises act traditionally; that is to say, they act always with an ethically responsible will. They represent vital morality, humanism. Being antitraditional, the Snopeses are immoral from the Sartoris point of view. But the Snopeses do not recognize this point of view; acting only for self-interest, they acknowledge no ethical duty. Really, then, they are amoral; they represent naturalism or animalism. And

the Sartoris-Snopes conflict is fundamentally a struggle between humanism
and naturalism.

As a universal conflict, it is important only philosophically. But it is
important artistically, in this instance, because Mr. Faulkner has dramatized it convincingly in the terms of particular history and of actual life
in his own part of the South—in the terms of his own tradition.

In *Sartoris,* which was published before *The Unvanquished* but which
follows it in historical sequence, the conflict is between young Bayard
Sartoris (the grandson of the Bayard Sartoris who was a youth in *The
Unvanquished*) and the Snopes world of the 1920's. "General Johnston
or General Forrest wouldn't have took a Snopes into his army at all," one
of the characters says; but, significantly enough, one Flem Snopes has come,
by way of local political usefulness, to be vice-president of old Bayard
Sartoris' bank. Young Bayard's brother, John, has been killed in a war;
but it is clear that it was a Snopes war and not a Sartoris war. Bayard
himself is extremely conscious of his family's doom; he feels cheated because he did not die violently, in the tradition, like his brother; finally, he
kills himself, taking up an aeroplane that he knows will crash.

The Snopes world has done more than oppose the Sartorises. It has
weakened them internally (as it weakened Rosa Millard) in using them
for its advantage; it has made them self-conscious, queer, psychologically
tortured. Bayard Sartoris has something of the traditional instinct for noble
and disinterested action, under a vital ethical code. But the strength is so
warped internally by the psychological effects of the Snopes world upon it,
and it is so alien to the habitual actions of that world, that it can only
manifest itself in meaningless violence, ending in self-destruction.

The same pattern recurs, varied somewhat and handled in miniature,
in the short story about the Sartorises—"There Was a Queen." Here the
real conflict centers in Narcissa Benbow, the widow of young Bayard
Sartoris, who has given herself to a detective in order to recover from his
possession a collection of obscene letters that one of the Snopeses had
written to her anonymously and afterwards stolen. The consciousness of
Narcissa's deed kills the embodiment of the virile tradition, old Miss Jenny
Sartoris (Mrs. DuPré). Narcissa's yielding to the detective is the result of
the *formalization* of one aspect of her traditional morality—her pride—
through the constant opposition of the Snopes world to it; this formalization allows the Snopes world to betray her into antitraditionalism by creating a situation in which she must make a formalized response. It is a
highly significant tactic. For the moment a tradition begins to be formalized

into a code, it commences to lose vitality; when it is entirely formalized, it is dead—it becomes pseudo-tradition.

As early as *Soldiers' Pay* (1926) the same theme is the basis for Mr. Faulkner's organization of experience; and it is the best possible indication of the urgency of the theme with him that it should be central in his first novel. Mahon, the old Episcopal clergyman, conscious of sin, tolerant of human weakness, is still unaware of the vital opponent to his formalized, and so impotent, tradition—the amorality with which history has surrounded him. Donald Mahon, his son, is brought home from the World War, dying; in him, the minister's code has faced antitraditional history. Because Donald is not dead, the conflict must continue; locally, it is between the preacher and Cecily Saunders (Donald's fiancée before he went to war) with her family and associates who are typical of the new Jazz Era. Obviously, Cecily's world of jazz and flappers and sleek-haired jelly-beans represents the same antitraditional historical movement that brought Flem Snopes into Bayard Sartoris' bank. The names and the settings are different; that is all.

In *The Sound and the Fury*, Quentin Compson represents all that is left of the Sartoris tradition. The rest of his family have either succumbed entirely to the Snopes world, like Jason Compson, or else have drugs to isolate them from it—Mr. Compson his fragments of philosophy, Uncle Maury his liquor, Mrs. Compson her religion and her invalidism, Benjy his idiocy. But Quentin's very body is "an empty hall echoing with sonorous defeated names."[1] His world is peopled with "baffled, outraged ghosts"; and although Quentin himself is "still too young to deserve yet to be a ghost," he is one of them. However, it is evident that Quentin's traditionalism is far gone in the direction of formalization, with its concomitant lack of vitality; he is psychologically kin to Bayard Sartoris and to Narcissa Benbow. When he discovers that his sister Candace has been giving herself to the town boys of Jefferson, Mississippi, and is pregnant, he attempts to change her situation by telling their father that he has committed incest with her. It is a key incident. Quentin is attempting to transform Candace's yielding to the amorality of the Snopes world into a sin, within the Sartoris morality; but the means he employs are more nearly pseudo-traditional and romantic than traditional; and he fails.

Quentin tells his father: "It was to isolate her out of the loud world

1. The quotations are from *Absalom, Absalom!*, the other novel in which Quentin appears; but they are necessary for an understanding of his function in *The Sound and the Fury*.

so that it would have to flee us of necessity." Precisely. The loud world is the Snopes world, with which the Compson house has become thoroughly infected and to which it is subject. Quentin is really *striving toward the condition of tragedy* for his family; he is trying to transform meaningless degeneracy into significant doom. But because his moral code is no longer vital, he fails and ends in a kind of escapism, breaking his watch to put himself beyond time, finally killing himself to escape consciousness. Only he is aware of the real meaning of his struggle, which sets up the dramatic tension in *The Sound and the Fury*.

In a way, Quentin's struggle is Mr. Faulkner's own struggle as an artist. In *Sartoris,* Mr. Faulkner wrote of the name: "There is death in the sound of it, and a glamorous fatality." Sartoris—all that the name implies— is the tragic hero of his work; it is doomed, like any tragic hero. But the doom toward which the Sartoris world moves should be a noble one. In *Absalom, Absalom!,* although apparently with great difficulty, as if he were wrestling with the Snopes world all the while, Mr. Faulkner finally achieves the presentation of a kind of "glamorous fatality" for the Sartoris world— embodied in Thomas Sutpen and his house.

The book is really a summary of the whole career of the tradition— its rise, its fatal defects, its opponents, its decline, and its destruction. The action is of heroic proportions. The figures are larger than life; but, as Mr. T. S. Eliot has suggested of Tourneur's characters, they are all distorted to scale, so that the whole action has a self-subsistent reality. And the book ends with a ritualistic purgation of the doomed house, by fire, which is as nearly a genuine tragic scene as anything in modern fiction.

For the first time, Mr. Faulkner makes explicit here the contrast between traditional (Sartoris) man and modern (Snopes) man, dissociated into a sequence of animal functions, lacking in unity under essential morality. One of the characters says of traditional men:

People too as we are, and victims too as we are, but victims of a different circumstance, simpler and therefore, integer for integer, larger, more heroic and the figures therefore more heroic too, not dwarfed and involved but distinct, uncomplex who had the gift of living once or dying once instead of being diffused and scattered creatures drawn blindly from a grab bag and assembled.

It was the world of these "diffused and scattered creatures" in which Quentin Compson lived; and it was the effort not to be "diffused and scattered"—to transform his own family's doom into the proportions of

the world of Sutpen and Sartoris—that led to his death. But it is significant
that it should be Quentin through whose gradual understanding the story of
Sutpen is told, and that it should be Quentin who watches the final destruction of Sutpen's house. For Sutpen's tradition was defective, but it was
not formalized as Quentin's was; and his story approaches tragedy.

*As I Lay Dying* stands a little apart from the rest of Mr. Faulkner's
novels, but it is based upon the philosophical essence of his Sartoris-Snopes
theme—the struggle between humanism and naturalism. The naïf hill folk
who appear in the book are poor and ungraceful, certainly; they are of low
mentality; sexually, they are almost animalistic. But when Anse Bundren
promises his dying wife that he will bury her in Jefferson, he sets up for
himself an ethical duty which he recognizes as such—though not in these
terms. It is the fulfillment of this obligation, in spite of constant temptation
to abandon it, and in spite of multiplied difficulties put in his way by nature
itself, that makes up the action of the novel.

Fundamentally, *As I Lay Dying* is a legend; and the procession of
ragged, depraved hillmen, carrying Addie Bundren's body through water
and through fire to the cemetery in Jefferson, while people flee from the
smell and buzzards circle overhead—this progress is not unlike that of the
medieval soul toward redemption. The allegories of Alanus de Insulis and
the visions of Sister Hildegard of Bingen would yield a good many parallels.
On a less esoteric plane, however, the legend is more instructive for us.
Because they are simpler in mind and live more remotely from the Snopes
world than the younger Sartorises and Compsons, the Bundrens are able
to carry a genuine act of traditional morality through to its end. They are
infected with amorality; but it is the amorality of physical nature, not the
artificial, self-interested amorality of the Snopeses. More heroism is possible among them than among the inhabitants of Jefferson.

2

So far I have been concerned mainly with exegesis, aiming to show
how fundamental the Sartoris-Snopes conflict is in Mr. Faulkner's novels.
To provide such exegesis of the six books that I have discussed, it is necessary to do violence to the fictions themselves, by abstraction. This is the
significant point, for criticism; because the necessity for abstraction is
evidence that, in these six books, the theme is really informed in the
fictions or myths.

The Sartorises and the Sutpens and the Compsons do not represent
the tradition in its various degrees of vitality, as *x, y,* and *z* may represent

a sequence of numbers in mathematics. They are people, in a certain way of life, at a particular time, confronted with real circumstances and with items of history. And their humanity (or their illusion of humanity, on a larger-than-life scale) is not limited, ultimately, by their archetypal significance. Moreover, in each book there is a dramatically credible fiction which remains particular and (sometimes with difficulty) coherent as action, even though the pattern is true, in a larger sense, as myth. In short, Mr. Faulkner's successful work has the same kind, though certainly not the same degree, of general meaning that is to be found in Dante's *Divina Commedia* or in the *Electra* of Sophocles. The only close parallel in American literature is the better work of Nathaniel Hawthorne, whom Mr. Faulkner resembles in a great many ways.

However, as I have suggested already, a literary and personal tension arises, for William Faulkner the artist, out of the same conflict that is central in his work. This tension sets up his crucial problem as an artist, and his failures result from it. In so far as he can sustain his inherent tradition, he is enabled to project the central conflict in the valid terms of myth. However, as a Sartoris artist in a Snopes world, he is constantly subject to opposition that tends to force him into the same kind of reactionary formalization of tradition that betrayed Narcissa Benbow as a character. When, because of the opposition and his reaction to it, Mr. Faulkner writes as *formal* traditionalist rather than as *vital* traditionalist, he writes allegory. Allegory might be defined, indeed, as formalized—and therefore dead— myth.

*Sanctuary,* which is unfortunately the most widely known and misunderstood of Mr. Faulkner's novels, is a failure of this kind. In simple terms, the pattern of the allegory is something like this: Southern Womanhood Corrupted but Undefiled (Temple Drake), in the company of the Corrupted Tradition (Gowan Stevens, a professional Virginian), falls into the clutches of amoral Modernism (Popeye), which is itself impotent, but which with the aid of its strong ally Natural Lust ("Red") rapes Southern Womanhood unnaturally and then seduces her so satisfactorily that her corruption is total, and she becomes the tacit ally of Modernism. Meanwhile Pore White Trash (Godwin) has been accused of the crime which he, with the aid of the Naïf Faithful (Tawmmy), actually tried to prevent. The Formalized Tradition (Horace Benbow), perceiving the true state of affairs, tries vainly to defend Pore White Trash. However, Southern Womanhood is so hopelessly corrupted that she wilfully sees Pore White Trash convicted and lynched; she is then carried off by Wealth (Judge

Drake) to meaningless escape in European luxury. Modernism, carrying in it from birth its own impotence and doom, submits with masochistic pleasure to its own destruction for the one crime that it has not yet committed—Revolutionary Destruction of Order (the murder of the Alabama policeman, for which the innocent Popeye is executed).

Here Mr. Faulkner's theme is forced into allegory, not projected as myth. In this sense, the book is a "cheap idea"—as Mr. Faulkner himself calls it in his preface to the Modern Library edition. Its defects are those of allegory in general. The characters are distorted, being more nearly grotesques than human beings; and they are not distorted to scale (Temple is only a type; Benbow is a recognizably human character, and so is Miss Reba, the keeper of the bawdy house); accordingly, the book lacks the "self-subsistent reality" which may be found in a work like *Absalom, Absalom!* It is powerful; and it contains some passages of bawdy folk humor that are of a high order of excellence; but it is fundamentally a caricature.

When *Light in August* appeared in England, an anonymous reviewer for *The Illustrated London News* suggested that it might be a parable of the struggle between good and evil. The notion is not entirely fanciful. But, more specifically, the book might be considered as an allegory based upon Mr. Faulkner's usual theme, with the clergyman, Hightower, standing for the Formalized Tradition. The simple-hearted Byron Bunch corresponds with the naïf traditionalist, Anse Bundren; Christmas, the mulatto, is a Snopes character, as is his partner, Lucas Burch, the seducer of Lena Grove. And the pregnant Lena might represent, vaguely, life itself, which Byron and Hightower are futilely attempting to protect from Lucas Burch and Christmas and their kind.

But the book is not so transparently allegorical as *Sanctuary*; indeed, it is a confused allegory in which realism is present as well. It fails, partly, because of this confusion, which never permits the two sides of the conflict really to join the issue. But it fails, even more clearly, because of the disproportionate emphasis upon Christmas—who ought to be the antagonist but who becomes, like Milton's Satan, the real protagonist in the novel.

This defines the second general type of failure in Mr. Faulkner's work: Mr. Faulkner is unable to sustain his traditionalism at all, and the forces of antitraditionalism become the protagonists.

The discussion reaches a dangerous point here. Since the time of Flaubert, at least, it has been customary to hold the view that one mark of a novelist's craft is his skill in creating all of his characters in the round and in maintaining an equal sympathy for all of them. However, it is not necessary to repudiate this view to suggest that there is a difference in kind between Flaubert's studies of human character in the behavior of the French bourgeois world and Mr. Faulkner's books, which are essentially myths, built around the conflict of two different worlds, to one of which Mr. Faulkner belongs as an artist, though he is of physical necessity a citizen of the other.

When one possesses traditional values of conduct, he has naturally a kind of hierarchy of sympathy, dependent upon the values, which makes him more or less sympathetic to characters in proportion as they are or are not traditional. Mr. Faulkner appears to maintain such a hierarchy in the greater part of his work; although he projects the characters of the Snopes world as clearly as he projects those of the Sartoris world, in his better books he is always seeing them and determining their proportionate stature from the Sartoris point of view.

But in *Light in August* the proportionate dramatic content of the characters is the reverse of the norm set up by the other books; and there is a corollary confusion of the whole scheme of traditional values. The Sartoris characters, like Hightower, are vague or typical; Christmas, the Snopes character, dominates sympathy, and his tortured amorality determines the ethical tone of the book. In proportion as Christmas becomes the protagonist, the Snopes world, with its total lack of values, seems to have supplanted the Sartoris values *within the artist himself,* although against his will. And the confused, malproportioned fiction, wavering between realism and allegory, seems to be the artistic issue of Mr. Faulkner's violent—but, in this case, unavailing—effort to maintain the Sartoris point of view in his work.

Mr. Faulkner never gives his whole consent to such a confusion of values. That he is not content to remain within the characters of his protagonists when they are antitraditional, but must go outside them for "purple passages," seems to be evidence of this fact. *Pylon* is a case in point. It is a study of the effect of machinery upon human beings; the aviators who people it are timeless and placeless; they stay drunk most of the time to aggravate their insensitiveness; they have oil in their veins instead of blood; flying is their obsession, and when they are not in the air they do not live at all. In short, they are artifacts of the Snopes world. Against the background of an airport opening and a Mardi-Gras carnival in a Southern city, they move like characters in an animated cartoon, performing incredible antics but never being alive. Unable to speak through them,

Mr. Faulkner speaks about them, in an androgynous prose-poetry that is not to be found anywhere else in his work. *Pylon* is his most conspicuous failure; and his imperfect sympathy with, and his inability to control, the protagonists, who should be the antagonists, seem to account for the failure. *Mosquitoes* fails for similar reasons. Here, however, the imperfect sympathy issues in satire—of the Snopes-world Bohemia that existed in the Vieux Carré section of New Orleans during the 1920's. Since this is Mr. Faulkner's second novel, and since it was written just after he had lived in the Vieux Carré himself, while he was still under thirty, it offers another clear indication of the centrality of his traditionalism. It shows how great is the distance separating him from many of his contemporaries, such as, let us say, Mr. Ernest Hemingway. For *Mosquitoes* makes it very plain that if Mr. Faulkner is of the "lost generation," it is only of the lost generation of Sartorises. But it shows, too, that Mr. Faulkner is not an Aldous Huxley and should not try to be one. He is primarily a mythmaker; and there can be no such thing as a satiric myth.

## 3

William Faulkner's latest novel, *The Wild Palms,* tells two entirely different stories, in alternating sections; but the stories are complementary in that they both derive from the conflict between humanism and naturalism.

For Harry, the young doctor, and Charlotte, his mistress, all humanistic morality is equated with the Snopes code of mere "respectability," into which morality has degenerated. Of that code, one of the characters says: "If Jesus returned today we would have to crucify him quick in our own defense, to justify and preserve the civilization we have worked and suffered and died . . . for two thousand years to create and perfect in man's own image." Charlotte and Harry are attempting to escape from the code into pure naturalism. Charlotte is natural, or amoral, Woman; with her, Harry becomes natural, amoral Man. They are constantly insisting upon the entirely physical nature of their love—and in no evasive terms. Their fear of any code amounts to an obsession: when they begin to feel as if they were married, living and working together in Chicago, they run off to a remote mining settlement in order to escape respectability. But Harry is conscious of doom: "So I am afraid. Because They [the forces of the code] are smart, shrewd, They will have to be; if They were to let us beat Them, it would be like unchecked murder and robbery. Of course we can't beat Them; we are doomed, of course. . . ." The fear is justified; for they are

defeated by the very naturalism to which they have fled: Charlotte dies
from the effects of an abortion that Harry attempts to perform on her.

The other story concerns a nameless convict, adrift in a small boat
on the Mississippi River during the flood of 1927. Like Harry and Charlotte, the convict exists in a realm of unchecked natural forces; but unlike
them, he has been put there against his will. With him in the skiff is a
pregnant woman whom he has been sent to rescue. Like Anse Bundren,
the convict is capable of genuine moral action; and his struggle with naturalism is based upon the ethical urge to return to his prison and to
carry back the woman he has saved. When he is finally captured, he says:
"Yonder's your boat and here's the woman"; with simple-minded tenacity,
he has fulfilled his ethical obligation.

Technically, the book fails; only the complementary themes connect
the two parts, and the connection is not strong enough for any sort of
fictional unity. Indeed, it is a pity that the two parts are printed together;
for the story of Charlotte and Harry is one of Mr. Faulkner's failures,
whereas the story of the convict is one of his successes.

Charlotte and Harry, fleeing the Snopes world but fleeing all codes,
too, are products of the antitraditional overbalancing in Mr. Faulkner
which yielded *Pylon*. And the failure of their story derives, like the failure
of that book, from the fact that in them the natural protagonist-antagonist
schematism of Mr. Faulkner's myth is reversed. Sympathy must be given
to them reluctantly; for though they are, as a matter of fact, running away
from the Snopes world, they are running away from the Sartoris world, too;
and, as Harry says, if they were to succeed, it would be like unchecked
robbery and murder. In defense of one's own humanism, one must not
yield entire sympathy to human beings who enter the realm of pure
animalism.

But the story of the nameless convict is an heroic legend, similar to
*As I Lay Dying*; it must be counted as one of Mr. Faulkner's definite
achievements. Moreover, it has a quality of gusty humor (a sense of the out-
rageously grotesque heroic, related to the humor of the "tall tales" in folk
literature) which is rarer in Mr. Faulkner's work but which is always impressive when it appears. It is to be found in some of the scenes of *Sanctuary*, notably in the gangster funeral and in the drunken "afternoon tea"
of the middle-aged harlots at Miss Reba's house. It shows up in some of the
short stories—"Spotted Horses," for example. And it appears in the
scenes of the convicts' alligator hunting in *The Wild Palms*. However, this

quality does not destroy, but serves rather to strengthen, the heroic legend as a whole.

### 4

William Faulkner's myth finds expression in work that is definitely romantic; when he comes near to tragedy, it is the tragedy of Webster. His art, like Webster's, is tortured. In form, each of his novels resembles a late-Elizabethan blank verse line, where the meter is strained, threatens to break, sometimes breaks, but is always exciting. He is an original craftsman, making his own solutions to his problems of form, often blundering, but occasionally striking upon an effect that no amount of studious craftsmanship could achieve. Consequently, like Dostoevsky, or like Miss Djuna Barnes in our own time, he is very special; and his work cannot be imitated except futilely, for he works within no general tradition of craft and hands on no tradition to his successors.

But Mr. Faulkner's difficulties of form derive, in part, from the struggle that he has to make to inform his material. The struggle is manifest, even in the prose itself. Discounting the results of plain carelessness in all of the books, the correlation between the fictions and the quality of the prose in Mr. Faulkner's books is instructive. It appears significant that *The Unvanquished* contains his least tortured and *Pylon* his most tortured prose.

He has worked to project in fiction the conflict between his inherent traditional values and the modern world; and the conflict has affected his fictional projection, so that all of his work is really a *striving toward* the condition of tragedy. He is the Quentin Compson or the Bayard Sartoris of modern fiction. He does not always fail; but when he does, his failure is like theirs—he ends in confused or meaningless violence. And for the same reasons: his heritage is theirs, and it is subject to the same opposition to which they are subject as characters. When he is partially successful, the result is tortured but major romantic art.

Now, in 1939, Mr. Faulkner's work may seem melodramatic. Melodrama differs from tragedy only in the amount of meaning that is subsistent in the pattern of events; and in our time the values of Mr. Faulkner's tradition are available to most men only historically, in the same way that, let us say, medieval values are available. The significance of the work as myth depends, then, upon the willingness of the reader to recover the meaning of the tradition—even historically.

# INTRODUCTION TO
## *THE PORTABLE FAULKNER*

MALCOLM COWLEY

### 1

WHEN THE WAR WAS OVER—the other war—William Faulkner went back
to Oxford, Mississippi. He had served in the Royal Air Force in 1918.
Now he was home again and not at home, or at least not able to accept
the postwar world. He was writing poems, most of them worthless, and
dozens of immature but violent and effective stories, while at the same time
he was brooding over his own situation and the decline of the South. Slowly
the brooding thoughts arranged themselves into the whole interconnected
pattern that would form the substance of his later novels.

This pattern, which almost all his critics have overlooked, was based
on what he saw in Oxford or remembered from his childhood; on scraps of
family tradition (the Falkners, as they spelled the name, had played their
part in the history of the state); on kitchen dialogues between the black
cook and her amiable husband; on Saturday-afternoon gossip in Courthouse Square; on stories told by men in overalls squatting on their heels
while they passed around a fruit jar full of white corn liquor; on all the
sources familiar to a small-town Mississippi boy—but the whole of it was
elaborated, transformed, given convulsive life by his emotions; until, by the
simple intensity of feeling, the figures in it became a little more than human,
became heroic or diabolical, became symbols of the old South, of war and
reconstruction, of commerce and machinery destroying the standards of the
past. There in Oxford, Faulkner performed a labor of imagination that has
not been equaled in our time, and a double labor: first, to invent a Mississippi county that was like a mythical kingdom, but was complete and living
in all its details; second, to make his story of Yoknapatawpha County stand
as a parable or legend of all the Deep South.

For this double task, Faulkner was better equipped by talent and background than he was by schooling. He was born in New Albany, Mississippi,

on September 25, 1897; he was the oldest of four brothers. The family soon moved to Oxford, where he attended the public school, but without being graduated from high school. For a year after the war, he was a student at the University of Mississippi, in Oxford, where veterans could then matriculate without a high-school diploma; but he neglected his classroom work and left without taking a degree. He had less of a formal education than any other good writer of his time, except Hart Crane—less even than Hemingway, who never went to college, but who learned to speak three foreign languages and studied writing in Paris from the best masters. Faulkner taught himself, largely, as he says, by "undirected and uncorrelated reading." Among the authors either mentioned or echoed in his early stories and poems are Keats, Balzac, Flaubert, Swinburne, Mallarmé, Wilde, Housman, Joyce, Eliot, Sherwood Anderson, and E. E. Cummings, with fainter suggestions of Hemingway (in a fishing scene), Dos Passos (in the spelling of compound words), and Scott Fitzgerald. The poems he wrote in those days were wholly derivative, but his prose from the beginning was a form of poetry; and in spite of the echoes it was always his own. He traveled less than any of his writing contemporaries. After a succession of odd jobs in Oxford, there was a brief period when he lived in New Orleans with Sherwood Anderson and met the literary crowd—he even satirized them in a very bad early novel, *Mosquitoes*; then he went to New York, where for a few unhappy months he clerked in a bookstore; in 1925 he took a long walking trip in Europe without settling on the Left Bank. Except for recent visits to Hollywood, the rest of his life has been spent in the town where he grew up, less than forty miles from his birthplace.

Although Oxford, Mississippi, is the seat of a university, it is even less of a literary center than was Salem, Massachusetts, during Hawthorne's early years as a writer; and Faulkner himself has shown an even greater dislike than Hawthorne for literary society. His novels are the books of a man who broods about literature but doesn't often discuss it with his friends; there is no ease about them, no feeling that they come from a background of taste refined by argument and of opinions held in common. They make me think of a passage from Henry James's little book on Hawthorne:

The best things come, as a general thing, from the talents that are members of a group; every man works better when he has companions working in the same line, and yielding to the stimulus of suggestion, comparison, emulation. Great things of course have been done by solitary workers; but they have usually been done with double the pains they would have cost if they had been produced in more genial circumstances. The solitary worker loses the profit of example and discussion; he is apt to make awkward experiments; he is in the nature of the case more or less of an empiric. The empiric may, as I say, be treated by the world as an expert; but the drawbacks and discomforts of empiricism remain to him, and are in fact increased by the suspicion that is mingled with his gratitude, of a want in the public taste of a sense of the proportion of things.

Like Hawthorne, Faulkner is a solitary worker by choice, and he has done great things not only with double the pains to himself that they might have cost if produced in more genial circumstances, but sometimes also with double the pains to the reader. Two or three of his books as a whole and many of them in part are awkward experiments. All of them are full of over-blown words like "imponderable," "immortal," "immutable," and "immemorial" that he would have used with more discretion, or not at all, if he had followed Hemingway's example and served an apprenticeship to an older writer. He is a most uncertain judge of his own work, and he has no reason to believe that the world's judgment of it is any more to be trusted; indeed, there is no American author who would be justified in feeling more suspicion of "a want in the public taste of a sense of the proportion of things." His early novels were overpraised, usually for the wrong reasons; his later and in many ways better novels have been obstinately condemned or simply neglected; and in 1945 all his seventeen books were out of print, with some of them unobtainable in the second-hand bookshops.

Even his warm admirers, of whom there are many—no author has a higher standing among his fellow novelists—have sometimes shown a rather vague idea of what he is trying to do; and Faulkner himself has never explained. He holds a curious attitude toward the public that appears to be lofty indifference (as in the one preface he wrote, for the Modern Library edition of *Sanctuary*), but really comes closer to being a mixture of skittery distrust and pure unconsciousness that the public exists. He doesn't furnish information or correct misstatements about himself (most of the biographical sketches that deal with him are full of preposterous errors). He doesn't care which way his name is spelled in the records, with or without the "u"—"Either way suits me," he said. Once he has finished a book, he is apparently not concerned with the question how it will be presented, to what sort of audience; and sometimes he doesn't bother to keep a private copy of it. He said in a letter, "I think I have written a lot and sent it off to print before I actually realized strangers might read it." Others might say that Faulkner, at least in those early days, was not so much composing stories for the public as telling them to himself—like a lonely child in his imaginary world, but also like a writer of genius.

2

Faulkner's mythical kingdom is a county in northern Mississippi, on the border between the sand hills covered with scrubby pine and the black earth of the river bottoms. Except for the storekeepers, mechanics, and professional men who live in Jefferson, the county seat, all the inhabitants are farmers or woodsmen. Except for a little lumber, their only product is baled cotton for the Memphis market. A few of them live in big plantation houses, the relics of another age, and more of them in substantial wooden farmhouses; but most of them are tenants, no better housed than slaves on good plantations before the Civil War. Yoknapatawpha County—"William Faulkner, sole owner and proprietor," as he inscribed on one of the maps he drew—has a population of 15,611 persons scattered over 2,400 square miles. It sometimes seems to me that every house or hovel has been described in one of Faulkner's novels; and that all the people of the imaginary county, black and white, townsmen, farmers, and housewives, have played their parts in one connected story.

He has so far written nine books wholly concerned with Yoknapatawpha County and its people, who also appear in parts of three others and in thirty or more uncollected stories. *Sartoris* was the first of the books to be published, in the spring of 1929; it is a romantic and partly unconvincing novel, but with many fine scenes in it, like the hero's visit to a family of independent pine-hill farmers; and it states most of the themes that the author would later develop at length. *The Sound and the Fury* was written before *Sartoris,* but wasn't published until six months later; it describes the fall of the Compson family, and it was the first of Faulkner's novels to be widely discussed. The books that followed, in the Yoknapatawpha series, are *As I Lay Dying* (1930), about the death and burial of Addie Bundren; *Sanctuary* (1931), always the most popular of his novels; *Light in August* (1932), in many ways the best; *Absalom, Absalom!* (1936) about Colonel Sutpen and his ambition to found a family; *The Unvanquished* (1938), a book of interrelated stories about the Sartoris dynasty; *The Wild Palms* (1939), half of which deals with a convict from back in the pine hills; *The Hamlet* (1940), a novel about the Snopes clan; and *Go Down, Moses* (1942), in which Faulkner's theme is the Negroes. There are also many Yoknapatawpha stories in *These Thirteen* (1931) and *Dr. Martino* (1934), besides other stories privately printed (like "Miss Zilphia Gant") or published in magazines and still to be collected or used as episodes in novels.

Just as Balzac, who seems to have inspired the series, divided his *Comédie Humaine* into "Scenes of Parisian Life," "Scenes of Provincial Life," "Scenes of Private Life," so Faulkner might divide his work into a number of cycles: one about the planters and their descendants, one about the townspeople of Jefferson, one about the poor whites, one about the Indians (consisting of stories already written but never brought together), and one about the Negroes. Or again, if he adopted a division by families, there would be the Compson-Sartoris saga, the still unfinished Snopes saga, the McCaslin saga, dealing with the white and black descendants of Carothers McCaslin, and the Ratliff-Bundren saga, devoted to the backwoods farmers of Frenchman's Bend. All the cycles or sagas are closely interconnected; it is as if each new book was a chord or segment of a total situation always existing in the author's mind. Sometimes a short story is the sequel to an earlier novel. For example, we read in *Sartoris* that Byron Snopes stole a packet of letters from Narcissa Benbow; and in "There Was a Queen," a story published five years later, we learn how Narcissa got the letters back again. Sometimes, on the other hand, a novel contains the sequel to a story; and we discover from an incidental reference in *The Sound and the Fury* that the Negro woman whose terror of death was described in "That Evening Sun" had later been murdered by her husband, who left her body in a ditch for the vultures. Sometimes an episode has a more complicated history. Thus, in the first chapter of *Sanctuary,* we hear about the Old Frenchman place, a ruined mansion near which the people of the neighborhood had been "digging with secret and sporadic optimism for gold which the builder was reputed to have buried somewhere about the place when Grant came through the country on his Vicksburg campaign." Later this digging for gold served as the subject of a story published in the *Saturday Evening Post:* "Lizards in Jamshyd's Courtyard." Still later the story was completely rewritten and became the last chapter of *The Hamlet.*

As one book leads into another, Faulkner sometimes falls into inconsistencies of detail. There is a sewing-machine agent named V. K. Suratt who appears in *Sartoris* and some of the later stories. By the time we reach *The Hamlet,* his name has changed to Ratliff, although his character remains the same (and his age, too, for all the twenty years that separate the backgrounds of the two novels). Henry Armstid is a likable figure in *As I Lay Dying* and *Light in August;* in *The Hamlet* he is mean and half-demented. His wife, whose character remains consistent, is called Lula in one book and Martha in another; in the third she is nameless. There is an Indian chief named Doom who appears in several stories; he starts as the father of Issetibeha and ends as his grandson. The mansion called Sutpen's Hundred was built of brick at the beginning of *Absalom, Absalom!* but at the end of the novel it is all wood and inflammable except for the chimneys. But these errors are comparatively few and inconsequential, considering the scope of Faulkner's series; and I should judge that most of them are afterthoughts rather than oversights.

All his books in the Yoknapatawpha saga are part of the same living pattern. It is this pattern, and not the printed volumes in which part of it is recorded, that is Faulkner's real achievement. Its existence helps to explain one feature of his work: that each novel, each long or short story, seems to reveal more than it states explicitly and to have a subject bigger than itself. All the separate works are like blocks of marble from the same quarry: they show the veins and faults of the mother rock. Or else—to use a rather strained figure—they are like wooden planks that were cut not from a log, but from a still living tree. The planks are planed and chiseled into their final shapes, but the tree itself heals over the wound and continues to grow. Faulkner is incapable of telling the same story twice without adding new details. In the present volume I wanted to use part of *The Sound and the Fury,* the novel that deals with the fall of the Compson family. I thought that the last part of the book would be most effective as a separate episode, but still it depended too much on what had gone before. Faulkner offered to write a very brief introduction that would explain the relations of the characters. What he finally sent me is the much longer passage here printed as an appendix: a genealogy of the Compsons from their first arrival in this country. Whereas the novel is confined to a period of eighteen years ending in 1928, the genealogy goes back to the battle of Culloden in 1745, and forward to the year 1945, when Jason, last of the Compson males, has sold the family mansion, and Sister Caddy has last been heard of as the mistress of a German general. The novel that Faulkner wrote about the Compsons had long ago been given its final shape; but the pattern or body of legend behind the novel—and behind all his other books—was still developing.

Although the pattern is presented in terms of a single Mississippi county, it can be extended to the Deep South as a whole; and Faulkner always seems conscious of its wider application. He might have been thinking of his own novels when he described the ledgers in the commissary of the McCaslin plantation, in *Go Down, Moses.* They recorded, he said, "that slow trickle of molasses and meal and meat, of shoes and straw hats and overalls, of plowlines and collars and heelbolts and clevises, which returned each fall as cotton"—in a sense they were local and limited; but they were also "the continuation of that record which two hundred years had not been enough to complete and another hundred would not be enough to discharge; that chronicle which was a whole land in miniature, which multiplied and compounded was the entire South."

## 3

"Tell about the South," says Quentin Compson's roommate at Harvard, a Canadian named Shreve McCannon who is curious about the unknown region beyond the Ohio. "What's it like there?" he asks. "What do they do there? Why do they live there? Why do they live at all?" And Quentin, whose background is a little like that of Faulkner himself and who sometimes seems to speak for him—Quentin answers, "You can't understand it. You would have to be born there." Nevertheless, he tells a long and violent story that he regards as the essence of the Deep South, which is not so much a mere region as it is, in Quentin's mind, an incomplete and frustrated nation trying to relive its legendary past.

The story he tells—I am trying to summarize the plot of *Absalom, Absalom!*—is that of a mountain boy named Thomas Sutpen whose family drifted into the Virginia lowlands, where his father found odd jobs on a plantation. One day the father sent him with a message to the big house, but he was turned away at the door by a black man in livery. Puzzled and humiliated, the mountain boy was seized upon by the lifelong ambition to which he would afterward refer as "the design." He too would own a plantation with slaves and a liveried butler; he would build a mansion as big as any of those in the Tidewater; and he would have a son to inherit his wealth.

A dozen years later, Sutpen appeared in the frontier town of Jefferson, where he managed to obtain a hundred square miles of land from the Chickasaws. With the help of twenty wild Negroes from the jungle and a French architect, he set about building the largest house in northern Mississippi, using timbers from the forest and bricks that his Negroes molded and baked on the spot; it was as if his mansion, Sutpen's Hundred, had been literally torn from the soil. Only one man in Jefferson—he was Quentin's grandfather, General Compson—ever learned how and where Sutpen had acquired his slaves. He had shipped to Haiti from Virginia, worked as overseer on a sugar plantation and married the rich planter's daughter, who had borne him a son. Then, finding that his wife had Negro blood, he had simply put her away, with her child and her fortune, while keeping the twenty slaves as a sort of indemnity.

In Jefferson, Sutpen married again. This time his wife belonged to a pious family of the neighborhood, and she bore him two children, Henry and Judith. He became the biggest cotton planter in Yoknapatawpha County, and it seemed that his "design" had already been fulfilled. At this moment, however, Henry came home from the University of Mississippi with an older and worldlier new friend, Charles Bon, who was in reality Sutpen's son by his first marriage. Charles became engaged to Judith. Sutpen learned his identity and, without making a sign of recognition, ordered him from the house. Henry, who refused to believe that Charles was his half-brother, renounced his birthright and followed him to New Orleans. In 1861, all the male Sutpens went off to war, and all of them survived four years of fighting. Then, in the spring of 1865, Charles suddenly decided to marry Judith, even though he was certain by now that she was his half-sister. Henry rode beside him all the way back to Sutpen's Hundred, but tried to stop him at the gate, killed him when he insisted on going ahead with his plan, told Judith what he had done, and disappeared.

But Quentin's story of the Deep South does not end with the war. Colonel Sutpen came home, he says, to find his wife dead, his son a fugitive, his slaves dispersed (they had run away even before they were freed by the Union army), and most of his land about to be seized for debt. Still determined to carry out "the design," he did not even pause for breath before undertaking to restore his house and plantation to what they had been. The effort failed and Sutpen was reduced to keeping a cross-roads store. Now in his sixties, he tried again to beget a son; but his wife's younger sister, Miss Rosa Coldfield, was outraged by his proposal ("Let's try it," he had said, "and if it's a boy we'll get married"); and later poor Milly Jones, with whom he had an affair, gave birth to a baby girl. At that Sutpen abandoned hope and provoked Milly's grandfather into killing him. Judith survived her father for a time, as did the half-caste son of Charles Bon by a New Orleans octoroon. After the death of these two by yellow fever, the great house was haunted rather than inhabited by an ancient mulatto woman. Sutpen's daughter by one of his slaves. The fugitive Henry Sutpen came home to die; the townspeople heard of his illness and sent an ambulance after him; but old Clytie thought they were arresting him for murder and set fire to Sutpen's Hundred. The only survival of the conflagration was Jim Bond, a halfwitted creature who was Charles Bon's grandson.

"Now I want you to tell me just one thing more," Shreve McCannon

says after hearing the story. "Why do you hate the South?"—"I don't
hate it," Quentin says quickly, at once. "I dont hate it," he repeats, speaking for the author as well as himself. *I dont hate it,* he thinks, panting in
the cold air, the iron New England dark; *I dont. I dont hate it! I dont
hate it!*

The reader cannot help wondering why this somber and, at moments,
plainly incredible story had so seized upon Quentin's mind that he trembled
with excitement when telling it and felt it revealed the essence of the Deep
South. It seems to belong in the realm of Gothic romances, with Sutpen's
Hundred taking the place of the haunted castle on the Rhine, with Colonel
Sutpen as Faust and Charles Bon as Manfred. Then slowly it dawns on you
that most of the characters and incidents have a double meaning; that
besides their place in the story, they also serve as symbols or metaphors
with a general application. Sutpen's great design, the land he stole from
the Indians, the French architect who built his house with the help of wild
Negroes from the jungle, the woman of mixed blood whom he married and
disowned, the unacknowledged son who ruined him, the poor white whom
he wronged and who killed him in anger, the final destruction of the mansion like the downfall of a social order: all these might belong to a tragic
fable of Southern history. With a little cleverness, the whole novel might
be explained as a connected and logical allegory, but this, I think, would
be going far beyond the author's intention. First of all he was writing a
story, and one that affected him deeply, but he was also brooding over a
social situation. More or less unconsciously, the incidents in the story
came to represent the forces and elements in the social situation, since the
mind naturally works in terms of symbols and parallels. In Faulkner's case,
this form of parallelism is not confined to *Absalom, Absalom!* It can be
found in the whole fictional framework that he has been elaborating in
novel after novel, until his work has become a myth or legend of the
South.

I call it a legend because it is obviously no more intended as a historical account of the country south of the Ohio than *The Scarlet Letter* was
intended as a history of Massachusetts or *Paradise Lost* as a factual description of the Fall. Briefly stated, the legend might run something like this:
The Deep South was settled partly by aristocrats like the Sartoris clan and
partly by new men like Colonel Sutpen. Both types of planters were determined to establish a lasting social order on the land they had seized from the
Indians (that is, to leave sons behind them). They had the virtue of living
single-mindedly by a fixed code; but there was also an inherent guilt in

their "design," their way of life; it was slavery that put a curse on the land and brought about the Civil War. After the War was lost, partly as a result of their own mad heroism (for who else but men as brave as Jackson and Stuart could have frightened the Yankees into standing together and fighting back?) they tried to restore "the design" by other methods. But they no longer had the strength to achieve more than a partial success, even after they had freed their land from the carpetbaggers who followed the Northern armies. As time passed, moreover, the men of the old order found that they had Southern enemies too: they had to fight against a new exploiting class descended from the landless whites of slavery days. In this struggle between the clan of Sartoris and the unscrupulous tribe of Snopes, the Sartorises were defeated in advance by a traditional code that kept them from using the weapons of the enemy. As a price of victory, however, the Snopeses had to serve the mechanized civilization of the North, which was morally impotent in itself, but which, with the aid of its Southern retainers, ended by corrupting the Southern nation.

Faulkner's novels of contemporary Southern life continue the legend into a period that he regards as one of moral confusion and social decay. He is continually seeking in them for violent images to convey his sense of despair. *Sanctuary* is the most violent of all his novels; it is also the most popular and by no means the least important (in spite of Faulkner's comment that it was "a cheap idea . . . deliberately conceived to make money"). The story of Popeye and Temple Drake has more meaning than appears on a first hasty reading—the only reading that most of the critics have been willing to grant it. Popeye himself is one of several characters in Faulkner's novels who represent the mechanical civilization that has invaded and partly conquered the South. He is always described in mechanical terms: his eyes "looked like rubber knobs"; his face "just went awry, like the face of a wax doll set too near a hot fire and forgotten"; his tight suit and stiff hat were "all angles, like a modernistic lampshade"; and in general he had "that vicious depthless quality of stamped tin." Popeye was the son of a professional strikebreaker, from whom he had inherited syphilis, and the grandson of a pyromaniac. Like two other villains in Faulkner's novels, Joe Christmas and Januarius Jones, he had spent most of his childhood in an institution. He was the man "who made money and had nothing he could do with it, spend it for, since he knew that alcohol would kill him like poison, who had no friends and had never known a woman"—in other words, he was the compendium of all the hateful qualities that Faulkner assigns to finance capitalism. *Sanctuary* is not a connected allegory, as one critic explained it, but neither is it a mere accumulation of pointless horrors. It is an example of the Freudian method turned backward, being full of sexual nightmares that are in reality social symbols. It is somehow connected in the author's mind with what he regards as the rape and corruption of the South.

In all his novels dealing with the present, Faulkner makes it clear that the descendants of the old ruling caste have the wish but not the courage or the strength to prevent this new disaster. They are defeated by Popeye (like Horace Benbow), or they run away from him (like Gowan Stevens, who had gone to school at Virginia and learned to drink like a gentleman, but not to fight for his principles), or they are robbed and replaced in their positions of influence by the Snopeses (like old Bayard Sartoris, the president of the bank), or they drug themselves with eloquence and alcohol (like Quentin Compson's father), or they retire into the illusion of being inviolable Southern ladies (like Mrs. Compson, who says, "It can't be simply to flout and hurt me. Whoever God is, He would not permit that. I'm a lady."), or they dwell so much on the past that they are incapable of facing the present (like Reverend Hightower of *Light in August*), or they run from danger to danger (like young Bayard Sartoris) frantically seeking their own destruction. Faulkner's novels are full of well-meaning and even admirable persons, not only the grandsons of the cotton aristocracy, but also pine-hill farmers and storekeepers and sewing-machine agents and Negro cooks and sharecroppers; but they are almost all of them defeated by circumstances and they carry with them a sense of their own doom.

They also carry, whether heroes or villains, a curious sense of submission to their fate. "There is not one of Faulkner's characters," says André Gide in his dialogue on "The New American Novelists," "who properly speaking, has a soul"; and I think he means that not one of them exercises the faculty of conscious choice between good and evil. They are haunted, obsessed, driven forward by some inner necessity. Like Miss Rosa Coldfield, in *Absalom, Absalom!* they exist in "that dream state in which you run without moving from a terror in which you cannot believe, toward a safety in which you have no faith." Or, like the slaves freed by General Sherman's army, in *The Unvanquished,* they blindly follow the roads toward any river, believing that it will be their Jordan:

They were singing, walking along the road singing, not even looking to either side. The dust didn't even settle for two days, because all that night they still passed; we sat up listening to them, and the next morning every few yards along the road would be the old ones who couldn't keep up any more, sitting or lying down and even crawling along, calling to the others to help them; and the others—the young ones—not stopping, not even looking at them. "Going to Jordan," they told me. "Going to cross Jordan."

All Faulkner's characters, black and white, are a little like that. They dig for gold frenziedly after they have lost their hope of finding it (like Henry Armstid in *The Hamlet* and Lucas Beauchamp in *Go Down, Moses*); or they battle against and survive a Mississippi flood for the one privilege of returning to the state prison farm (like the tall convict in "Old Man"); or, a whole family together, they carry a body through flood and fire and corruption to bury it in the cemetery at Jefferson (like the Bundrens in *As I Lay Dying*); or they tramp the roads week after week in search of men who had promised but never intended to marry them (like Lena Grove, the pregnant woman of *Light in August*); or, pursued by a mob, they turn at the end to meet and accept death (like Joe Christmas in the same novel). Even when they seem to be guided by a conscious purpose, like Colonel Sutpen, it is not something they have chosen by an act of will, but something that has taken possession of them: Sutpen's great design was "not what he wanted to do but what he just had to do, had to do it whether he wanted to or not, because if he did not do it he knew that he could never live with himself for the rest of his life." In the same way, Faulkner himself writes not what he wants to, but what he just has to write whether he wants to or not.

### 4

He is not primarily a novelist: that is, his stories do not occur to him in book-length units of 70,000 to 150,000 words. Almost all his novels have some weakness in structure. Some of them combine two or more themes having little relation to each other, like *Light in August,* while others, like *The Hamlet,* tend to resolve themselves into a series of episodes resembling beads on a string. In *The Sound and the Fury,* which is superb as a whole, we can't be sure that the four sections of the novel are presented in the most effective order; at any rate, we can't fully understand and perhaps can't even read the first section until we have read the other three. *Absalom, Absalom!* though pitched in too high a key, is structurally the soundest of all the novels in the Yoknapatawpha series; but even here the author's attention shifts halfway through the book from the principal theme of Colonel Sutpen's ambition to the secondary theme of incest and miscegenation.

Faulkner is best and most nearly himself either in long stories like "The Bear," in *Go Down, Moses,* and "Old Man," which was published as half of *The Wild Palms,* and "Spotted Horses," which was first printed separately, then greatly expanded and fitted into the loose framework of *The Hamlet*—all three stories are included in this volume; or else in the Yoknapatawpha saga as a whole. That is, he is most effective in dealing with the total situation that is always present in his mind as a pattern of the South; or else in shorter units that can be conceived and written in a single burst of creative effort. It is by his ·best that we should judge him, like every other author; and Faulkner at his best—even sometimes at his worst—has a power, a richness of life, an intensity to be found in no other American novelist of our time. He has—once more I am quoting from Henry James's essay on Hawthorne—"the element of simple genius, the quality of imagination."

Moreover, he has a brooding love for the land where he was born and reared and where, unlike other writers of his generation, he has chosen to spend his life. It is ". . . this land, this South, for which God has done so much, with woods for game and streams for fish and deep rich soil for seed and lush springs to sprout it and long summers to mature it and serene falls to harvest it and short mild winters for men and animals." So far as Faulkner's country includes the Delta, it is also (in the words of old Ike McCaslin)

This land which man has deswamped and denuded and derivered in two generations so that white men can own plantations and commute every night to Memphis and black men own plantations and ride in jim crow cars to Chicago and live in millionaires' mansions on Lake Shore Drive, where white men rent farms and live like niggers and niggers crop on shares and live like animals, where cotton is planted and grows man-tall in the very cracks of the sidewalks, and usury and mortgage and bankruptcy and measureless wealth, Chinese and African and Aryan and Jew, all breed and spawn together.

Here are the two sides of Faulkner's feeling for the South: on the one side, an admiring and possessive love; on the other, a compulsive fear lest what he loves should be destroyed by the ignorance of its native serfs and the greed of traders and absentee landlords.

No other American writer takes such delight in the weather. He speaks in various novels of "the hot still pine-winey silence of the August afternoon"; of "the moonless September dust, the trees along the road not rising soaring as trees should but squatting like huge fowl"; of "the tranquil sunset of October mazy with windless wood-smoke"; of the "slow drizzle of November rain just above the ice point"; of "those windless Mississippi

December days which are a sort of Indian summer's Indian summer"; of January and February when there is "no movement anywhere save the low constant smoke . . . and no sound save the chopping of axes and the lonely whistle of the daily trains." Spring in Faulkner's country is a hurried season, "all coming at once, pell mell and disordered, fruit and bloom and leaf, pied meadow and blossoming wood and the long fields shearing dark out of winter's slumber, to the shearing plow." Summer is dust-choked and blazing, and it lasts far into what should be autumn. "That's the one trouble with this country," he says in *As I Lay Dying.* "Everything, weather, all, hangs on too long. Like our rivers, our land: opaque, slow, violent; shaping and creating the life of man in its implacable and brooding image."

And Faulkner loves these people created in the image of the land. After a second reading of his novels, you continue to be impressed by his villains, Popeye and Jason and Joe Christmas and Flem Snopes; but this time you find more place in your memory for other figures standing a little in the background yet presented by the author with quiet affection: old ladies like Miss Jenny DuPré, with their sharp-tongued benevolence; shrewd but kindly bargainers like Ratliff, the sewing-machine agent, and Will Varner, with his cotton gin and general store; long-suffering farm wives like Mrs. Henry Armstid (whether her name is Lula or Martha); and backwoods patriarchs like Pappy MacCullum, with his six middle-aged but unmarried sons named after the generals of Lee's army. You remember the big plantation houses that collapse in flames as if a whole civilization were dying, but you also remember men in patched and faded but quite clean overalls sitting on the gallery—here in the North we should call it the porch—of a crossroads store that is covered with posters advertising soft drinks and patent medicines; and you remember the stories they tell while chewing tobacco until the suption is out of it (everything in their world is reduced to anecdote, and every anecdote is based on character). You remember Quentin Compson not in his despairing moments, but riding with his father behind the dogs as they quarter a sedge-grown hillside after quail; and not listening to his father's story, but still knowing every word of it, because, as he thought to himself, "You had learned, absorbed it already without the medium of speech somehow from having been born and living beside it, with it, as children will and do: so that what your father was saying did not tell you anything so much as it struck, word by word, the resonant strings of remembering."

Faulkner's novels have the quality of being lived, absorbed, remembered rather than merely observed. And they have what is rare in the

novels of our time, a warmth of family affection, brother for brother and
sister, the father for his children—a love so warm and proud that it tries
to shut out the rest of the world. Compared with that affection, married
love is presented as something calculating, and illicit love as a consuming
fire. And because the blood relationship is central in his novels, Faulkner
finds it hard to create sympathetic characters between the ages of twenty
and forty. He is better with children, Negro and white, and incomparably
good with older people who preserve the standards that have come down
to them "out of the old time, the old days."

In his later books, which have attracted so little attention that they
seem to have gone unread, there is a quality not exactly new to Faulkner—
it had appeared already in passages of *Sartoris* and *Sanctuary*—but now
much stronger and no longer overshadowed by violence and horror. It is a
sort of homely and sober-sided frontier humor that is seldom achieved
in contemporary writing (except by Erskine Caldwell, another Southerner).
The horse-trading episodes in *The Hamlet,* and especially the long story of
the spotted ponies from Texas, might have been inspired by the Davy
Crockett almanacs. "Old Man," the story of the convict who surmounted
the greatest of all the Mississippi floods, might almost be a continuation of
*Huckleberry Finn.* It is as if some older friend of Huck's had taken the
raft and drifted on from Aunt Sally Phelps's farm into wilder adventures,
described in a wilder style, among Chinese and Cajuns and bayous crawling
with alligators. In a curious way, Faulkner combines two of the principal
traditions in American letters: the tradition of psychological horror, often
close to symbolism, that begins with Charles Brockden Brown, our first
professional novelist, and extends through Poe, Melville, Henry James (in
his later stories), Stephen Crane, and Hemingway; and the other tradition
of frontier humor and realism, beginning with Augustus Longstreet's
*Georgia Scenes* and having Mark Twain as its best example.

But the American author he most resembles is Hawthorne, for all
their polar differences. They stand to each other as July to December, as
heat to cold, as swamp to mountain, as the luxuriant to the meager but perfect, as planter to Puritan; and yet Hawthorne had much the same attitude
toward New England that Faulkner has toward the South, together with a
strong sense of regional particularity. The Civil War made Hawthorne feel
that "the North and the South were two distinct nations in opinions and
habits, and had better not try to live under the same institutions." In the
Spring of 1861, he wrote to his Bowdoin classmate Horatio Bridge, "We
were never one people and never really had a country."—"New England,"

he said a little later, "is quite as large a lump of earth as my heart can really take in." But it was more than a lump of earth for him; it was a lump of history and a permanent state of consciousness. Like Faulkner in the South, he applied himself to creating its moral fables and elaborating its legends, which existed, as it were, in his solitary heart. Pacing the hillside behind his house in Concord, he listened for a voice; you might say that he lay in wait for it, passively but expectantly, like a hunter behind a rock; then, when it had spoken, he transcribed its words—more slowly and carefully than Faulkner, it is true; with more form and less fire, but with the same essential fidelity. If the voice was silent, he had nothing to write. "I have an instinct that I had better keep quiet," he said in a letter to his publisher. "Perhaps I shall have a new spirit of vigor if I wait quietly for it; perhaps not." Faulkner is another author who has to wait for the spirit and the voice. Essentially he is not a novelist, in the sense of not being a writer who sets out to observe actions and characters, then fits them into the architectural framework of a story. For all the weakness of his own poems, he is an epic or bardic poet in prose, a creator of myths that he weaves together into a legend of the South.

# WILLIAM FAULKNER

### ROBERT PENN WARREN

MALCOLM COWLEY'S editing of *The Portable Faulkner*[1] is remarkable on two counts. First, the selection from Faulkner's work is made not merely to give a cross section or a group of good examples but to demonstrate one of the principles of integration in the work. Second, the introductory essay is one of the few things ever written on Faulkner which is not hagridden by prejudice or preconception and which really sheds some light on the subject.

The selections here are made to describe the place, Yoknapatawpha

Reprinted with permission from *The New Republic*, August 12, 1946, pp. 176-80, and August 26, 1946, pp. 234-37.
1. *The Portable Faulkner*, edited by Malcolm Cowley. New York: Viking Press.

County, Mississippi, which is, as Cowley puts it, "Faulkner's mythical kingdom," and to give the history of that kingdom. The place is the locale of most of Faulkner's work. Its 2,400 square miles lie between the hills of north Mississippi and the rich, black bottom lands. It has a population of 15,611 persons, composing a society with characters as different as the Bundrens, the Snopeses, Ike McCaslin, Percy Grimm, Temple Drake, the Compsons, Christmas, Dilsey, and the tall convict of *The Wild Palms.* No land in all fiction lives more vividly in its physical presence than this mythical county—the "pine-winey" afternoons, the nights with "a thin sickle of moon like the heel print of a boot in wet sand," the tremendous reach of the big river in flood, "yellow and sleepy in the afternoon," and the "little piddling creeks, that run backward one day and forward the next and come busting down on a man full of dead mules and hen houses," the ruined plantation which was Popeye's hang-out, the swamps and fields and hot, dusty roads of the Frenchman's Bend section, and the remnants of the great original forests, "green with gloom" in summer, "if anything actually dimmer than they had been in November's gray dissolution, where even at noon the sun fell only in windless dappling upon the earth which never completely dried."

And no land in all fiction is more painstakingly analyzed from the sociological standpoint. The descendants of the old families, the descendants of bushwackers and carpetbaggers, the swamp rats, the Negro cooks and farm hands, bootleggers and gangsters, peddlers, college boys, tenant farmers, country storekeepers, county-seat lawyers are all here. The marks of class, occupation, and history are fully rendered and we know completely their speech, dress, food, houses, manners, and attitudes. Nature and sociology, geography and human geography, are scrupulously though effortlessly presented in Faulkner's work, and their significance for his work is very great; but the significance is of a conditioning order. They are, as it were, aspects of man's "doom"—a word of which Faulkner is very fond—but his manhood in the face of that doom is what is important.

Cowley's selections are made to give the description of the mythical kingdom, but more important, they are made to give its history. Most critics, even those who have most naïvely or deliberately misread the meaning of the fact, have been aware that the sense of the past is crucial in Faulkner's work. Cowley has here set up selections running in date of action from 1820 to 1940. The first, "A Justice," is a story about Ikkemotubbe, the nephew of a Chickasaw chief who went to New Orleans, where he received the name of *du Homme,* which became Doom; who came

back to the tribe to poison his way to the Man-ship; and who, in the end
(in Faulkner's "history" though not in "A Justice" itself), swaps a mile
square of "virgin north Mississippi dirt" for a racing mare owned by
Jason Lycurgus Compson, the founder of the Compson family in Mississippi. The last selection, "Delta Autumn," shows us Isaac McCaslin, the
man who brings the best of the old order, philosopher, aristocrat, woods-
man, into the modern world and who gives the silver-mounted horn which
General Compson had left him to a mulatto woman for her bastard son
by a relative of McCaslin's. In between "A Justice" and "Delta Autumn"
fall such pieces as the magnificent "Red Leaves," the profoundly symbolic
story called "The Bear," the Civil War and Reconstruction stories, "Rain"
(from *The Unvanquished*) and "Wash," "Old Man" (the story of the
tall convict from *The Wild Palms*), and the often anthologized "That
Evening Sun" and "A Rose for Emily," and the brilliant episode of "Percy
Grimm" (from *Light in August*). There are other pieces included, but
these are the best, and the best for showing high points in the history
of Yoknapatawpha County.

Cowley's introduction undertakes to define the significance of place
and history in Faulkner's work, that "labor of imagination that has not
been equaled in our time." That labor is, as he points out, a double labor:
"first, to invent a Mississippi county that was like a mythical kingdom,
but was complete and living in all its details; second, to make his story of
Yoknapatawpha County stand as a parable or legend of all the Deep
South." The legend—called a legend "because it is obviously no more
intended as a historical account of the country south of the Ohio than
*The Scarlet Letter* was intended as a history of Massachusetts"—is, as
Cowley defines it, this:

The South was settled by Sartorises (aristocrats) and Sutpens (nameless, ambitious men) who, seizing the land from the Indians, were determined to found an enduring and stable order. But despite their strength
and integrity their project was, to use Faulkner's word, "accursed" by
slavery, which, with the Civil War as instrument, frustrated their design.
Their attempt to rebuild according to the old plan and old values was
defeated by a combination of forces—the carpetbaggers and Snopeses
("a new exploiting class descended from the landless whites"). Most of
the descendants of the old order are in various ways incompetent: they
are prevented by their code from competing with the codeless Snopeses,
they cling to the letter and forget the spirit of their tradition, they lose
contact with the realities of the present and escape into a dream world of

alcohol or rhetoric or gentility or madness, they fall in love with defeat
or death, they lose nerve and become cowards, or they, like the last Jason
in *The Sound and the Fury,* adopt Snopesism and become worse than any
Snopes. Figures like Popeye (eyes like "rubber knobs," a creature having "that vicious depthless quality of stamped tin," the man "who made
money and had nothing he could do with it, spend it for, since he knew
that alcohol would kill him like poison, who had no friends and had never
known a woman") are in their dehumanized quality symbols of modernism,
for the society of finance capitalism. The violence of some of Faulkner's
work is, according to Cowley, "an example of the Freudian method turned
backward, being full of sexual nightmares that are in reality social symbols.
It is somehow connected in the author's mind with what he regards as
the rape and corruption of the South."

This is, in brief, Cowley's interpretation of the legend, and it provides
an excellent way into Faulkner; it exactly serves the purpose which an
introduction should serve. The interpretation is indebted, no doubt, to
that of George Marion O'Donnell (the first and still an indispensable study
of Faulkner's theme), but it modifies O'Donnell's tendency to read Faulkner with an allegorical rigidity and with a kind of doctrinal single-minded-
ness.

It is possible that the present view, however, should be somewhat
modified, at least in emphasis. Although no writer is more deeply committed to a locality than Faulkner, the emphasis on the Southern elements
may blind us to other elements, or at least other applications, of deep
significance. And this is especially true in so far as the work is interpreted
merely as Southern apologetics or, as it is by Maxwell Geismar, as the
"extreme hallucinations" of a "cultural psychosis."

It is important, I think, that Faulkner's work be regarded not in
terms of the South against the North, but in terms of issues which are
common to our modern world. The legend is not merely a legend of the
South, but is also a legend of our general plight and problem. The modern
world is in moral confusion. It does suffer from a lack of discipline, of
sanctions, of community of values, of a sense of a mission. It is a world
in which self-interest, workableness, success, provide the standards. It
is a world which is the victim of abstraction and of mechanism, or at least,
at moments, feels itself to be. It can look back nostalgically upon the old
world of traditional values and feel loss and perhaps despair—upon the
world in which, as one of Faulkner's characters puts it, men "had the gift
of living once or dying once instead of being diffused and scattered creatures

drawn blindly from a grab bag and assembled"—a world in which men were, "integer for integer," more simple and complete.

If it be objected that Faulkner's view is unrealistic, that had the old order satisfied human needs it would have survived, and that it is sentimental to hold that it was killed from the outside, the answer is clear in the work: the old order did not satisfy human needs—the Southern old order or any other—for it, not being founded on justice, was "accursed" and held the seeds of its own ruin in itself. But even in terms of the curse the old order, as opposed to the new order (in so far as the new is to be equated with Snopesism), allowed the traditional man to define himself as human by setting up codes, concepts of virtue, obligations, and by accepting the risks of his humanity. Within the traditional order was a notion of truth, even if man in the flow of things did not succeed in realizing that truth. Take, for instance, the passage from "The Bear":

"All right," he said. "Listen," and read again, but only one stanza this time and closed the book and laid it on the table. "She cannot fade, though thou has not thy bliss," McCaslin said: "Forever wilt thou love, and she be fair."

"He's talking about a girl," he said.

"He had to talk about something," McCaslin said. Then he said, "He was talking about truth. Truth is one. It doesn't change. It covers all things which touch the heart—honor and pride and pity and justice and courage and love. Do you see now?"

The human effort is what is important, the capacity to make the effort to rise above the mechanical process of life, the pride to endure, for in endurance there is a kind of self-conquest.

When it is said, as it is often said, that Faulkner's work is "backward-looking," the answer is that the constant ethical center is to be found in the glorification of the human effort and of human endurance, which are not in time, even though in modernity they seem to persist most surely among the despised and rejected. It is true that Faulkner's work contains a savage attack on modernity, but it is to be remembered that Elizabethan tragedy, for instance, contained just such an attack on its own special "modernity." (Ambition is the most constant tragic crime, and ambition is the attitude special to an opening society; all villains are rationalists and appeal to "nature" beyond traditional morality for justification, and rationalism is, in the sense implied here, the attitude special to the rise of a secular and scientific order before a new morality can be formulated.)

It is not ultimately important whether the traditional order (Southern or other) as depicted by Faulkner fits exactly the picture which critical historical method provides. Let it be granted, for the sake of discussion, that Faulkner does oversimplify the matter. What is ultimately important, both ethically and artistically, is the symbolic function of that order in relation to the world which is set in opposition to it. The opposition between the old order and the new does not, however, exhaust the picture. What of the order to come? "We will have to wait," old Ike McCaslin says to the mulatto girl who is in love with a white man. A curse may work itself out in time; and in such glimpses, which occur now and then, we get the notion of a grudging meliorism, a practical supplement to the idealism, like Ike McCaslin's, which finds compensation in the human effort and the contemplation of "truth."

The discussion, even at a larger scope and with more satisfactory analysis, of the central theme of Faulkner would not exhaust the interest of his work. In fact, the discussion of this question always runs the risk of making his work appear too schematic, too dry and too complacent when in actual fact it is full of rich detail, of shadings and complexities of attitude, of ironies and ambivalences. Cowley's introduction cautions the reader on this point and suggests various fruitful topics for investigation and thought. But I shall make bold—and in the general barrenness of criticism on Faulkner it does not require excessive boldness—to list and comment on certain topics which seem to me to demand further critical study.

*Nature.* The vividness of the natural background is one of the impressive features of Faulkner's work. It is accurately observed, but observation only provides the stuff from which the characteristic effects are gained. It is the atmosphere which counts, the poetry, the infusion of feeling, the symbolic weight. Nature provides a backdrop—of lyric beauty (the meadow in the cow episode of *The Hamlet*), of homely charm (the trial scene of the "Spotted Horses" story from the same book), of sinister, brooding force (the river in "Old Man" from *The Wild Palms*), of massive dignity (the forest in "The Bear")—for the human action and passion. The indestructible beauty is there: "God created man," Ike McCaslin says in "Delta Autumn," "and He created the world for him to live in and I reckon He created the kind of world He would have wanted to live in if He had been a man."

Ideally, if man were like God, as Ike McCaslin puts it, man's attitude toward nature would be one of pure contemplation, pure participation in its great forms and appearances; the appropriate attitude is love, for with Ike

McCaslin the moment of love is equated with godhood. But since man "wasn't quite God himself," since he lives in the world of flesh, he must be a hunter, user, and violator. To return to McCaslin: God "put them both here: man and the game he would follow and kill, foreknowing it. I believe He said, 'So be it.' I reckon He even foreknew the end. But He said, 'I will give him his chance. I will give him warning and foreknowledge too, along with the desire to follow and the power to slay. The woods and the fields he ravages and the game he devastates will be the consequence and signature of his crime and guilt, and his punishment.'"

There is, then, a contamination implicit in the human condition—a kind of Original Sin, as it were—but it is possible, even in the contaminating act, the violation, for man to achieve some measure of redemption, a redemption through love. For instance, in "The Bear," the great legendary beast which is pursued for years to the death is also an object of love and veneration, and the symbol of virtue, and the deer hunt of "Delta Autumn" is for Ike McCaslin a ritual of renewal. Those who have learned the right relationship to nature—"the pride and humility" which young Ike McCaslin learns from the half-Negro, half-Indian Sam Fathers—are set over against those who have not. In "The Bear," General Compson speaks up to Cass McCaslin to defend the wish of the boy Ike McCaslin to stay an extra week in the woods: "You got one foot straddled into a farm and the other foot straddled into a bank; you ain't even got a good hand-hold where this boy was already an old man long before you damned Sartorises and Edmondses invented farms and banks to keep yourselves from having to find out what this boy was born knowing and fearing too maybe, but without being afraid, that could go ten miles on a compass because he wanted to look at a bear none of us had ever got near enough to put a bullet in and looked at the bear and came the ten miles back on the compass in the dark; maybe by God that's the why and the wherefore of farms and banks."

Those who have the wrong attitude toward nature are the pure exploiters, the apostles of abstractionism, the truly evil men. For instance, the very opening of *Sanctuary* presents a distinction on this ground between Benbow and Popeye. While the threat of Popeye keeps Benbow crouching by the spring, he hears a Carolina wren sing, and even under these circumstances tries to recall the local name for it. And he says to Popeye: "And of course you don't know the name of it. I don't suppose you'd know a bird at all, without it was singing in a cage in a hotel lounge, or cost four dollars on a plate." Popeye, as we may remember, spits in the spring (he hates nature and must foul it), is afraid to go through the woods ("Through

all them trees?" he demands when Benbow points out the short cut), and
when an owl whisks past them in the twilight, claws at Benbow's coat with
almost hysterical fear ("It's just an owl," Benbow says. "It's nothing but
an owl.")

The pure exploiters, though they may gain ownership and use of a
thing, never really have it; like Popeye, they are impotent. For instance,
Flem Snopes, the central character and villain of *The Hamlet,* who brings
the exploiter's mentality to Frenchman's Bend, finally marries Eula Varner,
a kind of fertility goddess or earth goddess; but his ownership is meaningless, for she always refers to him as "that man" (she does not even have a
name for him), and he has only got her after she has given herself willingly
to one of the bold, hotblooded boys of the neighborhood. In fact, nature
can't, in one sense, be "owned." Ike McCaslin, in "The Bear," says of the
land which has come down to him: "It was never Father's and Uncle
Buddy's to bequeath me to repudiate, because it was never Grandfather's to
bequeath them to bequeath me to repudiate, because it was never old
Ikkemotubbe's to sell to Grandfather for bequeathment and repudiation.
Because it was never Ikkemotubbe's father's father's to bequeath Ikkemotubbe to sell to Grandfather or any man because on the instant when Ikkemotubbe discovered, realized, that he could sell it for money, on that
instant it ceased ever to have been his forever, father to father, to father,
and the man who bought it bought nothing."

The right attitude toward nature is, as a matter of fact, associated
with the right attitude toward man, and the mere lust for power over
nature is associated with the lust for power over other men, for God gave
the earth to man, we read in "The Bear," not "to hold for himself and his
descendants inviolable title forever, generation after generation, to the ob-
longs and squares of the earth, but to hold the earth mutual and intact
in the communal anonymity of brotherhood, and all the fee He asked was
pity and humility and sufferance and endurance and the sweat of his face
for bread." It is the failure of this pity which curses the earth (the land
in Faulkner's particular country is "accursed" by chattel slavery, but slavery
is simply one of the possible forms of the failure). But the rape of nature
and the crime against man are always avenged. The rape of nature, the mere
exploitation of it without love, is always avenged because the attitude which
commits that crime also commits the crime against men which in turn exacts
vengeance, so that man finally punishes himself. It is only by this line of
reasoning that one can, I think, read the last page of "Delta Autumn":

This land which man has deswamped and denuded and derivered in two generations so that white men can own plantations and commute every night to Memphis and black men own plantations and ride in jim crow cars to Chicago to live in millionaires' mansions on Lake Shore Drive; where white men rent farms and live like niggers and niggers crop on shares and live like animals; where cotton is planted and grows man-tall in the very cracks of the sidewalks, and usury and mortgage and bankruptcy and measureless wealth, Chinese and African and Aryan and Jew, all breed and spawn together until no man has time to say which one is which nor cares . . . . No wonder the ruined woods I used to know don't cry for retribution! he thought: The people who have destroyed it will accomplish its revenge.

The attitude toward nature in Faulkner's work, however, does not involve a sinking into nature. In Faulkner's mythology man has "suzerainty over the earth," he is not of the earth, and it is the human virtues which count—"pity and humility and sufferance and endurance." If we take even the extreme case of the idiot Snopes and his fixation on the cow in *The Hamlet* (a scene whose function in the total order of the book is to show that even the idiot pervert is superior to Flem), a scene which shows the human being as close as possible to the "natural" level, we find that the scene is the most lyrical in Faulkner's work: even the idiot is human and not animal, for only human desires, not animal, clothe themselves in poetry. I think that George Marion O'Donnell is right in pointing to the humanism-naturalism opposition in Faulkner's work, and over and over again we find that the point of some novel or story has to do with the human effort to find or create values in the mechanical round of experience—"not just to eat and evacuate and sleep warm," as Charlotte Rittenmeyer says in *The Wild Palms,* "so we can get up and eat and evacuate in order to sleep warm again," or not just to raise cotton to buy niggers to raise cotton to buy niggers, as it is put in another place. Even when a character seems to be caught in the iron ring of some compulsion, of some mechanical process (the hunted Negro of "Red Leaves," the tall convict of *The Wild Palms,* Christmas of *Light in August*), the effort may be discernible. And in Quentin's attempt, in *The Sound and the Fury,* to persuade his sister Caddy, who is pregnant by one of the boys of Jefferson, to confess that she has committed incest with him, we find among other things the idea that "the horror" and "the clean flame" would be preferable to the meaninglessness of the "loud world."

*Humor.* One of the most important remarks in Cowley's introduction is that concerning humor. There is, especially in the later books, "a sort of

homely and sober-sided frontier humor that is seldom achieved in contemporary writing." Cowley continues: "In a curious way, Faulkner combines two of the principal traditions in American letters: the tradition of
psychological horror, often close to symbolism, that begins with Charles
Brockden Brown, our first professional novelist, and extends through Poe,
Melville, Henry James (in his later stories), Stephen Crane and Hemingway; and the other tradition of frontier humor and realism, beginning with
Augustus Longstreet's *Georgia Scenes* and having Mark Twain as its best
example." The observation is an acute one, for the distortions of humor
and the distortions of horror in Faulkner's work are closely akin and
frequently, in a given instance, can scarcely be disentangled.

It is true that the most important strain of humor in Faulkner's work
is derived from the tradition of frontier humor (though it is probable that
he got it from the porches of country stores and the courthouse yards of
county-seat towns and not from any book), and it is true that the most
spectacular displays of Faulkner's humor are of this order—for example, the
"Spotted Horses" episode from *The Hamlet* or the story "Was." But there
are other strains which might be distinguished and investigated. For example, there is a kind of Dickensian humor; the scene in the Memphis
brothel from *Sanctuary,* which is reprinted here under the title "Uncle Bud
and the Three Madams," is certainly more Dickensian than frontier. There
is a subdued humor, sometimes shading into pathos, in the treatment of
some of the Negro characters and in their dialogue. And there is an irony
ranging from that in the scene in *Sanctuary* where Miss Reba, the madam,
in offended decency keeps telling Temple, "Lie down and cover up your
nekkidness," while the girl talks with Benbow, to that in the magnificently
sustained monologue of Jason at the end of *The Sound and the Fury.*

In any case, humor in Faulkner's work is never exploited for its own
sake. It is regularly used as an index, as a lead, to other effects. The humor
in itself may be striking, but Faulkner is not a humorist in the sense, say,
that Mark Twain is. His humor is but one perspective on the material and
it is never a final perspective, as we can see from such an example as the
episode of "Spotted Horses." Nothing could be more wide of the point than
the remark in Maxwell Geismar's essay on Faulkner to the effect that Faulkner in *The Hamlet* "seems now to accept the antics of his provincial morons,
to enjoy the chronicle of their low-grade behavior; he submerges himself
in their clownish degradation." All the critic seems to find in Mink Snopes'
victim with his lifelong devotion to the memory of his dead wife, and in
Ratliff with his good heart and ironical mind and quiet wisdom, is comic
"descendants of the gangling and giggling Wash Jones."

*The Poor White.* The above remark leads us to the not uncommon misconception about the role of the poor white in Faulkner's work. It is true that the Snopeses are poor whites, descendants of bushwackers (and therefore outside society, as the bushwhacker was outside society, had no "side" in the Civil War but tried to make a good thing of it), and it is true that Snopesism represents a special kind of villainy and degradation, the form that the pure doctrine of exploitation and degradation takes in the society of which Faulkner writes, but any careful reader realizes that a Snopes is not to be equated with a poor white. For instance, the book most fully about the poor white, *As I Lay Dying,* is full of sympathy and poetry. There are a hundred touches like that in Cash's soliloquy about the phonograph: "I reckon it's a good thing we ain't got ere a one of them. I reckon I wouldn't never get no work done a-tall for listening to it. I don't know if a little music ain't about the nicest thing a fellow can have. Seems like when he comes in tired of a night, it ain't nothing could rest him like having a little music played and him resting." Or like the long section toward the middle of the book devoted to Addie Bundren, a section which is full of eloquence like that of this paragraph: "And then he died. He did not know he was dead. I would lie by him in the dark, hearing the dark land talking of God's love and His beauty and His sin; hearing the dark voicelessness in which the words are the deeds, and the other words that are not deeds, that are just the gaps in people's lacks, coming down like the cries of geese out of the wild darkness in the old terrible nights, fumbling at the deeds like orphans to whom are pointed out in a crowd two faces and told, That is your father, your mother." Do these passages indicate a relish in the "antics of his provincial morons"?

The whole *As I Lay Dying* is based on the heroic effort of the Bundren family to fulfill the promise to the dead mother, to take her body to Jefferson; and the fact that Anse Bundren, after the heroic effort has been completed, immediately gets him a new wife, the "duck-shaped woman" with the "hard-looking pop-eyes," does not negate the heroism of the effort nor the poetry and feeling which give flesh to the book. We are told by one critic that "what should have been the drama of the Bundrens thus becomes in the end a sort of brutal farce," and that we are "unable to feel the tragedy because the author has refused to accept the Bundrens, as he did accept the Compsons, as tragic." Rather, I should say, the Bundrens may come off a little better than the latter-day Compsons, the whining mother, the promiscuous Caddy, the ineffectual Quentin, and the rest. The Bundrens, at least, are capable of the heroic effort, and the promise is fulfilled. What the conclusion indicates is that even such a

fellow as Anse Bundren (who is not typical of his family, by the way), in
the grip of an idea, in terms of promise or code, is capable of rising out
of his ordinary level; Anse falls back at the end, but only after the prop
of the idea and obligation have been removed. And we may recall that
even the "gangling and giggling Wash Jones" has always been capable of
some kind of obscure dream and aspiration (his very attachment to
Sutpen indicates that), and that in the end he achieves dignity and manhood.

The final and incontrovertible evidence that Snopes is not to be
equated with poor white comes in *The Hamlet* (though actually most of the
characters in the book, though they may be poor, are not, strictly speaking, "poor whites" at all, but rather what uninstructed reviewers choose
to call by that label). The point of the book is the assault made on a solid
community of plain, hard-working small farmers by Snopeses and Snopesism. Ratliff is not rich, but he is not Flem Snopes. And if the corruption
of Snopesism does penetrate into the communtiy, there is no one here
who can be compared in degradation and vileness to Jason of *The Sound
and the Fury,* the Compson who has embraced Snopesism. In fact, Popeye and Flem, Faulkner's best advertised villains, cannot, for vileness
and ultimate meanness, touch Jason.

*The Negro.* In one of Faulkner's books it is said that every white child
is born crucified on a black cross. Remarks like this have led to a gross
misconception of the place of the Negro in Faulkner's work, to the notion
that Faulkner "hates" Negroes. For instance, we find Maxwell Geismar
exclaiming what a "strange inversion" it is to take the Negro, who is the
"tragic consequence," and to exhibit him as the "evil cause" of the failure
of the old order in the South.

This is a misreading of the text. It is slavery, not the Negro, which
is defined, quite flatly, as the curse, over and over again, and the Negro
is the black cross in so far as he is the embodiment of the curse, the reminder of the guilt, the incarnation of the problem. That is the basic
point. But now and then, as a kind of tangential irony, we have the notion,
not of the burden of the white on the black, but of the burden of the
black on the white, the weight of obligation, inefficiency, and so on, as
well as the weight of guilt (the notion we find in the old story of the
plantation mistress who, after the Civil War, said: "Mr. Lincoln thought
he was emancipating those slaves, but he was really emancipating me").

For instance, we get hints of this notion in "Red Leaves": one of
the Indians, sweating in the chase of the runaway Negro who is to be

killed for the Man's funeral, says, "Damn that Negro," and the other
Indian replies, "Yao. When have they ever been anything but a trial and
a care to us?" But the black cross is, fundaméntally, the weight of the
white man's guilt, the white man who now sells salves and potions to
"bleach the pigment and straighten the hair of negroes that they might
resemble the very race which for two hundred years had held them in
bondage and from which for another hundred years not even a bloody
civil war would have set them completely free." The curse is still operative,
as the crime is still compounded.

The actual role of the Negro in Faulkner's fiction is consistently one
of pathos or heroism. It is not merely, as has been suggested more than
once, that Faulkner condescends to the good and faithful servant, the
"white folks' nigger." There are figures like Dilsey, but they are not as
impressive as the Negro in "Red Leaves" or Sam Fathers, who, with the
bear, is the hero of "The Bear." The fugitive, who gains in the course of
the former story a shadowy symbolic significance, is told in the end by
one of the Indians who overtake him, "You ran well. Do not be ashamed,"
and when he walks among the Indians, he is "the tallest there, his high,
close, mud-caked head looming above them all." And Sam Fathers is the
fountainhead of wisdom which Ike McCaslin finally gains, and the repository of the virtues which are central for Faulkner—"an old man,
son of a Negro slave and an Indian king, inheritor on the one hand of
the long chronicle of a people who had learned humility through suffering
and learned pride through the endurance which survived suffering, and on
the other side the chronicle of a people even longer in the land than the
first, yet who now existed there only in the solitary brotherhood of an
old and childless Negro's alien blood and the wild and invincible spirit
of an old bear."

Even Christmas, in *Light in August,* though he is sometimes spoken
of as a villain, is a mixture of heroism and pathos. He is the lost, suffering, enduring creature (the figure like Sam Fathers, the tall convict of
*The Wild Palms,* or Dilsey in *The Sound and the Fury*), and even the
murder he commits at the end is a fumbling attempt to define his manhood, is an attempt to break out of the iron ring of mechanism, to lift
himself out of "nature," for the woman whom he kills has become a
figure of the horror of the human which has surrendered the human
attributes. (We may compare Christmas to Mink Snopes in *The Hamlet*
in this respect: Mink, mean and vicious as he is, kills out of a kind of

warped and confused pride, and by this affirmation is set off against his kinsman Flem, whose only values are those of pure Snopesism.)

Even such a brief comment on the Negro in Faulkner's work cannot close without this passage from "The Bear":

"Because they will endure. They are better than we are. Stronger than we are. Their vices are vices aped from white men or that white men and bondage have taught them: improvidence and intemperance and evasion— not laziness: evasion: of what white men had set them to, not for their aggrandizement or even comfort but his own—" and McCaslin

"All right. Go on: Promiscuity. Violence. Instability and lack of control. Inability to distingish between mine and thine—" and he

"How distinguish when for two hundred years mine did not even exist for them?" and McCaslin

"All right. Go on. And their virtues—" and he

"Yes. Their own. Endurance—" and McCaslin

"So have mules:" and he

"—and pity and tolerance and forbearance and fidelity and love of children—" and McCaslin

"So have dogs:" and he

"—whether their own or not or black or not. And more: what they got not only from white people but not even despite white people because they had it already from the old free fathers a longer time free than us because we have never been free—"

And there is the single comment under Dilsey's name in the annotated genealogy of the Compsons which Faulkner has prepared for the present volume: "They endured."

*Technique.* There are excellent comments on this subject by Cowley, Conrad Aiken, Warren Beck, Joseph Warren Beach, and Alfred Kazin, but the subject has not been fully explored. One difficulty is that Faulkner is an incorrigible and restless experimenter, is peculiarly sensitive to the expressive possibilities of shifts in technique and has not developed (like Hemingway or Katherine Anne Porter—lyric rather than dramatic writers, artists with a great deal of self-certainty) in a straight line.

Provisionally, we may distinguish in Faulkner's work three basic methods of handling a narrative. One is best typified in *Sanctuary,* where there is a tightly organized plot, a crisp, laconic style, an objective presentation of character—an impersonal method. Another is best typified by *As I Lay Dying* or *The Sound and the Fury,* where each character unfolds in his own language or flow of being before us—a dramatic method in that the author does not obtrude, but a method which makes the subjective reference of character the medium of presentation. Another is best typified by "Was," "The Bear," or the story of the tall convict in *The Wild Palms,* where the organization of the narrative is episodic and the sense of a voice, a narrator's presence (though not necessarily a narrator in the formal sense), is almost constantly felt—a method in which the medium is ultimately a "voice" as index to sensibility. The assumptions underlying these methods, and the relations among them, would provide a study.

Cowley's emphasis on the unity of Faulkner's work, the fact that all the novels and stories are to be taken as aspects of a single, large design, is very important. It is important, for one thing, in regard to the handling of character. A character, Sutpen, for instance, may appear in various perspectives, so that from book to book we move toward a final definition much as in actual life we move toward the definition of a person. The same principle applies to event, as Conrad Aiken has pointed out, the principle of the spiral method which takes the reader over and over the same event from a different altitude, as it were, and a different angle. In relation to both character and event this method, once it is understood by the reader, makes for a kind of realism and a kind of suspense (in the formal not the factual sense) not common in fiction.

The emphasis on the unity of Faulkner's work may, however, lead to an underrating of the degree of organization within individual works. Cowley is right in pointing out the structural defect in *Light in August,* but he may be putting too much emphasis on the over-all unity and not enough on the organization of the individual work when he says that *The Hamlet* tends to resolve into a "series of episodes resembling beads on a string." I think that in that novel we have a type of organization in which the thematic rather than the narrative emphasis is the basic principle, and once we grasp that fact the unity of the individual work may come clear. In fact, the whole subject of the principle of thematic organization in the novels and long stories, "The Bear," for instance, needs investigation. In pieces which seem disjointed, or which seem to have the mere tale-teller's improvisations, we may sometimes discover the true unity if we think of the line of meaning, the symbolic ordering, and surrender ourselves to the tale-teller's "voice." And it may be useful at times to recall the distinction between the formal, forensic realism of Ibsen as opposed to the fluid, suggestive realism of Chekhov.

*Symbol and Image.* Cowley and O'Donnell have given acute readings of the main symbolic outline of Faulkner's fiction, but no one has yet devoted himself to the study of symbolic motifs which, though not major, are nevertheless extremely instructive. For instance, the images of the hunt, the flight, the pursuit, such as we have in "Red Leaves," *The Wild Palms,* the episode of "Percy Grimm" in *Light in August,* "The Bear," "Delta Autumn," "Was," and (especially in the hordes of moving Negroes) in *The Unvanquished.* Or there is the important symbolic relationship between man and earth. Or there is the contrast between images of compulsion and images of will or freedom. Or there is the device of what we might call the frozen moment, the arrested action which becomes symbolic, as in the moment when, in "An Odor of Verbena" (from *The Unvanquished*), Drusilla offers the pistols to the hero.

*Polarity.* To what extent does Faulkner work in terms of polarities, oppositions, paradoxes, inversions of roles? How much does he employ a line of concealed (or open) dialectic progression as a principle for his fiction? The study of these questions may lead to the discovery of principles of organization in his work not yet defined by criticism.

The study of Faulkner is the most challenging single task in contemporary American literature for criticism to undertake. Here is a novelist who, in mass of work, in scope of material, in range of effect, in reportorial accuracy and symbolic subtlety, in philosophical weight can be put beside the masters of our own past literature. Yet this accomplishment has been effected in what almost amounts to critical isolation and silence, and when the silence has been broken it has usually been broken by someone (sometimes one of our better critics) whose reading has been hasty, whose analysis unscholarly and whose judgments superficial. The picture of Faulkner presented to the public by such criticism is a combination of Thomas Nelson Page, a fascist and a psychopath, gnawing his nails. Of course, this picture is usually accompanied by a grudging remark about genius.

Cowley's book, for its intelligence, sensitivity, and sobriety in the introduction, and for the ingenuity and judgment exhibited in the selections, would be valuable at any time. But it is especially valuable at this time. Perhaps it can mark a turning point in Faulkner's reputation. That will be of slight service to Faulkner, who, as much as any writer of our place and time, can rest in confidence. He can afford to wait. But can we?

# WILDERNESS AND CIVILIZATION:
# A NOTE ON WILLIAM FAULKNER

URSULA BRUMM

1

AMONG the many analogues to the Bible in William Faulkner's last book *A Fable* is one to the well-known words of I Corinthians 13:8 "Charity never faileth":

> Rapacity does not fail, else man must deny he breathes. Not rapacity: its whole vast glorious history repudiates that. It does not, cannot, must not fail. Not just one family in one nation privileged to soar comet-like into splendid zenith through and because of it, not just one nation among all the nations selected as heir to that vast splendid heritage; not just France, but all governments and nations which ever rose and endured long enough to leave their mark as such, had sprung from it and in and upon and by means of it became forever fixed in the amazement of man's present and the glory of his past; civilization itself is its password and Christianity its masterpiece; Chartres and the Sistine Chapel, the pyramids and the rock-wombed powder-magazines under the Gates of Hercules its altars and monuments, Michelangelo and Phidias and Newton and Ericsson and Archimedes and Krupp its priests and popes and bishops; the long deathless roster of its glory—Caesar and the Barcas and the two Macedonians, our own Bonaparte and the great Russian and the giants who strode nimbused in red hair like fire across the Aurora Borealis, and all the lesser nameless who were not heroes but, glorious in anonymity, at least served the destiny of heroes—the generals and admirals, the corporals and ratings of glory, the batmen and orderlies of reknown, and the chairmen of boards and the presidents of federations, the doctors and lawyers and educators and churchmen who after nineteen centuries have rescued the son of heaven from oblivion and translated him from mere meek heir to earth to chairman of its board of trade . . . it is in and from rapacity that he [man] gets, holds, his immortality . . . (259-60)

This is, indeed, the focal point of *A Fable,* summing up in a sweeping rhetorical passage the whole history of human effort and achievement

Reprinted with permission from *Partisan Review,* Summer, 1955, pp. 340-50.

and finding it all rooted in rapacity: trade, government, war, art, Christianity, all of civilization. It is against this tremendous edifice of human endeavor that the Corporal, the Christ figure of the *Fable,* is juxtaposed in his great passive act of refusing to fight. He is a representative of the mass of unambitious, silent people, who have no stake in any of it, and only "endure." Christ in Faulkner's vision is the "mere meek heir to earth," who, "with his humility and pity and sacrifice," has not even converted the world to Christianity; "It was pagan and bloody Rome that did it"; and his modern reincarnation, the Corporal, is one of Faulkner's tragic heroes who, as Malraux has said, stand up against the irremediable and are crushed by it. He does not save anybody. He is the hero in his role as opponent of civilization.

So far it seems that readers and reviewers of *A Fable* have been saved from the shock of recognizing the ferocity of Faulkner's vision because they have approached it with the traditional interpretation of the Bible, adapting the novel to it. The truth is that it is absolute heresy. The same shock is due to all who adhere to the idea of civilization as the accumulated result of the best human efforts, which is perhaps somewhat in danger of becoming corrupted or of exercising a corrupting influence on innocent virtue. But Faulkner's view is a far cry from Rousseau's petulant argument that civilization corrupts virtue and morals; it is a wholesale indictment of civilization as rapacious, seeing its best fruits precisely a sublimation of this, its innermost nature.

This is not a new turn of thought in Faulkner's work. It has been latent in it for a long time, at first more as a feeling than a formulated thought, but already clearly emerging in *Go Down, Moses.* Moreover, there is a latent hostility, a deep-seated suspicion of civilization which has been present, if submerged, in American literature since its early times. It can be found in many of its writers—flippantly in Mark Twain, who lets Huck say in the end: "But I reckon I got to light out for the territory ahead of the rest, because Aunt Sally she's going to adopt me and civilize me, and I can't stand it"—although it has never been conceived and articulated so radically. But in one form or another it has given to American realism from Crane and Dreiser to Hemingway its characteristic bluntness and the vigor of absolute, if undefined, conviction.

The first American proponent of this feeling was James Fenimore Cooper, although in this as in other things he never quite recognized the full implication of what he was saying. It is, of course, Leatherstocking and his friends who are the spokesmen of this philosophy. In *The Pioneers* the young hunter says, "The wolf of the forest is not more rapacious for his prey than man is greedy of gold"; and Leatherstocking cries, "This comes from settling a country!" when he sees the cruel, greedy slaughter of the pigeons. "The wickedness and waste of the settlements" is a stock phrase of his, which is contrasted to his own unambitious and rightful life in the wilderness. Cooper, so different from Faulkner in all other respects, is indeed the writer closest to him in this trend of thought. *Go Down, Moses* and the Leatherstocking tales, above all *The Pioneers* and *The Prairie,* belong side by side in this peculiarly American tradition.

It has been pointed out by various critics[1] that Cooper in his *Pioneers* and *Prairie* described a crucial stage of American history: the receding of the wilderness before the victorious and irresistible onslaught of civilization. This is also a significant part of the American experience. In this struggle, Cooper's sympathies were divided. In part against his own convictions, he created Leatherstocking with unfailing sympathy to represent what he felt was, after all, a lost cause. He himself was convinced "that the time will come when the civilization of America will look down on that of any other section of the world."

Nevertheless he gave to Leatherstocking's cause all the persuasiveness (and a bit more) possible to this character. There are a number of statements in Natty's remarkable eloquence which are made again and again; some of them not really proving very much, but made nevertheless with a stubborn and forceful insistence. One is Leatherstocking's age and the long time he has been living in the forest; and that he is kinless, without wife or children, and solitary; another one is the complaint about the greediness of the settlers, their wickedness and wasteful manners. Opposed to that is the "rule" of the forest, an unwritten law to kill only as much as is necessary for one's subsistence: one should not "fish and hunt out of rule"; because God has put the animals into the wilderness and he "won't see the waste of his creatures for nothing." Finally there is the question of the land. Whose property is it rightfully? A disconcerting question under the circumstances, it persistently crops up at various stages of these "romances." Leatherstocking insists that it should be there for all men to use reverently.

These are the facts which by emphasis and reiteration are implanted in the reader's mind. The same elements, with some modification of Faulknerian rhetoric, can be found in *Go Down, Moses.* There also exists a

1. H. N. Smith, *Virgin Land* (Cambridge, 1950), p. 58 ff. R. H. Pearce, "The Leatherstocking Tales Re-examined," *South Atlantic Quart.,* Oct. 1947.

curious affinity between the persons whom the two writers have made to represent the closest communion with the wilderness: Cooper's Leather-stocking and Faulkner's Sam Fathers, son of a Chickasaw chief and a Negro slave, who initiates Isaac McCaslin to the woods. It is an affinity which stems not from literary tradition but from similar symbolic aims. Both are old, illiterate but wise, solitary, kinless, childless, without property, and are held by the others in the veneration of an almost extinct species. Their deaths coincide with the death of the wilderness, it is a waning away, as if they are taken back into nature, "When I am gone," says the dying Leather-stocking, "there will be an end to my race."

This is at least the way in which Cooper first conceived Leatherstock-ing; later he rejuvenated him, but although he tried hard to get him into wedlock, he did not succeed. It has been shown by H. N. Smith in *Virgin Land* how the convention of the romance and Cooper's own social prej-udice hindered that; but actually Cooper had already sinned against both by creating this character and giving him a dominant role. Above all, it was the symbolic significance invested in Leatherstocking, weightier than Cooper himself realized, which refused to be destroyed: Leatherstocking as well as Sam Fathers had to be and remain solitary to serve their symbolic function. To start a family, to provide and procreate, would have severed their bonds to the wilderness and involved them in all the activities bearing the burden and the taint of civilization. Sterile in their solitariness, they are the representatives of a dying giant: the wilderness.

## 2

It has been said that America is a country without a pre-history.[2] In another sense, however, America is the unique case of a country whose pre-history, the wilderness, is still with us, in remnants at least, and men who are living now, or only a hundred years ago, wrote about it from experience. It has been described by writers so different as Cooper, Mel-ville and Faulkner, to mention only three, in almost identical terms: they have seen the primeval forest, as it existed at the beginning of time, and could never forget it. "How should a man who has lived in towns and schools know anything about the wonders of the woods?" says Cooper. "No, no, lad; there has that little stream of water been playing among these hills *since He made the world,* and not a dozen white men have ever laid eyes on it." And Melville, following the same train of thought: ". . . there came into

2. F. G. Friedmann, "America: A Country without Pre-History," *Partisan Review,* March-April 1952.

the mind of Pierre thoughts and fancies never imbibed within the gates of towns; but only given forth by the atmosphere of primeval forests, which with the eternal ocean, are the only unchanged objects remaining to this day, from those that *originally met the gaze of Adam.*" And Faulkner, who juxtaposes the saga of the McCaslins against this primeval "doomed wilderness whose edges were being constantly and punily gnawed at by men with plows and axes": "There was some of it left, although now it was two hundred miles from Jefferson when once it had been thirty. He watched it, not being conquered, destroyed, so much as retreating since its purpose was served now and *its time an outmoded time.*" It is un-historical, prehistoric time.

Surely, to all these writers this was a tremendous experience, whether in reality or in imagination, and neither Rousseau nor any other European could have explained it to them. It is an experience wholly autochthonous, and actually the more clearly and genuinely realized the less the mind is influenced by European ideas of nature or the picturesque. What they are trying to get at is not Emerson's nature, philosophically conceived and inspired by European thought, which "wears the color of the spirit," but this raw breath of the wilderness that modern Europeans never knew, in whose countries every patch of woods has been cared for hundreds of years. Their sense of nature has fed only on these thoroughly cultivated forests, which are really parks compared to the American wilderness. It seems therefore inaccurate to speak of this American experience in terms taken from European history of thought: both romanticism and primitivism belong to a frame of mind which craves to reach back to a state of nature actually lost long ago. But to these Americans the wilderness was still there, receding but still existing, and they tried to catch its last breath and to convey its sense of life, a remnant from the world's beginnings: a-historic, un-human, and almost incomprehensible. When Cooper tries to describe the wilderness he does so in the conventional language of his time. But he is really most expressive when he abandons it under the impact of a powerful experience. "What do you see when you get up there?" Leatherstocking is asked. " 'Creation,' said Natty, dropping the end of his rod into the water and sweeping one hand around him in a circle, 'all creation, lad.' " Faulkner gives us a sense of wilderness, not any character's impression of it. The words he uses to present it are: tremendous, brooding, sentient, attentive or inattentive, impartial, omniscient. He gives not so much a symbolization, as an impersonation, in the bear, the snake, or the buck, whom Sam Fathers hails with "Oleh, Chief, Grandfather."

For "there was something running in Sam Fathers' veins which runs in the veins of the buck too." In other words, America's pre-history, the wilderness, is now in the process of being transformed into myth, and the bear and Sam Fathers are taking the parts of the trolls, the giants and the Rubezahls of Europe.

This deep attachment of the wilderness, to untouched, timeless nature, reflects on the attitude toward civilization, its inevitable enemy and destroyer. Here again is a genuinely American experience for which Europe has no counterpart: the destruction of the wilderness by civilization in one short, dramatic act taking less than a man's lifetime. There is, to be sure, a sentimentality in this feeling for the wilderness: only as doomed and vanquished could it be lamented and loved so much by writers who necessarily, just by picking up pen and paper, have to confess themselves as part of the civilization they accuse. But love and art feed well on contradictions; and it is inevitable that the wilderness, achieving the revenge of the weak and the vanquished, should engage the imagination of the American writer in order to achieve its immortality with a vengeance. Cooper saw and described with sad anger the slaughter of the pigeons. To kill them, the settlers fire a cannon which otherwise is used for the celebrations of the 4th of July; and one wonders how much symbolical weight Cooper wanted to apply by that. He did not face the question whether it is the "wickedness" of the settlers, or civilization as such, which is to blame. Back in his mind there seems always to be the possibility of an ideal solution in which good settlers take the preachings of Leatherstocking to their heart and respect and preserve nature. In that sense he can in the end somewhat inconsistently celebrate Leatherstocking as "the foremost in that band of pioneers who are opening the way for the march of the nation across the continent." Not so Faulkner, who recognizes the inevitable, tragic conflict. His sorrow about the vanishing of the wilderness is as acute and more articulate than Cooper's, and he comes to a conclusion which to my knowledge no European has ever drawn with such severity: at the root and beginning of civilization and all its achievements is rapacity, and civilized man has to bear the burden of this guilt always and everywhere.

If this is, in the end, a critique of the empire builders, it is at bottom a questioning of the basis of our civilization: property, specifically the property of the land. Even the property-minded Cooper felt uneasy about this question and could not help dealing with it. Clumsily he used it as the nail on which to hang his plot of the *Pioneers*; and the property of the land, or rather its "dispossession," is a topic of discussion between Indians and whites throughout the Leatherstocking tales. Again, American experience is here sharper, more dramatic, and above all more recent than that of any of the European nations, for most of whom a similar act of dispossession and appropriation has happened at least as far back as the migration of tribes, and therefore cannot sting the awareness of a modern writer very acutely.

Ownership of the land is the basic theme of the stories in *Go Down, Moses*. The book relates the story of a family, the McCaslins, their white and their black branch, narrated not in novel form but in more or less long short stories (the most substantial being "The Bear") which are focused on various members and events in the family history. This is their common background: Old Carothers McCaslin bought his land "with white man's money" from the Indian chief Ikkemotubbe, who in turn possessed it by treachery. (There is no sentimentalizing about the Indians here; they share the guilt.) McCaslin "tamed and ordered or believed he had tamed and ordered (the wilderness) for the reason that the human beings he held in bondage and in the power of life and death had removed the forest from it and in their sweat scratched the surface of it to a depth of perhaps fourteen inches in order to grow something out of it which had not been there before and which could be translated back into money. . . ." The ownership of the land through money as well as its use for money and profit-making are part of the guilt, because God created the earth to hold it "mutual and intact in the communal anonymity of brotherhood."

Two of McCaslin's grandsons figure prominently in these stories: Isaac McCaslin, the only white descendant in the male line, and the Negro Lucas Beauchamp, son of McCaslin's son by a black mistress. Isaac, who who was initiated to the wilderness, and manhood and huntership, by Sam Fathers, inherits the land but relinquishes it to his cousin Edmonds, a son of old McCaslin's daughter (it seems all good heroes of Faulkner have to give up their inheritance):

"I can't repudiate it. It was never mine to repudiate. It was never Father's and Uncle Buddy's to bequeath me to repudiate because it was never Grandfather's . . . because on the instant when Ikkemotubbe discovered, realized that he could sell it for money, on that instant it ceased ever to have been his forever, father to father to father, and the man who bought it bought nothing."

Isaac McCaslin pays back, and increases, to his black cousins the money intended for them by his grandfather in atonement of his guilt. After he has given up the land, he possesses "but one object more than he could wear and carry in his pockets and his hands at one time and that was an iron cot and the stained lean mattress which he used camping in the woods for deer and bear or for fishing or simply because he loved the woods." He takes up the trade of a carpenter, "because if the Nazarene had found carpenting good for the life and end He had assumed and elected to serve, it would be all right too for Isaac McCaslin." Isaac, who renounces the rapacity and guilt of property is in that sense a forerunner of the Corporal in *A Fable,* though without quite realizing as yet that this is a renunciation of civilization and all it implies. However, we find him in such close communion with the wilderness that this in itself is already a repudiation of civilization; and he rejects the responsibility of keeping the farm, which his wife demands of him. But like the Corporal, he only establishes an example of refusal; he saves nobody but himself perhaps.

The McCaslin saga is another of Faulkner's representations of the story of the South: the ownership of the land by one man (the white man) under exclusion of another (his black cousin) results in tension and guilt, and this is the famous "curse" of the South. But not only of the South. Already in *Go Down, Moses* allusion is made to the rapacity of the westward expansion, and the plantation is made symbol of exploitation on world-historic scale: ". . . on down through the tedious and shabby chronicle of His chosen sprung from Abraham, and of the sons of them who dispossessed Abraham, and of the five hundred years during which half the known world and all it contained was chattel to one city as this plantation and all the life it contained was chattel and revokeless thrall to this commissary store and those ledgers yonder. . . ." The plantation and its system symbolizes Roman imperialism.

### 3

It seems that Faulkner's work invites interpretations in terms of various anti-theses. *A Fable,* as we have seen, makes a basic division between the meek of the earth and the ambitious, rapacious but creative ones, who participate in the works of civilization. Many critics who have dealt with Faulkner have tried to explain his entire writings by tracing in them a pair of anti-theses: traditionalism against anti-traditionalism, the Sartoris world against the Snopes world, sickness against primitivism,[3] humanism against animalism, etc. Sensitive critics have, of course, been aware that none of these scholastic schemes can really encompass Faulkner's turbulent imagination. Nevertheless, the conception of Faulkner as a traditionalist,

3. M. Backman, "Sickness and Primitivism," *Accent,* Winter 1954.

who hates and castigates the "anti-traditional" forces, represented chiefly by the Snopeses, prevails in most discussions of his work. It is along this line that some of the best and most influential essays on Faulkner have been written: as G. M. O'Donnell's "Faulkner's Mythology," from which Malcolm Cowley took off in his introduction to the *Portable Faulkner*. Robert Penn Warren, in turn, somewhat more cautiously, continued Cowley's thoughts.[4] But O'Donnell had been the first to run into difficulties and miss the point when he interpreted *Light in August* in accordance with this theory.

Actually, it should always have been clear that Faulkner never was a traditionalist in any accepted sense of the term. His attachment to the South, like Quentin Compson's in *Absalom, Absalom!*, is one of tormented love but not of admiration. Although he frequently went far enough back into history, he never chose to concentrate on Southern society in its happier ante-bellum days; or to hold it up as a model for preservation. He always shows a tradition in the process of going to pieces, and probes into the past for the causes. In the causal complexity there is always at bottom the same thing: a guilt of rapacity and greediness which has corrupted the tradition right at its starting point, an inevitable sin in man's civilizing efforts. In others words: tradition itself is part of the curse, it is its continuance through time; and history for Faulkner is really nothing but a working out of the guilt, either by atonement, as in the case of Isaac McCaslin, or by disasters administered as punishment. They are not disasters of a blind fate, but proceeding logically from the guilt and brought about by the same spirit which created the guilt. Justice in Faulkner is always done by self-inflicted punishment. "No wonder the ruined woods I used to know don't cry for retribution! he thought: The people who have destroyed it will accomplish its revenge."

Sutpen's downfall is a perfect illustration of this. But he is not the only sinner; the McCaslins, Sartorises, Compsons, and all the other aristocratic planters of the South, also acquired their land by devious means. Faulkner has developed this idea slowly. When he wrote *Absalom, Absalom!*, published in 1936, he made Sutpen an outsider, who with crueller methods imitates the already established planters in order to found a dynasty of his own. But in *Go Down, Moses* (1942) he shows that the older families had the same doubtful beginning, and the system of a Southern plantation can serve as symbol for the exploitation of ancient

4. All three essays reprinted above.

Rome. And by 1954, in *A Fable,* Faulkner sees the same guilt, which
cursed the South, in all civilization.

The stories of *Go Down, Moses,* particularly "The Bear," "Old
People," and "Delta Autumn," when discussed critically, are usually put
under the heading of "primitivism." Ironically enough, this is done
primarily with the same arguments used for Faulkner as traditionalist,
namely his hate for the mechanized aspects of modern civilization: the
auto, the machine, the gadgets.

A few months ago, Faulkner wrote a letter to the *New York Times*
about the crash of an Italian airliner trying to make an instrument landing
at Idlewild Airport in bad weather. The pilot, William Faulkner maintains,
"was victim of that mystical, unquestioning, almost religious awe and
veneration in which our culture has trained us to hold gadgets—any gadget
if it is only complex enough and cryptic enough and costs enough." The
pilot crashed, in Faulkner's opinion, because he did not dare to rely on his
experience, his instinct, or "the seat of his pants." "We all had better
grieve for all people beneath a culture," he says, "which holds any
mechanical (gadget) superior to any man simply because the one, being
mechanical, is infallible, while the other, being nothing but man, is not
just subject to failure but doomed to it."

The imaginative parallel to this letter is to be found in "The Bear,"
where Isaac McCaslin in search for Old Ben realizes that he has to relinquish all the gadgets with which civilization has provided him: first the
gun, but that is not enough; he has to leave his old silver watch and the
compass too. Only then is he able to meet the bear, "epitome and apotheosis of the old wild life." The question is whether this and all it implies is
"primitivism," or not rather a form of humanism, since it is marked by a
reliance on the purely human qualities under exclusion of all the mechanical inventions with which civilization has armed mankind. And the
rejection of civilization, whether in *A Fable,* or in *Go Down, Moses,* is
not linked to savagery or paganism. It means a closer communion with
the wilderness, and at the same time leads both the Corporal and Isaac
McCaslin to an *imitatio Christi.* His shadow had already been invoked
in *The Sound and the Fury* and *Light in August.* He now becomes more and
more dominant; not the son of God or the founder of Christianity, but
Christ the archetype of man suffering, and of those who expiate the guilt
of civilization by renunciation of the power and the privilege: Quentin
Compson, Isaac McCaslin, and the Corporal.

# III. The Work:

## Studies of Method and Language

## WILLIAM FAULKNER: THE NOVEL AS FORM

### CONRAD AIKEN

THE FAMOUS REMARK MADE TO MACAULAY—"Young man, the more I consider the less can I conceive where you picked up that style"—might with advantage have been saved for Mr. William Faulkner. For if one thing is more outstanding than another about Mr. Faulkner—some readers find it so outstanding, indeed, that they never get beyond it—it is the uncompromising and almost hypnotic zeal with which he insists upon having a style, and, especially of late, the very peculiar style which he insists upon having. Perhaps to that one should add that he insists *when he remembers* —he can write straightforwardly enough when he wants to; he does so often in the best of his short stories (and they are brilliant), often enough, too, in the novels. But that *style* is what he really wants to get back to; and get back to it he invariably does.

And what a style it is, to be sure! The exuberant and tropical luxuriance of sound which Jim Europe's jazz band used to exhale, like a jungle of rank creepers and ferocious blooms taking shape before one's eyes,— magnificently and endlessly intervolved, glisteningly and ophidianly in motion, coil sliding over coil, and leaf and flower forever magically interchanging,—was scarcely more bewildering, in its sheer inexhaustible fecundity, than Mr. Faulkner's style. Small wonder if even the most passionate of Mr. Faulkner's admirers—among whom the present writer honors himself by enlisting—must find, with each new novel, that the first fifty pages are always the hardest, that each time one must learn all over again *how* to read this strangely fluid and slippery and heavily mannered prose,

Reprinted with permission from *The Atlantic Monthly,* November, 1939, pp. 650-54.

and that one is even, like a kind of Laocoön, sometimes tempted to give it up.

Wrestle, for example, with two very short (for Mr. Faulkner!) sentences, taken from an early page of *Absalom, Absalom!*

Meanwhile, as though in inverse ratio to the vanishing voice, the invoked ghost of the man whom she could neither forgive nor revenge herself upon began to assume a quality almost of solidity, permanence. Itself circumambient and enclosed by its effluvium of hell, its aura of unregeneration, it mused (mused, thought, seemed to possess sentience as if, though dispossessed of the peace—who was impervious anyhow to fatigue—which she declined to give it, it was still irrevocably outside the scope of her hurt or harm) with that quality peaceful and now harmless and not even very attentive— the ogreshape which, as Miss Coldfield's voice went on, resolved out of itself before Quentin's eyes the two half-ogre children, the three of them forming a shadowy background for the fourth one.

Well, it may be reasonably questioned whether, on page thirteen of a novel, that little cordite bolus of suppressed reference isn't a thumping aesthetic mistake. Returned to, when one has finished the book, it may be as simple as daylight; but encountered for the first time, and no matter how often reread, it guards its enigma with the stony impassivity of the Sphinx.

Or take again from the very first page of *The Wild Palms*—Mr. Faulkner's latest novel, and certainly one of his finest—this little specimen of "exposition": "Because he had been born here, on this coast though not in this house but in the other, the residence in town, and had lived here all his life, including the four years at the State University's medical school and the two years as an intern in New Orleans where ( a thick man even when young, with thick soft woman's hands, who should never have been a doctor at all, who even after the six more or less metropolitan years looked out from a provincial and insulated amazement at his classmates and fellows: the lean young men swaggering in the drill jackets on which —to him—they wore the myriad anonymous faces of the probationer nurses with a ruthless and assured braggadocio like decorations, like flower trophies) he had sickened for it." What is one to say of that—or of a sentence only a little lower on the same page which runs for thirty-three lines? Is this, somehow perverted, the influence of the later Henry James—James the Old Pretender?

In short, Mr. Faulkner's style, though often brilliant and always interesting, is all too frequently downright bad; and it has inevitably offered an all-too-easy mark for the sharpshooting of such alert critics as Mr. Wyndham Lewis. But if it is easy enough to make fun of Mr. Faulkner's obsessions for particular words, or his indifference and violence to them, or the parrotlike mechanical mytacism (for it is really like a stammer) with which he will go on endlessly repeating such favorites as "myriad, source-less, impalpable, outrageous, risible, profound," there is nevertheless something more to be said for his passion for overelaborate sentence structure.

Overelaborate they certainly are, baroque and involuted in the extreme, these sentences: trailing clauses, one after another, shadowily in apposition, or perhaps not even with so much connection as that; parenthesis after parenthesis, the parenthesis itself often containing one or more parentheses—they remind one of those brightly colored Chinese eggs of one's childhood, which when opened disclosed egg after egg, each smaller and subtler than the last. It is as if Mr. Faulkner, in a sort of hurried despair, had decided to try to tell us everything, absolutely everything, every last origin or source or quality or qualification, and every possible future or permutation as well, in one terrifically concentrated effort: each sentence to be, as it were, a microcosm. And it must be admitted that the practice is annoying and distracting.

It is annoying, at the end of a sentence, to find that one does not know in the least what was the subject of the verb that dangles *in vacuo*— it is distracting to have to go back and sort out the meaning, track down the structure from clause to clause, then only to find that after all it doesn't much matter, and that the obscurity was perhaps neither subtle nor important. And to the extent that one *is* annoyed and distracted, and *does* thus go back and work it out, it may be at once added that Mr. Faulkner has defeated his own ends. One has had, of course, to emerge from the stream, and to step away from it, in order properly to see it; and as Mr. Faulkner works precisely by a process of *immersion,* of hypnotizing his reader into *remaining immersed* in his stream, this occasional blunder produces irritation and failure.

Nevertheless, despite the blunders, and despite the bad habits and the willful bad writing (and willful it obviously is), the style as a whole is extraordinarily effective; the reader *does* remain immersed, *wants* to remain immersed, and it is interesting to look into the reasons for this. And at once, if one considers these queer sentences not simply by themselves, as monsters of grammar or awkwardness, but in their relation to the book as a whole, one sees a functional reason and necessity for their being as they

are. They parallel in a curious and perhaps inevitable way, and not without
aesthetic justification, the whole elaborate method of *deliberately withheld
meaning,* of progressive and partial and delayed disclosure, which so often
gives the characteristic shape to the novels themselves. It is a persistent
offering of obstacles, a calculated system of screens and obtrusions, of
confusions and ambiguous interpolations and delays, with one express
purpose; and that purpose is simply to keep the form—and the idea—
fluid and unfinished, still in motion, as it were, and unknown, until the
dropping into place of the very last syllable.

What Mr. Faulkner is after, in a sense, is a *continuum.* He wants
a medium without stops or pauses, a medium which is always *of the moment,* and of which the passage from moment to moment is as fluid and
undetectable as in the life itself which he is purporting to give. It is all
inside and underneath, or as seen from within and below; the reader must
therefore be steadily *drawn in*; he must be powerfully and unremittingly
hypnotized inward and downward to that image-stream; and this suggests,
perhaps, a reason not only for the length and elaborateness of the sentence
structure, but for the repetitiveness as well. The repetitiveness, and the
steady iterative emphasis—like a kind of chanting or invocation—on certain relatively abstract words ("sonorous, latin, *vaguely* eloquent"), have
the effect at last of producing, for Mr. Faulkner, a special language, a
conglomerate of his own, which he uses with an astonishing virtuosity, and
which, although in detailed analysis it may look shoddy, is actually for
his purpose a life stream of almost miraculous adaptability. At the one
extreme it is abstract, cerebral, time-and-space-obsessed, tortured and
twisted, but nevertheless always with a living *pulse* in it; and at the other
it can be as overwhelming in its simple vividness, its richness in the actual,
as the flood scenes in *The Wild Palms.*

Obviously, such a style, especially when allied with such a *concern*
for method, must make difficulties for the reader; and it must be admitted
that Mr. Faulkner does little or nothing as a rule to make his highly complex "situation" easily available or perceptible. The reader must simply
make up his mind to go to work, and in a sense to cooperate; his reward
being that there *is* a situation to be given shape, a meaning to be extracted,
and that half the fun is precisely in watching the queer, difficult, and often
so laborious evolution of Mr. Faulkner's idea. And not so much idea,
either, as form. For, like the great predecessor whom at least in this regard
he so oddly resembles, Mr. Faulkner could say with Henry James that it
is practically impossible to make any real distinction between theme and

form. What immoderately delights him, alike in *Sanctuary, The Sound and the Fury, As I Lay Dying, Light in August, Pylon, Absalom, Absalom!* and now again the *The Wild Palms,* and what sets him above—shall we say it firmly—all his American contemporaries, is his continuous preoccupation with the novel *as form,* his passionate concern with it, and a degree of success with it which would clearly have commanded the interest and respect of Henry James himself. The novel as revelation, the novel as slice-of-life, the novel as mere story, do not interest him: these he would say, like James again, "are the circumstances of the interest," but not the interest itself. The interest itself will be the use to which these circumstances are put, the degree to which they can be organized.

From this point of view, he is not in the least to be considered as a mere "Southern" writer: the "Southernness" of his scences and characters is of little concern to him, just as little as the question whether they are pleasant or unpleasant, true or untrue. Verisimilitude—or, at any rate, *degree* of verisimilitude—he will cheerfully abandon, where necessary, if the compensating advantages of plan or tone are a sufficient inducement. The famous scene in *Sanctuary* of Miss Reba and Uncle Bud in which a "madam" and her cronies hold a wake for a dead gangster, while the small boy gets drunk, is quite false, taken out of its context; it is not endowed with the same *kind* of actuality which permeates the greater part of the book at all. Mr. Faulkner was cunning enough to see that a two-dimensional cartoon-like statement, at this juncture, would supply him with the effect of a chorus, and without in the least being perceived as a change in the temperature of truthfulness.

That particular kind of dilution, or adulteration, of verisimilitude was both practised and praised by James: as when he blandly admitted of *In the Cage* that his central character was "too ardent a focus of divination" to be quite credible. It was defensible simply because it made possible the coherence of the whole, and was itself absorbed back into the luminous texture. It was for him a device for organization, just as the careful cherishing of "viewpoint" was a device, whether simply or in counterpoint. Of Mr. Faulkner's devices, of this sort, aimed at the achievement of complex "form," the two most constant are the manipulation of viewpoint and the use of the flashback, or sudden shift of time-scene, forward or backward.

In *Sanctuary,* where the alternation of viewpoint is a little lawless, the complexity is given, perhaps a shade disingenuously, by violent shifts in time; a deliberate disarrangement of an otherwise straightforward story. Technically, there is no doubt that the novel, despite its fame, rattles a little; and Mr. Faulkner himself takes pains to disclaim it. But, even done with the left hand, it betrays a genius for form, quite apart from its wonderful virtuosity in other respects. *Light in August,* published a year after *Sanctuary,* repeats the same technique, that of a dislocation of time, and more elaborately; the time-shifts alternate with shifts in the viewpoint; and if the book is a failure it is perhaps because Mr. Faulkner's tendency to what is almost a hypertrophy of form is not here, as well as in the other novels, matched with the characters and the theme. Neither the person nor the story of Joe Christmas is seen fiercely enough—by its creator— to carry off that immense machinery of narrative; it would have needed another Popeye, or another Jiggs and Shumann, another Temple Drake, and for once Mr. Faulkner's inexhaustible inventiveness seems to have been at fault. Consequently what we see is an extraordinary power for form functioning relatively *in vacuo,* and existing only to sustain itself.

In the best of the novels, however,—and it is difficult to choose between *The Sound and the Fury* and *The Wild Palms,* with *Absalom, Absalom!* a very close third,—this tendency to hypertrophy of form has been sufficiently curbed; and it is interesting, too, to notice that in all these three (and in that remarkable *tour de force, As I Lay Dying,* as well), while there is still a considerable reliance on time-shift, the effect of richness and complexity is chiefly obtained by a very skillful fugue-like alternation of viewpoint. Fugue-like in *The Wild Palms*—and fugue-like especially, of course, in *As I Lay Dying,* where the shift is kaleidoscopically rapid, and where, despite an astonishing violence to plausibility (in the reflections, and *language* of reflection, of the characters) an effect of the utmost reality and immediateness is nevertheless produced. Fugue-like, again, in *Absalom, Absalom!* where indeed one may say the form is really circular— there is no beginning and no ending properly speaking, and therefore no *logical* point of entrance: we must just submit, and follow the circling of the author's interest, which turns a light inward towards the center, but every moment from a new angle, a new point of view. The story unfolds, therefore, now in one color of light, now in another, with references backward and forward: those that refer forward being necessarily, for the moment, blind. What is complete in Mr. Faulkner's pattern, *a priori,* must nevertheless remain incomplete for us until the very last stone is in place; what is "real," therefore, at one stage of the unfolding, or from one point of view, turns out to be "unreal" from another; and we find that one among other things with which we are engaged is the fascinating sport of trying to separate truth from legend, watching the growth of legend from truth, and finally reaching the conclusion that the distinction is itself false.

Something of the same sort is true also of *The Sound and the Fury* —and this, with its massive four-part symphonic structure, is perhaps the most beautifully *wrought* of the whole series, and an indubitable masterpiece of what James loved to call the "fictive art." The joinery is flawless in its intricacy; it is a novelist's novel—a whole textbook on the craft of fiction in itself, comparable in its way to *What Maisie Knew* or *The Golden Bowl*.

But if it is important, for the moment, to emphasize Mr. Faulkner's genius for form, and his continued exploration of its possibilities, as against the usual concern with the violence and dreadfulness of his themes— though we might pause to remind carpers on this score of the fact that the best of Henry James is precisely that group of last novels which so completely concerned themselves with moral depravity—it is also well to keep in mind his genius for invention, whether of character or episode. The inventiveness is of the richest possible sort—a headlong and tumultuous abundance, an exuberant generosity and vitality, which makes most other contemporary fiction look very pale and chaste indeed. It is an unforgettable gallery of portraits, whether character or caricature, and all of them endowed with a violent and immediate vitality.

"He is at once"—to quote once more from James—"one of the most corrupt of writers and one of the most naïf, the most mechanical and pedantic, and the fullest of *bonhomie* and natural impulse. He is one of the finest of artists and one of the coarsest. Viewed in one way, his novels are ponderous, shapeless, overloaded; his touch is graceless, violent, barbarous. Viewed in another, his tales have more color, more composition, more grasp of the reader's attention than any others. [His] style would demand a chapter apart. It is the least simple style, probably, that was ever written; it bristles, it cracks, it swells and swaggers; but it is a perfect expression of the man's genius. Like his genius, it contains a certain quantity of everything, from immaculate gold to flagrant dross. He was a very bad writer, and yet unquestionably he was a very great writer. We may say briefly, that in so far as his method was an instinct it was successful, and that in so far as it was a theory it was a failure. But both in instinct and in theory he had the aid of an immense force of conviction. His imagination warmed to its work so intensely that there was nothing his volition could not impose upon it. Hallucination settled upon him, and he believed anything that was necessary in the circumstances."

That passage, from Henry James's essay on Balzac, is almost word for word, with scarcely a reservation, applicable to Mr. Faulkner. All that is lacking is Balzac's greater *range* of understanding and tenderness, his greater freedom from special preoccupations. For this, one would hazard the guess that Mr. Faulkner has the gifts—and time is still before him.

# WILLIAM FAULKNER'S STYLE

### WARREN BECK

NO OTHER contemporary American novelist of comparable stature has been as frequently or as severely criticized for his style as has William Faulkner. Yet he is a brilliantly original and versatile stylist. The condemnations of his way of writing have been in part just; all but the most idolatrous of Faulkner's admirers must have wished he had blotted a thousand infelicities. However, an enumeration of his faults in style would leave still unsaid the most important things about his style. There is need here for a reapportionment of negative and positive criticism.

It is true that the preponderant excellences of Faulkner's prose, when recognized, make his faults all the more conspicuous and irritating. And under criticism Faulkner has not only remained guilty of occasional carelessness, especially in sentence construction, but seems to have persisted in mannerisms. On the other hand, his progress as a stylist has been steady and rapid; his third novel, *Sartoris,* while still experimenting toward a technique, was a notable advance over his first two in style as well as in theme and narrative structure, and in his fourth novel, *The Sound and the Fury,* style is what it has continued to be in all his subsequent work, a significant factor, masterfully controlled. This growth has been made largely without the aid of appreciative criticism, and in the face of some misunderstanding and abuse of the most dynamic qualities in his writing. It is quite possible that Faulkner would have paid more attention to the critics' valid objections if these had not been so frequently interlarded with misconceptions of his stylistic method, or indeed complete insensitivity to it.

Repetition of words, for instance, has often seemed an obvious fault. At times, however, Faulkner's repetitions may be a not unjustifiable by-product of his thematic composition. Some of his favorites in *Absalom, Absalom!*—not just Miss Rosa's "demon," which may be charged off to her own mania, nor "indolent" applied to Bon, but such recurrent terms as effluvium, outrage, grim, indomitable, ruthless, fury, fatality—seem to intend adumbration of the tale's whole significance and tone. Nor is the reiteration as frequent or as obvious here as in earlier books; perhaps Faulkner has been making an experiment over which he is increasingly gaining control.

Faulkner often piles up words in a way that brings the charge of prolixity. He has Wilbourne say of his life with Charlotte in Chicago,

it was the mausoleum of love, it was the stinking catafalque of the dead corpse borne between the olfactoryless walking shapes of the immortal unsentient demanding ancient meat.

However, these word-series, while conspicuous at times, may have a place in a style as minutely analytical as Faulkner's. In their typical form they are not redundant, however elaborate, and sometimes their cumulative effect is undeniable—for example, the "long still hot weary dead September afternoon" when Quentin listens to Miss Rosa's story. Colonel Feinman, the wealthy exploiter of impecunious aviators, had as secretary "a young man, sleek, in horn rim glasses," who spoke "with a kind of silken insolence, like the pampered intelligent hateridden eunuchmountebank of an eastern despot," and here the amplification redounds to the significance of the whole scene. Quite often, too, these series of words, while seemingly extravagant, are a remarkably compressed rendering, as in the phrase "passionate tragic ephemeral loves of adolescence."

In fairness it must be noted too that Faulkner's later work never drops to the level of fantastic verbosity found in the thematic paragraph introducing his second novel, *Mosquitoes*. Nor does he any longer break the continuum of his narrative with rhapsodies like the notable description of the mule in *Sartoris,* a sort of cadenza obviously done out of exuberance. In the later books profuseness of language is always knit into the thematic structure. Thus the elaborate lyrical descriptions of the sunrise and of a spring rain in book three of *The Hamlet* furnish by their imagery and mood a sharp, artistically serviceable contrast to the perversion of the

Reprinted with permission from *American Prefaces,* Spring, 1941, pp. 195-211.

idiot Ike Snopes, and as such they deepen the melancholy perspective from which this episode is observed.

Faulkner's studied use of a full style and his sense of its place in the architectonics of an extended and affecting narrative is well displayed in the last chapters of *Light in August,* chapter nineteen closing with the first climax, of Joe Christmas' death, poetically expressed; chapter twenty closing similarly in the second and more comprehensive climax of Hightower's final vision; and then chapter twenty-one, which completes the book, furnishing a modulation to detached calm through the simply prosaic, somewhat humorous account, by a new and neutral spokesman, of the exodus of Lena and Byron into Tennessee. Indeed, one of the best indexes to the degree of Faulkner's control of eloquence is in a comparison of the novels' conclusions—some of them in a full descriptive style, as in *Soldiers' Pay, Sartoris, Sanctuary,* and to a degree in *The Sound and the Fury* and *The Unvanquished;* more of the novels closing with a meaningful but plainly stated utterance or gesture of a character, as in *Mosquitoes, As I Lay Dying, Pylon, Absalom, Absalom!, The Wild Palms,* and *The Hamlet* —(the last that wonderful "Snopes turned his head and spat over the wagon wheel. He jerked the reins slightly. 'Come up,' he said.") This ratio suggests that while Faulkner does not avoid elaboration, neither is he its slave.

Faulkner's diction, charged and proliferate though it may be, usually displays a nice precision, and this is especially evident in its direct imagery. An example is in the glimpse of Cash, after he has worked all night in the rain, finishing his mother's coffin:

In the lantern light his face is calm, musing; slowly he strokes his hands on his raincoated thighs in a gesture deliberate, final and composed.

Frequently, however, Faulkner proceeds in descriptive style beyond epithet and abstract definition to figurative language. Having written,

It is just dawn, daylight: that gray and lonely suspension filled with the peaceful and tentative waking of birds.

he goes on in the next sentence to a simile:

The air, inbreathed, is like spring water.

The novels abound in examples of his talent for imaginative comparisons; for instance, the hard-boiled flier Shumann, dressed up:

He wore a new gray homburg hat, not raked like in the department store cuts but set square on the back of his head so that (not tall, with blue eyes in a square thin profoundly sober face) he looked out not from beneath it but from within it with open and fatal humorlessness, like an early Briton who has been assured that the Roman governor will not receive him unless he wear the borrowed centurion's helmet.

There is nothing unique, however, in Faulkner's use of direct and forceful diction or fine figurative image. What is most individual in his style is its persistent lyrical embroidery and coloring, in extended passages, of the narrative theme. In this sense Faulkner is one of the most subjective of writers, his brooding temperament constantly probing and interpreting his subject matter. Thus his full style is comprehensive in its intention. He may often be unfashionably rhapsodic, but he seldom falls into the preciosity that lingers over a passage for its own sweet sake. Definition of his story as a whole and the enhancement of its immediate appeals to the imagination are his constant aims.

The latest of Faulkner's novels demonstrates the grasp he has developed upon all the devices of his style. *The Hamlet* is a sort of prose fantasia; the various episodes employ colloquial tall stories, poetic description, folk humor, deliberate reflective narration, swift cryptic drama, and even a grotesque allegory, of Snopes in hell. Differing in tone from the elegiac brooding of *Light in August,* or the exasperated volubility of *Pylon,* the modulant intricacy and fusion of *Absalom, Absalom!,* the tender directness of *The Unvanquished,* or the eloquent turbulence of *The Wild Palms, The Hamlet* seems an extravaganza improvised more freely in a more detached mood, the author apparently delighting in the realizations of varied subject-matters through the flexibilities of his multiform style.

A number of passages in *The Hamlet* give precise indications of Faulkner's purpose as a stylist, inasmuch as they are reworkings of material released as short stories in magazines from four to nine years before the novel's publication. "Spotted Horses," which appeared in *Scribner's* for June, 1931, contains in germ Flem Snopes' whole career in *The Hamlet.* The story is in first person; Ratliff is the reciter, but he is not quite the shrewd and benevolent spectator he becomes under the touches of Faulkner's own descriptions in the third-person narrative of the novel. The short story moves faster, of course, sketching the drama more broadly and making no pause for brooding lyrical interpretation. Faulkner's omniscient narration of the episode is almost twice as long as Ratliff's simple monologue, and rises to an altogether different plane of conception and diction. The contrast is almost like that between a ballad and a tone poem.

This difference, which certainly must indicate Faulkner's free and considered choice and his fundamental aethetic inclination, can be defined by a comparison of parallel passages from the horse-auction scene, when the Texan tries to hold one of the animals and continue his salestalk. The Scribner short story, with Ratliff as first-person narrator, reads as follows:

"Look it over," he says, with his heels dug too and that white pistol sticking outen his pocket and his neck swole up like a spreading adder's until you could just tell what he was saying, cussing the horse and talking to us all at once: "Look him over, the fiddle-headed son of fourteen fathers. Try him, buy him, you will get the best—" Then it was all dust again, and we couldn't see nothing but spotted hide and mane, and that ere Texas man's boot-heels like a couple of walnuts on two strings, and after a while that two-gallon hat come sailing out like a fat old hen crossing a fence. When the dust settled again, he was just getting outen the far fence corner, brushing himself off. He come and got his hat and brushed it off and come and clumb onto the gate post again.

In the novel the parallel passage has been recast in the third person thus:

"Look him over boys," the Texan panted, turning his own suffused face and the protuberant glare of his eyes toward the fence. "Look him over quick. Them shoulders and—" He had relaxed for an instant apparently. The animal exploded again; again for an instant the Texan was free of the earth, though he was still talking: "—and legs you whoa I'll tear your face right look him over quick boys worth fifteen dollars of let me get a holt of who'll make me a bid whoa you blareyed jack rabbit, whoa!" They were moving now—a kaleidoscope of inextricable and incredible violence on the periphery of which the metal clasps of the Texan's suspenders sun-glinted in ceaseless orbit, with terrific slowness across the lot. Then the broad clay-colored hat soared deliberately outward; an instant later the Texan followed it, though still on his feet, and the pony shot free in mad, stag-like bounds. The Texan picked up the hat and struck the dust from it against his leg, and returned to the fence and mounted the post again.

Obviously the difference is not only quantitative but qualitative. Instead of Ratliff's "that old two-gallon hat come sailing out like a fat old hen crossing a fence" there is Faulkner's "the broad claycolored hat soared deliberately outward"; Ratliff sees "that ere Texas man's bootheels like a couple of walnuts on two strings," but Faulkner shows a "kaleidoscope of inextricable and incredible violence on the periphery of which the metal clasps of the Texan's suspenders sun-glinted in ceaseless orbit with terrific slowness across the lot." This latter represents the style Faulkner has chosen to develop; he can do the simpler and more objective narration, but when given such an opportunity as in the amalgamating of these magazine stories into a novel, he insists on transmuting the factual-objective into the descriptive-definitive colored by his imagination and elaborated by his resourcefulness in language.

In its typical exercise this style gives image only incidentally and exists primarily to enhance and sustain mood. Thus Wilbourne's first approach to the house where his meeting with Charlotte is to begin their passionate and disastrous love story is set in this key:

. . . they entered: a court paved with the same soft, quietly rotting brick. There was a stagnant pool with a terra-cotta figure, a mass of lantana, the single palm, the thick rich leaves and the heavy white stars of the jasmine bush where light fell upon it through open French doors, the court balcony —overhung too on three sides, the walls of that same annealing brick lifting a rampart broken and nowhere level against the glare of the city on the low eternally overcast sky, and over all, brittle, dissonant and ephemeral, the spurious sophistication of the piano like symbols scrawled by adolescent boys upon an ancient decayed rodent-scavengered tomb.

The reporter's mood of anxious inquiry and the frustration which is thematic in *Pylon* are both represented as he telephones:

Now he too heard only dead wirehum, as if the other end of it extended beyond atmosphere, into cold space; as though he listened now to the profound sound of infinity, of void itself filled with the cold unceasing murmur of aeonweary and unflagging stars.

This organic quality of Faulkner's style, sustaining through essentially poetic devices an orchestration of meaning, makes it impossible to judge him adequately by brief quotation. In the description of Temple's first hours in Madam Reba's brothel, for instance, the thematic recurrence from page to page to subjectively interpreted imagery builds up in a time continuum the mood of the girl's trance-like state of shock and also the larger fact of her isolation in the sordid. First,

The drawn shades, cracked into a myriad pattern like old skin, blew faintly on the bright air, breathing into the room on waning surges the sound of Sabbath traffic, festive, steady, evanescent. . . .

and then, three pages further,

The shades blew steadily in the windows, with faint rasping sounds. Temple began to hear a clock. It sat on the mantel above a grate filled with fluted green paper. The clock was of flowered china, supported by four china nymphs. It had only one hand, scrolled and gilded, halfway between ten and eleven, lending to the otherwise blank face a quality of unequivocal assertion, as though it had nothing whatever to do with time.

and then, two pages further,

In the window the cracked shade, yawning now and then with a faint rasp against the frame, let twilight into the room in fainting surges. From beneath the shade the smoke-colored twilight emerged in slow puffs like signal smoke from a blanket, thickening in the room. The china figures which supported the clock gleamed in hushed smooth flexions: knee, elbow, flank, arm and breast in attitudes of voluptuous lassitude. The glass face, become mirror-like, appeared to hold all reluctant light, holding in its tranquil depths a quiet gesture of moribund time, one-armed like a veteran from the wars. Half past ten o'clock. Temple lay in the bed, looking at the clock, thinking about half-past-ten-o'clock.

Yet side by side with this richly interpretative style there exists in almost all of Faulkner's work a realistic colloquialism, expressing lively dialogue that any playwright might envy, and even carrying over into sustained first-person narrative the flavor of regionalism and the idiosyncrasies of character. In the colloquial vein Faulkner's brilliance is unsurpassed in contemporary American fiction. He has fully mastered the central difficulty, to retain verisimilitude while subjecting the prolix and monotonous raw material of most natural speech to an artistic pruning and pointing up. *Sanctuary,* for an example, is full of excellent dialogue, sharply individualized. And Faulkner's latest book[1] not only contains some of his most poetic writing but has one of his best talkers, Ratliff, both in extended anecdote in monologue and in dramatic conversations. Ratliff's reflective, humorous, humane, but skeptical nature, a triumph in characterization, is silhouetted largely out of his talk about the hamlet's affairs.

Faulkner also can weave colloquial bits into the matrix of a more literary passage, with the enlarging effect of a controlled dissonance. Thus Quentin imagines Henry Sutpen and Charles Bon, at the end of the war, Charles determined to marry Judith, Henry forbidding; and then into Quentin's elaboration of the scene breaks the voice of his father, continuing the story, giving its denouement in the words vulgarly uttered by Wash Jones:

(It seemed to Quentin that he could actually see them. . . . They faced one another on the two gaunt horses, two men, young, not yet in the world,

1. *The Hamlet* (New York, 1940) [editor's note].

not yet breathed over long enough, to be old but with old eyes, with un-
kempt hair and faces gaunt and weathered as if cast by some spartan and
even niggard hand from bronze, in worn and patched gray weathered
now to the color of dead leaves, the one with the tarnished braid of an
officer, the other plain of cuff, the pistol lying yet across the saddle bow
unaimed, the two faces calm, the voices not even raised: *Dont you pass the
shadow of this post, this branch, Charles;* and *I am going to pass it,
Henry*)—and then Wash Jones sitting that saddleless mule before Miss
Rosa's gate, shouting her name into the sunny and peaceful quiet of the
street, saying, "Air you Rosie Coldfield? Then you better come on out yon.
Henry has done shot that durn French feller. Kilt him dead as a beef."

Master of colloquialism in dramatic scene though he is, Faulkner
sometimes lays aside this power in order to put into a character's mouth
the fullest expression of the narrative's meaning. The mature Bayard
Sartoris, looking back to Civil War times, telling the story of his boyhood
and youth in *The Unvanquished,* opens what is Faulkner's most straightforward narrative, and his only novel related throughout by one character in
first person, in this strain:

Behind the smokehouse that summer, Ringo and I had a living map. Although Vicksburg was just a handful of chips from the woodpile and the
River a trench scraped into the packed earth with the point of a hoe, it
(river, city, and terrain) lived, possessing even in miniature that ponderable
though passive recalcitrance of topography which outweighs artillery,
against which the most brilliant of victories and the most tragic of defeats
are but the loud noises of a moment.

At times it seems as though the author, after having created an unsophisticated character, is elbowing him off the stage, as when the rustic Darl
Bundren sees "the square squat shape of the coffin on the sawhorses like a
cubistic bug," or as when in the short story, "All The Dead Pilots," the
World War flier John Sartoris is characterized as having a vocabulary of
"perhaps two hundred words" and then is made to say,

. . . I knew that if I busted in and dragged him out and bashed his head
off, I'd not only be cashiered, I'd be clinked for life for having infringed the
articles of alliance by invading foreign property without warrant or something.

For the most part, however, the transcending of colloquial verisimilitude
in the novels is a fairly controlled and consistent technique, the characters
Faulkner most often endows with penetration and eloquence being his

philosophical spectators. Undoubtedly his chief concern, though, is with a lyric encompassment of his narrative's whole meaning rather than with the reticences of objective dramatic representation.

Thus many of his characters speak with the tongues of themselves and of William Faulkner. As Quentin and his Harvard roommate Shreve evolve the reconstruction of Thomas Sutpen's story which constitutes the second half of *Absalom, Absalom!,* Quentin thinks when Shreve talks, "He sounds just like father," and later, when Quentin has the floor, Shreve interrupts with "Don't say it's just me that sounds like your old man," which certainly shows that Faulkner realizes what he is doing. Actually he does make some differences among these voices: Miss Rosa rambles and ejaculates with erratic spinsterish emotion, Mr. Compson is elaborately and sometimes parenthetically ironic, Quentin is most sensitively imaginative and melancholy, Shreve most detached and humorous. What they have in common is the scope and pitch of an almost lyrical style which Faulkner has arbitrarily fixed upon for an artistic instrument. The justification of all such practices is empirical; imaginative writing must not be judged by its minute correspondence to fact but by its total effect; and to object against Faulkner's style that men and women don't really talk in such long sentences, with so full a vocabulary so fancifully employed, is as narrowly dogmatic as was Sinclair Lewis, in *Main Street,* insisting that Sir Launcelot didn't actually speak in "honeyed pentameters."

Typical instances of Faulkner's endowing his characters with precise diction and fluency may show that on the whole it is not an unacceptable convention. Thus Wilbourne's full and finished sentence,

We lived in an apartment that wasn't bohemian, it wasn't even a tabloid love-nest, it wasn't even in that part of town but in a neighborhood dedicated by both city ordinance and architecture to the second year of wedlock among the five-thousand-a-year bracket.

though it is not stylistically rooted in his manner as characterized up to this point, is not inconsistent with his personality and sensibilities, and it does get on with the story. Equally acceptable is Ratliff's remark about the platitudinous family-fleeing I. O. Snopes,

What's his name? that quick-fatherer, the Moses with his mouth full of mottoes and his coat-tail full of them already half-grown retroactive sons?

Its keen diction and nice rhythm are not essentially false to Ratliff, but only an idealization in language of the percipient humorous sewing-machine salesman the reader already knows. The same is true of those tumbling floods of phrases, too prolonged for human breath to utter, with which the reporter in *Pylon* assaults the sympathies of editor Hagood; they are not so much a part of dialogue as an intense symbol of the pace of racing aviation and the reporter's frantic concern for his protégés among the fliers.

It is interesting to note that Faulkner's full style somewhat resembles older literary uses, such as the dramatic chorus, the prologue and epilogue, and the *dramatis personae* themselves in soliloquy and extended speech. The aim of any such device is not objective realism but revelation of theme, a revelation raised by the unstinted resourcefulness and power of its language to the highest ranges of imaginative outlook. No wonder that with such a purpose Faulkner often comes closer than is common in these times to Shakespeare's imperial and opulent use of words. If unfortunately his ambition has sometimes led Faulkner to perpetrate some rather clotted prose, perhaps these lapses may be judged charitably in the light of the great endeavor they but infrequently flaw.

More particularly Faulkner's full sentence structure springs from the elaborateness of his fancies ramifying in descriptive imagery. Thus editor Hagood, perpetually beset by small annoyances and chronically irritated by them, drops himself wearily into his roadster's low seat,

. . . whereupon without sound or warning the golfbag struck him across the head and shoulder with an apparently calculated and lurking viciousness, emitting a series of dry clicks as though produced by the jaws of a beast domesticated though not tamed, half in fun and half in deadly seriousness, like a pet shark.

Another typical source of fullness in Faulkner's sentences is a tendency to musing speculation, sometimes proceeding to the statement of alternative suggestions. Thus Miss Rosa speaks of wearing garments left behind by the eloping aunt in "kindness or haste or oversight," that doing its bit in a sentence well over three hundred words long. Such characteristic theorizing may run to the length of this postscript to a description of Flem Snopes:

. . . a thick squat soft man of no establishable age between twenty and thirty, with a broad still face containing a tight seam of mouth stained slightly at the corners with tobacco, and eyes the color of stagnant water, and projecting from among the other features in startling and sudden paradox, a tiny predatory nose like the beak of a small hawk. It was as though the original nose had been left off by the original designer or craftsman and the unfinished job taken over by someone of a radically different school or perhaps by some viciously maniacal humorist or perhaps by one who had only time to clap into the center of the face a frantic and desperate warning.

Even the most elaborate and esoteric of these speculations are not limited to third-person narrative; Faulkner's pervasive subjectivity injects such abstractions too, as well as extended imagery, into the reflections and speech of many of his characters, again most typically those who contemplate and interpret the action of the stories, who act as chorus or soliloquize. Here too the device proves itself in practice. When such characters brood over the events, painstakingly rehearsing details, piling one hypothesis upon another, their very tentativeness creates for the reader the clouded enigmatic perspective of reality itself. Thus Miss Rosa's account, with reinterpretation imposed upon memory, of Sutpen's driving in to church with his family:

It was as though the sister whom I had never laid eyes on, who before I was born had vanished into the stronghold of an ogre or a djinn, was now to return through a dispensation of one day only, to the world which she had quitted, and I a child of three, waked early for the occasion, dressed and curled as if for Christmas, for an occasion more serious than Christmas even, since now and at last this ogre or djinn had agreed for the sake of the wife and the children to come to church, to permit them at least to approach the vicinity of salvation, to at least give Ellen one chance to struggle with him for those children's souls on a battleground where she could be supported not only by Heaven but by her own family and people of her own kind; yes, even for the moment submitting himself to redemption, or lacking that, at least chivalrous for the instant even though still unregenerate.

The foregoing examples, however, do not illustrate Faulkner's style at its most involved, as in this passage from Quentin's consciousness, while he listens to Miss Rosa's reconstruction of the Sutpen family history:

It should have been later than it was; it should have been late, yet the yellow slashes of mote-palpitant sunlight were latticed no higher up the impalpable wall of gloom which separated them; the sun seemed hardly to have moved. It (the talking, the telling) seemed (to him, to Quentin) to partake of that logic- and reason-flouting quality of a dream which the sleeper knows must have occurred, stillborn and complete, in a second, yet the very quality upon which it must depend to move the dreamer (verisimilitude) to credulity—horror or pleasure or amazement—depends as completely upon a formal recognition of and acceptance of elapsed and yet-elapsing time as music or a printed tale.

By its parentheses and involution and fullness this last sentence illustrates that occasionally extreme eccentricity most often and most rightfully objected to in its author's style. At the same time this sentence may give a key to Faulkner's entire method and typify its artistic purposefulness—to create "that logic- and reason-flouting quality of a dream," yet to depend upon the recognized verisimilitude of "elapsed and yet-elapsing time." Such a product is not necessarily mere nightmare; it is often a real quality of experience at its greatest intensity and acuteness. In his most characteristic writing Faulkner is trying to render the transcendent life of the mind, the crowded composite of associative and analytical consciousness which expands the vibrant moment into the reaches of all time, simultaneously observing, remembering, interpreting, and modifying the object of its awareness. To this end the sentence as a rhetorical unit (however strained) is made to hold diverse yet related elements in a sort of saturated solution, which is perhaps the nearest that language as the instrument of fiction can come to the instantaneous complexities of consciousness itself. Faulkner really seems to be trying to give narrative prose another dimension.

To speak of Faulkner's fiction as dream-like (using Quentin's notion as a key) does not imply that his style is phantasmagoric, deranged, or incoherent. Dreams are not always delirium; and association, sometimes the supplanter of pattern, can also be its agent. The dreaming mind, while envisaging experience strangely, may find in that strangeness a fresh revelation, all the more profound in that the conventional and adventitious are pierced through. Similarly inhibitions and apathies must be transcended in any really imaginative inquiry, and thus do Faulkner's speculative characters ponder over the whole story, and project into cumulative drama its underlying significations. Behind all of them, of course, is their master-dreamer; Faulkner's own dominating temperament, constantly interpreting, is in the air of all these narratives, reverberant. Hence no matter how psychological the story's material, Faulkner never falls into the mere enumeration which in much stream-of-consciousness writing dissolves all drama and reduces the narrative to a case history without the shaping framework of analysis, or even to an unmapped anachronistic chaos of raw consciousness. Faulkner is always a dynamic story-teller, never just a reporter of unorganized phenomena. His most drastic, most dream-like use of stream-of-consciousness, for instance, in *The Sound and the Fury,* is not only limited to the first two sections of the book, but it sketches a plot which in the lucid sections that follow gradually emerges clear-cut.

As clear-cut, at least, as Faulkner's stories can be. Here again is illustrated the close relation of his style to his whole point of view. If Faulkner's sentences sometimes soar and circle involved and prolonged, if his scenes become halls of mirrors repeating tableaux in a progressive magnification, if echoes multiply into the dissonance of infinite overtones, it is because the meanings his stories unfold are complex, mysterious, obscure, and incomplete. There is no absolute, no eternal pure white radiance in such presentations, but rather the stain of many colors, refracted and shifting in kaleidoscopic suspension, about the center of man's enigmatic behavior and fate, within the drastic orbit of mortality. Such being Faulkner's view of life, such is his style.

To this view the very rhythm of Faulkner's prose is nicely adjusted. It is not emphatic; rather it is a slow prolonged movement, nothing dashing, even at its fullest flood, but surging with an irresistible momentum. His effects insofar as they depend on prose rhythms are never staccato, they are cumulative rather than abrupt. Such a prose rhythm supplements the contributions of full vocabulary and lengthy sentence toward suspension rather than impact, and consequently toward deep realization rather than quick surprise. And the prolonged even murmur of Faulkner's voice throughout his pages is an almost hypnotic induction into those detailed and darkly colored visions of life which drift across the horizons of his imagination like clouds—great yet vaporous, changing yet enduring, unearthly yet of common substance. It might be supposed that his occasionally crowded and circumlocutory style would destroy narrative pace and consequence. Actually this hovering of active imagination, while employing the sustained lyricism and solid abstraction which differentiate Faulkner from the objective realist, furnishes the epitome of drama. The whole aim is at perspective, through the multiple dimensions of experience, upon a subject in that suspension which allows reflection. The accomplishment is the gradual, sustained, and enriched revelation of meaning; in Faulkner's novels drama is of that highest form which awaits the unfolding of composite action, characterization, mood, and idea, through the medium of style.

Faulkner himself probably would admit the relative inadequacy of instrument to purpose, would agree with Mr. Compson in calling language "that meager and fragile thread by which the little surface corners and edges of men's secret and solitary lives may be joined for an instant." Faulkner perhaps has no greater faith in the word than have his contemporaries who have partially repudiated it, but instead of joining that somewhat paradoxical literary trend, he seems determined to exploit an imperfect device to the uttermost within the limits of artistic illusion. Thus although in certain passages he has demonstrated his command of a simplified objective method, he has not made it his invariable device, nor does he allow its contemporary vogue to prevent his using words in the old-fashioned way for whatever they are worth descriptively and definitively.

Faulkner's whole narrative method, as described, may seem to be a retrogression in technique. Two main tendencies in modern fiction have been toward a more and more material dramatic presentation, depending simply upon the naming of objects and acts and the reporting of speech, and on the other hand, toward an ostensibly complete and unbroken reproduction of the free flow of consciousness. These methods have produced books as radically different as *The Sun Also Rises* and *Ulysses,* yet they have elements in common. In both types the author attempts to conceal himself completely behind his materials, to give them the quality of integral phenomena, and in line with this purpose the style aims at pure reproduction, never allowing definition and interpretation from any detached point of view. These have been honest attempts, a great deal of fine craftsmanship has gone into them, and some of the products have been excellent in their kind. Yet at their most extreme these have been movements in the one direction toward bareness, impoverishment, and in the other toward incoherence. Confronted by the imperfections and confusions of the present scene, and made hyperskeptical by deference to scientific method, the writers who have attempted absolute objectivity (whether dramatic or psychological, whether in overt event or stream of association) have sometimes produced what looks like an anti-intellectual aesthetic of futility and inconsequence. So in another sense Faulkner's narrative technique, particularly as implemented by his full style, instead of being a retrogression may represent one kind of progression through the danger of impasse created by too great submission to vogues of photographic or psychographic reproduction.

Yet Faulkner's is not altogether a return to an older expressiveness, not a complete departure from the modern schools of Hemingway and Joyce. In his colloquial passages he is quite as objectively dramatic as the one, in his rehearsal of the fantasies of acute consciousness he follows the other—and it should be remembered that he is superlatively skillful at both, so that it cannot be said that he puts these objective methods aside because he cannot use them. Furthermore, Faulkner is fond of employing in extended passages one of the favorite modern means of objectivity in fiction, the first-person narrator, using the device toward its most honored modern purpose, the attainment of detached perspective and the creation of realistic illusion concerning large vistas of the story. In short, there is no method in modern fiction which Faulkner does not comprehend and use on occasion. Fundamentally Faulkner's only heterodoxy by present standards of style is his fullness, especially as it takes the form of descriptive eloquence or abstraction and definitiveness. What is stylistically most remarkable in his work is the synthesis he has effected between the subtleties of modern narrative techniques and the resources of language employed in the traditionally poetic or interpretative vein. That such a synthesis is feasible is demonstrated in the dynamic forms of his novels, and it may be prelude to significant new developments in the methods of fiction.


# THE CREATION OF THE REAL
# IN WILLIAM FAULKNER

## JEAN-JACQUES MAYOUX

If there is a true anthology piece in all the work of Faulkner, the first page of *Sanctuary* is surely it.

From beyond the screen of bushes which surrounded the spring, Popeye watched the man drinking. A faint path led from the road to the spring. Popeye watched the man—a tall, thin man, hatless, in worn gray flannel trousers and carrying a tweed coat over his arm—emerge from the path and kneel to drink from the spring.

The spring welled up at the root of a beech tree and flowed away upon a bottom of whorled and waved sand. It was surrounded by a thick growth of cane and brier, of cypress and gum in which broken sunlight lay sourceless. Somewhere, hidden and secret yet nearby, a bird sang three notes and ceased.

In the spring the drinking man leaned his face to the broken and myriad reflection of his own drinking. When he rose up he saw among them the shattered reflection of Popeye's straw hat, though he had heard no sound.

Reprinted with permission from *Études Anglaises,* February, 1952, pp. 25-39. Translated by Frederick J. Hoffman, with the assistance of the author.

He saw, facing him across the spring, a man of under size, his hands in his coat pockets, a cigarette slanted from his chin. His suit was black, with a tight, high-waisted coat. His trousers were rolled once and caked with mud above mud-caked shoes. His face had a queer, bloodless color, as though seen by electric light; against the sunny silence, in his slanted straw hat and his slightly akimbo arms, he had that vicious depthless quality of stamped tin.

Behind him the bird sang again, three bars in monotonous repetition: a sound meaningless and profound out of a suspirant and peaceful following silence which seemed to isolate the spot, and out of which a moment later came the sound of an automobile passing along a road and dying away.*

Reading this passage one is aware of a completely real presence, such as one finds in first-rank novels (I think first of all of Dostoevsky, particularly of *Crime and Punishment*): that is, the scene does not affect us as if set in a book or through words; it is before us; rather, it surrounds us. It is around us as though we were in the process, not so much of living it as of dreaming it. Let us examine the passage a little more closely, and try to determine how Faulkner makes us visualize it, what devices he uses; we might also try to discover his way of seeing, what is traditionally called his world vision.

First of all, a scene such as this at the very beginning of a work is quite rare. Faulkner saves the reader from all of the usual approaches; there are none of the customary introductions to place and character. Some kind of adaptation is performed by our minds, and we ourselves appear to have dropped into the scene by accident, as though we had come upon it while strolling along. This is the first quality of the "presence," this illusion which leads the reader directly into the scene instead of simply putting it on display before him.

Moreover, there is an interchange of subjective awareness among the participants that enables us to go directly to the scene and to forget the author. He has not said ten words when, in the very first phrase, the responsibility of observing is shifted to the first character. "Popeye watched the man drinking." The two men, one designated by a vulgar nickname, the other no more than an obscure shadow, suffice as a kind of mutual inventory of the situation. This is true even though we well know that neither Popeye nor Benbow perceives very much; the symbol of the reflections in the water is relevant. In its superb economy, this passage succeeds in rendering the scene (having first set us within it) by merely setting down

* Except when specified, quotations are from first American editions [editor's note].

the data enabling us to find our bearings; Faulkner does not intellectually abstract the scene, but absorbs it into a *moment* keyed to a peculiar emotional note and quality. It is a moment bewitched. Faulkner at times reminds us of Conrad—for example, in *Absalom, Absalom!*. He had read widely in Conrad's works, and may have found in him a type of method which he made his own (such as putting the narrator into the tale). Here in the opening pages of *Sanctuary,* he seems to communicate a quality of atmosphere, not dissimilar from that one breathes (or barely senses) in Conrad. It is produced by a subtle grouping of disagreeable sensations: the inordinate stillness of a character in relation to another who does not see him; a numbness undisturbed even by the bubbling of the spring; the sleeping sun, in the silence, which is of course accentuated by the three notes of the bird and the strange and elusive sound of the automobile.

At the center the two characters stand. One is barely sketched, as is appropriate to his weak nature (suggested by the very absence of features and the vagueness of outline); the other, at this first meeting, is already entirely *present,* in the full meaning of the word. Certain characteristics of this actuality are perhaps simply "realistic" and relate to the situation, to the external world. The rest is part of a system of symbols, and especially of sharply expressive physiognomic signs (deliberately emphasized by Faulkner), to be repeated throughout the book. There is nothing extraneous, nothing haphazard, in Popeye, nothing accidental; even the description of his clothes is purposeful: the scanty black suit and over-tight jacket are a reflection of the crazy moron.

Our attention is drawn to his face: the all but missing chin, melted away like that of a wax doll left too close to a fire; the eyes, like two small soft rubber knobs, the little doll hands. But even before we see those features we get the first impact from his pallor, as though we were seeing him in a strong electric light. And we here notice a characteristic that is common to all of Faulkner's work, his effort to clarify by a *correspondence,* an overemphatic analogy, a particularity of appearance repeated endlessly and completed by an *as if,* a *like,* or some such phrase.

At first it seems as though Faulkner pursues these analogies for his own sake: they are a part for him of the profound identity of his characters, they are essential to his meaning. The metallic analogy is attached to Popeye from the beginning, worked over, represented in implausible yet convincing combinations, as when (Signet edition, 138) he compares Popeye's fingers to steel that nevertheless has the cold lightness of aluminum. Each time the analogy is orientated so precisely that there will be no mistake about it; for example, in this present case, the point in question is an inhuman quality, an irreducible appearance of the metal, so communicated that Popeye appears at once metallic and fragile, with a brittleness equally inhuman.[1]

The primary quality of this text is the effect of immediacy; and because, as in a dream (if the sensation is strong enough), nothing can be questioned any more, the effect of that quality grows upon us. The effect of immediacy is strengthened by the obstacle it overcomes; and, accepting the unusual, we experience the uneasy feeling that in literature sometimes suggests the disturbance of a dream.

The strongly expressive system of physical signs through which Popeye's strangeness is conveyed marks him for a drama developing in time; in addition we experience from it something akin to the impression produced by the sight of witchcraft. This latter affects our sensibility much more fully and profoundly than any limited development of events could. This complexity of impressions comes and radiates from the very first scene.

Frequently, as here, in Faulkner we get a sense of the unusual principally because of a peculiarity of appearance. In some such way the protagonist of the Grumby episode (in *The Unvanquished*) appears as though in a dream, with this same oddity of excessive smallness: ". . . his neat little fine made boots, . . . his little feet side by side . . . and his two hands on his knees as small as a woman's hands and covered with a light mat of fine black hair right down to the finger nails. . . ." (189-90) The description of his handwriting presents the man vividly to us: ". . . something else written beneath it in a hand neat and small and prettier than Granny's, only you knew that a man had written it; and while I looked at the dirty paper I could see him again, with his neat little feet and his little black-haired hands. . . ." (203)

For another example, Rosa Coldfield in *Absalom, Absolom!* (in her case the odd is for once harmless) sits, dressed in the mourning she has worn for 43 years, looking like a character of the Douanier Rousseau, "bolt upright in the straight hard chair that was so tall for her that her legs hung straight and rigid as if she had iron shinbones and ankles, clear of the floor with that air of impotent and static rage like children's feet. . . ." (Modern Library, 7) ". . . the wan haggard face watched him above the faint tri-

---

1. Page 136, Signet edition: "his arms had a fragile appearance: no larger than a child's, dead, hard, light as a stick. . . ." Page 139: "The little arms of Popeye, light and rigid as aluminum. . . ."

angle of lace at wrists and throat from the too tall chair in which she resembled a crucified child. . . ." (8)

This is the way Quentin Compson sees her and pictures her. Also in *Absalom, Absalom!,* Sutpen, the most striking of Faulkner's heroes, has his character elaborately developed by several intermediate imaginations (Rosa, General Compson, his son, Quentin his grandson); he emerges realized in a series of apparitions and revealing aspects. The element of strangeness, perhaps too easily given in some instances, is absent here. Sutpen's peculiar quality is more subtly suggested.

At first he appears as the stranger, who looks "like an explorer say, who not only had to face the normal hardship of the pursuit which he chose but was overtaken by the added and unforeseen handicap of the fever. . . ." "A man with a big frame but gaunt now almost to emaciation, with a short reddish beard which resembled a disguise and above which his pale eyes had a quality at once visionary and alert, ruthless and reposed in a face whose flesh had the appearance of pottery, of having been colored by that oven's fever either of soul or environment, deeper than sun alone beneath a dead impervious surface as of glazed clay." (32-33)

Later he is defined and described in a different way:

He was not portly yet, though he was now getting on toward fifty-five. The fat, the stomach, came later. It came upon him suddenly, all at once [the year after his failure to marry Rosa] . . . as though what the negroes and Wash Jones, too, called the fine figure of a man had reached and held its peak after the foundation had given away and something between the shape of him that people knew and the uncompromising skeleton of what he actually was had gone fluid, and, earthbound, had been snubbed up and restrained, balloonlike, unstable and lifeless, by the envelope it had betrayed. (80-81)

Refined, subtle, savagely ingenious, absurd: however one may wish to call this analysis of Sutpen, it indicates Faulkner's dualism, his feeling that the body and the self exist in an unstable relation, often ironic never casual. In spite of herself, Rosa Coldfield is only what her body makes her: "this small body . . . with its air of curious and paradoxical awkwardness like a costume borrowed at the last moment and of necessity for a masquerade which she did not want to attend. . . ." (65) The body denotes lack, failure, defeat and even madness, but it also indicates the power of the will to live. In any case, the description offers the external signs of an essential being, perhaps even of a conflict of essences.

There are no meaningful physical classes or types in Faulkner to which individuals may be ascribed, such as one finds in D. H. Lawrence: instinctive and sensitive brown-skinned people, for example, or idealistic, insensitive ill-adapted blondes, etc. . . . ; Faulkner gives us no systematic classification of physical appearances, but instead offers quite separate insights into individuals. He is interested, not in anything specifically physical, but in something like a *language of the body,* suggested in traits, gestures, manners. From it comes the matter of taking the gesture as a kind of alphabet. In *The Wild Palms,* Harry, in desperate need of help for his mistress, lays his hand upon the arm of a Puritan doctor; the doctor has stifled since birth all impulses of instinctive or sensual life, let along passionate intensities. His inner life has always depended upon reassuring formulas. The doctor reacts to this "impure contact" and rejects the guilty hand, "not exactly as if it has been a spider or a reptile or even a piece of filth, but rather as if he had found clinging to his sleeve a piece of atheistic or Communist propaganda. . . ." (280) Contrary to what would occur in a physiognomic system, it is not the physical peculiarity of gesture which makes motivation clear, but a precise and thorough investigation of the motive which makes the gesture meaningful. But one essential quality of his characters is their frequent reflex actions, which are extraordinarily revealing.

This is true throughout of those astonishing partners, Popeye and Temple Drake. Her psychic disorder reduces her body to behaving in the grotesque manner of a lifeless jumping jack; thus, her head "began to move. . . . It turned on to an excruciating degree, though no other muscle moved, like one of those papiermâché Easter toys filled with candy, and became motionless in that reverted position. Then it turned back, slowly. . . ." (81) As for Popeye, he acts as though he had no control of himself, almost as if he were demented; the fear, vice, and cruelty that are his nature are expressed in the gestures not so much of an automaton as in those of a beast. When Temple induces in him an erotic delirium, she hears him "begin to make a whimpering sound . . . his bluish lips protruding as though he were blowing upon hot soup, making a high whinnying sound like a horse. . . ." (191)

I have said that in the characters of Faulkner, the relation between consciousness and body is curiously strained. One can even say that at the point where they join the characters suffer a double anguish. First, there is a *sensation of imminence,* which I have analyzed elsewhere.[2] An abnormal

2. In *Cahiers du collège philosophique, La Profondeur et le Rhythme* (Arthaud, 1948), "Le Temps et la Destinée chez William Faulkner," pp. 303-31.

tension of the self which is directed entirely toward its body leads to giving the feeling that interior time, instead of passing away in some fashion or other, accumulates irresistibly, rolls up like a spring, up to the fatal point of release, even if the event seems to be entirely exterior and entirely compelling—which this preparation and this appeal strongly deny. At moments of the greatest tension, the line breaks; in some way the consciousness goes one way, the body another. Quite literally the character (Temple, Christmas, Rosa—each of us will think of examples) does not know what is being done even at the moment his or her body is doing it. The passionate intensities of those moments are marked in Faulkner's novels by the disorders which are striking symptoms of them. I have suggested elsewhere that in these circumstances the consciousness loses its close relationship with the body, that it gets out of order, erratically moves ahead or lags behind the act, the attitude, the state of the body. After the event, after the disaster, there is a new form of anguish: Temple's, for example, with its complex symbols, the empty time of a defunct clock, and the secret hemorrhage. This hemorrhage is a form of the consciousness of the body, curiously frequent in Faulkner:—the slow flowing of the blood, while the broken personality drifts toward physical or moral destruction. It is almost as if the character, by the betrayal of the body which has literally become a stranger, has found itself cast adrift standing on melting ice amidst a river, on the way to nothingness.

Faulkner's search for the most expressive way of representing his characters leads him to try all kinds of literary technique. Sometimes he finds models in the work of his contemporaries: a choral procedure, more or less *unanimiste*; interior monologues which are halfway individual and halfway collective (as in *Soldiers' Pay*); a succession of personal angles of vision (as in *As I Lay Dying* and *The Sound and the Fury*); impressionist and expressionist techniques inspired by the cinema or Dos Passos, as in *Pylon*. In all of these manners he pursues his own proper object, the direct communication of a complex and sorrowful human reality, in respect to which he feels nothing like artistic detachment. Wyndham Lewis devoted some hostile but intelligent pages to him in *Men Without Art,* at a time when Faulkner was many years away from the Nobel Prize. Lewis appreciated his satiric gift ("The moralist with a corn-cob"), and he showed what strength the satirical determination gave certain scenes, for example that of the collegians meeting Horace Benbow in a train. Faulkner is usually concerned with a scene of no more than three or four characters, though there is often a vague hint of epic themes in the background. When he cares to, however, he shows extraordinary skill in his treatment of a multitude. In these scenes the rhythm of his symbolism changes: a sign here, a hint there, given in rapid succession, help both to bring individuals to life and vividly to present the group with its group tics and automatisms.

One sometimes regrets that he has not used this gift more often, or has not produced more of his searching caricatures of individuals, creating extraordinary *"drôles de corps."* These vivid portrayals serve to complement the characters found in a more sinister world; they are equally predetermined, and are scarcely less menacing to man, despite the extremely comical detail. Has not the world of the grotesques been ever thus, since Bosch and Breughel? This is the world of the enormous, the shapeless Senator Snopes, whose skin looks as though it had been dry-cleaned rather than washed. As in many other places, we note here the tendency of Faulkner's analogies to bring the organic and the inorganic close together. Again, in *Sanctuary,* the dogs of Miss Reba seem to have been dry-cleaned rather than washed. And as for her, the landlady of the brothel, she too has many a symbolic trait: round, swollen, "pneumatic," with her asthmatic joviality, and with her two dogs, too white and beribboned, trailing along with her. Miss Reba, Faulkner's greatest comedy success, is in a tradition which derives at once from Dickens and from Maupassant. Another memorable character, the reporter of *Pylon,* a dissolute and eager skeleton, moves through the densest of crowds, "as a playing card." The difficulty, surely overcome here, of integrating such drolleries within a somber symbolic pattern probably prevents them from recurring frequently in his work.[3]

On the one hand there is a drama in Faulkner which unfolds in time; even if this time should also be often upset, confused, and inverted, as we shall see. On the other hand, beyond this level of action there is the world of the imagination. If we go back to re-examine his texts, we find our suspicions verified, that the characters have a quite unusual way of appearing and disappearing; they do not behave as do the actors in some human comedy. They rise to the surface, they *are materialized.* I use the word advisedly.

In this way Sutpen appears: "Out of quiet thunderclap he would abrupt

3. As these pages were going to the printers, I had a chance to examine the selection of critiques titled *William Faulkner: Two Decades of Criticism* (Edited by F. J. Hoffman and Olga W. Vickery). In one of the critical essays, "William Faulkner: The Novel as Form," Conrad Aiken remarked of the great burlesque scene in which Reba, "Uncle Bud" and the little boy are presented, that this two dimensional caricature does not have the same reality as the book but plays its "choral" role perfectly.

(man-horse-demon) upon a scene peaceful and decorous as a schoolprize water color, faint sulphur-reek in hair, clothes and beard. . . ." (8)

". . . that Sunday morning in June in 1833 when he first rode into town out of no discernible past. . . ." (11)

". . . the other men sitting with their feet on the railing of the Holston House gallery looked up, and there the stranger was. He was already halfway across the Square when they saw him, on a big hard-ridden roan horse, man and beast *looking as though they had been created out of thin air. . . .*" (31-32)

Faulkner's stories are full of these apparitions. Most of these cases have a double aspect: in regard to the temporal dimension of the drama, the appearance represents the insertion of a disturbing element in a community accustomed to ordinary affairs. The ensuing adventure is an outgrowth of this appearance, as in a Hardy or a Lawrence novel. But there is a more profound aspect. That odor of sulphur does not belong solely to Rosa's vision, it has a specific meaning; if once we leave the temporal dimension, those characters are *manifestations,* they express forces which they believe they are using and of which they are at once the plaything and the agent. They are thus evil forces, anti-human and destructive, even of their own instruments. If we push our investigation further, we find that these characters evince a tonality which shows them to belong to an affective system, neither logical nor chronological. Because the characters, the places, the acts are caught and held together in an affective fusion, we have the impression of a poet's quest of an obscure wholeness. In all of the mature works of this writer (I might say, of this poet), whether we accept it or not, he offers us what appears to be an entirely unified vision.

* * *

Let us return once more to that first scene, which has helped us to determine so many points. Of the two characters, one is an agent, a destroyer, a manifestation; the other is an inadequate and mediocre person, one of those who can only stand by, nursing more or less abnormal and ineffectual passions, to observe the behavior of the live and the monstrous one. He is an observer-voyeur; through him we grasp most of the novel's reality. He is the melancholy chorus; despite his blundering efforts to participate, he is powerless to change it.

The observer is more or less present in all of Faulkner's books. He may be a type of voyeur, or he may be the hero of the plot; or at the end of the drama, he might prove to have been the means of revealing its meaning (this last is true of Quentin in *Absalom, Absalom!*). He is surely something more than an easy contrivance to add to the illusion, to make things more real; even though he is a voyeur, he takes part in the action, in such a way as not to be merely an objective observer; he has absorbed the situation into his imagination and feeling.

There are many examples of the character as sensitive and sorrowful witness in Faulkner's books, the man who desperately tries to understand and to make sense of the situations he observes: Judge Benbow, impotent and inadequate, a bondslave to two bitches, his wife and his stepdaughter (*Sanctuary*); the good Byron Bunch, son of a long line of timid and puny beings, which both life and the novel have in abundance (*Light in August*); the reporter of *Pylon,* who chooses to aggravate his illness by drinking, so that he can the more quickly abolish despair, yet retains his curiosity like a ravenous hunger, at the same time as he is a prey to an absurd passion for a pilot's moll. One might add that if there is one of them who speaks, expounds, tries to appraise the toughness and complexity of this human knot which holds him in fascination, there is another who listens. Characters, plot, chains of causes, fury of forces rise in ghostly fashion not in one but among several imaginations. And the ghost ends by appearing more real than the reality itself from which it apparently comes, but of which one may query whether it ever existed, so that the fictional creation emerges as true reality.

What is "experience," really? How indeed do we determine the reality of immediate, direct action, of even the most violent gesture, even of those directly designed to cut and to destroy? This is probably why one cannot escape the narrow limits of direct experience. To the limits of personal experience we add what we learn, imagine, what is transmitted to us; "reality" is enlarged in all directions into one vast legend. This process is the true identifying mark of the human.

In the matter of the Civil War, for example, sweeping through space and time in the whole of *Absalom, Absalom!* or *The Unvanquished*:[4] what is, and where is, its reality, the characters ask themselves. They look for it in rumor, in news, in the men whose deaths are announced, in others who come back. All of this scarcely produced objective and coherent reality; it suggests the battle of Waterloo as described in *Chartreuse*. Charles Bon, who dies, whom Henry Sutpen has killed, is surrounded by such unreality in himself and in his death, which Rosa vainly tries to comprehend:

4. "We knew there was a war. . . . However, we had no proof of it." (*The Unvanquished*)

"You see, I never saw him. I never even saw him dead. I heard an echo, but not the shot; I saw a closed door but did not enter it . . . I remember how as we carried him down the stairs and out to the waiting wagon I tried to take the full weight of the coffin to prove to myself that he was really in it. And I could not tell." (150-51) ". . . Three women put something into the earth and covered it, and he had never been." (153)

In any case, just who was Charles Bon, as he is evoked by Quentin Compson's father? Bon, with his sardonic disdain, his vague and impenetrable character, seems ". . . a myth, a phantom: something which [Henry, Judith, and Ellen] engendered and created whole themselves; some effluvium of Sutpen blood and character, as though as a man he did not exist at all." (104)

One may see the point of definition I wish to reach, or rather the point I need to reach, in order to understand Faulkner—these characters are *representations*. Bon is an extreme case, but he is not an exception. They are less existing beings as such than emanations. The characters who puzzle over their meaning, like Shreve and Quentin of *Absalom, Absalom!*, are engaged in an act of discovery. Consider, for example, the two young men of *Absalom, Absalom!*, in their dormitory room, truly a *"camera obscura."* Shreve the stranger, the pure spectator, does not simply listen to Quentin, but also takes his share in the creation of Bon; he too seeks for the symbols and signs needful to the meaning; he describes a dining room, gives the traits of a character, corrects a point of detail which appears unsuitable. "Your father *is mistaken*. According to him, it is Bon who was wounded. But that isn't so." It is a *tragedia dell'arte* which the "past" offers our imagination.

One would think that such characters as Bon depended entirely upon those who imagined them, or even that they were mere tricks of the mind. On the contrary, nothing is so remarkable as the persistence of their impact; this is a true sign of Faulkner's creative power. As obscure and unaccountable shapes these characters haunt the present, they live in us. "It is as though," Faulkner says somewhere, "nothing ever passed away," at least not the great horrors, the great terrors of the past. This ghostly survival pervades everything connected with the Sutpen saga. Consider, for example, the frenetic shrieks of the vision-haunted Judith (these children raised by the demon Sutpen remind one of the children of Henry James's *Turn of the Screw*); her screaming, as she urges on her father's savage Negroes, resounds seventy years afterward in an unappeased air. The impression is of a past in pain inflicted upon a present in pain and upon ever troubled souls; it is a past one must some day purge. The primary step in achieving this great catharsis is to penetrate this opaque past to the depth of its human reality.

Faulkner starts off from a present, a present that can be so choked by a stagnant past that there is no place in it for the future. This helps to explain the particular form his creation takes. The past is the unconscious mind of the present; it is a question not of invention but of a resurgence forcefully stimulated by an emotional need, not logical nor tied to chronology. The Faulkner drama is not in the past, it is a *psychodrama* of the present. Quentin, with Shreve as his partner, attempts to reconstruct the drama of Sutpen and of the Civil War, with the aid of the memories of his grandfather, of his father and of Rosa. But he does not need to assume it; he is *inside* it: ". . . his very body was an empty hall echoing with sonorous defeated names; he was not a being, an entity, he was a commonwealth." (12)

Quentin committed suicide at the end of *The Sound and the Fury*. It is perhaps an error of Faulkner's genius, to have linked the identity of that neurotic with the young man in *Absalom, Absalom!* who makes so strong and so clear-sighted an effort to move into the past, to which he endeavors to restore a meaning as he recreates it. One needs, it seems to me, to forget the other Quentin while searching for the meaning of *Absalom, Absalom!*. Our narrator, however terrifying his nervous tension might be, should have made a nobler end, more stoical, more appropriate to his imagination.

If we explore further the comparison of *The Sound and the Fury* and *Absalom, Absalom!,* it seems to me we will note a progress from one to the other. In the first, Faulkner poses to himself the problem of preserving past reality which he calls before us in its emotional and concrete quality; he wants as little as possible to translate sensation into perception. This problem he solves with great ingenuity; but ingenuity in literature, even though it were managed by Sterne, has a weakening effect and is ill suited to tragedy. Thus, the past of the Compson family reappears first without chronology, without logic, without coherence, without a chance of all that; we sense it first as a quality of pure affectivity, as a continuous present, such as it is supposed to be in the mind of the idiot Benjy, and as the associations of ideas in an idiot's power can call to light.

Scarcely less affective, and colored by the same emotional associations as the first section of *The Sound and the Fury,* there are the monologue and actions of Quentin at Harvard in their progress as of the day when he will commit suicide because the sister he has loved is a bitch. Logic and even metaphysics on this occasion have been restored, but in this delirium there is still no clear sense of chronology. This last element is restored in the passages devoted to Jason, who reviews the same family history at the level of his debased soul. By now we are impervious, however; there is no risk that we should take this story as external matter of fact. In it there have been two monolithic, massive apprehensions; Jason's alone can not really affect them; the author himself, when finally he comes personally to pursue the tale, finds it the easier to preserve its intense character not to let its reality degenerate into realism.

Faulkner seems at that stage to have risked anti-realism: perhaps because of a natural affinity with such writers as Strindberg, perhaps because of their influence, he has tried expressionistic and violent techniques, the non-realism of which was in danger (as in the absurd interior monologue of the idiot deaf-mute) of falling into an affectation of anti-realism. In my opinion, this was not his way.

\* \* \*

Let us return to the question of narrators, our witnesses, to the choral or the solitary presentation of an imagined reality.

Between Faulkner and his intermediaries, among themselves, and between them and the actors in the plot, all relations are possible, all angles, all superpositions. Faulkner manages all of these with growing ease; as a skillful writer handles by turns, in units deftly loosened and subtly rejoined, the direct style and the indirect. In the same manner, Faulkner, in movements more and more subtle, can by turns bring the characters toward us in a fragment of interior monologue: as when in *Absalom, Absalom!* Quentin expresses the weariness he feels in his being condemned to relive again and again the obscure and atrocious drama of Sutpen and the South; or when Rosa, unable to put a stop to her persistent monologue, lets the same tale unroll itself in the long psalmodic chant of her memory. Or again Faulkner can accompany from behind their tormented thoughts; can follow along with them, in a rhythm as expressive as and less deceptive than the interior monologue, the gestures they watch themselves make, the feelings of which they are vaguely aware: such as Christmas or Hightower in *Light in August,* or Harry in the last pages of *The Wild Palms.*

All of this forces our attention upon that sole reality which constitutes the creation of the real by the imagination; it undoubtedly never acts, even though in face of the "real," except by the acts and rhythms of memory. The novelist ordains these acts and these rhythms—it is the role of literature, Faulkner says in part, to give coherence to life—but it is not surprising that, within the novels, he allows the consciousness free play. In *Old Man* the convict relives his adventure among his comrades, so much that he is a prey to nervous twitches that repeat the quality of the evoked experience, by a sort of Einfühlung that makes his body and mind the very scene of his drama. In this way, as he is drifting in his canoe, ". . . a town . . . appears suddenly in the telling as it probably appeared in actuality. . . ." (172) Just in the midst of the passage, when he is most seriously disturbed, calm returns to him. "And now when he told this, despite the fury of element which climaxed it, it (the telling) became quite simple. . . ." (174) He rolls his cigarette peacefully without spilling the crumbs of tobacco, and the rest of the tale "seemed to reach his listeners as though from beyond a sheet of slightly milky though still transparent glass, as something not heard but seen. . . ." (174)

What decisive points of contact occur between a past that is totally obscure and a present, almost real, tangible, objective, represented by the room at Harvard, or a prison cell, the Compson apartment, or whatever, the characters set in it acting as if they were before a crystal bowl, breathing the cold of the night or the heat of the day? By what decisive thrusts does the past burst into the present, as do the fragments of Proust's absolute memory? Now between these points, the imaginations at work strive to re-establish a continuity, availing themselves of every chance in successive illuminations, groping onward, putting forward then dropping a conjecture so that the past changes in the very process of its being determined, at any rate provisionally.

Certain experiences do not let "the past" disappear; traumatic shocks block the flow of time, even though there is no visible destruction; so Rosa, in 1909, is stopped at 1865 and 1869; again and again she finds that four or five scenes recur to her mind, two especially, the key scenes of her history and of the Sutpen legend.

The first is truly in its two stages the great, decisive scene of the book: there is the moment when Henry Sutpen appears before his sister, who is preparing to try on the wedding dress made of such pitiful tatters as are available in a time of distress; at this moment he announces to her that he has killed Charles Bon, the fiancé he had once presented to her. Then comes the moment when Rosa arises in the midst of this devastation and is checked by the hand of the mulatto woman Clytemnestra, half-sister of Henry and Judith, barring her from the stairway, as from a forbidden secret.

Again, there is the last scene, where Sutpen, in insulting the daughter

of his obscure vassal, the *poor white,* Wash Jones, because she gave him
a daughter and not a son, wipes out an entire life of fanatic and savage
loyalty and goads Jones into killing him.

Now, the sense of these scenes is that they represent arrests of the
consciousness and of vital rhythm; they are in themselves, too, curiously
stilled. Henry, the disheveled soldier of the defeated army (his hair has been
cut by the hacking of a sabre), rises before his sister, who holds the useless
dress before her shabby under-clothing; Rosa, the hand of the mulatto
woman arresting her drive; moments like these are touched by the wand of
a black fairy, tragic and in their immobility almost sculptural. These visions
close in upon an act of violence, and solemnizing it, confirm Faulkner's
orientation toward an idealistic conception.

At the beginning of *Light in August* a beautiful phrase describes the
voyage of Lena and the long peaceful and monotonous succession of
changes, of day into night and night into day. She travels in identical
wagons, anonymous and deliberate, "as though through a succession of
creakwheeled and limpeared avatars, *like something moving forever and
without progress across an urn.*" (Modern Library, 6)

May we risk the suggestion that here we find ourselves before that
Greek vase in terms of which Keats made his profession of idealism, as
well as before the immobility of the instant and of movement itself: even
if here is the simple living consciousness that offers the illusion of stillness,
instead of its being simply art whose role is to arrest life in stillness.

"Thou still unravished bride of quietness," the poet says of the eternal
fiancée whom the outstretched arms of the lover, however near, will never
reach. "Unravished nuptial," says Faulkner of the soul of Judith in her
wedding preparations—contrasted, as the only intangible reality, with the
absence that comes from every consummation,[5] with inevitable widowhood.

Faulkner plays it constantly, this game of the consciousness with its
bizarre "instantaneities" that are always on the point of being transformed
into absolutes. The buggy of Miss Rosa advances in this way: ". . . the
dustcloud in which the buggy moved not blowing away because it had been
raised by no wind and was supported by no wind and was supported by no
air but *evoked, materialized* about them, *instantaneous* and *eternal.* . . ."

A strange fantasy in *Intruder in the Dust* begins with an evocation
of that September morning when everybody prepares the hogs for killing
on the same evening; the hogs are vaguely disturbed: ". . . by nightfall the
whole land would be hung with their spectral intact tallowcolored empty

5. In the story, "The Bear," one of the characters reads and comments upon this
ode: "Listen: 'She cannot fade, though thou hast not the bliss. . . .' "

carcasses immobilised by the heels in attitudes of frantic running as though full tilt at the center of the earth." (4) Later we encounter "the land's living symbol—a formal group of ritual almost mystic significance identical and monotonous as milestones . . . the beast the plow and the man integrated in one foundationed into the frozen wave of their furrow tremendous with effort yet at the same time vacant of progress, ponderable immovable and immobile like groups of wrestling statuary. . . ." (147)

These passages suggest an idealism which one ought not label too easily. And yet . . . through separate existences, forces push their way, show themselves and *are embodied*. Let us return to our key scene, to Rosa faced with Henry's murder of Charles, stopped in her drive by Clytemnestra, finding before her the face she assumes is Henry's: "Because it was not Henry's face. It was Sutpen face enough, but not his; Sutpen coffee-colored face enough there in the dim light, . . . not approaching, not swimming up out of the gloom, but already there, rocklike and firm and antedating time and house and doom and all. . . ." (136)

And of the son of Charles and of the octoroon, ". . . this child with a face not old but without age, as if he had had no childhood, . . . as if he had not been human born but instead created without agency of man or agony of woman . . . as if he were the delicate and perverse spirit-symbol, immortal page of the ancient immortal Lilith. . . ." (196)

This final presence before the world—it is not important to know by how many stages of narrators it is relayed—is only the presence of the imagination to itself, and perhaps in fact absence from the world, if the world does exist. The language, the "metaphysical" style of the writer, perhaps decadent, is indefensible from the point of view of correctness or of clarity, but it is marvelously proper for showing the unity of an interior and a qualitative world. As for this vision reality is perhaps only the concrete vesture of ideas, similarly in the style, these concrete details are united to abstractions, in the most singular combinations, and lend them a strange life; one recalls the "succession of creak-wheeled and limpeared avatars" of Lena. In the same spirit Cash the carpenter is making Addie's coffin, "sawing the long hot yellow days up into planks and nailing them to something. . . ." (Modern Library, 355) If finally ideas and representations are what make up the human world (as the "metaphysicals" thought), there is no separation between the most concrete, the most physical of sensations and abstractions of all degrees; inversely, none of all this concreteness is simply "physical" or "material," and cosmic relations are implied in every sensation.

In all that is abstract, everything is charged with the physical, the immediate; in all concrete particulars, everything is charged with the highest abstractions; and the extraordinary range of Faulknerian adjectives describes this arc.

No vain conceit, no affectation is implied by Faulkner when he writes in *Pylon* of the new aerodrome of *New Valois,* built upon the mud of a lagoon, as "the flat triangle of land, reconquered and tortured, restored by the slow violence of machines to the air and to the flickering of the light. . . ." Here William Faulkner moves into the company of Sir Thomas Browne.

A strange writer, Faulkner is as Protean as the most characteristic vision of our divided times; he is contradictory and one might even call him incomprehensible if it were not possible to overcome his contradictions. I believe one can do so, and I think it possible finally to bring into relation all of the elements of his genius. The Faulknerian reality, as his genius has recreated it, is certainly not what critical conventions associate with the term *realism,* if by that term one means a sort of photography or a photographic montage of the external world. My force, Théophile Gautier said once in this connection, comes from the fact that I am a man for whom the external world exists. The power of Faulkner comes from his being a man for whom finally nothing exists beyond the interior world. In art, but in philosophy as well (for this uncouth artist is a philosopher, though perhaps without his knowing it), he is an idealist, for whom as for Berkeley *esse est percipi,* for whom all takes place in the consciousness and between consciousnesses. Dr. Johnson kicked a stone to demonstrate the independent existence of matter. For Faulkner the mystery is not thus resolved, but remains untouched. Like Keats, like Mallarmé, like Proust, like Joyce, this idealist belongs to the Platonic tradition; he does not see any matter other than materializations, signs, symbols, of forces which are transformed into existences. Reality is thus presented in a double aspect. It is powerfully significant in that it reflects the play of forces, the strongest of which emerge from the shadows toward which they constantly draw back our effort. It is very illusory, since our consciousness seizes nothing but manifestations. Thus on the one hand we have this so vigorous representation of a world charged with meaning, and with an astonishing wealth and variety of physiognomic appearances, whether of men or places or gestures, or of the scenes containing them. On the other hand, we have all those hints that remind us that it is also a kind of dream, more often even a nightmare.

Faulkner is as American as Kafka is Judeo-German. Thus their symbolic and dreamlike reality is as different as it can be; perhaps we should try to assess the differences. One senses, for example, that in Faulkner we are before the dream of a reality, and in Kafka, before the reality of a dream. Once this difference is established, we are free to insist upon the qualitative and affective aspect of Faulkner's world. He reflects and expresses the anguish of a disintegrating class and society, of various representatives of that society and of a class thrown by the waves of history beyond reality (as a fish might be thrown out of water), and wandering in its mind in a lost world. This is not to reduce but to define the authenticity of his feverish and barbaric vision.

# THE EDGE OF ORDER: THE PATTERN
# OF FAULKNER'S RHETORIC

## WALTER J. SLATOFF

IN WILLIAM FAULKNER's short story "Delta Autumn," Ike McCaslin says that "the heart dont always have time to bother with thinking up words that fit together."[1] In *Absalom, Absalom!*, when Charles Bon leaves for college, Faulkner describes him as "almost touching the answer, aware of the jig-saw puzzle picture integers of it waiting, almost lurking, just beyond his reach, inextricable, jumbled, and unrecognizable yet on the point of falling into pattern which would reveal to him at once, like a flash of light, the meaning of his whole life" (313). The integers never do fall into place for Charles Bon. Much the same can be said about Benjy and Quentin

Reprinted with permission from *Twentieth Century Literature,* October, 1957, pp. 107-27.
1. William Faulkner, *Go Down, Moses* (Random House, 1942), p. 348; hereafter abbreviated *GDM*. Other abbreviations and editions of Faulkner's works used here are as follows. *AA: Absalom, Absalom!* (New York: Modern Library, 1951); *AILD: As I Lay Dying* (New York: Modern Library, 1946); *CS: Collected Stories* (New York: Random House, 1950); *H: The Hamlet* (New York: Random House, 1940); *ID: Intruder in the Dust* (Random House, 1948); *LIA: Light in August* (New York: Modern Library, 1950); *MCS: Mirrors of Chartres Street* (Minneapolis: Faulkner Studies, 1953); *P: Pylon* (London: Chatto and Windlus, 1935); *RN: Requiem for a Nun* (New York: Random House, 1950); *S: Sanctuary* (New York: Modern Library, 1932); *SF: The Sound and the Fury* (New York: Modern Library, 1946); *WP: The Wild Palms* (New York: Random House, 1939).

Compson, Darl Bundren, Gail Hightower, Thomas Sutpen and numerous other characters in Faulkner's novels.

Every Faulkner novel in some way provides the reader with the problem of fitting pieces together, and many readers of Faulkner feel with respect to the meanings of the novels much as Charles Bon did about the meaning of his life. Much Faulkner criticism has been devoted to explaining, both in particular novels and in his works in general, how the pieces do fit together, the patterns of meaning they do form. A good many such patterns have been discovered and offered as the essential meanings of the novels and of Faulkner's vision as a whole.

In this paper I wish to suggest that in many ways and on many levels Faulkner seems very anxious to keep pieces from fitting together, and that this is a crucial aspect of his work. It has been generally recognized that the purpose of some of Faulkner's structural complexities is to keep his material in a state of flux or suspension. But it has also generally been thought and argued or assumed that these suspensions are finally resolved, that by the ends of the novels the jig-saw picture puzzle integers do fall into place. There is much evidence, I think, that Faulkner is willing and even anxious to leave most of them in a high degree of suspension, or at least a suspension that cannot be resolved in logical or rational terms. Nor has it been recognized how very much his moment to moment presentation of experience involves a juxtaposition of elements which do not seem to fit together and which to some degree resist synthesis or resolution.

1

A remarkably frequent and persistent phenomenon in Faulkner's writing is his presentation of opposed or contradictory suggestions. In some instances the contradictions are more apparent than real; in others they seem quite real. I shall not try to distinguish between them. My purpose here is simply to suggest something of the number and variety of things which are presented in conflicting terms. Again and again, for example, Faulkner describes objects and events in terms which at once suggest motion and immobility. A large number of wagons, buggies, and engines are described as moving "without progress" or with an effect of "nomotion." The carcasses of hogs hang "immobilized by the heels in attitudes of frantic running" (*ID*, 4). Rosa Coldfield and Clytie face one another: "I motionless in the attitude and action of running, she rigid in that furious immobility" (*AA*, 140). Psychological conditions are often similarly rendered. When the schoolbell rings, Quentin Compson's "insides would move, sitting still. *Moving sitting still"* (*SF*, 107). "Though Joe had not moved since he entered, he was still running" (*LIA*, 187). Frequently the contradictory suggestions are compressed into phrases like "poised and swooping immobility," "terrific immobility," or "dynamic immobility."

Sound and silence, also, are frequently presented as existing simultaneously. Silence often seems not so much the absence of sound as a container for it, a presence even while the sounds are occurring. We read of a "silence filled with the puny sounds of men" (*LIA*, 259) and "a sound . . . which silence itself, seemed to find strange and hard to digest" (*MCS*, 19-20). Very frequently, just as he gives maximum simultaneity and compression to motion and immobility in images like "dynamic immobility," Faulkner compresses the suggestions of sound and silence to the condition of oxymoron. Thus, again and again we find phrases like "crashing silently," "exploded soundlessly," "soundless yelling," and "quiet thunderclap." On at least three occasions Faulkner sets up, in effect, double oxymorons of sound and silence, the most compact being "soundless words in the pattering silence" (*CS*, 899).

Perhaps the most common physical and psychological conditions presented by Faulkner are ones which simultaneously contain elements of quiescence and turbulence. A flood is likely to exhibit a calm, still surface above its raging currents or to suggest "fury in itself quiet with stagnation" (*AILD*, 458). Fights commonly occur in silence or in tranquil surroundings. Characters, even the most violent and tormented, are most apt to possess quiet or calm exteriors, to exhibit furious immobility or quiet rage, or to behave with quiet fury or calm violence. When their tension or torment has become unbearable they may, like a farmer in *The Hamlet,* become "calm and contained and rigidly boiling" (222), or they may like the dietitian in *Light in August* and Wilbourne in *The Wild Palms,* be described as going calmly and quietly mad.

Opposed suggestions are not at all confined to these areas. In every Faulkner novel an astonishing number and variety of characters and events are described in oxymoronic or near oxymoronic terms. Here is a small sampling from two of Faulkner's novels which may give some idea of the pervasiveness of the phenomenon and of the variety of contexts in which it occurs.

In *Light in August,* Doc Hines is "paradoxically rapt and alert at the same time" (323) and has the ability "to flux instantaneously between complete attention that does not seem to hear, and that comalike bemusement in which the stare of his apparently inverted eye is as uncomfortable as though he held them [his companions] with his hand" (334). His wife's face is at the same time "peaceful and terrible" and her attitude is "at once like a rock and like a crouching beast" (348). The face of Hightower, with whom the Hineses are talking, is "at once gaunt and flabby" (77). The Sunday morning service in the church in which he once preached has a "stern and formal fury" (321). He hears singing from the church: "a sound at once austere and rich, abject and proud" (65). When he resigns his pulpit "the town was sorry with being glad" (60). Joe Christmas' feet are capable of moving at "deliberate random" (291). He can "hear without hearing them wails of terror and distress quieter than sighs all about him" (293). Lena Grove gives Armstid, Winterbottom, and Armstid's wagon a glance which is at once "innocent and profound" (7). Later she and the wagon come slowly together "without any semblance of progress" (10). She passes fields and woods "at once static and fluid" (24).

In *The Hamlet* Will Varner is "at once active and lazy" (6). His son Jody wears a costume which is "at once ceremonial and negligee" (11). Tull has a "gentle, almost sad face until you unravelled what were actually two separate expressions—a temporary one of static peace and quiet overlaying a constant one of definite even though faint harriedness" (10). Armstid's eyes are "at once vague and intense" (331). After his illness Ratliff emanates "a sort of delicate robustness" (78). Ab Snopes' homestead is a "cluttered desolation" (54). Eula Varner seems to exist in a "teeming vacuum" (107). At the age of eleven, sitting on the schoolhouse steps eating a cold potato, she "postulated that ungirdled quality of the very goddesses in . . . Homer and Thucydides: of being at once corrupt and immaculate, at once virgins and the mothers of warriors and of grown men" (128). She is "at once supremely unchaste and inviolable" (131). Her admirers depart "seething and decorous" and ride in "furious wordless amity" (150). Houston and the girl he is to marry are "chained irrevocably . . . not by love but by implacable constancy and invincible repudiation" (237). Up to a point their struggle, "for all its deadly seriousness . . . had retained something of childhood, something both illogical and consistent, both reasonable and bizarre" (239).

Some of Faulkner's oxymorons are brilliant and completely justified by their context; others seem mechanical or excessive. I am not here concerned with discriminating between them. What I wish to emphasize is their remarkable frequency and variety, remarkable even in our contemporary literary environment which prizes paradox and linguistic shock. More than anything else, I believe, that baffling figure can help to illuminate Faulkner's work. Not only does its abundance indicate a good deal about Faulkner's general intentions and effects, but the figure, itself, in miniature and extreme form contains or suggests many of the most important qualities of his art and vision.

Like Faulkner's writing in general, the oxymoron involves sharp polarity, extreme tension, a high degree of conceptual and stylistic antithesis, and the simultaneous suggestion of disparate or opposed elements. Moreover, the figure tends to hold these elements in suspension rather than to fuse them. Both terms of an oxymoron are in a sense true. One's recognition that the contradiction is apparent rather than real does not eliminate the tension between the terms, for the conflicting elements remain. Neither negates the other. The oxymoron, on the one hand, achieves a kind of order, definiteness, and coherence by virtue of the clear and sharp antithesis it involves. On the other, it moves toward disorder and incoherence by virtue of its qualities of irresolution and self-contradiction. Its validity is usually intuitive and emotional rather than logical or intellectual. It does not so much explore or analyze a condition as render it forcefully. Traditionally it has often been used to reflect desperately divided states of mind.

## 2

Any oxymoron to some degree defies our customary intellectual desire for logical resolution, for even when we see beyond the contradiction, it still leaves us with the conflicting assertions. But many of Faulkner's oxymorons (e.g., "vague and intense") leave us with especially insoluble suspensions. They involve so complete or balanced a contradiction that they not only oppose our desire for resolution, but remain in opposition to it; no amount of thought and analysis can move us beyond the suspension of opposed elements. In the traditional oxymoron such as "cruel kindness" or "living death" at least a partial resolution is usually possible because one of the opposing elements is given subordinate emphasis either by context or by logical or grammatical subordination. Faulkner, on the other hand, seems especially fond of juxtaposing contradictory terms of equal rank and emphasis, and often further blocks resolution by the prefatory phrase "at once" (e.g., "at once corrupt and immaculate"). That he may be indifferent to the effects even when his oxymorons do involve logical or grammatical subordination is suggested by his apparently synonymous use of "implacable weariness" and "weary implacability" (*H,* 254-255). The essential purpose and effect of most of Faulkner's oxymorons, I believe, is not to force the reader to grasp a reality or unity beneath an apparent contradiction but to leave him with the tension of the contradiction itself. We are to feel and to continue to feel, for example, that the struggle between Houston and his wife had in it "something both illogical and consistent, both reasonable and bizarre."

I have stressed this as much as I have because I wish to show as conclusively as I can that Faulkner frequently seems willing and even anxious to leave his reader with suspensions which are not resolvable in rational terms. This is not to say that he always does so nor does it prove that his novels as wholes are similarly unresolvable, but it does suggest that his novels may be more ambiguous and more resistant to rational analysis than has often been supposed. This possibility is strengthened by the many other aspects of his presentation which resist rational analysis and leave us with an unresolved suspension of varied or opposed suggestions.

A large number of Faulkner's extended metaphors, for example, have these qualities. This partial description of the sermon of the visiting preacher in *The Sound and the Fury* is characteristic.

He tramped steadily back and forth . . . hunched, his hands clapsed behind him. He was like a worn small rock whelmed by the successive waves of his voice. With his body he seemed to feed the voice that, succubus like, had fleshed its teeth in him. And the congregation seemed to watch with its own eyes while the voice consumed him, until he was nothing and they were nothing and there was not even a voice but instead their hearts were speaking to one another in chanting measures beyond the need for words, so that when he came to rest against the reading desk, his monkey face lifted and his whole attitude that of a serene, tortured crucifix that transcended its shabbiness and insignificance and made it of no moment, a long moaning expulsion of breath rose from them, and a woman's single soprano: "Yes, Jesus!" (310).

In context the passage has considerable emotional force and conveys a sense of the minister's power and effect on the congregation. On the other hand, it is full of opposed and varied suggestions which resist rational integration. We shift from naturalistic description to a simile in which the preacher is likened to a rock and his voice to waves. The voice then acquires teeth, and "succubus like" (i.e., like an *evil* spirit!) consumes him. Is the ugliness of the image intentional, we wonder. Does Faulkner perhaps add teeth because they are in antithesis to the "suck" suggestion of "succubus"? The minister and the congregation become "nothing" but still have hearts. There is no voice, but the hearts "speak" to one another, although without words. We are then reminded of the naturalistic monkey face immediately before the preacher's figure (which was a "rock," fleshly food, "nothing," and a speaking "heart") becomes suggestive of a crucifix, at once "serene" and "tortured," "that transcended its [the attitude's? the crucifix's?] shabbiness and insignificance." Upon close examination even the general nature of the experience of the congregation is perplexing, because there is the implication of a peaceful speaking of hearts and then of release of tension. Faulkner's mixed metaphors of this sort are not simply occasional accidents, for in general he makes no effort to keep them consistent and often makes use of the most "mixed" for his most important communications. And as in the oxymoron, the irresolvable elements are not accidental but seem an integral part of structure. Comparable to these mixed metaphors in effect are Faulkner's frequent synesthetic images which may be considered psychological oxymorons. Typical examples are "dark cool breeze" (*SF,* 149), "visibility roaring soundless down about him" (*H,* 195), and "walked out of their talking" (*LIA,* 9).

Less obvious, perhaps, but equally common are the conflicting suggestions which often occur in Faulkner's extended presentations of characters and events. A relatively compact illustration is the episode in *Light in August* in which McEachern attacks Joe Christmas in the dancehall.

Before this episode, what has been emphasized, above all, about McEachern is his absolute sense of self-righteousness, and the calm, heavy, methodical quality of all of his actions, even his violent ones. When he realizes that Joe has climbed out of his room and gone off to what he is sure is lechery, he saddles "his big, old, strong white horse" and goes down the road at a "slow and ponderous gallop" (176). So far he is still very much in character. Faulkner then inserts a suggestion of speed by means of metaphor: ". . . the two of them, man and beast, leaning a little stiffly forward as though in some juggernautish simulation of terrific speed though the actual speed itself was absent, as if in that cold and implacable and undeviating conviction of both omnipotence and clairvoyance of which they both partook known destination and speed were not necessary" (176-177). When McEachern reaches the dancehall, however, Faulkner has him move with actual speed. He dismounts "almost before the horse had stopped. He did not even tether it. He got down, and in the carpet slippers and the dangling braces and his round head and his short, blunt, outraged beard ran toward the open door" (177). In the next paragraph Faulkner goes on to describe him as thrusting through the dancers, and running toward Joe and the waitress, and then thundering "Away, Jezebel! . . . Away, harlot!" (178)

McEachern's disarray and uncontrolled running and thunderous shouting provide an emotional climax of strong impact and intensity; but they
may come as rather a shock to the understanding of the reader in view of
Faulkner's earlier characterizations of the man as utterly deliberate and controlled (124-34). The next paragraph reads:

Perhaps it did not seem to him that he had been moving fast nor that his
voice was loud. Very likely he seemed to himself to be standing just and
rocklike and with neither haste nor anger while on all sides the sluttishness
of weak human men seethed in a long sigh of terror about the actual representative of the wrathful and retributive Throne. Perhaps they were not
even his hands which struck at the face of the youth whom he had nurtured
and sheltered and clothed from a child, and perhaps when the face ducked
the blow and came up again it was not the face of that child. But he could
not have been surprised at that, since it was not that child's face which he
was concerned with: it was the face of Satan, which he knew as well. And
when, staring at the face, he walked steadily toward it with his hand still
raised, very likely he walked toward it in the furious and dreamlike exaltation of a martyr who has already been absolved, into the descending chair
which Joe swung at his head, and into nothingness. (178)

We begin with what appears not to be the real version of what happened
but the way it appeared to McEachern. But the passage slips gradually
toward what is presumably a statement of what did happen, and the final
picture we have is of the McEachern we knew earlier, who, staring at
Joe-Satan, walks "steadily" toward the raised chair "in the furious and
dreamlike exaltation of a martyr." In a generally emotive way we are satisfied by the suggestiveness and general movement of the passage. If we stop
to reflect, however, we wonder how the event did happen, which image of
McEachern to accept: the one of a ponderous and deliberate man whose
conviction is such that speed is not necessary; the one suggested by the
hanging braces, carpet slippers, the running and thundering rage; or the one
of a convinced and peaceful and yet somehow furious martyr? We wonder
what McEachern is like. We wonder, also, whether McEachern has been
killed. The final description of him offers no resolution: "He looked quite
peaceful now. He appeared to sleep: bluntheaded, indomitable even in
repose, even the blood on his forehead peaceful and quiet" (178). This
final statement is typical of many of Faulkner's endings to situations and
even to whole works. It is effective emotionally and dramatically but does
not resolve questions which the earlier presentation has raised for the
understanding. There is a suggestion of resolution, in this case supplied by
the emphasis upon peace and quiescence. At the same time, however, there

remain tensions and opposing suggestions, here provided by the unquiet words "bluntheaded," "indomitable," and "blood."

One of the most striking and widely commented upon aspects of Faulkner's writing is his use of marathon sentences whose structure and syntax are often perplexing or obscure. Here is a fragment of a sentence from *Go Down, Moses,* a sentence which runs for over a page and a half. Among sentences and fragments of this type, it is one of the least complex. Contextually, the sentence and fragment would seem to be important, for they presumably communicate a significant part of Ike McCaslin's education and experience.

. . . a boy who wished to learn humility and pride in order to become skillful and worthy in the woods but found himself becoming so skillful so fast that he feared he would never become worthy because he had not learned humility and pride though he had tried, until one day an old man who could not have defined either led him as though by the hand to where an old bear and a little mongrel dog showed him that, by possessing one thing other, he would possess them both; and a little dog, nameless and mongrel and many-fathered, grown yet weighing less than six pounds, who couldn't be dangerous because there was nothing anywhere much smaller, not fierce because that would have been called just noise, not humble because it was already too near the ground to genuflect, and not proud because it would not have been close enough for anyone to discern what was casting that shadow and which didn't even know it was not going to heaven since they had already decided it had no immortal soul, so that all it could be was brave even though they would probably call that too just noise. (295-296)

We may note first, that all but one of the clauses beginning "because," "since," or "so that," are deliberate non-sequiturs. Moreover, the final statement about the dog's bravery is not consistent with the statement about his fierceness. In one instance the existence of a quality depends upon what people call it; in the other it does not. At the same time, in opposition to the illogicality, there is a promise of clarity, order, and logicality, a frequent characteristic of Faulkner's writing. The description of the dog pretends to be a definition (presumably of "the one thing other") arrived at through careful exclusion and negation. Further promise of clarity and simplicity is made by the cause and effect terminology, antithesis, persistent parallelism, and general division of things into simple pairs. There is also the promise communicated by the suggestion that the mongrel dog showed Ike that "*one* thing" (italics mine) would solve his problem of gaining humility and pride.

The passage quoted is characteristic of many of Faulkner's other structures, also, in its shifts in tone. The context of the description of the dog is serious. Presumably our understanding of the nature of the dog is essential to our understanding of the nature of pride and humility, and to our understanding of Ike. The surrounding passages are serious. The description of the dog's qualities, however, is largely playful.

As in many other passages close scrutiny leads only to further difficulties. There is first the hurdle of the oxymoron "humility and pride." We are then told that the possession of one thing "other" would enable Ike to possess both qualities. If the one thing other is "bravery" (we cannot be sure), we may wonder why Faulkner communicates it so ambiguously, and may wonder about the relationship between bravery, humility, and pride. Our understanding of that relationship is not aided by the fact that the dog, who has the bravery, is described specifically as neither humble nor proud. When we read further we are led to Keats' "Ode on a Grecian Urn" and to the statement that *"Truth is one. It doesn't change. It covers all things which touch the heart—honor and pride and pity and justice and courage and love"* (297), a statement which McCaslin indicates ought to clarify things for Ike. Even if one is not troubled by the meanings of the words "covers" and "touch" and does not wonder whether such qualities as hatred and greed "touch" the heart, one must certainly wonder why humility is missing from the list. A few lines later Faulkner drops this subject and moves to a "discussion" of the curse on the land.

Again Faulkner's presentation has left us with tensions and questions we cannot resolve. I have dwelt upon the difficulties structures of this sort pose for the understanding, and have emphasized their resistance to analysis, because I wish to make clear that they may be organized not merely so as to make intellectual resolution difficult but so as to discourage it and make it impossible, just as synesthetic images make precise sense localization impossible and many of Faulkner's oxymorons make logical resolution impossible. The difficulties in the way of understanding are often not resolvable nor meant to be.

The preceding illustrations show some of the ways by which Faulkner keeps his reader from fitting things together. Instead of moving toward synthesis and resolution, his presentation often provides a suspension of varied or opposed suggestions. Two specific devices which further contribute to this suggestive suspension warrant mention.

The first is the frequent use of "perhaps" and "maybe," and other inconclusive or conjectural terms or phrases in describing motivations, thoughts, and events. The second is that which Warren Beck has labelled "the statement of alternative suggestions"[2] "The woman had never seen him but once, but perhaps she remembered him, or perhaps his appearance now was enough."[3] Sometimes the juxtaposed alternatives are so important and so divergent that a choice would be of immense philosophic and practical significance, as in *Go Down, Moses* where McCaslin says that the Bible was written to be read "by the heart, not by the wise of the earth because *maybe they dont need it or maybe the wise no longer have any heart*" (260, italics mine). On occasion the alternatives are diametrically opposed:

It was as if only half of her had been born, that mentality and body had somehow become either completely separated or hopelessly involved; that either only one of them had ever emerged, or that one had emerged, itself not accompanied by, but rather pregnant with, the other. (*H*, 109)

Note the complete opposition of the alternatives "completely separated" and "hopelessly involved." If we substitute "at once . . . and" where Faulkner has used "either . . . or," the result is an oxymoron. Even as worded in the text, however, the passage is, in effect, an oxymoron, because no real choice is offered. As is true for almost all of Faulkner's "alternative" suggestions, we are to keep in mind both alternatives; no choice or resolution is possible.

### 3

Faulkner's novels, of course, are far more complex than the structures we have been looking at, and I certainly do not wish to suggest that the kinds of qualities I have been illustrating fully explain or describe them. I do contend, however, that they resemble these structures more closely than has generally been recognized. They have certain kinds of unity and resolution, of course, but in many ways they remain insoluble. Obviously, a thorough or conclusive study of the novels is impossible here. I can do little more than suggest something of the extent to which they are suspensions of the sort I have indicated. Apart from the evidence we have already seen which suggests this possibility, and apart from internal evidence I shall consider later, there is also some external evidence that Faulkner might regard too much coherence as a kind of failure.

In a recent interview Faulkner is quoted as saying:

2. Warren Beck, "William Faulkner's Style," see above.
3. *LIA*, 177. Note that the phrasing "had never seen him but once," communicates almost a double suggestion. Compare "had seen him but once," or "had seen him once only."

I was asked the question who were the five best contemporary writers and how did I rate them. And I said Wolfe, Hemingway, Dos Passos, Caldwell and myself. I rated Wolfe first, myself second. I put Hemingway last. I said we were all failures. All of us had failed to match the dream of perfection and I rated the authors on the basis of their splendid failure to do the impossible. I believed Wolfe tried to do the greatest of the impossible, that he tried to reduce all human experience to literature. And I thought after Wolfe I had tried the most. I rated Hemingway last because he stayed within what he knew. He did it fine, but he didn't try for the impossible.

A moment later he adds:

I rated those authors by the way in which they failed to match the dream of perfection. . . . This had nothing to do with the value of the work, the impact or perfection of its own kind that it had. I was talking only about the magnificence of the failure, the attempt to do the impossible within human experience. (New York *Times Book Review,* Jan. 30, 1955)

There are ambiguities in Faulkner's statement, but it strongly suggests that he would consider full coherence a sign of weakness and something to be avoided. That is, he not only places a higher value[4] upon the effort to do the *impossible* than upon accepting human and artistic limitations, but he also seems to measure the effort by the extent of the failure. His works show, in part, I believe, an active quest for "failure."

It is no accident that every one of Faulkner's experiments with form and style—his rapidly shifting points of view, his use of more or less incoherent narrators such as Benjy, Quentin, Darl, Rosa Coldfield, and Gavin Stevens, his disordered time sequences, his juxtapositions of largely independent stories, his unsyntactical marathon sentences, his whole method, as Conrad Aiken puts it, "of deliberately withheld meaning, of progressive

4. I am aware that Faulkner has said that his rating "had nothing to do with the value of the work." The whole tenor of the statement, however, indicates that he does attach high value to the quest for the impossible and to the magnificent failure. His very choice to rate the authors in those terms is an affirmation of the value of those terms. It may be argued that by saying that his rating had nothing to do with value, Faulkner only intends to qualify his earlier statement. But, in fact, the statement about value contradicts his earlier rhetoric and content, both, and involves an unwillingness to commit himself fully to the meaning of that rhetoric and content or to the consequences of his choice to rate the authors in the terms he did. Similar sorts of self contradiction are present in Faulkner's introduction to the Modern Library Edition of *Sanctuary,* in his Foreword to *The Faulkner Reader,* and a bit less obviously, in his Nobel Prize speech and various other public utterances. That this is true suggests that his literary use of ambiguity may be a matter of temperament as well as of conscious artistic intent.

and partial and delayed disclosure"—is a movement away from order and coherence. And it is no accident that every one of Faulkner's novels involves one or more of these experiments and that in most of the novels we find all of them.

It is important to recognize, also, that the effects of Faulkner's fragmentation of material are usually quite different from those produced by others who have used similar techniques. In works like *The Ring and the Book* and the Japanese film *Rashomon* various perspectives are thrown upon the same central event. In *Mrs. Dalloway* and *Ulysses* the seemingly unconnected experiences and events are occurring at the same time or on the same day. That is, either event, time or point of view is held constant. In *The Sound and the Fury, As I Lay Dying,* and *Absalom, Absalom!,* on the other hand, none of these is constant. The various narrators touch upon a few of the same events, but the selection of events seems determined essentially by the particular interests and obsessions of the narrator. In *The Sound and the Fury,* for example, neither Benjy nor Jason throws light on the incest theme which dominates the Quentin section. And Quentin, on the other hand, is dead before many of the events take place which are crucial in the lives of Benjy and Jason. In *Absalom, Absalom!* the various narrators emphasize quite different aspects and periods of Sutpen's history. As a result the reader feels less sense of pattern and equilibrium than in the first named works, is less able to group his thoughts and feelings about a common center.

Particularly indicative of Faulkner's intentions, I think, is the fact that when he does present explicit interpretations of events or analytic commentaries on them he always takes pains to make them either suspect, inconclusive, or incoherent. On many occasions he will narrate or describe an action in perfectly conventional and logical sequence, but his interpretive or philosophic passages are almost invariably disordered. I think we can go so far as to say that the more explanatory or intellectual the content, the less the coherence. The dominant characteristic, in fact, of Faulkner's intellectuals—and it is they, of course, who offer most of the interpretations—is their tendency to be incoherent. The most intellectual character in Faulkner's novels, and probably his favorite commentator, is Gavin Stevens, a Ph.D. from Heidelburg. And, as has been generally recognized, it is his statements which usually provide the greatest resistance to rational understanding. Here, for example, is a part of his final commentary, and the final explicit commentary of any sort, on the meaning of the events in *Intruder in the Dust.* Gavin is talking to his nephew Charles

Mallison who has been chiefly responsible for saving the Negro Lucas Beauchamp from being lynched.

> . . . what's out yonder in the ground at Caledonia Church was Crawford Gowrie for only a second or two last Saturday and Lucas Beauchamp will be carrying his pigment into ten thousand situations a wiser man would have avoided and a lighter escaped ten thousand times after what was Lucas Beauchamp for a second or so last Saturday is in the ground at his Caledonia church too, because that Yoknapatawpha County which would have stopped you and Aleck Sander and Miss Habersham last Sunday night are right actually, Lucas' life the breathing and eating and sleeping is of no importance just as yours and mine are not but his unchallengeable right to it in peace and security and in fact this earth would be much more comfortable with a good deal fewer Beauchamps and Stevenses and Mallisons of all colors in it if there were only some painless way to efface not the clumsy room-devouring carcasses which can be done but the memory which cannot—that inevictible immortal memory awareness of having once been alive which exists forever still ten thousand years afterward in ten thousand recollections of injustice and suffering, too many of us not because of the room we take up but because we are willing to sell liberty short at any tawdry price for the sake of what we call our own which is a constitutional statutory license to pursue each his private postulate of happiness and contentment regardless of grief and cost even to the crucifixion of someone whose nose or pigment we dont like and even these can be coped with provided that few of others who believe that a human life is valuable simply because it has a right to keep on breathing no matter what pigment its lungs distend or nose inhales the air and are willing to defend that right at any price, it doesn't take many three were enough last Sunday night even one can be enough and with enough ones willing to be more than grieved and shamed Lucas will no longer run the risk of needing without warning to be saved:" (*ID,* 243-244).

Fortunately Faulkner has other voices besides that of Gavin. But these other voices do not negate or encompass Gavin's so much as stand in suspension with it.

Probably the most crucial indication of Faulkner's intentions is the fact that the endings of all his novels not only fail to resolve many of the tensions and meanings provided in the novels but also seem carefully designed to prevent such resolution. Above all, they leave unresolved the question of the meaningfulness of the human efforts and suffering we have witnessed, whether the sound and the fury is part of some larger design or whether it has signified nothing in an essentially meaningless universe.

Consider, for example, the final section of *The Sound and the Fury,* which is perhaps Faulkner's most unified and tightly woven novel. By the end of the first three sections we have seen various parts of the history of the Compson family through the eyes of three of its members—respectively, the idiot Benjy, the sensitive and romantic but neurotically obsessed Quentin, and the practical, materialistic and self-pitying Jason. And we are groping for some larger perspective, context, or pattern under which to view and interpret the unhappy events we have been witnessing. Faulkner has suggested a number of these. The title of the book has suggested strongly that there is no pattern, and Mr. Compson's nihilistic philosophy reinforces this, as does the seemingly chaotic order of events. Opposed to this, however, is our natural disinclination to accept such a view and our awareness of Faulkner's at least partial approval of Benjy, Quentin, Caddie, Mr. Compson, and Dilsey and his disapproval of Mrs. Compson, Herbert, and Jason. And there is also our recognition of several more or less recurrent motifs which encourage us to look for pattern and significance. But the search has sent us in varying directions, none of which has been clearly or conclusively marked. Some of the events have seemed chiefly in accord with a socio-economic antithesis between an old and new culture of the general sort pointed out by the O'Donnell, Cowley, Warren line of criticism. Some of the events and emphases have suggested interpretation in terms of clinical or even specifically Freudian psychology. We have been strongly encouraged, also, to interpret events in relation to Christian myth and ideology, in relation to concepts of time, and in relation to Shakespearian tragedy.

At the same time we are not sure what attitude we are to take toward the disintegration of the family. In the first two sections Benjy and Quentin have reported events in such a way that we see and feel their pathetic rather than ludicrous or ironic side. We are somewhat aware that Benjy is sub-human and that his suffering is not of an order that requires the highest kind of sympathy, and Quentin's posturing and extreme Romanticism at times seem comic, but essentially we are led to see them both as suffering individuals, to feel considerable compassion for them and to take their predicaments very seriously. In the third section, however, narrated by Jason, the tone has been essentially comic and satiric. Not only does Jason come through as a largely comic character but his narration tends to bathe the whole Compson history in a somewhat comic light which at least temporarily blinds us to the poignancy and pathos of it. We are much more detached than in the earlier sections, less serious. We want to see

Jason made a fool of and we are not especially moved by the plight of his niece Quentin. Had the novel ended with this section we would view the Compson history largely with a sense of grim amusement, as a tale of sound and fury signifying that the human condition is essentially hopeless and not worth much thought or compassion.

The final section, narrated from an omniscient and objective point of view, begins with a focus and emphasis that seems to offer a kind of implicit interpretation and resolution, one in accord with the sentiments and mood of Faulkner's Nobel Prize speech. The strong emphasis on Dilsey's fortitude, decency, and Christian humility and on her comprehensive view of time, as numerous critics have pointed out, provides a context for the unhappy events, a perspective from which to view them and a way to feel about them. On the other hand, this episode does not so much offer a synthesis or interpretation as a general vantage point and degree of moral affirmation. It does not help us to understand most of the particulars of the Compson story any better, to illuminate, say, the character and motives of Quentin and Caddie. Nor does it in any but a peripheral way relate to the socio-economic context of the story. And although it asserts the relevance of Christianity to the story it does not really clarify the nature of that relevance nor make clear how seriously we are to take the Christian context. Still, its tone and general tenor do provide a general way of looking at and feeling about the story and a sense of resolution.

But—and it is a very crucial "but" which most interpreters of the novel have ignored—the emphasis on Dilsey and her trip to church is at the beginning of the final section, and is only one of several emphases in that section. It is followed by the lengthy description of Jason's vain and tormenting pursuit of Quentin which provides a very different perspective, mood, and set of feelings. We are back in a realm of sound and fury, even of melodrama. We do not see Jason from the large perspective we have just shared with Dilsey, but respond to his frustration and defeat with a grim amusement and satisfaction only slightly leavened by pity. Nor does his defeat appear in any way an affirmative thing, for the "heroine" who has eluded him seems equally doomed. Dilsey and her church recede into the landscape and seem barely relevant to Jason's predicament.

The final part of the last section emphasizes Benjy's misery and the callousness and swagger of Dilsey's grandson, Luster, as he torments Benjy, first by taking his bottle, then by shouting Caddie, and finally by driving around the square in the wrong direction. We are reminded for a moment of Dilsey's decency and faith but only to feel its ineffectualness, for neither she nor the church service has touched Luster. The book closes with the carriage ride of Luster and Benjy: with our attention focused on a young Negro whose main desire is to show off, and on an idiot, capable of serenity or anguish but little more than that. Faulkner emphasizes his terrible agony as Luster throws his world into disorder by going around the square in the wrong direction. Jason comes rushing across the square, turns the carriage around and hits both Luster and Benjy. Benjy becomes serene again as the carriage moves in its usual direction and things flow by smoothly from left to right, "each in its ordered place."

It is a powerful ending and a fitting one in its focus on Benjy and its application to the general theme of order and disorder which runs through the novel. But it is an ending which provides anything but a synthesis or resolution, and it leaves us with numerous conflicting feelings and ideas.

We are momentarily relieved and pleased by the cessation of Benjy's suffering but we are troubled by the fact that it has been achieved by Jason who cares nothing for Benjy and is concerned only with maintaining an external and superficial decorum. And we can hardly draw any real satisfaction from the serenity and order because the serenity is the "empty" serenity of an idiot and the order that demanded by an idiot. The general tenor of the episode is in accord with Mr. Compson's pessimism rather than Faulkner's Nobel Prize speech, for everything in it suggests the meaninglessness and futility of life.

This final scene does not negate the moderate affirmation of the Dilsey episode, nor does it really qualify it. Rather it stands in suspension with it as a commentary of equal force. We feel and are intended to feel, I think, that the events we have witnessed are at once tragic and futile, significant and meaningless. We cannot move beyond this. Nor does the final section help us to resolve whether the Compsons were defeated essentially by acts of choice or by some kind of doom, or whether the doom was chiefly a matter of fate or of psychological aberration or of socio-economic forces. And it is worth noting that if we do accept as a primary motif the opposition between an older and newer culture we face the impossibility of choosing between them. Our sympathies, like Faulkner's, are with the old, but the best representatives of it in this book are a drunkard, a suicide, and a lost and lonely woman. And between what they are and what Jason is there seems no middle ground offered.

In short, the ending seems designed not to interpret or to integrate but to leave the various elements of the story in much the same suspension in which they were offered, and to leave the reader with a high degree of emotional and intellectual tension.

The endings of Faulkner's other novels are similar. Two brief illustrations will have to suffice. *As I Lay Dying* ends with Pa's acquisition of new teeth and a new wife, a cynical, almost farcical note which suggests that all of the pain and struggle and even heroism of the Bundrens was for nothing, that shiftlessness and ineptitude triumph over all, and that we do not take the story very seriously. At the same time, however, the fact that the family did succeed in its task and the emphasis on the patience and sanity of Cash, as well as the presentation of much of the story suggests that what we have witnessed is significant, even epic, and worthy of the highest seriousness of response. The fate of Darl generates further intellectual and emotional conflict, which Faulkner strengthens in a number of ways. He has Cash speculate inconclusively about the question of Darl's insanity, and neither he nor we can get beyond the feeling that we "ain't so sho that ere a man has the right to say what is crazy and what ain't" (*AILD*, 515). But we are far more disturbed than Cash, for unlike Cash we do not misinterpret Darl's bitter laughter when Cash says he will be better off at the insane asylum at Jackson. Our response is further complicated by Faulkner's emphasis on Darl's humane concern about Cash's bad leg and by the terrible ambiguity of Darl's laughter and reiterated "yes's" as he is taken away to Jackson. Moreover, these uncertainties reflect back through the novel, for Darl has been the dominant narrator of the book and perhaps the most sympathetic character. As in *The Sound and the Fury* the ending, far from helping us to order or resolve the suspension of multiple suggestions and points of view presented in the book, seems designed to preserve that suspension in all its complexity and even to make it more complex. There is nothing which points firmly or clearly toward any one way of thinking or feeling about the things we have seen. Above all, the ending suggests that the story we have been told is highly significant and worthy of serious contemplation and emotion and that it signifies nothing and deserves primarily a bitter laugh.

At the very end of *Absalom, Absalom!* there are, in effect, four commentaries on the meaning of the whole Sutpen story. The first is provided by the picture of the last Sutpen, the idiot boy Jim Bond, lurking around the ashes and gutted chimneys that are the remnants of Sutpen's mansion, howling until someone would drive him away (376).

The second is provided by the end of Mr. Compson's letter, the first part of which we have read two hundred odd pages earlier (173-174), a letter which is obviously and carefully ambiguous and irrelevant so far as any ordering of the story is concerned. The third commentary is that of Shreve, who summarizes the story with brutal and flippant absurdity: " 'So it took Charles Bon and his mother to get rid of old Tom, and Charles Bon and the octoroon to get rid of Judith, and Charles Bon and Clytie to get rid of Henry; and Charles Bon's mother and Charles Bon's grandmother to get rid of Charles Bon. So it takes two niggers to get rid of one Sutpen, don't it?' " (377-378) He then observes that everything is taken care of except that " 'You've got one nigger left. One nigger Sutpen left,' " and he briefly erects this Negro into a symbol of Southern guilt (378, 11, 11-14). Following this he revels in paradox: the Jim Bonds conquer the western hemisphere and turn white, but still remain Jim Bonds, " 'and so [note the pseudo logic] in a few thousand years, I who regard you will also have sprung from the loins of African kings. Now I want you to tell me just one thing more. Why do you hate the South?' " (378). And the final commentary:

"I dont hate it," Quentin said, quickly, at once, immediately; "I dont hate it," he said. *I dont hate it* he thought, panting in the cold air, the iron New England dark; *I dont. I dont! I dont hate it! I dont hate it!*

It is difficult to conceive of an "ending" which would provide less ordering and resolution. For not only is there no resolution on a cognitive level, but we are also confronted with the differing tones of the four "commentaries," and the terrible emotional ambivalence of Quentin's final outburst. We "end," then, with a psychological oxymoron of simultaneous love and hate, with internal conflict and self-contradiction. It is an intense and powerful ending, and a proper one to seal off and preserve the complex suspension of elements the book has presented. But it is also a pitiful ending. It is pitiful in that Shreve and Quentin seem to have been so little instructed by their immense labor of imagination. It is pitiful (and among many other things, perhaps, Faulkner is saying this, too) in its varied assertions that so much energy, effort, and pain have come to so little: to a lone idiot, an ironic letter, a brutally flippant commentary and act of cruelty to a roommate, and a bewildered cry of pain. It is, above all, pitiful because by it, Faulkner again demonstrates his unwillingness to step beyond the sanctuary of the paradox, to make himself, as do a number of his characters, the clarifying "gesture," which might enable him and us to move beyond that bewildered cry of pain.

Faulkner's other novels exhibit the same avoidance of resolution, the same intent to present suggestive suspensions rather than rationally integrated wholes. In *The Wild Palms,* where Faulkner alternates the chapters of two completely independent narratives, and in *Requiem for a Nun,* where he juxtaposes sections of broad historical narrative with the acts of a play, and in *Light in August,* where he juxtaposes three largely discrete stories, these suspensions become most amorphous. The greatest degree of resolution is offered, perhaps, by *Intruder in the Dust,* whose plot is relatively uncomplicated, and where there is very little doubt cast upon the propriety or justice of the boy's effort to save Lucas Beauchamp. On the other hand, with respect to the motivation for the effort, and the meaning of it, Faulkner is far from conclusive, and in the final chapter of the novel he complicates the context of the entire event by shifting his focus to the evils of mechanization and standardization. His final re-emphasis upon Beauchamp's almost comic pride and pedantry and his own almost comic treatment of the final scene further complicate our reaction to the story. Works whose ambiguities of content and tone have been especially overlooked in critical discussion are *Pylon,* the tall convict section of *The Wild Palms,* "The Bear," and the play in *Requiem for a Nun.*[5]

## 4

As the reader is undoubtedly aware, I have used the terms "suspension" and "resolution" quite loosely and have made no careful effort to distinguish between what is resolved and what is not or between the kinds of elements left in suspension or between valid and invalid kinds

5. In discussing the end of *RN,* one critic writes: "Stevens is rightly and necessarily silent as the inarticulate, uneducated Nancy says simply 'Believe.' Nancy is herself the visible sign which Temple had sought, the concrete illustration of what is meant by 'Believe' " (Olga Vickery, "Gavin Stevens: From Rhetoric to Dialectic," *Faulkner Studies* II [Spring, 1953], 4). Mrs. Vickery overlooks the final exchange between Temple and Stevens at the end of the book by which Faulkner, characteristically, avoids resolution. Walking out of the jail Temple speaks: " 'Anyone to save it [reference obscure]. Anyone who wants it. If there is none, I'm sunk. We all are. Doomed. Damned.' " To this Gavin Stevens responds: " 'Of course we are. Hasn't He been telling us that for going on two thousand years?' " (286). If anything, Nancy has believed that man will or can be "saved" (278). Stevens' statement not only qualifies Nancy's by its content and tone but leaves us with what is virtually an oxymoron, for the very use of the "He" contradicts the statement that we are all damned. His statement also suggests that he has not really grown and developed, as Mrs. Vickery has argued.

of irresolution. To make these distinctions seems to me a crucial and exceedingly complex problem for future Faulkner criticism. My primary purpose here has been to show that there is a problem, that the irresolution runs both wide and deep. I would like also to suggest some explanations for it.

So far I have written as though Faulkner's ambiguity and irresolution were entirely deliberate, strictly a matter of artistic intent, rather than one of temperament or general irrationalism or mere lack of concern about rational coherence. Up to a point, I think this is actually the case and that we may understand much of the ambiguity and irresolution as serving or reflecting two general intentions.

Conrad Aiken has suggested that what Faulkner is after, in part, is a "medium without stops or pauses," an "image stream" toward which the reader "must be powerfully and unremittingly hypnotized," and he suggests that this intent to hypnotize accounts, perhaps, not only for the length and elaborateness of Faulkner's sentence structure but for his repetitiveness as well.[6] It is very likely that Faulkner's frequent resistance to rational analysis also contributes to this hypnotic effect. Some passages from Edward Snyder's *Hypnotic Poetry*[7] strongly suggest this. Professor Snyder notes that in actual hypnosis the stimuli used "are such as to fix the attention while retarding mental activity," (25) and he concludes that the same retardation of mental activity is helpful in producing the less complete hypnoidal state which he calls "emotional trance," a state in which the subject's emotional susceptibility is highly intensified (32-33). In his Foreword to Snyder's book, the psychologist James Leuba writes that Snyder has "demonstrated the existence of a type of poetry which owes its attraction to a method of composition, the effect of which is to limit the intellectual activity, i.e., to induce a state of partial trance, and thereby to free in some measure the emotional life from the trammel of critical thinking." (x)

Whether Faulkner actually induces a state of partial trance is not especially important here. But it does seem likely that the purpose and effect of much of his presentation is to free the emotional life from the "trammel" of critical thinking, so that like the preacher in *The Sound and the Fury,* who is also in a sense a hypnotist, he might speak directly to the "heart." To some extent, we can say of Faulkner, as McCaslin says was true for God, that he "didn't have His Book written to be read by what

6. Conrad Aiken, "William Faulkner: The Novel as Form," see above.
7. *Hypnotic Poetry: A Study of Trance-Inducing Techniques in Certain Poems and its Literary Significance* (Philadelphia: University of Pennsylvania Press, 1930).

must elect and choose, but by the heart" (*GDM,* 260). I do not mean to equate the word "heart" entirely with the words "emotive" or "hypnotic," and Faulkner's own use of the word is ambiguous, but there is no doubt that he sees the heart essentially as an organ of feeling and as antithetic to the head, and that he regards it, and not the head, as the way to truth. "Ideas and facts," he has said in a recent interview, "have very little connection with truth."[8] We give ourselves "mind's reason[s]," says McCaslin, "because the heart dont always have time to bother with thinking up words that fit together" (*GDM,* 348). A generally non-intellectual intention is suggested also by Faulkner's statements that "I must try to express clumsily in words what the pure music would have done better,"[9] and that "I think people try to find more in my work than I've put there. I like to tell stories, to create people, and situations. But that's all. I doubt if an author knows what he puts in a story. All he is trying to do is to tell what he knows about his environment and the people around him in the most moving way possible."[10]

An effort to reach the heart, or to "lift" it, as Faulkner sometimes puts it, by bypassing or retarding mental activity explains certain of Faulkner's obstacles to rational comprehension, but there is much that it does not explain, for Faulkner is not so consistent or complete an irrationalist or even non-intellectual as such an explanation implies. His ambiguity and irresolution must also be understood as asserting and reflecting a view of life. It is a difficult view to define, and the nature of it is such that it is almost impossible to draw a dividing line between the view and temperament. A statement by Warren Beck is helpful toward defining this view of life.

If Faulkner's sentences sometimes soar and circle involved and prolonged, if his scenes become halls of mirrors repeating tableaux in a progressive magnification, if echoes multiply into the dissonance of infinite overtones, it is because the meanings his stories unfold are complex, mysterious, obscure, and incomplete. There is no absolute, no eternal pure white radiance in such presentations, but rather the stain of many colors, refracted and shifting in kaleidoscopic suspension, about the center of man's enigmatic behavior and fate, within the drastic orbit of mortality. Such being Faulkner's view of life, such is his style.[11]

8. Jean Stein, "The Art of Fiction XII: William Faulkner," see above.
9. Jean Stein, "The Art of Fiction."
10. Cynthia Grenier, "The Art of Fiction: An Interview with William Faulkner," *Accent,* XVI (Summer, 1956), 171.
11. Beck, "William Faulkner's Style."

Professor Zink asserts that "at its best, form in Faulkner's art constitutes a living effort to penetrate and to realize in art an ineffable complexity."[12]

Certainly, these critics are right that Faulkner's form often suggests and seeks to communicate a view of life as enigmatic and ineffably complex. To a large extent his shifts in tone and point of view, his avoidance of resolution, and his various obstacles to rational understanding, may be viewed as an effort to present life and experience in such a way as to make facile interpretation impossible. The meaning of the stories of Sutpen and Joe Christmas and others, Faulkner is saying, is largely ambiguous. Whether they are free agents or pawns, heroes or villains, is ambiguous, just as it is uncertain whether the tall convict is a hero or fool, whether Darl Bundren is a seer or madman, and whether the desperate struggles of the convict, the Bundrens, and others are tragic or comic, significant or futile. They are presented as both and neither, just as simple entities like faces are conceived in the both and neither terms of the oxymoron, and just as Quentin's reaction to the Sutpen story, and to the South, in general, is a both and neither combination of love and hate. Whether there is a God or not is problematical, and if there is, whether he is Jehovah, Christ, Satan, Joker, Umpire, Chess Player, or Life Force. The only certainty that exists, Faulkner sometimes suggests, is that man will "endure," but whether he will endure by virtue of his soul or his folly Faulkner does not make clear, not is it clear whether enduring means primarily to suffer or to transcend time.

But these descriptions are inadequate, for they leave out important qualities of Faulkner's feeling about life which are inseparable from his view.

You get born and you try this and you dont know why only you keep on trying it and you are born at the same time with a lot of other people, all mixed up with them, like trying to, having to, move your arms and legs with strings only the same strings are hitched to all the other arms and legs and the others all trying and they dont know why either except that the strings are all in one another's way like five or six people all trying to make a rug on the same loom only each one wants to weave his own pattern into the rug; and it cant matter, you know that, or the Ones that set up the loom would have arranged things a little better, and yet it must matter because you keep on trying. . . . (*AA,* 127)

12. Karl E. Zink, "William Faulkner: Form as Experience," *The South Atlantic Quarterly,* 53 (July, 1954), 384.

The words are Judith Sutpen's but the passage communicates more clearly than any other, I believe, the essence of Faulkner's view of life and feeling toward it. The passage suggests not only the complex and enigmatic qualities of life, but the sense of life as conflict, tension, and frustration, which persistently informs Faulkner's presentation. Above all, it suggests the intense contradictory feelings which, more than anything else, I think, explain Faulkner's attitude toward life and toward his own art: "it can't matter, you know that . . . and yet it must matter." It cannot have meaning and yet it must. The statement does not simply describe a dual perspective—"seems sometimes to matter, sometimes not," nor an uncertainty— "may or may not matter," nor even a paradox—"does and does not matter." The simultaneous "can't" and "must" suggests a desperately divided and tormented perspective and condition of mind which tries to move simultaneously and intensely toward both order and chaos, and which understandably seizes upon the figure which most nearly moves in both directions, the oxymoron.

This divided view and feeling about the meaningfulness of life and effort accounts, undoubtedly, for Faulkner's frequent explicit and implicit coupling of terms like "empty" and "profound," "futile" and "tragic," and for statements such as "the substance itself [life] not only not dead, not complete, but in its very insoluble enigma of human folly and blundering possessing a futile and tragic immortality" (*P,* 82), and "profound and irrevocable if only in the sense of being profoundly and irrevocably unimportant" (*P,* 109). It helps us to understand Faulkner's seemingly obsessive assertion and denial of immortality and to account for his often perceptive idiots and incoherent intellectuals. It accounts, in part, for his failure to pursue thoroughly many of the ideas and meanings which he has suggested; even more, for his ability to urge certain meanings intensely and then to ignore them or to contradict them with equal intensity, for his use of form both to illuminate and obscure. It is a view and feeling which, in general, makes it necessary for him to try continuously to affirm and deny, to illuminate and obscure, the meaning of his own artistic creations and the significance of the lives and experiences he presents. It accounts, perhaps, for his inability finally to commit himself, and for his ability to treat art both as a plaything and a dedication. Undoubtedly it helps to explain the utterly divergent critical estimates and interpretations of his work. Finally, I believe, it accounts in large measure for the peculiarly compelling and disturbing power of his works, for it reminds us of the similar schizophrenia within ourselves which we have worked hard to bury.

Generally skeptical views of life, or dual perspectives in which life appears in some ways meaningful and in some ways meaningless, are not uncommon, are certainly comprehensible, and have informed much great art, including that of Shakespeare. Metaphysical poetry and Jacobean drama, at times, seem to suggest a division of feeling, as well as of view, about life's meaningfulness which is as intense as Faulkner's. There is still, however, an important difference. Whatever the tensions and opposing suggestions, explicit or implicit, in a poem by Donne or a play by Webster, one feels behind them, I think, a governing mind which never really doubts the validity of its own ideas and perceptions or the possibility if not the existence, of a moral universe in which such ideas and perceptions are relevant, which never abandons the effort to order its thoughts and emotions. Like many modern artists Faulkner has no such certainty.

Unlike any other moderns of comparable stature, however, Faulkner's uncertainty also embraces his art. Joyce, Virginia Woolf, and even Kafka have never really doubted the validity of art and have used it always to resist and to recreate as well as to reflect the dissolving worlds they saw and felt about them. They remain committed to order and reason. There have been some writers and painters, the surrealists and dadaists, who have not resisted, whose uncertainty or despair has led them to deny reason, whose desperation has led them to protest against disorder with disorder. A part of Faulkner remains intensely committed to art and order, and seeks desperately, and of course, paradoxically to find a way by which art can order equally intense convictions that life and art do and do not matter. A part of him is content with disorder.

Faulkner is more of an irrationalist than many of his critics have been willing to accept, but less of one than he, himself, has often suggested by his numerous explicit antitheses of head and heart and by his varied assertions that "ideas and facts have very little connection with truth." It is only partially true that he "didn't have His Book written to be read by what must elect and choose but by the heart" (*GDM,* 260). For the mere act of reading Faulkner requires a large intellectual effort and much of his appeal is clearly intellectual. Like most of the other elements of his work, his irrationalism is not a consistent or systematic thing, not a clearly governing principle of organization; it, too, becomes part of a suspension and will not fall clearly into place. Perhaps the best term for Faulkner is "non-rationalist."

But finally, I do not think we can adequately explain the kinds of tensions and suspensions we find in Faulkner's work except in terms of temperament. For, at bottom, his works seem governed not so much by a view of life, or by a particular gap in his thought and feeling, or by particular principles of organization as by his temperament;[13] that is, by the particular compound of intellectual and emotional inclinations, tendencies, and responses that characterize his mental life and shape his reactions to experience. It is his temperamental responses rather than any theories or ideas or particular torments, which he undoubtedly trusts to produce and to order his art. One fundamental quality of that temperament is its response to tension and opposition. Another is perhaps best described as a tendency toward profusion. It is this which no doubt helps to account for the remarkable scope of his fictional creation, but also for what surely must be criticized as an overabundance of effects and suggestions. Related to his inability or unwillingness to set limits on abundance, but yet to be distinguished from that quality, is his tendency to avoid commitment. It is this, as has no doubt been apparent, which most troubles me, from a human as well as an aesthetic point of view. For, surely, if there are to be any distinctions in art and life between responsibility and irresponsibility, indeed, any distinctions at all, we must insist that man can and must make choices. In both the form and content of Faulkner's works there is often the assertion or implication that man does not need to make choices. "You don't need to choose," says McCaslin. "The heart already knows" (*GDM,* 260). We do need to choose. There is, of course, also, in Faulkner the frequent implication that we do need to choose, and Ike, himself, does seem to make a terribly important choice by relinquishing his land. By suggesting, finally, that Ike both did and did not choose,[14] Faulkner, too, has made a choice, the choice which he can rarely resist, and which, I feel, seriously limits his stature, the choice not to choose.

13. Any work of art, no doubt, reflects the temperament of its author, and in some ultimate sense is governed by it. In Faulkner's case, however, I am suggesting that the relationship between his art and temperament is a far more immediate, direct, and pervasive one than is true for most novelists.
14. See *GDM,* 288, 309, 310.

# FAULKNER: THE WORD AS
# PRINCIPLE AND POWER

## FLORENCE LEAVER

SINCE THE PUBLICATION of George O'Donnell's article, "Faulkner's Mythology," in *The Kenyon Review* (1939) and Malcolm Cowley's "Introduction" to *The Portable Faulkner* (1946), few readers doubt that the Yoknapatawpha novels constitute a myth. These two critics based their analysis upon the narrative element, upon the dovetailing of the pieces of the total story, not always precisely, from novel to novel. It has not been sufficiently stated, however, that the mythical quality is produced, also, by the author's style, deriving from what Wellek and Warren call "mythic thinking—thinking in poetic vision," a kind of thinking which drives a writer to the very edge of what language can do.

Much of what has been written about Faulkner's style has stressed the involuted sentence patterns. A prime source of his power, however, is his sense of the word—a substantial factor in giving eloquence and mythical quality to his work. Faulkner explores the language: he employs seldom-used words; he coins words when the language seems inadequate; he uses the word as motif and for the accumulative effect of repetition; he dares to use feelingly and freely abstract nouns with strong associational meanings; and in order to increase intensity, which is his key mood, he makes use of negative words of ultimate degree.

Faulkner is extremely conscious of words as tools, although he does not trust them. In *Absalom, Absalom!* he calls language "that meager and fragile thread . . . by which the little surface corners and edges of men's secret and solitary lives may be joined for an instant now and then. . . ." Only the "little surfaces" touch, however, for there is small trust in words really to communicate. In *As I Lay Dying*, Addie Bundren, listening to the hammering together of her own coffin, recalls her betrayal by her minister-lover's words: "That was when I knew words are no good; that words don't

Reprinted with permission from the *South Atlantic Quarterly*, Autumn, 1958, pp. 464-76.

ever fit what they are trying to say at." Again she calls a word "just a shape
to fill a lack" and says later:

... I would think how words go straight up in a thin line, quick and harmless, and how terribly doing goes along the earth, clinging to it, so that after
a while the two lines are too far apart for the same person to straddle from
one to the other. ...

Perhaps it is this distance between the deed and the word, the idea without
form and the form which it must take, however imperfectly, which accounts for Faulkner's intensity, his attempt to make words do more than
they can do—to find *logos* for *mythos*.

It is his distrust of words which makes him critical of rhetoric as a
way of life. Two of his characters, in particular, are extraordinarily articulate men—Horace Benbow and Gavin Stevens. Benbow says that he
has "always been ordered by words," and Faulkner labels him with the
phrase "delicate futility." Stevens, much given to dialectic, ironically
spends his time talking while more practical people—often women, children, or Negroes—do the deeds he talks about. Both of these men intel-
lectualize: the doers act upon intuition, common sense, and folk wisdom.
As Uncle Ephraim in *Intruder in the Dust* says to Chick:

Young folks and women, they ain't cluttered. They can listen. But a
middle-year man like your paw and your uncle [Gavin Stevens] they can't
listen. They ain't got time. They're too busy with facks. In fact, you mought
bear this in mind. ... If you ever needs anything done outside the common run, don't waste yo time on the menfolks; get the womens and children to working at it.

R. L. Ramsey writes in the preface to a study of Mark Twain's
vocabulary that the discovery of a "great original" writer's ways with the
English language leads to a realization of the vitality of that language. It
is also true that a thorough vocabulary study of such an original writer as
William Faulkner yields valuable insight into the writer: his emotional
and intellectual quality, the tensions which may underlie his literary
concept, and clues to his view of man and the universe. Consider, for
example, four Faulknerian practices particularly concerned with the word,
sampled sketchily from the abundant data in his novels: (1) his use of
abstract words, chiefly nouns; (2) his special words of intensity—"negative
ultimates"; (3) his coined compounds; (4) his repetitions of certain
words from chapter to chapter and from book to book.

Faulkner's use of abstract words is a factor in his eloquence. He refuses to accept at face value the contemporary faith in concrete words. He can and does expertly use them at will, writing meticulously objective reports of the simplest actions, such as Lucas's counting out his money at the end of *Intruder in the Dust,* but unlike his contemporaries, Faulkner dares to generalize, to utter judgment upon evil doing, and to evaluate an act, in words, in the larger context of man's long journey and destiny. In such passages his eloquence mounts and mounts. He knowingly faces the inadequacy of language; he knowingly confronts the impossibility of understanding the imponderables. Making use of abstract terms around which have clustered untold associations, he makes language transcend itself by hypersuggestion. Admittedly, complex syntax is often an agent in the process, but he frequently uses simple structure for these judgments. Any structure would lose power without these spine-tingling abstract words.

Faulkner's feeling about such words is very different from that of Mr. Hemingway, who says, in the character of Frederick Henry:

. . . I was always embarrassed by the words sacred, glorious, and sacrifice and the expression in vain. . . . There were many words that you could not stand to hear and finally only the names of places had dignity. Abstract words such as glory, honor, courage, or hallow were obscene beside.

Some of the very words which Hemingway seems to fear Faulkner uses repeatedly—an interesting observation in light of the fact that of all contemporary American writers these two, as Lionel Trilling expresses it, have a

cogency in the degree that the confronting emotions go deep, or in the degree that the old pieties are firmly held and the new exigencies strongly apprehended. . . .

In the work of both men the cogency is a function not of their conscious but of their unconscious minds.

Yet one writer favors the clean-cut, sparse, objective expression; the other explores many avenues between concept and vehicle and glories in the abstract word.

In the Sartoris-Compson-Snopes myth appear repeatedly such words as *honor, pride, courage, vanity, sacrifice, endurance, destiny, abnegation, outrage, repudiation, humility, despair;* what Faulkner calls "the old agonies, terror, impotence, and hope"; and over and around all, what D. H. Lawrence designates "that beautiful northern word," *doom.* The

pairings of certain abstract words in paradoxical phrases give expression
to some of the thematic tensions in the whole Yoknapatawpha story—such
phrases as "glamorous and old disastrous things," "glamorous fatality,"
"defeat and glory," "travail and glory," "leashed violence," "brooding
violence of temporary repose," "doomed immortality and immortal doom,"
and "childlike . . . incompetence and paradoxical reliability." These phrases
and their like hold the soul-searing compulsions of the Sartoris-Compson
element, the ineffectual wrath of the white farmer group, the impotent
revulsion of both these groups toward the Snopeses, and the black-white
tension.

By the rhetoric of abstractions Faulkner repeatedly impregnates the
simplest acts with cosmic significance. One thinks of the two small boys
of *The Unvanquished,* a black and a white—young Bayard Sartoris and
Ringo, his "boy"—building of earth, wood-chips, and water a map of
Vicksburg in the summer of 1863. Remembering their panting efforts to
supply the dry map with water from a distant well by carrying a leaky
bucket at breakneck speed, Bayard long years after recognizes

the two of us needing first to join forces and spend ourselves against a common enemy, time, before we could engender between us and hold intact
the pattern of recapitulant mimic furious victory like a cloth, a shield between ourselves and reality, between us and fact and doom.

Labove, the young schoolteacher in Frenchman's Bend (*The Hamlet*),
studying far into the night, is "measuring the turned pages against the
fleeing seconds of irrevocable time like the implacable inching of a leaf-
worm." Eight-year-old Eula Varner's entrance into Labove's schoolroom is
a "moist blast of spring's liquorish corruption, a pagan triumphal pros-
tration before the supreme primal uterus." The abstract words in such
phrases are not substitutes for the concrete, nor could they be, but they
define, evaluate, and interpret the specific situation or character, lift it
from its earthbound state to universal significance, and ponder the human
dilemma. Phrases like these, of which there are a great number, are, without a doubt, one of the means by which the Yoknapatawpha County story
becomes myth.

Another vocabulary practice frequently encountered in Faulkner is
the use of what may be called negative ultimates. They begin with a
negative prefix, or, as in a few cases, they end in *less.* They create a
sense of negation by the very nature of the prefix or suffix but beyond
that, they variously suggest other areas of meaning. Note six of these

areas, categorized after examination of several hundred usages, with a few words to illustrate each area:

(1) The inability to comprehend, to believe, or to do—*impotent, uncomprehending, incredulous, incapable.* (2) Absolute fixity, inaccessibility, or immutability—*immobile, impenetrable, ineradicable, impervious, implacable.* (3) Predetermination and hopelessness (closely allied with the previous classification)—*inescapable, inexorable, irrevocable, unavoidable, irremediable, inevitable.* (4) Lacking physical substance—*impalpable, sourceless, weightless, intangible, substanceless.* (5) Immeasurability—*unplumbable, inexhaustible, insatiable, illimitable, interminable, unfinishability.* (6) The absence of a quality which itself in context has negative connotation—*unillusion, unhaste, unreluctance, unregret, unimpatience, undefeat.*

The function of these "negative ultimates" is the creation of an overpowering negative intensity which traps the characters, boxing them in with their own ignorance, impotence, or bafflement in an incomprehensible world which, in spite of the land's fecundity, holds violence and terror. These words express, too, the characters' profligacy of misdirected energy, on the one hand, or, on the other, blind or instinctive identification with nature. Lena Grove (of *Light in August*), in complete harmony with earth's life forces, is *unshakable* in her fidelity; she has *unflagging* faith; her body is *shapeless* and *immobile*; she "sits quite still, hearing and feeling the implacable and immemorial earth," in response to the movements of her unborn child. Houston, however, (*The Hamlet*) flees at sixteen from the "immemorial trap of love," becomes "inevitably sophisticated" and "invincibly incorrigible," is "possessed of a strong lust . . . for that fetterless immobility called freedom," is caught in the trap of love at last, and grieves in "indomitable fidelity" at his wife's death. The two had been "chained irrevocably . . . by implacable constancy and invincible repudiation."

One might say that these "ultimates," together with certain abstract word motifs attached to many characters, transform man, through the heightening of his passions and energies, into a creature of intensity. While retaining corporeal identity, he at the same time is hyperbolized into pure quality. Young Bayard, for instance, becomes despair beyond grief; Ratliff, uncanny shrewdness; Aunt Jennie, indomitability, even to the angle of her bonnet; Mink Snopes, blind fury; Eula Varner, voluptuous sexuality; and Flem Snopes, invulnerable cupidity. In becoming, at one level, pure quality, the characters are suitable inhabitants of a mythical world, where pure quality is an essential—even in a literary mythical world. To the extent that the characters approach pure quality they take on something of the archetypal—a state most easily seen, perhaps, in Eula Varner, who is potentially the Great Mother, the abiding earth, the primal life force.

A third aspect of the Faulknerian use of words is the coinage of compounds, of which there are a fantastic number. They can be classified on the basis of their grammatical structure, but more important is their semantic and emotional function. The largest group by far, of a total of several hundred examined, consists of those combining a noun with a participle and expressing instrument or agency. Those depicting man or man-made objects as agent are illustrated by *thumb-polished* (coins), *knife-gnawed* (bench), *heel-gnawed* (porch), *torch-disturbed* (darkness), and *razor-hedged* (crap-game); but overwhelmingly larger is the group expressing the agency of nature. A few of these are *dusk-filled* (study), *day-granaried* (leaf), *sun-impacted* (dust), *swamp-hatched* (butterfly), *shadowbitten* (darkness), *bug-swirled* (lamp), and *hill-cradled* (village).

Immediately evident is the conciseness achieved by these compounds. *Sun-impacted* is three words shorter than *impacted by the sun,* and besides its economy, there is a momentary intellectual-emotional stimulus not present in the denotative phrase. *Day-granaried,* expressed in referential language, would require even more words and would lose more imaginative quality, since it not only expresses agency but also sharpens the imagery, as do such words as *razor-hedged* and *heel-gnawed.*

Another group consists of those compounds basically metaphoric, such as *wire-taut* (wariness), *broom-tailed* (horses), *stringstraight* (path), *diamondsurfaced* (respectability), *patinasmooth* (earth), *boardflat* (coat tails). The practice of making metaphor by compound is a distinctly poetic device, since the poet seeks the strictest economy and precise imagery. One remembers Keats's "leaf-fringed legend" and "spectre-thin youth," Browning's "precipice-encircled" castle in the "wind-grieved Apennine." In our own time there are, among a thousand others, Dylan Thomas' "lamb-white days" and his "springful of larks." Likewise in Faulkner, not only is conciseness served, but also a whole imaginative concept. He began as a poet; he is still a poet, a "maker" with and of words, sometimes joining two such shockingly incongruous words as *cocoon* and *casket* to make an adjectival modifier, *cocoon-casket,* for "marriage-bed of youth."

Still another group of compounds seem to serve only to intensify sensory impressions: *head-nuzzling* (forceps), *coffin-smelling* (gloom), *cadaverface, spreadkneed* (McEachern), and *worm-glut.* A few seem to be formed on the basis of sound, as *glitter-glare, grumble-gutted, pinewiney.*

Some of the most interesting compounds, including *mote-palpitant, miasmal-distillant, Augusttremulous, pollenwroiled, confettiswirl* (of raging facetiae), and *heatshimmer* develop an effect of never-ending nebulous motion—a kind of pulsation like the awakening of life, or sometimes, perhaps, like life's dissolution, by particles, still floating. The tightly packed images in these words assist in the intensification of the natural forces in Yoknapatawpha County. The great emphasis upon nature in all the compounds extends the fecund earth theme and fills the story with a sense of wonder at the intensity of "myriad" life and the cycle of eternal change from origin to dissolution. Man, too, is a part of this cycle. In "The Bear," young Ike McCaslin at Sam Fathers's grave understands that the knoll was

no abode of the dead because there was no death, not Lion and not Sam: not held fast in earth but free in earth and not in earth but of earth, myriad yet undiffused of every part, leaf and twig and particle, air and sun and rain and dew and night, acorn oak and leaf and acorn again, dark and dawn and dark and dawn again in their immutable progression, and, being myriad, one. . . .

Thus man and earth things take their places in the cycle according to an invariable and awesome pattern. Primitive or literary, a myth is created by, and in turn creates, a sense of wonder, a sense of the marvelous. Neutralization of nature has no place in myth; it is the enemy of wonder and of the sublime, which alone gives birth to *pietas,* natural piety. Earth in this myth is never neutral; it may be unfriendly, and even its fecundity is "violent," but man is always aware of its eternal progression of growth and death and growth again.

Central in the Yoknapatawpha story is the fecund earth—challenge to man, his charge to keep, and not only the stage of life, but its source, too. The word *fecund,* along with *myriad* and *seethe* (another favorite), keeps the reader constantly reminded of the fecundity idea; the earth *seethes* with *myriad* life. One hears the soft sounds of growth and the *sibilance* of insects, smells the breeze carrying the odor of "turned earth and crabapple," feels the cool dew and lies in the "drenched myriad life of grasses." Joe Christmas, lying on his belly on the "neversunned earth," feels it "strike, slow and receptive, against him through his clothes" and there is "in his nostrils the damp rich odor of the dark and fecund earth." Impotent, frustrated Quentin, walking the cold streets of Cambridge, thinks of the "violent fecundity" of his South.

The word *fecund* is attached to woman, too; in fact, woman and earth are equated here, the woman-land equation creating another list of frequently repeated words—*moon* compounds. As land produces cyclically, woman produces cyclically; the moon in this myth measures both. The moon controls the tides; Faulkner writes of the "ebb periods" of woman. Faulkner's moon is not the chaste Artemis who brought Acteon to his death for looking upon her nudeness, but Diana of the yellow harvest moon, goddess of fertility, represented, as Frazer wrote, "in her sanctuary on the Aventine . . . by an image copied from the many-breasted idol of the Ephesian Artemis, with all its crowded emblems of exuberant fecundity." In *The Hamlet* the neighbors who welcomed the recently married Houston back to the village remarked how "the house had been completed exactly in time to catch the moon's full of April through the window where the bed was placed." In the despair of grief beyond hope after his wife's violent death, Houston stripped the new house of the things that reminded him most of her. He had

only the stove, the kitchen table he ate from, and the cot he had substituted for the bed beneath the window. The moon was full on that first night he slept on the cot too, so he moved the cot into another room and then against a north wall where the moon could not possibly reach him. . . .

Scenes in the mythical county are described as *moony, moon-dappled, moon-blanched, moon-shadowed, moon-gleamed,* and even *moonbitten.* While the men are vainly chasing the spotted horses after the Vanity Fair of the horse sale, Faulkner ironically uses the word *moon* or some compound of it ten times in five pages; even the deserted scene of the sale is *moon-drenched.* As if to clinch his point of nature's rich fertility versus man's desiccated ventures, he shows Ratliff and his companions treading the *moon-blanched* dust to Varner's house in the *moonlight* where the fertility goddess, Eula Varner Snopes, stands in the window "full in the moon" . . . "not even doomed, just damned," for she is married to an impotent man. The potential fecundity of nature and of woman has been violated.

Another side of woman gives rise to a different list of compounds, for she may be diverted from her natural function by promiscuity or sterility. The child Joe Christmas noted the *womansmelling* garments as he hid in the "pinkwomansmelling obscurity behind the curtain" in the *womanroom.* In this setting there are such words as *womanflesh, womanfilth, womansign, womanevil, womangarments,* and *womansinning.* To balance these are *mansmelling, manstale, manshape, manvoice,* and *mansense,* all of them derogatory, or at least, not laudatory.

Of course, these compounds are thematic in function, for their final effect, as they relate earth and woman to fulfilment, is to insist that the novelist is concerned with vital, teeming life. Those recording the failure in productivity reflect a judgment upon that failure, and the two lists juxtaposed extend the continuing American theme of fertility, natural and symbolic, which is the concern of Henry Adams in "The Virgin and the Dynamo," of much of Walt Whitman's work, of more of Melville than has been generally realized, and of T. S. Eliot in *The Waste Land* and elsewhere.

The fourth of Faulkner's practices to be discussed here is the repetition of certain words, from chapter to chapter and from novel to novel. One learns to expect in many contexts such words as *myriad, effluvium, miasmic, annealing, immemorial, immolate,* and *endure.* There are "myriad candles," "myriad scent," "myriad odors of waxing spring," "myriad silence," "myriad flickering fire." There are "voices myriad out of all time," "hot myriad silences in the breathless night," "myriad anonymity," "the myriad waking life of grasses," and "the myriad glitter" of John Sartoris's sword. The repeated use of this word and others, such as *miasmic* and *effluvium,* serve to bedim the outlines of the Faulkner geography and the things in it by enveloping them in a kind of mist, as they cloy the senses with excess or elude them with indefiniteness, for Yoknapatawpha County, nostalgic kingdom of lost glory, like Ike McCaslin's bear, must not and cannot be clearly defined, in spite of Mr. Faulkner's map naming himself "sole owner and proprietor." It is right that a mythical county, whose story transcends plot, should have a tenuous outline in time and space. *Myriad* suggests countless; *immemorial* and *endure* suggest timelessness; *miasmic* and *effluvium,* vaporous, misty; even the word *immolate* in its root meaning denotes the sprinkling of the innumerable grains of sacrificial meal. The sum of these impressions is a feeling of the illusory, the shadowy, the indefinite.

Others of the repetitions in these novels are clearly motifs, which sometimes develop into symbols. I have mentioned the repeated abstract words used as character signs, such as *despair* for young Bayard. In the Quentin section of *The Sound and the Fury* four powerful word motifs contain the tragic elements of the narrative: *door,* used twenty-five times; *sister,* twenty-nine times; *honeysuckle,* twenty-seven times; and *water,* forty-eight times. These words, embodying the incest theme, the too-sweet honeysuckle memories, and the compulsion to death by water, dominate by repetition the movement of the hundred-page section. Add to this the time motifs— *watch, clock,* and *chimes*—and Quentin's tragic conflict is complete. By indirection, using these words which simultaneously serve as motifs to lead the reader and as symbols to reveal Quentin's extremely disturbed state, the novelist has achieved masterful control of a complex and highly charged situation. By choosing three words at least (*door, sister, water*) which have Biblical or psychological associations, he has added to the injected overtones of mythical dimension.

*Endure,* which, beyond its time content, is an often-repeated word supporting the fecundity theme, is applied to the land, the woman, and the Negro. These three endure neglect, abuse, and violence, but they go on and on. In the famous "Appendix" to *The Portable Faulkner* the novelist felt the need of only two words after the name of Dilsey, woman *and* Negro: "They endured." Uncle Gavin, Harvard-Heidelberg philosopher-lawyer, says:

. . . the ones named Sambo, . . .they can stand anything . . . not all white people can endure slavery and apparently no man can stand freedom. . . . But the people named Sambo survived the one and who knows? they may even endure the other. . . .

Out of the many repetitions of *endure* develops the inference that patient endurance is a virtue and a strength able to meet formidable adversaries because it can wait. The land endures, like the Negro, because of patient acceptance and because it is fecund. In "Tomorrow," a short story, we are told of "the poor soil, the little tilled and barren patches of giant corn and cotton which somehow endured, as the people they fed somehow endured."

On the other hand, there is a force in both man and nature which rejects patient endurance. Not all men till the barren patches in submission; some break themselves unwillingly upon them. To turn casually through the novels, noting the many repetitions of such words as *violent* and *savage,* with their derivatives; of *fury, destruction, dissolution, flagellation, laceration, rage, outrage,* and their like is to infer an emphasis away from peace of spirit, even to active rebellion against life as it is. There is a common compulsion to violence. Many characters seem driven, not to placid acceptance, but to a stubborn, fighting submission to their fate, with seemingly no hope and no purpose. One thinks of Armstid at the end of *The Hamlet,* digging for gold beyond the hope of finding it; of Judith and Rosa in *Absalom, Absalom!*; of Sutpen and his doomed Hundred; of Quentin's long inner struggle before suicide; of young Bayard's despair beyond grief; of Houston living with the ghost of his love; and of Joe Christmas, torn by the black-white war within.

In conclusion, it seems evident that these observations on Faulkner's extraordinary verbal resources reveal his emotional and intellectual quality, the basic tensions at the core of his story, his poetic quality; and they certainly suggest his concept of man and his world. His characteristic mood, intensity, depends no more, and perhaps less, upon sentence structure than upon word choice. *Sanctuary, Sartoris,* and *The Unvanquished,* for instance, where the intensity is as high as in any of the other books, make little use of the involuted sentence pattern, but the practices I have listed are there.

In addition to the scope of the Yoknapatawpha narrative, it is the intensity that extends the story beyond mere happening. It is the intensity which creates a violent world inhabited by people of violent emotions and powerful frustrations. Like Van Gogh, who, impatient with his brush, squeezed his violent yellows thickly from tube to canvas, Faulkner, to create his mythic world, discards the more ordinary use of language and draws from some inner rage, or at least, from some deep concern. He bears out this conclusion in his statement published in *College English,* October, 1957, in answer to the question, "Mr. Faulkner, would you say that much writing is the result of unrest in the writer?"

I think [he replied] it's all a result of unrest in the writer. I think the writer is demon-driven, that he can't be at peace unless he is trying to take the sorry, shabby world which he finds and . . . can't change . . . physically, . . . to create a world of his own in which people are braver or better blackguards or better heroes or more chaste or better villains than he finds in the world around him. He's demon-driven, I think.

So Faulkner's "mythic thinking" drives him to an intensity achieved not only by his "deliberately withheld meaning" and his complex syntax, but also by the use of abstract words of high associational meaning, his hyperbolic words and hyperbole through repetition, his coined compounds for compression, and his use of "negative ultimates." All these practices help to create a sense of wonder, without which no myth remains myth. Here, Nature, in her profligate fertility, is not neutralized, making man an alien, an outsider, but is hyperbolized into a great primal, immeasurable force, of which man is always aware. Within the violent scene there is the wilderness serene as Eden, and the wilderness theme runs like a clear stream through the land. Man may placidly harmonize with Nature or in fury destroy himself upon it, but it is deserving of his wonder. Within the limitations imposed by the very nature of language itself, *mythos* has found *logos* in these novels and made way for *pietas,* whose prerequisite is a sense of wonder.

# IV. The Work

*Studies of Individual Novels*

## A. "The Time of Genius"

## MIRROR ANALOGUES IN

## *THE SOUND AND THE FURY*

LAWRANCE THOMPSON

THE CONCEPT of holding a mirror up to nature suggests an attractive, but thorny, path across the history of ideas, because that trope has lent itself to so many conflicting usages and interpretations. Yet the persistent allusions to mirrors in *The Sound and the Fury* would seem to invite the reader to notice that Faulkner has adapted the ancient literary mirror device and mirror principle to his own peculiar purposes, as a means of reflecting various kinds of correspondences, antitheses, parallelisms, analogues—even as a means of illuminating certain thematic concerns which are implicit throughout the total action. At the risk of oversimplifying Faulkner's elaborately developed meanings, I propose to present in ascending order of significance a few mirror allusions and mirror devices, in the hope that such a progression may increase our awareness of certain basic meanings.

Perhaps the first hint or foreshadowing occurs when the idiot Ben touches a place on a wall where a mirror used to be. During the late afternoon of Ben's thirty-third birthday his Negro guardian, Luster, leads him into this experience:

"We went to the library. Luster turned on the light. The windows went

Reprinted with permission from *English Institute Essays, 1952* (New York, Columbia University Press, 1953), pp. 83-106.

black, and the dark tall place on the wall came and I went and touched it. It was like a door, only it wasn't a door.

"The fire came behind me and I went to the fire and sat on the floor, holding the slipper. The fire went higher. It went onto the cushion in Mother's chair."

Although each of those images in that passage has important associations for Ben, this initial allusion to "the dark tall place on the wall" must strike the first reader as being mysterious, even meaningless, except that the tantalizing phrase does have the effect of creating a tension of interest, a focus of attention, which sharpens the response of the reader to later pertinent passages. For example, the superficial tension is completely resolved when Jason subsequently gives his recollection of a similar situation, and views it from a decidedly different angle.

I went on into the living room. I couldn't hear anything from upstairs. I opened the paper. After awhile Ben and Luster came in. Ben went to the dark place on the wall where the mirror used to be, rubbing his hands on it and slobbering and moaning. Luster begun punching at the fire.

"What're you doing?" I says. "We dont need any fire tonight."

"I trying to keep him quiet," he says.

Even this superficial clarification does not help us to understand the significance to Ben of that "dark place on the wall where the mirror used to be" before some of the furnishings were sold. But through Ben's stream-of-consciousness associations evoked by that "dark place" and that fire, Faulkner proceeds to develop a gradually revealing series of analogues, involving Ben and his sister Caddy and his mother at about the time he had been repudiated by his family through the act of changing his name from Maury to Benjamin. Two brief passages may be quoted to suggest the still enigmatic allusions to mirrors.

"Versh set me down and we went into Mother's room. There was a fire. It was rising and falling on the walls. There was another fire in the mirror."

Next, and again by association, Ben is reminded of Caddy. " 'Come and tell Mother goodnight.' Caddy said. We went to the bed. The fire went out of the mirror."

The specific meaning of that final sentence is obvious: as Ben's angle of vision changed, he could no longer see the reflection of fire in the mirror. But the immediate context suggests a symbolic value for that sentence: as Ben turns from Caddy to his mother he suffers a sense of loss which may be symbolized by the disappearance of the reflected fire. His next associational memory dramatizes several reasons why Ben may well have suffered a sense of loss whenever he turned from Caddy to his mother.

I could see the fire in the mirror too. Caddy lifted me up.

"Come on, now." she said. "Then you can come back to the fire. Hush now."

. . . . "Bring him here." Mother said. "He's too big for you to carry."

"He's not too heavy." Caddy said. "I can carry him."

"Well, I don't want him carried, then." Mother said. "A five year old child. No, no. Not in my lap. Let him stand up."

"If you'll hold him, he'll stop." Caddy said. "Hush." she said. "You can go right back. Here. Here's your cushion. See."

"Dont, Candace." Mother said.

"Let him look at it, and he'll be quiet." Caddy said. "Hold up just a minute while I slip it out. There, Benjy. Look."

I looked at it and hushed.

"You humour him too much." Mother said. "You and your father both. You dont realize that I am the one who has to pay for it. . . ."

"You dont need to bother with him." Caddy said. "I like to take care of him. Dont I, Benjy."

"Candace." Mother said. "I told you not to call him that. . . . Benjamin." she said. "Take that cushion away, Candace."

"He'll cry." Caddy said.

"Take that cushion away, like I told you." Mother said. "He must learn to mind."

The cushion went away.

"Hush, Benjy." Caddy said.

"You go over there and sit down." Mother said. "Benjamin." She held my face to hers.

"Stop that." she said. "Stop it."

But I didn't stop and Mother caught me in her arms and began to cry, and I cried. Then the cushion came back and Caddy held it above Mother's head. She drew Mother back in the chair and Mother lay crying against the red and yellow cushion.

"Hush, Mother." Caddy said. "You go upstairs and lay down, so you can be sick. I'll go get Dilsey." She led me to the fire and I looked at the bright, smooth shapes. I could hear the fire and the roof. . . .

"You can look at the fire and the mirror and the cushion too," Caddy said.

In that little dramatic action is ample evidence that Caddy, motivated by her compassion for her younger brother, has eagerly given Ben the kind of motherly attention previously denied to him because of his own mother's inadequacies. Tenderly, solicitously, Caddy has discovered ways of appealing to Ben's limited responses, to satisfy his instinctive and unreasoning hunger for orderliness, peacefulness, serenity. The fire, the red-yellow cushion, the smooth satin slipper are only a few of the objects used by Caddy to provide him with values which are positive to him because they are somehow sustaining. Then Caddy has also taught Ben the pleasure of multiplying these positive values through their reflections in the mirror. Because she has heightened his awareness of all those symmetrical visions of "bright, smooth shapes" which comfort him, it might be said that Caddy herself has become for Ben a kind of mirror of all his positive values, framed in love: her love for him and his love for her.

Ben's seemingly chaotic reverie in Part One of *The Sound and the Fury* is so contrived by Faulkner as to focus attention, not merely on fragments of the entire Compson story, but particularly on Ben's all-absorbing love for the Caddy who was and (like the mirror) is now gone. Her presence was Ben's joy; her absence his grief; her possible return his hope. The arrangement of these fragments in Part One enables Faulkner to withhold conclusive information as to how it happened that the finely sensitive and mothering child Caddy has so completely disappeared. The reader's tension of interest concerning that question is gradually resolved through various later uses of mirror analogues which disclose related aspects of Faulkner's complex theme.

Throughout *The Sound and the Fury* Faulkner employs the convention of using some of his characters to serve as mirrors of other characters; mirrors set at different angles so that they provide contrasting angles of vision. For example, we have already had occasion to observe two contrasting images of Ben: the image reflected in the articulated consciousness of Caddy, as differing from the image reflected in the articulated consciousness of Mrs. Compson. Although various characters in the narrative reflect various images of Ben, all these images may be reduced to two roughly antithetical categories: most of the characters view Ben as a disgrace, a menace, or at least as a slobbering idiot. By contrast, those who genuinely love Ben (particularly Caddy and the Negro servant Dilsey) insist that Ben has certain particular and extraordinary powers of perception. As Roskus phrases it, "He know lot more than folks thinks." Repeatedly Ben is represented as having the instinctive and intuitive power to differentiate between objects or actions which are life-encouraging and others which are life-injuring, and these are used by Faulkner to symbolize the antithesis between good and evil. In this limited sense, then, Ben serves as a kind of moral mirror, in which the members of his own family may contemplate reflections of their own potentialities, their own moral strengths and weaknesses. Most of them naturally refuse to acknowledge this power in Ben, because they do not wish to see themselves in any light other than that of self-justification.

Appropriately, Caddy is represented as having the greatest sensitivity to her brother's power of serving as a kind of moral mirror, and her sensitivity is heightened by her unselfish love for him. Faulkner develops this aspect of Ben's significance in four episodes which illuminate the progressive phases of Caddy's growth. When she is old enough to be interested in adolescent courtship, she discovers that Ben's unreasoning reaction against the smell of perfume gives her a sense of guilt and prompts her to wash herself clean—a primitive ritual repeatedly correlated with Ben's potential for serving as moral agent and moral conscience in his family. Later, when Ben escapes from the house one night, to find Caddy and Charlie kissing in the swing on the lawn, Caddy leaves Charlie, ostensibly to quiet Ben, but also because Ben has again evoked in her a sense of guilt.

We ran out into the moonlight, toward the kitchen. . . . Caddy and I ran. We ran up the kitchen steps, onto the porch, and Caddy knelt down in the dark and held me. I could hear her and feel her chest. "I wont." she said. "I wont anymore, ever. Benjy. Benjy." Then she was crying, and I cried, and we held each other. "Hush." she said. "Hush. I wont anymore." So I hushed and Caddy took the kitchen soap and washed her mouth at the sink, hard.

The third time when Ben in represented as a moral mirror occurs as Caddy returns home immediately after her first complete sexual experience. In that scene Faulkner correlates two implicit analogues which complement each other: first, the analogue of Ben as a moral mirror; secondly, the analogue between simple physical vision and conscious moral vision, suggested by the persistent recurrence of the word "eyes" and the cognate words, "looking" and "seeing," as Ben again evokes in Caddy a deeper sense of guilt.

Caddy came to the door and stood there, looking at Father and Mother. Her eyes flew at me, and away. I began to cry. It went loud and I got up. Caddy came in and stood with her back to the wall, looking at me. I went toward her, crying, and she shrank against the wall and I saw her eyes and I cried louder and pulled at her dress. She put her hands out but I pulled at her dress. Her eyes ran. . . . We were in the hall, Caddy was still looking at me. Her hand was against her mouth and I saw her eyes and I cried. We went up the stairs. She stopped again, against the wall, looking at me and I cried and she went on and I came on, crying, and she shrank against the wall looking at me. She opened the door to her room, but I pulled at her dress and we went to the bathroom and she stood against the door, looking at me. Then she put her arm across her face and I pushed at her, crying.

Each of these three closely related episodes (involving Ben as moral mirror and also involving the symbolic and penitent ritual of washing away guilt with water) is associated in Ben's recollection with his ultimate re-action, at the time of Caddy's fake wedding, where the sense of guilt was ironically washed away with champagne until the celebration was terminated by Ben's unreasoning and bellowing protest. This fourth episode represents the end of the period in Ben's life when Caddy had been able to help him by bringing relative order out of his relatively chaotic experience, and the end of the period when Ben had served as moral mirror for Caddy. Notice that these two endings are obliquely suggested by reiterative mirror imagery in Quentin's recollection of that incident which broke up the wedding celebration.

She ran right out of the mirror, out of the banked scent. Roses. Roses. . . . Only she was running already when I heard it. In the mirror she was running before I knew what it was. That quick, her train caught up over her arm she ran out of the mirror like a cloud, her veil swirling in long glints her heels brittle and fast clutching her dress onto her shoulder with the other hand, running out of the mirror the smells roses roses the voice that breathed o'er Eden. Then she was across the porch I couldn't hear her heels then in the moonlight like a cloud, the floating shadow of the veil running across the grass, into the bellowing.

Caddy goes away after the fake wedding ceremony, leaving a double image of herself as reflected in the consciousness of her family. The reader's initial image of Caddy has been that reflected repeatedly in the consciousness of Ben: the sensitive and mothering Caddy whose love for Ben evoked his love for her and gave meaning to his life. That image remains. Antithetically, the second image of Caddy is that soon reflected (with only minor variations) in the consciousness of Mrs. Compson, Quentin, and Jason: the image of the member of the family whose fall from innocence is said to have brought a peculiar disgrace on the entire family; a disgrace considered equal to, or even greater than, that of Ben's idiocy. Gradually, however, the reader appreciates that Mrs. Compson, Quentin, and Jason, each motivated by different kinds of need for self-justification, have first made a scapegoat of Ben and have then made a scapegoat of Caddy, so that they may heap on these two scapegoats the ultimate blame for the disintegration within the Compson family. Although this suggests one further aspect of Faulkner's complex theme, further elaboration of this central meaning may be postponed until we have considered other varieties of mirror analogues.

In Part Two of *The Sound and the Fury* Faulkner gradually suggests antithetical contrasts between Ben's preoccupation with mirrors and Quentin's preoccupation with mirrors. At one point in his reverie Quentin makes this sequence of observations.

I could smell the curves of the river beyond the dusk and I saw the last light supine and tranquil upon the tideflats like pieces of broken mirror . . . Benjamin the child of. How he used to sit before that mirror. Refuge unfailing in which conflict [was] tempered silenced reconciled.

Quentin is (if we may borrow a phrase which Faulkner affords to Quentin himself) "a sort of obverse reflection" of Ben. By contrast with Ben's instinctive response to objects used to symbolize positive values in human experience, Quentin serves to dramatize a consciously willed and obsessive love for negative values which are life-injuring, life-destroying, and which in turn, are nicely symbolized by his elaborately planned act of suicide by drowning. Throughout *The Sound and the Fury* a recurrent motif, suggested by the title itself, is the traditional convention of conflict between order-producing forces and chaos-producing forces in human experience, here represented in part by the gradual drift of the Compson family from remembered dignity and order toward disgrace and chaos. Quentin is represented as one whose disordering self-love motivates not only his masochistic delight in creating inner chaos but also his erotic lust for his own death. Structurally, then, the juxtaposition of Ben's thirty-third birthday against Quentin's death day accentuates the contrasting life-visions symbolized by Ben (who is ironically the shame of the Compsons) and by Quentin (who is ironically the pride of the Compsons). The two brief passages which constitute, respectively, the end of Ben's day and the beginning of Quentin's day may be quoted to suggest, once again, Faulkner's fondness for the technical principle of antithesis, here used to illuminate obliquely the basic ways in which these two brothers serve as obverse reflections of each other. Ben's day ends with these words:

Caddy held me and I could hear us all, and the darkness, and sometimes I could smell. And then I could see the windows, where the trees were buzzing. Then the dark began to go in smooth, bright shapes, like it always does, even when Caddy says that I have been asleep.

There, implicitly, recurs the thematic suggestion that Ben, with the aid of Caddy, has developed the ability to find within himself the power to convert even darkness into a pattern of meaningful and soothing symmetry, serenity, order: "refuge unfailing, in which conflict [was] tempered silenced reconciled," as Quentin phrased it. By contrast, Quentin begins his day with an irritated resentment of sunlight and with an insistence on finding within himself the power to convert even the life-giving value of sunlight into a reminder of time. After the manner of his father, Quentin has already endowed time with ugly and chaotic significance: "When the shadow of the sash appeared on the curtains it was between seven and eight o'clock and then I was in time again, hearing the watch."

For immediate purposes the pivotal image there is "shadow," an image subsequently enriched by Faulkner to represent Quentin's *alter ego,* his own reflected image of himself, developed by Quentin as an elaborate mirror analogue. Quentin's reasoning, obliquely suggested by his numerous references to his own mirror analogue, may be paraphrased briefly. To achieve his willed act of self-destruction, he is aware that he must cope with that other side of self which is represented by his physical being or body, which intuitively or instinctively clings to life while resisting the death-will of his mind. To insult and belittle that resisting other-self (the body), Quentin identifies his body with his sun-cast shadow. Because the sun is repeatedly represented as creating the shadow of his body, this shadow might be considered poetically as the body's tribute to the life-giving power of the sun. But this is exactly the kind of tribute which Quentin wishes to deny. His inverted attitude toward the instinctive life-wish of his body is nicely reflected in the following poetic sentence, so rich in suggested extensions of meanings: "There was a clock, high up in the sun, and I thought about how when you don't want to do a thing, your body will try to trick you into doing it, sort of unawares."

At first glance, this echo of the traditional body-versus-spirit antithesis suggests Quentin's warped Calvinistic Presbyterian heritage. On reconsideration, it becomes obvious that the thing which Quentin does not want to do is to live; that which his body tries to do is to resist Quentin's obsessive and erotic lust for death. Consequently Quentin perversely views the body's natural death-resistance as the body's attempt to "trick" him. This inverted concept evokes his further conviction that he must counterattack that body-impulse by managing somehow to subdue and "trick" his shadow. Four very brief utterances of Quentin's may be quoted here to demonstrate the ironically enriching effects achieved by Faulkner in permitting this shadow-reflection of Quentin's body to represent Quentin's other-self opponent.

[1] I stepped into the sunlight, finding my shadow again.

[2] Trampling my shadow's bones into the concrete with hard heels. . . .

[3] The car stopped. I got off, into the middle of my shadow . . . trampling my shadow into the dust.

[4] The wall went into shadow, and then my shadow, I had tricked it again.

Obviously, Quentin's ultimate tricking of his "shadow" must be the destruction of his body in the planned act of suicide by drowning. In developing the double significance of this act (as being desired by the will and as being not desired by the body), Faulkner makes pertinent use of Quentin's initial experience on a bridge over the Charles River, where he stands contemplating his own shadow mirrored on the surface of the water below.

The shadow of the bridge, the tiers of railings, my shadow leaning flat upon the water, so easily had I tricked it that it would not quit me. At least fifty feet it was, and if I only had something to blot it into the water, holding it until it drowned, the shadow of the package like two shoes wrapped up lying on the water. Niggers say a drowned man's shadow was watching for him in the water all the time. . . . I leaned on the railing, watching my shadow, how I had tricked it. I moved along the rail, but my suit was dark too and I could wipe my hands, watching my shadow, how I had tricked it.

Later, from another bridge, Quentin blindly contemplates another symbolic shadow: the trout, instinctively fulfilling its potentialities as it swims against the destructive element in which it has its being.

I could not see the bottom, but I could see a long way into the motion of the water before the eye gave out, and then I saw a shadow hanging like a fat arrow stemming into the current. Mayflies skimmed in and out of the shadow of the bridge just above the surface. . . . The arrow increased without motion, then in a quick swirl the trout lipped a fly beneath the surface. . . . The fading vortex drifted away down stream and then I saw the arrow again, nose into the current, wavering delicately to the motion of the water above which the Mayflies slanted and poised. . . . Three boys with fishing poles came onto the bridge and we leaned on the rail and looked down at the trout. They knew the fish. He was a neighborhood character. . . . "We dont try to catch him anymore," he said. "We just watch Boston folks that come out and try."

That little parable or implicit mirror of meaning, wasted on Quentin, helps to correlate several different aspects of Faulkner's steadily developing emphasis on the value of certain kinds of instinctive response in human experience. There is even a suggested analogy between the instinctive action of the trout and the instinctive action of the sea gull which Quentin also blindly contemplates: each in its own discrete element instinctively uses the current or stream of its own element to achieve poise, even as the Mayflies do. Consider these two quotations in their relation to each other.

. . . rushing away under the poised gull and all things rushing.
. . . the arrow again, nose into the current, wavering delicately to the motion of the water above which the Mayflies slanted and poised.

Quentin's element is time, and instead of building on his own innate and instinctive potentialities for achieving poise against the motion of "all things rushing," he is represented as having deliberately chosen to pervert and destroy those potentialities. The trout, the gull, the Mayflies, along with Ben, make available to the reader the kinds of metaphorical "mirrors" of meaning which Quentin refuses to understand. By contrast with Ben, Quentin has a tendency to use all mirrors (literal or figurative) to multiply negative values, particularly those disordered and chaotic values symbolized by the reflection of his own death-obsessed face. On the evening of his death day, as he continues his chaotically systematic ritual of death courtship, Quentin momentarily finds in a window of a trolley car a mirror of things broken: "The lights were on in the car, so while we ran behind trees I couldn't see anything except my own face and a woman across the aisle with a hat sitting right on top of her head, with a broken feather in it."

Having established that mirror-image of the trolley car window, Faulkner subsequently develops extensions of meaning from it. Quentin, after returning to his dormitory room to clean himself up for death, stands before a conventional mirror, brushing his hair, troubled at the thought that Shreve, his roommate, may return in time to spoil his plans. Or perhaps, he thinks, Shreve may be coming in to town on a trolley, just as Quentin is again going out on another trolley, and if so their faces will be momentarily juxtaposed and separated only by the two windows and the space between. The elliptical passage containing hints of these thoughts is of particular interest here, because it suggests a basic mirror principle, namely, Quentin's use of phrases which have only a superficial value for him, but a far deeper thematic suggestion for the reader. Here is the passage.

While I was brushing my hair the half hour went. But there was until the three quarters anyway, except supposing seeing on the rushing darkness only his own face no broken feather unless two of them but not two like that going to Boston the same night then my face his face for an instant across the crashing when out of the darkness two lighted windows in rigid fleeing crash gone his face and mine just as I see saw did I see.

The potentials of meaning which go far beyond Quentin's immediate meaning there may be passed over to let us concentrate particularly on that striking phrase, less applicable to Shreve than to the total action of Quentin: "seeing on the rushing darkness only his own face." That again strongly suggests not only the conflict between Quentin's two opposed consciences but also the total contrast between Quentin's uses of mirrors and Ben's uses of mirrors.

Faulkner's most elaborately contrived mirror analogue, in the presentation of Quentin's death day, stands out as technically different from any mirror analogue we have yet considered. It is a figurative or symbolic mirroring of the meaning of a past action in a present action: the parallelism between the way Quentin plays big brother to the little Italian girl and the way Quentin previously played big brother to Caddy. Another kind of "broken mirror" effect is achieved by scattering through the entire episode involving the Italian girl evoked fragments of memories concerning earlier and related episodes involving Quentin and Caddy. This twofold sequence of analogous actions is much too long to be analyzed here. Yet it deserves to be mentioned as an extremely important example of a mirror analogue, in which Faulkner at least suggests that Caddy's love for her younger brother Ben and for her older brother Quentin was soiled, stained, and perverted by Quentin's self-love until Caddy, trying to keep up with her brother, got into trouble. To a large degree, Quentin is represented as having been personally responsible for the change which occurred in the character of Caddy. Yet, even as Quentin rejects as ridiculous the charge of the Italian brother, "You steela my sister," so he also rejects and ignores even the suggestions made by his own conscious or subconscious associations that he was, indeed, in some way responsible for what happened to Caddy. In this immediate context there is a highly ironic significance in the fact that Caddy should have chosen to name her daughter Quentin, even though her brother was not physically the father of her child.

Faulkner seems to have saved two oblique and "gathering" metaphors or symbolic actions for use in the concluding pages of *The Sound and the Fury,* and in this context it may be permissible to consider those two actions as mirror analogues, figuratively speaking. The first of these occurs in the episode involving Dilsey and Ben at the Easter service in the Negro church, and Faulkner begins it by making technical use, once again, of two contrasting or antithetical attitudes toward one person, namely, the monkey-faced preacher, who undergoes a metamorphosis, as he loses himself in the meaning of an action symbolizing self-sacrificial love:

And the congregation seemed to watch with its own eyes while the voice consumed him, until he was nothing and they were nothing and there was not even a voice but instead their hearts were speaking to one another in chanting measures beyond the need for words, so that when he came to rest against the reading desk, his monkey face lifted and his whole attitude that of a serene, tortured crucifix that transcended its shabbiness and insignificance and made of it no moment, a long expulsion of breath rose from them.

Faulkner would seem to be dramatizing in that symbolic action a key aspect of his central theme, always pivoting, as it does, on various possible meanings for the single word "love." For that reason the responses of Dilsey and Ben to that action are pertinent.

Dilsey sat bolt upright, her hand on Ben's knee. The tears slid down her fallen cheeks, in and out of the myriad coruscations of immolation and abnegation and time. . . . In the midst of the voices and the hands Ben sat, rapt in his sweet blue gaze. Dilsey sat bolt upright beside, crying rigidly and quietly in the annealment and the blood of the remembered Lamb.

The second of these gathering metaphors also illuminates and accentuates the implicit thematic antithesis between two kinds of vision. This time the extensions of meaning are ironically suggested through Luster's saucy analogy between how he does something and "how quality does it." While entertaining Ben by taking him for his customary ride to the cemetery on Easter Sunday, Luster decides to show off, for the benefit of some loitering Negroes. He merely proposes a simple violation of a simple law when he says, "Les show dem niggers how quality does it, Benjy." Instead of driving around the monument in the accustomed way, he starts Queenie the wrong way. Ben, instinctively feeling the difference between right and wrong even in such a trivial situation, begins to bellow and continues until the minor chaos of that situation (ironically corrected by Jason, out of mere embarrassment) has given way to the ritual of orderly return. So the total action of the narrative ends with the implicit and symbolic reiteration of the part Ben has played throughout, in terms of the antithesis between the human power to create chaos and the human power to create order.

Queenie moved again, her feet began to clop-clop, steadily again, and at once Ben hushed. Luster looked quickly back over his shoulder, then he drove on. The broken flower drooped over Ben's fist, and his eyes were empty and blue and serene again, as cornice and façade flowed smoothly once more, from left to right; post and tree, window and doorway, and signboard, each in its ordered place.

Faulkner's choice of title deserves to be viewed figuratively as suggesting one further kind of mirror analogue, because the attitude of Macbeth, as dramatized in the familiar fifth-act soliloquy, nicely reflects an important element in the attitudes of Faulkner's three major protagonists of chaos, Mrs. Compson, Quentin, and Jason. All of these characters have this much in common: each is intent on self-pitying self-justification. All are certain that they have become victimized by circumstances beyond their control, and all of them project outward on life their own inner chaos, which has its roots in a perversion of love, through self-love. Similarly, in the fifth act, Macbeth is represented as refusing to recognize that he has been in any way to blame, or responsible, for what has happened to him. Instead, he also projects his own inner chaos outward, self-justifyingly, to make a scapegoat of the whole world, even of time, and to view life itself as a walking "shadow." Now consider the ironies of situation implicit in that passage which Faulkner's title suggests as a pertinent mirror of the attitudes not only of Quentin and Jason but also of Mr. and Mrs. Compson.

> Tomorrow, and tomorrow, and tomorrow,
> Creeps in this petty pace from day to day,
> To the last syllable of recorded time.
> And all our yesterdays have lighted fools
> The way to dusty death. Out, out, brief candle!
> Life's but a walking shadow, a poor player
> That struts and frets his hour upon the stage,
> And then is heard no more. It is a tale
> Told by an idiot, full of sound and fury,
> Signifying nothing.

Finally, the meaning of Faulkner's total structure may be suggested by one last mirror analogue. As narrator, he would seem to be intent on

achieving a high degree of detachment by arranging his four separate parts
in such a way that they do not tell a story in the conventional sense. Faulkner neither invites nor permits the reader to look directly at the total
cause-and-effect sequence of events, as such. Instead, each of the four
parts provides a different aspect, a different view, a different angle of
vision, a different reflection of some parts of the story. Each of these four
structural units, thus contiguous, hinged, set at a different angle from
the others, might be called analogous to those hinged and contiguous haber-
dashery mirrors which permit us to contemplate the immediate picture reflected in any single one of those mirrors, and then to contemplate secondary or subordinate pictures which are reflections of reflections in each
of the separate mirrors.

In Faulkner's four structural mirrors (the four parts), the first picture
(or pictures) may be said to be provided through Ben's reflecting angle
of vision. Although the reader's initial impression of Ben's reverie may,
indeed, provide a sense that the tale is told by an idiot, signifying nothing,
the ultimate impression is that Ben's angle of vision concentrates our attention symbolically on certain basic and primitive powers of perception,
available even to an idiot; powers of perception which enable even a severely handicapped individual to create, from his own experience and with
the aid of his instincts and intuitions, some forms of order which can give
positive values to human experience.

Structurally, the second set of pictures is provided through Quentin's
reflecting angle of vision. This time, although the reader's early impression of Quentin's reverie may provide a preliminary sense of a highly
sensitive and Hamlet-like character, who views himself as intent on holding up to nature his own idealistic mirror, the ultimate impression is that
Quentin's angle of vision reflects, by contrast with Ben's, several important aspects of the negative or obverse side of Faulkner's theme. Psychologically unbalanced by his own inner and outer conflicts, Quentin is
represented as being partly responsible not only for what has happened to
himself but also for what has happened to some other members of his
family. He has permitted his warped and warping ego to invert exactly
those basic and primitive and positive values symbolized by that which
Ben instinctively and intuitively cherished.

The third set of images is provided by Jason's reflecting angle of
vision, and even though Jason sees himself as the only sane Compson,
the reader quickly becomes convinced that Jason's sadistic scale of values
is more nearly analogous to the values of Iago than to those of the almost

Hamlet-like Quentin. The irony of the total situation involving Jason culminates in a ridiculously fine burlesque of poetic justice when Faulkner permits Jason's golden fleece of Caddy to be avenged by Caddy's daughter's golden fleece of Jason. Even as Caddy's brother Quentin has somehow been at least partially responsible for the moral degeneration of Caddy, so Jason is represented as being at least partially responsbile for the moral degeneration of Caddy's daughter.

The fourth set of images is provided through Dilsey's reflecting angle of vision. Implicitly and symbolically there is an analogous relationship between Dilsey's emphasis on certain basic, primary, positive values throughout and Ben's intuitive sense of values. Thus, the positive angles of vision, mirrored by Ben and Dilsey most sharply in the first and fourth structural parts of *The Sound and the Fury,* may be considered literally and symbolically as bracketing and containing the two negative angles of vision mirrored by Quentin and Jason in the second and third parts. Taken in this sense, the structural arrangement of these four hinged mirrors serves to heighten the reader's awareness of Faulkner's major thematic antithesis between the chaos-producing effects of self-love and the order-producing effects of compassionate and self-sacrificial love in human experience.

# TIME IN FAULKNER:
## *THE SOUND AND THE FURY*

### JEAN-PAUL SARTRE

THE READER OF *The Sound and the Fury* is at first struck by the oddities of its technique. Why has Faulkner broken up the time of his story and disarranged the fragments? Why does the mind of an idiot provide the first window opened on Faulkner's imaginary world? The reader is tempted to look for points of reference and to re-establish the chronology

Reprinted by permission of Librairie Gallimard, Paris, from *Situations* I, "Le Bruit et la Fureur" (Paris: Gallimard, 1947), pp. 70-81. Originally published in *La Nouvelle Revue Française*, June and July, 1939. Translated by Martine Darmon, with the assistance of the editors.

for himself: "Jason and Caroline Compson had three sons and a daughter. The daughter, Caddy, was seduced by Dalton Ames and driven to find a husband. . . ." But he stops here, because he notices that he is telling another story. Faulkner did not first think in terms of an orderly narrative and then shuffle the parts like a pack of cards; he could not have told the story in any other way. In the classical novel, the action has a focus: for example, the murder of the Karamazov father, or the meeting between Edouard and Bernard in *The Counterfeiters*. It would be futile to look for this kind of focus in *The Sound and the Fury*: is it Benjy's castration? Caddy's unfortunate love affair? Quentin's suicide? Jason's hatred for his niece? Each episode, once it has been grasped, invokes others—in fact, all the other episodes connected with it. Nothing happens, the story does not progress; rather, we discover it behind each word as an oppressive and hateful presence, varying in intensity with each situation. It is a mistake to think of these anomalies as mere exercises in virtuosity; the novelist's aesthetic always sends us back to his metaphysic. The critic's task is to bring out the author's metaphysic before evaluating his technique. And it is obvious that Faulkner's is a metaphysic of time.

It is man's misfortune to be confined in time. ". . . a man is the sum of his misfortunes. One day you'd think misfortune would get tired, but then time is your misfortune. . . ."[1] This is the true subject of the novel. And if the technique adopted by Faulkner seems at first to be a negation of time, that is because we confuse time with chronology. Dates and clocks were invented by man: ". . . constant speculation regarding the position of mechanical hands on an arbitrary dial which is a symptom of mind-function. Excrement Father said like sweating." (96) To reach real time, we must abandon these devices, which measure nothing: ". . . time is dead as long as it is being clicked off by little wheels; only when the clock stops does time come to life." (104) Quentin's breaking his watch has, therefore, a symbolic value; it forces us to see time without the aid of clocks. The time of the idiot, Benjy, is also unmeasured by clocks, for he does not understand them.

As for Faulkner's concept of the present, it is not a circumscribed or sharply defined point between past and future. His present is irrational in its essence; it is an event, monstrous and incomprehensible, which comes upon us like a thief—comes upon us and disappears. Beyond this present, there is nothing, since the future does not exist. One present, emerging from the unknown, drives out another present. It is like a sum that we

1. *The Sound and the Fury* (New York: Modern Library, 1946), p. 123.

compute again and again: "And . . . and . . . and then." Like Dos Passos, but with greater subtlety, Faulkner makes his story a matter of addition. Even when the characters are aware of them, the actions, when they emerge in the present, burst into scattered fragments: "I went to the dresser and took up the watch, with the face still down. I tapped the crystal on the corner of the dresser and caught the fragments of glass in my hand and put them into the ashtray and twisted the hands off and put them in the tray. The watch ticked on."(99) The other characteristic of Faulkner's present is *suspension.** I use this word, for lack of a better one, to indicate a kind of arrested motion in time. In Faulkner, there is never any progression, nothing which can come from the future. The present does not contain in itself the future events we expect—as it seems to when I say that the friend I have been waiting for finally appears. On the contrary, to be present is to appear without reason and to be suspended. Faulkner does not see this suspension in abstract terms; he perceives it in things themselves and tries to make it felt. "The train swung around the curve, the engine puffing with short, heavy blasts, and they passed smoothly from sight that way, with that quality about them of shabby and timeless patience, of static serenity. . . ."(106) And again: "Beneath the sag of the buggy the hooves neatly rapid like the motions of a lady doing embroidery, *diminishing without progress* like a figure on a treadmill being drawn rapidly offstage."[2] Faulkner appears to arrest the motion at the very heart of things; moments erupt and freeze, then fade, recede and diminish, still motionless.

However, this fugitive and incomprehensible state can be grasped and made verbal. Quentin can say: I broke my watch. But when he says it, his gesture will be *past.* The past can be named and described. Up to a certain point it can be fixed by concepts or intuitively grasped. We have already noted, in connection with *Sartoris,* that Faulkner always shows us events when they are already completed. In *The Sound and the Fury,* everything occurs in the wings; nothing happens, everything has happened. This is what enables us to understand that strange formula of one of the heroes: "I am not is, I was." In this sense also, Faulkner can make of man a being without future, "sum of his climactic experiences," "sum of his misfortunes," "sum of what have you." At every instant we draw a line, since the present is nothing but disordered rumor, a future already

* The French word is *l'enfoncement,* for which the word *suspension* seemed the most suitable translation, in view of the context. [translator's note]
2. *Ibid.,* p. 143. Italics mine.

past. Faulkner's vision of the world can be compared to that of a man sitting in a convertible looking back. At every moment shadows emerge on his right, and on his left flickering and quavering points of light, which become trees, men, and cars only when they are seen in perspective. The past here gains a surrealistic quality; its outline is hard, clear and immutable. The indefinable and elusive present is helpless before it; it is full of holes through which past things, fixed, motionless and silent, invade it. Faulkner's soliloquies make us think of plane flights made rough by air pockets; at every point the consciousness of the hero "falls into the past" and rises once more, to fall again. The present does not exist, it becomes; everything *was.* In *Sartoris,* the past was seen in terms of "stories" because it consisted of a store of familiar memories and because Faulkner had not yet found his technique. In *The Sound and the Fury* he is more experimental and therefore less certain. But his preoccupation with the past is so strong that he sometimes disguises the present—and the present makes its way in the shadows, like an underground river, to reappear only when it has become past. Thus, Quentin is not even conscious of having insulted Bland, for he is reliving his quarrel with Dalton Ames.[3] And when Bland hits him, the fight is identified with the past fight between Quentin and Ames. Later, Shreve will *relate* how Bland struck Quentin; he will describe the scene because it has become history—but when it was taking place in the present it was nothing more than a shadowy and obscure event. I have been told of an old school principal whose memory had stopped like a broken watch; it remained forever fixed at his fortieth year. Though he was sixty, he was not aware of his age; his last memory was of the schoolyard and his daily rounds in the playground. Thus he interpreted his present by means of this fixed past and he walked around his table, convinced that he was watching students at their play. Faulkner's characters behave in a similar fashion. Worse than that, their past is not ordered according to chronology but follows certain impulses and emotions. Around some central themes (Caddy's pregnancy, Benjy's castration, Quentin's suicide) innumerable fragments of thought and act revolve. Hence the absurdity of chronology, of "the round and stupid assertion of the clock." The order of the past is the order of the heart. We must not believe that the present event, after it has gone, becomes the most immediate of our memories. The shift of time can submerge it at the bottom

3. *Ibid.,* pp. 178-184. Cf. p. 179, the dialogue with Bland inserted in the middle of the dialogue with Ames: "did you ever have a sister did you," and the inextricable confusion of the two battles.

of memory or leave it on the surface. Only its own intrinsic value and its relevance to our lives can determine its level.

This, then, is the nature of Faulkner's time. How valid is it? This indefinable present; these sudden invasions of the past; this affective order, opposed to the rational order which, though chronological, lacks reality; these memories, monstrous and recurring; these fluctuations of the heart—don't we recognize in them Marcel Proust's lost and recaptured time? I am aware of the differences; I know, for instance, that in Proust, salvation lies in time itself, in the total recovery of the past. For Faulkner, on the contrary, the past is unfortunately never lost; it is always there, almost as an obsession. Mystical ecstasies are our only means of escaping from the temporal world; and a mystic is always a man who wants to forget something: his Self, or more generally, language or formal representation. Faulkner wants to forget time: ". . . Quentin, I give you the mausoleum of all hope and desire; it's rather excruciating-ly apt that you will use it to gain the reducto absurdum of all human experience which can fit your individual needs no better than it fitted his or his father's. I give it to you not that you may remember time, *but that you might forget it now and then for a moment* and not spend all your breath trying to conquer it. Because no battle is ever won, he said. They are not even fought. The field only reveals to man his own folly and despair, and victory is an illusion of philosophers and fools."[4] Because he has forgotten time, the hunted Negro in *Light in August* suddenly achieves a strange and unnatural happiness: "It's not when you realize that nothing can help —religion, pride, anything—it's when you realize that you don't need any aid."[5] But for Faulkner, as for Proust, time is above all that which isolates. We remember the lovers in *Les Plaisirs et les Jours,* holding on to their passions which they are afraid will pass, which they know will pass. The same anguish is found in Faulkner: ". . . people cannot do anything that dreadful they cannot do anything very dreadful at all they cannot even remember tomorrow what seemed dreadful today . . ."[6] and ". . . a love or a sorrow is a bond purchased without design and which matures willynilly and is recalled without warning to be replaced by whatever issue the gods happen to be floating at the time. . . ."[7] Proust really *should have* employed a technique like Faulkner's; that was the logical outcome

4. *Ibid.*, p. 95. Italics mine.
5. *Light in August* (New York: Modern Library, 1950), p. 99.
6. *The Sound and the Fury*, p. 99.
7. *Ibid.*, p. 196.

of his metaphysic. Faulkner, however, is a lost man, and because he knows that he is lost he risks pushing his thought to its conclusion. Proust is a classicist and a Frenchman; and the French lose themselves with caution and always end by finding themselves. Eloquence, a love of clarity and a rational mind led Proust to preserve at least the appearance of chronology.

We can find the real reason for their similarities in a widely shared literary preoccupation. Most of the great contemporary writers—Proust, Joyce, Dos Passos, Faulkner, Gide, and Virginia Woolf—have tried, each in his own way, to mutilate time. Some have deprived it of past and future and reduced it to the pure intuition of the moment; others, like Dos Passos, make it a limited and mechanical memory. Proust and Faulkner have simply decapitated it; they have taken away its future—that is to say, the dimension of free choice and act. Proust's heroes never undertake anything: they foresee, yes, but their previsions, like day-dreams that put reality to flight, cling to them and therefore they cannot go beyond the present. The Albertine who appears is not the one we expected, and the interlude proves to be only a small, inconsequential agitation, limited to an instant. As for Faulkner's heroes, they never foresee: the car takes them away, as they look back. The approaching suicide which throws its dark shadow over Quentin's last day is not in the realm of human choice. Quentin cannot, for one second, conceive of the possibility of *not* killing himself. The suicide is an issue already determined, something which he approaches blindly without either desiring or conceiving it: ". . . you seem to regard it merely as an experience that will whiten your hair overnight so to speak without altering your appearance at all. . . ." Suicide is not consciously chosen, for it is inevitable. In losing its character of the possible, it ceases to exist in the future; it has become part of the present, and all Faulkner's art aims to suggest to us that Quentin's soliliquy and his last walk *are already* his suicide. I believe we can explain in this fashion a curious paradox: Quentin thinks of his last day as being in the past, like someone who remembers. But who is it that remembers, since the last thoughts of the hero almost coincide with the sudden eruption and destruction of his memory? The answer lies in the novelist's skill in choosing the particular moment of the present from which he describes the past. Like Salacrou in *L'Inconnue d'Arras,* Faulkner has chosen for his present the infinitesimal instant of death. Thus, when Quentin's memory begins to enumerate his impressions ("Through the wall I heard Shreve's bed-springs and then his slippers on the floor hishing. I got up. . . ."), *he is already dead.* So much art and, in fact, so much dishonesty only aim to compensate for the author's lack of any intuitive knowledge of the future. Everything, and in particular the irrationality of time, in Faulkner now becomes clear. Since the present is the unexpected, the unshaped future can be determined only by an excess of memories. We realize that duration is "man's own misfortune." If the future has reality, time moves from the past and draws near the future; but if the future is suppressed, time is no longer that which separates, which cuts the present off from itself: ". . . you cannot bear to think that someday it will no longer hurt you like this. . . ." Man spends his life struggling against time; and, acid-like, time corrodes man, tears him from himself and keeps him from realizing his humanity. Everything becomes absurd: "[Life] is a tale told by an idiot, full of sound and fury, signifying nothing."[8]

But is the time of man without a future? I can see that the nail, the clod of earth, the atom live in a perpetual present. But is man only a thinking nail? If we begin by plunging him into universal time, the time of nebulae and of planets, of tertiary formations and of animal species, as in a bath of sulfuric acid, the answer is obvious. It is nevertheless true, if we believe that time can be imposed from the outside, that a consciousness thus tossed from instant to instant would be a consciousness *first* and temporal *afterwards.* Consciousness can be "in time" only if it becomes time by that movement itself which makes it consciousness; to use Heidegger's phrase, it must "become time." In that case, it is no longer possible to stop man at each successive moment and to define him as the "sum of what have you." On the contrary, the nature of consciousness implies that it is projected into the future; we can understand what it is only by what it will become; it is determined in its present being by its own potentialities. This is what Heidegger calls "the silent strength of the possible." You won't recognize in yourself the Faulknerian man, a creature deprived of potentiality and explained only by what he was. If you try to fix your consciousness and examine it, you will see that it is hollow; you will find only futurity. I am not even talking about your plans or expectations; but the very gesture that you notice in its passing has meaning for you only if you project its completion outside itself, outside yourself, into the not-yet. The cup with its bottom which you do not see but which you could see, at the end of a movement not yet made—this white sheet of paper with its hidden verso which you could see if you turned the sheet— these, and all the stable and massive objects which surround us, extend their most immediate and solid qualities into the future. Man is not the

8. *Macbeth,* Act V, scene v.

sum of what he has, but the totality of what he does not yet have, of what he could have. And if we are thus immersed in the future, is not the irrational brutality of the present diminished? The event does not pounce upon us like a thief, since it is by its very nature a future-that-has-been. And is it not the task of the historian who explains the past to inquire first into its future? I am afraid that the absurdity Faulkner finds in human life was originally placed there by him. Not that life is not absurd, but that it has an absurdity different from what Faulkner ascribes to it.

Why have Faulkner and so many other writers chosen this particular absurdity, which is so far from the creative imagination and from truth? We must look for the reason in the social conditions of our present life. Faulkner's despair seems to me to be anterior to his metaphysic; for him, as for all of us, the future is barred. All that we see, all that we live through, incites us to say: "It can't last much longer"; we cannot, however, conceive of any change but a violent one. We live in a time of incredible revolutions, and Faulkner uses his extraordinary art to describe a world dying of old age, with us gasping and choking in it. I like his art, but I don't believe in his metaphysic. A barred future is still a future. "Even if human reality has nothing more 'ahead,' even if it has 'closed its accounts,' its being is still determined by this 'anticipation of itself.' " The loss of all hope, for example, does not deprive human reality of all possibilities; it is simply "a way of *being* in terms of those possibilities."[9]

# THE DIMENSIONS OF CONSCIOUSNESS:
## *AS I LAY DYING*

OLGA W. VICKERY

As I LAY DYING possesses basically the same structure as *The Sound and the Fury* but in a more complex form. Instead of four main sections, three of which are dominated by the consciousness of a single character, there are some sixty short sections apportioned among fifteen characters. Each

9. Heidegger, *Sein und Zeit.*

Reprinted with permission from *The Novels of William Faulkner* (Louisiana State University Press, 1959), pp. 50-65.

of these brief chapters describes some part either of the funeral preparations or of the procession itself, even as it explores and defines the mind of the observer from whose point of view the action is described. Accordingly, the clear sweep of the narrative is paralleled by a developing psychological drama of whose tensions and compulsions the characters themselves are only half-aware. The need to co-operate during the journey merely disguises the essential isolation of each of the Bundrens and postpones the inevitable conflict between them. For the Bundrens, no less than the Compsons, are living each in a private world whose nature is gauged in relation to Addie and to the actual events of the journey to Jefferson. The larger frame of reference, provided in *The Sound and the Fury* by the impersonal, third person narration of the fourth section, is here conveyed dramatically through eight different characters who comment on some aspect of the funeral in which they themselves are not immediately involved. Their diverse reactions to and judgments of the Bundrens chart the range of social responses, passing from friendliness to indifference to outraged indignation.

As in *The Sound and the Fury,* each private world manifests a fixed and distinctive way of reacting to and ordering experience. Words, action, and contemplation constitute the possible modes of response, while sensation, reason, and intuition form the levels of consciousness. All of these combine to establish a total relationship between the individual and his experience; for certain of the characters in *As I Lay Dying,* however, this relationship is fragmented and distorted. Anse, for example, is always the bystander, contemplating events and reducing the richness of experience to a few threadbare clichés. In contrast, Darl, the most complex of the characters, owes his complexity and his madness to the fact that he encompasses all possible modes of response and awareness without being able to effect their integration. It is Cash, the oldest brother, who ultimately achieves maturity and understanding by integrating these modes into one distinctively human response which fuses words and action, reason and intuition. In short, the Bundren family provides a locus for the exploration of the human psyche in all its complexity without in the least impairing the immediate reality of character and action.

The different levels of consciousness are rendered by Faulkner through variations in style ranging from the dialect of actual speech to the intricate imagery and poetic rhythms of the unconscious. When the characters are engaged in conversation or concerned with concrete objects, the vocabulary used is limited and repetitious and the style is realistic and colloquial.

These same qualities, though to a lesser extent, characterize the expression of conscious thought, for whatever a person is aware of, he articulates in his habitual way, which in a number of instances involves a groping for words. There is, however, some loss of immediacy and vividness since on this level language strives to achieve the impersonal order and clarity of reason rather than the concreteness of sensation. With the unconscious or intuitive, the personal element is at once restored and transcended. Making its appeal to emotion and imagination, the language of the unconscious relies heavily on symbols with their power to evoke rather than to define reality. Thus, Faulkner is able to indicate the particular combination of sensation, reason, and intuition possessed by each of his characters as well as their range of awareness through a subtle manipulation of language and style.

Quite naturally, the three modes of response to experience—words, action, and contemplation—are implemented not by the style but by the series of events with which the characters are confronted. Each of the Bundrens is concerned with Addie's death and with her funeral, events which are by no means identical. As Doctor Peabody suggests, the former is a personal and private matter: "I can remember how when I was young I believed death to be a phenomenon of the body; now I know it to be merely a function of the mind—and that of the minds of the ones who suffer the bereavement." (368)[1] Thus, it is Addie not as a mother, corpse, or promise but as an element in the blood of her children who dominates and shapes their complex psychological reactions. Their motivation lies within her life, for she is the source of the tension and latent violence which each of them feels within himself and expresses in his contacts with the rest of the family. Obsessed by their own relationships to Addie, they can resolve that tension only when they have come to terms with her as a person and with what she signifies in their own consciousness.

In contrast to her death, her funeral is a public affair, participated in and, indeed, supervised by the neighbors as well as the family. On this level she is simply the corpse which must be disposed of in accordance with a long established ritual of interment. While the neighbors prepare themselves to comfort the bereaved, the Bundrens are expected to assume the traditional role of mourners, a role which carries with it unspoken rules of propriety and decorum. Only Anse, for whom Addie never existed as an individual, finds such a role congenial. His face tragic and composed, he easily makes the proper responses to condolences and recites his

1. Numbers indicate page references to the Modern Library edition, 1946.

litany of grief, though somewhat marred by his irrepressible egotism. There is even a sense in which Anse thoroughly enjoys the situation since as chief mourner he is, for once in his life, a person of importance. It is not, however, that simple for Addie's sons, who find that the conventions of mourning and burial can neither channel nor contain their grief. Thus, Cora Tull, the self-appointed champion and arbiter of propriety, finds that each of them fails, at some point, to behave in a fitting manner.

Because the agonizing journey to Jefferson does fulfill the promise to Addie, because it does reunite her in death with her family, some critics have seen in it an inspiring gesture of humanity or a heroic act of traditional morality. In reality, however, the journey from beginning to end is a travesty of the ritual of interment. Any ritual, as Addie herself suggests, can become a travesty, even though it has been ordained and sanctioned in its fixed order from the beginning of time. Since there is no virtue attached simply to the meticulous repetition of its words and gestures, it is the individual who must give meaning and life to ritual by recognizing its symbolic function. But the spirit which should give meaning to Addie's funeral is either absent, as in Anse and Dewey Dell, or in conflict with it, as in Cash and Darl. As this becomes clear, the series of catastrophes that befall the Bundrens becomes a source of macabre humor, for it is only when the ritual is disengaged from its symbolic function that the comic aspect becomes apparent.

Awareness of the difference between empty and significant ritual, framed in terms of the word and the act, dominates Addie Bundren's dying thoughts. She concludes that any experience—love, marriage, motherhood, bereavement—can be either an intensely felt reality or a mere conventional form of speech and behavior. The ritual of the word attempts to impose an order and a significance on experience, while the ritual of the act allows them to emerge from it. While Anse talks about his trials and his grief, Cash, Darl, and Jewel, each in his own way, express the meaning of love and bereavement through their actions which frequently come in conflict with accepted and acceptable forms of behavior. This contrast, sustained throughout the funeral journey, is a confirmation of Addie's perception of "how words go straight up in a thin line, quick and harmless, and how terribly doing goes along the earth, clinging to it, so that after a while the two lines are too far apart for the same person to straddle from one to the other." (465) Words need not, however, be empty providing they are grounded in non-verbal experience. It is when this condition is not met that they tend to be separated from and ultimately to replace the act. There are, as Addie realizes, both "the words [that] are the deeds, and the other words that are not deeds, that are just the gaps in peoples' lacks." (466)

Addie and Anse themselves represent the two polar opposites of action and words which must be meshed if their relationship is to be meaningful. The word by itself leads to a paralysis of the ability to feel and act; the act by itself results in excessive and uncontrolled responses to various stimuli both internal and external. Addie and Anse, however, are not able to effect this fusion of word and act. Because they are "husband" and "wife," Anse feels no need to establish a personal relationship which would give significance to those words and to the ritual of marriage. He is completely blind to Addie's intense desire for life and to her conviction that language is a grotesque tautology which prevents any real communication.

The birth of Cash confirms her feeling that words are irrelevant and that only physical experience has reality and significance. Through the act of giving birth she becomes part of the endless cycle of creation and destruction, discovering that, for the first time, her "aloneness had been violated and then made whole again by the violation." (464) Yet accepting Cash as the sign of her own passionate involvement in experience implies a total rejection of Anse who is now father as well as husband in name only. Because Addie accepts the fact that she and Anse live in different worlds, her second child, Darl, comes as the ultimate and unforgivable outrage. Addie, however, quickly disowns the thought of Anse as the deliberate agent of her betrayal; they have both been "tricked by words older than Anse or love." (464) Precisely what these words are is not clear, but what they signify for Addie is quite apparent. Primarily, she realizes that the ritual of the word does have its repercussions in the world of experience, and on this basis she is able to distinguish between the empty words of Anse and the words which are deeds.

Her sudden and brief affair with Whitfield constitutes Addie's attempt to explore this new relationship between words and acts, for it encompasses even as it differentiates between two quite distinct conceptions of sin. As a word, sin is the opposite of virtue and leads inevitably to damnation. It is this aspect which Addie stresses when she thinks of sin as garments which she and Whitfield wear in the face of the world and which they remove "in order to shape and coerce the terrible blood to the forlorn echo of the dead word high in the air." (466) But as an act, sin may be a step toward salvation. Accordingly, Whitfield becomes "the instrument ordained by God who created the sin, to sanctify that sin He had created." (466) The adultery thus becomes a moral act, not, of course, in the sense of "good" or "virtuous," but in the sense that it re-establishes the reality of moral conduct and of the relationship between God and man. This reality is neither linguistic nor factual in character; instead, it consists of the possible, the hypothetical, the conceivable, all, in short, that follows from the capacity for unrestricted choice. Significantly, Addie sees in Jewel, the child of her sin, a sign of grace: " 'He is my cross and he will be my salvation. He will save me from the water and from the fire. Even though I have laid down my life, he will save me.' " (460) Through sin Addie seeks to find and enact her own humanity, and if her solution seems extreme, so is her provocation. For the alternative, as she sees it, is the moral myopia of those who live by words "because people to whom sin is just a matter of words, to them salvation is just words too." (468)

After her desperate effort to explore and encompass the potentialities of life in one intensely felt act, she is ready to set her house in order. She consciously and deliberately gives Anse Dewey Dell to "negative" Jewel and Vardaman to replace him. Yet in a deep and profound sense, Anse can never claim or share in the lives of any of his children and this gives her a final moment of exhilarated realization: "My children were of me alone, of the wild blood boiling along the earth, of me and of all that lived; of none and of all." (467) Through her, life itself has effected its own continuance and in that process the mother-child relationship has its roots. Two of the children, however, are hers in an additional sense, for she has chosen them for a relationship that is personal as well as maternal. There is an unspoken understanding between herself and Cash. The same understanding, though no longer peaceful, exists between her and Jewel. In both cases the relationship is simple and direct, uninterrupted by conventional expressions of familial sentiments.

The circumstances of the birth of her children establish the level of their awareness of Addie and the mode of their response to and participation in her burial. Through an unconscious identification with her, they faithfully reproduce, though in varying degree, her very moods as well as her attitude to the external world. Jewel comes closest to recreating one aspect of her character, while Dewey Dell and Vardaman, the children reserved for Anse, seem least directly involved with her as a person. The structure of *As I Lay Dying* in which the progression is centrifugal as well as linear implements this pattern. Centrifugally, each section establishes the relationship between Addie and the character whose thoughts and observations are being recorded. Linearly, each section contributes to the sequence of actions and events which constitutes the plot. Furthermore, the separation of word and deed which Addie has recounted is dramatized in the journey to Jefferson. Anse undertakes a moral pilgrimage but solely on the verbal level. Inarticulate except when he is cursing, it is Jewel who rushes into action each time there is a new barrier to be overcome or a new catastrophe to be countered. The rest of the family move between these two extremes.

Because Anse lives by words alone, Addie has no influence over him except when she ironically exacts a promise which is a word but which will compel him to act. All that saves him from equating the deed with the word and the intention with the achievement of it is his own desire for new teeth and Jewel's savage determination to perform the promised act. At the first sign of difficulty he falls back on his inexhaustible stock of moral platitudes to isolate himself effectively from the horrors of the journey, to avoid any exertion on his part, and to maneuver others into acting for him. Incapable of formulating any plan or initiating any action, he depends on his sons to overcome each new obstacle. If they fail, there are always the neighbors to come to his rescue. Certainly the neighbors can do nothing but help when confronted by his covert pleas couched in the language of forbearance: " 'I ain't asking you to risk your mule. It ain't your dead; I am not blaming you.' " (436) His words create an image of himself as the meek and magnanimous victim forgiving a cruel and heartless world. To refuse him help after this is to admit the validity of his remarks and therefore, by implication, their own hardheartedness. They see through his verbal camouflage, but since it is based on emotional and moral clichés to which the response is predetermined, they are helpless before it.

From the beginning the distance between what Anse says and what he does is ironically and humorously emphasized. The irony is, however, most apparent in the scene of Addie's burial. Having had his promise to her fulfilled for him, he makes a short funeral oration. His words and his sentiments as he expresses his grief, though a trifle marred by self-pity, are appropriate to the occasion and to his role as chief mourner: " 'The somebody you was young with and you growed old in her and she growed old in you, seeing the old coming on and it was the one somebody you could hear say it don't matter and know it was the truth outen the hard world and all a man's grief and trials. You all don't know.' " (511) But it is simply a verbal sincerity, unrelated to the act and therefore to the kind of truth that arises out of and touches the heart directly and immediately. Lacking these, his words, like his expression, constitute "a monstrous burlesque of all bereavement." (394) The lament for Addie is followed by his unwillingness to buy a shovel for digging her grave; and even before her body has been placed in it, he has found a new wife to reassure him in his old age. These ironic incongruities are profoundly in keeping with Anse's character. Cushioned by words and conventional sentiments against the harsh impact of reality, he is the only one of the Bundrens completely unchanged by Addie's death or by the funeral journey. The horrors which drive Darl into insanity and leave their mark on the others pass him by so that he avoids agony and insight alike.

In contrast to his father, Cash undergoes certain very clear and definite changes as a result of Addie's death and funeral. Apparently reflecting Addie's rejection of words at the time of his birth, Cash begins by being silent, absorbed in his work, and curiously remote from the tensions and violence of the rest of the family. It is only after something concrete has been accomplished that he speaks. As a carpenter, Cash is concerned with working with his hands and building well; as Addie's son, he uses those hands and that skill to express what she means to him. Thus, the construction of the coffin becomes an act of love, understood as such by Addie, in which emotion tempered by reason is manifested in a concrete form. The sense of proportion which guides his hands also distinguishes his behavior and makes him the inevitable peacemaker in the family. Yet admirable as these characteristics are, Cash is, at the outset, a curiously stiff and one-sided figure. By devoting all his energy to and expressing his emotions through his work, he leaves no room for the cultivation of imaginative or linguistic potentialities. If Anse represents words without action, Cash is action in search of a word. Accordingly, a whole realm of human awareness and response is closed to him.

Cash does, however, develop a more comprehensive understanding of himself and his world. His exclusive preoccupation with concrete tangible objects yields to a more flexible, imaginative vision. The violence he suffers is, if not the cause, then the means of this profound transformation. The twice broken leg and the pain which he accepts without protest, as Addie had accepted the violence of his birth, pave the way for the extension of his range of awareness and for his increased sensitivity both to events and to people. The process is accelerated by the fact that his traditional mode of response, constructive action, is suddenly denied him. Lying helplessly on the coffin, his leg encased in cement and jarred by every turn of the wheel, he is forced to seek new forms of expression.

The increasing range of Cash's awareness is suggested by his growing sympathy with Darl. Facing the flooded river, they "look at one another with long probing looks, looks that plunge unimpeded through one another's eyes and into the ultimate secret place." (439) In that moment crossing the river becomes more than a problem of finding ways and means; Cash begins to realize that the prolonged journey is, in effect, destroying the significance it should affirm. During their stay at the Gillespies', Cash and Darl once more share the same revulsion and repudiation of the family's obsession with fulfilling the letter of the promise to Addie. Although it is Darl who sets fire to the barn, Cash accepts the responsibility as his own because he is the elder and because he too had contemplated the same violent act. Accepting this responsibility is one more step in his recognition of the complexity of those moral and emotional qualities which inhere in men's actions. Accordingly, he alone comprehends that the judgment of Darl's attempt to destroy the coffin and of Jewel's grim effort to save it must depend upon whether the body is viewed realistically or symbolically. Darl's action issues from his conviction that the corpse has long since become an offense to God and man, Jewel's from the equally strong emotional conviction that the coffin contains his mother. Combined with his own firm foundation in action and the concrete details of his trade, this increase of sensitivity and imaginative perception makes Cash the one character in the novel who achieves his full humanity in which reason and intuition, words and action merge into a single though complex response.

Darl, the second son and the most complicated of the Bundrens, faithfully reflects and dramatizes Addie's attitude at the time of his birth. She had believed, a belief later qualified, that reality lay only in physical experience and that the word and the act were polar opposites. Feeling Darl to be an outrage, she had denied him a place in her affections and in her world. Consequently, Darl's is a world of consciousness exclusively, and this, of course, renders his connection with the external world increasingly precarious and insecure. He exists in a kind of limbo where the firm, defining shape of objects and of people is continually dissolving. Only by a painful process of reasoning can he establish the physical existence of himself, his mother, and the loaded wagon: "Yet the wagon *is,* because when the wagon is *was,* Addie Bundren will not be. And Jewel *is,* so Addie Bundren must be. And then I must be, or I could not empty myself for sleep in a strange room." (396) This attempt to define objective reality is an index of Darl's separation from it.

But the same absence of defining and limiting outline permits Darl to penetrate the minds of others and to intuit those secret thoughts of which they themselves are scarcely aware. Twice, while he himself is absent, he apprehends the actions of Cash, Anse, and Dewey Dell as they cluster around the dying Addie and describes them with startling vividness. And at every moment he is able to expose, with merciless accuracy, the secret thoughts and motives of others. He knows that Jewel is the son of Addie's sin, a fact with which he repeatedly taunts the latter by asking, "Who is your father, Jewel?" More important, he knows that the horse Jewel caresses and curses is a surrogate for Addie. Similarly, he is aware of Dewey Dell's pregnancy. In both cases his knowledge forces them to face certain facts about themselves and their world. Unwilling to do so, Jewel relieves his mounting frustration in the violence of curses, while Dewey Dell finds temporary release in a fantasy of murder. Both join in the vicious physical attack on Darl when they arrive in Jefferson. Addie's rejection of him is thus repeated: with the exception of Vardaman, who is too young to know what is happening, each of the Bundrens contributes to the decision to send Darl to Jackson. As Cash's final, unacrimonious assessment suggests, the rejection is inevitable: "This world is not his world; this life his life." (532)

As Darl loses contact with the external world and with objective reality, his resemblance to Vardaman becomes more pronounced. When the wagon reaches the Gillespies', their sections are juxtaposed five times. The two of them have reached an understanding which is beyond logic and reason. Just before the fire their attitudes toward Addie become identical: as Vardaman states in one scene and Darl repeats in the next, Addie is stirring in her coffin. Darl's own intention becomes clear as he informs Vardaman that she is asking God " 'to hide her away from the sight of man. . . . So she can lay down her life.' " (495) Their shared delusion suggests that for both of them the world of fantasy has become as real as the concrete facts which we call reality.

Yet Darl's delusion is grounded in the conviction that the funeral has become an unbearable travesty of filial piety. Addie's imagined but not unreasonable request prompts him to abandon his usual role as spectator. Thought and action are fused, though in a particularly violent way. Depending on one's point of view, his action becomes a sign either of a deranged mind or of an acute moral sensibility, an ambiguity recognized by Cash who reflects: "Sometimes I ain't so sho who's got ere a right to say when a man is crazy and when he ain't. Sometimes I think it ain't none of us pure crazy and ain't none of us pure sane until the balance of us talks him that-a-way." (510) Action, the basis of individual moral conduct, is subject to social judgments and these are implemented through langauge. Hence, though Cash understands and is sympathetic to Darl's gesture of protest, he is forced to conclude that society's judgment is the only possible one.

Although Jewel is the most closely connected with Addie and the most active during the journey, only one section is devoted to his stream of consciousness. The reason for this is that his world is least accessible to public scrutiny since it consists of a welter of emotions, centering on Addie, which cannot be communicated. These emotions are not subjected to the control of reason but are translated immediately into actions which, unlike Cash's carefully planned moves, are the products of spontaneous reflexes. Whether the results of such actions are destructive or constructive in any given instance is a matter of chance. Thus, his is the blame for perpetuating the horrors of the journey and his the credit for forcing it to a successful conclusion. It is significant that when the stimulus to action is removed, when Addie's corpse is buried and Darl committed to an insane asylum, Jewel's fury subsides except for brief spasms of irritation caused by some word or gesture of Anse's.

Because Jewel is himself largely unconscious of his own motives and emotional compulsions, it is Darl who expresses them. As Darl keeps reiterating, Jewel has no father. Addie, then, becomes the sole center of his emotional life. There is, however, no way in which Jewel's violent feelings can be channelled into socially acceptable rituals. Seeing, as usual, only the surface meaning of actions, Cora Tull mistakes his despair for indifference. But when Jewel's own thoughts are revealed, they are seen to be devoted entirely to Addie. He imagines the two of them defiantly and violently isolated from the world and its interference. Most of Jewel's subsequent actions are, in effect, attempts to make this fantasy a reality and so to claim exclusive possession of Addie. Dewey Dell, Vardaman, and Anse, he simply ignores; but each time he meets Cash it is to override the latter's caution with his own impetuous activity. As for the neighbors, they are kept at a distance by his coldness and his deliberate insults. Even the genuinely helpful and sympathetic Tull is repulsed. Only Darl cannot be excluded from his private world and he is finally eliminated by being sent to Jackson.

This process of exclusion merely intensifies Jewel's emotional attachment to Addie without providing a release for it. The latter he finds in the wild horse which he tames and on which he can lavish his love and inflict his hatred. Because the horse is actually his possession, he can and does isolate himself and it from all contact with others. No one except himself is permitted to feed, care for, or even touch it. In a sense, the horse perpetuates Addie's emotional relationship with Jewel. Because of this identification, Jewel insists on bringing the horse with him despite Anse's protests and Darl's oblique taunts. And when he finally sells it to pay for a new team, the full intensity of his feeling reverts to Addie. This explains why he is almost prevented by his concern for the horse from rescuing Addie's coffin out of the river, whereas during the fire all his energies are directed solely toward saving it.

In sharp contrast to Jewel, Dewey Dell seems the least concerned with Addie's death and funeral. Addie, however, had revealed the same impersonal and unemotional attitude toward Dewey Dell when she stated that she had given Dewey Dell to Anse in order to "negative" Jewel. In a way, Dewey Dell has no need of Addie because she herself is recreating Addie's past and discovering that pregnancy is both a state of mind and a physical fact, both a word and an action. But unlike Addie, she is determined, if possible, to effect their separation. Thus, she will not name her condition even to herself because to do so would be to transfer her pregnancy from her private world of awareness to the public world of fact.

Yet it is only by admitting the physical reality of her pregnancy and by making it, at least to some extent, public that she can do anything to terminate it. The problem is focussed for her by the presence of Peabody. By destroying the physical evidence of her pregnancy, Peabody would become a witness to its reality, a reality which would be perpetuated in his consciousness. She avoids telling Peabody, but Darl, unfortunately, already knows. Her desire to destroy Darl and with him his knowledge is first expressed in fantasy: "I rose and took the knife from the steaming fish still hissing and I killed Darl." (423) This is followed by her savage physical attack on him and by her determination to have him sent to Jackson. Darl's departure does not, of course, solve anything for Dewey Dell, but it does postpone the need for immediate decision and action. Because there is no one present who knows of her pregnancy, she can act, for the time being, as if it did not exist. As she sits on the wagon, placidly munching a banana, her mind relapses into its normal state, that of the minimal level of conscious thought.

The limitations of Vardaman's mind are of a different order; they are those of the youngest child, who is bewildered by a phenomenon completely new to him. Out of the various sensations that he experiences and the facts that he observes while Addie is dying, he attempts to define for himself the meaning of death. He can do this only by constructing analogies to what he already knows or remembers. But because Vardaman is limited largely to sensations, he is not able to pass from the concrete to the general and abstract. What begins as an analogy ends as an identification. Addie and the fish are linked by death and therefore, according to his own particular logic, what happens to one happens to the other: "Then it wasn't and she was, and now it is and she wasn't. And tomorrow it will be cooked and et and she will be him and pa and Cash and Dewey Dell and there won't be anything in the box and so she can breathe." (386) Eventually the dead fish and the dead mother fuse into a single thought: "My mother is a fish." Knowing that he himself is the cause and instrument of the fish's death, Vardaman seeks to find the agent responsible for Addie's death. Selecting Doctor Peabody, he gains his revenge by mistreating the doctor's horses.

Still arguing from analogy, Vardaman remembers the lack of air in the corn crib and assumes that his mother, now confined in the coffin, must feel a similar lack. Drilling holes in the coffin thus becomes a reasonable and humane act, an expression of his concern for his mother. Though certain of Vardaman's acts seem to border on the insane, he himself is not. He is a child, sensitive and even intelligent, who is exposed to a tremendous shock. And in meeting it, he has neither precedent nor advice to guide him. It is, therefore, almost inevitable that he should arrive at a distorted conception of death and that his actions, having their source in that concept, should appear grotesque and incongruous. Certainly Vardaman suffers from a delusion but an understandable one since it permits him to dissociate his mother from the horrors of physical death and decay: *"My mother is not in the box. My mother does not smell like that. My mother is a fish."* (483)

Through the interaction of the characters the complexity of the central situation is evoked, and through an understanding of those complexities, the motivation and hence the credibility of the characters is established. At the end, we see them in terms of their relationship to Addie and to each other, "sitting bolt upright in [their] nakedness, staring at one another and saying 'Now is the truth.' " (433) The private world of each of the Bundrens has been exposed, partly by their own actions and partly by Darl's constant probing. With his departure and the burial of Addie's corpse, the period of tension ends. The new wife, the gramophone, the memory of the toy trains, and the bananas do not replace Addie, but they do indicate a shift in the family's focus of consciousness. It is through the inception of such new patterns that the characters seek to avoid too close, protracted, and painful a scrutiny of the meaning of life and death.

Addie's death and her funeral are construed in terms of the family's varied levels and modes of consciousness, but they also possess a wider frame of reference, for the actions of the Bundrens project both death and funeral into the public world. It is in his capacity of responding to the Bundrens and their funeral procession that Faulkner introduces his eight reverberators. Mosely and MacGowan reveal two contrasting attitudes to Dewey Dell's pregnancy. The former responds to her request for pills with self-righteous moral indignation; the latter unhesitatingly takes advantage of what he conceives to be an essentially comic situation. Between them they indicate the range of possible social reactions to and judgments of her condition. Quite obviously, neither Mosely nor MacGowan is concerned with Dewey Dell as a person; they respond only to the fact that she is clearly somewhat stupid, pregnant, and unmarried.

In Samson, Armstid, and Tull, the purely social and moral judgment is tempered by personal knowledge of the Bundrens. They are, in fact, themselves implicated to some extent in the funeral. There is a kind of humororus despair in their frustrating knowledge that Anse has and will continue to take advantage of their neighborliness. Tull, for example, remarks: "Like most folks around here, I done holp him so much already I can't quit now." (360) Each of these men describes a stage in the journey to Jefferson in terms of his contribution to it. Significantly, as individuals, they are appalled by the horrifying physical aspects of Addie's decaying body; but as neighbors, they feel obligated to offer their help in continuing the journey. With the burning of Gillespie's barn, however, the limits of neighborliness are reached.

In contrast to the three men, Cora Tull and Whitfield see the Bundrens solely in terms of their own ethical systems. It is fitting, therefore, that Addie's soliloquy, with its emphasis on the separation of the word and the act, should be flanked by their moralizing and empty rhetoric. Fearing that he will be forced at last to face Anse, Whitfield is intent upon finding the right words for framing his confession. Yet the moment he learns that Addie has not betrayed their secret, all thoughts of confession leave his mind. He is once more free to act as if he had never violated the moral code of his community since the public world is still unaware of his guilt. As for the sin against God, a verbal apology is sufficient: "He will accept the will for the deed, Who knew that when I framed the words of my confession it was to Anse I spoke them, even though he was not there." (469) Confession, repentance, and even penance are carried out in his mind, thereby obviating any necessity of embracing them in an act. Anse's own formula of verbal evasion is thus, ironically, turned against him.

Whitfield's account of his relationship with Addie is rendered wholly in terms of ethical and religious clichés from which all human passion and meaning has been carefully deleted. Similarly, everything about Addie, her family, and her death is but another moral lesson to be interpreted by Cora Tull as she elbows her way to heaven. Having learned her ethics by rote, Cora has no difficulty in affixing praise and blame or in predicting salvation or damnation for all whom she meets. Though she consigns Addie and her family to the latter category, she is consistently and determinedly helpful. Her help, however, is offered in the name of duty not love, and it is meant, whether she realizes it or not, to be one more step in establishing her own virtue and her own right to salvation. Kindness such as Cora's is essentially selfish, debasing both the giver and the recipient and destroying the possibility of any personal relationship between them. In her eyes even family ties are moral rather than emotional. As a result, Cora is totally unaware, in any real sense, of those agonizing and exalting human experiences which stand outside her rigid system of ethics, resisting and disrupting its smooth simplification of existence.

Of all the characters who observe and comment on the actions of the Bundrens, Doctor Peabody is the most judicious. Although Tull's remarks often contain shrewd assessments of specific events, it is Peabody who grasps their broader significance. His insight is the result of long and varied experience with people compelled to face the realities of pain, suffering, and death. Thus, when he makes separate evaluations of life, love, and death, his statements serve as a general guide for interpreting the actions of the family. His is the compassionate but detached vision of the country doctor-cum-philosopher. Yet when he is suddenly confronted with the Bundrens in Jefferson, he loses his philosophic objectivity. Overwhelmed by the massing of concrete horrors and sensations, he reacts with bitter indignation.

While acting as reverberator for the actions of the Bundrens, these eight characters offer release from the tension through humorous or ironic remarks. Because only the actions of the Bundrens and not their thoughts and emotions are perceived, they become grotesques. What is horror and pain for the family becomes farce for those who are not themselves involved and who merely observe with the physical eye. For the Bundrens, the journey seethes with unresolved tensions; for the townspeople of Mottson, it is only a ridiculous or macabre spectacle. This intermingling of humor and horror, which is part of the very texture of *As I Lay Dying*, issues out of the Bundrens' conviction that their actions are eminently reasonable and out of the spectators' conviction that the Bundrens and their coffin have long since passed beyond the realm of reason, logic, or even commonsense. The juxtaposition of the two views gives rise to a complicated and ambivalent feeling of hilarity and despair. Confronted with the irrational, the rational mind finds itself bewildered and uneasy, indignant and outraged, or simply wryly amused. As the funeral journey is prolonged, all these attitudes are exhibited.

The interplay of seriousness which reaches toward tragedy and of humor which is practically farce is part of the complete success of *As I Lay Dying*. In a sense, it reinforces the theme of the separation of words and acts by insisting on at least these two modes of response to the same set of characters and events. At the same time, it precludes any easy generalizations about the funeral journey itself. Any event or series of events elicits various and, at times, contradictory responses. The meaning of an experience as distinct from a word exists in the consciousness of the individual observer. Accordingly, it is only when one becomes conscious of the mingling of humor and pathos, of the relation of the Bundrens to Addie, and of the observers to the action that the full complexity of *As I Lay Dying* is plumbed and Faulkner's easy mastery of it recognized.

# THE STILLNESS OF
## *LIGHT IN AUGUST*

### ALFRED KAZIN

*Light in August* begins unforgettably with a pregnant young woman from Alabama sitting beside a road in Mississippi, her feet in a ditch, her shoes in her hand, watching a wagon that is mounting the hill toward her with a noise that carries for a half mile "across the hot still pine-winey silence of the August afternoon." She has been on the road for a month, riding in a long succession of farmwagons or walking the hot dusty roads with

Reprinted with permission from *Twelve Original Essays on Great American Novels*, edited by Charles Shapiro (Detroit: Wayne State University Press, 1958), pp. 257-83.

her shoes in her hand, trying to get to Jefferson. There, she firmly expects, she will find her lover working in a planing mill and ready to marry her, and there—that is the big city—she will put her shoes on at last.

This opening chapter, so dry and loving in its pastoral humor, centering on the picture of Lena and her precious burden being carried in one wagon or another, by one farmer after another, to her hoped-for destination in a husband, ends sharply on the outskirts of Jefferson, from which she can see smoke going up from a burning house. It is the house of Joanna Burden, who has just been murdered by Joe Christmas. The images that have crowded us—the dust and heat of the unending road; the young woman continually amazed at how far a body can go; the serenity of her face, "calm as a stone, but not hard"; the "sharp and brittle crack and clatter" of identical and anonymous wagons "weathered and ungreased wood and metal"; the mules plodding in a steady and unflagging hypnosis; the drowsy heat of the afternoon; Lena's faded blue dress, her palm leaf fan, her small bundle in which she carries thirty-five cents in nickels and dimes, and the shoes that she takes off and carries in her hand as soon as she feels the dust of the road beneath her feet—all these, we soon discover, provide us with that foundation in the local and the provincial, the earth and the road which man must travel on it, against which are set images of fire and murder, of aimless wandering and of flight, embodied in the figure who soon enters the book and dominates it in his remorseless gray anonymity. Joe Christmas does not even have a name of his own, only a mocking label stuck on him at the orphanage where he was deposited one Christmas Eve. "Joe Christmas" is worse than any real name could be, for it indicates not only that he has no background, no roots, no name of his own, but that he is regarded as a *tabula rasa,* a white sheet of paper on which anyone can write out an identity for him and make him believe it.

It is the contrast of Lena Grove and Joe Christmas, of the country girl and the American wanderer, who is a stranger even to himself, the ultimate personification of modern loneliness, that frames the book— literally so, since Lena Grove begins and ends it, while Joe Christmas' agony and crucifixion are enacted as within a circle round which he runs in an effort to catch up with himself. When he finds that he cannot run out of this circle and stands still at last in order to die, the book comes back to Lena Grove and ends on her ritualistic procession up the road with her baby and Byron Bunch—Faulkner's version of the Holy Family. By the time we have finished *Light in August,* we have come to feel that the real greatness of Faulkner in this book (and indeed of his extraordinary compassion) lies in the amazing depth which he brings to this contrast of which American writers—particularly in the South—are so fond: between the natural and the urban, between Lena Grove's simplicity and the world in which Joe Christmas walks all city pavements with the same isolation and indifference, eats at the coldly smooth wooden counter, and is murdered. Faulkner even leads up to a strange and tortured fantasy of Joe Christmas as Lena Grove's still unnamed son. There is virtually an annunciation to Lena, in the moving last phase of the book when Lena, delivered of her child just as Joe Christmas is running for his life, hears Mrs. Hines, Christmas's grandmother, calling the baby "Joey"— he who is a "nigger" murderer, and whom Lena has never seen. The reader comes to this with a shock, only because of Faulkner's reckless, desperate eagerness to wrest all the possible implications from his material, to think it out interminably, since there is no end to all one's possible meditations round and round the human cycle. One of the conflicts of which the book is made—between life and anti-life, between the spirit of birth and the murderous abstractions and obsessions which drive most of the characters—is in Faulkner himself, in his attempt to will his painful material into a kind of harmony that it does not really possess.

But in any event, it is Lena who opens the book, Lena's world, Lena's patience, that set the ideal behind the book—that world of the permanent and the natural which Joe Christmas seeks all his life without knowing that he does, and seeking it, runs full tilt into the ground. "Light in August" is itself a country saying: light as a mare or cow is light after delivery. And it is this world of Lena Grove from Doane's Mill—the tiny hamlet too small for any post-office list, though Lena, living in the backwoods, had not seen it until her parents died—with the sound of the wagon wheel taking her away from it, that becomes in the book not merely a world that Faulkner celebrates but a mythic source of strength. As indeed it is. For it is this intense sense of the earth, this superb registering of country sights and sounds as the stillness is broken by the creaking and lumbering wagon coming up the hill, that is the secret of Southern writing. In his attachment to the irretrievable, in his obstinate feeling for the earth, the good Southern writer makes so much writing in America seem as shallow as if it had been composed by a young instructor in English sitting in his study surrounded by manuals on the great novels. Albert Camus, talking appreciatively about Southern novelists, once remarked to a friend of mine that what he liked about their books was "the dust and the heat."

And to the man from North Africa, with his memories of the blazing world described in *Noces,* that world into which Paris can never enter, Faulkner's sense of local color must be especially moving. But after all, it is this sense of place that is the great thing about American writing. It is the "mossy scabs of the worm fence, heap'd stones, elder, mullein and pokeweed" in *Song of Myself*; the landscape that in *Walden* seems always to be reflected in water; the strong native sense of the here and now that is the basis of Emerson's esthetic; the edge of the world seen from Hemingway's Michigan woods; "reading the river" in *Life on the Mississippi* and *Huckleberry Finn*; the "snow, the real snow" seen only beyond Chicago that Scott Fitzgerald described so rapturously in his memories of Midwesterners in Eastern colleges going home for Christmas. And if we ask what is so remarkable about that sense of place which is, after all, essential to imaginative writing, the answer is that we Americans are in fact just the opposite of the homogeneous mass we are always trying to be, and that what distinguishes American writing is exactly the fact that we are strangers to each other and that each writer describes his own world to strangers living in the same land with himself.

Now of all parts of the United States the South is certainly the strangest to the others; it is, in fact—or used to be—a separate nation. And almost all the good Southern writers have this sense of local color to an extreme, for to the degree that the South is what it is because of its rural background, its "backwardness," its isolation, its comparatively homogeneous white population—to that degree does the American's need to value and venerate his own region or place as the only escape from American bigness, American smoothness, American abstractness, American slogans, the juggernaut of American progress, find (at least it used to find) its deepest expression in the South. Even poverty, which in America certainly is a disgrace, becomes in Southern writing a sign of the natural man (Huckleberry Finn) or the earth-mother (Lena Grove). And, as so often happens in Southern writing—for sensitive Southerners are likely to feel that they are lost in the modern industrial world and, in mourning their traditional homeland, to see the immediate world around them as damned—Faulkner's pictures of the impersonal modern world, the opposite of Lena's sacred grove, are lurid. As Lena is all fertility, so the others are all barrenness. Destruction, fire, obsession, inhumanity, anonymity, the "friction-smooth" wooden counter at which Joe Christmas eats, the hard cold eyes of Bobbie the prostitute and Mame the madam and Max the pimp—these against the images of locality, the farmers in their faded and patched but clean overalls, and of time, the wagon along the road and the "heelgnawed porch" of the country store around which farmers sit. As soon as we get to Jefferson, we catch the typical dialectic of life and anti-life, the contrast of birth and destruction on which the book is built, in the fact that the slow patient rhythms of Lena, the wagon, the road, are immediately followed by the whine of the saw in the planing mill, the reiteration of *smooth*. The world is narrowing down to the contest between the good Christian laborer, Byron Bunch, the very essence of the common ordinary good man, and those who, like Lena's seducer, have either taken on a name which is not their own, "Brown," a name too conventional even to be *his* name, or who, like Joe Christmas, have no name to begin with.

This contrast is familiar enough in Southern opinion, and one can find the same horror of miscegenation, of uprooting, of the city man's anonymity, in any expression of Southern agrarianism. But Faulkner does not stop at the abstraction of the alien: he carries it on, he carries it out to astonishing lengths. And it is this intensity of conception that makes the portrait of Joe Chrismas so compelling rather than believable, that makes him a source of wonder, of horror, yet above all of pity, rather than of pleasure in the creation of a real human being. For Joe Christmas remains, as he is born, an abstraction; from the moment he appears, "there was something definitely rootless about him, as though no town nor city was his, no street, no walls, no square of earth his home." He comes to work in the only clothes he has, a serge suit and a white shirt; and Byron Bunch, watching him, knows that Joe Christmas "carried his knowledge with him always as though it were a banner, with a quality ruthless, lonely, and almost proud." So from the moment Joe Christmas appears, he is seen as what others say about him, he is only a thought in other people's minds. More than this, he is looked at always from a distance, as if he were not quite human, which in many ways he is not.

*We* see Joe Christmas from a distance, and this distance is the actual space between him and his fellows. It is also the distance between the name "Joe Christmas," which is clownish, and the actual suffering of someone who has to live up to the non-humanity of his name, to the obsession (founded on hearsay, not on actual evidence) that his father had "some" Negro blood in him. Joe Christmas, then, is really "man" trying to discover the particular kind of man he is. He is an abstraction created by the racist mania of his grandfather, a former preacher whose tormented life is spent insisting that Negroes are guilty in the eyes of God and must serve white men. When his daughter ran away with a "Mexican" circus hand, Doc Hines not only killed the man, and after his daughter died in childbirth on Christmas Eve, left the baby on the steps of an orphanage, but later took a job as a janitor in the orphanage in order to make sure that his "nigger" grandson would never be allowed to contaminate anyone. This obsession about race goes hand in hand with a Calvinist obsession of the elect and of the hopeless sinfulness of others, an obsession which is found both in Joe Christmas' rigidly doctrinaire foster-father, Calvin McEachern, and in his future mistress, Joanna Burden, a descendant of New Hampshire Puritans who remains in the South though she is the sworn enemy of its ways. All these obsessions about purity and guilt are, Faulkner indicates, the remnants of an inhuman religion that has added bigotry and arrogance to the curse of slavery. They are the symbols of a church that has lost its spiritual function and that has been deserted by the Reverend Gail Hightower, who spends his days in endless reveries of the South's irretrievable glory. The obsessions are all summed up in the fate of Joe Christmas, who is trying to become *someone,* a human being, to find the integrity that is so ripely present in Lena Grove. Lena does not have to try; her symbol is the wheel on the road. Joe Christmas' is flight: flight on the same road, but flight toward himself, which he cannot reach, and away from hatred of himself, which he cannot escape. Only his pursuers catch up with him, to murder and to castrate him.

Joe Christmas is an abstraction seeking to become a human being. In the race-mad South, many a Negro—and Mexican, and Jew—is turned into an abstraction. But this man is *born* an abstraction and is seeking to become a person. He is an orphan, brought up in a foundling home, who in earliest childhood is watched by his own grandfather as if he were a caged beast. He is then bribed by the dietitian, whom he has heard making love with the interne, as if he knew enough to betray her. He is adopted by a farmer who re-names him, lectures him, starves him, beats him for not learning the catechism. He is robbed and beaten by the pimp of the prostitute with whom he has fallen in love. He is constantly treated by his Negrophile mistress, Joanna Burden, as if his own personality were of no account and is beseeched in her sexual transports as "Negro." And finally, after being starved, betrayed, flogged, beaten, pursued by bloodhounds, he is castrated. The essential picture behind Joe Christmas is his grandfather's carrying him to the orphanage and then from it in a savage parody of loving care. Joe Christmas is nothing but the man things are done to, the man who has no free will of his own, who is constantly seeking a moment of rest ("When have I ever eaten in peace?") and who looks for an identity by deliberately provoking responses that will let him be *someone,* if only as a white man among Negroes, or as someone calling himself a Negro in an effort to shock the white prostitute he has just slept with. His passivity, his ability to lend himself to situations and to people who will "carry" him for a while, is immense and pitiful.

Joe Christmas is the most solitary character in American fiction, the most extreme phase conceivable of American loneliness. He is never seen full face, but always as a silhouette, a dark shadow haunting others, a shadow upon the road he constantly runs—a foreshadowing of his cruci-fixion, which, so terrible and concentrated is his suffering, already haunts the lives of others like a black shadow. For, almost *because* he does not look it, he becomes the "Negro," or the thought of, the obsession with, Negroes in the minds of those who, looking at Joe Christmas, can think of nothing else. And Joanna Burden, whose abolitionist grandfather was murdered in the South, whose whole life has been an obstinate carrying on, deep inside Mississippi, of her family's coldly abstract espousal of Negroes, shows us how much of an abstraction Joe Christmas is when she makes love crying to him "Negro! Negro!" Whether the "Negro" represent the white man's guilt or the white man's fear, he is always a thought in the white's mind, and—in the South—an obsession. So Joanna Burden, who befriends him, and Doc Hines, who hates him, come to see in him the cause of guilt that is finally the image of guilt. "I thought," Joanna says to her lover,

of all the children coming forever and ever into the world, white, with the black shadow already falling upon them before they drew breath. And I seemed to see the black shadow in the shape of a cross. And it seemed like the white babies were struggling, even before they drew breath, to escape from the shadow that was not only upon them but beneath them, too, flung out like their arms were flung out, as if they were nailed to the cross.

And she quotes her father:

"In order to rise, you must raise the shadow with you. But you can never lift it to your level. I see that now, which I did not see until I came down here. But escape it you cannot. The curse of the black race is God's curse. But the curse of the white race is the black man who will be forever God's chosen own because He once cursed Him."

The grounds of this obsession, then, can be a compassion for the Negro that is as profound as hatred, and equally removed from brotherhood.

This compassion seems to me the essence of Faulkner's approach to Joe Christmas, and the triumph of the book is Faulkner's ability to keep his leading character a shadow, and yet to make us feel all his suffering. Compare Joe Christmas with the types of the Northerner, the city man, the "stranger" in Southern writing, to say nothing of the Negro, and you realize that where so many neo-orthodox Southern literary critics are hysterically fearful of the "stranger," Faulkner, by a tremendous and moving act of imagination, has found in Joe Christmas the incarnation of "man"— that is, of modern man, reduced entirely to his unsupported and inexplicable human feelings. There are no gods in Faulkner's world; there are only men—some entirely subject to circumstances, some protesting against them, and some even moved to change them. The hero of *A Fable* is of the last; Joe Christmas is of the first. He is human to us because of the experiences he undergoes, but his passivity is so great that he is finally a body castrated, a mere corpse on a dissection table—or someone whose body has been turned into the host, material for a ritual, so that his last agony will earn him the respect he never earned while he was alive. He is not, like the Christ of *A Fable,* a man who gives new meaning to life; like Benjy in *The Sound and the Fury,* he is an incarnation of human suffering, unable to speak—except in the tremendous action near the end of the book when he stops running from his pursuers and waits for them, and attains in this first moment of selfhood, the martyrdom that ends it.

We see Joe Christmas always from a distance. This distance from ourselves to him seems to me the key to the book, for it explains why Joe exists for us principally as a man who is described, not seen. He is so far away that we cannot see him; he is reported to us. And this distance is filled with the stillness of a continuous meditation. *Light in August* tells a story of violence, but the book itself is curiously soundless, for it is full of people thinking to themselves about events past. As soon as Lena Grove arrives in Jefferson, at the end of the first chapter, the story of Joe Christmas comes to us through flashbacks, through talk by the other men at the planing mill, through a whole chapter of summary biography, Chapter VI, through rumors and gossip of the townspeople, and at the very end, when Joe Christmas' whole story is put together for us, by Gavin Stevens' telling a stranger about the grandparents. Almost everything we learn about Joe Christmas comes to us in the form of hearsay, accusation, the tortured memories of others; even his death is told as an incident in the life of his murderer, Percy Grimm. All these reports about the stranger sufficiently suggest his alienation. But in themselves they also create that stillness, that depth of meditation into which all the characters are plunged. This meditation begins in Joe Christmas himself, who in his distance from other men is constantly trying to think himself back to life, and who, without knowing exactly how his ordeal began—and certainly not why— finds himself like a caged animal going over and over the same ground. We hear him talking to himself, and we follow his slow and puzzled efforts to understand the effect of his actions upon others. We see him as a child in the orphange, eating the toothpaste, frightening the dietitian out of her wits because he is staring straight at her trying to understand what she is accusing him of. We watch him walking the path between his cabin and Joanna Burden's house for his meals, thinking out everything he finds between the four walls of her kitchen. Finally we watch him running, and thinking deliriously in his flight, until, in that magnificent and piercing scene near the end of his flight, he falls asleep as he runs. The pressure of thought, the torture of thought, is overwhelming—and useless—since Joe Christmas does not know who he is and so cannot locate the first cause of his misery. But still he thinks, he broods, he watches, he waits. And it is this brooding silence in him, fixed in attention over he knows not what, that explains why he is so often described in the book as looking like a man in prayer—even like a "monk." There is a strange and dis- turbing stillness about him that eases him, more swiftly than most men, into the stillness of non-being.

The stillness of the book has, of course, an immense reverberation within it. Describing Doc Hines, Faulkner notes about him "a quality of outworn violence like a scent, an odor," and the actual violence of Joe Christmas is always felt about him even when he sits rigidly still at counters like a man in prayer. When Joe's past history is run off in the rapid newsreel style of Dos Passos, one feels not only his personal in- significance, but the just leashed violence of American life of which Joe is, in his way, completely the creature:

He stepped from the dark porch, into the moonlight, and with his bloody head and his empty stomach hot, savage, and courageous with whiskey, he entered the street which was to run for fifteen years.

The whiskey died away in time and was renewed and died again, but the street ran on. From that night the thousand streets ran as one street, with imperceptible corners and changes of scene, broken by intervals of begged and stolen rides, on trains and trucks, and on country wagons with he at twenty and twenty-five and thirty sitting on the seat with his still, hard face and the clothes (even when soiled and worn) of a city man and the driver of the wagon not knowing who or what the passenger was and not daring to ask.

Yet it is a stillness of thought that generally pervades the book, in the form of enormous meditations by which Faulkner tries to lift his material into place. The stillness is interrupted by shooting, burning, beating, the barking of bloodhounds and Percy Grimm's mutilation of Joe Christmas, which interrupts the pervading stillness like the sound which nails must make when they are driven into wood through human flesh. Yet, just behind this obvious figure of the Roman soldier torturing Christ, there is a pastoral world. As Irving Howe has noted, the arrangement of the book "resembles an early Renaissance painting—in the foreground a bleeding martyr, far to the rear a scene of bucolic peacefulness, with women quietly working in the fields." Despite its violence, *Light in August* is one of the few American novels that remind one of the humanized and tranquil landscape in European novels. Its stillness is rooted in the peaceful and timeless world which Lena Grove personifies and in which she has her being. It is the stillness of the personal darkness inside which Joe Christmas lives. But his stillness is also the sickly, after-dark silence of the Reverend Gail Hightower sitting in his study, with his stale clothes and stale thoughts, going over and over the tragedy of his life, his grandfather's "glorious" death, his wife's desertion and suicide—and finally and typically summing it all up into a stale round of human illusion and defeat. Faulkner wishes us to understand that Hightower finally cuts the gordian knot of his thoughts when he delivers Lena's baby and is struck down by Percy Grimm as he stands between him and Joe Christmas. But Hightower, whether brooding out upon the street, or sitting behind the green lamp in his parlor when he receives Byron Bunch, his only visitor, enlarges the stillness, increases its weight, by personifying what is immediately present in the book, and throughout Faulkner's novels—the Southern effort to explain, to justify, and through some consummation in violent physical action even to lighten, the burden of this obsession with the past.

Hightower, by general consent, is one of the failures of the book: he is too vague, too drooping, too formless, in a word too much the creature of defeat and of obsession, to compel our interest or our belief. But this is so partly because Hightower is both a surrogate figure for Faulkner's meditations and a kind of scapegoat on whom Faulkner can discharge his exasperation with Southern nostalgia and the endless searching in the labyrinths of the past for the explanation of the Southern defeat and of the hold it keeps on the descendants of the Confederate aristocracy. Hightower is a failure because Faulkner both uses and parodies him. Because of the absurdly literal symbolism of his name, his constant watchful position behind the green lamp, his useless reveries, he is never on the same scale with the other characters, who are equally obsessed by the past, but who function on the plane of some positive action. Hightower not only lives by his thoughts; he has no life but his thoughts. We miss in him the life-like element of violence (the only possible end to characters so entirely formed of reverie) that we find in Joanna Burden's degeneration, in Joe Christmas' hatred, in Percy Grimm's fanaticism, in Doc Hines's mania. Hightower, acting in various sections of the book as a foreground observer, brings to them not merely a stillness but a deadness which intervenes between us and the other characters. This shapeless, ghostly body of thought has its symbolic place in the mind of Hightower. For just as his life is over, and he has no function but to brood, so Faulkner has signified in Hightower that wholly retrospective, watchful concern, not with the past but with their bondage to the past, that seems to be the essence of what Faulkner's characters are always thinking about.

Joe Christmas, Joanna Burden, Gail Hightower—each of these is the prisoner of his own history, and is trying to come to terms with this servitude in his own mind. None of them can ever lift themselves out of the labyrinth by taking thought. But in this effort to think man's life out of the circumstances that enclose it, Faulkner sees the condition of man. Man is engulfed in events that are always too much for him. Hightower, listening to Byron Bunch make plans for Lena's confinement, thinks: "It is because so much happens. Too much happens. That's it. Man performs, engenders, so much more than he can or should have to bear. That's how he finds out that he can bear anything. That's it. That's what is so terrible. That he can bear anything, anything." Endurance, as we know, is the key-word in Faulkner's system of values. At least this was so up to *A Fable.* There, as Faulkner himself has told us, the highest value is represented not by the young Jewish pilot officer who says, "This is terrible. I refuse to accept it, even if I must refuse life to do so"; not by the old French quartermaster general who says, "This is terrible, but we can weep and bear it," but by the English battalion runner who says, "This is terrible, I'm going to do something about it." *Light in August* does not arrive at this step. Man never thinks of changing the world; it is all he can do to get a grip on it, to understand some part of what has happened to him and to endure all of it. Any release that occurs is a purely individual one, as when Hightower finally frees himself, in the one profoundly unselfish act of his life, by delivering Lena's baby. In the freshness of the early morning, after Lena has given birth, Hightower feels that he is in touch with the earth again—the symbol throughout the book of rightness, authenticity, peace. But the earth is not his life, as it is Lena Grove's. Man's highest aim in this book is to meet his destiny without everlasting self-concern. Yet this profoundly tragic cast to *Light in August,* so much like a Hardy novel in the implacable pattern that unrolls against a country background and the inarticulate stillness of its leading characters, is matched by Faulkner's ironic awareness that man, in his endless brooding over events, can never stop, that the event is nothing compared with the speculation that follows and in a sense replaces it. One of the most revealing phrases in Faulkner's rhetoric is: "not that"—it is not peace, not an end, that his people ever want. The violence may be "outworn," but it is the human passion. He describes his chorus, the townspeople, scurrying around Joanna Burden's house after her murder, looking "for someone to crucify":

But there wasn't anybody. She had lived such a quiet life, attended so to her own affairs, that she bequeathed to the town in which she had been born and lived and died a foreigner, an outlander, a kind of heritage of astonishment and outrage, for which, even though she had supplied them at last with an emotional barbecue, a Roman holiday almost, they would never forgive her and let her be dead in peace and quiet. Not that. Peace is not that often. So they moiled and clotted, believing that the flames, the blood, the body that had died three years ago and had now just begun to live again, cried out for vengeance, not believing that the rapt infury of the flames and the immobility of the body were both affirmations of an attained bourne beyond the hurt and harm of man. Not that.

We can never let the event go, for that would mean an end to the human history that is lived in retrospection. Just as Faulkner's language is full of words, like "avatar" and "outrage," which are really private symbols left over from his unceasing meditation, and just as his style is formed from the fierce inner pressure of problems which give no solution, so the actual texture of *Light in August* suggests, in the tension and repetition of certain verbal motifs, that man can never quite say what the event originally meant, or what he is to think of it now. Language never quite comes up to the meaning of events. To adapt Faulkner's phrase, it is not that, or that. The townspeople exist in *Light in August,* as in so many Faulkner novels, to ask questions whose very function is to deny the possibility of an answer. Faulkner's grim, sarcastic asides show that he views language as in some basic sense unavailing. The astounding repetition of

certain key phrases and verbal rhythms in his work signifies his return
back and back on the question.

Call the event history, call it the Fall: man is forever engaged in
meditating, not the past itself, for that would bring knowledge, but man's
guilt, for that may bring freedom. Guilt, not history, is the nightmare
from which all of Faulkner's deepest characters are trying to escape. The
guilt arises from man's endless complicity in his own history, as when the
innocent, gravely staring child that Joe Christmas was, ate toothpaste and
listened to the dietitian making love. Hightower is guilty because his sickly,
foolish nostalgia for his grandfather's one day of glory made him unavail-
able to his own wife, who committed suicide; Joanna Burden feels so guilty
that she has remained an alien in the Southern town in which she was
born, accepting her isolation as the price of her identification both with
her Abolitionist forebears, who were shot down in the South, and with
the Negroes, on whom a curse must have been laid. Even Doc Hines and
Percy Grimm murder in order to "clean" life of the stain that Negroes
have put on it, for as the Negroes were cursed by God, so they have
cursed life, and the maniac "saviors" of Southern racial purity have to
save their hallowed country from contagion. But just as no one of them can
really distinguish the hate they feel for others from self-accusation, so no
one can say with whom guilt began, where the ultimate human crime was
committed. The paths which lead back to the human past are endless
through the human brain, and sitting at his study window after he has
gained new self-respect by delivering Lena's baby and by standing up to
Percy Grimm, the dying Hightower still ruminates, goes over and over
the past, as "the final copper light of afternoon fades" and "the world
hangs in a green suspension in color and texture like through colored
glass." The everlasting reverie begins again, but now the wheel of life that
brought Lena Grove to Jefferson begins to slow down, runs into sand,
"the axle, the vehicle, the power which propels it not yet aware." These
memories are endless and the style in which they are described is over-
colored in a way that shows how static action often becomes in Faulkner's
work, how much it serves as the raw material for reflection, which is why
he can lavish so many Joycean compound words on objects which do not
seem to move of their own accord, but to be rallying points in Faulkner's
tortured concern with guilt.

Guilt is endless; in the labyrinths of the mind, there is turning, but
no deliverance. Like T. S. Eliot, Faulkner is a favorite today because he
takes his stand on human guilt; this is the side of ourselves that we can

recognize, and, curiously, stand by; for in this alone, as we feel, is the possibility of our freedom. When men feel so wretchedly small before their own past, they must be guilty. So runs the legend. This is the argument behind Faulkner's novels: of the God who made Yoknapatawpha County. In the beginning, life was free and good and natural; but something inexplicable, a curse, was put on it. Perhaps the curse is nothing more than man's effort to get the better of events that are "too much for us"; the evil lies in arrogance. Doc Hines hears God addressing him personally, ordering him to act for Him. Calvin McEachern, Joe Christmas' adopted father, starves and beats him because he cannot memorize portions of the catechism on order. "He asked that the child's stubborn heart be softened and that the sin of disobedience be forgiven him also, through the advocacy of the man whom he had flouted and disobeyed, requesting that the Almighty be as magnanimous as himself, and by and through and because of conscious grace." Even Joanna Burden tries to play God to her Negro charges. *Light in August* is one of the sharpest criticisms of Calvinism ever written, but unlike so many Southern writers on Puritanism, Faulkner knows that the same religion is found in Doc Hines and Joanna Burden. The guilt that is the mainstay of their faith is embodied in the assumption of excessive authority by fathers, law-givers, teachers, ministers. Everyone wants to play God to the orphan Joe Christmas. In Faulkner's eyes, life is an ironic and tragic affair that is beyond human rule and mis-rule; but Calvinists like Doc Hines and Calvin McEachern, the children of Calvinists like Joanna Burden, even murdering simon-pure "patriots" like Percy Grimm, take life in their hands, they dominate and they murder. Joe Christmas is their favorite pupil; he is the man "things are done to." His final ignominy comes when his mistress, Joanna Burden, regarding him in her new phase as a Negro charge to be "brought up," tells him that she wants him to go to school so that he can become a lawyer. And it is at this point that he breaks. It is this point that has always been the signature of the everlasting victim. Other men are the law-givers; the law is passed out to him, through him, inflicted on him. And so finally he murders and dies, a pure victim, shot, castrated, treated like a thing. It is the final ignominy. But in the very unattainability of his suffering, in its inexpressibility, is the key to his healing power over others. For where life exists so much in the relation of master to man, of the elect to the sinner, the only possible consummation man can ever reach, for Joe Christmas as for Uncle Tom, is in the final consistency of his suffering, in a fate so extreme that it becomes a single human word which men can read. This is what Faulkner means in that exalted passage after Joe Christmas' immolation:

> . . . when they saw what Grimm was doing one of the men gave a choked cry and stumbled back into the wall and began to vomit. Then Grimm too sprang back, flinging behind him the bloody butcher knife. "Now you'll let white women alone, even in hell," he said. But the man on the floor had not moved. He just lay there, with his eyes open and empty of everything save consciousness, and with something, a shadow, about his mouth. For a long moment he looked up at them with peaceful and unfathomable and unbearable eyes. Then his face, body, all, seemed to collapse, to fall in upon itself, and from out the slashed garments about his hips and loins the pent black blood seemed to rush like a released breath. It seemed to rush out of his pale body like the rush of sparks from a rising rocket; upon that black blast the man seemed to rise soaring into their memories forever and ever. They are not to lose it, in whatever peaceful valleys, beside whatever placid and reassuring streams of old age, in the mirroring faces of whatever children they will contemplate old disasters and newer hopes. It will be there, musing, quiet, steadfast, not fading and not particularly threatful, but of itself alone serene, of itself alone triumphant.

Joe Christmas has attained the stillness that will finally allow us to see him. Of sufferings alone is he made, and in this sense, and in this sense alone, is he a figure whose condition is so total that he reminds us of Christ in the sense of Christ's integrality. That tortured and would-be Christian philosopher, Simone Weil, understood this when she found that *malheur,* affliction, could become so much in itself that she felt riven to the universe by bonds of pain. The arch-victim may not be a "martyr," as students of totalitarianism have noticed; but there is a kind of suffering in our time which is so extreme that it becomes an integral *fact* of the human condition. Father Zossima bowed down to Dmitri Karamazov because of all the affliction he would undergo. So marvellous is Faulkner's compassion, he can visualize in the man who was nothing but a victim, the shadow thrown from the Cross of Christ, who was nothing, as it were, but Himself. Men are men because events are always "too much" for them; Joe Christmas became one with his life in that extreme moment when even he had no longer to search out the past. The figure on the Cross is the most tremendous interventive symbol in history; the castrated man on the floor has only one free power in his life—to stop running at last and to face his murderer. Faulkner intends no parody; he is moved by the likeness of totality to totality. But neither is he a Christian. There is no redemption; there is not even in *A Fable*—but there man has the courage to redeem circumstances by denying their fatality. In *Light in August,* the past is not merely exigent; it is malicious, the spirit of pure bad luck, a god-like force that confronts man at every turn with everything he has been, and so seems to mock and to oppose him. This spirit is called "The Player": Lena's seducer, "Brown," still running away from her at the last, sends a Negro boy to the sheriff for the reward money he has earned in informing on Joe Christmas, but knows despairingly that he will never see the money.

"He wont do it. He cant do it. I know he cant find him, cant get it, bring it back." He called no names, thought no names. It seemed to him now that they were all just shapes like chessmen—the negro, the sheriff, the money, all—unpredictable and without reason moved here and there by an Opponent who could read his moves before he made them and who created spontaneous rules which he and not the Opponent, must follow.

This is the Opponent that Joe Christmas decides finally not to elude again, the "Player" who moves Percy Grimm unerringly from position to position:

He was beside the ditch now. He stopped, motionless in midstride. Above the blunt, cold rake of the automatic his face had that serene, unearthly luminousness of angels in church windows. He was moving again almost before he had stopped, with that lean, swift, blind obedience to whatever Player moved him on the Board. He ran to the ditch.

All things are fated; man is in any place because the Player moved him there. Our past sets up the positions into which we fall. This is why Joe Christmas' grandmother, Mrs. Hines, utters the most significant lines in the book when, at the end, she pitifully cries:

"I am not saying that he never did what they say he did. Ought not to suffer for it like he made them that loved and lost suffer. But if folks could maybe just let him for one day. Like it hadn't happened yet. Like the world never had anything against him yet. Then it could be like he had just went on a trip and grew man grown and come back. If it could be like that for just one day."

And it is in these terms that we come to understand why Joe Christmas, in running away from a past that he cannot escape, seems constantly to be looking back as he runs. Not only is no one free of his past; he even has, at the most critical moments, the sense of not moving at all, but of being silently lifted from position to position. It is because of this curious effect of immobility in Faulkner's characters as they run (as if they were held up in the air by wires) that Faulkner can lavish such idle poetic largesse upon them: can see in a Percy Grimm that "serene, unearthly luminousness of angels in church windows," and at various points throughout the book emphasized Joe Christmas' rigid likeness to a man in prayer. Even the countrymen in overalls move at one point "with almost the air of monks in a cloister." The reason is that all these characters are lost in contemplation as they are moved here and there by the Player. There is no free action for anyone; everyone is carried, as Lena Grove was carried to Jefferson in a whole succession of farmwagons, by the fate that was and so shall be.

Faulkner's world is grim—a world in which the past exerts an irresistible force, but against which there is no supernatural sanction, no redeeming belief. He believes in original sin, but not in divine love, and he is endlessly bemused by the human effort to read fate or to avoid it. The highest reach of his belief is the effort to become "a saint without God" (Albert Camus), but this is a point not yet tried for in *Light in August.* Correspondingly, there is great power in his work, but little color, and *Light in August,* for all its brilliance, somehow wears the lack-lustre look of the year in which it was published, 1932. It is a grim book, and the countryside described in it already has the pinched, rotted look that one sees in so many depression novels about the South. The greatest fault of the book is its over-schematic, intellectualized past. Although Faulkner himself has lived more like Joe Christmas than like the Sartorises, he is socially far from the world of Joe Christmas and Lena Grove, and there are tell-tale signs in the novel that it is written *down*—for Faulkner, too much from his head down, and about people whom he tends to generalize and to over-praise, as if he saw them only as symbols rather than as entirely complex beings. And it is a simple fact that the opening of *Light in August* is so beautiful that nothing after quite comes up to it.

On the other hand, it is one of Faulkner's greatest books, and although it does not have the blazing directness of *The Sound and the Fury* (a book written more directly out of Faulkner's own experience), it has much of the creative audacity which is Faulkner's highest ideal in art. With this book, published in 1932, Faulkner completed a period of extraordinary fertility. He was only thirty-five; since 1929, he had published, in rapid order, *Sartoris, The Sound and the Fury, As I Lay Dying, Sanctuary,* and *Light in August*. It was a period of tremendous creative power. When he was recently in Japan, Faulkner said of this period:

I think there's a period in a writer's life when he, well, simply for lack of any other word, is fertile and he just produces. Later on, his blood slows, his bones get a little more brittle, his muscles get a little stiff, he gets perhaps other interests, but I think there's one time in his life when he writes at the top of his talent plus his speed, too. Later the speed slows; the talent doesn't necessarily have to fade at the same time. But there's a time in his life, one matchless time, when they are matched completely. The speed, and the power and the talent, they're all there and then he is . . . 'hot.'

*Light in August* comes out of that "one matchless time." The only possible objection one can have to the book is the number of implications which Faulkner tries to bring out of his material—for just as the characters' own lives are "set" for them to mull over, so Faulkner constantly mulls over them, wringing a poetry that has grandeur but also an intensity of contemplation that is sometimes more furious in expression than meaningful in content. If we see Faulkner's narrative method as essentially recollective, in the form of individual meditation over past events, we can recognize the advantage he has over most "naturalistic" writers and we understand why Faulkner refers to himself as a "poet." For what makes the portrait of Joe Christmas so astonishing is the energy of imagination lavished upon it, the consistency of texture that derives from the poet's sense that he has not only to *show,* in the modern realistic sense, but to *say*— that is, to tell a story which follows from his contemplation of the world, and which preserves in the nobility of its style and in the serene independence of its technique, the human victory over circumstances.

It is this that makes us hear Faulkner's own voice throughout the book, that allows him to pull off the tremendous feat of making us believe in a character who in many ways is not a human being at all—but struggling to become one. And this, after all, is the great problem of the novelist today. Joe Christmas is an incarnation not only of the "race problem" in America, but of the condition of man. More and more, not merely the American novel, but all serious contemporary novels, are concerned with men who are not real enough to themselves to be seriously in conflict with other men. Their conflicts, as we say, are "internal"; for they are seeking to become *someone*. Joe Christmas lives a life that is not only solitary but detached. He lives in society physically, but actually he is concerned only with the process of self-discovery, or of self-naming, even of self-legalization. This is a fate which, as we know, can be as arduous and deadly as that of the classic heroes. But in Joe Christmas' case, there is no conflict from positions of strength, no engagement between man and man—only the search of the "stranger," *l'étranger,* to become man.

## JOE CHRISTMAS: THE HERO IN THE MODERN WORLD

### JOHN L. LONGLEY, JR.

**1**

ARISTOTLE has not defined pity and terror," said Stephen Dedalus. "I have. Pity is the feeling which arrests the mind in the presence of whatsoever is grave and constant in human sufferings and unites it with the human sufferer. Terror is the feeling which arrests the mind in the presence of whatsoever is grave and constant in human sufferings and unites it with the secret cause." Stephen's definition is appropriate, for different as he is from Joe Christmas, they are alike in being heroes who are distinctly modern and who must make their way in a cosmos that is violent, chaotic, and absurd.

Of course, not everyone will be willing to accept the word "tragic" in connection with the works of William Faulkner, or, indeed, with anything in the literature of this century. Some readers do not like his work at all and say so. Many have confessed that they find it difficult to understand. The objections will vary with the individual, but the major factors in the dissatisfaction are not at all difficult to discover. One factor is the "difficulty" of the style; the non-stop sentences and the obliqueness of presentation. In a very basic sense, the ultimate meaning of the book has not reached the reader. Another factor, of course, is hostility: hostility to Faulkner's region and/or his matter, or a simple quarrelsome disagreement with a view of life that is not the reader's own. And much of the hostility has been generated by bad criticism.

No purpose is served by rehearsing the melancholy and incredible

Reprinted with permission from *Virginia Quarterly Review,* Spring, 1957, pp. 233-49.

history of Faulkner criticism, but it may be helpful to point out how the criticism arrived at its present position. Even though at rare intervals the casually inserted adjective "tragic" began to creep into Faulkner criticism fairly early, the critics were largely engaged in hot sniffing after the slightest scent of deviation from either their own particular sub-Marxian theories of socio-economic determinism or from that view which insists that all is for the best in this best of all possible worlds. The deviations were not difficult to discover, and the critics held them aloft with loud cries of horror and dismay. But now the tide has turned, and Faulkner is finally established as a traditional moralist and is usually granted a comprehensive and tragic view of mankind. Most critics today would agree that Sutpen and John Sartoris, especially when viewed in their dynastic patterns, are tragic heroes in the grand and traditional classic mold. They are, of course, located in a remote and more "heroic" time, when presumably there existed that scope of action and choice large enough for heroic gesture. There is some evidence that Faulkner is deliberately using the matter of Greek tragedy, as in the names in the story of Sutpen.

But I do not for a moment wish to suggest that Mr. Faulkner is primarily interested in writing tragedy to prescription. There is probably no writer living who cares less what the professors say of his work. And, as we know, tragedy ground out in conformity to a set prescription has almost without exception failed to become tragic. Tragedy is autochthonous and mantic, and set prescriptions for these conditions cannot be written; they must be achieved in another way. One is reminded of Jane Harrison's admission: "Great things in literature, Greek plays for example, I most enjoy when behind their bright splendors I see moving darker and older shapes." It is this kind of infinitely extended suggestivity, the waking of universal echoes, that the better work of Faulkner so conspicuously has and the work of so many modern writers—for instance, Arthur Miller—so conspicuously lacks.

It is not the purpose of this essay to rack Joe Christmas on the bed of any one or another Procrustean theory of tragedy and demand that he fit it. It will, rather, use the much lazier method of hindsight: begin with the *fait accompli* of the response and the emotion which the better work of Faulkner arouses in the reader, and attempt to account for it. It is my contention that this feeling is the authentic pity and terror; the twin poles of tragic katharsis.

But even assuming Faulkner's possession of a tragic sensibility and granting him the ability to shape it into art, how can the very long jump to Joe Christmas as tragic hero be made? There are perhaps two possible approaches, and perhaps both of them should be used: to what extent is Christmas authentically tragic by traditional criteria, and to what extent can it be shown that he is tragic by some entirely modern, different set of criteria which apply? Vastly oversimplified, the modern protagonist should be one who is typical of the age and not so remote from typical human beings as to make emotional identification difficult for the spectator. In some highly symbolic fashion, the modern hero must typify the major myths and problems of our century. In a cosmos where all is chaos and all standards have disappeared, he will very likely be destroyed as a result of his failure to define himself correctly in relation to that cosmos. Lastly he must embody the perpetual human constants which are the property of any age. Bypassing for a moment the very interesting second possibility, let us examine Christmas in the light of traditional, classic tragic criteria. At first glance, this procedure appears unpromising.

Granting his acts of persistence, his arrogance and pride, how can Christmas be called noble? How can he be said to be illustrious in rank and fortune? Above all, how can a human so conditioned, so utterly predestined to violence and death ever be called free: free to choose and free to act or not act? It is my belief that this is precisely the point.

Aristotle awarded the palm for classic tragedy to the *Oedipus Tyrannos* of Sophocles. If this is not quite the same thing as saying that Oedipus is the most perfect example of the tragic protagonist, perhaps he will do for comparison. Everyone knows his tragic story, at least in outline, for it is one of the ironies of history that he has given his name to the folklore of psychology. In that same folklore, in the modern world, we give tacit agreement to the belief that human free will is all but impossible. In the Greek world, once the oracle had spoken, who was ever so hopelessly "predestined" as Oedipus?

But, as everyone also knows, that is not it at all. To vastly oversimplify, Oedipus becomes tragic only because he does strive against the prediction. Resolved to know, he goes to the oracle himself and hears with his own ears the dire prophecy repeated. He runs away. His hubris lies not in the running but in boasting that he has escaped and has become king of Thebes by his own strength and cunning. His confidence unbroken, he is convinced he can save Thebes again as he did before. He pronounces the curse on the unknown polluter of the city, and as the process of ferreting out the guilty one goes on, Oedipus' search becomes one of finding out his own identity. But even as the dark hints begin to accumulate, and Jocasta has guessed the

truth, he boasts of his contempt for oracles and prophecy; his father is still
alive and his mother is far away. He will trust only that god-like strength
and cunning that has made him tyrannos—"first of men." As the flawlessly
plotted action unfolds, there comes the crushing peripateia: all along he
had been nearer home than he knew.

We could say that Oedipus' fault lies in trying to beat the rap. But
again, everyone knows that his tragedy has to mean more than this; that
this expenditure of human striving and achievement and suffering has to
stand for something grave and constant in the eternal human condition. It is
very true that his is the classical hubris; the sin of pride and arrogance and
over-confidence in his own ability. But far more to our purpose, we can
say it is a failure to achieve self-knowledge, a failure of self-definition.
Oedipus was saddled with an incredibly horrible, inevitable future; he had
not asked for it and had done nothing to deserve it; it was all "decided" before he was born. But he persists, and demands to know the truth. Bernard
Knox has noted how in the original there is the constant cruelly ironic inter-
running of "Oedipus" and "Oidi" ("swell," as with pride and arrogance)
and "Oida" ("I know"), words that are all too often in Oedipus' mouth.
At the beginning of the play there is too much that he does not know, and at
the end there is too much that he does. It is in the interweaving of guilt and
innocence, in the willing of his own actions against the pressure of his destiny; in the godlike insistence on knowing *who* he is and in the crushing
ruin that this knowledge brings him to, that the tragic glory of Oedipus lies.

Consider another hero. About his birth there is mystery also. He too
is spirited away as an infant because dreadful things are whispered about
him, and he too is brought up by foster-parents whom he leaves hurriedly
for fear he may have killed his foster-father. In a very direct way, it can be
said that his very begetting caused the death of his real father. He brings
terrible shame, agony, and death to his real mother. After a great deal of
wandering, he returns to that part of the world which, unknown to him, was
the scene of his begetting and birth. Early in life he was given a free choice
of two lines of conduct, one of which will remove him from all danger to
himself. He persists in the other because it is necessary to the terms of his
own definition of himself. He lives connubially with an older woman, who
as a result of his drive toward self-definition dies a horrible death. The
fearful rumors about him break out afresh. There is an old, mad visionary
who claims to have special insight into the truth about him, and as a result,
his fellowmen are convinced he is a ritual pollution in the community.
Pursued by them, he is harried for days and is eventually sacrificed in a

particularly horrible ritual murder. He was saddled with an incredibly horrible, inevitable curse; he had not asked for it and had done nothing to deserve it; it was all "decided" before he was born. The second hero is, of course, Joe Christmas.

2

If the fall of Oedipus comes as the direct result of his terribly mistaken idea of who he is and his insistence on finding out, then the death of Christmas is a result of his insistence that he already knows who he is, and his persistence in the demand for the right to be himself; to live on the terms of his own self-definition. To state the paradox in another way, the classic tragic protagonist such as Oedipus, Othello, Hamlet, or Macbeth rejoices in an existence which allows him a superb scope of action in which to achieve self-realization, including knowledge, even though in this same drive toward self-fulfillment he destroys himself. The modern tragic protagonist, such as the heroes of a Dostoevsky, a Conrad, a Kafka, a Faulkner, a Hemingway or a Warren must use all his intelligence, his strength, his luck, merely to travel the tightrope between Cosmic Chaos on the one hand and Cosmic Absurdity on the other. He can trust in nothing, hope for nothing, and accept nothing at face value until he has tried it on the test of his own pulses. He may have heard of Determinism, but does not believe in it; in the face of those joyous theories of self-exculpation formulated by present-day psychology and sociology which presumably give the individual the right to scream "It's not my fault! It's not my fault!" his preference is much nearer the dreadful freedom of the Existentialist: since existence is prior to essence, the individual is totally free, and totally accountable for his own view of things, for with total freedom comes total responsibility.

In the case of Joe Christmas, Faulkner takes pains to make this freedom absolute. Here we must be blunt: previous critical opinion seems almost never to have been aware of that freedom. Partly because, one supposes, the term "conditioning" is now a household word, it was decided that Christmas is the helpless victim of his own conditioning. But surely it is obvious that the wellspring of all his actions is his refusal to surrender to that conditioning. The conditioning is well documented, but in the first mention of him his significant quality is his rootlessness, his freedom from the customary restraints of job, property, wife, children, and taxes. Straw hat on head and razor in pocket, he is ready for a journey of one mile or a thousand.

One of Faulkner's clearest strokes of genius is in leaving the question of Christmas' possible Negro blood unanswered. We, no one, will ever know if he has it or not. If he does have it, the percentage is very small, which not only adds to the irony, but leaves him free to "pass" if he chooses. Although various characters in the novel make statements, and very positive statements, about the matter, the author never commits himself. Christmas is putatively a Negro child at the orphanage largely through the efforts of Old Doc Hines, but he is adopted and brought up as a white child by the McEacherns. ("He dont look no more like a nigger than I do," says a white character.) This is probably the most crucial point in the book: Christmas is free to choose what he will be. Precisely as Oedipus, he must find out who and what he is. One remembers a scene in the orphanage: Old Doc Hines is recalling how the five-year-old Christmas has begun following the Negro yard-boy around:

. . . until at last the nigger said, 'What you watching me for boy? and he said, 'How come you are a nigger?' and the nigger said, 'Who told you I am a nigger, you little white trash bastard?' and he says, 'I aint a nigger,' and the nigger says, 'You are worse than that. You dont know what you are. And more than that, you wont never know. You'll live and you'll die, and you wont never know. . . .'

But he must know. As with his determination to keep his own name, and because he is free, he cannot let others tell him how and what to be. All his life, people attempt to force him to be what they insist he must be: McEachern's beating him to inculcate worship of the Moloch-Jehovah; Mrs. McEachern's sickening attempts to make him as cringing as herself; Joanna Burden's final insistence that he "become a nigger." His method is active. In the fifteen years of wandering he tries life as a black man, living with Negroes, and as a white man attempting to live with whites. But ultimately he chooses to be neither—he will simply be himself. Until the very end, the community cannot decide for sure what he is; their deep distrust grows from his refusal to declare himself one *or* the other, in a social pattern where this is the most important distinction of all. He will insist on his right to simply be; he has defined himself and has fought hard for the definition. The murder of Joanna Burden and his own death are the fruit of that insistence.

Granted he has freedom and choice, what about rank and fortune? The hero, like Oedipus and Macbeth, makes his own. Christmas' distinction lies in the strength of his proud, ruthless, arrogant, cold self-sufficiency, as rigid as that of a Richard or an Ahab, and more adequate to the strain

placed upon it than Macbeth's. As with any modern hero, the simple fact
that he is still alive may be as much good fortune as he can expect. It is
more important for our purposes to prove he is typically human.

Part of the difficulty in understanding Christmas again lies in the form
and structure of the novel. The sequence of telling is such that he is first
seen as the utterly sinister alien, and is revealed early in the book as a
brutal murderer. It is only as the flashbacks begin to unfold and we see
him as a child and youth that we are made aware of his simple humanity.
Presented for the most part at a distance, his inmost thoughts and feelings
are not often enough open to us, but at rare intervals a momentary flash
of insight will give a total revelation. We see the denial of love and belong-
ing in the orphanage and the beatings by McEachern, and the effect of
these is of course cumulative, but one of the revealing flashes comes when
he hears that his name will be changed:

"He will eat my bread and he will observe my religion," the stranger
said. "Why should he not bear my name?"

The child was not listening. He was not bothered. He did not especially care, anymore than if the man had said the day was hot when it
was not hot. He didn't even bother to say to himself *My name aint Mc-
Eachern. My Name is Christmas.* There was no need to bother about that
yet. There was plenty of time.

We are shown the idyllic relationship with Bobbie, the stunted and no-
longer-young waitress who is a working prostitute in her spare time. His
slipping away from the McEachern farm to be with her is part of his program of defiance, but it is truly, at least at the beginning, the adolescent's
first tentative awe-struck discovery of the body of the beloved and all its
possibilities. Again, just before the dawn of the day on which he will
murder Joanna Burden, when the pressures that will compel either murder
or complete surrender are building past endurance, he muses:

. . . it seemed to him, sitting on the cot in the dark room, that he was hearing a myriad of sounds of no greater volume—voices, murmurs, whispers:
of trees, darkness, earth; people: his own voice; other voices evocative of
names and times and places—which he had been conscious of all his life,
without knowing it, which were his life, thinking *God perhaps and me not
knowing that too* He could see it like a printed sentence, fullborn and already dead *God loves me too* like the faded and weathered letters on a last
years's billboard *God loves me too.*

His humanity and perhaps even his own completely tragic awareness
of his situation are revealed in that incredible week in which we run with

him while he eludes mobs, sheriff, deputies, Lucas, and bloodhounds. All that has gone before in the novel is brilliantly recapitulated as Christmas, still wrapped in the rags and tatters of his self-sufficiency and pride, works himself slowly away from the violence of the attack on the Negro church toward his tragic reconciliation with his fate, his acceptance of the price of the risk of the human condition. The incidents of his life which have "predestined" him toward the proud denial of his own humanity are echoed. Aware, as perhaps never before, of the simple joy of merely being alive and breathing, he watches another day begin:

It is just dawn, daylight; that gray and lonely suspension filled with the tentative and peaceful waking of birds. The air, inbreathed, is like spring water. He breathes deep and slow, feeling with each breath himself diffuse in the neutral grayness, becoming one with loneliness and quiet that has never known fury or despair. 'That was all I wanted,' he thinks, in a quiet and slow amazement. 'That was all, for thirty years. That didn't seem to be a whole lot to ask in thirty years.'

Perhaps the right to live one's life is not too much to ask. But Christmas' dilemma is the truly tragic one. He is caught not between clear-cut right and wrong, but between right and right. Rejected, feared, hated; he has sought and been proud of that rejection and fear; but pushed too far he has gone too far, and unable to reconcile conflicting responsibility, he has committed a brutal murder. Now he must accept responsibility for the freedom of choice he exercised in his actions and pay the price of that freedom. But, because he is truly tragic, he will not practice a mere lethargic passivity, and wait for the men with the dogs to come up and shoot him. He will actively seek his human reconciliation; his problem is how to begin to get back inside the human community. It is not easy; he has been isolated for too many years. He waits in the dawn for a farmhouse to come alive and the men to leave for the fields. Then he approaches the farm wife, who recognizes him, and he quietly, from a respectful distance, asks: "Can you tell me what day this is? I just want to know what day this is."

Even though the white woman sends him away, the symbolism is clear. He wants to begin again by re-accepting the limitations of one of the most human and communal inventions: time. The next step involves a basic human need and social ritual. Having violently rejected the offer of food on a number of symbolic occasions, he approaches a Negro cabin to ask for a meal.

. . . He was sitting at a table, waiting, thinking of nothing in an emptiness, a silence filled with flight. Then there was food before him, appearing suddenly between long, limber black hands fleeing too in the act of setting down the dishes. It seemed to him that he could hear without hearing them wails of terror and distress quieter than sighs all about him, with the sounds of the chewing and the swallowing. 'It was a cabin that time,' he thought. 'And they were afraid. Of their brother afraid.'

This is not enough. Rejected and feared by Negroes as well as whites, he shaves himself carefully with the razor, the murder weapon, and strikes across country to Mottstown. Given a ride on a wagon by a Negro youth who does not know who he is, he reviews his life:

. . . he is entering it again, the street which ran for thirty years. It had been a paved street, where going should be fast. It had made a circle and he is still inside of it. Though during the last seven days he has had no paved street, yet he has travelled farther than in all the thirty years before. And yet is still inside the circle. 'And yet I have been farther in these seven days than in all the thirty years,' he thinks. 'But I have never got outside that circle. I have never broken out of the ring of what I have already done and cannot ever undo,' he thinks quietly, sitting on the seat, with planted on the dashboard before him the shoes, the black shoes smelling of Negro: that mark on his ankles that gauge definite and ineradicable of the black tide creeping up his legs, moving from his feet upward as death moves.

One is tempted to abandon the story for the fascination of peeling back the layers of meaning in the symbol. At first, the obvious meaning seems brutal and shocking, but it must be recalled that for thirty centuries or so the black-white, light-dark, Apollonian-Dionysian, rational-irrational opposition has existed in Western civilization. If this were the only meaning, its use would be forgivable but little more. It should be remembered that Christmas gleefully exchanged his own shoes for these, worn by a Negro woman, to throw the bloodhounds off the scent. (At this stage Christmas, like Oedipus, is full of devices.) But there is another meaning, far more important. Now, completely alone, he is feared and rejected by black and white alike. Urged on by the frantic greed of Lucas Burch and the fanatic madness of Old Doc Hines, the white community considers him a Negro, hunts him as a Negro, and will lynch him as a Negro. Continuing to wear the shoes, he looks at that mark ". . . moving upward from his feet as death moves." No one has ever been able to compel him to choose, black or white; but now the murder is the result of that refusal. While choice of action remains (which may not be long), he will choose his means of reconciliation. Had he chosen sooner, or had he merely gone away as he was also free to do, Joanna Burden would not be dead and he would not be about to die. As surely as he sees the blackness (his acceptance of Negro status) creep up his body, as surely his body is sinking into the darkness, the extinction, of death. He walks quietly about the streets of Mottstown until he is captured.

At this point only the last of the tragedy remains to be played out. It may be felt that Christmas is unable to sustain his resolution, that his breaking away from the officers only to be shot and castrated by Percy Grimm is an artistic defect on the part of the writer. But Oedipus and Lear have moments toward the end when the old rage and arrogance blaze out; Antigone, St. Joan, Richard, all have moments when human fear of absolute extinction overwhelms human integrity. The moment is there for a conscious artistic purpose: to give us that ultimate awareness of pity and terror by reminding us that the protagonist is not a hollow tragic mask, but a living human being only a little less lucky than ourselves. And there is a further meaning: free to the end, Christmas has held on to his life until the proper moment has come to give it, the moment most filled with meaning.

As Gavin Stevens says, no one will ever know what Christmas hoped for from Hightower, but that it was the conflict in his blood that let him run but would not let him escape; that made him snatch up the pistol but would not let him kill Grimm with it. Stevens has his opinion of Christmas' origin, as do various others, but by this time it does not seem to matter. The meaning has taken on almost universal significance. It is the light-dark opposition that is in the blood of all of us; the savage pull between bright rationality and the instinctiveness and bestiality of the darkness that leads to irrationality and death.

Few scenes in modern literature have the speed and inevitable on-ward sweep of the chapter in which Percy Grimm pursues Christmas and kills him. Taken merely as the realistic evocation of a scene, the writing is superb: the shots, the shouting; the blind rushes and clotted confusion of the mob; the added detail of the fire siren, a characteristic sound of our time, screaming the rise and fall of its meaningless message; the early resolution of the pursuit into a personal contest between Christmas and Grimm. The rendition of Grimm as a type is as merciless as anything of the sort ever done. He is Faulkner's equivalent of the classic Nemesis or the Furies; machine-like, unerring, impersonal, mindless.

As the narrative continues, Christmas runs into Hightower's house still holding the pistol he has snatched up on the way. He could kill Grimm easily, but with nothing more to lose by an additional killing, he does not; this is his final gesture of human reconciliation. Grimm empties the magazine of the automatic into Christmas' body, but this is not all.

When the others reached the kitchen they saw the table flung aside now and Grimm stooping over the body. When they approached to see what he was about, they saw that the man was not dead yet, and when they saw what Grimm was doing one of the men gave a choked cry and stumbled back into the wall and began to vomit. Then Grimm too sprang back, flinging behind him the bloody butcher knife. "Now you'll leave white women alone, even in hell," he said. But the man on the floor had not moved. He just lay there, with his eyes open and empty of everything but consciousness, and with something, a shadow, about his mouth. For a long moment he looked up at them with peaceful and unfathomable and unbearable eyes. Then his face, body, all, seemed to collapse, to fall in upon itself, and from out the slashed garments about his hips and loins the pent black blood seemed to rush like a released breath. It seemed to rush out of his pale body like the rush of sparks from a rising rocket; upon that black blast the man seemed to rise soaring into their memories forever and ever. They are not to lose it, in whatever peaceful valleys, beside whatever placid and reassuring streams of old age, in the mirroring faces of whatever children they will contemplate old disasters and newer hopes. It will be there, musing, quiet, steadfast, not fading and not particularly threatful, but of itself alone serene, of itself alone triumphant. Again from the town, deadened a little by the walls, the scream of the siren mounted toward its unbelievable crescendo, passing out of the realm of hearing.

They are not to lose it, nor, I think, are we. In Stephen Dedalus' terms, we feel pity and terror to a degree that is almost unbearable. No one knows why we feel these emotions, or even less why the tragic spectacle is so compelling. It may be that it is better that we don't know. Behind the stark shapes of Grimm and Christmas outlined against the blinding light of August we seem to see the darker shapes of human sacrifice and mutilation that go back beyond the earliest human history. Certainly, as Nietzsche claimed, the tragic emotions lurk in the dark, irrational part of the blood, and very likely the rational mind wants nothing to do with them. "Pity is the feeling which arrests the mind in the presence of whatsoever is grave and constant in human sufferings and unites it with the human sufferer." We feel with Joe Christmas because he is the modern Everyman. In a cosmos where the only constants are absurdity and instability, we have the right to expect anything except rationality. Any one of us could become

the victim. His suffering far transcends the time and place and means
Faulkner has used, and comes to stand for everything that is grave and
constant in the human condition.

"Terror is the feeling which arrests the mind in the presence of whatsoever is grave and constant in human sufferings and unites it with the
secret cause." The union with the secret cause is almost as terrible as the
suffering itself, because it gives a moment of true insight into ourselves.
Part of this insight is perfectly symbolized in *Light in August* when the
injured Hightower, in a scene that might have come straight out of
Dostoevsky, is working himself toward complete self-knowledge. As the
wheel of his memory turns on and on, he comes to realize that his own
cold selfishness, his absorption in the Confederate grandfather, has caused
his wife's disgrace and death. As the crowd of faces in his memory struggle
to come into focus, one of them becomes the dead face of Christmas, but
the focus is not clear; another face is struggling with that face, struggling to
become clear and be recognized. Suddenly it emerges: it is the face of
Percy Grimm; gunman, mutilator, avenging fury, lyncher extraordinary.
Hightower never saw either of them before the lynching, but their terrible
failure and terrible guilt are somehow the direct result of his own failure
to live up to his humanity. Somewhere at the root of the secret cause of
things as they are, we are all related; we are all involved. We are all
responsible because we are all a part of mankind. So far as the rational
mind goes, the union with the secret cause is a moment of awareness, of
realizing that grave and constant human suffering is truly constant. Once
we achieve this awareness, the acceptance of the tragic human situation,
with all its absurdity and irrationality, becomes possible, and with the acceptance come the emotions of peace and tranquility.

Yet the union with the secret cause has another side, which is less
commendable. This emotion, which we are not so willing to let swim up to
conscious awareness, can be curtly put as "There but for the Grace of
God. . . ." The hero has fallen, but we, for the moment at least, are
safe. Let society pick its victims as it pleases, so long as the victim is not I.
It is in just this area of playing upon our deep, instinctual fears and mis-
givings that Faulkner has succeeded in achieving favorable comparison with
classic tragedy. It was impossible to put the Furies believably on the stage,
but Faulkner found the perfect equivalent in the lynch mob, which in one
way or another elicits a strong emotion in all of us, or better still, a mixed
one. In an age where the very name of Oedipus has been explained away,
tamed, and embalmed in the clinic; where almost no one can truly feel

why Macbeth should think the murder of a king to be so much worse than any murder, and where no one believes in such an absurdity as an ancestral curse, the beholder is simply asked: "Did Joe Christmas inherit a curse?" Or rather, it is not necessary to ask, since we know. Faulkner has used the subconscious fear of mutilation and distrust of miscegenation that lurks in all of us, the love of and response to violence and death, the simultaneous love and hate of the loved one, to arouse these emotions or their equivalents in us. We love the violence and evil because we acquiesce in them. No doubt these emotions are despicable, but no doubt the emotions aroused by the spectacle of what Oedipus had done were despicable also. The doctor who tamed the legend of Oedipus and rechristened it a complex only found out very late what the Christian world had known all along: when there are guilt and filth in the human psyche, the only possible remedy is to cast them out.

3

This essay has dealt only with the analysis of Joe Christmas as a modern tragic protagonist. It has hardly mentioned the many other excellences of the novel *Light in August,* leaving completely out of consideration the tragic situations of Joanna Burden and Hightower, who are also classic examples of the tragedy of isolation, strongly complementing the situation of Christmas. This study does not bring up the very skillfully handled elements of humor or comic relief, nor even mention by name Lena Grove, who is Faulkner's equivalent of the Shakespearian norm of humanity. There is no mention of Byron Bunch, who is as surely a comic hero as Christmas is a tragic one. But they are not properly matter for the subject of this essay.

Tradition tells us that the Greeks demanded that each trilogy submitted in the great dramatic contests be accompanied by an outrageous and lewd satyr-play, which preferably would burlesque the very elements and events just presented as tragedy. Perhaps some such comic relief is essential. After the human emotions have endured all they can, after the katharsis, something has to sustain us until we can touch down on earth again. Perhaps this is the explanation of the bawdy, almost folksy humor of the Lena-Byron episode in the last chapter of *Light in August,* so often dismissed with bewilderment or anger as an artistic botch. The direct experience of pity and terror is a little like being caught up in a cyclone, or to use another metaphor, like being at the heart of what goes on in a thermonuclear explosion. In contemplating the question "When will I be blown up?" the author of *Light in August* has always been willing to risk a small side bet on mankind. This risk and this faith are also a part of the tragic paradox. The Greeks knew, as did the Elizabethans after them, that once the mushroom cloud has blown away and the fallout has ceased to fall, there is always that continuing residue of humanity. It, as the author would no doubt say, will endure.

# THE DESIGN AND MEANING OF
## *ABSALOM, ABSALOM!*

ILSE DUSOIR LIND

ABSALOM, ABSALOM! is a unique fictional experiment—unique in relation to Faulkner's other novels and to modern fiction generally. Indeed, it is not too much to claim that in point of technique it constitutes the last radical innovation in fictional method since Joyce. A "difficult" work, its difficulties do not inhere in verbal subtleties or in excessive refinement of perception, but in the strain imposed upon attention and sensibility in comprehending its monumental design.

Broadly stated, the intention of *Absalom, Absalom!* is to create, through the utilization of all the resources of fiction, a grand tragic vision of historic dimension. As in the tragedies of the ancients and in the great myths of the Old Testament, the action represents issues of timeless moral significance. That Faulkner here links the decline of a social order to an infraction of fundamental morality cannot be doubted. Sutpen falls through innate deficiency of moral insight, but the error which he commits is also socially derived and thus illustrates the flaw which dooms with equal finality the aspirations of a whole culture. Events of modern history, here viewed as classic tragedy, are elevated through conscious artistry to the status of a new myth.

Every reader of the novel is struck by its curiously heightened pitch, its brooding intensity, its poetic language, and the endless recapitulations which have the effect almost of incantation. What has not yet been studied

Reprinted with permission from *PMLA*, December, 1955, pp. 887-912.

is the relation of style and structure to the larger plan of execution. An exploration of unprecedented depth and scope into the meaning of history, the novel possesses throughout techniques proportionate to its ends. Only by considering form and meaning in organic interrelationship can we hope to discover the conception underlying this vast and strangely compelling tragic vision.

## 1

The characters themselves are projected on a scale larger than life. As Mr. Compson puts it, musing on the differences between then and now, we see "in this shadowy attenuation of time [people] possessing now heroic proportions, performing their acts of simple passion and simple violence, impervious to time and inexplicable." Sutpen "abrupts" onto the scene as "demon," devil, with "faint sulphur-reek still in hair, clothes and beard," "ogre-shape," "fiend," "blackguard." His stature is heroic: the towns-people feel that, "given the occasion and the need, this man can and will do anything." His face is "like the mask in Greek tragedy." He is the chief actor on the stage, "still playing the scene to the audience, [while] behind him Fate, destiny, retribution, irony—the stage manager . . . was already striking the set and dragging on the synthetic spurious shadows and shapes of the next one." Community opinion chants the chorus to his actions: ". . . in steady strophe and anti-strophe: *Sutpen. Sutpen. Sutpen. Sutpen.*"

Even in his decline, his proportions are projected on a scale enlarged by wide mythological reference. He is not the "widowed Agamemnon" that he should be, but "ancient, stiff-jointed Pyramus." He is an "ancient varicose and despairing Faustus," an enfeebled Abraham relegating the punishment of his sins to his children's children. His death is by the scythe, "symbolic laurel of a Caesar's triumph." And not least, in his anguished recognition of the unavailability of his rightful heir for the fulfillment of his design, he is, by ironical allusion to the title of the book, King David of Jerusalem, to whom it was promised that God would build him a house and establish his kingdom forever.

Of his brood, "begot with the fecundity of dragon's teeth," it can equally be said that they were "not articulated into this world." They are drawn with a curious flatness; their gestures are formalized, almost choreographic, wholly determined by the exigencies of the theme. Behind Judith's mask we never penetrate. Credited with her father's demonic will, she enacts her role for motives that we are not given to know. Like

Antigone, she dignifies the rejected brother with the appropriate rites of burial; as with Greek tragic heroines, generally, her individual psychology is not explored. She is the righteous Judith of the Old Testament, "the same as a widow without ever having been a bride," dedicated under self-assumed and uncommunicated compulsion to single-handed restoration of the moral order.

Henry Sutpen and Charles Bon exist only to perform the parts assigned to them—Bon to pursue the acknowledgment which can never be his; Henry to commit, under circumstances which convey its poignancy to the fullest, the inevitable fratricide. They are the Biblical Absalom and Ammon in mortal conflict over a sister; they are Polyneices and Eteocles, sons of the cursed family of Oedipus, separated by their claims to power and doomed to mutually inflicted extinction.

The literary associations here suggested for Judith, Henry, and Charles are not, as in the case of Sutpen, made by direct allusion, but that such association is intended to magnify the tragic aura is evident in the choice of a name for Sutpen's Negro daughter. Sutpen called her Clytemnestra, Mr. Compson tells us, in confusion with the more appropriate Cassandra. Remote, inscrutable, unspeaking, she exists as the pure, abstract embodiment of the theme, "in the very pigmentation of her flesh representing that debacle which [says Miss Rosa] had brought Judith and me to what we were and which made of her (Clytie) what she declined to be just as she had declined to be that from which its purpose had been to emancipate her." Identifying herself with Sutpen worth while still fulfilling the menial role allotted to one of her blood, she is the essence of that division which spells disaster for the man and social order which begot her: ". . . presiding aloof upon the new, she deliberately remained to represent . . . the threatful portent of the old." As an individual she remains unknown. Her actions, like those of Charles Bon, Charles Etienne Bon, and Jim Bond, serve primarily to illuminate—not her own psychology —but the psychological, social, and moral aspects of the Negro-white conflict.

To be sure, Charles Bon and his son become better known to us than do Clytie or Judith, but the compulsions which drive them are sketched with bold strokes; the Bons are not rounded characters. Comparing Charles Etienne Bon with Joe Christmas of *Light in August* (they are identical types), the deliberate chiaroscuro of Faulkner's characterization becomes apparent. An intimate and compassionate understanding of the psychodynamics of Joe Christmas is a major goal of *Light in August;* his "case history" is therefore minutely documented. For Charles Etienne Bon, however, the psychodynamics are indicated in almost code form. The reader, crediting the unalterability of inner psychological drives as such, accepts his strivings as inevitable. Our compassion for him derives from the recognition of the conflicts by which he is torn, rather than from personal identification with him as an individual.

If the characters in the Sutpen story remind us of Greek actors and epic Biblical figures, so does the action itself recall the events of ancient tragic myth. A synopsis of the Sutpen legend would read like one of the summaries of Greek myths conveniently placed as prologue to modern translations of Greek plays. The continuing (though loose) analogies which exist between Sutpen and Oedipus, Sutpen's sons and Eteocles and Poly- neices, Judith and Antigone, suggest that the Oedipus trilogy might have served as a general guide in the drafting of the plot.[1] At the same time, Sutpen's fall and the obliteration of his house bring to mind the great myth of man's original fall from innocence and the visitations of Divine justice upon third and fourth generations. Old Testament violence evoking God's wrath is recaptured here in a legend of father turning against son, son against father, and brother against brother.

What endows the novel as a whole with a sense of overpowering urgency is its surcharged atmosphere of doom. This pressure derives in part from the blind psychological forces by which all the characters are driven. But fate itself is felt to be the agent of personal and historical doom. The Greek sense of fate, specifically, is invoked. Slavery goes against the will of the gods; or, as it is stated in more exact terms, slavery goes against nature. In Haiti, where the earliest instance of this moral viola- tion takes place, it is "as if nature held a balance and kept a book and offered recompense for the torn limbs and outraged hearts even if man did not." Buried in the soil, the bones and blood of the first Haitian slaves "still cried out for vengeance." The undoing of Sutpen's false ambition illustrates the operation of retributive justice in the human drama; the fall of the South is its larger social representation.

## 2

The Sutpen tragedy as communicated in the novel has no "objective" existence. It is the collective product of the workings of the minds of three

1. Eugene O'Neill, 5 years earlier, had discussed the possibility of using "one of the old legend plots of Greek tragedy as the basis for a modern psychological drama" in which he hoped to "achieve a modern psychological approximation of the Greek sense of fate which would seem credible to a present-day audience and at the same time prove emotionally affecting." Introd. to *Mourning Becomes Electra*, Wilderness Ed. (New York, 1934), II, xiii.

major narrators, abetted by the collaboration of a fourth. The Sutpen tragedy is the novel's center of dramatic interest, but the narrators are the center of the novel. In the execution of this double focus Faulkner exercises the full play of his genius.

The story of Sutpen exists in local recollection. The four narrators take the local story and transmit it through what they are and through their relation to it. The Sutpen tragedy, with its magnitude, power, and intensity, is thus synthesized by Faulkner from the psychic bias of each narrator. Projecting their distortions upon their narrations, he achieves a reality which rests upon unreality. When the reader first encounters Sutpen and his kin, he suspects a distortion in the manner of Miss Rosa's presentation of the story, but he cannot measure its degree because he knows as yet so little about her. As the legend grows through the narrators' successive contributions, his capacity to estimate the various degrees of distortion increases. However, such is the ordering of the narrative that the magnification of events occurs always in advance of an understanding of the distortions which cause it. The reader is consequently affected sensibly before he can react intellectually. He knows that the narrators' conjectures are often in point of literal fact impossible, but he is forced to give them provisional credence; in so doing, he is taken in despite his reservations. Thus it is that the incredible tragedy of Sutpen's ambition and fall is brought into being. The heroic enlargement, the urgency, and the aura of relentless doom, are endowed by the narrators who create it.

Miss Rosa, whose shrill, belated, and misguided cry for vengeance opens the tale at its highest pitch, is a frustrated spinster. She is both physically and psychically misshapen. Venting upon Sutpen's image the accumulated tension of a lifetime of hallucinated isolation, she pictures Sutpen as the incarnation of demonic energy, positing horrendous crimes, "too dark to talk about," as the cause of the disasters which have overtaken Sutpen and his kin. A belief in his foredoomed obliteration is to her a psychological necessity, a means by which she can visit upon Sutpen vicariously her unquenchable private outrage and relieve her preternaturally developed sense of guilt. A Methodist steward's daughter, she endows her notion of an avenging fate with the coloration of a wrathfully righteous Lord, pondering "what our father or his father could have done before he married our mother that Ellen and I would have to expiate . . . what crime committed that would leave our family cursed to be instruments not only for that man's destruction, but for our own." Her portions of the narrative, hysterical and disordered, generate the tension and fatality which span the entire legend. It is her madness which endows Sutpen with supernatural vitality and her perverted moralism which invokes the certainty of his destruction.

Mr. Compson brings to his narration a seeming repose and expansiveness which is a welcome counterbalance to Miss Rosa's blind subjectivity. Enlightened, informed, comprehensive in his judgments, Mr. Compson at first arouses the confidence of the reader as an unbiased narrator. His ironic eye easily pierces the romanticisms, enthusiasms, and self-deceptions of others. A skeptic in religion, a rationalist in his general approach to life, a shrewd analyst of the social scene, his elaboration gives the legend an apparent foundation in fact. But his observations have dubious validity; they are the projections of a profound spiritual resignation. His world-weariness, his love of paradox, his fascination with the exotic, all suggest that he has absorbed the *malaise* of *fin de siècle* decadence into his private philosophy. The cast of his imagination is unhealthily voluptuous. Only his love for the refinements of eroticism could do justice to the institution of octoroon mistresses in New Orleans. His skepticism is bottomless; he is a fatalist because he is at heart a defeatist. His grandiloquent allusions to "the horrible and bloody mischancing of human affairs," and to the "blank face of oblivion to which we are all doomed," endow his narrations with the atmosphere of moral gloom. He sustains the aura of catastrophe which Miss Rosa's forebodings initiated.

Quentin's efforts at legendizing are marked by a febrile intensity which charges the entire last section with renewed emotion. The passionate delivery of the Bon-Henry conflict derives wholly from Quentin's morbid involvement. Aroused by the question of incest which the Bon-Henry-Judith relationship poses, Quentin shapes the story in the terms of his own vicarious incest wishes and creates the doomed Henry as an image of himself.

Shreve, whose youthful curiosity and romanticism make him a suitable collaborator in the Bon-Henry legend, projects the fraternal affection, mildly homosexual in basis, which exists between his roommate and himself. Not otherwise involved, he serves chiefly as instigator, prodding his curiosly obsessed Southern roommate into the reluctant fulfillment of his narrative function.

Through their acts of narration, the narrators reveal themselves. Miss Rosa's impossible romanticism is betrayed by her image of the ideal lover (the Bon-Judith courtship), her obsession with sin in her ascription of evil to Sutpen. Mr. Compson's effeteness is established in the very play of his rhetoric, in his perverse delight in what is mildly shocking, and in his sardonic asides. Quentin's psychology is depicted through his creation of Henry to no less degree than Henry's through Quentin.

The narrators frame the legend as well as relate it. Their unhappy condition arouses the question which the tragedy they create must answer. They live in a world of ghosts—the shades of the past. Miss Rosa is in pursuit of a ghost. Mr. Compson has surrendered himself to them; he has nothing to give his son except tales of the past, redolent of grandeur and defeat, but without meaning. During the period over which the legendizing takes place, we see Quentin sink progressively into self-willed oblivion. The past engulfs him; he cannot stay its flood. Miss Rosa drags him on her mission; his father refuses to stop talking. Quentin makes feeble efforts at resistance: he doesn't want to accompany Miss Rosa; he would rather not hear any more about Sutpen; he shuts his ears to his father's endless hypothesizing. During much of the legendizing he is "not even listening." But he is propelled by a momentum which is beyond his own power to check.

It is Quentin's tragedy, above all, which the Sutpen tragedy must finally illuminate. "Too young to deserve yet to be a ghost, but nevertheless having to be one for all that, since he was born and bred in the deep South," he is doomed through some cause antecedent to his own existence, the victim of some larger fatality marked for the deep South itself.

All of the major narrators are born and bred in the South. Their relationship to the Sutpen tragedy is immediate: their own ancestors appear in the background. Mr. Compson and Quentin are descended from the General Compson of the tale, whose independence and humanity set him apart from his fellow citizens of aristocratic status. In the Sutpen story, he transcends the narrowness of his class, accepting Sutpen into the community, attending his wedding, and befriending him in his crisis. He comprehends the limitations of Sutpen's nature, yet he is not alienated from him in human affection. To Charles Etienne Bon, Sutpen's Negro grandson, he accords equal sympathy. He knows the hopelessness of his plight, yet intercedes for him with the law and attempts personal assistance. In him the best of the Old South, as opposed to the "minimum of logic and morality," which governed the aspirations of the class of men represented by Sutpen, is symbolized.

Quentin and Mr. Compson are General Compson's heirs, the inheritors not only of his broad intelligence and conscience, but also of the altered social status which the Civil War brought about. Retaining the refinements of culture and sensibility perpetuated in family tradition, but deprived through historical circumstance of a proper field in which they may be exercised, Mr. Compson and Quentin are both rendered incapable of action. Their feelings towards Negroes are, like their ancestor's, personal and humane; no trace of prejudice or condescension is to be found in their narrations or conversational interchanges. They lack aggressiveness completely. Mr. Compson's manner of coping with life is through intellectual analysis undertaken from the refuge of personal retreat; Quentin, as the unfortunate heir of his spiritual bankruptcy and further declined status, is equipped only with excessive sensibility and illusion.

Miss Rosa is implicated in the legend in a different way, through the direct impingement of Sutpen's drives upon her life, and through the place of her father in implementing Sutpen's design by providing him with an acceptable marital alliance. The part played by Southern Protestantism in lending support to caste ambitions is depicted in the behavior of Mr. Coldfield. Denying slavery in principle, abetting it in practice, and in general substituting morbid righteousness for warm humanity, Mr. Coldfield's religiosity—and its contribution to Negro-white tensions—is a representation, in condensed form, of all that was set forth on this theme in *Light in August*. He lends money for Sutpen's dubious financial speculations (symbolizing the involvement of Southern planters with Northern finance), while detaching himself from the consequent moral responsibility. His impossible stand on the issues involved in the War leads to his complete withdrawal and ultimate self-annihilation.

From the atmosphere of cold abstraction and proud near-poverty in which she was raised, Miss Rosa derives not only her distorted view of life, but the social pretentiousness of a would-be aristocrat. Her repeated assertions that Sutpen "wasn't even a gentleman," and her claim that "the Coldfields are qualified to reciprocate whatever particularly signal honor marriage with anyone might confer on them," betray her actual social position. Her prejudices against Negroes are intensified by her repressions and by her need to sustain a false sense of social superiority. In youth, she refused to touch the objects with which Clytie had come in contact; at one point in the story, the shock of physical contact with Sutpen's Negro daughter sickens her with revulsion. Time does not lessen her snobbery or her prejudices; it merely fixes them into reflexes. The form of address she employs to the last of Sutpen's enfeebled kin: "You nigger. . . . You ain't any Sutpen," reveals that even as late as 1913 there was no end in sight of the vicious continuum of Negro-white tension. If the Compsons survive as the undeserving victims of the conflict brought on over the Negro issue, Miss Rosa remains as a pitiable reminder of the persistence of its causes.

The thematic link between the created tragedy and the narrators who project it is reinforced by many interspersed observations about the present-ness of the past and the pastness of the present. There is, to begin with, the identity of place: "Quentin breathed the same air in which those church bells had rung on that Sunday morning in 1833." There is continuity of blood: Mr. Compson recognizes, in these figures from an earlier era, "people in whose living blood and seed we ourselves lay dormant and waiting." Most binding of all is the psychic bond with a dead past. The cord which ties Quentin to the past has never been severed. Struggling futilely to free himself, Quentin succumbs in a hopeless concession to interrelatedness in which no individual identity remains: "Maybe nothing ever happens and is finished . . . maybe it took Father and me both to make Shreve or Shreve and me both to make Father or maybe Thomas Sutpen to make all of us."

The narrators themselves, lost in their private obsessions and viewing the Sutpen story only partially through their individual distortions of vision, do not see the meaning of the tragedy in which they play a part nor its relation to the one they have made. Only the reader has a full view of the stage. He sees, as it were, two tragedies on a single theme, simultaneously enacted. The curtain lifts on a play within a play: on the inner stage, the Sutpen drama; on the outer, the larger social tragedy involving the narrators. The second creates the first, and the first serves to convey the second. They are brought to their overwhelming finale together, but not without the reminder that, although catastrophe has been portrayed, life goes on. Shreve, the Canadian, remote from the involvements of either South or North, remains to the last uncomprehending and unaffected. His levity intensifies Quentin's ordeal by contrast, but it also affords a means by which the conjoined tragedies can be placed in detached perspective. The inclusion of his "normal" view toward the end of the novel is analogous to the placement of the Dilsey section in *The Sound and the Fury* and the furniture dealer's story in *Light in August*. Subtly mediating the return to reality, Faulkner demonstrates his own hold upon it and proves his absolute command of the means by which imaginative reality is brought into being.

### 3

One of the most remarkable achievements of the novel is the maintenance of suspense. The reader knows the outlines of Sutpen's history from

Miss Rosa's first account; in each subsequent narration the local myth of his strange rise and fall is told again and again, until through sheer repetition it takes on the quality of a familiar legend. Yet knowing the outcome of Sutpen's ambition, the reader's anticipation of what each new redactor will bring to the tale is not diminished. In fact, suspense mounts steadily.

The problem of creating suspense when treating well known legendary characters was a crucial one for Greek dramatists. Individual playwrights met the challenge by providing new details of interpretation or by selecting, from among the wealth of divergent stories already existing about the same figure, a new conclusion which resolved the contradictions of varying versions or which embodied the particular moral which the dramatist wished to illustrate. "The element of uncertainty which could be produced by these means," one classical scholar has asserted, was "perhaps the most important single factor in the suspense of any Greek play."[2]

We cannot know whether Faulkner availed himself of the scholarly hints which might have been serviceable to his purpose; nor is it our present object to inquire into his sources. The value of the analogy which can be drawn between Faulkner's method of creating suspense and the practise of the Greek dramatists is that it enables us to see how the sequence of narrations gains momentum.

If we grant, as indeed we must, that Miss Rosa, Mr. Compson, and Quentin are the creators of the Sutpen myth, each spinning his version of the legend out of his own psyche, then their three differing interpretations might be compared to a display of the talents of three Greek dramatists composing tragedies about the same mythical figure, each poet having access to his predecessor's interpretation and adding new insights and flourishes of his own. The last composer would be in the position to contribute the most; suspense would consist in the expectation that he solve the questions which earlier versions had raised.

The most prominent inconsistency in the three narrators' versions relates to Sutpen's motivation for the act which brought about his downfall. The question upon which all the narrators brood successively is: Why did Sutpen forbid the marriage of Bon and Judith? (The motive of Henry's murder of Bon hinges on the answer to this question.) It was the mystery of Sutpen's opposition to Bon which confounded Miss Rosa. "I saw Judith's marriage forbidden without rhyme or reason or shadow of excuse," she says, hinting at demonism as the only possible explanation.

2. William Flint, Jr., *The Use of Myths to Create Suspense in Extant Greek Tragedy* (Concord, N. H., 1922), p. 6.

Mr. Compson gropes in equal futility for an answer to this question; he guesses that an "eighth part negro mistress" was the basis of Sutpen's denial and Henry's subsequent murder of Bon. It was the "morganatic ceremony" which—he conjectures—aroused Sutpen and shocked Henry. Elaborating this theory in fond detail, he nevertheless is forced to abandon it as wide of the mark. "It's just incredible," he finally concedes. "It just doesn't explain. . . . They are there, yet something is missing."

We thus await Quentin's resumption of the task of providing a more satisfactory account of Sutpen's motivation. Bringing the new information that Bon was Sutpen's son (a fact which he had been told by his grand-father but had not shared with his father), Quentin constructs with Shreve the legend of the outcast brother, the son who renounced his birthright, and the incestuous love triangle.

But even this will not wholly serve. Assuming that both Henry and Bon guess their blood relationship, Quentin explores the incest theory with an intensity of interest possible only to one of his morbid sensibility and finds it still insufficient. Suppose Bon and Henry surmised the incestu-ous objection, Quentin considers, how would Henry react? He would oppose the sin at first, but he would reconsider. His identification with both Bon and Judith would cause him to override the objections of conscience. He would sanction the unlawful union between his idolized older brother and his adored female counterpart. Thus, the basis of Sutpen's objection must have exceeded even this, to account for Henry's strange and abrupt reversal. Quentin and Shreve continue their conjuring.

They reinvoke Sutpen, and five fatal words dropped from his lips serve at last to resolve everything. They are spoken to Henry and relate to Bon: ". . . his mother was part negro." This final revelation, held for the very close of the legend, casts into sudden order all the hitherto unaligned clues in the versions of the various narrators and clinches the moral of the tragedy. That scene in the cold early dawn in which Charles, not knowing the news Henry has brought from Sutpen, places his cloak about his younger brother's shoulders in the last gesture of tenderness which can ever be possible between them, is the high point of pathos in the entire drama. The love of a brother for a brother, represented as so ideal in quality that it could surmount even the test of the incest conflict, is altered in an instant to blindly obliterative hate. The slight fraction of Negro blood, whose denial was Sutpen's crime, is sole cause. Now at last we know what turned father against son, son against father, and brother

against brother. The language and allusions which elevate this compas-
sionately rendered Cain-Abel conflict are appropriately Biblical.

The placement of the narrations in a sequence of cumulative revela-
tions is supplemented by more familiar suspense-building devices. Accomplished action precedes cause throughout. In Chapters I through VI, Sutpen appears as heroic, demonic, purposive and inscrutable; Chapter VII first
presents him as the baffled, limited and compulsive mortal that he is.
Henry's murder is cited as fact beginning with Chapter I; the circumstances
and motive are not provided until Chapter VIII. Miss Rosa's ravings are
suspect as hysterical from her earliest remarks in Chapter I; not until Chapter V do we learn how to discount her assertions in the light of her own
psychology. Sutpen is buried (Chapter VI) before we are admitted to a
view of his murder (Chapter VII); the murder itself is recounted in all its
violence without our knowing what really provoked it (the sex of Milly's
baby). Effect-cause sequence is worked into all the action and characterization.

The promise of an easy moral also lures the reader on from the opening pages. Quentin's first thought is that Sutpen's story will tell him (italics
his): *"why God let us lose the war: that only through the blood of our men
and the tears of our women could He stay this demon and efface his name
and lineage from the earth."* We must make our way through almost the
entire novel to modify this view and to extend it properly to the whole social
class which Sutpen and his design epitomize. The most direct statement of
this modification is made when Wash awaits the citizenry who will pass
judgment on his murder of Sutpen. He "felt them gathering . . .—the curious
and the vengeful—men of Sutpen's own kind, who used to eat at his
table . . .—men who had led the way, shown the other and lesser ones
how to fight in battles . . .—who had galloped also in the old days arrogant
and proud on the fine horses about the fine plantations—symbol also of
admiration and hope, instruments too of despair and grief." In his profound
and tragic disillusionment, he sees them with new eyes: ". . . and maybe for
the first time in his life [Mr. Compson comments] he began to comprehend
how it had been possible for the Yankees or any other army to have
whipped them."

Gothic mystery is also used to engage our curiosity and heighten our
sense of horror. The entire novel is framed in a macabre search. When the
book opens, Miss Rosa asks Quentin to help her find out who is now living
in that decaying, almost-deserted old house. The answer to this question,
bringing before us the sight of Henry's "wasted yellow face . . . wasted

hands crossed on the breast as if he were already a corpse," closes the legend. As a device it is melodramatic, excessive. But it achieves its purpose without taking us off our course. The rotting mansion is the house of the past; the death-in-life of Henry is Quentin's own.

## 4

The literary style of the novel is in keeping with its high tragic aim. We habitually think of Faulkner as having a single style because all of his writings bear his markedly individual stamp, but this is to overlook the consciously contrived effects within his various works. In *The Sound and the Fury,* four distinct styles are employed, all scrupulously differentiated, and the short stories are a record of endless stylistic experimentation.

All the narrators speak in two voices—their own idiom, when engaged in casual conversation with each other, and the highly stylized orations in which they serve as narrators of the legend. (For Quentin, a third style, stream-of-consciousness, is also maintained.) Miss Rosa's decorum as a Southern maiden lady is conveyed in her initial address to Quentin: "Because you are going away to attend the college at Harvard. . . . Maybe you will enter the literary profession as so many Southern gentlemen and gentle women too are doing now and maybe some day you will remember this and write about it." When later she deviates from this drawing-room propriety to use such overt sexual imagery as "a metabolism of the spirit . . . in which the stored accumulations of long time burn, generate, create and break some maidenhead of the ravening meat," or to describe herself in adolescence as "all polymath love's androgynous advocate" (which simply means that she fell in love with love)—we may well wonder what has happened to dictional verisimilitude.

The difference is consistent, however; the actual Quentin is represented by his polite "Yessums" and "Nomes"; the narrator Quentin by Faulkner's own characteristically sonorous, Latinate prose. Shreve, as the Canadian and college youth, speaks an amusingly bluff, deprecating slang. When he collaborates in the creation of the Bon legend, however, the distinguishing features of his personal idiom disappear. The differences are not arbitrary. By means of a few strokes of realistic dialogue, the narrators are established as real; once established, they become the instruments for Faulkner's own poetic formulation of his material. Thus, while we must take each narration in its own terms, making allowance for the disposition of the teller, all the mythologizing is unified by the dominance of a single rhetorical style.

Decanting the poetic essence from his carefully wrought vessels, Faulkner himself is everywhere and nowhere. As in the great tragedies of Shakespeare, poetized philosophy—observations upon love, life, death, nature—finds, as it were, objective utterance through *dramatis personae* who speak in elevated poetic diction. Such diction—the blank or heroic verse appointed for tragedy—was an established convention in the sixteenth and seventeenth centuries. For modern writers, however, no such resource exists; original expedients have had to be devised to suit the needs of heroic enlargement. Melville's rhetorical prose was one such device; Maxwell Anderson's modernized blank verse another. If, as Emily Dickinson has observed, "the abdication of belief/ makes the behavior small," so too, it may be argued, does the use of a realistic prose style in compliance with an outlook of "scientific" objectivity. The declining vitality of much realistic writing of the twenties and thirties—of Farrell's fiction, for example, which was also intended to convey the power of relentless forces—is in part a reflection of the inadequacy of realism for tragic themes.

The rhetorical style of *Absalom, Absalom!* is essential to its conception, excessive as it may at times appear when it fails in that perfect felicity in which rhetoric is never questioned. The use of polysyllabics and involved —usually periodic—sentences, while natural to the author, is not a surrender to the line of least resistance. Prefixes and suffixes, especially those containing liquids and nasals in combination with vowels, lend sonorous enrichment; sentence units into which are enfolded a series of phrases and clauses which must be gathered sequentially into the mind before the release of meaning afforded in a final verb, are a means of approximating poetic rhythm in prose medium.

The unceasing flow of language gives the effect, as in *Moby-Dick,* of being tapped under pressure from unconscious or supraconscious sources; the richness of poetic imagery and literary association enlarges its power at every turn. In addition to the allusions already cited, Faulkner echoes familiar lines of deeply tragic import from *Hamlet, Macbeth* and from A. E. Housman. The intention of heroic enlargement is discernible throughout: Sutpen's wife is a Niobe; Bon a Lothario, a Lancelot, and a hero out of the Arabian Nights; the young Confederates are the Virgins of Priapus; Sutpen builds "Camelots and Carcassonnes," and performs "Herculean" labors.

The many memorable utterances, taking the form of maxim-like gems or sustained metaphors, will perhaps remain as the novel's greatest permanent attraction. Miss Rosa's sections particularly reflect this poetizing tendency. Her incisive capsule definitions of hope, defeat, sanity, madness, penury, endurance, etc., dropped parenthetically into the pauses of her breathless self-justification, are poetry in all but metre. They are reminiscent, in manner as well as idea, of the penetrating formulations of Emily Dickinson. And indeed, the concept of Miss Rosa as a kind of Emily (one is reminded of that cryptic title, "A Rose for Emily"), may have entered into Faulkner's creation of her: Miss Rosa was the local poetess. Mr. Compson's *bon mots* tend more toward the definition of social concepts and customs, though his range, too, includes timeless psychological verities.

Such imaginative reaches are attained variously by almost all the speakers: Gen. Compson on morality viewed as a baking recipe, Judith on life as the weaving of a pattern into a carpet, Bon on existence as a conjugation of the verb *to be,* Quentin on the interpenetration of all historical events—these are eternally pertinent and consummately expressed.

Many general observations of a philosophic nature are stated in such a way as to reinforce the tragic theme directly, as the definition of the verbal communication, for example, which is brief enough to cite by way of illustrating the aphoristic quality that is often attained: ". . . language, that meagre and fragile thread . . . by which the little surface corners and edges of man's secret and solitary lives may be joined for an instant now and then before sinking back into the darkness where the spirit cried for the first time and was not heard and will cry for the last time and will not be heard either." Spoken by Gen. Compson to Quentin in connection with Sutpen's regret at not having learned French before going to Haiti, it arises so naturally from the situation that the reader has no special sense of the intrusion of the author's eloquence. Placed within the dramatic frame, made to flow from narrations which are maintained at a consistently elevated level of expression, such *sententiae* belong, like the novel itself, to a grand tradition of noble utterance.

5

Nothing which is told or conjectured by the narrators, however distorted, is without thematic relevance. Since their projections are determined by their own psychological and social past, and since the Sutpen story throws additional light upon that past, the meaning of what they tell reflects at least doubly and must be read throughout for its multiple import. Even the false leads, while they delay our otherwise too hasty discovery of Sutpen's motive, are significant. They tell what *might* have occurred; their usefulness lies in their conjectural plausibility. For example, although in actuality Henry did not object to Bon's marriage to the octoroon mistress, it is likely that as a young Sutpen he would have. This theoretical probability— raised by Mr. Compson and later disproved by other facts—in its very error is valuable as a thematic datum. For "there is a might-have-been which is more true than truth," as Miss Rosa symptomatically puts it. Out of guess and conjecture, snatches of old story, the narrators build their tragedy. Perhaps none of it is true; or perhaps it is the only truth. How can truth be known except by conjecture? Quentin remarks, "If I had been there, I could not have seen it this plain."

Through the reciprocal interplay of narrators and the story they tell, the issues created by racial subordination are considered in many aspects and driven home through the working out of numerous parallels and re-capitulations. For purposes of analysis, two coordinate levels of the theme may be differentiated: the problem of blood as it figures in the Sutpen tragedy, and the issue of slavery as it affected the history of the South.

In the Sutpen tragedy, one of the most striking recurrent patterns expressing the theme is the problem of legal marriage, an obvious crux in a society where continuing class superiority depends on strict differentia-tion of blood. In fact, as Mr. Compson reminds us, sexual relationships between Negro women and white men were never honored by law. The license which recorded the marriage of Bon and his mistress was a meaning-less document, "vesting no new rights in no one [*sic*], denying to none the old." For, as Compson has Bon explain to Henry during the time when both young men assume that Bon is white, the ceremony was a mere ro-mantic ritual, unenforceable by the octoroon. For "this woman, this child, are niggers."

When Sutpen, in conformity to the "design," dishonors his legal tie to his first fractionally Negro wife, convincing himself that the claims of morality have been appeased by a financial settlement, his first crime against humanity is committed. According to law he has done, as he re-peatedly argues, more than was demanded of him. But there are obligations of heart and feeling of which Sutpen is unaware. The true nature of his "abysmal and purblind" innocence is appropriately commented upon by Gen. Compson (speaking through Quentin): ". . . because it was that innocence again . . . which believed that the ingredients of morality were like the ingredients of a pie or cake and once you had measured them and balanced them and mixed them and put them into the oven it was all finished and nothing but pie or cake could come out."

That innocence, a "minimal" response to the human spirit and its needs, Sutpen never outgrows. He marries Ellen not for love, but because he is ready to acquire the furniture for his house, "not the least of which furniture was the wedding license."

When Bon appears as the suitor to Judith, he comes as the instrument of vengeance for the outraged heart of his mother. Sutpen immediately knows him for his own son, and worse, knows that he is part Negro. Acknowledge him he feels he cannot; yet without acknowledgement there is no basis for objection to his marriage to Judith. "Fogbound" in this dilemma, Sutpen forbids the marriage without any reason, hoping that time itself will veer the curve of events within the orbit of his ambition.

But he fails to reckon with love. Judith and Henry both love Bon, and their self-sacrificing loyalty is as fixed as Sutpen's will. Alienated from his father because of the seeming unreasonableness of his opposition, Henry renounces his patrimony in favor of Bon, and in so doing deprives Sutpen of the sole object of his matrimonial endeavor—a suitable heir. Desperate, Sutpen plays his trump card (the information that Judith's suitor is part Negro), but again he miscalculates. Henry's prejudices are more deeply ingrained than his own, which have a purely practical basis in his ambition. What Sutpen had wished was merely to have Bon stopped; Henry murders him. Now both sons are lost, and Sutpen's incapacity for feeling has caused the death of Charles, the exemption of Henry from meaningful existence, the unbrided widowhood of Judith, and all the ills which are yet to befall the remaining Bon descendants.

His inability to locate his error dooms him to a repetition of his sins. At best, he can think only in terms of some practical mistake, some miscalculation in "strategy" which threw him off the "schedule" he had set himself for the completion of his project. The actual source of his frustrations remains concealed from him; he questions neither the limitations of his own rationalism nor the justice underlying the design itself. "Whether it was a good or bad design is beside the point," he tells Quentin's grandfather; "the question is, Where did I make the mistake in it . . .?" After the destruction of the design in Henry's flight from justice, he is chary of any new marital commitment which does not guarantee in advance the suitable heir of which he feels that he has been defrauded. Hence his retraction of his proposal to Miss Rosa. His cold-blooded proposition—"let's try it and if it's a boy and it lives, we'll get married"—enkindles in her the wrath which still burns after forty-three years. Hence, too, his holding off with Milly until after he knows the outcome of her delivery. When Wash is compelled to absorb the finality of Sutpen's dishonorable intentions toward

Milly, the bottom drops out of his world. His smiting down of Sutpen at this point is an appropriate vengeance against an overstepping—almost beyond credibility—of the bounds of generally understood humanity.

In their attitudes toward Negro-white marriages, Sutpen's children reflect the views of the class in which they have been reared. At least so Mr. Compson, reasoning from the axioms of Southern upper-class mores, offers for conjecture. His mythologizing completes the symmetry of the marriage pattern. According to him, the puritanical Henry was less offended by the voluptuousness of Bon's erotic tie to the octoroon mistress than by the implied insult to Judith of even a "morganatic" ceremony. Judith herself is pictured years later as reminding Etienne Bon that the "paper . . . between you and one who is inescapably negro . . . can be put aside." The point is clear: where caste rules prevail, affection and intimate relationships between "whites" and those of "tainted" blood cannot be recognized or sanctioned. The effect of such denial to those involved is, of course, vicious. Arbitrary rejection from those most binding of all ties, familial and marital love, breeds psychic outrage, and psychic outrage breeds personal revolt. The human psyche has its own mechanics of vengeance.

The exclusion of the Negro from another fundamental relation, participation as an accepted member in the social community with his fellows, adds further impetus to negative compulsions. This variation of the theme is also elaborately patterned. All the Sutpens accept the doctrines of racial supremacy as such, with no thought as to their origins, rightness, or possibility of modification under special circumstances. When Sutpen learns of his wife's part-Spanish, part-Negro ancestry, he ousts her without entertaining even momentarily the possibility of suppressing the knowledge of her origins, the traces of which were so invisible as to have successfully deceived him.

Judith, Clytie, Henry, and Miss Rosa similarly perpetuate the race assumptions derived from plantation culture. Clytie and Judith keep young Charles Etienne Bon scrupulously isolated from Negro companions, in an excess of good intention which has dire results. Clytie is depicted as trying literally to scrub the faint ivory tinge from his young skin. Henry, for all his delicacy of conscience, succumbs ironically at the last to the simple murderous reflexes of his class: his brother may marry his sister, but a "nigger" must be shot dead. Miss Rosa's prejudices are rabid, as has already been shown.

The indignation of the denied Sutpens, exhausting itself for lack of a more assailable object in wanton violence or destructive self-spite, is traced to its final obliteration from consciousness in the idiocy of Jim Bond. The well-bred mother of Bon never comes to terms with her dismissal. "Paranoic" in her enraged irreconcilability, she lives as the true Clytemnestra of the tale, appeasing her lust for vengeance at last. The genteel Charles Bon does not leave the scene without making final show of his outrage, in terms appropriate to his upbringing. His sudden determination to marry Judith against Henry's command, after his long submission to the outcome of Henry's internal debate, is touched off by the realization that he has been rejected by Sutpen and Henry, not as a man, or even as Judith's brother, but *in toto*—as Negro. "So it's the miscegenation, not the incest, that you can't bear," he reasons summarily, freezing in the instant of this awareness into stony recalcitrance. Defiance and counter-retaliation are the cause of his removing Judith's picture from his wallet and replacing it with that of his octoroon wife. (Shreve's foolish interpretation of this act gives ironic heightening to its real poignance.) Charles's gesture says, in effect, that if he is to be none of theirs, they will be none of his. In flaunting Henry's will, Charles invites his own death; yet before he is killed he succeeds in giving at least token return for the psychic blow he has received.

Charles Etienne Bon, whose spiritual rebellion is signalized in his establishment at Sutpen's Hundred of an anthropoid wife and in his rampages of uninhibited inebriation, reenacts his father's symbolic gestures with greater vehemence, in response to the more sustained psychic and social pressure which he has had to endure. Raised as white but self-identified as Negro, he treads that special path to Gethsemane which is reserved for the Joe Christmases of this world.

The blight of slavery is rendered with supreme effectiveness in terms of another pattern which appears recurrently in the Sutpen legend—the effect of race division upon the "common man" in the South—the poor white. Sutpen and his father were of this class; so too were Wash and Milly. The power of caste aspiration to blot the true ties of human kinship from recognition is brought fully home when it is remembered that Sutpen, who was incapable of according to Milly the accommodations provided even for a beast, had himself had a sister whose illegitimate child was born in an outbuilding. In Sutpen's sister's case, however, no vengeance was sought upon the defaulting male; the girl simply climbed back into the wagon with her child and rejoined the family.

But the mountain society from which the Sutpens descended lacked the conditions which fostered perpetual tensions of social status. A primitive community, men within it were judged on the basis of individual strength

and courage, not upon the ownership of goods or upon spurious differenti-
ations between the quality of their blood and that of certain of their fellows.
In the mountain where young Sutpen lived "the land belonged to anybody
and everybody and so the man who would go to the trouble and work to
fence off a piece of it and say 'this is mine' was crazy; and as for objects,
nobody had any more of them than you did."

The gradual descent from this mountain paradise to a society, "where
a few men not only had the power of life and death and barter and sale
over others, but had living human men to perform . . . [those tasks] which
no man ever has or will like to do," constitutes the fall of the Sutpens and
their kind from grace. The Biblical allusions which pervade the descent
heighten the contrast between mountain "innocence" and the spiritual depravity of a slave society.

The gradual corruption of the mountain-folk is traced step by step.
When Sutpen's hard-drinking father enters a tavern now, he is "not even
allowed to come in by the front door." At one place "a huge bull of a
nigger, the first black man, slave, they had ever seen," ejects him. (The
doorway barred to inferior whites, with a Negro standing in enforcement of
the distinction, is itself a recurrent symbol. Just so, the Negro butler turns
away young Sutpen, and Clytie later bars admission to Wash.) Soon Sutpen's father needs to find outlet for inexplicable tensions in the empty
triumphs of "whupping Pettibone's niggers." The passive, seemingly mocking docility of the slaves challenges in the white man his sense of personal
worth, causing him to strike out in random violence, not against Negroes as
individuals, but at their "balloon faces." The women, too, are affected; it
shows in a "certain flat level silent way" Sutpen's sisters and other women
of their kind had "of looking at niggers . . . with a kind of speculative an-
tagonism."

Young Sutpen's own loss of "innocence" takes place before that white
door of the great house of the plantation owner, where—under the stare
of the "nigger monkey"—he first felt, like Adam in Paradise, the shameful
inadequacy of his natural garb ("his patched overalls and no shoes"). That
single, contemptuous glance of the slave at the door altered his whole spiritual condition. The refusal of the Negro to hear his message or give him ad-
mittance provided the negative impetus upon which his entire design was
constructed. Indescribably moving is the account of young Sutpen's attempt, in his retreat to the woods for clarity of thought, to adapt himself to
his new sinful awareness by the use of his logical faculties. What makes this
effort all the more touching is that the labored advances of his circumscribed

reason are logical, undeflected by self-commiseration, and brought to a conclusion leading to action.

In his ordeal of social initiation, Sutpen learns—at a rate faster than his capacity for emotional assimilation—that there are differences "not only between white men and black ones," but between "white men and white," not measurable in the rudimentary tests of manhood with which he is familiar, like "lifting anvils or gouging eyes or how much whiskey you could drink." Sensing exactly where his own naked worth places him in this new system of values, Sutpen is outraged to the very depths of his being. His first impulse is to shoot the "man in the hammock," whose indifferent luxurious- ness is the symbol of everything which has disordered his simple world. But his reason tells him that nothing can be accomplished by direct assault. It "ain't a question of rifles," he painfully concludes: ". . . to combat them you have got to have what they have that made them do what that man did." Accepting the fruits of this logic, Sutpen sets himself to the labors indicated. The path of social conformity which he chooses, however, proves a straight descending route to perdition.

After our imaginative participation in Sutpen's ordeal, we can never be wholly alienated from him in sympathy. We cannot hate him, any more than Quentin can "hate" the South. The family stock from which Sutpen derived was the class of settlers released to America from penal servitude in Old Bailey, and from this bit of genealogy we may assume for young Sutpen a meager heritage of humanistic values. The governing influence of his mother upon the movements of the family (it was she who directed them westward, and it was not until after her death that they "slid" down the mountain), ceased in Sutpen's early adolescence. The effects of caste splendor upon his impressionable mind shortly thereafter were fatal. The ideals which guided him in life were thus inadequate in their origins and too soon crystallized from experience. "Courage" and "shrewdness" without humanity will not serve to found a family any more than they will afford a stable basis for a culture.

Within their understandable limitations, however, Sutpen's qualities are admirable. His private integrity, manifested in innumerable small ways —his refusal to malign his first wife, his unwillingness to accept favors he cannot return, his establishment of man-to-man superiority over his slaves in sportsmanlike physical combat (as opposed to anonymous raids in the darkness, typical of others of his class), his searching for faults in his own acts rather than blaming others or Fate for his disappointments, his purposive adherence in conduct to the illuminations of his reason—these virtues confirm the largeness of his stature.

To be sure, he never becomes an integrated member of his community. Yet this is an adverse reflection upon the community as well as upon Sutpen. Their first response to his entry was a watchful defensiveness of their own privileged status: they attempted to halt his architectural enterprise by having him placed under arbitrary arrest, and they incited a mob (which later dispersed "like rats") to bombard his bride with vegetable refuse. Over the years "the town . . . had merely assumed armistice rather than accepting and assimilating." Only General Compson gives him friendship, and it is he whom Sutpen honors with his confidence. Sutpen fights in the war for "four honorable years"; afterwards, he refuses flatly to be coerced into joining one of the armed secret groups which terrorize the country. To the deputation which calls upon him he speaks his mind with fearlessness and essential rightness: ". . . that if each man in the South . . . would see to the restoration of his own land, the general land and South would save itself."

In his independence and strength, he is truly heroic; in the tragic flaw of his nature he resembles the great tragic heroes of literature. Unlike Macbeth or Lear, however, he never gains insight into his fault. Like Oedipus, rather, he is driven to new evils by forces which antedate his birth and which are beyond the sphere of his conscious governing. He is the modern tragic hero, insofar as art can represent him, a man felt to be circumscribed by psychological and social conditions, however large his abilities and aspirations.

His tragic fate is reiterated in the plight of his unheroic foil, Wash Jones. Weak, cowardly, compliant, Wash nevertheless also knows the longings of the poor white to rise above his class and senses the derision of the Negroes for his familiarity with the plantation owner. Sutpen he takes for no less than "God himself." Wash, too, has an innocence to lose—the belief that because Sutpen is brave and a big plantation owner, he is capable of being human in considerations touching his design. ("But you are brave," he says to Sutpen prayerfully in submitting to the aged man's seduction of his granddaughter. "That's where it's different.") In his childlike adulation he believes that whatever the aged Sutpen driven to madness by the frustrations of his ambition may do, he will "make hit right" with the fifteen-year-old Milly.

The incredulity of his disillusionment equals that of the boy not accepted as a simple human boy by the "monkey" at the white door: "I kaint have heard what I know I heard," he utters. "I just know it. I just know I

kaint." Wash's thought, before he cuts his swath of corpses, is the despairing cry of a heart too young in the knowledge of this world's treachery to
support the staggering burden: "Better if his kin and mine too had never
drawn the breath of life on this earth. Better that all who remain of us be
blasted from the face of it."

Thus the results of caste ambition, as they affect the relations of whites
to whites as well as of whites to Negroes, are illustrated in the Sutpen
tragedy.

## 6

The Sutpen tragedy is the means of conveying the larger social tragedy.
In its broader outlines, the Sutpen tragedy is in many ways analogous to the
social. Sutpen had two sons: one white, the other Negro. He denied the
Negro; fratricide resulted. The Civil War, too, was a fratricidal conflict
caused by denial of the Negro. In the passage which designates the Mississippi River as the "geological umbilicus" of the continent, uniting Quentin
and Shreve in a "sort of geographical substantiation," the brotherhood of
North and South is established explicitly.

Sutpen's sin, his failure of humanity, is the equivalent in personal
terms of the sin of plantation culture, its failure to accept the brotherhood
of all mankind. Both failures are provided with the suggestion of an ancestry.
Sutpen's progenitors go back to the criminal element in England; slavery,
when first introduced into the West Indies, was begun by men "whom the
civilized land and people had expelled": "whose thinking and desires had
become too crass to be faced and borne longer," and who had been set,
"homeless and desperate upon the lonely ocean." In the description of Haiti
as "the half-way point between what we call the jungle and what we call
civilization," we are not far from Mr. Compson's description of the half-
civilized Methodist South: "(. . . Sutpen and Henry and the Coldfields too)
who have not quite yet emerged from barbarism, who two thousand years
hence will still be throwing off the yoke of Latin culture and intelligence
from which they never were in any great permanent danger to begin with."

The social tragedy is conveyed through the Sutpen tragedy concretely
as well as abstractly. As the biggest single plantation owner in the county,
Sutpen is the very incarnation of the Old South. In describing the conception, attainment, and destruction of Sutpen's design, Faulkner shows the
tragedy of that society in terms of the presiding theme.

The social panorama which first unfolds itself to young Sutpen's eye
when he descends the mountain is of "a country all divided and fixed and

neat with people living on it all divided and fixed and neat because of what color their skins happened to be and what they happened to own." The division upon which the planation system rests is seen as already established. He sees "niggers working in the fields . . . while fine men sat fine horses and watched them." Poor whites find miscellaneous work in connection with the plantations, getting their overalls and calico dresses from the "plantation commissary," or on store credit, and taking shelter in cabins "not quite as well kept up and preserved as the ones the nigger slaves lived in." The poor whites are physically less well provided for than the Negroes, but their dwellings are "nimbused with freedom's bright aura." In the theoretical concession to worth which freedom implies lies their torment. Only the exceptionally strong and ruthless of purpose, like Sutpen, could accept the challenge to equality with the men who sat the fine horses. Their more typical responses of indignation, blocking the road to an oncoming carriage or throwing dust after its proud wheels, were purely symbolic.

During the years in which Sutpen completes his house, obtains the appropriate wife, and raises to near adulthood the two perfectly suitable heirs of his caste ambitions, plantation society is depicted as reaching the pinnacle of civilized refinement in manners, arts, dress, ceremony and entertainment. The exquisiteness of these attainments is in part symbolized in the beauty of the house itself, its grace deriving from the enforced labors of the French architect and from the objects which go to furnish it: the crystal chandeliers, the candelabra, the tapestries, silver, linen, Damask, crystal, Wedgewood, carpets, and—above all—the great formal white door with its fanlight "imported pane by pane from Europe." (Shreve's garbled review of "crystal tapestries and Wedgewood chairs" is final evidence of the hopelessness of his ever comprehending this aspect of Quentin's cultural past.) Sutpen's marble monument, imported from Italy and brought past the Civil War blockade to be toted in the regimental forage wagon all the way from Charleston, symbolizes a sense of social grandeur and dignity which had become so completely assimilated by the upper classes as to be projected for immortality.

Sutpen's wife, Ellen, the vacuous "butterfly" who chaperones for Judith and Bon a courtship of patterend walks in a formal garden, is the female who presides over the rituals of refined existence. The shopping expeditions with her marriageable daughter, during which she would "finger and handle and disarrange and then reject . . . the meagre fripperies and baubles" of local shops, conveys the luxury of taste made possible by plantation prosperity. Henry's social experience, a round of hunting and cockfighting, amateur horse racing, and dancing at "other plantations almost interchangeable with his own," is the model of socially prescribed leisure. Judith's pattern, likewise, is conveyed by "riding habits" and "ball gowns." The library of the magnificent house, decked in the consummate festiveness of Southern Yuletide, is the scene where the gentlemanly young Henry renounces his birthright in favor of the even more gentlemanly, New Orleans-bred Bon, whose poised indolence and silken dressing gown had first won him his country brother's idolatry.

The image of that society is captured in briefly-sketched word pictures which are as conventional and set as old-time calendar prints. The slave belongs in this picture, and he is never omitted. There are the ladies going to church "with house negroes to carry the parasols and flyswishes . . . moving in hoops among the miniature broadcloth of the . . . little boys and pantelettes of the little girls." There is the evocation of Southern Christmas in a view of the plantation houses "with . . . holly thrust beneath the knockers . . . eggnog and toddy . . . and blue unwinded wood smoke standing above the plastered chimneys of the slave quarters." There is "music at night— fiddle and triangle among the blazing candles." On such occasions the best champagne is "dispensed out of the burlesqued pantomime elegance of Negro butlers." When the young Confederates make their farewells for battle, after an evening of waltzing with their crinolined ladies, the view of their departure includes their grooms and "body servants." The glory and romance are conveyed unforgettably, but the shadow of the slave haunts the scene. As Ellen and Judith return in their carriage from a triumphant shopping expedition, they ride with "an extra nigger on the box with the coachman to stop every few miles and build a fire and re-heat the bricks on which Ellen and Judith's feet rested."

The extent to which the entire social superstructure is set upon treacherous foundations is hinted at repeatedly. Graciousness prevails, but at too great a remove from the elementary facts of life. Private and colonel, on the eve of enlistment, are united in honor and pride. They "call each by their given names . . . one man to another above the suave powdered shoulders of the women." But they do so as gentleman to gentleman, "not . . . as one farmer to another across a halted plow in a field."

The delicacy of consideration accorded the young gentlewomen is not truly earned. Mr. Compson distinguishes three types of females in the society: "the virgins whom gentlemen someday married, the courtesans to whom they went while on sabbaticals to the cities, [and] the slave girls and women upon whom that first caste rested and to whom in certain cases it doubtless owed the very fact of its virginity." He describes the simple commandeering of the slave girls from the fields; no more respect was accorded the well kept octoroon mistresses, like Bon's, who for all their loyalty and careful nurturing were valuable only as "commodities." Except for the selective interest of the white man in these few, Mr. Compson has Bon explain to Henry, they "would have been sold to any brute for the price . . . body and soul for life . . . [to be used] with no more impunity than he would dare to use an animal." In their incredible beauty and helplessness, these women are "the supreme apotheosis of chattelry."

Upon the maintained difference between slave-girl and gentlewoman, slave laborer and gentleman, plantation society rested. Yet how different were Henry and the young men of his class from their darker-skinned contemporaries? It is Mr. Compson who asks this question and gives the answer: ". . . only in the surface matter of food and clothing and daily occupation any different from the Negro slaves who supported them—the same sweat, the only difference being that on the one hand it went for labor in the fields where on the other it went for the spartan pleasures which were available to them because they did not have to sweat in the field."

From the utmost heights comes the fall to utter devastation, economically, socially and spiritually. The war is lost, and not merely because of the superior strategy and numbers of the enemy, but through the transposition into military terms of the very flaw by which the society was marred, through "generals . . . who should not have been generals . . . who were generals not through training or aptitude . . . but, by divine right to say 'Go there' conferred upon them by an absolute caste system."

Girls of Judith's kind, created by "a hundred years of careful nurturing . . . by the tradition in which Thomas Sutpen's ruthless will had carved a niche," must now dress the "self-fouled bodies of the strange injured and dead," must learn to tend household without money or servants, to harness the mule, and go clad in faded gingham. The house, too, must surrender its objects of beauty and pride, "giving of itself in slow driblets of furniture and carpet, linen and silver."

Sutpen comes home to find "his plantation ruined, fields fallow . . . taxes and levies and penalties sowed by United States marshals . . . and all his niggers gone." Defeat has brought about a leveling of whites; Wash Jones, who never before would have dared, now freely crosses the threshold. Sutpen is reduced to running a country store with Wash. His persistence in his design becomes fantastic.

Most devastating is the spiritual alteration in the people. The gallantry of those who were the first to go is contrasted strikingly with the sullenness of those who were the first to come home: ". . . not all of them tramps, ruffians, but men who had risked and lost everything, suffered beyond endurance and had returned now to the ruined land, not the same men who had marched away but transformed . . . into the likeness of that man who abuses from very despair and pity the beloved wife or mistress who in his absence has been raped." Frustrated and embittered, these men strike fear into their compatriots who remained. During the era of carpetbaggers, they organize into night raiders, draining off in these excesses the "suppurations" of defeat. The more reflective exist, like Bon, "mindless and irrational companion and inmate of a body which . . . is still immersed . . . in recollections of old peace" but in whom consciousness enforces the knowledge that "what Was is one thing and now it is not because it is dead, it died in 1861."

Forty years later the Sutpen mansion, symbol of a social design, still stands. Its "rotting portico and scaling walls" bespeak "some desolation more profound than ruin." Three generations of Sutpen had met doom within it; three generations of Southerners, brooding upon the mystery of its decay, had lived within the shadow of its prefigured annihilation. The desolation of the mansion is the key to Quentin's own, and in the story of a design that failed we may read the meaning of the decline of the South. And more: this novel, which holds an instant in history timeless and infinite in sombre implication, is a new revelation of "the dark and simple heart of things,"[3] pulsing forever in the world. All human history in its recurrence of error and anguish is represented in the myth of Quentin, Sutpen, and the South. In this fall of a man, a house, a class, and a culture, we know again, with terrifying nearness, the inexorability of "fate." Hybris and its punishment, sin and atonement, psychological compulsions and their proliferating destructiveness—these concepts, ancient and modern, endow *Absalom, Absalom!* with the poetic reality of classic moral tragedy.

3. *Mosquitoes* (New York, 1927), p. 340.

## B. The Edge of Yoknapatawpha

# UNITY OF THEME AND STRUCTURE IN *THE WILD PALMS*

### JOSEPH J. MOLDENHAUER

WHEN FAULKNER's double novel, *The Wild Palms,* appeared in 1939, its peculiarity of structure—the alternating chapters of two long stories whose plots, characters, settings, and themes seemed completely unrelated—provoked a number of reviewers to express bewilderment and outright dissatisfaction with the work as a whole. They were virtually unanimous in their praise of one of the tales, "Old Man," and unenthusiastic though not bitterly hostile toward the other, "Wild Palms." But they gravely denounced the coupling of the stories as arbitrary, artificial, and detrimental to both narratives.[1] Conrad Aiken raised his voice in the wilderness when he admired the book's "fugue-like alternation of viewpoint";[2] but he did not suggest the relationship between this structure and the themes and characters of the stories. The novel's publication history appeared to bear out the reviewers' conclusions: Signet Books, after having published "Old Man" and "Wild Palms" in separate volumes, issued them between one set of covers, but without alternation of chapters, in 1954. Modern Library has recently reprinted "Old Man" with "Spotted Horses" and "The Bear" in one volume.[3] And Malcolm Cowley shared the majority opinion when in his introductory notes to *The Portable Faulkner,* which contains "Old Man" as an independent selection, he wrote that this story is more effective than "Wild Palms" and "gains by standing alone."[4]

Among the inevitable results of the contemporary "discovery" of

1. See Anonymous, "When the Dam Breaks," *Time,* January 23, 1939, pp. 45-46; Clifton Fadiman, "Mississippi Frankenstein," *The New Yorker,* January 21, 1939, pp. 68-69; and Ben Ray Redman, "Faulkner's Double Novel," *Saturday Review of Literature,* January 21, 1939, p. 5.
2. Conrad Aiken, "William Faulkner—The Novel as Form," *The Atlantic,* 165 (November, 1939), p. 653. Alfred Kazin, in "A Study of Conscience" (*Books,* January 22, 1939, p. 2), admires the coupling but offers only superficial justifications for it.
3. William Faulkner, *Three Famous Short Novels* (New York, 1958).
4. Malcolm Cowley, ed., *The Portable Faulkner* (New York, 1946), p. 540.

Faulkner has been a renewed interest in *The Wild Palms*. "Old Man" and "Wild Palms" have been studied individually, and critical attempts to explain the curious form of the original edition have in the past decade produced several imaginative though somewhat unconvincing hypotheses. In any case, it has been firmly established that the reader should recognize *The Wild Palms* as a structural experiment and that each of the stories might be profitably read in terms of the other.

"Old Man," with its chronological plot and seeming lack of philosophical complexity, has always been the more popular work. Early critics were quick to appreciate the fundamentally allegorical qualities of this story: the nameless protagonist, the parable-like beginning, the heavy elements of fate and coincidence, the archetypal material of a voyage on water, and the ostensibly direct moral recommendation of the hero, who endures cyclopean hardships with singleness of mind and will. While "Old Man" is not so systematic an allegory as *Pilgrim's Progress,* it will survive comparison with works like *Mardi* and *Huckleberry Finn.* (The *Time* reviewer quite shrewdly entitled it "a kind of hysterical *Huckleberry Finn*,[5] and Cowley extended the comparison in his *Portable Faulkner* notes.) Moreover, "Old Man" has much in common with Faulkner's earlier saga, *As I Lay Dying,* particularly that the physical obstacles faced by the voyagers in each tale are so huge and frustrating that they give the work an integral quality of grotesque humor. An allegorical reading of "Old Man" is unquestionably enlightening; but Faulkner's pairing of "Wild Palms" with the river tale suggests that the former story might set limits of interpretation upon the latter.

What has unfortunately been overlooked is that "Wild Palms" itself contains many allegorical elements. It also portrays a physical and spiritual voyage. Fate and coincidence are highly instrumental to its plot. The name of the protagonist, Harry Wilbourne, embraces rich denotative possibilities, among which are "will burn" (will suffer some infernal punishment), "burning with will," and "bourne-ed (limited) by will." Just as "Old Man" invites comparison with *Huckleberry Finn* (although the dominant values of Mark Twain's novel are in fact inverted in "Old Man"), "Wild Palms" might easily be called a hysterical or inverted *Scarlet Letter*. While the symbolic content of Faulkner's story can be in part traced to such disparate sources as Dante[6] and Hemingway,[7] the characterizations and the theme—

5. Anon., "When the Dam Breaks," p. 46.
6. That is, the Paolo and Francesca Canto (V) of the *Inferno*.
7. See especially "Hills Like White Elephants," *The Short Stories of Ernest Heming-*

the complex, often destructive demands upon one another of the physical or spiritual or psychological elements in man—are immediately suggestive of Hawthorne's novel. Furthermore, Faulkner's double-edged use of allegorical materials, with its accompanying delight in the manipulation of points of view, is at least a close cousin to Hawthorne's method. Both writers employ the moral and aesthetic weapon of puritanism, the concept of correspondence between the emblem and the thing symbolized, in making critical judgments upon the puritan's own mental anatomy. In effect, they ironically reverse allegorical expectations to illustrate the awesome pitfalls which allegorical thinking and moral preconceptiqn place in the way of human sympathy.

In both "Wild Palms" and "Old Man" the relationship of the protagonist to the moral framework of Southern puritanism is of central importance. Neither story was intended to stand alone, and if they are separated one sacrifices not simply a clever structural device but a vital dimension of meaning. It is in the interaction of the two equivocally allegorical tales, one, like *The Scarlet Letter,* approaching fearful tragedy, and the other, like *Huckleberry Finn,* verging upon burlesque in its humor, that the reader must seek any final statement by the novelist.

## 2

Harry Wilbourne is a renegade medical intern whose tortured and fatal romance with a married woman, Charlotte Rittenmeyer, forms the substance of "Wild Palms." Although he is introduced in the first chapter of the novel, the nature of his problem remains a mystery until two chapters later, when the story has its chronological beginning. Meanwhile the reader is given two other characters against whom to measure Wilbourne: the convict-protagonist of "Old Man" and the point-of-view character of chapter one. The latter is a doctor from whom Harry and Charlotte have rented a cabin on the gulf shore where she succumbs to blood-poisoning contracted in an abortion attempt. The product of a "provincial protestant"[8] upbringing, a domineering father, and an acceptable though mediocre medical education, the doctor has stepped into his father's practice, taken the wife

---

*way* (New York, 1938), p. 373. H. Edward Richardson has discussed similarities between "Wild Palms" and *A Farewell to Arms* in his article, "The 'Hemingwaves' in Faulkner's 'Wild Palms,'" *Modern Fiction Studies,* 4 (Winter, 1958-1959), pp. 357-360.

8. Faulkner, *The Wild Palms* (New York: Random House, 1939), p. 9. Subsequent references to *The Wild Palms* are to page numbers in this edition and will be cited parenthetically in the text.

his father chose for him into the house his father had built, and slept with her in the same childless bed for twenty-three years. While he suspects, with grim righteousness, that his tenants are not married, he does not openly declare this suspicion to his monochromatic wife because "They both knew that, once it was said aloud between them, he would turn the renters out" (9).

Aware that Charlotte is ill, the "doctor in the Doctor" is professionally curious; but the Baptist in the Doctor, zealous to perceive moral absolutes and violations from a safe distance, believes he can discern "the truth already, the shadowy indefinite shape of truth, as though he were separated from the truth only by a veil" (6). Called to the cabin when Charlotte suffers a hemorrhage, he learns that Harry himself had performed the abortion. The doctor's shock and revulsion almost outweigh his orthodox wrath: *"I thought you were the lover,"* he thinks; *"There are rules! Limits! To fornication, adultery, to abortion, crime. . . . To that of love and passion and tragedy which is allowed to anyone lest he become as God Who has suffered likewise all that Satan can have known"* (280). In his unwilling proximity to these massive sins, the doctor suggests what Charlotte had told Wilbourne before they began their troubled odyssey: that for the selfless lover there is a basic identity between sex and moral dedication, that " 'love and suffering are the same thing and that the value of love is the sum of what you have to pay for it and any time you get it cheap you have cheated yourself' " (48).

The doctor's function in the story is a complex one: he is neither in diametric contrast to Wilbourne nor merely the man whom Harry might have become if he had obeyed his own tradition and training. Although the doctor undeniably typifies the conventional and barren future from which Harry had thought he was escaping, he also serves as a full representative of those very moral scruples which prevent Wilbourne's happiness and which subconsciously—but inexorably—drive him to failure in the abortion. In Wilbourne, Faulkner presents as deliberate a psychoanalytic study as that of Quentin Compson in *The Sound and the Fury*. And Harry is not, as several critics have assumed, a well-meaning innocent whose desire for a sincere romantic relationship with Charlotte is thwarted by the forces of nature or society.[9] Nor is he, as one hypothesis has it, an Adamic figure corrupted by an insatiable paramour,[10] indeed, the reverse seems to be the

9. Richardson, p. 357; William Van O'Connor, *The Tangled Fire of William Faulkner* (Minneapolis, 1954), pp. 104-110; and, by implication, W. R. Moses, "The Unity of *The Wild Palms," Modern Fiction Studies*, 2 (Autumn, 1956), pp. 125-131.
10. Irving Howe, *William Faulkner* (New York, 1952), p. 173.

case. The same Puritan preoccupation with a fixed moral and social order which has molded the doctor lies behind Wilbourne's incapacity to enjoy the pagan freedom Charlotte offers him, behind his masochistic and self-defeating efforts to refute that order, and behind his final eager acceptance of the sentence pronounced by an outraged gulf-town court. Fearful of physical love and unable to escape or obey his conscience, Harry Wilbourne follows a course of frenzied self-punishment which culminates in his blundering and compulsive murder of Charlotte.

Harry's father had worked his way through medical school and expected his son, who chose to follow the paternal calling, likewise to reap the fruits of thrift and industry. Harry pursues his education under the constant dread of failure and the constant burden of poverty. The frugality of his "monastic life" in New Orleans demands that he renounce love and even its surrogate and partner, imagination. Still virgin on his twenty-seventh birthday, he thinks of "the empty years . . . for the passionate tragic ephemeral loves of adolescence, . . . which had not been for him"; but, he concludes, *"I do not need it; by next year or two years or five years . . . I will not even need to want it"* (34). A fellow intern, pitying him, subdues Harry's conscience, "the guardian of the old trained peace and resignation . . . the grim Moses" (35), and persuades him to come to a party. Here he meets Charlotte, a passionate sculptress whose dissatisfaction with her conventional marriage is as honest as it is painful for her husband. Harry is attracted by her yellow eyes, her candor, and her strong dignity; she is struck with sympathy for his poverty and inexperience. Wilbourne's exposure and initiation to love are neatly rendered in the description of the garden at the artist's home where he meets Charlotte. The passage displays Faulkner's impressive control of Freudian symbolism as he renders the scene from a point of view close to Wilbourne's:

Flint jerked the bell again, again nothing came of it. "It's not locked, anyway," Wilbourne said. It was not, they entered: a court paved with the same soft, quietly rotting brick. There was a stagnant pool with a terracotta figure, a mass of lantana, the single palm, the thick rich leaves and the heavy white stars of the jasmine bush where light fell upon it through open French doors, the court balcony—overhung too on three sides, the walls of that same annealing brick lifting a rampart broken and nowhere level against the glare of the city on the low eternally overcast sky, and over all, brittle, dissonant and ephemeral, the spurious sophistication of the piano like symbols scrawled by adolescent boys upon an ancient decayed rodent-scavengered tomb. (36-37)

On their second meeting Harry and Charlotte admit their love for one another; she holds out to him a brave new world of sensual freedom. But circumstances threaten to forestall the affair. A hotel tryst fails because of Charlotte's aversion to secrecy and guilt, which she fears will corrupt their love. Moreover, they lack funds to support themselves. Despite her emotional intensity, Charlotte is eminently practical; she decides that they must not meet again. By fantastic coincidence Harry now finds a wallet containing nearly thirteen hundred dollars in a trash bin. His first impulse, significantly, is to return the wallet. He walks to the post office in order to mail the treasure to its owner, with an ascetic's glee at having saved himself *"at least forty-five minutes of time that otherwise would have been filled with leisure"* (52). But the post office is closed, and hours later the opportunity which the money affords finally dawns upon him. He informs Charlotte that they will be able to leave New Orleans.

Even at the outset of his adventure with Charlotte, Harry reveals the sense of guilt which will cause his tragic failure. On the train to Chicago, he reflects upon the morality of his deeds, and while he maintains disbelief in "sin," his definition of iniquity has a relentless inherent Puritanism of its own: *"You are born submerged in anonymous lockstep with the teeming anonymous myriads of your time and generation; you get out of step once, falter once, and you are trampled to death"* (54). Yet to Charlotte love is a religion complete in itself. She invokes the Sermon on the Mount as she suggests to Harry that they consummate their relationship immediately. For her the act will be a symbolic repudiation of conventional society and its inherited burden of remorse. As Wilbourne follows her down the aisle to a compartment he believes that "everyone in the car must have known their history" and discerned their "aura of unsanctity" (60). After they have established residence in Chicago Charlotte provides a theological definition of love: it must be " 'Either heaven, or hell: no comfortable safe peaceful purgatory between for you and me to wait in until good behavior or forbearance or shame or repentance overtakes us.' " It is a gift, she continues, some form of divine grace: " 'They say that love dies between two people. That's wrong. . . . It just leaves you, goes away, if you are not good enough, worthy enough. It doesn't die; you're the one that dies' " (83). In terms of Wilbourne's preconceptions it is an inner appetite, a shameful flaw. The Chicago sojourn is for him a period of continual introspection. He tries to talk himself into accepting Charlotte's theory of love (84-85), but his very self-consciousness makes the possibility of such a conversion preposterous.

A hard-bitten journalist named McCord, who admires the sincerity of

Charlotte's convictions, assists the lovers in their rebellion from society when destitution compels them to leave the city. He takes them to an unoccupied cabin on a Wisconsin lake, but before returning to Chicago he recognizes Wilbourne's Puritan dilemma: " 'You haven't even got the courage of your fornications, have you?' " He admonishes Harry to " 'Stop thinking about yourself and think about Charlotte for a while' " (101). If this is impossible, he offers to send Charlotte back to New Orleans, leaving Wilbourne to " 'eat through your hundred bucks and then move into the woods and eat ants and play Saint Anthony in a tree and on Christmas you can take a mussel shell and make yourself a present of your own oysters' " (103). McCord's last remark is of course an acute analysis of Wilbourne's latent wishes. While Charlotte roams the woods with her sketch-pad and water-colors and sunbathes naked every day, Harry sleeps in the cabin almost constantly. When awake he lies on the bed, "not even thinking but merely existing in a drowsy and foetuslike state" (110). Wilbourne is likewise passive in their lovemaking. He can neither enjoy Charlotte completely nor summon the strength to leave her.

This qualified idyll comes to an end as winter approaches. Harry is suddenly resentful of nature itself for having conspired against him to make him unaware of his moral position: *"I have been seduced to an imbecile's paradise by an old whore; I have been throttled and sapped of strength and volition by the old weary Lilith of the year"* (114-115). Foetuslike submission has not solved Wilbourne's problem. Without an organizing moral equation the relationship has become meaningless for him. Charlotte had hoped to return to prelapsarian innocence through sensuality; she had addressed him as "Adam" and had not hidden her body; and now Harry urges in vain that she return to Chicago alone, leaving him to live (as McCord had predicted) like a hermit in the woods.

Once again in the city, Charlotte finds work in a department store and Wilbourne sits at home writing erotic confession stories for the pulp magazines. This occupation, which he pursues with zest and intensity, is a means by which he can shamefully record his own preoccupations with sin, and, in making them public, indulge in the exhibitionist's self-degradation. He writes while Charlotte sleeps and retires when she arises, adding celibacy to exhibitionism. But even this arrangement proves unsatisfactory when he is rewarded by society, with money and respectability, for his very act of self-punishment. The city has provided a *"routine even of sinning, an absolution even for adultery"* (126). Harry concludes that they must leave Chicago, and he accepts a position as a doctor at a Utah mining camp.

Immediately before their departure for this weird snowbound place, Wilbourne holds a lengthy conversation with McCord. Toasting "freedom" with a glass of ginger-ale, he unwittingly portrays the irony of his ineffectual quest. McCord warns Harry that his flight to Utah in midwinter is simply further imprisonment; but Wilbourne, as if to convince the journalist that he has been enlightened, launches into a violent denunciation of society and its values—which are, as we know, his own: " 'what we call the prime virtues—thrift, industry, independence,' " he says, breed " 'all the vices—fanaticism, smugness, meddling, fear, and worst of all, respectability' " (133). Because " 'There is no place for [love] in the world today' " (136), Wilbourne's noble ambition is to reconstruct love by escaping civilization, to establish a moment of perfection and "solitude" in the sexual act. Finally, in a dithyrambic outburst, Harry names McCord and Charlotte as the "parents" of some sacred awareness in him and requests McCord's blessing. The journalist, realizing that selfishness and self-deception underlie all Wilbourne's declarations and that Harry's own limitations, rather than the pressures of society, have stunted the romance, replies, " 'Take my curse' " (141).

The Utah episode once more demonstrates Harry's inability to find emotional peace with Charlotte. It can best be understood as a nightmare attempt to purify and punish himself and his lover. When the snows begin to melt in spring, Charlotte conceives through a contraceptive accident and pleads with Wilbourne to perform an abortion upon her. The bankruptcy of the mine owners has again made the lovers destitute, and Charlotte argues that " 'I can starve and you can starve but not it. So we must, Harry' " (205). But in the light of Wilbourne's obsession, the prospect of a child is a blessing. Like Hester's Pearl in *The Scarlet Letter* the baby will be a visible sign, for all society to see, of his guilt and sin with Charlotte. He refuses to perform the operation and takes Charlotte to Texas, where he unsuccessfully seeks employment in order to support the child when it arrives. In desperation he tries to " 'set up as a professional abortionist' " (208), offering to accept cases from licensed physicians as an ironic alternative to operating on Charlotte. But he has promised her that he will comply with her request if he has not found work by the fourth month, and he is held to his word. Like his search for a job, the abortion is "inherent with its own negation" (219). He later explains his failure in these terms: *"A miser would probably bungle the blowing of his own safe too. Should have called in a professional, a cracksman who didn't care, didn't love the very iron flanks that held the money"* (297). But the analogy is not an adequate explanation. Wilbourne's dilemma precludes a successful abortion. The reason for the "failure" lies in his compulsive need to punish himself and Charlotte for their life of what he has believed all the while to be sin. Charlotte's brooding apathy, so apparent to the doctor in chapter one, results not only from her fear of death but also from her subtle recognition that her lover has sacrificed her in chastizing himself.

Charlotte's last request is that Harry run away. But he remains with her in the cabin, and when the ambulance and sheriff arrive (both had been called by the doctor), Wilbourne asks to be handcuffed. After her death he is sentenced by a provincial jury and a righteous judge to fifty years of hard labor at a prison farm. His rejection of a chance for suicide presented by Charlotte's husband serves as a final affirmation of his wish to enjoy the full pain of punishment. *"Yes,* he thought, *between grief and nothing I will take grief"* (324).

3

On one of the infrequent occasions when Faulkner has spoken publicly about his double novel he called it a story of "two types of love."[11] In "Old Man" as in "Wild Palms," the central theme is the conflict between freedom (or sex) and the demands of a restrictive moral framework. The convict possesses a simple, unfathomable puritan ideology, and he has acquired security and dignity at a Mississippi prison farm. When during the great flood of 1927 he is sent onto the river to rescue a trapped woman, he finds himself in a world of violent, inexplicable nature, of mechanical force, and he struggles almost blindly to fulfill the duty with which he has been entrusted. The convict does not take advantage of his freedom. He does not even comprehend it, for he is in fact less free on the river than at the farm. No thought of escape disturbs his inner serenity, and upon his return, weeks later, he accepts an additional prison sentence with equanimity, even gratitude.

Imagination, the cause of Wilbourne's defection from his internship, is directly responsible for the convict's imprisonment. A voracious reader of detective fiction, he had studied tales of banditry with Calvinistic diligence, "taking the good from each and discarding the dross as his workable plan [for a train robbery] emerged" (24). The robbery was a fiasco:

11. Lavon Roscoe, "An Interview with William Faulkner," *The Western Review,* 15 (Summer, 1951), p. 300.

he entered the train carrying a toy pistol and dark lantern and wearing a mask, and was captured instantly by the trainmen. After seven years at Parchman, he still feels outrage "not at the men who had foiled his crime, not even at the lawyers and judges who had sent him here, but at the writers" of crime stories whom he had accepted, with "outspoken good faith" (23), as spokesmen of the truth. And now the convict has willingly renounced imagination and the "fluid world of his time" (25) just as the young Wilbourne renounced the world of sex which he believed he could never afford. The convict has discovered at the prison farm a suitable environment for the exercise of those virtuous ambitions and the attainment of those imperative spiritual goals whose symbol—money—he had sought when planning the robbery.

Because the convict strikes deep roots at Parchman, he comes to consider the "fluid" world illusory, and the simple duties of the farm become the substance of reality. Parchman has been his home "almost since childhood"; here he is accepted by mules and men; here he is respected. He thinks of

his own character (Two years ago they had offered to make a trusty of him. He would no longer need to ploy or feed stock, he would only follow those who did with a loaded gun, but he declined. "I reckon I'll stick to plowing," he said, absolutely without humor. "I done already tried to use a gun one time too many.") his good name, his responsibility not only toward those who were responsible toward him but to himself, his own honor in the doing of what was asked of him, his pride in being able to do it, no matter what it was. (166)

Sheltered from the temptations of the appetites or the imagination, the convict enjoys an anchorite's limited horizons and unimaginable bliss.

As if with a will of its own, the flood wrenches the convict from his monastic existence; he and his fellow prisoners are assigned to strengthen a crumbling river-bank. Although he had worked the soil for years in the shadow of the levee, he had, significantly, never seen the Mississippi, the "Old Man" which serves as a violent epitome of the "fluid" social world the convict had abjured. Even in its backwaters, the flood resembles "a rifle bullet the width of a cotton field" (145); a cresting wave is like "the mane of a galloping horse" (156); the swirling eddies are "iron-like and shifting convolutions like an anaconda" (145); and against this backdrop of lawless energy men are reduced to "cattle," "dogs," and "ants." Confronted with this spectacle, the convict is bewildered, his concept of the earth's stability undermined like the levees themselves. When a deputy asks him to row through the flooded farmland behind the levee to rescue a stranded woman, he assures himself that he will not have to go " 'nowhere out yonder' " on the raging and incomprehensible Mississippi, and then accepts the task with his customary stoicism.

The skiff presently enters a flooded bayou. Caught in the current, it whirls with unexpected violence, overturns, and with the convict grasping its sterns, sweeps madly downstream. In an initial attempt to identify himself as the stable center of an unhinged universe the convict seems "to see the trees and sky rushing past with vertiginous speed." But he soon realizes his own helplessness and envies the trees that they were "fixed and secure in something" (144). Unable to explain nature's violation of his stability, he responds with intense moral resentment. He has become a "toy and pawn on a vicious and inflammable geography" (162), and while he still struggles—as he is to struggle for seven weeks—to impose his will upon nature, his efforts are ludicrously unrewarding. The skiff rights itself in colliding with a snag, and the convict, his nose broken by the impact, manages to crawl aboard. Then he tries to paddle against the current, which spins the boat through a wide circle and again dashes it against the snag, hurling the convict flat on his face in the bloody bilge. Lying there in "a kind of abject meditation," he thinks that he "would have to get up sometime, . . . just as all life consists of having to get up sooner or later and then having to lie down again sooner or later after a while" (147). But a voice interrupts his reveries, and in the branches of the snag above he sees the woman he had been sent to save. She is big with child.

Taking the woman into the skiff, the convict attempts to complete his assignment, but he is again unable to propel or even maneuver the boat, and they are soon swept into the Yazoo River. He now paddles *with* the current, in the direction he believes to be downstream, furiously seeking "people, houses, something, anything he might reach and surrender his charge to and turn his back . . . on all pregnant and female life forever and return to that monastic existence of shotguns and shackles where he would be secure from it" (153). For the woman has already come to symbolize to him the realm which he had denied as illusory and chaotic: the maddening and terrific flood is but a larger emblem of the mechanical fecundity which she embodies. But the river changes its course, destroying any last measure of the convict's belief in the order of external experience. Whereas the Yazoo had previously been backing up, away from the "Old Man," its current is now reversed by the mass of water which has broken through the levees above and which rushes in a huge crest back toward the Mississippi. Baffled and exhausted, the convict huddles blindly in the bow as the skiff is swept past Vicksburg and onto the Father of Waters.

Two days pass, and the convict still obeys only his sense of obligation to the authority which has sent him into this unimaginable wilderness of water. His immediate aim is to "get rid of the woman, the belly, . . . in the right way" (161). But the endeavor fails when the convict is twice fired upon, first by a gang of criminals in a shanty boat and again by a group of soldiers at a landing below Baton Rouge. Implacable nature, no longer satisfied that he simply endure, now forces him to participate in its progress. On a half-flooded and snake-infested Indian burial mound the woman bears her child with the assistance of the convict. He displays the same grudging sense of obligation as that with which he struggles to preserve the boat and himself on the river, and he feels the "same outrageous affronting of a condition purely moral, the same raging impotence to find any answer to it" (229). Looking down upon the infant, he recognizes the fundamental affinity between sex and nature, the antithesis to his settled existence at Parchman: *"This is what severed me violently from all I ever knew and did not wish to leave and cast me upon a medium I was born to fear, to fetch up at last in a place I never saw before and where I do not even know where I am"* (231).

Because the paddle has unaccountably disappeared, the travellers must spend another week on the mound, subsisting on drowned animals, while the convict painstakingly burns a tree into a makeshift oar. He at first avoids and finally almost ignores the water mocassins, which represent all that is loathesome and destructive in the "fluid world." His relationship to the snakes parallels his struggle with the river: rather than attempting to kill them, he simply strives to maintain his moral posture, for he is as unresponsive to evil as to freedom. During the next fortnight he and the woman live in the marshes behind the levee with a Cajun alligator hunter who takes the convict into a hunting partnership. It is a grotesque pastoral interlude in the convict's odyssey. He takes a naïve pleasure of workmanship in killing alligators, not with a gun, but with knife and club, to the amazement and admiring glee of the Cajuns. The reptiles, like the "Old Man" itself, are beyond his comprehension, and he identifies them as merely a large and powerful breed of livestock. *"After all,"* he thinks, preparing to attack the first one, *"a man cant only do what he has to do, with what he has to do it with, with what he has learned, to the best of his judgment. And I reckon a hog is still a hog, no matter what it looks like"*

(258). This is surely a profound protestantism. Although the obligation to complete his mission still dominates his consciousness, he decides with surprise that he enjoys making money. But even this small pleasure, by which Faulkner gives some human depth to the allegorical outlines of the convict, is cut short by the implacable river. "Cosmic violence" descends on him again; the "cosmic joker" (264) causes the flood to resume and drives the convict and his charges back into the skiff. Two weeks later, seven weeks after he had set out to rescue the woman, he lands the skiff at his point of departure, finds a law officer, and announces that his job is finished.

But the convict has been officially declared dead, and, as an emissary from the governor tells the perplexed warden, he "doesn't belong" at Parchman. The warden is posed with two alternatives. He can classify the convict's absence as an escape or dismiss the deputy who had reported him dead. Since the deputy wields considerable political influence, he chooses the least painful course: " 'They are going to have to add ten years to your time,' " he tells the convict, who replies, " 'All right, . . . If that's the rule' " (331). He accepts with quiet pleasure the security of his closed universe, a realm without violence and without women.

While Harry Wilbourne tries to burst moral limits and plunge into freedom and sex, the convict struggles to avoid involvement in that "fluid world" and to return to the greater freedom of his circumscribed life at the prison farm. It is precisely because Harry shares the moral orientation of the doctor and the convict that he defeats himself; it is precisely because of the convict's total and slavish commitment to his moral code that he manages to endure the blows of the cosmic joker. Moreover, nature (or sex) and time are centrally related in both "Old Man" and "Wild Palms." Each protagonist's efforts to make time meaningful serve to illuminate the conflict between inner moral compulsion and external reality. At the chronological beginning of "Wild Palms," Harry believes that his ascetic dedication to the goal of a medical career has somehow placed him outside of time (33), but his very concern with lost youth illustrates his dissatisfaction. Charlotte offers him passion and suffering as a means to redeem time and to nullify its mechanical progress. At first Harry agrees: at the moment of sexual fulfillment, as he later tells McCord, he finds himself in "eclipse" and "outside of time" (137). At the lake with Charlotte, hounded by the guilt of self-violation, he ponders the "timeless void into which the individual days had vanished" (114) and realizes that he must impose some kind of temporal order upon the future. He discovers that he can use "the dates of and intervals between Charlotte's menstrual periods" as the basis for his calendar, delighting in the paradox that "Nature the unmathematical, the overfecund, the prime disorderly and illogical and patternless spend-thrift" will be forced to "prove his mathematical problem for him" (114). When Wilbourne delivers his parting sermon to McCord in the railroad station, the two men stand beneath a clock whose "ubiquitous and syn-chronized face, oracular admonitory and unsentient" (131), sharpens the irony of Harry's proclamation about "freedom" and "love." And when, during Charlotte's pregnancy, Wilbourne fails to find employment, the means of casting her condition into moral perspective are reduced to one: the abortion will be botched; then it will be simply a matter of time before her death. Harry is convicted of manslaughter and sentenced to hard labor at Parchman " 'for a period of not less than fifty years' " (321). Time will, at last, acquire moral dimension through memory and guilt and grief.

Behind his mules in the rich fields, the convict is unaware of temporal progress because his temptationless existence allows him to disclaim his criminal youth in the "living and fluid world" as insubstantial. After he has been swept away in the bayou, the deputy, presuming him dead, displays his ignorance of the convict's orientation by saying " 'He's free. He's done served his time' " (80). Just as the convict is actually imprisoned, not liberated, by the river, he is also cast into a time scheme which is destruc-tive and therefore morally unsatisfactory. The "Old Man," as C. P. Swig-gart suggests, is itself a symbol for the mechanical passage of time; and the convict is related to Thomas Sutpen of *Absalom, Absalom!* and the Bundrens of *As I Lay Dying* in his struggle to deny this mechanical move-ment by "sheer perseverance of will."[12] Time challenges him to prove his immunity, and the demands of the river are relentless. As in "Wild Palms" the urgent passage of time is linked to the woman's reproductive function. "Time: that was his itch now" (169), the narrator remarks as the woman goes into labor. The additional ten-year sentence levied upon the convict when he returns to Parchman is not, from his point of view, punitive. Paradoxically, ten years of "time" in prison will be another decade of free-dom from the demands of the world outside, a world which exists in *in-significant* time. When a fellow convict rails at the warden's apparent in-justice, declaring that " 'It's them ten more years that hurt. Ten more years to do without a woman,' " the protagonist answers with implicit dis-agreement and grave scorn, " 'Women—!' " (339)

12. C. P. Swiggart, "Moral and Temporal Order in *The Sound and the Fury*," *Sewanee Review*, 111 (Spring, 1953), p. 231.

## 4

Irving Howe, who in his *William Faulkner* made the first serious effort
to explain and justify the alternation of chapters in *The Wild Palms*, submitted the following pattern for the interweaving of plot elements:[13]

| "The Wild Palms" | "Old Man" |
|---|---|
| 1. Failure of abortion, Charlotte close to death. | 2. Convict leaves for flood. |
| 3. Flashback: Charlotte and Harry leave New Orleans. | 4. "Lost" in flood. |
| 5. Flashback: drifting from country to Chicago. | 6. Drifting with pregnant woman on flood waters. |
| 7. Flashback: haven in a mining camp. | 8. Haven with Cajun. |
| 9. Charlotte's death, Harry's imprisonment. | 10. Return to prison. |

Howe supplements his design with this statement: "Even a glance at the . . .
parsing of the novel should show rough parallels between the stories and
the possibility that if taken together they might yield a tone of dissonant
irony which neither could alone. . . . Each story charts an escape from
confinement to a temporary and qualified freedom, and then to an ultimate,
still more confining imprisonment."[14] But his conceptions of "freedom"
and "imprisonment" and his reading of the two stories as basically identical
in moral statement cast severe limitations upon his search for "dissonant
irony," and his argument that "the two parts of the book are genuinely
bound together by theme and atmosphere"[15] does not thoroughly convince
the reader of the need for chapter alternation. Howe even lowers his colors
somewhat in the last paragraph of his essay: "Probably of little use to anyone but himself, Faulkner's device . . . may be judged a *tour de force* that
partly works."[16]

In an article entitled "The Unity of 'The Wild Palms,' " W. R. Moses
presents the provocative idea that "Themes—and plots are . . . mirror twins
of an almost embarrassing degree of similarity."[17] He picks up Howe's
equation of the "drifting" motifs of chapters five and six, and observes that

13. Howe, p. 176.
14. *Ibid.*, p. 177.
15. *Ibid.*, p. 172.
16. *Ibid.*, p. 178.
17. Moses, p. 125.

"the convict struggles to escape a material flood," whereas "Harry and Charlotte struggle to remain immersed in an immaterial one, which in spite of its immateriality is just as destructive as the raging Mississippi."[18] This promising hypothesis is weakened, however, by the critic's strained efforts to discern symbolic parallels.[19] He neatly isolates three instances of mirror-contrast but fails to exploit their inherent meaning. Despite his early promise that the reading of the two stories as a single novel with a double plot is "a rich experience," he does not assay the wealth.

Yet Moses' pairing of episodes and Howe's parsing of chapters hold great value; once the fundamental ironic contrast between the stories is appreciated, the plot-alternations justify themselves. To Howe's schematization of the literary design I should like, then, to add the ideas I have developed in my study:

| "Wild Palms" | "Old Man" |
|---|---|
| 1. Major characters introduced; not identified or fully named. Major symbol (wind) presented. Charlotte near death. Doctor contrasted with Harry. | 2. Major character introduced; identified but not named. Major symbol (river) suggested. Convict contrasted, by implication, with Harry. |
| 3. Flashback: chronological beginning of lovers' journey; Harry willingly renounces his monastic life for what he believes will be freedom. Harry's guilt stressed toward end of episode. | 4. Chronological beginning of convict's journey; convict unwillingly thrown into the river or imprisoning reality. Irony of convict's "freedom" stressed at end of episode. |
| 5. Flashback: Harry and Charlotte feel repressed in Chicago and go to Wisconsin. Harry tries to abandon Charlotte but cannot. Another failure to reconcile guilt and sensuality in Chicago. Lovers leave for Utah, seeking again for freedom. | 6. Convict burdened by woman; river frustrates his efforts to return to levee. Convict tries twice to surrender, is twice rejected and fired upon. Convict defeated in efforts to abandon his "freedom." |
| 7. Flashback: Charlotte becomes pregnant. | 8. Convict helps woman bear child. |

18. *Ibid.*, p. 128.
19. For instance, his equation of Charlotte's yellow eyes with the yellow flood waters; *ibid.*, pp. 126-127.

Unsuccessful search for employment in Texas.

Harry punishes himself and Charlotte with shoddy operation. Return to gulf coast for final four days of "freedom."

9. Charlotte dies.

Harry given fifty years in prison to enjoy remorse for his freedom.

Successful employment with Cajun.

"Cosmic joker" punishes convict as flood resumes.

Return to Parchman and "imprisonment."

10. Convict victimized by law officers.

Convict given ten years in prison for his "escape" from the levee.

Not only the "mirror opposites" of plot but the consistent ironic contrasts of motivation, incident, and theme are revealed by this structural representation. The relative simplicity and directness of "Old Man" may be seen, moreover, to throw the tragedy of "Wild Palms" into sharp relief. In spite of the heavy ironies which appear in a comparative reading of the stories and Faulkner's apparent sympathy with the convict rather than Wilbourne, it is clear that "Old Man" serves primarily to parody the tragic theme of the other tale. Faulkner's major concern seems to be with Wilbourne, a credible modern character whose incubus—guilt—is the author's special interest. On the other hand, the convict in "Old Man" is really a grotesque, a petrified man, an automaton who manages to reject experience and flee from the problem of existence. With his neurotic indecisiveness, Wilbourne fails not because he is diametrically opposed to the "successful" convict but because neither resource, the convict's faith in the divinity of rules or Charlotte's faith in the power of love to deny all rules, is accessible to him. Harry's tragedy (the thesis of the novel) is caused not by the implacable forces of external nature nor by Charlotte's "powerful sexual needs," (as Howe has said) but by his own inner weakness. His struggle throughout the story is internal. "Old Man" serves as the antithesis of the novel; the convict succeeds because his struggle is almost purely external; his morality and mentality are all of a piece; his herculean duel with the river is never tragic. Irving Howe has provided this working definition of the Faulknerian tragic theme: "cursed by the tragic need to compromise his freedom, man can still redeem himself through a gesture which may not mitigate his defeat but will declare his humanity in defeat."[20] While "Wild Palms" clearly meets the requirements of this formula, the other story just as clearly avoids them. Its mode is the comic.

20. Howe, p. 103.

The reading of *The Wild Palms* which I have presented seems, finally, to harmonize with Faulkner's latest and most challenging statement about the book. Asked by an interviewer whether he had brought the two stories together for "any symbolic purpose," Faulkner replied:

That was one story—the story of Charlotte Rittenmeyer and Harry Wilbourn[e], who sacrificed everything for love, and then lost that. I did not know it would be two separate stories until after I had started the book. When I reached the end of what is now the first section of *The Wild Palms,* I realized suddenly that something was missing, it needed emphasis, something to lift it like counterpoint in music. So I wrote on the *Old Man* story until *The Wild Palms* story rose back to pitch. Then I stopped the *Old Man* story at what is now its first section, and took up *The Wild Palms* story until it began again to sag. Then I raised it to pitch again with another section of its antithesis, which is the story of a man who got his love and spent the rest of the book fleeing from it, even to the extent of voluntarily going back to jail where he would be safe. They are only two stories by chance, perhaps necessity. The story is that of Charlotte and Wilbourne.[21]

## C. The Land And Its People

## THE WILDERNESS THEME IN FAULKNER'S "THE BEAR"

### WILLIAM VAN O'CONNOR

INEVITABLY, as Faulkner has grown older, the problems of his region have become more and more profoundly intertwined with his own commitments and ideals. To a reporter who interviewed her about Faulkner at the time of the Nobel Award, Mrs. Calvin Brown, who had known Faulkner since he was a boy, said, "I think Billy is heartbroken about what he sees, heartbroken about the deterioration of ideals." She felt he has also suffered, as all intelligent Southerners do, over their "confusion and mixed-up emotions . . . about the race question." The book most frequently quoted by critics examining Faulkner's attitudes about modern society and, inevitably, about the race question is *Go Down, Moses.*

21. Jean Stein (interviewer), "The Art of Fiction XII: William Faulkner," *The Paris Review,* no. 12 (Spring, 1956), p. 43.
    Reprinted with permission from *Accent,* Winter, 1953, pp. 12-20.

This book marks a profound shift in his work. In place of the sense of doom, of tragic inevitabilities, or of an Old Testament harshness, one finds a sense of hopefulness, a promise of salvation. There are in *Go Down, Moses* two loosely related strands of subject matter—the life of the ascetic Isaac McCaslin, the hunter, and the life of Lucas Beauchamp, the son of the mulatto slave who in turn had been the son of Carothers McCaslin, Isaac's grandfather.[1]

The antecedents of Isaac are explained in "Was," the humorous story in which we learn that Uncle Bud and Uncle Buck, Isaac's father, refused to profit from slavery. Isaac himself figures dominantly in "The Old People," "The Bear," and "Delta Autumn."[2] Two chapters are devoted to Lucas Beauchamp and his family, "The Fire and the Hearth" and "Go Down, Moses." Both of these sections, however, relate more directly and intimately to the action in *Intruder in the Dust,* a later novel, than to the chapters devoted to Isaac. The theme implicit in the sections devoted to Lucas Beauchamp is white injustice to the Negro, and the theme implicit in those devoted to Isaac is the nobility of character to be learned from life in the wilderness. In "The Bear" Faulkner attempts to bring the two subject matters and therefore the two themes together, with the wilderness theme dominating.

Immediately preceding "The Bear" is "The Old People," which develops the wilderness theme and introduces us to the significant figure of Sam Fathers, the son of a Negro slave and Ikkemotube or Doom, a Chickasaw chief. He and his mother had been sold to Carothers McCaslin, Ike's grandfather.[3] After the death of Joe Baker, also a Chickasaw, Sam Fathers asks permission to live by himself at the Big Bottom, the hunting grounds on the Tallahatchie River, a way of recapturing the spirit of the wilderness which flows in his blood. He is joined there during the hunting expeditions by General Compson, Major de Spain, Boon Hogganbeck (who also has

1. "Pantaloon in Black," which is an ironic story of white misunderstanding of the terrible excess of human feeling in a young Negro, a tremendously moving story, falls outside the two strands of subject matter. As an indication of the re-use that Faulkner makes of his materials it may be noted that this story is recapitulated briefly in *Requiem for a Nun.*
2. Isaac had appeared as an incidental character in an early story, "A Bear Hunt" (not included in *Go Down, Moses*), a comic story which has no thematic relationship to "The Bear."
3. Sam Fathers makes an earlier appearance in "A Justice," in *These Thirteen,* in which his paternity is attributed not to Ikkemotube but to a man named Crawford, or Crayfishford. Incidentally, the Sam Fathers of "The Old People" is a stronger, more independent character, more aware of his Indian antecedents than of his slave heritage, than the Sam Fathers of "The Bear."

Indian blood, but not from a chief), and others. When Isaac kills his first
deer, Sam marks his face with the blood, teaching him to respect and love
what he kills. *"I slew you; my bearing must not shame your quitting life."*
(As an old man in "Delta Autumn," Ike recalls the story and elaborates its
meaning.) On the same day Ike is shown with Sam, waiting to shoot at a
deer they know will return to bed for the night. But at another stand above
them they hear a shot, followed by a hunter's horn, and they know Walter
Ewell has killed the deer. But Sam tells Ike to wait, and this is what
they see:

> Then it saw them. And still it did not begin to run. It just stopped for
> an instant, taller than any man, looking at them; then its muscles suppled,
> gathered. It did not even alter its course, not fleeing, not even running, just
> moving with that winged and effortless ease with which deer move, passing
> within twenty feet of them, its head high and the eye not proud and not
> haughty but just full and wild and unafraid, and Sam standing beside the
> boy now, his right arm raised at full length, palm-outward, speaking in that
> tongue which the boy had learned from listening to him and Joe Baker in
> the blacksmith shop, while up the ridge Walter Ewell's horn was still blow-
> ing them in to a dead buck.
> "Oleh, Chief," Sam said. "Grandfather."

When Isaac tells his cousin McCaslin Edmonds the story the latter confirms it, and we infer that the shade of the deer is to be interpreted as the
spirit of the wilderness, related not merely to Sam but to all men if they
could but rediscover it, and the symbol of an abundant earth eager to
produce. "The Old People," then, is a preliminary probing of the subject
of the wilderness and man's relationship to it.

The first version of "The Bear,"[4] much simpler than the revised
version, is the story of the young Ike's initiation as a hunter and his growing awareness of what is to be learned from the wilderness, symbolized by
the bear, Old Ben. His two mentors are Sam Fathers and his own father
(in the revised version it is his cousin McCaslin Edmonds, sixteen years
his senior and the joint heir with Ike of the McCaslin farm). Old Ben is
an epitome, an apotheosis of the old wild life known to the Chickasaws
before man hacked away at the forest and before they sold a part of it to
Jason Lycurgus Compson or any one else. Nature should be free and
abundant. No one has the right to own or sell it. Sam tells Ike that Old

4. This was published in *The Saturday Evening Post*, 214 (May 9, 1942), 30-31, the
same year the revised version was published as a part of *Go Down, Moses,* but
obviously it had been written earlier.

Ben won't allow himself to be seen until, without a gun and without giving in to his fear, Ike learns to relinquish himself to the wilderness. This the boy does learn, even to giving up his watch and compass.

Then he saw the bear. It did not emerge, appear; it was just there, immobile, solid, fixed in the hot dappling of the green and windless noon, not as big as he had dreamed it, but as big as he had expected it, bigger, dimensionless, against the dappled obscurity, looking at him where he sat quietly on the log and looked back at it.

Then it moved. It made no sound. It did not hurry. It crossed the glade, walking for an instant into the full glare of the sun; when it reached the other side it stopped again, and looked back at him across one shoulder while his quiet breathing inhaled and exhaled three times.

Then it was gone. It didn't walk into the woods, the undergrowth. It faded, sank back into the wilderness as he had watched a fish, a huge old bass, sink and vanish into the dark depths of its pool without even any movement of its fins.

Several years later, Ike sees the bear again. On one occasion he has with him a little mongrel, "of the sort called by Negroes a fyce," which tries to attack Old Ben. Ike drops his gun and chases the fyce, picking it up immediately in front of the bear, which without attacking disappears. Then the boy realizes that he has not wanted to shoot the bear. Talking about it with his father he comes to realize that the bear represents a "wild immortal spirit," related to the endurance, humility and courage of the hunter in his contest with the wilderness. Old Ben had a fierce pride in his liberty—

Who at times even seemed deliberately to put that freedom and liberty in jeopardy in order to savor them, to remind his old strong bones and flesh to keep supple and quick to defend and preserve them.

In Sam Fathers, Ike had seen in addition to the wild invincible spirit of the bear inherited from his Chickasaw blood the pride and humility of the Negro, the rewards of endurance and suffering. And from the little fyce he has also learned courage. Ike's father (who, incidentally, is not identified as the elderly Uncle Buck of "Was" or of the revised version of "The Bear") sums up the meaning of the boy's meetings with Old Ben: "Courage, and honor, and pride," his father said, "and pity, and love of justice and of liberty. They all touch the heart and what the heart holds becomes the truth." This in general is the meaning of the story—Old Ben is the wilderness, the mystery of man's nature and origins beneath the forms of civilization; and man's proper relationship with the wilderness teaches him liberty, courage, pride and humility.

The bear, as Frazer and others have pointed out,[5] has been treated reverently by primitive hunters. In seeing him walk upright, leave footprints much like a man's, sit up against a tree, and employ a wide range of facial expressions and yet belong to a non-human wilderness, these hunters must have thought the bear a kind of bridge between man as a rational and conscious creature and man as a physical creature dependent on and involved in that same mysterious nature. Obviously the bear almost begs to be treated as a symbol in stories dealing with man's relationship with nature, especially those stories that present the physical world and the creatures in it as sacramental, as manifestations of a holy spirit suffusing all things and asking that man conduct himself in piety and with reverence. The latter view permeates Faulkner's "The Bear."

Such a view is defensible. It recurs throughout literature, having perhaps its most notable expression in English in the poetry of Blake and Coleridge. But it does invite one to sentimentalize nature and it has no very good answer for those who ask how respectful one should be of a bear or any other creature that wantonly would crush one's head or rip off one's limbs. It invites, that is, the puzzled or angry recognition in *Moby-Dick* that the beautiful white polar bears should be killers. Some such reservations as these, which must lurk in the mind of even the sympathetic reader, do not destroy Faulkner's story, but they modify one's enjoyment of it. One gives it sympathy but only partial credence.

In general there are two major changes in the revised "The Bear." It incorporates an earlier story, "Lion"[6]—not completely successful in its own terms—which tells how Boon Hogganbeck kills the bear when it tries to kill Lion, the courageous dog, and it presents Isaac McCaslin not only

5. It seems likely the Faulkner got the hint for his story from T. B. Thorpe's "The Big Bar of Arkansas," *The Spirit of the Times* (1841). The following are passages which suggest the similarities between the two stories: (1) "Only one pup came near him, and he was brushed out so totally with the bar's left paw, that he entirely disappeared. . . ." (2) "Yes, the old varmit was within a hundred yards of me, and the way he walked *over that fence* — stranger, he loomed up like a *black mist,* he seemed so large, and he walked right towards me. I raised myself, took deliberate aim, and fired. Instantly the varmint wheeled, gave a yell, and *walked through the fence like a falling tree would through a cobweb.*" (3) [The bar, like Old Ben, took to taking hogs whenever it wanted to. This causes the hunter to want to destroy the bar. But he has trouble shooting him, as though the bar's life were charmed. Finally he kills him, too easily, as it seems to the hunter.] "There is something curious about it, I could never understand, — and I never was satisfied at his giving in so easy at last. Perhaps he had heard of my preparations to hunt him the next day, so he jist come in, like Capt. Scott's coon, to save his wind to grunt with in dying; but that ain't likely. My private opinion is, that that bar was an *unhuntable bar, and died when his time come.*"
6. *Harper's,* 172 (December, 1935), pp. 67-77.

in childhood but in his mature years as a noble hunter and as a Christ-like figure who repudiates the land because it has been cursed by slavery.

In the revised version of "The Bear" Old Ben is falsely suspected of wantonly destroying domestic animals, thus making it justifiable that the hunters track him down to kill him. In terms of the wilderness theme, two possible reasons for the bear's action suggest themselves: one, the wilderness even in its primeval form is evil as well as good, but there is no justification or preparation for this in the story; second, the wilderness simply seems to be taking revenge on man. This latter interpretation is clearly suggested by the unsympathetic descriptions of the lumbering interests cutting into the forest. (In "Delta Autumn" there is this: "No wonder the ruined woods I used to know don't cry for retribution! he thought: The people who have destroyed it will accomplish its revenge.")

In the first version of "The Bear" the spirit of the wilderness, of course, dominates the action. Although in a lesser degree, the story has, as already implied, a kind of *Midsummer Night's Dream* atmosphere: there are difficulties and stupidities, but they are under the aegis of Titania and Oberon and at the end no irreconcilable conflicts will remain. Occasionally we hear the voice of hard reality like that of Theseus or of stupidity like that of Bottom, but ultimately their words belong to the realm of moonlight. Because the hunt is not solely a painless ritual under the aegis of the wilderness spirit, Faulkner has considerable difficulty in incorporating or assimilating the action of "Lion" into the action of "The Bear." Often the hunt demands violence and cruelty. And the hunt, to the extent that animals are not killed out of a need for food, is a violation of the sacramental view of the world implicit in the wilderness theme.

In "Lion" the bear had no symbolic significance. He was simply a creature to be hunted, and there was nothing sacred about him. The theme grew out of the dog as hunter, not the bear as wilderness. "Lion was like the chiefs of Aztec and Polynesian tribes who were looked upon as being not men but both more and less than men. Because we were not men either while we were in camp: we were hunters and Lion the best hunter of all."[7] In other words, Lion is the ruthless, non-human spirit of the kill. At the beginning of section two of the revised "The Bear" there is this isolated sentence about thirteen-year-old Ike's attitude toward Lion: "So he should have hated and feared Lion." The isolated sentence seems to be

7. In "Lion," unlike "The Bear," the story is told from the point of view of a boy who is *not* Ike McCaslin. Ike himself is the boy's mentor, giving him the sort of advice Sam (who does not appear) gives Ike in both versions of "The Bear."

a plant, suggesting but without explaining to the reader how the apotheosis of Lion is not contradicting the apotheosis of Old Ben. But as a matter of fact, it does contradict it. If Ike is the voice of the wisdom to be learned from the wilderness, then indeed he should have been opposed to the spirit represented by Lion.

But, first, a look at the main action of "Lion." At the center of the story are Lion and Boon Hogganbeck, who is presented pretty much as mindless or childlike and inefficient, possibly to suggest the degeneracy of the old wild spirit of the Indians. Boon is filled with admiration for the untamable Lion. In the killing of the bear Lion is mortally wounded. Boon then kills the bear with a knife, and although wounded himself carries Lion to a doctor who sews him up but cannot save him. The next year Major de Spain declines to hunt in the Big Bottom and the boy perceives the reason: Major de Spain can not bring himself to revisit the ground where Lion, the spirit of bravery and courage, has been destroyed. With the death of Lion the spirit of the hunt, the challenge and the chase, has left the woods. But the conclusion of "Lion," a brilliantly done scene in itself (which is repeated in the revised "The Bear"), does not seem to be the inevitable resolution of the previous actions: despite Major de Spain's decision, the boy visits the woods at the regular hunting season and sees Boon sitting under a tree, hammering violently at a section of his old worn-out gun. Above Boon in the tree the squirrels are racing madly, frantic from the sounds Boon is making in beating of the stock of his gun. Boon's "walnut face" is "wild and urgent and streaming with sweat," and as the boy goes up to him Boon screams at him in "a hoarse, strangled voice: 'Get out of here! Don't touch them! Don't touch a one of them! They're mine!' " Presumably we are to infer that not merely the spirit of nobility but also the spirit of comradeship and mutual help among the hunters has disappeared with the death of Lion, and that Boon's insistence is civilization's almost hysterical insistence on "mine!" But if so, Lion himself, who is ruthless courage, not generosity, is hardly a good symbol of these virtues. Old Ben, on the other hand, in his role as majestic overseer of the wilderness, is a more appropriate symbol, and Boon's crazy violence in the revised "The Bear," in which Old Ben himself is destroyed, seems better motivated.

In section IV of the revised version, Faulkner makes an even stronger effort than he had through the symbolic figure of Sam Fathers to unite the two major themes of *Go Down, Moses,* the proper relationship to nature which is to be learned from the wilderness and the injustice to the Negro. The section is about as long as the remaining sections taken together. For the most part it is new material but it incorporates from the first version the meaning of Old Ben as symbol, here giving the remarks made by Ike's father to Ike's cousin, McCaslin Edmonds.

But the section is not exclusively devoted to the boy Ike's learning the significance of the wilderness theme; it is primarily about Ike at twenty-one refusing to inherit property stained by the guilt of slavery, and it is about Ike's subsequent life. There are long conversations between the cousins, at the end of which we know of Grandfather McCaslin's mulatto heirs and their sometimes terrible sufferings, of the country after the Civil War, of McCaslin Edmonds' attempts to help the mulatto heirs, of Ike's marriage to a woman who is unhappy because of his refusal to inherit his share of the family property, and of his living as a carpenter, in what some critics seem to consider an imitation of Christ.

In spite of this new material, the reader has only scattered glimpses of the adult Isaac McCaslin, and is never wholly certain what he is to make of him. More than likely he will see Isaac, at least in part, as far too passive a protester of injustice. Ike never seems a particularly good representative of the virtues to be learned from the wilderness because he is ineffectual or inactive in contexts where the virtues he has learned in the wilderness, particularly the respect for liberty, might motivate him to some positive action. For example, he allows McCaslin Edmonds to put a monthly payment in his bank account, the profit from the land he repudiates, and he allows his cousin to meet the family's and therefore Isaac's own obligations to Carothers McCaslin's mulatto heirs. Isaac would absolve himself not merely from the guilt but from the obligations contingent upon the guilt.

In "Delta Autumn," the final section or story in *Go Down, Moses,* we see Ike, now in his seventies, immediately confronted by an instance of racial injustice. The evil of old Carothers McCaslin is repeated: Roth Edmonds, the grandson of McCaslin Edmonds, has a child by a mulatto granddaughter of James Buchanan, whose parents had been owned by Uncle Buck and Uncle Bud. Earlier in "Delta Autumn" Ike has been explaining that the right attitude towards nature, for instance, not killing does and not exploiting the land, leads to having the right attitude toward man. But that this does not relate to the present world becomes clear when Ike is more than a little horrified to discover that the Negress would like to marry the father of her child. *"Maybe in a thousand or two thousand years in America,* he thought. *But not now! Not now!"* As a gesture or token of his good will and of his hopes for the future Ike gives her for the illegitimate child the hunting horn inherited from General Compson. But Ike's silent exclamation that it will take one thousand or two thousand years before such a marriage could take place makes it quite clear that the theme of the wisdom to be derived from the wilderness, even in its great prophet Ike, is merely juxtaposed against the theme of the injustice to the Negro. It merely acknowledges, it does not materially modify the injustice.

The inconsistencies in Ike as a character are merely a manifestation of the more general inconsistency that inheres in Faulkner's attempt to treat the subject of slavery and injustice to the Negro in relation to the wilderness theme. Civilization is not an idyllic wilderness nor even an idyllic pastoralism; and slavery and injustice are in the context of civilization. The wilderness, however much civilization can learn from it, has to give way for fields and towns, and the problems of civilization, involving not merely complex struggles for status or power or acceptance but also the abuse or destruction of many things that are beautiful in their natural or original state, are much more subtle than they are in the mythic wilderness of which Ike dreams.

Faulkner's treatment of the theme of the wilderness in the first version of "The Bear" is moving, almost hallucinatory in its power to convince us of the existence of a world of no sin, no evil, no injustice. It does convince us, at the least, of the need for us to contemplate such an ideal world. But Faulkner is not willing, apparently, to allow the implications of the wilderness theme, its power to purify, to work as a leaven inside the subject or theme of injustice to the Negro. The treatment of the spirit of the wilderness has no real relevance beyond acknowledging a former and continuing wrong. It relates to a world not merely prior to slavery but prior to civilization. It is a kind of neurotic dream—an escape from, rather than an attempt to solve, the present injustice.

# THE THEME AND STRUCTURE
## OF FAULKNER'S *THE HAMLET*

### T. Y. GREET

WILLIAM FAULKNER'S novel *The Hamlet* has received less critical attention and, perhaps, less critical intelligence than any other of his major

Reprinted with permission from *PMLA*, September, 1957, pp. 775-90.

works. The reasons for this neglect are rather easily stated. Published in 1940, Faulkner's only significant novel between *Absalom, Absalom!* in 1936 and *Go Down, Moses* in 1942, *The Hamlet* differs considerably from the novels of the "major phase," 1929–1936. It comes at a point in the development of the Yoknapatawpha Cycle when the early conflict between legend and reality which so disturbed Quentin Compson had been largely resolved, and it is concerned with themes that had earlier been of peripheral interest. It presents as protagonists a class of Yoknapatawphans who are relative newcomers to the cycle. These things together—the lessening of tension and the use of new material—are reflected in the unique tone of *The Hamlet,* which led Malcolm Cowley to entitle his review of the novel "Faulkner By Daylight."[1] Further, since the novel is leisurely in its narrative method and relatively lucid in its style, it does not at first glance seem to demand or merit the sort of exhaustive readings which have been given, say, to *The Sound and the Fury.* Finally, with the major exception of Robert Penn Warren, almost none of the critics has been willing to recognize the book as a novel at all. Cowley speaks of its structure as that of "beads on a string."[2] John Arthos calls the book Faulkner's "most remarkable writing" but adds that it "falls into at least four separate stories . . . there is no real unity."[3] O'Connor, Howe, Campbell and Foster have all dealt with and appreciated various aspects of the novel but it remains the chief enigma of the cycle.[4]

This brief review of the criticism suggests some of the problems raised by *The Hamlet* and indicates the value, first, of attempting to place the novel in the geographical and thematic context of the Yoknapatawpha Cycle. To suggest that the dwellers of Frenchman's Bend have not been treated earlier in the cycle is to err in fact if not in principle. The Snopes family appears as early as the Civil War (Ab in *The Unvanquished*) and as late as 1929 (Senator Clarence in *Sanctuary*), so that the narrative of Flem Snopes's ascendancy in *The Hamlet* has ramifications extending both backward and forward into the cycle.[5] As for the setting, the stage of *The*

1. *New Republic,* 102 (April 15, 1940), p. 510.
2. Introd., *The Portable Faulkner* (New York, 1949), p. 18.
3. "Ritual and Humor in the Writings of William Faulkner," *William Faulkner: Two Decades of Criticism*, Frederick J. Hoffman and Olga Vickery (eds) (East Lansing, Mich., 1951), p. 113.
4. Viola Hopkins, "Meaning and Form in Faulkner's *The Hamlet*," *Accent*, 15 (Spring 1955), pp. 125-144, provides an extended and provocative treatment.
5. Nor are the Snopeses the only persons from the Bend who are dealt with elsewhere. Suratt, who becomes Ratliff, is a companion of Bayard Sartoris and appears in several short stories. Cora and Vernon Tull, Bookwright, and the Armstids all play minor roles

*Hamlet,* with its piney hills and red bluffs, is isolated almost as if by Snopesian design. The people of the Bend, with few exceptions, are "rednecks" and sharecroppers, ready victims of whichever Snopes or Varner is, for the season, providing them "furnishings." In Frenchman's Bend, Faulkner has created a "control condition" where Flem can practice his wiles before moving on to the less susceptible society of Jefferson.

The milieu of *The Hamlet,* though it differs from that of Faulkner's other works, is nonetheless part and parcel of Yoknapatawpha County, and the same is true of the novel as it relates thematically to the cycle. After disposing in *Absalom, Absalom!* of Quentin Compson's tortured search for reality, Faulkner turned from his major theme, that of man's relations with himself, to a minor aspect of that theme, the problem of man's relations to the land. The years from 1936 to "The Bear" in 1942 are in a sense transitional ones during which Faulkner seems to have been formulating the credo of Isaac McCaslin, many of whose ideas are implicit in *The Hamlet.* A sense of the richness and inviolability of the land pervades much of Faulkner's earlier work, especially the Indian stories, *Absalom, Absalom!* and *Old Man,* but not until *The Hamlet* does it become the dominant interest. Here, in the symbols of Eula and the cow, the conflict between Flem and Ratliff, Faulkner relates the minor theme most significantly to the major one. Only as he learns properly to value emotion, to venerate nature, will man recover his integrity and achieve a meaningful relationship with his fellows.

That the novel is itself a part of the greater unity of the cycle is thus clear, and it is now possible to refute such comments as those of Cowley and Arthos by relating the apparently diverse elements of the novel to each other. Robert Penn Warren in an early study of the book provides the first and, perhaps, most cogent defense of its structural integrity: "The structure of the book depends on the intricate patterning of contrasts, for instance the contrast of the Flem-Eula story with the Houston-wife story. . . . Flem stands outside the scale which runs from idiot to Houston, from groping animalism to secret poetry; in his cunning, he stands beyond appetite, passion, pride, fidelity, exploiting all of these things."[6] The development of the novel is governed, however, by a yet more significant contrast, that between reason and emotion. This conflict, of recurrent inter-

in other novels and, in a sense, the world of *As I Lay Dying* is that of *The Hamlet.* Faulkner's treatment of Flem and Eula in *The Town* has no appreciable bearing on my reading here of *The Hamlet.*
6. "The Snopes World," *Kenyon Review,* 3 (Spring 1941), p. 256.

est in American literature at least since Melville and Hawthorne, has been implicit in other works of Faulkner as well. Jason IV in *The Sound and the Fury* is made despicable largely because he possesses none of the compassion which gains our sympathy for the ineffectual Quentin. Even Isaac McCaslin fails at last because he has forgotten all he ever knew about love,[7] and again and again, as between Chick Mallison and Gavin Stevens, Faulkner's sympathies lie chiefly with children, with women, with "primitives" who retain in its most elemental degree the ability to respond with sincere emotion.

In still later works, especially *Requiem for a Nun* and *A Fable,* this theme has been so dominant as almost to obscure art, and it is in *The Hamlet* that it receives, though obliquely, its fullest and most effective treatment. One may think of the structure of the novel as a single, undeviating line opposed and crossed by many, always fore-shortened, lesser lines. The central line denotes Flem's rise, his progress along a coldly rational plane, "beyond appetite," from a clerkship in Varner's store to his victory over Ratliff. The opposing lines, ineffectual but sharply drawn, indicate those points at which Ratliff, Flem's only possible antagonist, attempts to forestall or mitigate the Snopes influence. Finally, the lines which rise from and return to the center denote actions stemming from passions foreign to Flem, actions which, nobly or violently conceived, prove futile when they come in contact with the rational plane. A concept of this sort leads, of course, to oversimplification, but the reading which follows will attempt to show how symbol, style, and tone serve to transform morality into art.

One of the primary sources of the critical confusion *The Hamlet* has caused is apparently its division into four books of approximately equal length and of rather sharply contrasting tones. Book I, which describes the arrival of Ab and Flem, the Varners' intimidation and Flem's symbolic ascension to Will's barrel chair, is the lightest and most objectively written of the four. These qualities result from the predominance in the first book of the point of view of V. K. Ratliff, whose function in the novel is a double one, that of participant and observer-commentator. Faulkner's characterization of him as a man "affable, courteous, anecdotal and impenetrable" with his "shrewd brown face"[8] may well be supplemented by Constance Rourke's description of the "Yankee peddlar": "The Yankee was never

7. "Delta Autumn," *Go Down, Moses* (New York, 1931), p. 363.
8. *The Hamlet* (New York, 1940), pp. 15-16. All subsequent references to the novel will appear in parentheses immediately following citations in the text.

passive, not the cracker-box philosopher seated in some dim interior, utter-ing wisdom before a ring of quiet figures; he was noticeably out in the world; it was a prime part of his character to be 'a-doin'. But though he often pulled strings, always made shrewd or caustic comments . . . he was seldom deeply involved in situations; even his native background was meagerly drawn. . . . Though he talked increasingly his monologues still never brimmed over into personal revelation."[9]

That these details are so readily applicable to Ratliff makes him one with such classic American humorists as Sam Slick, Seba Smith, and Sut Lovingood. Critics have found him influenced chiefly by G. W. Harris' Sut and Augustus B. Longstreet's *Georgia Scenes*. Investigation of both these sources shows, however, that the influences are only general and suggests that attention might best be given to the nature rather than the genesis of Ratliff's humor.[10] In the first book of the novel he has two ex-cellent opportunities to practice his forte, the humorous narrative, when he describes Ab's first triumph over Major de Spain and his later defeat at the hands of Pat Stamper in a horse trade. The first and more immediately significant story is related to Jody Varner as he rides confidently to Ab's with a rent contract. Ratliff is seeking to bait Jody and the structure and tone of the narrative are clearly purposeful.

As Jody glares down in "protuberant and speechless horror," Ratliff seizes on every detail which will dehumanize Ab. If his portrait of the Snopeses is no less "cruel" than his effort to intimidate Jody, it is con-tinually lightened by comic devices of style and method. The circumlocu-tion and litotes are harrowing: "Well . . . I don't know as I would go on record as saying he set ere a one of them afire. . . . You might say that fire seems to follow him around, like dogs follows some folks." Ab's daughters become grotesque, "strapping girls," not simply "like a pair of heifers," but in a comic extension and reversal of the figure, "like a pair of heifers just a little too valuable to hit hard with a stick" (14, 16). The pace of the narrative is slow, and Jody champs helplessly as Ratliff delights in his hyperboles, rustic comparisons, and comic juxtapositions. These and the other devices, characteristic of such humorists as Twain and Longstreet, are couched in an idiom reminiscent of Huck Finn's and Sut Lovingood's,

9. *American Humor: A Study of the National Character* (New York, 1931), pp. 29-30.
10. William Van O'Connor, *The Tangled Fire of William Faulkner* (Minneapolis, 1954), is best on sources. John Arthos, "Ritual and Humor," and Harry M. Campbell and Ruel E. Foster, *William Faulkner* (Norman, Okla., 1951), are best on humor generally.

greatly moderated, of course. The whole tone of Ratliff's discourse is, in fact, colored by the vocabulary, the area of comparisons, and the grammatical accuracy to which he is restricted in expressing his keen insights. The manner of his speech as much as its matter lends to his reports and comments the veracity which gives them value.

In his second anecdotal narrative, of Ab's being duped by Pat Stamper, Ratliff, aware now of Flem's threat, seems almost regretful of his first characterization of Ab. Reminiscently, and in a tone different from that of the De Spain story, Ratliff speaks of Ab in the days before he was "soured," when he relished a sharp trade and was capable of a certain resignation when defeated. This story has been related by O'Connor to "The Horse Swap" of *Georgia Scenes,* but it is in tone and structure far superior to its possible source. The second of many short stories to be incorporated into *The Hamlet,* this has undergone less revision than any other and may well have provided the sharpest early conception of Ratliff's manner.[11] In its present context the story is chiefly important for its introduction of at least two elements which later are to be significant. At two points in the novel horses act to determine the actions or fates of characters: Houston's wife is killed by a stallion, and the havoc of Book IV is wrought by Flem's "spotted ponies." Here the horse is an object purely of humor, free of menace, and of no symbolic value beyond that of representing a dominant passion which sets up a conflict between Ab and his wife. She herself is the second significant element. As Warren notes, much of the novel is concerned with the lives of various pairs of "lovers," and Ab and Mrs. Snopes are the first of them. Ab in his trading uses money which she has set aside for a cream separator, just as Henry Armstid is later to use his wife's meager savings to buy one of Flem's ponies; but not even a distaff Snopes can be expected to show Mrs. Armstid's resignation, and Ab's wife caps the comedy by swapping the cow for a separator which she can operate only with borrowed milk. The pattern, then, is one of parallels and, more importantly, contrasts. Flem's touch has yet to "sour" events. Only with his emergence does the horse become a destroyer, the wife a helpless victim.

Ratliff is quick to perceive that it is not Ab's headstrong pride or his vengefulness which must be feared. Rather it is Flem's utter lack of sensibility, his irresistible and amoral logic. When he returns after an absence of some six months to discover that a plague of Snopeses has descended on the Bend, Ratliff seeks to counter Flem's wiles. If one pauses, however,

11. "Fool About a Horse," *Scribner's Magazine,* 100 (August 1936), pp. 80-86.

to look at his opponent, the fact of his only moderate success will be better understood. Campbell and Foster have pointed out the significance of the Snopes names (104–105), and in image after grotesque image Faulkner creates about Flem and the rest an impression of animal greed and amorality. Flem "lurked among the ultimate shadows" of the store "with a good deal of the quality of a spider of that bulbous blond omnivorous though non-poisonous species" (66–67). I. O. has "a talkative weasel's face" and a "voice voluble and rapid and meaningless like something talking to itself about nothing in a deserted cavern" (74).

Such images, many of them extended to comic extremes, reveal the essential vacuousness of those to whom they apply. In his continual mention of Flem's costume, especially the machine-made bow tie, Faulkner seems to be striving for the same tone (66).[12] These things together, the brutality and depthlessness, suggest cardinal facts about the Snopeses with the exceptions of Eck, Ike, and Mink. One need not look to them for an awareness of conventional restraints or for any mode of conduct motivated by other than animal opportunism. Had Ratliff acknowledged these facts in time, he might have triumphed. Even Jody Varner, however, himself shrewd, is able to say as late as Book IV that St. Elmo Snopes, who may stand as a symbol for the tribe, is "worse than a goat," *likely* to devour the Bend, store, gin, and all (364).

Ratliff achieves little success with his first counterattack, which oddly enough utilizes goats. Thus Book I, dominated by his detached ironies, the arid setting, the sterile interplay of calculating minds, ends with Flem alone at the annual settlement, boarding at Varner's and, most importantly, symbolically enthroned in Will's barrel chair at Old Frenchman's Place. Already about his seat can be heard the distant rumble of the passions to which his advent will give rise. For the first time one learns that there is a conflict between Mink and Jack Houston over a cow that has wandered into the latter's fields. But we live in a rational world and are not greatly concerned. Flem has won, but so far he has broken only man's law; nature is still inviolate.

The undeviating line of Flem's rise is now fixed, but it is not until Book II that the full significance of his rational victory is made clear. Earlier Faulkner has mentioned Jody's sister, Eula, who impassively dominates the second book and, transformed into a symbol, becomes central to the meaning of the novel. At her second appearance she suggests "some

12. Suggestive also is Faulkner's description of I. O., who wears spectacles without lenses, a dickey, and a coat with shirt cuffs attached (229).

symbology out of the old Dionysic times," and immediately the tone of the novel changes (107). Jody, his sister's and, unwittingly, nature's protector, says of her that "Soon as she passes anything in long pants she begins to give off something. You can smell it!" (112) And this aura of fecundity permeates not only the dry air of the Bend but the style of the novel.

Little summary of Eula's comatose career is necessary. When she is eight, Jody insists on the girl's entering the village school and persists in his endeavor until her quality, like that of "the very goddesses in Homer and Thucydides," has transformed the "wooden desks and benches" of the school "into a grove of Venus," the hapless teacher, Labove, into a satyr (128, 130). Eula in the schoolroom abrogates "the whole long sum of human thinking and suffering which is called knowledge, education, wisdom" (131). But Labove, even as late as his third year of teaching, hesitates to go with his graduating law class to a brothel because "He still believed . . . the white magic of Latin degrees, which was an actual counterpart of the old monk's faith in his wooden cross" (133). Irresistibly, though he knows it is to be his "Gethsemane . . . and his Golgotha too," Labove is drawn back by Eula to the Bend. Under her influence his transformation into satyr begins: his legs are described as "haired-over like those of a faun" (134).

His iron will does not break, however, until the end of the sixth year when Labove becomes aware of Eula's symbolic significance, seeing the "fine land rich and fecund and foul and eternal and impervious" deeded to a husband who will be "a dwarf, a gnome, without glands or desire" (134–135). Goaded by this sense of waste, Labove finally assaults Eula, but fails because at the instant of his act "something furious and cold, or [of ?] repudiation and bereavement both, blew in him." Reason, morality, reassert themselves; his violence is made meaningless as Eula dismisses him: "Stop pawing me . . . You old headless horseman Ichabod Crane" (137–138).

This is in 1890 and for three years, the center of an ever more mature, more intensely watchful circle of admirers, she remains inviolate. Then appears Labove's antithesis, Hoake McCarron, the embodiment, in his dashing buggy, of the aggressive male principle. James G. Frazer points out that the earth goddess, "she who fertilizes nature must herself be fertile, and to be that she must necessarily have a male consort," and observes that the "marriage of the goddess is always a central rite."[13]

13. *The Golden Bough* (New York, 1937), I, p. 39; II, p. 129 ff.

Hoake is an admirably chosen consort, and Faulkner's treatment of Eula's seduction gives it certainly a central status. If rationality pervades the first book, then utter moon-struck madness is the tone of the second, where in passages rich with suggestive diction, assonance, and image Faulkner describes the frustration of Eula's suitors, who at last succeed in waylaying her with Hoake, breaking his arm in the melee. Later, symbolically, Eula must support his injured side to facilitate her ritual impregnation.

After the relief of a comic scene which reveals the Varners' total unawareness of the true nature of their tragedy, Flem's triumph ensues. Hoake, fearful of convention, has fled; the Varners, bound by it, must find a husband; and Will, in the central irony of the novel, chooses the sterile Flem, even deeding him Old Frenchman's Place and purchasing the wedding license. The earth goddess has been sacrificed to the pagan and from this point Eula's face is not only beautiful but "damned"— damned by the rational blindness which does not perceive, in the words of Ike McCaslin, that the land is no man's to bequeath to another, that as soon as anyone discovered "he could sell it for money, on that instant it ceased ever to have been his . . . and the man who bought it bought nothing."[14]

That Faulkner intends Eula's seduction to have great significance is clear from the elegiac lament which follows her marriage. The Bend becomes a village "without grace, forsaken, yet which wombed once by chance and accident one blind seed of the spendthrift Olympian ejaculation and did not even know it, without tumescence [the word hints at a miraculous birth] conceived and bore." The nymph and the symbolic buggies are departed and there remains only "the word, the dream and the wish of all male under the sun capable of harm" (169). This is the crux of the novel, that the favor of the gods—Love, Fertility—has been sacrificed to rational opportunism.

The union of Anchises with Venus produced Aeneas and inaugurated a golden age. The daughter of Eula and Hoake is barely mentioned in the novel, and of their union comes only tragedy. Ratliff, returning at the end of the "doomed and dying" summer of Eula's departure with Flem for Texas, enters a wasteland where "the very hot, vivid air . . . seemed to be filled with the slow laborious plaint of laden wagons." His regret is bitter that Eula could not have been "the unscalable sierra . . . for no man to conquer scot-free or even to conquer at all," and he is outraged at

14. "The Bear," *Go Down, Moses*, p. 257.

"the useless squandering . . . as though the gods themselves had fun-
nelled all the concentrated bright wet-slanted unparadised June onto a
dung-heap, breeding pismires" (181–182).

Ratliff's humorous detachment, under the pressure of this awareness,
has deserted him; but Constance Rourke notes that "humor bears the
closest relation to emotion," often "rising like a rebirth of feeling from
dead levels after turmoil."[15] Thus Ratliff's bitterness is suddenly transformed, and he conjures a vision of Flem in Hell, comically triumphant
over Satan himself. But this humor is that of a new Ratliff, no longer
gentle in his ironies. In his fantasy he seizes on the elements of the Snopes-
Varner conflict and incorporates them with embellishments into an extended and accurate analogy which serves as a turning point on the humorous level as Eula's marriage does on the serious one.[16]

Flem's victory—from tenancy, to barrel chair, to Satan's throne—is
now complete, and he disappears from the scene during the whole of
Book III. The Fisher King is gone and life in the wasteland seeks to re-
new itself, but the passions which rise during the summer of his absence
are perverse, virulent, destructive. The vague threat to sanity posed by
the conflict between Mink Snopes and Jack Houston at the end of the
first book breaks in Book III into violence, after Mink loses a suit for the
recovery of his cow. Ratliff is at the store when I. O., Mink's self-styled
attorney, emerges, offering him only the comfort of typically vapid aphor-
isms. Mink turns on him with a fierce obscenity, "——t," an epithet
which suggests the heightened tone of the events that center about the
cow.

For instance, Ratliff, still rankled by the sacrifice of Eula, seizes at
once on I. O.'s idiom for the most scathing comment he has yet made:
"Snopes can come and Snopes can go, but Will Varner looks like he is
going to snopes forever. Or Varner will Snopes forever—take your pick.
What is it the fellow says? off with the old and on with the new; the
old job at the old stand, maybe a new fellow doing the jobbing but it's the
same old stern getting reamed out?" (185). Here, in his first use of
word play and sharp irony, Ratliff abandons humor and deliberately
seizes on wit as his weapon. This form, forged by the critical intelligence,

15. *American Humor,* p. 10.
16. It is worth noting that B. A. Botkin, *A Treasury of American Folk Humor* (New
York, 1949), pp. 80-81, tells the story of a "Snopes" who went to Hell and was imprisoned under a washpot. Later, a visitor starting to lift it was stopped by the Devil's
shouting. "Don't lift that pot! We have Old Man Cobb under there and if you let
him out he'll foreclose a mortgage on all hell in the first crop season!"

untempered by sympathy, now becomes his favorite mode, a fact which serves to guage his increasing bitterness and frustration. Thus all is now distorted, and when Ratliff's tirade is interrupted by a bid to watch some salacious occurrence in Mrs. Littlejohn's barn, our expectations are of the worst.

This event, the nature of which is revealed only slowly, has almost the significance of Eula's seduction and marriage in the thematic development of the novel. Hoake, the goddess' consort, is with sudden and tragic irony replaced by Ike Snopes, idiot; and the "shape of love" is transformed grotesquely into that of a cow. But the ironies here stem not only from diminution. As Faulkner develops one of his most brilliant symbols, Ike's relation with the cow becomes a metaphor of love, sharply contrasting with Flem's "courtship" of Eula.

Ike woos the cow at length, but only wins her after rescuing her from the inferno of a brush fire. Even in this, however, he is almost thwarted as a fear-crazed horse materializes out of the flames, "the wild eyes, the yellow teeth, the long gullet red with ravening gleeful triumph . . . the fierce dragon-reek of its passage, blasting at his hair and garments" (197). Four times, as Ike moans with pain, the horse rushes out at him, but he braves the monster, until he is finally discovered by Houston, who cries furiously to the cow, "Git on home, you damned whore!" The word shocks us into a rational perception and emphasizes by contrasts all that follows. On his way home Ike loses a coin which Houston has given him, but he refuses to search for it, this un-Snopeslike rejection marking him as a courtly lover who accepts no material compensation. Immediately afterward, however, he returns and leads the cow from her stall. He has braved the dragon and in the idyll which follows he rejoices in his reward.

Not only do these events suggest the medieval romance but so does the tone in which they are treated. Eula was often described in bovine terms, but the cow is Astarte, "maiden, meditant, shame-free"; and Ike, weaving for her clumsy garlands, is devout priest and swain together. The style, purple as any in modern prose, has the richness of Spenser. Campbell and Foster note this episode as being a striking example of Faulkner's "surrealistic" humor and point out that the style, so much richer than its objective content, adds much to this effect (97–98). But the style does even more. It elevates the lovers again into symbols, encouraging the reader to seek in myth and legend for its rationale. Indeed these two lovers, "orginal, in the womb-dimension, the unavoidable first and the inescapable last, eyeless," seem at times archetypes, but the style has a surer justification (212). In the wasteland any love, though it conventionally be a perverse one, is a promise of redemption, worth a prothalamion.

The quality and intent of this style are apparent as Faulkner describes Ike's walk to a farm from which he pilfers feed, when he observed

that dawn, light . . . is from the earth itself suspired. Roofed by the woven canopy of blind annealing grass-roots . . . dark in the blind dark of time's silt and rich refuse—the constant and unslumbering anonymous wormglut . . . —Troy's Helen and the nymphs and the snoring mitred bishops . . . —it wakes, upseeping . . . first, root; then frond by frond, from whose escaping tips like gas it rises and disseminates and stains the sleep-fast earth with drowsy insect-murmur; then . . . it upward bursts . . . Far below, the gauzy hemisphere treads with herald cock . . . Vanes on steeples groove the southwest wind, and fields for plowing, since sunset married to the bedded and unhorsed plow, spring into half-furrowed sight . . . Then the sun itself . . . The silent copper roar fires the drenched grass and flings long before him his shadow prone for the vain eluded treading; the earth mirrors his antic and constant frustration . . . (207-208)

The poetic quality here—derived chiefly from parallelisms, repetitions, periods, and assonances—establishes the emotional rhythm of the entire idyll. The primordial quality of the moment before dawn is conveyed chiefly through evocations of darkness, lethargy, and enriching decay. The classical and medieval allusions especially suggest the permanence and fecundity of nature until, after the carefully wrought, richly detailed transition, they give way to the sun and bucolic reality. The implications of fertility are then made explicit, so that the progress is from slumbering potency to inchoate and, finally, aroused desire. The symbolic and objective levels of Ike's experience are perfectly merged.

But this love, the most elemental and purest emotion of the novel, is, like Eula's, truncated. After Houston recovers the cow, he takes it to Mrs. Littlejohn as a gift for Ike. It is not long until Lump, Ike's uncle, has pulled a plank off the barn and it is to this vantage point that Ratliff has earlier been invited. He shows deep concern, and Mrs. Littlejohn retorts, "So that's it . . . It's all right for it to be, but folks mustn't know it, see it?" Ratliff's reply epitomizes the conflict of the novel: "Was, . . . because it's finished now. . . . You don't need to tell me he aint got nothing else. I know that. . . . just as I know that the reason I aint going to leave him have what he does have is simply because I am strong enough to keep him from it. I am stronger than him. Not righter. Not any better, maybe. But just stronger" (226–227). Mrs. Littlejohn suggests that Ratliff is guilty of the same fear of convention which has sacrificed Eula; though acknowledging the injustice of his attitude, he nonetheless embraces it. Ratliff, the rational, the conventional, overbears Ike, the passionate, the natural. Ratliff is as humane, perhaps as good, as a man may be, but the ravished land will be redeemed by an act of love, not of righteousness.[17] Rain is described but once in *The Hamlet*: it falls on Ike and his beloved (210–211).

Ratliff achieves his purpose through I. O., who fears the effects of a family scandal on his position as teacher. In a comic travesty on the workings of the rational mind, one sees Snopes parrying Snopes in a ridiculous effort to preserve honor. More seriously, the cow, "the shape of love," has become merchandise to be haggled over, and we have on the comic level the same moral blindness Mrs. Littlejohn has condemned: "The Snopes name. . . . That's got to be kept pure as marble" (231–234).

This thwarting of Ike's passion has its parallel in the bitter outcome of Mink Snopes' murder of Jack Houston. Earlier, Ratliff has said of Mink "this here seems to be a different kind of Snopes like a cottonmouth is a different kind of snake" (104). But he is wrong. Mink, like Houston, is virile and proud; both men are capable of creative action, and it is only within a Snopesian context that their passions lead ironically to self-destruction. This episode is chiefly significant in that during Mink's ordeal, nature, twice violated, becomes actively hostile. It seeks not only to obstruct Mink but to inform against him. First, of course, there is the hound; then the shotgun is cast up from the slough into which Mink his thrown it; and, finally, after he believes the hound dead, circling buzzards seem intent on betraying him.

Still, there is a richness here, even though it be somber. After Mink's imprisonment to await trial, nature, in the bonds of winter, becomes sterile. At no other point in the novel is winter described, but now much is made of it. It is "the winter from which the people as they became older were to establish time and date events," and trains, unpeopled, rushed "without purpose through the white and rigid solitude" (296, 301).

17. Viola Hopkins views Ratliff's decision as an "act of conscience," which Faulkner sees as "one of the conditions of humanity." As she further points out, "Ratliff is certainly the chief spokesman and defendant of an ethical, humane tradition" ("Meaning and Form," pp. 135, 130); but I would suggest that his defensive attitude and Mrs. Littlejohn's comment justify my censure. Florence Leaver, "The Structure of *The Hamlet*," *Twentieth Century Literature*, (July 1955), pp. 77-84, holds Mrs. Littlejohn to be morally superior even to Ratliff.

Here the novel reaches its point of deepest negation. During the summer that follows, however, this bitterness is moderated by the injection, again, of frontier humor, by the lessening of tensions, and by Ratliff's admission of defeat at Flem's game. In May, Flem arrives from Texas with a string of wild ponies. These animals and their sale dominate the fourth book and are important because, given demonic proportions, they act as catalysts and serve to clarify two aspects of the theme: the destructive nature of purely acquisitive instincts and the susceptibility of acquisitive man to rational manipulation.

The horse has already been seen as a symbolic barrier between Ab and his wife, Ike and the cow. Lucy Pate has been killed by the stallion which Houston bought "as if for a wedding present to her," almost as if "that blood and bone and muscles represented that polygamous and bitless masculinity which he had relinquished" (246–247). Now these incidents become more meaningful. For every man in the Bend the ponies are a fatal temptation. Ratliff alone demurs, "You folks can buy them critters if you want to. But me, I'd just as soon buy a tiger or a rattlesnake."

Ratliff's skepticism is immediately justified as the ponies become a center of catastrophe. The most important injury, if we are finally to understand the horse as symbol, is done the Armstid family. Henry Armstid so desires one of the animals that he deprives his "chaps" of food that he may purchase it and cruelly flogs his wife for having failed in its capture. Later, when the ponies break free, Henry is trampled, his leg fractured; but his fate is less significant than the intensity of his desire. It is not necessary to see the horse, as do Russell Roth and Phyllis Hirshleifer, as a symbol of abnormal sexuality.[18] When one recalls how Henry and his wife, after the death of a mule, were forced to spell each other in the traces, he recognizes that in the economy of the Bend ownership of a horse represents not only affluence but a factor of survival as well. Further, to outwit one's opponents in a horse trade is to gain the immediate respect of one's peers. Corollary to this is the fact that to own and trade in horses is a purely masculine prerogative: that "bitless masculinity" which is relinquished not only in marriage but in subjugation of any sort. For these reasons, and not because they are a "symbolic disclosure of misdirected sexual energy," the horses are demonized as agents of destruction (Roth, 204).

The auction culminates in a violent competition for the possession of

18. "The Centaur and the Pear Tree," *Western Review*, 16 (Spring 1952), pp. 199-205; "As Whirlwinds in the South," *Perspective*, 2 (Summer 1949), pp. 225-238.

a pony, a last token of irresponsible individuality. Amid all the hysteria, however, the fecund imperturbability of setting serves continually to recall the symbolic values of Eula and the cow. The night of the ponies' escape is brilliant with moonlight which earlier, for Houston and Lucy, had possessed a magic quality: "they observed the old country belief that the full moon of April guaranteed the fertilizing act" (248). Near Mrs. Littlejohn's is a pear tree "now in full and frosty bloom, the twigs and branches . . . standing motionless and perpendicular above the horizontal boughs like the separated and upstreaming hair of a drowned woman" (316). After Armstid's accident, Ratliff and the others go to Varner's to fetch Will. There Eula opens an upstairs window and looks down upon them: "to those below what Brunhilde, what Rhinemaiden on what spurious river-rock of papier-mache, what Helen returned to what topless and shoddy Argos, waiting for no one." (349–350).

Later, returning to Mrs. Littlejohn's the men observe the pear tree: " 'Look at that tree,' Varner said. 'It ought to make this year, sho'." Then he adds that "A moon like this is good for every growing thing outen the earth," and relates the folk belief that "if a woman showed her belly to the full moon after she had done caught [as Mrs. Varner had when carrying Eula], it would be a gal" (351).

In the pear tree a "mockingbird's idiot reiteration pulsed and pearled," and with the addition of this detail Faulkner's intention becomes clear. In a series of synecdoches the whole theme of the novel seems to be implied. The moon pours its magic rays onto a land where, for the moment, man is given up to the pursuit of a bootless freedom. The pear tree is like a drowned woman sleeping, but it is sure to "make," suffer a sea change. Eula, however damned, remains inviolate, a goddess supreme over a sterile domain. The bird's song is an "idiot reiteration," to which the pear tree is insensible, just as Eula is insensible to "that man," just as the earth is insensible to the "thin and urgent cries and the brief and fading bursts of galloping hooves." Yet, Will pauses amid the chaos to remark on the burgeoning of nature, to recount a fertility legend, and we realize that the blight will somehow pass. The earth endures and in man's acknowledgment of this lies his hope for restoration.[19]

Essentially, *The Hamlet* culminates in the stampede of the ponies:

19. I have relied here, to some extent, on Roth. He, however, emphasizes the sexual implications of the symbolism, tending, perhaps, to distort its context. See also Harry M. Campbell, "Mr. Roth's Centaur and Faulkner's Symbolism," *Western Review*, 16 (Summer 1952), pp. 320-321.

from the ensuing chaos only Flem and the land emerge unaltered. The suit against Flem which is brought by Armstid and the Tulls miscarries because of a legal technicality and Lump's perjury. In sharp contrast Mink, who has proudly refused counsel, comes to trial in Jefferson and is convicted of murder. There is another sort of culmination, too, in Mink's words as he cries into the crowded courtroom, "Is Flem Snopes in this room? Tell that son of a bitch――" (382). Again an epithet crystallizes our reactions and, this time, prepares us for the final act, Ratliff's own fall.

So far in the novel Ratliff's involvement, which followed Eula's marriage, has been in minor "holding actions." After the injustice to Mrs. Armstid, Bookwright half expects Ratliff to return her money as he had Ike's, and his rejoinder is the bitterest of the novel: " 'I could have,' he said. 'But I didn't. . . . Besides, I wasn't protecting a Snopes from Snopeses; I wasn't even protecting a people from a Snopes. I was protecting something that . . . wouldn't know how to hurt no man even if it would . . . I never made them Snopeses and I never made the folks that can't wait to bare their backsides to them. I could do more, but I won't. I won't, I tell you!' " (367). Ratliff is making here his sharpest rejection of human sympathy. Later, Gavin Stevens' rational skepticism leads almost to tragedy, which is averted only by Charles Mallison's emotional intervention. Ratliff is a transitional figure; his faith in man shaken, he begins to abjure responsibility, foreshadowing, perhaps, Isaac McCaslin's withdrawal. Ratliff's pride, however, proves of a sort which precedes a fall. Himself ensnared, his sympathies will be renewed and deepened.

Ratliff's purchase of Old Frenchman's Place is made plausible not only by his loss of detachment. Afflicted already with a fatal acquisitiveness, he too readily trusts Will Varner's judgment. Varner formerly spent much of his time sitting alone at the Place, as if guarding something, and Ratliff "declined to believe that Varner ever had been or ever would be stuck with anything; that if . . . he kept it, it was too valuable to sell" (179). Also he had become infected by Henry's madness and the general atmosphere of irrational excitement. By his naïve negotiations with Flem, his superstitious use of a divining rod, his hysterical digging, Ratliff shows himself for a time transformed by money-lust and guilt: they "slept again . . . while noon came and the creeping and probing golden sun at whose touch they turned and shifted as though in impotent nightmare flight from that impalpable . . . burden" (411). It is this guilt, however, Ratliff's self-awareness, which permits reason once more to function. Perceiving Flem's arch deception and almost as if relieved that his turn has come and gone, Ratliff recovers his equanimity.

At the same time, thanks ironically to Ratliff's having deeded him interest in a restaurant, Flem sets out for Jefferson, and only Henry remains as a grotesque reminder of the madness generated by the ponies. His emotion, perverted by deprivation and by Flem's injustice, has made him a notorious attraction. Henry digs himself "back into that earth which had produced him to be its born and fated thrall forever until he died," and as he does so, Flem pauses in his progress toward new conquests to contemplate the token of his first: Henry "got back into the trench and began to dig. Snopes turned his head and spat over the wagon wheel. He jerked the reins slightly. 'Come up,' he said" (420–421). This juxtaposition of Henry, the earth, and Flem objectifies the central irony toward which the novel has been directed: All men are thralls to the earth, but in his respect for his servitude lies man's chief hope of endurance through human sympathy and mutual respect.

This thesis is developed on two levels, the mythic and objective. On the primary level as major symbols stand Eula and the cow, while on the secondary are Flem and Ratliff; and out of the parallel and conflicting development of these levels the novel grows. Through the implication of symbolic event and style, Faulkner leads us to expect that Eula merits reverence as the embodiment of fertility. Proper understanding of this symbol demands, however, a sloughing off of such accretions as traditional morality and destructive individualism. Thus Labove fails because the instinctive rightness of his desire is repudiated by his overly developed rational will. Thus the horses rise again and again as barriers between man and woman, as sources of catastrophe.

The goddess is betrayed because she exists in a world predominantly self-conscious. Flem, whose utter lack of passion makes him irresistible on the rational level, can neither conceive of nor respect the values which Eula embodies. The Varners, though capable of pity and reverence, abet Flem in his corruption by sacrificing love on the sterile altar of conventional morality.

The result of this profanation is chaos. Eula is transformed into the cow and love becomes perverse; the fist fights of Eula's suitors become a murderous quarrel between Mink and Houston. Flem triumphs while Ike, Houston, and Mink, all capable of love, are deprived or destroyed. Even the earth, in the grip of winter, becomes sterile; and finally the humane, objective Ratliff shares the guilt of the Varners as he works the destruction of the cow, the last vestige in the land of "the shape of love."

These rich passions at rest, Flem returns to manipulate those which remain, offering the horse as a symbol of the self-respect which has been so damningly compromised. The consequent release of desire results in havoc, for Henry in madness. But now the moon-drenched earth gives promise of recovery, of endurance; the violence is but an "idiot repetition." With Ratliff's fall, justice, taking only Henry as its toll, seems to have worked itself out.

This didactic summary puts baldly ideas which Faulkner reveals only by indirection. Emphasis on theme and structure at the expense of the novel's many other facets has been the result of an effort to order apparent chaos. Most of all, Faulkner's humor has received less than due attention, though it is through humor—Ratliff's ironic comments, Faulkner's grandiose distortions—that the events of the novel are for the most part made acceptable. Humor states truth obliquely, leaving us to wonder whether it means what it says; it flanks our defenses so that often it is only later, with a degree of shock, that we concede its point. The development of *The Hamlet,* like that of *The Waste Land,* is contrapuntal. The myth gains immediacy from its juxtaposition with the contemporaneous, the rational; conversely, in a series of ironic contrasts, the contemporaneous derives meaning, universality, from its juxtaposition with myth. By indirection, Faulkner thus achieved in *The Hamlet,* to a higher degree than in any succeeding work, an effective union of art and morality.

# D. The Nobel Prize and After

## THE STOCKHOLM ADDRESS

### WILLIAM FAULKNER

I FEEL that this award was not made to me as a man but to my work—a life's work in the agony and sweat of the human spirit, not for glory and least of all for profit, but to create out of the materials of the human spirit something which did not exist before. So this award is only mine in trust. It will not be difficult to find a dedication for the money part of it commensurate with the purpose and significance of its origin. But I would like to do the same with the acclaim too, by using this moment as a pinnacle from which I might be listened to by the young men and women already dedicated to the same anguish and travail, among whom is already that one who will some day stand here where I am standing.

Our tragedy today is a general and universal physical fear so long sustained by now that we can even bear it. There are no longer problems of the spirit. There is only the question: When will I be blown up? Because of this, the young man or woman writing today has forgotten the problems of the human heart in conflict with itself which alone can make good writing because only that is worth writing about, worth the agony and the sweat.

He must learn them again. He must teach himself that the basest of all things is to be afraid; and, teaching himself that, forget it forever, leaving no room in his workshop for anything but the old verities and truths of the heart, the old universal truths lacking which any story is ephemeral and doomed—love and honor and pity and pride and compassion and sacrifice. Until he does so, he labors under a curse. He writes not of love but of lust, of defeats in which nobody loses anything of value, of victories without hope and, worst of all, without pity or compassion. His griefs grieve on no universal bones, leaving no scars. He writes not of the heart but of the glands.

Until he relearns these things, he will write as though he stood alone and watched the end of man. I decline to accept the end of man. It is easy enough to say that man is immortal simply because he will endure; that when the last ding-dong of doom has clanged and faded from the last worthless rock hanging tideless in the last red and dying evening, that even then there will still be one more sound: that of his puny inexhaustible voice, still talking. I refuse to accept this. I believe that man will not merely endure: he will prevail. He is immortal, not because he alone among creatures has an inexhaustible voice but because he has a soul, a spirit capable of compassion and sacrifice and endurance. The poet's, the writer's, duty is to write about these things. It is his privilege to help man endure by lifting his heart, by reminding him of the courage and honor and hope and pride and compassion and pity and sacrifice which have been the glory of his past. The poet's voice need not merely be the record of man, it can be one of the props, the pillars to help him endure and prevail.

# AN AMERICAN INTERPRETATION
# OF EXISTENCE:
# FAULKNER'S *A FABLE*

HEINRICH STRAUMANN

## 1

FOR THE EUROPEAN READER, William Faulkner's *A Fable* (1954) is the most important novel the American writer has written. At the same time it is the most significant work of an epic cast in English since the Second World War and belongs among those rare works to which the standard of a century may unhesitatingly be applied.

These are strong assertions, and it is proper to examine them more closely. First, it should be established that expressions such as "touching," "harmonious," "beautiful" have not been used. When *Robinson Crusoe* was published, no critic thought of regarding that work mainly as literature, much less of investing it with such attributes. Faulkner's novel is a powerful and moving book in the sense that Tolstoy's *War and Peace* is powerful and moving; it is also a philosophically loaded book, probably more difficult than *Moby-Dick*. And it confuses the reader because idea and event on the various levels of symbolic, allegorical, and imitative presentation appear now separated, now closely interwoven. Indeed, for precisely this reason its critical reception in America was not at all uniform. Certain skeptical voices made no secret of their uncertainty as to its meaning.[1]

Reprinted with permission from *Anglia*, 1955, pp. 484-515. Translated by Grace A. Goodman and Olga W. Vickery.

1. One of the most understanding reviews up to this time is Philip Blair Rice's "Faulkner's Crucifixion," in the *Kenyon Review,* Autumn, 1954, p. 660 ff. In it among other things, remote connections with the theology of Reinhold Niebuhr and Paul Tillich are spoken of. Brilliant, but scarcely doing justice to the matter, is R. W. Flint's review in the *Hudson Review,* Winter, 1955, p. 602 ff.

After the completion of the present work, the article by the noted American lyric poet Delmore Schwartz appeared in *Perspectives,* no. 10, Winter, 1955, p. 126 ff. It contains a penetrating discussion of the novel, which is characterized as "a masterpiece, a unique fulfillment of Faulkner's genius." Schwartz also takes up several points which are considered as crucial in the present article, but his argument stresses the problem of a (monistically considered) belief in humanity and the conquest of fear.

This is, to be sure, nothing new for Faulkner and it is easily explicable. Perhaps one need only examine the anthology of critical opinions about Faulkner's work, *William Faulkner: Two Decades of Criticism,* to get a picture of the astonishingly divergent interpretations and evaluations of the author. This is particularly true of the time between the two World Wars, while in the last ten years, especially since the Nobel Prize award of 1950, the attitude of the critics, though certainly no more uniform, has been in essence considerably more respectful. The striking increase of publications on Faulkner in recent years testifies to the growing desire for analysis of his work. Several books and dozens of articles, some very significant, have appeared in America; and Europe, especially France, is increasingly concerned with him.[2]

This can only mean that something is involved in Faulkner's presentation which only recently has been considered as particularly significant; in other words, the early Faulkner so far outstripped his time that he can only now be comprehended by criticism, while the present Faulkner is once more a considerable distance ahead. Thus, twenty years ago the discussion of *Light in August* (1932) was primarily concerned with what could be directly grasped of the story: the race question in the American South, the problem of the vagrant, the moral confusion of certain characters, the "trueness to life" of the presentation. Since then the critical approach has shifted decisively. The realistic, the psychological, the sociological facts are mentioned no longer or only incidentally. Instead the problem of the inner estrangement of the individual from society is regarded as essential; the position of the man of mixed blood, at first unrecognized, is interpreted as a symbol of the loneliness of man in general; the ethical question is focussed on the limits of human endurance; the complexity of the narrative is discussed as a necessity of form.[3] In short, the interpretation has shifted from the surface to the interior, thereby certainly doing more justice to the book and to Faulkner's earlier work in general.

Now, perhaps it is directly because of this shift in emphasis that recently *A Fable* could confuse critics. For neither a clear-cut structural

2. See on this subject Maurice Edgar Coindreau, "William Faulkner in France," *Yale French Studies,* no. 10 (1953), p. 85 ff. as well as Thelma M. Smith and Ward L. Miner, *Transatlantic Migration: The Contemporary American Novel in France* (Durham, N.C., 1955).
3. Cf. Cleanth Brooks, "Notes on Faulkner's *Light in August,*" in the *Harvard Advocate,* 135, Nov. 1951, a number which contains several other noteworthy articles on Faulkner; further, see Richard Chase's "The Stone and the Crucifixion: Faulkner's *Light in August,*" in *Kenyon Review,* Autumn, 1948.

analysis nor a radically symbolic interpretation can penetrate to the center of the work, although both are probably indispensable to the recognition of essential aspects of it. Rather, problems of mimesis, of allegory, of tone or level of style, and primarily of a certain world-view emerge in a way and to a degree scarcely found in Faulkner's earlier works.[4] Any attempt to comprehend the whole cannot evade the question of the nature of all these elements as well as their mutual interweavings.

## 2

It is usual to begin the consideration of a novel with the plot. In this case, that would be the events which center on the mutiny of a French and British unit on the Western front in the First World War, and which show a similarity, to be sure only remote, with the historical incident of General Nivelle's offensive in the spring of 1917. But this self-same point of departure, however much it claims and is supposed to claim the attention of the reader, is overshadowed by something else, that is, by the discussion among those who have to decide the fate of the mutineers. In these discussions is located the philosophical center of the work, and from this center the way leads to all other aspects of the novel, including the development of the action, characters, and levels of style. For this very reason it is something new in Faulkner—indeed, one can say that the author has never before taken up so meaningful a position on the problem of human existence as here. A clearly tragic world order is presented: tragic because it is shown in successive pairs of opposites each of which is absolutely irresolvable, and hence the whole allows room neither for the idea of completion nor for reconciliation.

The first and most important pair of opposites is that of the commander-in-chief of the Allied forces and the corporal who sets off the mutiny. If their relation to each other and to the total pattern is comprehended, the other problems almost solve themselves. Critics could say with ostensible justice that the commander-in-chief is almost inconceivable as a human being. He is a unique condensation of the most praiseworthy human characteristics: just, wise, serene, friendly, even loving. He has the highest intelligence and self-control, the keenest insight into the inner relationships of events, and in addition he is connected by birth with the most influential, most powerful, and wealthiest French families. His career

4. The expressions "mimesis" and "level of style" have been taken over, appropriately I hope, from Erich Auerbach's *Mimesis: Representation of Reality in Western Literature* (Bern, 1946).

brings him from the military academy first to a remote post in Morocco, then to Asia Minor, where, through a barely hinted at affair with a native girl, a son is born to him. He knows, of course, of his son's existence, but he never sees him until the decisive moment. The son is none other than the corporal who sets off the mutiny in the French regiment, is taken prisoner and faces execution. An incredible number of qualities are given to the son, as they are to the father, only this time they are those of the man who stands lowest in the social hierarchy: endless patience, the incomprehensible strength to endure and capacity to suffer, goodness, forbearance, and forgiveness. The son is brought by his half-sisters, Marya and Marthe, first to the coast of Asia Minor and then, through the marriage of Marthe to a French colonial soldier, to France. There the four manage a farm near St. Mihiel until the war breaks out and the son, after forming a relationship with a prostitute (Magdalena) in Marseille, is sent to the front as a corporal. In his extreme simplicity (he cannot even read) and anonymity he seems to be omnipresent in the army: superiors repeatedly identify him with soldiers who have been declared killed and buried.

From these short sketches it is immediately apparent that a purely realistic interpretation of the two main figures cannot do justice to the novel. Neither the piling up of the aforementioned qualities nor the position in which the antagonists find themselves is plausible by ordinary human standards. However, neither would a purely figurative interpretation succeed, even though the allegorical parallel with the events of Holy Week is made clear enough. For example, the corporal has in the regiment his twelve disciples: one, Polchek, betrays him; another, Pierre Bouc, denies him; a third, Paul, represents him during a temporary absence. He is executed at the same time as a murderer and a thief; he has his crown of barbed wire, and his body is hidden by the three women, Marya, Marthe, and Magdalena. However, just as the commander-in-chief corresponds but little to the historical Marshal Foch or, despite certain similarities, to Pontius Pilate, so the corporal is far from being directly equated with Christ. Rather, these similarities are intended, on the one hand, to bring out the intensity of the basic concern, and, on the other hand, to establish the validity of the statements in relation to our own terrible reality and our own highest scale of values.

And this actually happens on the level of dialectic. First the comander-in-chief has to confer with the Allied generals and the German delegates about the events. What was impossible during four years of war has become possible through the mutiny of a French regiment: a conference between enemy commanders, who realize instantly that the war must not under any circumstances end in this way lest the whole significance of the military hierarchy and its concepts of honor break down. The French division commander in whose unit the mutiny occurred refuses to compromise: he demands the execution of the entire regiment and therefore of himself. This is the consequence, simultaneously exciting horror and working up to the grotesque, of a position which in itself is quite commendable, but which is carried to an extreme of rigidity. The shooting of the division commander, undertaken by three American volunteers since no French soldier can be expected to do it, is one of the most horrifying episodes in the book. It represents the conversion of the concept of honor into something subhuman.

In the talk between the Allied generals and the German delegates, the contrast is brought out in sociological terms. While the decision as such is scarcely mentioned, so much the more is said of British dilettantism as compared to German professionalism in warfare. The German general pays his respects to the concept of honor by shooting the German pilot who is ordered to set him down behind the enemy lines and who must therefore surrender his plane. Further, the human side of the affair is brought out and simultaneously connected with the metaphysical in the contrast between the commander-in-chief and the quartermaster-general, who have remained friends since their time together in the military academy. To the quartermaster-general, it is intolerable to know that one must make common cause with the enemy in order to finish off a group of honest compatriots. But he cannot get around the arguments of the commander-in-chief, who points out that among the mutineers themselves there is a traitor, that is, that something "bad" has crept into the "good" intentions; that the agreement with the enemy is the only alternative to certain chaos, and that it is precisely his execution that will prove the corporal neither lived nor died in vain. Here the dualistic nature of things is made so clear that it becomes a commentary on events which have already happened and been narrated and at the same time prepares us for the still higher plane of that which is to come.

This is the encounter between the commander-in-chief and the corporal, between the judge and the one who is to be judged, between father and son. In their long talk practically the only one to express himself is the commander-in-chief, whom we have known until now as a rather silent man: it is his most impressive attempt to persuade the corporal to yield his position. He casts all values into the scales to weigh them in his favor; he promises the corporal freedom, the possibility of moving unhindered through the universe; he offers him the whole world in the sense of a unique abundance of power; and finally he very simply presents to him the beauty of life itself as a temptation. All these offers are accompanied by cogent reasons, among which the statement that they both, commander-in-chief and corporal, are articulations of opposing terms of existence is the most important one. This is most concisely expressed in the commander's reference to himself as "champion of this mundane earth" (348) and to the corporal as, therefore, a champion "of an esoteric realm of man's baseless hopes and his infinite capacity—no: passion—for unfact" (348).[5] The corporal declines all these offers with the sole, scarcely articulated reason that the suffering of others would still not be helped. Although an unbridgeable gulf between the world of the commander-in-chief and that of the corporal does exist, they do have one important point of contact, namely, the conviction that mankind in its madness will continue to exist in spite of all horrors that the future may bring. For this future existence the commander-in-chief uses the word "prevail" and the corporal, "endure," whereby the distance between "prevailing" and "enduring" within the same existence is made clear.[6]

In the interpretation of this encounter one is first inclined to see the parallel with the temptation of Christ by Satan, and this is by no means to be rejected. However, for the comprehension of the whole, to do so would be an unjustified simplification, for in addition to the similarity there are the differences which cannot be disregarded. Of these only the most striking need be mentioned, namely, that the general is not only the corporal's father but also his highest superior. In fact, this very relationship is of particular significance for the further clarification of the underlying meaning. What is involved is a dualistic view of the world rooted in the profoundest depths and of literally Manichean proportions. A light and a dark principle is immanent in all the orders and values of existence. The commander-in-chief is none other than the origin and source of this double principle. He unites in himself qualities which can lead to the best as well as to the worst. He has godlike as well as satanic traits. He exercises the highest authority, which, on the one hand, means order and the confinement of chaos, but which, on the other hand, can

5. The page numbers are those of the original American edition by Random House, New York, 1954.
6. The same expressions concluded the famous speech which Faulkner delivered on December 10, 1950, on the occasion of receiving the Nobel Prize. See above.

destroy the lives of hundreds of thousands. He is the law, which seeks justice and simultaneously produces suffering. He has wisdom, which means not only knowledge but also temptation. Indeed, from him arise those very powers which directly challenge him and his principle: the powers of pure goodness, love, and hope, which, however, can only be expressed in rebellion against his control and which consequently have a dual nature. The essential point is that these powers can neither change anything of the original order nor effect any kind of deliverance from evil. There is suffering and endurance and perhaps hope but no question of the certainty of salvation. This constitutes a marked difference from Christian thought, which should be remembered in any consideration of Faulkner's pattern of ideas. Rather, we may speak of his intellectual affinity with the Stoics, for the very phenomenon of suffering and the ability to endure that gives outline to so many of Faulkner's works is here too in the foreground of all events and finds its ultimate significance in the corporal's final word "endure."[7]

It is not accidental that the two other most important characters in the book regard endurance as the highest value: the commander-in-chief, in an interior monologue immediately before the crucial decisions are made (239 and 242), and the British messenger, about whom we shall talk later, in his conversation with the Negro (203). For this reason alone one cannot speak of a really pessimistic world view, terrible as the separate events may be. But in addition there is that distinctive level of style, often approaching humor, which can also be found in Faulkner's other works. It is the direct accompaniment of a basically ironic mood which in its turn rests squarely on the knowledge of the inevitability of suffering and the conviction that mankind has the power to endure it. These intricate patterns are for many, especially American readers, the most pleasing side of the author, and their connection with the principle of the two-fold meaning of all things, a connection based as it were on natural laws, is evident. Indeed, most remaining aspects of the work follow from this basic attitude with conclusive logic.

## 3

For the sequence of events, the strongest formative element is the principle of duality, both in the sense of parallels and doubling and also

7. Charles Anderson has already pointed to this before the publication of *A Fable* in his article "Faulkner's Moral Center," in *Études Anglaises*, January, 1954, p. 48 ff.

of the interplay of persons, motives, and actions. Apart from the already mentioned pairs of opposites—commander-in-chief/corporal, commander-in-chief/quartermaster, German general/Allied generals—one is struck by the characteristic duality of the main theme, the mutiny. By the side of the French regiment for whose refusal to attack the corporal and his twelve followers are responsible, there is a British unit in which two days later something similar happens. The differences are, however, significant. While we learn almost no details of the past history of the French mutineers and outside of the war-weariness we know nothing of their reasons, there is in the British unit a quite definite and complex situation which requires some analysis.

The first decisive incident is the one in which the British soldiers, leaving their weapons behind, climb out of the trenches, with the idea of joining the German troops opposite them, who do the same thing. Instantly British and Germans are placed under concentric fire by the batteries which lie farther back, in accordance with the agreement of the troop leaders for this situation, so that the mutineers are completely annihilated. Therefore, while the mutiny among the French remains a mere "omission," it becomes with the British and Germans a definite "commission."

Furthermore, among the British, two contrasting characters play a special role: a runner and a sentry. The runner is a former officer, who has himself demoted to the ranks because he believes he can endure the wretchedness of war only by suffering with the anonymous mass. He forces his own demotion by committing an offence against public decency, that is, for the sake of a moral protest he must commit an immoral act—an example of the duality and irony of meaning. As a runner he hears not only of the passive resistance of the French regiment and the conference of the enemy army leaders, but he is also a witness to the strange authority which the sentry exercises over his comrades in the British unit. It consists of the fact that the sentry, through something that would normally be regarded as an insurance swindle, practically holds his comrads in bondage. He lends them small sums of money which they pay back in installments, and in return they appoint him beneficiary of their military insurance policies for the term of the loan. The sentry therefore speculates coldbloodedly on the highest possible casualty list for his unit. This is the obverse image of the sway that the French corporal has over his own comrades; on the one side brotherly kindness, on the other naked egotism. And it is grimly ironic that their effect is identical. For it is essentially this insane gambling that impels the runner to persuade the soldiers to mutiny. The fact that he also desperately though ineffectually tries to destroy their secret society by this means is again a reversal of the proceedings among the French, where an unspoken agreement already seems to exist among the mutineers. He is, further, in natural opposition to the sentry, who from the start has only curses for his reflections. Again we are confronted by an inversion of ethical values in that the humanly appealing but legally irresponsible act of the runner stands opposed to the humanly repugnant but legally permissible one of the sentry.

Of the numerous further examples of duality as a principle of structure we need only cite the following, which is at the same time related to the question of personal or professional honor. In the early stage of his career in Morocco the commander-in-chief sacrifices a Foreign Legionnaire in order to avert an armed conflict with an Arabian tribe. Although the author clearly states that the Legionnaire is a common criminal, even a murderer, it is nevertheless made evident that the commander-in-chief's action is shrewd and far-sighted since by it order and peace can be preserved though it cannot be approved from the standpoint of strict honor. What the commander-in-chief here performs in miniature is later repeated "in large" in his handling of the mutiny.

The concept of the ability to endure also is reversed in certain significant incidents connected with the problem of honor. One example is the episode of the young American pilot who, out of deepest conviction, has enlisted in the British air force. He is a witness as a German aircraft lands on the British airfield. His mission ought to be to attack this plane, and he tries to do so, only to perceive to his bewilderment that he is shooting blank ammunition. Other unusual events confirm his belief that this has been ordered by higher authorities. His bewilderment increases when he ultimately learns why the enemy plane is allowed to make a landing and for what purpose the troop commanders have met. He hears of the mutiny of the British battalion that was placed under bombardment; everything becomes mere appearance to him; the meaning of his existence, erected on a belief in honor and integrity of action, collapses; the values that alone give his life meaning do not exist; he seizes the pistol to put an end to his life. Here also is a significant detail: his flight dress is singed in one place by phosphorescent ammunition. It does only a little damage, but it goes on corroding slowly and constantly in the fabric, and causes an overpowering stench: a small leitmotif for the slow disintegration and destruction which recurs throughout the work.

The case of the priest is quite similar. His mission is to persuade the

French corporal, before his execution, to renounce the idea of personal suffering in connection with which the necessity of an order embodied in the institution of the Church becomes significant. Only here the collapse is enacted in the short span of a personal conversation. After the priest fails in his argument, including the appeal to life itself, his system of belief is shaken to its foundations. His whole existence has become meaningless and unbearable, and so he too chooses suicide.

In the fact that admirable, well-meaning men experience this collapse of meaning and are incapable of enduring it lies that irony which lends to the Faulkner world its dual nature and which is still to be discussed. First, however, a further essential element in the structure of the novel must be considered: the motif of "The Stranger in the Crowd."

## 4

Faulkner's novel begins and ends with mob scenes from which individuals emerge as strangers who have gone astray. This motif also recurs twice in the course of the story, so that it appears in quadruple variation, to which a fifth is added, enacted, to be sure, on an entirely different plane. The story begins with the description of the crowd which gathers in the French city where the Allied headquarters are located to see the arrival of the captive French mutineers as well as the troop commanders who are to decide their fate. An apathetic, shapeless, anonymous mass waits for an event unable to do more than just suspect its importance: "one vast tongueless brotherhood of dread and anxiety" (3)—a gigantic symbol for a passive mankind which has to accept happiness or disaster in speechless anxiety.

In this crowd is a young woman, whose strange individuality is noticed only because she almost collapses from exhaustion. She is, as is revealed later, the fiancée of the corporal, who himself appears as a stranger among strangers, as he moves past the crowd, chained in the lorry. The woman is supported by another unknown, who gives her some bread and arouses the suspicion of a sergeant on duty because he has knowledge of the mutiny. No names are given. At the end of the scene, after the crowd has dispersed, the young woman stays behind in silent despair, alone.

These few indications already convey the tight interweaving of motifs, moods, and symbols which is so consistently carried out in this story. The fact that no names are given strengthens the impression of strangeness which emanates from these characters and simultaneously indicates their universal validity. Both are of significance for the comprehension of the whole. Above all, however, a feeling of unutterable isolation is produced through the events which take place around these few nameless people in the nameless mass. It is perhaps strongest here in the beginning of the story where it determines the level of style for the theme of suffering and the ability to endure which is articulated by the same events.

The same motif-groups and mood appear in varying strengths in the remaining four places in the story. The first elaborates the situation (120–39) in which the crowd continues to await the development of events silently and passively and only once turns purposelessly against that section of the camp where the mutineers are held captive. This time it is the crowd whose uncertain emotional impulses are noted; the strangers who appeared in the first scene are not mentioned here. Instead individual military figures are introduced into the story, but again only in such a way that the impression of indefiniteness is preserved: sentries are changed, couriers come and go, the arrival of the division commander and a staff officer is observed. But here too the element of strangeness is present: the prison compound is guarded by Senegalese, doing their duty carelessly, impenetrably, fatalistically.

The third time (212–23) the individuals emerge more distinctly from the same waiting crowd. A name, Marthe, is even given for one of the corporal's two half-sisters, and we learn of the other young nameless woman's relationship to the corporal. But this elucidation goes hand in hand with the stress on the foreign origin of the women, who are moreover threatened with actual violence by the crowd which has become hostile. The isolation of the individual is, as it were, replaced by his expulsion by a group whereupon the motif of suffering clearly assumes the meaning of "endure."

The fourth mob scene takes place in characteristic inversion in the completely different setting of a small city in the American South in connection with the story of the stolen racehorse. More about this later.

In a level of style once again entirely different basically the same motif group appears at the end of the novel as in the beginning. This is the fifth mob scene. Years after the end of the war, the commander-in-chief is carried to his grave in Paris, accompanied by the representatives of all the powers and the whole population of France. This time it is a respectful though as before anonymous crowd which has turned out in immense numbers for this event. At the instant that the funeral procession arrives at the grave of the Unknown Soldier, a stranger rushes out of the crowd, throws his war medal on the coffin, breaks into incoherent words about the fate of mankind and national slogans, until he is beaten down by the crowd and arrested by the police. A second unknown supports him, and then come the final sounds of laughter and tears with which the book closes.

This closing scene naturally contains a great deal more than merely a variation on the theme of "The Stranger in the Crowd," but characteristically this very motif is used once again in order to bring together the intellectual outlines of the work. There are the characteristic little brush strokes indicating the symbolic references which will be further discussed later: sabre, medal, blood on the corner of the mouth, scars, all point to what lies farther back in the story and establish the connection with the ideas of Power, Honor, Suffering, and Endurance. Slowly and with some effort we learn from certain signs that we should know both the strangers. One of them is the British runner who forced his own demotion; knowing about the proceedings at the front and hoping for a mystic brotherhood, he was about to call on his unit to lay down its arms, and was severely wounded in the barrage. The other, supporting him, is the quartermaster-general whose pleas to the commander-in-chief for an understanding of the mutineers were rejected. Together they have the last word in the work: the eternal, nameless rebel, the Man, who knows of our struggles, who knows how to renounce outward honor, who has suffered most terribly, who is not afraid to give expression to his confused truth, who spits blood and at the same time laughs—and the other, the helper, aware of duty, honestly anxious and conscientious, but always standing in second place, the eternal adjutant, so to speak, who is not concerned with laughter.

This is the dual image that appears most impressively once again in this most critical place: in effect, our existence cannot be interpreted from a single point of view but only as a duality. There will always be one power which wants order, and one which rebels against it; there will always be a crowd and an individual who is threatened by it; there will always be one who struggles and endures, and one who helps and reconciles; there will always be weeping and laughing, difficult though they are to distinguish now and then; the one, indeed, sometimes takes the place of the other inasmuch as he who endures knows how to laugh, and he who helps, weeps. And here also the irony becomes apparent in this huge and never resolved drama, though, to be sure, in such a way that only the reader is supposed to know of it: the corpse of the commander-in-chief is conveyed to the grave of the Unknown Soldier, the symbol of valor, sacrifice, and national honor. Who, however, lies in this grave? None other than the corporal who was responsible for the mutiny of the French regiment and who was executed on the order of the very same man whose remains are now being brought to him as the last, highest honor. Are we to laugh or cry?

## 5

Actually, in *A Fable* pain and laughter merge into one another in almost imperceptible fashion: just as, frequently, the incipient laughter suddenly sticks in the reader's throat, so the horror turns into laughter. One can probably say that Faulkner's irony attains its subtlest value in this work both as a structural element that conditions events and as a factor determining the level of style in numerous episodes.

Irony as an element which conditions events is most pronounced in the story of the sentry as a jockey and in the episodes after the death of the corporal. The former is perhaps the most difficult part of the book for the non-American. First of all, one is struck by its minuteness of detail. To the characterization and explanation of a mere subordinate figure are devoted about sixty pages, that is, a full seventh of the total length. At first the events related in it seem scarcely relevant for the whole. The jockey in the Southern states saves a famous racehorse out of a railroad accident and with the animal, healed but running on only three legs, wins numerous races in smaller towns; a Negro and a youth help him. Upon the urging of the legal owner the law finally intervenes and terminates the affair.

One might think this episode a mere digression intended mainly to do justice to the comic element. And indeed, as he himself informs us in his preface, Faulkner published this section first as a separate unit in a special edition. This demonstrates that the story is capable of standing alone. It is, however, also of significance for the novel as a whole, éven if the relationships are not readily discernible. The quite special nature of these relationships can best be expressed in musical terms as "keeping close to the main theme in another key and instrumentation"—keeping in mind, of course, that it is scarcely probable that we have here a conscious principle of composition.

The jockey, an Englishman with a Cockney accent, is a stranger in America. This is noted several times both directly and with the veiled Faulkner humor: "A small bandy-legged foreigner who could barely speak English" (157, similarly father on, 162, 189, etc.). He is a stranger, who, however, is successful in such an unusual and legally dubious manner that the mob favors him. Just as later in the deadly peril of war he speculates on the casualty list of his unit, thereby binding his comrades to him, so here he wins his races under the constant risk of being arrested with a stolen horse, and thus wins the admiration of the spectators so that even such groups as the Baptists and the Freemasons make him one of them. The motif of the Stranger and the Crowd is here given a comical variation. We are amused because something of intrinsic importance (a portion of mankind acting in accordance with high ideals) is directly connected with a slight and morally disreputable affair.

The same motif appears a second time. The police succeed in arresting the Negro and his boy, who have accompanied the jockey on his racing trips. A silent mob assembles in front of the prison of the small American town, giving the impression that the dangerous and alarming mood could develop which precedes an act of lynch-justice. But just the opposite happens. The crowd demands the release of the Negro, on condition, to be sure, that he leave town, since "rich negroes are unwelcome there" (189). This is a deliberately paradoxical variation of our motif of the Stranger in the Crowd, and its liberating effect rests on the familiar principle of the relaxation of a dramatically pointed situation.

It does not, however, happen by accident that the mob appears as a helper here. In reversing the expected manner of representation the motif undergoes a doubling. The jockey is taken in by the Freemasons and draws the Negro with him, and the Negro, who belongs to the Baptists, baptizes the jockey, so that both belong to two great organizations. From this, at the outbreak of war, comes the connection with the American relief organization in France, financed by an American woman whose son was killed as a volunteer at the front. The relief organization is finally named *Les Amis Myriades et Anonymes à la France de Tout le Monde,* and the Negro and his boy are active in it in Paris. This is actually a theatrically handled group sequence of the stranger-and-secret-society motif. In addition, technically the episode becomes a feasible part of the war front story.

Furthermore, the problem of the contrast of order and mutiny also has its parallel in the episode of the stolen horse. After the horse vanishes onto the small racetracks, the legal owner in New York sets the authorities in motion to regain possession of his property. But he does not succeed. Though the commissioned official of the American police department tries his hardest, he suddenly realizes the pursuit is hopeless in view of the popularity of the horse-thief, and tries to convince the owner of the uselessness of the undertaking. The owner, for his part, attempts to keep him on the job by offering to increase the reward, but the latter takes the side of the "persecuted." Here the author himself indicates a comparison with the

British runner and subsequent mutineer (158). Also present in the official's discussion with the owner is the motif of temptation, reminiscent of the scene between the commander-in-chief and the corporal. However, because of the triviality of the object of the dispute, everything has a level of style which keeps the reader amused and amazed.

Finally, even a weak echo of the theme of suffering and the ability to endure can be noted, though transferred to a dumb animal. The racehorse, cause and occasion of the whole episode, before the beginning of his triumphal tour is so injured in a train accident that he remains lame in one leg even after his recovery. Nevertheless, he runs from victory to victory. The animal suffers, endures, and wins. The notion of a lame animal who is still able to run has something perplexing if not almost mad or grotesque about it, not unlike the impression which, at the end of the book, the British runner arouses with his gruesome scar and the threadbare dinner jacket. In addition to the parallel, however, there is also the contrast: the jockey kills the horse as it is on the point of being returned to the hands of the legal owner. He cannot endure the thought that it might be used as mere breeding material. What remains for men a lasting and eternally recurring state is for an animal a solitary event.

In contrast to the complexity of the jockey-and-racehorse episode, the irony connected with the events centering on the mortal remains of the corporal is grimly consistent in its level of style. It is a question of three separate crucial episodes which, however, all point directly to the corporal's death. The first shows how Marthe and Marya, the corporal's half-sisters, and his fiancée are given possession of his body after the execution, and bring him back by wagon and train to their farm in St. Mihiel near Verdun in order to bury him there under an old beech tree. The transportation takes place without hindrance, since it was so ordered by the supreme authority. The suspension of hostility still prevails as a consequence of the agreement among the opposing troop leaders. Finally, however, a day after the burial, a barrage of unheard of ferocity begins: the beech is shattered; a huge shell crater appears on the burial place; only splinters remain of the coffin; the body has disappeared. Again the analogy with the empty grave of Christ is evident, but the irony of the causal connection is just as important. The same supreme power which takes the greatest care to ensure in due order a grave for the executed man is also responsible for its destruction: from one and the same source come preservation and annihilation.

The second episode stands, in its turn, in a sort of inverse analogy

to the first. After the start of the official truce, a non-commissioned officer
and twelve soldiers carry out the order to bring a body out of the mass
graves of Verdun to Paris for the projected grave of the Unknown Soldier.
The first part of their assignment they carry out successfully. On the way
back, however, a peasant woman, under the delusion that it is her dead
son, demands the body from them in return for money and they agree to
the proposition. The substitute which has become necessary is offered them
by a peasant who has just ploughed up the body of a fallen Frenchman
while cultivating his field in the neighborhood of St. Mihiel. No one knows
that it is the mortal remans of the corporal and mutineer which now are
laid to rest in the grave of the Unknown Soldier.

Again, the irony consists first of all in the fact that an order from the
supreme authority, as it were, crosses itself up. What the men in unison
with the state power honor as a symbol of resistance against the enemy and
of the highest sacrifice for the Fatherland is in reality the incarnated pure
brotherly love which has just been destroyed by precisely this power. Such
an exchange becomes possible because the individual yields in crucial moments to some sort of weakness which in itself need not necessarily be a
negative trait. In the double bargain concerning the corpse lies a macabre
atrocity. We are not used to having people treat the remains of a human
being as if it were some casual object. But the behavior of the soldiers is
in complete harmony with what four years of a murderous war must evoke
in a man: a sort of objective attitude to death, which almost appears as
"gallows humor" and which together with other means serves to keep fear
away. It is, then, no accident that the one place in the whole book where
drunken soldiers are portrayed is connected with this exhuming episode.
Indeed, the first bargain is really determined by a desire for alcohol. But
just as important is the fact that the peasant woman who wants to get
possession of the body suffers from the illusion that it is her son. Her illusion has for her become reality, and this constitutes an antithesis to the
public's attitude concerning the grave of the Unknown Soldier. In handing
over the corpse to her, the soldiers fulfill a humanly understandable even
if completely foolish wish. Their deed is inextricably compounded from
the best as well as lesser motives, thereby giving it that dual nature with
which all important events in this work are endowed.

The third episode is concerned with the visit of two strange figures to
the farm of the corporal's half-sisters. The one asks for a snack, tries to
pay for it with thirty coins, and on departure stands for an instant in the
doorway so that he looks as though he were hanging from a rope. We

know it is Polchek, who belonged to the corporal's group and betrayed him. The other is an Englishman, badly injured in the war, in a tattered dinner jacket, who carries off in addition to his own two medals the third, which belonged to the corporal. We learn incidentally that the corporal's young fiancée has gone back to Marseille in order—once again as a prostitute—to earn money to support her mother; and that Marthe's husband has died.

Faulkner here once more takes up several threads, both to indicate the future fate of some important characters and to prepare us for the final scene beside the grave of the Unknown Soldier. Theme and level of style are matched. The corporal's fiancée suffers and endures as she has suffered and endured in the past. Marthe remains the provident, methodical, capable wife, accompanied by her simple-minded but clear-sighted sister, Marya. Marya recognizes the traitor without denying him the right to hospitality, since she knows that he cannot escape his own suffering and fate. This is one of the very few indications in the work which allows us to conclude that the author has a normative point of view about one of his characters. While deceit and blasphemy, swindling and prostitution, theft and even manslaughter must be accepted as part of the bargain and endured as phenomena of an immutably dualistic world order, the traitor is in a class by himself. He will put an end to his own life just as, at the other end of the scale, the airman and the priest can no longer endure their lives. In both cases the decision depends on a certain interpretation of honor which is here worked out reciprocally.

The Englishman is a strange figure. Only after he tells of his injury and of how he found the way to the sisters, do we know that he must be the runner, the same man who had himself demoted in order to be nearer to the suffering of his comrades and who was responsible for the outbreak of the mutiny in the British unit. It is almost more of a supposition than a certainty because what formerly was a strong, athletic figure is now a tattered cripple with only one eye, one ear, one leg, and with one corner of the mouth stiffened to a scar. He can, however, still laugh, and he laughs spontaneously with the simple and clear-sighted Marya, who gives him the corporal's medal. And then he sets out again on the road, painful and yet patient on his crutches: "not lonely: just solitary, invincible single" (431).

It is apparent that in this presentation mimetic and symbolic elements mingle in a unique way. The events themselves are on the very edge of the explicable and succeed each other, so to say, causelessly but still com-

pletely naturally. Marya knows why the stranger with the crutches comes
although she has never seen him. The laughter of the two has no reference
to anything tangible; the medal changes hands without our learning why.
Inevitably the result is that we ponder more about the meaning of these
actions than if they took place in a causal sequence. At the same time
several essential traits emerge. Marya has the power of intuitive knowledge
and in her simplicity she understands more than other people. She thus
becomes a clear-out symbol of absolute understanding. We already know
the runner as one who rebels against force although he himself must use
force, who struggles until he is mutilated and is willing to endure all suffering. Now he encounters for the first time absolute understanding, an intuition into the relationship of things, the "sancta simplicitas," and with it he
can raise himself above the misery of the world. He sees the irony of the
way the world is ordered, and gains the power and the right to laugh. Only
after this does he receive the medal, the badge of honor of one who had
to die for his faith in the brotherhood of men. And now he will continue
on his lonely way as stranger and as one who understands.

## 6

The details just observed belong to what may be called the network
of symbolic references in *A Fable*. It consists of a great number of apparently unimportant elements, which together with the intellectual and
motivational parts of the structure, nevertheless evoke an impression of a
comprehensive unity of composition, a unity which is greater than in most
other novels of Faulkner and his contemporaries. There are, moreover,
two distinct layers to be distinguished, in which the specific elements take
on more or less meaning as symbols according to the strength of their figurative nature.

Direct symbols, that is, symbols bound up with Christian and Western
tradition, are the repeatedly mentioned names and events connected with
the passion of Christ. These serve to place the aim of the author in the
same human and metaphysical perspective, and at the same time to show
in relief the complex of suffering and endurance. In addition there are signs
which always embody certain values and which appear here in their
natural role, namely, the sabre and the medal. But in certain situations
these symbols achieve a new meaning through allusion. The division commander, Gragnon, in whose unit the mutiny occurs, hands over his sabre
to his superior as a suitable expression of his demotion. This sabre appears
several more times in the course of the story, most impressively perhaps

when the anonymous crowd in the headquarters city awaits the arrival of the troop leader and recognizes "the longish object" (134) which the escorting staff officer carries under his arm. The crowd knows instantly what is involved when a division commander is under arrest, and it breaks out into a sound which carries its own symbolic meaning. The sabre is the recognized symbol not only of the honor of arms but also of the epitome of power, of rank, and of the war. And the fact that the division commander no longer commands it contains the concise theme of the collapse of order and its consequences.

In contrast to this uncomplicated symbol, the medal appears considerably more complex. In itself it is a military distinction, bestowed for bravery against the enemy. With Faulkner, however, it assumes still another meaning: it is the visible sign of injustice, suffering, and torment endured in the terror of war. A medal is first mentioned almost incidentally in the scene in which the division commander thinks of his past before he enters the headquarters. He recalls an incident in which one of his aides, at the sacrifice of his life, had warned the passengers in a coach of an artillery attack, and had been posthumously decorated. The theme of sacrifice is voiced and is characteristically connected immediately with the undertone of grim irony which anticipates a further theme: the medal can never be placed with the aide's corpse for the simple reason that it, as later that of the corporal, is not to be found. This episode, short as it is, has in addition its own special relevance, since among the passengers in the coach is the American woman in whose organization the Negro friend of the jockey works. Thus, the medal already serves to hold together several elements of the story.

The second mention of a military distinction occurs in the beginning of the story of the runner, who voluntarily has himself demoted and then conceals the decoration since he wants to remain an anonymous soldier (65). In this closer association with the group the first hint is given of the possible trouble which the runner could make in his new position, and which indeed later actually assumes the form of mutiny. Thus, here too the symbol is connected with elements which are crucial for the action.

The third medal is the corporal's, taken from him immediately before his execution by a non-commissioned officer who later gives it to Marthe (384). It is the tragic climax of the whole, once again sounding the disturbing note of irony: the sign of honor is removed at the instant when the passion attains its completion. And finally the same medal, which is saved by the two half-sisters in St. Mihiel, passes over into the hands of the British runner (431), who at the end of the story throws it on the coffin at the burial of the commander-in-chief. These two scenes, whose crucial significance we have already discussed, are thus prepared for not only through certain courses of action and intellectual concepts but equally through a slow and careful charging of the symbolic objects.

We have thus reached a second level of meaning, namely, those numerous examples of motives and plot divisions which first appear to be ordinary mimetic constructional elements and only through repetition assume by degrees the character of recurring motifs or symbols. The most easily recognizable motifs are perhaps the repeatedly mentioned mud-covered uniforms of the soldiers or, in contrast to this, the tattered tuxedo of the runner, symbol of his origin and rank in society, cast off by him but still not wholly to be denied. How the moldering airsuit of the young American officer, referred to time and again, in the end becomes a symbol of the decay and destruction of religious value has already been described. Similarly, the groaning noise which the waiting crowd raises at the appearance of the mutineers and later of the division commander gradually becomes an expression of that dull and silent suffering which in certain moments is heard not only by fellow men but also by those in authority without, however, the possibility of anything further being done about it.

The motif-group of food, drink, and spoon which appears repeatedly and which is given peculiar stress is far from easy to interpret. At the very beginning of the story we learn how the corporal's young fiancée obtains a piece of bread from an unknown person, which she spits out again while chewing as she sees her beloved, a prisoner, go by on the lorry (18). The three women are abused by the crowd as they approach a group to share a meal with it, and one of the crowd throws a spoon at them which mysteriously disappears. The next day the vanished spoon is the object of complaint that is even brought to the attention of the commander-in-chief, whereupon it reappears. The commander-in-chief, the division commander, the troop leaders, as well as the captured mutineers are depicted in detail while eating and drinking. This is also true of Polchek, the betrayer, and the British runner during their visit to the sisters, where, moreover, a spoon is once more mentioned, though knife and fork never appear in this context.

These examples affect all ranks, and there is in them something of the nature of Communion, which, according to the attitude of the participant, produces a redemptive or a hardening effect. The quality of Communion appears most unmistakably and in most direct analogy to Holy Week in the last common meal of the thirteen mutineers in prison where the treachery of Polcheck becomes evident and Pierre denies the corporal. Amid tension and release and tinged with the grotesque, the mealtime of the troop leaders proceeds, as does that of the two visitors in St. Mihiel. An atmosphere of silence, loneliness, and also an awareness of their responsibility surrounds the meals of the commander-in-chief and the division commander. Outspoken hardness, even hostility, confronts us in the attitude of part of the waiting crowd when a basket with foodstuffs is overthrown and the incident of the spoon occurs.[8] It seems as if, in their gross violation of the most elementary principles of decency, unique resources, at the very least, would have to be invoked to bring this group of human beings to order again. Here also the element of irony and the grotesque is not lacking. The commander-in-chief apparently attributes to the disappearance of the spoon such great significance that he sends out an adjutant with a whole company to search in the streets for it, knowing already that one of the sisters will produce it (273, 284). Perhaps it is going too far to think here of the concept of the wanton gods, but at least the notion of the highest being concerned with the smallest and most commonplace is present and this necessarily raises a serious matter in the sphere of humor.

In this connection one may also point to some of those elements of Faulkner's style which are especially close to the other aspects of his art. For a long time Faulkner's narrative technique and style were usually related to the allusions and associations of the stream of consciousness technique, and in fact his best known early works, especially *The Sound and the Fury* (1929), are strongly indebted to this manner of writing. In a greatly modified way, this is still the case even in *A Fable,* for here also are those feverish page-long sentences which set whole series of ideas in vibration. However, this time the ordering hand has become much more visible. What earlier often had a wearying effect because the relevance for the whole was not apparent has now been given direction and is filled with tension. The following example is taken from the scene at the beginning of the story when the crowd in the little French garrison city stands waiting for the arrival of the arrested mutineers and recognizes the thirteen ringleaders on the last truck:

8. In the Eastern Church the communion wine is taken with a spoon. Whether Faulkner knows of this custom is not certain.

Then you saw that four of the thirteen were really foreigners, alien not only by their gyves and isolation to the rest of the regiment but, against the whole panorama of city and soil across which the lorry was rushing them— the faces of four mountain men in a country which had no mountains, of peasants in a land which no longer had a peasantry; alien even among the other nine among whom they were chained and shackled, since where the other nine were grave and watchful and a little—not too much—concerned, three of the four who were not Frenchmen were merely a little puzzled, alert too, almost decorous, curious and interested: the mountain peasants whom they resembled, entering for the first time a strange valley market town, say; men overtaken suddenly by an uproar in a tongue which they had no hope of comprehending and, indeed, not much interest in, and therefore no concern in its significance—three of the four who were not Frenchmen, that is, because now the crowd itself had discerned that the fourth one was alien still somehow even to the other three, if only in being the sole object of its vituperation and terror and fury. (16-17)

The theme is that of the Crowd and the Stranger. The element of strangeness is expressed directly through words such as "alien," "foreigner," "strange," "not Frenchmen," "no hope of comprehending," etc; indirectly, though with equal force, through the opposites: land/city, peasantry/mar-kettown; and finally through certain characteristic associations: "mountain men in a country which had no mountains, peasants in a land which no longer had a peasantry"; that is, concrete things in a surrounding to which they no longer belong. In this case, the alienation is indicated not only through the sharpness of the contrast but also through a special gradation. Relevant here is the just mentioned "no longer" that signifies a relation which is conceivable but no longer in existence, as well as (before the beginning of our quotation) the stress placed first on the thirteen out of the whole number of the regiment, then on the four out of the thirteen, and finally on the one out of the four. This gradation is further emphasized through the distinctions observed in the behavior of the captives. The nine are grave, attentive, and concerned; the four rather surprised by it all, a little puzzled, even curious and interested, so that the calm behavior of the one (the corporal) whose description is still to follow is then seen in really sharp contrast to the movement of the raging crowd. Appropriately the method of doubling and of a kind of contrasted intensification is em-ployed: doubling in the expressions "gyves and isolation," "city and soil," "chained and shackled," and in the already mentioned pairs of opposites; intensification in the expressions "grave and watchful and a little—not too much—concerned," and in the clear logical progression of "an uproar in a tongue which they had no hope of comprehending and, indeed, not much interest in, and therefore no concern in its significance." The successive qualifications in the style are achieved, among other things, by the introduction of negation-particles, that is, a positive is expressed by a negative. This is a stylistic device so striking in Faulkner that one can have scarcely any doubt about its reference to a basically dualistic world view.

### 7

The whole work combines extraordinary pertinence for our time with unusual validity in the statements. The world of the war, not only as a sequence of events to be regarded mimetically but also as a symbol for the eternal suffering of mankind, is by itself an idea whose power cannot be avoided by modern man. All our cares have here been put into epic form. No order without force, no justice without power, no power without destruction, no loyalty without betrayal, no faith without doubt, no union without loneliness, no constancy without weakness, no Christ without Judas, no God without Satan. The dualism that Faulkner attributes to the whole world order belongs to that concept of tragedy which rests on the irresolvable contrasts of existence, yet allows no room for a real despair. The collapse of the American flier and the suicide of the priest are actions which follow from the over-refining of an illusionary idealism. They are the catastrophes of those who cannot endure the irony of the dualistic scale of values. And indeed endurance is precisely the one single highest value that Faulkner does not question by a contrast to its own category. Endurance is terribly hard, but it is the solution of sensitive men in the incessant strife between the opposing forces. And he who can endure also learns to understand, and he who can understand can also laugh. The laughter may often be filled with bitterness and horror, but it is also the occasion for and the indication of a momentary liberation from the weight of existence. Faulkner's irony borders on humor as well as on pathos.

The intellectual conception of the whole would not alone establish the book as a literary masterpiece. What makes it this is the absolute fusion of the philosophical with the epic development. The techniques of doubling, inversion, parallel structure, and opposition, in plot, characters, and single motifs are omnipresent but so handled that one becomes conscious of them only through a close analysis of events. Otherwise one simply gains a forceful total impression of what was designated here as duality. Battle-scene and armistice, front line and rear base, general and non-commissioned officer, crowd and individual, stranger and home, man and animal, communion and execution, burial and exhumation are contrasted in such a way that again and again an equilibrium of events is attained.

And finally we have to do with that rare form of action which is indebted to the real as well as to the symbolic in such a way that the two spheres merge almost imperceptibly. Parts of the action and characters such as the past history of the sentry as jockey, the execution of the French division commander, and the characterization of the American pilot at first appear to belong completely to mimesis and its crudest forms. In contrast, there are those elements of the same sort which can scarcely be interpreted mimetically, but must be regarded as openly symbolic, such as the encounter between the commander-in-chief and the corporal, their characterization, and all the episodes which are directly modelled on the events of the Passion. Between these two poles the rest revolve; that is, most of the events can be read either as a realistic account of a deeply moving war story or as an extensive allegory of the structure of existence held together by a whole network of real and symbolic references.

Faulkner's work confirms a trend which has become exceedingly significant in American intellectual life, and simultaneously gives it a new degree of projection. It is the remolding of the unalloyed realism of the period between the wars into something that could be called symbolic mimesis. It is found in numerous works of the younger authors such as Truman Capote, Wright Morris, Ralph Ellison, Jean Stafford, Paul Bowles, as well as in playwrights such as Tennessee Williams, Arthur Miller, and Robert Anderson, and in lyric poets such as Robert Lowell and Theodore Roethke. Hemingway's *The Old Man and the Sea* also belongs here. Even in the American literary essay, the tendency to a synthesis of the concrete and the symbolic way of thinking can be seen. Furthermore, this goes hand in hand with a negative evaluation of all attitudes tending to illusion, of which the new concern with Scott Fitzgerald's work is characteristic. What raises Faulkner's book above all this, however, is the all-embracing nature of his subject-matter, the suspension of his intellectual magnetic field between Manichaeism, Stoicism, and Christianity, and the meaningful references which are thoroughly worked out down to the smallest detail. It is a milestone in the history of American literature.

# FAULKNER'S CRUCIFIXION

## PHILIP BLAIR RICE

FROM THE OPENING PARAGRAPHS of *A Fable,* it is evident that Faulkner is tackling a larger and more serried canvas than he has attempted hitherto:

Long before the first bugles sounded from the barracks within the city and the cantonments surrounding it, most of the people in the city were already awake. They did not need to rise from the straw mattresses and thin pallet beds of their hive-dense tenements, because few of them save the children had even lain down. Instead, they had huddled all night in one vast tongue-less brotherhood of dread and anxiety, about the thin fires of braziers and meagre hearths, until the night wore at last away and a new day of anxiety and dread had begun. . . .

Even before the bugles' echoes died away, the warrened purlieus were already disgorging them. A French or British or American aviator (or a German either for that matter, if he had had the temerity and the luck) could have watched it best: hovel and tenement voiding into lane and alley and nameless *cul-de-sac,* and lane and alley and *cul-de-sac* compounding into streets as the trickles became streams and the streams became rivers, until the whole city seemed to be pouring down the broad boulevards converging like wheel spokes into the *Place de Ville,* filling the *Place* and then, pressed on by the weight of its own converging mass, flowing like an unrecoiling wave up to the blank gates of the *Hôtel* where the three sentries of the three embattled nations flanked the three empty flagstaffs awaiting the three concordant flags.

Here is something more overtly on a universal scale than a crowd of Yoknapatawpha County farmers converging upon Jefferson for a trial or a lynching. We have a sense of torrential commotion, of the unplanned but purposeful movement of a whole population, which in turn is emblematic of Humanity. And we know that the burden of its past and the meaning of its present existence are at stake, for we are told at once that the original regiment was raised in this district by one of Napoleon's marshals, and that all of these people are kin of the doomed men. Dread,

Reprinted with permission from *The Kenyon Review,* Autumn, 1954, pp. 661-70.

anxiety and doom: these have set the torrent in motion. The people press
into the unnamed city; they meet the cavalry and the cavalry gives way.
The camera's eye focuses on a mounted officer seeking to extricate himself,
then on a ragged young woman who has fainted. A sergeant asks for bread;
she at first refuses then devours it. Immediately we are shown a kind of
communion.

Evidence accumulates that this is no ordinary uprising. An open car
makes its way through the packed streets. It flies the pennon of the generalissimo of the Allied armies and contains the three high commanders.
British, American and French. It is followed by lorries crowded with the
doomed regiment, then by one holding exactly thirteen soldiers in French
uniform, manacled and chained. The eye focuses on four of them, not
Frenchmen but foreigners, mountain men, and finally on one of these,
against whose calm face the crowd raises its voices and shakes its fists:
the sacrificial Victim, the Christ-figure whom we are already awaiting.
The woman who took the bread spews it out at the man who gave it to her,
then runs after the lorry and stops in front of the *Hôtel de Ville*—"a slight
woman, not much more than a girl, who had been pretty once, and could
be again, with sleep and something to eat and a little warm water and
soap and a comb, and whatever it was out of her eyes, standing in the empty
*Place,* wringing her hands." We are into the Passion Week; the stage
is set for the Crucifixion, but it comes only after a long telling of what has
gone before.

What Faulkner is trying to say in the book is matter for perplexity on
a first reading, and far from pellucid thereafter; it will almost certainly be
distorted wilfully by reviewers with axes of their own to grind. Yet his
explicit message—for so it must be roundly named—is put in the novel
itself in almost the same summary words in which he stated it in his Nobel
Prize speech and in his Foreword to *The Faulkner Reader.* It is clear at
least that Faulkner is totally engaged by this message, that for him it represents the consummation of "a life's work in the agony and sweat of the
human spirit." That he has failed to find adequate incidents, agonists and
symbols to realize it dramatically and poetically is a conviction that grows
steadily and painfully upon the reader; that he has failed to dominate the
intellectual problems with which he has been struggling—for the book
cannot be taken as other than an effort at something like a social, a theological, a philosophical novel—is quite as evident. On the terms it sets for
itself, the book demands to be judged not merely against the background
of the author's own work, nor that of the current American novel, but by

comparison with such awesomely mentionable names as Melville, Tolstoy, Dostoevsky and Mann.

In seeking a larger scene, Faulkner has gone back to the only setting besides Mississippi which has deeply involved him before: the First World War. The central fable is the mutiny of a French regiment on the Western front in May, 1918. Three thousand men refuse to make an attack whose purpose is shadowy even to its commanding general, but lay down their weapons. The Germans refuse to counter-attack, and the war is stalled. The Allied generals, frightened by the prospect of peace and their own unemployment, communicate with the German command, which sends over by plane, through a fake barrage of blank anti-aircraft shells, one of its generals to negotiate the resumption of hostilities. The agitation spreads: a British and a German battalion lay down their arms, but on leaving the trenches are cut down by shells. The generals on both sides have got matters under control, and the war goes on.

True to the title of the book, Faulkner is not bothered by realistic canons of probability. The military implausibility of this main incident is exceeded by the garishness of the sub-plots. The Messiah who incites the mutiny is revealed later to be the natural son of the Allied generalissimo, and was born in a stable thirty-three years ago to a Balkan peasant woman. As a young man, he has found his way to France, married a Marseille whore (recipient of the bread in the opening scene), and become a corporal in the French army. The mutiny has been prepared by agitation within the Allied ranks and by mysterious absences of the corporal and his squad of twelve behind the German lines; their activity has been an open secret among the enlisted men, and wholly concealed from the officers. The second mutiny is carried out with the connivance of an elderly American Negro, groom and lay preacher, who bobs up fantastically in France and is given rare honors and privileges as head of *Les Amis Myriades et Anonymes à la France de Tout le Monde*. He persuades the British battalion to mutiny by giving them the sign of the Masonic order into which they have been "initiated" by the preacher's former associate in felony, a cockney groom who is now a private in the front lines and money-lender to the battalion. We are given a long and rhapsodic cut-back to a pre-war incident, the theft of a crippled champion race horse by the two grooms, who save him from the stud and dodge Federal marshals for months, winning quarter races with him throughout the South. They have defied the law to realize the essence of his horseness, and to re-enact the immortal pageant-piece of the tender legend which was the crowning glory of man's own legend beginning when his first paired children lost well the world and from which paired prototypes they still challenged paradise, still paired and still immortal against the chronicle's grimed and blood-stained pages: Adam and Lilith and Paris and Helen and Pyramus and Thisbe and all the other recordless Romeos and their Juliet's, the world's oldest and most shining tale limning in grief the warp-legged foul-mouthed English horse-groom as ever Paris or Lochinvar or any else of earth's splendid reapers. . . .

Faulkner summons to the telling of this secondary fable of profane love such warmth and lyricism that it makes his primary story of Christian *agape* seem cold and tenuous by contrast. The taking of the horse, we are told with hyperbole, was "not a theft, but a passion, an immolation, an apotheosis." In consequence, it may seem that Faulkner makes love for horse more vivid than love for man. He also renders the motivation of the two grooms more convincing than that of the corporal-Messiah, who is scarcely better individualized than the beam of white light by which Christ is represented on stage and screen; in fact, we are left room to take the corporal to be animated quite as much by an Oedipus complex as by dedication to the Kingdom of Heaven.

The allegory of the Passion Week is carried out with minute detail. Among the Thirteen are a Judas and a Peter (named Pierre). The corporal's entourage includes, besides his Magdalen, a Marya and a Marthe. There is a Last Supper, and a Temptation of the corporal by his father, the generalissimo, who offers him not only life and liberty but the world. The Messiah is shot lashed to a post between two robbers, and his head is crowned with barbed wire. There is a densely ironic Resurrection when the traitor's body is exhumed and reburied beneath the Arc de Triomphe as the Unknown Soldier. These are only a few of the correspondences with the Gospel story, many of which are more veiled.

However labored the retelling of the Christ story, the book leaves no doubt that Faulkner's possession by it is profound and shaking. The precise nature of his religious commitment is less easy to determine. His Christianity is not of a conventional sort, though without doubt it will be both welcomed as such and repudiated as a "failure of nerve"; nor is it an orthodox one, though it has much in common with certain types of neo-orthodox and existential theology. Neither can it bulwark the Church Visible, which Faulkner with some allowance for exceptions assigns to the ranks of Caesarism and Rapacity. Faulkner's is most likely a humanistic—

or, more accurately, a non-supernaturalistic—rendering of the Christian symbolism, and it offers no theodicy and no other-worldly beatitude. In his Nobel Prize speech and in his Foreword to *The Faulkner Reader,* he has defined his crystallizing purpose as a writer: "to uplift man's heart," "to say No to death," to show that "at least we are not vegetables," to help man to "teach himself that the basest of all things is to be afraid"; and he has summed up his credo quite simply—for our understanding of the novel, much too simply—in words that have already reverberated widely:

I decline to accept the end of man. It is easy enough to say that man is immortal simply because he will endure: that when the last ding-dong of doom has clanged and faded from the last worthless rock hanging tideless in the last red and dying evening, that even then there will still be one more sound: that of his puny inexhaustible voice, still talking. I refuse to accept this. I believe that man will not merely endure: he will prevail. He is immortal, not alone because he alone among creatures has an inexhaustible voice, but because he has a soul, a spirit capable of compassion and sacrifice and endurance.

Both the corporal and the Negro preacher echo part of this credo, but a part only. Asked if he is an ordained minister, the Negro replies:

"I dont know. I bears witness."
"To what? God?"
"To man. God dont need me. I bears witness to Him of course, but my main witness is to man."
"The most damning thing man could suffer would be a valid witness before God."
"You're wrong there," the Negro said. "Man is full of sin and nature, and all he does dont bear looking at, and a heap of what he says is a shame and a mawkery. But cant no witness hurt him. Some day something might beat him, but it wont be Satan."

For all the primitive Christian attitudes which Faulkner expresses sympathetically—humility, a mystique of suffering, *agape,* victory through passive resistance—it is neither his Messianic figure nor the apostles who utter the crowning article in his credo, that man will not merely endure but prevail, but, by a breath-taking reversal, the generalissimo, who functions as both Pontius Pilate and Tempter, and is functionally the supreme representative of Caesarism. The generalissimo is, indeed, an ambiguous figure from the beginning. Scion of a noble family and the *Comité de Ferrovie,* the most brilliant graduate of St. Cyr, he refuses as a young officer to take the

direct road to a mashal's baton but chooses for a hermitage a desert post
in North Africa where he flouts his superiors by preventing a desired
colonial war. We hear of him afterwards in a Tibetan Lamasery and on his
mysterious Balkan excursion; he reappears without explanation decades
later as supreme commander in the war. He is compared to St. Anthony,
but he is an anchorite of military austerity and patriotic devotion. And he
engineers the quelling of the mutiny and the continuance of the war.

It is, then, with the surprise of shock that in the last conversation between father and son we hear the generalissimo expressing the more
difficult faith in man, one which survives even the acceptance of the inevitability of wars and the multiplication of the Frankenstein machines which
make man's plight ever less controllable and his wars more devastating.
He says to the corporal at the end of the Temptation scene:

"Afraid? No no, it's not I but you who are afraid of man; not I but you who
believe that nothing but a death can save him. I know better. I know that
he has that in him which will enable him to outlast even his wars; that in
him more durable than all his vices, even that last and most fearsome one;
to outlast even this next avatar of his servitude which he now faces: his en-
slavement to the demonic progeny of his own mechanical curiosity, from
which he will emancipate himself by that ancient tried-and-true method by
which slaves have always freed themselves: by inculcating their masters
with the slaves' own vices—in this case the vice of war and that other one
which is no vice at all but instead is the quality-mark and warrant of man's
immortality: his deathless folly. . . ."

And it is the old marshal rather than the Messiah who ventures an
apocalypse—not of a New Jerusalem where lion and lamb will lie down
together but of an endless blood-letting and even the final devastation of
the planet. Man, he forsees, will endure through all this, though the
prophecy has to invoke science fiction to support the faith:

". . . already the next star in the blue immensity of space will be already
clamorous with the uproar of his debarkation, his puny and inexhaustible
voice still talking, still planning; and there too after the last ding dong of
doom has rung and died there will still be one sound more: his voice, planning to build something higher and faster and louder; more efficient and
louder and faster than ever before, yet it too inherent with the same old
primordial fault since it too in the end will fail to eradicate him from the
earth. I dont fear man. I do better: I respect and admire him. And pride: I
am ten times prouder of that immortality which he does possess than ever
he of that heavenly one of his delusion. Because man and his folly—"

"Will endure," the corporal said.

"They will do more," the old general said proudly. "They will prevail. —Shall we return?"

Although this is the last explicit word on the subject, we should not in consequence accept the marshal as the author's final spokesman. It is possible to take the corporal's subsequent apotheosis as the Unknown Soldier to be a forecast of the victory of Christ over Caesar; the incident has too much irony, however, for us to be happy about such a construction: the undying flame beneath the Arc de Triomphe after all commemorates devotion to country and therefore, in terms of Faulknerian Christianity, to Caesar. Nor, I believe, can we simply take the generalissimo to be the devil or the devil's advocate and treat the scene as the equivalent of the Grand Inquisitor section of *The Brothers Karamazov,* though the partial correspondence is obvious. Against this interpretation obtrudes not only the fact that it is the marshal who voices, even though for radically different reasons, the author's belief that man will not merely endure but prevail, but also the fact that he is the Messiah's father, and consequently stands to him in the relation of the first person of the Trinity, however much we must depart from the orthodox conceptions of this. The puzzle is heightened by the difference between the passage in the novel and the affirmation in the Nobel Prize speech. The former says that man will prevail because of his magnificent pride and folly; the latter says he will prevail because of his compassion and sacrifice (endurance is comprised in both versions).

To try to resolve this puzzle would get us into theological and moral questions which Faulkner himself steers clear of and probably has never confronted in abstract terms. One way out would be to construe the ending as a monstrous irony and nothing more: a forecast of the defeat of Christian virtues and even a repudiation of them. Another way, which would also account for the fusion of God and Satan in the ambivalent person of the generalissimo, would take the heretical tack—in Faulkner's case we cannot rule out the likelihood of some kind of heresy—that the New Covenant has not fulfilled and superseded the Old but inverted it; in which case Faulkner would be leaving open the Nietzschean possibility that a second transvaluation of values is called for. Still a third choice would be that of Barthian neo-orthodoxy: the victory of Christ over Caesar is purely otherworldly and not even a partial redemption of man in time and history. None of these solutions fits the novel.

From a European writer of Faulkner's stature we would expect in the treatment of such a theme, even if no answer, at least a sharper and richer debate in contemporary theological and philosophical terms than Faulkner gives us: there is a considerable amount of debate in the book, but it tapers off into nebulous language. Lionel Trilling has commented at length and penetratingly on both the limitations and the partial advantages that Faulkner and Hemingway as representative American writers exhibit because of their chosen and even vaunted "indifference to the conscious intellectual tradition of the time." Faulkner's explicit handling of ideas, outside as well as within the domain of theology, is usually amateurish. When, for example, as happens repeatedly in the novel, a cause is assigned to the war, it is the familiar simplification current in the 1920's: that it was an international conspiracy of the munitions makers and the generals. The generalissimo could, speaking in character, have introduced some needed complications, but he does not do so.

In trying to get some kind of foothold on the implicit ideational purport of the book, we can at least note some remote parallels to doctrines of such theologians as Tillich and Niebuhr. For the former, man's precarious triumph consists in his Courage to Be, which includes the courage to face anxiety and the eventual non-being in time which is his individual destiny: the Christ figure as the "concrete absolute" is the paradigm for this courage. For both theologians, man's redemption is not an ultimate victory of the Christian message in time, but both a timeless realization and a never-ending battle to wring some approximation to it from the relativities of history.

We can't be confident as to what intellectualized beliefs if any undergird the novel, and it is useless to conjecture what Faulkner would say if he articulated them fully. What we are compelled to do is to ask what sort of vision has been earned by the raw experience that the author has put into his work beyond the half-explicit formulations. The new book is not a simple about-face from Faulkner's previous writing, but has a positive continuity with it. Aside from his "primitives"—such as the frontiersmen and Indians who represent a golden age that is gone beyond recovery—in his fiction of the South two kinds of characters chiefly have dignity: Negroes and unreconstructed aristocrats. Faulkner's allegiance is divided between the two sets of virtues which they exhibit. His sympathies are enlisted both by the virtues of slave-morality and those of master-morality (each in a Mississippian rather than a Nietzschean version), without his being able to commit himself wholeheartedly to either. His Negroes, the insulted and injured yet faithful, alone are "Christians," and they have found a way to endure while accepting their status as victims. The un-vanquished among the Sartorises and Compsons do not endure literally; in fact they come to an early end. But they achieve a kind of immortality by style and gesture, through a code of honor. Their self-destructive pride and bravado make them live in the imaginations of men. Both sets of characters in their different ways endure and prevail. That such classic qualities as reason, moderation, disciplined imagination and political acumen can also help man to survive and intermittently triumph is nowhere acknowledged by Faulkner, though they are sometimes approximated in his sturdier but less glamorous characters, usually poor whites by origin. Anything Greek in Faulkner's world is of the Saturnian reign and the Dionysian rebellion: Apollo and Athene are absent from his pantheon.

When Faulkner leaves the microcosm of Yoknapatawpha for the great world of contemporary society, he maintains the same attitudes at whatever cost of oversimplification. The suffering servant is now the common soldier or the European peasant; the man of deathless folly is the army flyer, the stunt pilot or the professional military leader. In *A Fable,* despite the violent and forced invocation of Christian allegory, it is possible to see why the triumph of man is proclaimed by the generalissimo, regardless of consistency with the Nobel Prize speech. For the aesthetic vision, of a high romantic mold, struggles to some kind of victory over the moral: the meek may inherit the earth, but the "aristocratic" virtues, however tarnished, hold the allegiance of the novelist.

Even though *A Fable* is an eccentric and dreamlike commentary on modern society, and artistically unachieved, it at times commands partial respect by the heat of the vision and the depth of the concern. It is brave in these days to have persisted in seeking some kind of faith in man. But for evidence of Faulkner's mastery we must return to those books in which his troubled spiritual questings had not burst the bounds of his resources. In this book only those sections are convincing that, like the episode of the racehorse and the doings of the airmen, are deeply imbued by the author's experience and encompassed by his intellect.

# SNOPES REVISITED

## STEVEN MARCUS

*The Town,* sequel to *The Hamlet* and the second part of a long-projected trilogy about the Snopes family, is the most interesting book William Faulkner has published in fifteen years. Though it falls short of being a success it manages to transcend many of the moral and rhetorical ineptitudes into which Faulkner's more recent work has lapsed. It is not, like *Intruder in the Dust,* a novel with a broken back, half narrative, half Dixiecrat sociology. Its technical adventuresomeness does not, as it did in *Requiem for a Nun,* obscure the novel's main line of interest. Nor is its preoccupation with the largest moral issues so ponderous, so abstract or so personal that *The Town* is continually being surrendered, as *A Fable* was, to that monologue of musing and ranting about universals which turns up whenever Faulkner's dramatizing impulse wears thin. *The Town* revives the direct, dramatic mode of *As I Lay Dying*—the story is presented through the consciousness of several characters. It is remarkable for the extraordinary and intelligent self-awareness it contains, and for the definitive moral and social criticism it represents.

Beginning where *The Hamlet* leaves off, *The Town* covers approximately the next twenty years of the Snopes history, ending sometime in 1927. Its scene is Jefferson, its subject the impact of Flem and his family on Jefferson, and the reciprocal impact of Jefferson upon them. In Jefferson, Flem, the closest thing in American literature to a perpetual-motion machine of connivance and chicanery, parlays his interests with the same secret and preternatural genius for making money that enabled him to outman the "old pirate" of Frenchman's Bend, Will Varner. He eliminates his partner in the ownership of a restaurant; he invests in real estate; he becomes manager of the town power plant; he continues to lend money usuriously to the tenant farmers on whom "the entire cotton economy of the county was founded and supported," and becomes a power among them. Using his father-in-law's influence with impenetrable deviousness, he gets himself elected vice president of one of Jefferson's two banks, finally be-

Reprinted with permission from *Partisan Review,* Summer, 1957, pp. 432-41.

comes its president, a deacon in the Baptist church, an unshakeably respectable "solitary widower," and owner and master of "the old de Spain house which he had remodeled into an ante-bellum Southern mansion." It is a great American story of success, and a typical one. Inside of forty years, Flem, son of an outlawed, bushwhacking tenant farmer from the back hills —"Scratch?" says Gavin Stevens, "Scratch was euphemism indeed for where he started from"—has transformed himself into a rich and responsible citizen in a respectable old community, a defender of "civic jealousy and pride," a pillar of society.

But the rise of Flem Snopes, which Irving Howe has described as "an inverted and sinister picaresque adventure," is only one of several stories which make up the novel's elaborate organization. Another and more continuous narrative concerns Eula, Flem's wife, and her affair with Manfred de Spain, saber-scarred veteran of the Spanish-American War, romantic, rakehell, former mayor of Jefferson, and after the death of Colonel Sartoris president of the bank. It is revealed in this book that Flem Snopes is impotent, and Eula, as we recall from *The Hamlet,* is a kind of bucolic Venus and Brünnhilde, one glimpse of whom is enough to send most men into nympholepsy. The affair of Eula and de Spain goes on for eighteen years within "a kind of outrageous morality of adultery . . . based on an unimpugnable fidelity"; they come together in a "simple unadulterated uninhibited immortal lust," one of those characteristically fateful and annihilating grand passions through which Faulkner has frequently expressed his sense of the limits of feeling, of emotions whose splendor of commitment and selflessness is inevitably accompanied by barrenness and isolation: de Spain is driven out of town and Eula shoots herself. Flem knows about the affair all along and effortlessly contrives to make it serve his monomaniacal ambition—the adultery of Eula and de Spain is in fact the wave on which Flem rides into respectable society. Faulkner's sense of the social immorality that allows Flem's schemes to succeed is particularly acute, and out of it emerges the extremely critical judgment on Jefferson life which the novel pronounces.

The only way Flem can hurt Eula is through her daughter Linda, who is ignorant of her mother's adultery and of the fact that Flem is not her father. It is her innocence (inexplicably, she loves Flem) that is to be protected at all costs from the truth and from the scandal and violence that a public exposure would create. For this reason Eula and de Spain are from the very beginning enlisted in Flem's intrigues, which would destroy them in any case. Eula in turn engages Gavin Stevens in the defense of her daughter and herself, and in effect of Flem too. Thus, Stevens, who has always thought of himself as the champion of the tradition opposing what Snopes stands for, becomes Flem's principal if unwilling ally. "Just say I represent Jefferson and so Flem Snopes is my burden too," he intones.

The third main subdivision of the narrative is composed of tales about the double dealings of Flem and other Snopeses who have drifted in his wake to Jefferson. In this respect *The Town* most closely resembles *The Hamlet,* which contains such consummately humorous stories as "Spotted Horses" and the horse-trading of Pat Stamper and Ab Snopes. *The Town* contains four such stories. Like "Spotted Horses," two of them—"Mule in the Yard" and "Centaur in Brass"—are reworkings of previously published material and are considerably improved by revision. They are longer, their style is more dense and their action more complete. "Mule in the Yard," I think, can now be read with "Spotted Horses" as one of the minor masterpieces of American literature. It tells about a certain enterprise of I. O. Snopes, who some ten years before the story's action begins bought mules for fifty dollars each, took them at night to a blind curve on the railroad where they were run down, and collected indemnity of sixty dollars a mule from the railroad company. His assistant in this business, a man named Hait, had managed to get himself killed one night along with a string of the mules. Hait's widow collected $8500 from the railroad's insurance company, and I. O. has been stewing for years because he never received what he calculated was his share of the money. One foggy day a mule of I. O.'s breaks into the widow Hait's tiny yard. Old Het, the peripatetic Negress from the poorhouse, is there; so are Mrs. Hait's cow and chickens, and so, soon, is I. O. A fantastic chase begins to flow around the house, and Faulkner's prose breaks forth with that unique, brilliant energy of perception which transforms the most chaotic and violent activity into fluid, comic grace.

"In the cellar, fore God!" old Het hollered. She didn't wait either. "Go round the other way and head him!" she said. And she said that when she and Mrs. Hait turned that corner, there was the mule with the flying halter once more seeming to float lightly onward on a cloud of chickens with which, since the chickens had been able to go under the house and so along the chord while the mule had to go around on the arc, it had once more coincided. When they turned the next corner, they were in the back yard again.

"Fore God!" Het hollered. "He fixing to misuse the cow!" She said it was like a tableau. The cow had come out of the shed into the middle of the back yard; it and the mule were now facing each other about a yard apart, motionless, with lowered heads and braced legs like two mismatched book-ends, and Snopes was half in and half out of the now-open cellar door on the coping of which the scuttle of ashes still sat. . . .

Passages like this remind us of one of Faulkner's essential sources of strength: the legacy of Mark Twain. Like Twain, Faulkner has learned to assimilate the folk culture of a part of the country to the literary tradition. He has been able to do so partly because of the nature of that culture, because it possessed in its actual life the complication of social and moral assumptions that a genuine folk culture always has and that makes it so accessible to traditional literary modes. But he could not have done it in the way he has without the precedent of Twain; it is difficult to conceive of Faulkner at his characteristic best without being reminded that Twain stands in the immediate background.

The other three stories, though not so memorable as "Mule in the Yard," are sustained with impressive intelligence and humor. In the last of them, for example, the extraordinary vignette with which the novel ends, Byron Snopes, who has embezzled a couple of thousand dollars from the bank and fled to Texas, ships four of his children by "a Jicarilla Apache squaw" to Flem. " 'They looked like snakes. Or maybe that's too strong too. Anyway, they didn't look like children; if there was one thing in the world they didn't look like it was children.' " Like Faulkner's idiots, these children are natural objects forced to inhabit a civilized world; the laws of their being are irrelevant to the conventions by which man lives, even such conventions as the Snopeses find it necessary to observe. Since their Snopesian inheritance has been enriched with Apache blood, they exist by a kind of essential destructiveness, a natural, inarticulate, unblinking aggressive appetite: they eat and they destroy. A five-hundred-dollar pedigreed Pekinese disappears inside of them; they almost perform an *auto da fé,* Apache style, with their cousin Clarence Snopes as victim; if they regard themselves as being imposed on "a switch knife with a six-inch blade" appears out of thin air. Flem packs them off to Frenchman's Bend, but since they destroy everything and everyone in sight there too, Flem, defender of civilization, is forced to ship them back to Texas and liberate himself and the town of the last of the ineducable Snopeses: he has run the others out or they have gotten rid of themselves. As they are about to be deported, Ratliff says: "Would either of you gentlemen like to go down with me and watch what they call the end of a erea, if that's what they call what I'm trying to say? The last and final end of Snopes out-and-out unvarnished behavior in Jefferson, if that's what I'm trying to say."

If the reader feels that this doesn't sound quite like Ratliff, he has come upon one of the major issues in Faulkner's literary development. The Ratliff of *The Hamlet* is one of Faulkner's most admirable creations, a subtle, ironic sensibility, a disinterested intelligence through which the problems of a corrupt yet civilized society in the process of being infiltrated by Snopeses—not foreigners, but home-bred products of that corruption— are voiced. It is largely through Ratliff that *The Hamlet* achieves a poise and control unequaled in any other of Faulkner's works. He was to Faulkner what Marlow was to Conrad, and when we say that we again recognize the distinction of Faulkner's accomplishment in *The Hamlet*. Itinerant sewing-machine agent, carrier of news, repository of local history, Ratliff, who has known the Snopeses from boyhood and can even sympathize with their predicament, wages a long-drawn-out campaign against them. He represents the novelist's conviction that if civilization and sanity are to be preserved they must be fought for constantly, even if one has to fight with one hand tied behind his back, since to defeat the Snopeses by their own methods would be to forfeit the very values one wishes to defend. Ratliff appears in *The Town* in a more limited and constrained way. He is one of three characters who tell the story, and his part is the smallest, amounting to only 30 of the novel's 370 pages. This reduction of Ratliff's role is partly a result of the shift in time and place of the novel. We are to understand that he does not possess in Jefferson the decisive knowledge that he and no one else possessed in Frenchman's Bend.

Because of this, two other characters take over the bulk of the narration; Gavin Stevens and Charles Mallison are the Jeffersonians, and we are meant to regard them as inheriting in some degree Ratliff's insight into the Snopes character and activity. Each of them is supposed to personify a successive generation with a particular awareness: Ratliff, born shortly after the Civil War; Stevens, Faulkner's own age, born near the end of the century; Mallison, Stevens' nephew, born around the time of the First World War. I say "supposed" because Faulkner's intention here is not fulfilled, is in fact overridden by the persistent failure of Gavin Stevens as character, intelligence and moralist: that part of the novel in which he is the dominant figure—the working out of the Flem-Eula-de Spain triangle —is absurdly sluggish, involuted and opaque. Although whenever he is juxtaposed to Ratliff, Stevens seems silly and in a sense impotent,[1] Faulk-

1. Faulkner suggests that impotence only in the most literary and high-falutin manner: ". . . now only the afternoon remained: the interminable time until a few minutes after half past three filled with a thousand indecisions which each fierce

ner is still too involved with him personally to admit that Stevens never was and never could be that fountainhead of moral enlightenment and of a gallant, embattled tradition which in the crisis of his culture and therefore of his art Faulkner needs to portray. In *The Town* Stevens is the same windbag he has always been, and his character continues to reveal what one can only call the coarseness and vulgarity of moral tone that have been so ruinous in Faulkner's more recent writing. "Harvard M.A. and a Ph. D. from Heidelberg and his hair beginning to turn white even at just twenty-five," Stevens is the most transparent of lay figures; he embodies an undisguised personal wish. It is he who goes along with what Leslie Fiedler has called the frozen and ossified grandiloquence of Faulkner's later style— and it is he who wrote the speech Faulkner delivered at Stockholm.

In *The Town,* however, Stevens is put to an additional use. Since his is the mind and the rhetoric with which Faulkner feels the strongest affinity, it is largely through him that we get a glimpse of Ratliff—his ruminative, melodramatic consciousness is the complicated filter through which Ratliff's clear intellect is allowed to trickle. Mallison, a decent and perspicacious young man, affords an even further rarification of this device; he is less obfuscating than his uncle, but further removed from the events of the narrative, and often we reach Ratliff only through Mallison, who has gotten to him through Stevens. This extreme refinement in point of view is inherently undramatic and indicates how exiguous Faulkner's direct grasp on experience can become. Yet it indicates too how insistently he feels the necessity of re-establishing that grasp, and how strenuously he labors toward it.

At moments *The Town* does somehow get to Ratliff, and thus to Snopes, and whenever it does we seem to have come upon life and intelligence again, for in *The Town* Ratliff spends a good part of his time retelling the stories that made up *The Hamlet.* They are not, however, quite the same stories. The order of narration and even the facts are different. "Spotted Horses" is related for what must be the third or fourth time now, but as a compressed and anecdotal aside to another larger story. The story of Eula Varner and McCarron is retold with interesting variations. In the first version she gives up her virginity on the front porch after she and McCarron have returned from being ambushed by the country bucks, and

---

succeeding harassment would revise. . . . And I was in time but just in time." The echo of Prufrock is clear enough, and a case for its relevance might even be made. It is a comment, however, on Faulkner's sense of Stevens that he has to resort to literature itself to attain the frailest impersonality or irony in his relation to him.

after her father has set McCarron's broken arm. As Ratliff recounts the story in *The Town,* they fall upon each other "on the still-hot field of the triumph; right there on the ground in the middle of the dark because somebody had to hold that skeered horse, with the horse standing over them and her likely having to help hold him up too off of that broke arm." The murderer of Houston by Mink Snopes is retold with the details of time and place slightly different from those in *The Hamlet.* In fact the whole treatment of time, of dating the events in the narrative, becomes a part of our response to the novel; on the evidence of both *The Hamlet* and *The Town* it is possible, for example, to locate "Spotted Horses" in 1891, in 1900, or in 1908.

Someone is bound to say that these repetitions are compulsive and a sign of Faulkner's waning invention; that the discrepancies of detail are a sign of his forgetfulness and carelessness as an artist; and that it is pedantry to pause over them or consider them in other ways. This might be true, but for me these variations and recurrences reveal something worth noting about Faulkner and his art: he is moving back in the direction of his singular genius. The analogy I should like to make in this connection is to the post-Homeric fragments; in those almost entirely lost cyclic poems the stories of *The Iliad* and *The Odyssey* were recreated and amplified with the same character of variation that one finds in *The Town* and in parts of Faulkner's other works. As one reads about them one gets a renewed sense of how one of the primal powers of literature is to raise mythology to the level of history, to treat the material of the imagination as if it were indistinguishable from the actuality it invades and transcribes. Faulkner is the only contemporary American writer who has a faculty for this; perhaps he is the only modern writer who has it at all. The stories he wrote over twenty-five years ago have become part of the given; he takes a past which he has created himself and deals with it as received reality. It is "out there," independent of his ministrations, waiting for him to record and recreate rather than invent. And as the degree of Faulkner's conviction about the historicity of his imagination seems positive, so, too, does the degree of his conviction about the authenticity and necessity of society, and the degree to which he seems able to represent concretely the deterioration in American life of those institutions and values which allow for the cultivation of the imagination and the spirit.

To have achieved this is to have achieved classical status. In *The Town,* however, we do not have the major achievement so much as we have the impulse to discover the condition in which that achievement is again possible. We find that impulse in Faulkner's effort to come at Ratliff and the Snopeses again, as we find the contradicting impulse in his continued attachment to the obscuring sensibility of Gavin Stevens. In his sense of the motives of Flem Snopes, for instance, Ratliff is sharply distinguished from Stevens. For Ratliff, Flem and the Snopeses are primarily *objects,* animals (rabbits, snakes, rats, ants are his metaphors for them), which are to be understood as phenomena of nature. Their intense spirituality, their passion and rapacity, are a direct animal response to the values of money and power which control society. Their spirituality is depraved just because their response to society, their instinctive understanding of power, is so untrammeled and precise, so unfettered by the hypocrisies of form and manner with which society disguises from itself the facts of its life. Some Snopeses, like Mink, the murderer, and Ab, the old man, are destroyed by their uncontrollable animality. Others, like Ike, the idiot, and like Eck, the good-natured fool, are destroyed because they aren't sufficiently endowed with the Snopes passion and shrewdness for survival. Still others, like Byron, Like I. O.'s son Montgomery Ward, and Like I. O. himself, expose their rapacity too nakedly and are driven out of society. One Snopes, Wallstreet Panic, even turns his passionate endowment against Snopesery, becomes a mortal enemy of Flem and dedicates himself to a fanatic honesty. Only Flem has made the perfect adjustment: he sees how much of the Snopes is hidden in almost everyone, in the men who possess money and power and in the men who do not, and it is upon their secret charge of resentment, avarice and aggressiveness that he works. He is successful because he understands society so completely and because he is willing to submit himself to the terms that it enjoins.

As Gavin Stevens contemplates him, however, Flem Snopes undergoes a transformation; he becomes part of that viscous flow of rhetoric which oozes from Stevens' mind like sap from a wounded tree. He ceases to be an object and becomes primarily a consciousness. Nothing could be more fatal to his integrity as a Snopes. He is "humanized" by Stevens; his motives are understood as almost unexceptionable—they become the motives which move Everyman. Stevens even begins to pity Flem when he considers his origins in underprivilege and his plight as cuckold. The Old Heidelbergian's rubric reads *nihil humanum alienum est,* and under his spell Flem and Eula become articulate and begin to speak in those orotund cadences with which Stevens—and Faulkner when he is Stevens—inflates all reality and makes everything in it a duplication of himself. Stevens is a true solipsist

—here is, I think, one of the clearest indications of the central imbalance in Faulkner's art—the kind of monster who effaces the actuality of others by imposing on them his own. By apologizing for or denying their animality, he not only misunderstands the Snopeses but dehumanizes them too. It is this misunderstanding and dehumanization that Ratliff tries to withstand, insisting that Flem's motives will not be understood if they are sociologized, that his desire for respectability is simply another form of his desire for power, that his success is a result of having beaten the Jeffersonians at their own game, a game few of them admit they play.

Out of this contention a third and broader understanding begins to take shape, through which we begin to make out the connections between the success of Flem, the impotence of Stevens, and the destruction of Eula and de Spain. Charles Mallison, educated by Ratliff and Stevens but un-involved with the Snopeses, expresses it, and it is, it seems to me, one of the most explicit and critical statements Faulkner has made about his culture. It is a negative judgment, a judgment of failure upon a culture being deva-stated from within by its own values—values it has always had, even in its palmiest days when there were giants in the Southern earth. It is a judg-ment that is rigorous and self-denying:

. . . ours a town established and decreed by people neither Catholics nor Protestants nor even atheists but incorrigible nonconformists, nonconform-ists not just to everybody else but to each other in mutual accord; a non-conformism defended and preserved by descendants whose ancestors hadn't quitted home and security for a wilderness in which to find freedom of thought as they claimed and oh yes, believed, but to find freedom in which to be incorrigible and unreconstructible Baptists and Methodists; not to escape from tyranny as they claimed and believed, but to establish one.

There is no other living American novelist who can write with this au-thority, the authority of truth lived with for a lifetime. The tyranny which the passage describes and which the novel enacts generates both the fatal, desperate passions of the Eulas and de Spains, and the meanness of spirit against which they batter themselves and which finally, meanly, extirpates them as it tends to extirpate most impulses toward sensibility, vitality and style. It is utterly appropriate that a Snopes should come to power in this culture; he is no harbinger of something new and alien, something out of the North, or part of the "coastal spew of Europe," but the fulfillment of a tradition, its native, purified, stripped-down product. Once again Faulkner has cut the ground out from under his apologists, for this too, he is telling us, belongs to the South, to an abiding and in the end perhaps dominating tradition.

Coming from someone as intensely implicated in the fate of his culture as Faulkner is, we must, I think, recognize again what a force for truth art can be, and how an artist who is faithful to his art is likely to be faithful to his intelligence and humanity as well. With all its imperfections, *The Town* represents a great novelist's dedication to those values—seriousness, wit, style—toward which his art aspires and by which it will again immortalize itself.

# A Selective Bibliography*

## I

### WORKS BY FAULKNER

*The Marble Faun.* Boston: The Four Seas Co., 1924.
*Soldiers' Pay.* New York: Boni and Liveright, 1926.
*Mosquitoes.* New York: Boni and Liveright, 1927.
*Sartoris.* New York: Harcourt, Brace, 1929.
*The Sound and the Fury.* New York: Jonathan Cape and Harrison Smith, 1929. Also (with *As I Lay Dying*) in New York: The Modern Library, 1946.
*As I Lay Dying.* New York: Cape and Smith, 1930. Also (with *The Sound and the Fury*) in New York: The Modern Library, 1946.
*Sanctuary.* New York: Cape and Smith, 1931. Also in New York: The Modern Library, 1932.
*These Thirteen.* New York: Cape and Smith, 1931.
*Light in August.* New York: Harrison Smith and Robert Haas, 1932. Also in New York: The Modern Library, 1950.
*A Green Bough.* New York: Smith and Haas, 1933.
*Doctor Martino and Other Stories.* New York: Smith and Haas, 1934.
*Pylon.* New York: Smith and Haas, 1935.
*Absalom, Absalom!* New York: Random House, 1936. Also in New York: The Modern Library, 1951.
*The Unvanquished.* New York: Random House, 1938.
*The Wild Palms.* New York: Random House, 1939.
*The Hamlet.* New York: Random House, 1940. Also in New York: The Modern Library, 1956.
*Go Down, Moses and Other Stories.* New York: Random House, 1942. Also in New York: The Modern Library, 1955.
*Intruder in the Dust.* New York: Random House, 1948.
*Knight's Gambit.* New York: Random House, 1949.
*Collected Stories of William Faulkner.* New York: Random House, 1950.
*Requiem for a Nun.* New York: Random House, 1951.
*A Fable.* New York: Random House, 1954.
*Big Woods.* New York: Random House, 1955.

* Items marked WF III are reprinted in this collection.

*The Town.* New York: Random House, 1957.
*The Mansion.* New York: Random House, 1959.


II

BIBLIOGRAPHIES AND CHECK LISTS

Beebe, Maurice. "Criticism of William Faulkner: A Selected Checklist with an Index to Studies of Separate Works," *Modern Fiction Studies,* 2 (Autumn, 1956), 150-164.

Daniel, Robert W. *A Catalogue of the Writings of William Faulkner.* New Haven: Yale University Library, 1942.

Daniel, Robert W., and John L. Longley, Jr. "Faulkner's Critics: A Selective Bibliography," *Perspective,* 3 (Winter, 1950), 202-208.

Meriwether, James B. "William Faulkner: A Check List," *The Princeton University Library Chronicle,* 18 (Spring, 1957), 136-158.

Perry, Bradley T. "Faulkner Critics: A Bibliography Breakdown," *Faulkner Studies,* 2 (Spring-Summer-Winter, 1953), 11-13, 30-32, 60-64.

————. "A Selected Bibliography of Critical Works on William Faulkner," *University of Kansas City Review,* 18 (Winter, 1951), 159-164.

Runyan, Harry. "Faulkner's Non-Fiction Prose: An Annotated Checklist," *Faulkner Studies,* 3 (Winter, 1954), 67-69.

Smith, Thelma M., and Ward L. Miner. "Faulkner Checklist and Bibliography," *Transatlantic Migration: The Contemporary American Novel in France.* Durham: Duke University Press, 1955. Pages 227-235.

Stallman, Robert W. "William Faulkner," *Critiques and Essays on Modern Fiction, 1920-1951,* John W. Aldridge (ed). New York: Ronald Press, 1952. Pages 582-586.

Starke, Aubrey. "An American Comedy: An Introduction to a Bibliography of William Faulkner," *Colophon,* 5 (1934), part 19.

Vickery, Olga W. "Bibliography," *William Faulkner: Two Decades of Criticism,* Frederick J. Hoffman and Olga W. Vickery (eds). East Lansing: Michigan State University Press, 1951. Pages 269-280.

Woodworth, Stanley D. "Sélection bibliographique d'ouvrages ou d'articles sur William Faulkner en France, 1931–1952," *La Revue des Lettres Modernes,* 4 (2ᵉ Trim., 1957), 191-196.

# III

## INTERVIEWS, IMPRESSIONS AND BIOGRAPHICAL ESSAYS

Alexander, Sidney. "The Nobel Prize Comes to Mississippi: How Yoknapatawpha County Sees Its Author," *Commentary,* 12 (Summer, 1951), 176-180.

Arban, Dominique. "Interview de William Faulkner," *Le Figaro Littéraire,* 5-6 (December 16, 1950), 1.

Bouvard, Loïc. "Conversation with William Faulkner," *Modern Fiction Studies,* 5 (Winter, 1959-60), 361-364.

Bradford, Roark. "The Private World of William Faulkner," *'48, the Magazine of the Year,* 2 (May, 1948), 83-84, 90.

Breit, Harvey. "A Walk with Faulkner," *New York Times Book Review* (January 30, 1955), 4, 12. Reprinted in *The Writer Observed.* Cleveland: World Publishing Co., 1956. Pages 281-284.

Brennan, Dan. "Journey South," *University of Kansas City Review,* 22 (Autumn, 1955), 11-16.

Brière, Annie. "Faulkner Parle," *Nouvelles Littéraires,* No. 1466 (October 6, 1955), 1, 6.

Buttitta, Anthony. "William Faulkner: That Writin' Man of Oxford," *Saturday Review of Literature,* 18 (May 21, 1938), 6-8.

Cantwell, Robert. "The Faulkners: Recollections of a Gifted Family," *New World Writing,* No. 2 (November, 1952), 300-315. WF III

Carter, Hodding. "Faulkner and His Folk," *The Princeton University Library Chronicle,* 18 (Spring, 1957), 95-107.

Chapsal, Madeleine. "A Lion in the Garden," *The Reporter,* 13 (November 3, 1955), 40.

Dominicus, A. M. "An Interview with Faulkner," *Faulkner Studies,* 3 (Summer-Autumn, 1954), 33-37.

Evans, Medford. "Oxford, Mississippi," *Southwest Review,* 15 (Winter, 1929), 46-63.

Green, A. Wigfall. "William Faulkner at Home," *The Sewanee Review,* 40 (Summer, 1932), 294-306. Reprinted in *William Faulkner: Two Decades of Criticism,* Frederick J. Hoffman and Olga W. Vickery (eds). East Lansing: Michigan State University Press, 1951. Pages 33-47.

Grenier, Cynthia. "An Interview with William Faulkner—September, 1955," *Accent,* 16 (Summer, 1956), 167-177.

Guth, Paul. "En Remontant avec Faulkner les chemins de la vie et ceux de l'écriture," *Le Figaro Littéraire,* 10 (October 8, 1955), 3.

Gwynn, Frederick L., and Joseph L. Blotner (eds). *Faulkner in the University.* Charlottesville: University of Virginia Press, 1959.

Gwynn, Frederick L., and Joseph L. Blotner (eds). "Faulkner in the University: A Classroom Conference," *College English,* 19 (October, 1957), 1-6.

————. "William Faulkner on Dialect," *University of Virginia Magazine,* 2 (Winter, 1958), 7-13; cont'd. in 2 (Spring, 1958), 32-37.

Howe, Russell Warren. "A Talk with William Faulkner," *The Reporter,* 14 (March 22, 1956), 18-20.

Jelliffe, Robert A., ed. *Faulkner at Nagano.* Tokyo: Kenkyusha Ltd., 1956.

Pivano, Fernanda. "Vita di Faulkner," *La Rassegna d'Italia,* 4 (June, 1949), 638-645.

Rascoe, Lavon. "An Interview with William Faulkner," *Western Review,* 15 (Summer, 1951), 300-304.

Smith, Bradley. "The Faulkner Country," *'48, the Magazine of the Year,* 2 (May, 1948), 85-89.

Smith, Marshall J. "Faulkner of Mississippi," *The Bookman,* 74 (December, 1931), 411-417.

Stein, Jean. "William Faulkner," *Paris Review,* 4 (Spring, 1956), 28-52. Reprinted in *Writers at Work.* Malcolm Cowley (ed). New York: Viking, 1958. Pages 119-141. WF III

Stone, Phil. "William Faulkner, the Man and His Work," *Oxford Magazine* (Oxford, Mississippi), Copy 1 (1934), 13-14; continued in Copies 2 and 3; unfinished.

Sullivan, Frank. "A Distinguished Commuter," *Saturday Review,* 34 (June 9, 1951), 4.

Young, Stark. "New Year's Craw," *The New Republic,* 93 (January 12, 1938), 283-284.

# IV

## CRITICAL BOOKS AND SPECIAL ISSUES OF PERIODICALS

### A.

Campbell, Harry Modean, and Ruel E. Foster. *William Faulkner: A Critical Appraisal.* Norman: University of Oklahoma Press, 1951.

Coughlan, Robert. *The Private World of William Faulkner*. New York: Harper, 1954.

Hoffman, Frederick J., and Olga W. Vickery (eds). *William Faulkner: Two Decades of Criticism*. East Lansing: Michigan State University Press, 1951.

Howe, Irving. *William Faulkner: A Critical Study*. New York: Random House, 1952.

Malin, Irving. *William Faulkner: An Interpretation*. Stanford: Stanford University Press, 1957.

Miner, Ward L. *The World of William Faulkner*. Durham: Duke University Press, 1952.

O'Connor, William Van. *The Tangled Fire of William Faulkner*. Minneapolis: University of Minnesota Press, 1954.

————. *William Faulkner*. (Pamphlets on American Writers, No. 3), Minneapolis: University of Minnesota Press, 1959.

Robb, Mary Cooper. *William Faulkner: An Estimate of his Contribution to the American Novel*. Pittsburgh: University of Pittsburgh Press, 1957.

Vickery, Olga W. *The Novels of William Faulkner: A Critical Interpretation*. Baton Rouge: Louisiana State University Press, 1959. (Chapter 4 in WF III)

Waggoner, Hyatt H. *William Faulkner: From Jefferson to the World*. Lexington: University of Kentucky Press, 1959.

Woodworth, Stanley D. *William Faulkner en France (1931-1952)*. Paris: M. J. Minard: Lettres Modernes, 1959.

Yndurain, Francisco. *La Obra de William Faulkner*. Madrid: Ateno (La Editora Nacional), 1953.

Zavaleta, C. E. *William Faulkner: Novelista Tragico*. Lima: Publicaciones del Instituto de Literatura de la Facultad de la Universidad Nacional Major de San Marcos, 1959.

### B.

*English Institute Essays, 1952*. New York: Columbia University Press, 1954. Essays on *The Sound and the Fury* by Cleanth Brooks, Carvel Collins, Perrin Lowrey, Lawrance Thompson. (Thompson in WF III)

*Faulkner Studies*, 1-3 (Spring, 1952-Winter, 1954).

*The Harvard Advocate* (William Faulkner Issue), 135 (November, 1951). Essays by Conrad Aiken, Cleanth Brooks, Carvel Collins, Leonard Doran, Pierre Emmanuel, Jerome Gavin, Albert Guérard, Alfred Kazin, Archibald MacLeish, John Crowe Ransom.

*The Mississippi Quarterly* (Special Issue: William Faulkner), 11 (Fall, 1958). Essays by David Applewhite, Raymond Bernberg, William

Doster, Scott Greer, Elmo Howell, B. R. McElderry, Hallet Smith, T. D. Young and Floyd C. Watkins.

*Modern Fiction Studies* (William Faulkner Special Number), 2 (Autumn, 1956). Essays by Melvin Backman, Robert Flynn, David L. Frazier, Roma A. King, W. R. Moses, Karl E. Zink.

*Perspective* (Faulkner), 2 (Summer, 1949). Essays by Ruel E. Foster, Phyllis Hirshleifer, Sumner C. Powell, Russell Roth, Ray B. West.

*Perspective* (Faulkner, No. 2), 3 (Autumn, 1950). Essays by Harry M. Campbell, Tommy Hudson, Olga Westland Vickery, Edgar W. Whan.

*The Princeton University Library Chronicle* (William Faulkner), 18 (Spring, 1957). Essays by Hodding Carter, Maurice E. Coindreau, Carvel Collins, George P. Garrett.

*La Revue des Lettres Modernes* (William Faulkner: Configuration Critique I), 4 (2e Trim., 1957). Translation of essays contained in *Modern Fiction Studies,* II (Autumn, 1956). Additional material by B. W. Cottrell, S. D. Woodworth, D. Torchiana.

*La Revue des Lettres Modernes* (William Faulkner: Configuration Critique II), 5 (Winter, 1958-59). Essays by Cyrille Arnavon, Roger Asselineau, Melvin Backman, Melvin J. Friedman, Maurice Le Breton, Stanley D. Woodworth. Reprinted essays by Warren Beck, Robert Penn Warren.

# V

# GENERAL STUDIES

D'Agostino, Nemi. "William Faulkner," *Studia Americani,* 1 (1955), 257-308.

Aiken, Conrad. "William Faulkner: The Novel as Form," *The Atlantic Monthly,* 164 (November, 1939), 650-654. Reprinted in his *A Reviewer's ABC: Collected Criticism from 1916 to the Present.* New York: Meridian, 1958. Pages 200-207. WF III

Allen, Charles A. "William Faulkner's Vision of Good and Evil," *Pacific Spectator,* 10 (Summer, 1956), 236-241.

Anderson, Charles. "Faulkner's Moral Center," *Études Anglaises,* 7 (January, 1954), 48-58.

Anonymous. "Une discussion sur Faulkner chez les étudiants communistes américains," *La Nouvelle Critique,* 1 (July-August, 1949), 87-96. Comments by Jack Kroner, Al Greenberg, Al Kutzig, the Editors.

Anonymous. "The Worldwide Influence of William Faulkner: Reports from Six Capitols," *The New York Times Book Review,* 64 (November 15, 1959), 52-53. Statements by Walter Allen, Celia Bertin, Max Frankel, Flora Lewis, Masami Nishkawa, Emilio Cecchi.

Archer, H. Richard. "Collecting Faulkner Today," *Faulkner Studies,* 1 (Fall, 1952), 42-43.

————. "The Writings of William Faulkner: A Challenge to the Bibliographer," *Papers of the Bibliographical Society of America,* 50 (3rd quart., 1956), 229-242.

Arthos, John. "Ritual and Humor in the Writing of William Faulkner," *Accent,* 9 (Autumn, 1948), 17-30. Reprinted in *William Faulkner: Two Decades of Criticism,* Frederick J. Hoffman and Olga W. Vickery (eds). East Lansing: Michigan State University Press, 1951. Pages 101-118.

Asselineau, Roger. "William Faulkner, Moraliste Puritain," *La Revue des Lettres Modernes,* 5 (Winter, 1958-59), 231-249.

Aymé, Marcel. "What French Readers Find in William Faulkner's Fiction," *The New York Times Book Review* (December 17, 1950), 4. Reprinted in *Highlights of Modern Literature,* Francis Brown (ed.). New York: Mentor, 1954. Pages 103-106.

Backman, Melvin. "Faulkner's Sick Heroes: Bayard Sartoris and Quentin Compson," *Modern Fiction Studies,* 2 (Autumn, 1956), 95-108.

————. "Sickness and Primitivism: A Dominant Pattern in William Faulkner's Work," *Accent,* 14 (Winter, 1954), 61-73.

Baiwir, Albert. "William Faulkner," *Le Déclin de l'individualisme chez les romanciers américains contemporains.* Paris: Librairie E. Droz, 1943. Pages 313-332.

Baker, Carlos. "William Faulkner: The Doomed and the Damned," *The Young Rebel in American Literature,* Carl Bode (ed). London: Heinemann, 1959. Pages 145-169.

Baker, James R. "The Symbolic Extension of Yoknapatawpha County," *The Arizona Quarterly,* 8 (Autumn, 1952), 223-228.

Baldanza, Frank. "Faulkner and Stein: A Study in Stylistic Intransigence," *Georgia Review,* 13 (Fall, 1959), 274-286.

Beach, Joseph Warren. "William Faulkner," *American Fiction, 1920-1940.* New York: Macmillan, 1941. Pages 123-169.

Beck, Warren. "Faulkner and the South," *Antioch Review,* 1 (Spring, 1941), 82-94.

————. "Faulkner's Point of View," *College English,* 2 (May, 1941), 736-749.

————. "A Note on Faulkner's Style," *Rocky Mountain Review,* 6 (Spring-Summer, 1942), 6-7, 14.

————. "William Faulkner's Style," *American Prefaces,* 6 (Spring, 1941), 195-211. WF III

Blumenberg, Hans von. "Mythos und Ethos Amerikas im Werk William Faulkners," *Hochland,* 50 (February, 1958), 234-250.

Boynton, Percy H. "The Retrospective South," *America in Contemporary Fiction.* Chicago: University of Chicago Press, 1940. Pages 103-112.

Breaden, Dale G. "William Faulkner and the Land," *American Quarterly,* 10 (Fall, 1958), 344-357.

Breit, Harvey. "A Sense of Faulkner," *Partisan Review,* 18 (January-February, 1951), 88-94.

————. "William Faulkner," *The Atlantic Monthly,* 188 (October, 1951), 53-56.

Brion, Marcel. "Les prix Nobel: Bertrand Russell et William Faulkner," *La Revue des Deux Mondes* (December 1, 1950), 529-538.

Brodin, Pierre. "William Faulkner," *Les Écrivains américains de l'entre-deux-guerres.* Montreal: Éditions Bernard Valiquette, 1945. Pages 147-170.

Brumm, Ursula. "Wilderness and Civilization: A Note on William Faulkner," *Partisan Review,* 22 (Summer, 1955), 340-350. WF III

————. "William Faulkner im alten Süden," *Weltstimmen,* 19 (May, 1950), 374-380.

Burgum, Edwin Berry. "William Faulkner's Patterns of American Decadence," *The Novel and the World's Dilemma.* New York: Oxford University Press, 1947. Pages 205-22.

Calvo, Lino Novas. "El Demonio de Faulkner," *Revista de Occidente,* 39 (January, 1933), 98-103.

Campbell, Harry M. "Structural Devices in the Works of Faulkner," *Perspective,* 3 (Autumn, 1950), 209-226.

Caraceni, Augusto. "William Faulkner," *Aretusa,* 2 (November, 1945), 23-28.

Cargill, Oscar. "The Primitivists," *Intellectual America.* New York: Macmillan, 1941. Pages 370-386.

Cecchi, Emilio. "Note sur William Faulkner," *Prospettive,* No. 7 (Spring, 1954), 80-93. Reprinted in *William Faulkner: Venti anni di critica,* Frederick J. Hoffman and Olga W. Vickery (eds). Parma: Guanda, 1957. Pages 102-114.

————. "William Faulkner," *Pan,* 2 (May, 1934), 64-70.

Chase, Richard. "Faulkner—The Great Years," *The American Novel and its Tradition.* Garden City: Doubleday Anchor Books, 1957. Pages 205-236.

Clément, Danielle, "Faulkner, prix Nobel," *Terre Humaine,* No. 2 (February, 1951), 122-127.

Coindreau, Maurice E. "On Translating Faulkner," *The Princeton University Library Chronicle,* 18 (Spring, 1957), 108-113.

———. "Les principaux Romans de William Faulkner," *Aperçus de Littérature américaine.* Paris: Gallimard, 1946. Pages 111-146.

———. "Quadrille américain," *Les Oeuvres nouvelles.* New York: Éditions de la maison française, 1942. Pages 139-164.

———. "William Faulkner," *La Nouvelle Revue Française,* 36 (June 1, 1931), 926-930.

———. "William Faulkner in France," *Yale French Studies,* No. 10 (Fall, 1952), 85-91.

Collins, Carvel. "Faulkner and Certain Earlier Southern Fiction," *College English,* 16 (November, 1954), 92-97.

———. "Faulkner's Reputation and the Contemporary Novel," *Literature in the Modern World,* William J. Griffin (ed). Nashville: George Peabody College for Teachers, 1954. Pages 65-71.

Cowley, Malcolm. "Introduction," *The Portable Faulkner.* New York: Viking Press, 1946. Pages 1-24. WF III

———. "An Introduction to William Faulkner," *Critiques and Essays on Modern Fiction, 1920-1951,* John W. Aldridge (ed). New York: Ronald Press, 1952. Pages 427-446.

———. "William Faulkner's Human Comedy," *The New York Times Book Review* (October 29, 1944), 4.

———. "William Faulkner's Legend of the South," *The Sewanee Review,* 53 (Summer, 1945), 343-361. Reprinted in *A Southern Vanguard,* Allen Tate (ed). New York: Prentice-Hall, 1947. Pages 13-27.

———. "William Faulkner Revisited," *Saturday Review of Literature,* 28 (April 14, 1945), 13-16.

Denoreaz, Michel. "William Faulkner ou le parti pris de la fausse réalité," *La Nouvelle Critique,* 3 (January, 1951), 74-84.

DeVoto, Bernard. "Witchcraft in Mississippi," *Saturday Review of Literature,* 15 (October 31, 1936), 3-4, 14. Reprinted in *Minority Report.* Boston: Little, Brown, 1940. Pages 209-218.

Dickmann, Max. "William Faulkner, escritor diabólico," *Revista de las Indias,* 13 (March, 1942), 107-116.

Doderer, Hans von. "Zur Technik des modernen amerikanischen Romans," *Die Neueren Sprachen,* Heft 6 (1958), 257-264.

Doran, Leonard. "Form and the Story Teller," *The Harvard Advocate,* 135 (November, 1951), 12, 38-41.

Doster, William C. "The Several Faces of Gavin Stevens," *The Mississippi Quarterly,* 11 (Fall, 1958), 191-195.

Douglas, Harold J., and Robert Daniel. "Faulkner and the Puritanism of the South," *Tennessee Studies in Literature,* 2 (1957), 1-13.

Downing, Francis. "An Eloquent Man," *Commonweal,* 53 (December 15, 1950), 255-258.

Duesberg, Jacques. "Un Créateur de Mythes: William Faulkner," *Synthéses,* 3 (December, 1949), 342-354.

Edgar, Pelham. "Four American Novelists," *The Art of the Novel.* New York: Macmillan, 1933. Pages 338-351.

Edmonds, Irene C. "Faulkner and the Black Shadow," *Southern Renascence: The Literature of the Modern South,* Louis D. Rubin Jr. and Robert D. Jacobs (eds). Baltimore: Johns Hopkins University Press, 1953. Pages 192-206.

Emmanuel, Pierre. "Faulkner and the Sense of Sin," *The Harvard Advocate,* 135 (November, 1951), 20.

Erval, François. "Faulkner après le prix Nobel," *Les Temps Modernes,* 8 (June, 1953), 2024-2030.

———. "Faulkner, deuxième manière," *Les Temps Modernes,* 10 (November, 1954), 750-754.

Fadiman, Clifton, "William Faulkner," *Party of One.* Cleveland: World Publishing Co., 1955. Pages 98-125.

Fäy, Bernard. "L'École de l'infortune," *Revue de Paris,* 44 (August, 1937), 644-665.

Fiedler, Leslie A. "William Faulkner: An American Dickens," *Commentary,* 10 (October, 1950), 384-387.

Flint, R. W. "Faulkner as Elegist," *The Hudson Review,* 7 (Summer, 1954), 246-257.

Foster, Ruel E. "Dream as Symbolic Act in Faulkner," *Perspective,* 2 (Summer, 1949), 179-194.

Frohock, W. M. "William Faulkner: The Private versus the Public Vision," *Southwest Review,* 34 (Summer, 1949), 281-294. Reprinted in *The Novel of Violence in America.* Dallas: Southern Methodist University Press, 1950. Pages 101-124.

———. "William Faulkner: The Private Vision," *The Novel of Violence in America,* 2nd ed. Dallas: Southern Methodist University Press, 1957. Pages 144-165.

Garrett, George P. Jr. "An Examination of the Poetry of William Faulkner," *The Princeton University Library Chronicle,* 18 (Spring, 1957), 124-135.

———. "Faulkner's Early Literary Criticism," *Texas Studies in Literature and Language,* 1 (Spring, 1959), 3-10.

Geismar, Maxwell. "William Faulkner: The Negro and the Female," *Writers in Crisis.* Boston: Houghton Mifflin, 1942. Pages 143-183.

———. "William Faulkner: Before and After the Nobel Prize," *American*

*Moderns: From Rebellion to Conformity.* New York: Hill and Wang, 1958. Pages 91-106.

Gérard, Albert. "Justice in Yoknapatawpha County: Some Symbolic Motifs in Faulkner's Later Writing," *Faulkner Studies,* 2 (Winter, 1954), 49-57.

————. "William Faulkner, Chroniqueur de l'Apocalypse," *La Revue Nouvelle,* 13 (January 15, 1951), 81-90.

————. "William Faulkner, ou le fardeau de l'homme noir," *La Revue Nouvelle,* 24 (October, 1956), 331-338.

Giles, Barbara. "The South of William Faulkner," *Masses and Mainstream,* 3 (February, 1950), 26-40.

Glicksberg, Charles I. "William Faulkner and the Negro Problem," *Phylon,* 10 (June, 1949), 153-160.

————. "The World of William Faulkner," *Arizona Quarterly,* 5 (Spring, 1949), 46-58.

Greet, Tom (T. Y.). "Toward the Light: The Thematic Unity of Faulkner's 'Cycle,'" *Carolina Quarterly,* 3 (Fall, 1950), 38-44.

Griffin, William J. "How to Misread Faulkner: A Powerful Plea for Ignorance," *Tennessee Studies in Literature,* 1 (1956), 27-34.

Guyard, Marius François. "Faulkner et le tragique," *Études,* 268 (February, 1951), 172-183.

Hamilton, Edith. "Faulkner: Sorcerer or Slave?" *Saturday Review,* 35 (July 12, 1952), 8-10, 39-41.

Harder, Kelsie B. "Charactonyms in Faulkner's Novels," *Bucknell Review,* 8 (May, 1959), 189-201.

————. "Proverbial Snopeslore," *Tennessee Folklore Society Bulletin,* 24 (September, 1958), 89-95.

Harnack-Fish, Mildred. "William Faulkner, ein amerikanischer Dichter aus grosser Tradition," *Die Literatur,* 38 (October, 1935), 64-67.

Hartwick, Harry. "The Cult of Cruelty," *The Foreground of American Fiction.* New York: American Book Co., 1934. Pages 160-166.

Hatcher, Harlan. "Ultimate Extensions," *Creating the Modern American Novel.* New York: Farrar and Rinehart, 1935. Pages 234-243.

Hayakawa, Hiroshi. "Negation in William Faulkner," *Studies in English Grammar and Linguistics: A Miscellany in Honor of Takanobu Otsuka,* Kazuo Araki and others (eds.). Tokyo: Kenkyusha, 1958. Pages 103-113.

Hicks, Granville. "Faulkner's South: A Northern Interpretation," *Georgia Review,* 5 (Fall, 1951), 269-284.

————. "The Past and the Future of William Faulkner," *The Bookman,* 74 (September, 1931), 17-24.

Hoadley, Frank M. "Folk Humor in the Novels of William Faulkner," *Tennessee Folklore Society Bulletin,* 23 (September, 1957), 75-82.

Hoffman, Frederick J. "Violence and Rhetoric" *The Modern Novel in America, 1900-1950.* Chicago: Henry Regnery, 1951. Pages 154-164.

Hogan, Patrick G. Jr. "Critical Misconceptions of Southern Thought: Faulkner's Optimism," *The Mississippi Quarterly,* 10 (January, 1957), 19-28.

Hopper, Vincent F. "Faulkner's Paradise Lost," *Virginia Quarterly Review,* 23 (Summer, 1947), 405-420.

Howe, Irving. "The South and Current Literature," *The American Mercury,* 67 (October, 1948), 494-503.

————. "The Southern Myth and William Faulkner," *American Quarterly,* 3 (Winter, 1951), 357-362.

————. "William Faulkner and the Negro," *Commentary,* 12 (October, 1951), 359-368.

Hudson, Tommy. "William Faulkner: Mystic and Traditionalist," *Perspective,* 3 (Autumn, 1950), 227-235.

Humphrey, Robert. "Faulkner's Synthesis," *Stream of Consciousness in the Modern Novel.* Berkeley: University of California Press, 1954. Pages 17-21, 64-70, 104-111, *et passim.*

Jackson, James Turner. "Delta Cycle: A Study of William Faulkner," *Chimera,* 5 (Autumn, 1946), 3-14.

Jacobs, Robert D. "Faulkner and the Tragedy of Isolation," *Hopkins Review,* 6 (Spring-Summer, 1953), 162-183. Reprinted in *Southern Renascence: The Literature of the Modern South,* Louis D. Rubin Jr. and Robert D. Jacobs (eds). Baltimore: Johns Hopkins University Press, 1953. Pages 170-191.

————. "How do *you* Read Faulkner?" *The Provincial,* 1 (April, 1957), 3-5.

Jaffard, Paul. "Le Double aspect de l'oeuvre de Faulkner," *Critique,* 9 (June, 1953), 496-507.

Juin, Hubert. "L'Univers clos de William Faulkner," *Esprit,* 24 (November, 1956), 704-715.

Kazin, Alfred. "Faulkner in his Fury," *The Inmost Leaf.* New York: Harcourt, Brace, 1955. Pages 257-273.

————. "Faulkner: The Rhetoric and the Agony," *Virginia Quarterly Review,* 18 (Summer, 1942), 389-402. Reprinted in *On Native Grounds.* New York: Reynal & Hitchcock, 1942. Pages 453-470.

————. "Faulkner's Vision of Human Integrity," *The Harvard Advocate,* 135 (November, 1951), 8-9, 28-33.

Kohler, Dayton. "William Faulkner and the Social Conscience," *College*

*English,* 11 (December, 1949), 119-127. Also appeared in *English Journal,* 38 (December, 1949), 545-553.

Leaver, Florence. "Faulkner: The Word as Principle and Power," *South Atlantic Quarterly,* 57 (Autumn, 1958), 464-476. WF III

Le Breton, Maurice. "Technique et psychologie chez William Faulkner," *Études Anglaises,* 1 (September, 1937), 418-438.

————. "Temps et personne chez William Faulkner," *Journal de psychologie normale et pathologique,* 44 (janvier-juin, 1951), 344-354.

Leibowitz, René. "L'Art tragique de William Faulkner," *Cahiers du Sud,* 17 (November, 1940), 502-508.

Lewis, Wyndham. "The Moralist with a Corn-cob: A Study of William Faulkner," *Life and Letters,* 10 (June, 1934), 312-328. Reprinted in *Men without Art.* London: Cassell, 1934. Pages 42-64.

Lind, Ilse Dusoir. "The Teachable Faulkner," *College English,* 16 (February, 1955), 284-287, 302.

Linn, Robert. "Robinson Jeffers and William Faulkner," *The American Spectator,* 2 (1933), 1. Reprinted in *The American Spectator Year Book,* George Jean Nathan, Ernest Boyd, and others (eds). New York: Frederick A. Stokes, 1934. Pages 304-307.

Litz, Walton. "William Faulkner's Moral Vision," *Southwest Review,* 37 (Summer, 1952), 200-209.

Machlachlan, John M. "William Faulkner and the Southern Folk," *Southern Folklore Quarterly,* 9 (June, 1945), 153-167.

MacLeish, Archibald. "Faulkner and the Responsibility of the Artist," *The Harvard Advocate,* 135 (November 1951), 18, 43.

MacLure, Millar. "William Faulkner: Soothsayer of the South," *Queen's Quarterly,* 63 (Autumn, 1956), 334-343.

Magny, Claude-Edmonde. "Faulkner ou l'inversion théologique," *L'Age du roman américain.* Paris: Éditions du Seuil, 1948. Pages 196-243.

Mayes, Martha. "Faulkner Juvenalia," *New Campus Writing, No. 2.* New York: Bantam Books, 1957. Pages 135-144.

Mayoux, Jean Jacques. "La Création du réel chez William Faulkner," *Études Anglaises,* 5 (February, 1952), 25-39. WF III

————. "Le Temps et la destinée chez William Faulkner," *La Profondeur et le rythme* (Cahiers du collège philosophique). Paris: B. Arthaud, 1948. Pages 303-331.

McClennan, Joshua. "William Faulkner and Christian Complacency," *Papers of the Michigan Academy of Science, Arts, and Letters,* 41 (1956), 315-322.

McCole, Camille J. "The Nightmare Literature of William Faulkner," *The Catholic World,* 141 (August, 1935), 576-583.

————. "William Faulkner: Cretins, Coffinworms, and Cruelty," *Lucifer at Large*. New York: Longmans, 1937. Pages 203-228.

McCorquodale, Marjorie K. "Alienation in Yoknapatawpha County," *Forum* (Houston), 1 (January, 1957), 4-8.

McGrew, Julia. "Faulkner and the Icelanders," *Scandinavian Studies,* 31 (February, 1959), 1-14.

McIlwaine, Shields. "Naturalistic Modes: The Gothic, The Ribald, and the Tragic," *The Southern Poor-White from Lubberland to Tobacco Road*. Norman: University of Oklahoma Press, 1939. Pages 217-240.

Meriwether, James B. "William Faulkner," *Shenandoah,* 10 (Winter, 1959), 18-24.

Merwin, W. S. "William Faulkner," *Nobel Prize Winners,* L. J. Ludovici (ed). Westport: Associated Booksellers, 1957. Pages 43-60.

Mohrt, Michel. "William Faulkner ou démesure du souvenir," *Preuves,* 4 (April, 1954), 8-14.

————. "William Faulkner ou une religion du temps," *Le Nouveau roman américain*. Paris: Gallimard, 1955. Pages 80-118.

Moloney, Michael F. "The Enigma of Time: Proust, Virginia Woolf, and Faulkner," *Thought,* 32 (Spring, 1957), 69-85.

Montenegro, Ernesto. "Interpetacion de William Faulkner," *Panorama,* 1 (Núm. 2, 1952), 71-75.

Morris, Wright. "The Function of Rage: William Faulkner." *The Territory Ahead*. New York: Harcourt, Brace, 1958. Pages 171-184.

————. "The Violent Land: Some Observations on the Faulkner Country," *Magazine of Art,* 45 (March, 1952), 99-103.

Nicholson, Norman. "William Faulkner," *Man and Literature*. London: S. C. M. Press, 1943. Pages 122-138.

————. "William Faulkner," *The New Spirit,* E. W. Martin (ed). London: Dobson, 1946. Pages 32-41.

O'Connor, William Van. "Faulkner's Legend of the Old South," *Western Humanities Review,* 7 (Autumn, 1953), 293-301.

————. "Hawthorne and Faulkner: Some Common Ground," *Virginia Quarterly Review,* 33 (Winter, 1957), 105-123.

————. "Rhetoric in Southern Writing: Faulkner," *Georgia Review.* 12 (Spring, 1958), 83-86.

————. "William Faulkner's Apprenticeship," *Southwest Review,* 38 (Winter, 1953), 1-14.

O'Donnell, George M. "Faulkner's Mythology," *Kenyon Review,* 1 (Summer, 1939), 285-299. WF III

O'Faolain, Sean. "William Faulkner: More Genius than Talent," *The Vanishing Hero: Studies in Novelists of the Twenties*. Boston: Little, Brown, 1956. Pages 73-111.

Oñis, Harriet de. "William Faulkner," *La Torre,* 3 (October-December, 1955), 11-26.

———. "William Faulkner y su Mondo," *Sur,* No. 202 (August, 1951), 24-33.

Penick, Edwin A. Jr. "The Testimony of William Faulkner," *The Christian Scholar,* 38 (June, 1955), 121-133.

Perdeck, A. "William Faulkner," *Critisch Bulletin,* 1934, 209-213.

Peyre, Henri. "American Literature through French Eyes," *Virginia Quarterly Review,* 23 (Summer, 1947), 421-437.

Portuondo, José Antonio. "William Faulkner y la conciencia sureña," *El Heroísmo Intelectual.* Mexico: Tezontle, 1955. Pages 73-81.

Pouillon, Jean. "Temps et destinée chez Faulkner," *Temps et roman.* Paris: Gallimard, 1946. Pages 238-260.

Prescott, Orville. "The Eminently Obscure: Mann, Faulkner," *In My Opinion.* Indianapolis: Bobbs-Merrill, 1952. Pages 75-91.

Pritchett, V. S. "The Hill-Billies," *Books in General.* New York: Harcourt, Brace, 1953. Pages 242-247.

Pusey, William Webb III. "William Faulkner's Works in Germany to 1940: Translations and Criticism," *The Germanic Review,* 30 (October, 1955), 211-226.

Rabi. "Faulkner et la génération de l'exil," *Esprit,* 19 (January, 1951), 47-65. Translated by Martine Darmon and reprinted in *William Faulkner: Two Decades of Criticism,* Frederick J. Hoffman and Olga W. Vickery (eds). East Lansing: Michigan State University Press, 1951. Pages 118-138.

Ransom, John Crowe. "William Faulkner: An Impression," *The Harvard Advocate,* 135 (November, 1951), 17.

Rascoe, Burton. "Faulkner's New York Critics," *The American Mercury,* 50 (June, 1940), 243-247.

Riedel, F. C. "Faulkner as Stylist," *South Atlantic Quarterly,* 56 (Autumn, 1957), 462-479.

Rolle, Andrew F. "William Faulkner: An Inter-disciplinary Examination," *The Mississippi Quarterly,* 11 (Fall, 1958), 157-159.

Rosati, Salvatore. "William Faulkner," *Nuova Antologia,* 345 (January 16, 1938), 225-230.

Roth, Russell, "The Brennan Papers: Faulkner in Manuscript," *Perspective,* 2 (Summer, 1949), 219-224.

———. "The Centaur and the Pear Tree," *Western Review,* 16 (Spring, 1952), 199-205.

———. "Ideas and Queries," *Faulkner Studies,* 1 (Summer, 1952), 23-26.

———. "William Faulkner: The Pattern of Pilgrimage," *Perspective,* 2 (Summer, 1949), 246-254.

Rousseaux, André. "Mystique et tragique de Faulkner," *Litterature du vingtième siècle,* 3. Paris: Albin Michael, 1949. Pages 238-246.

Runyan, Harry. "Faulkner's Poetry," *Faulkner Studies,* 3 (Summer-Autumn, 1954), 23-29.

Sandeen, Ernest. "William Faulkner: Tragedian of Yoknapatawpha," *Fifty Years of the American Novel,* Harold C. Gardiner (ed). New York: Scribners, 1952. Pages 165-182.

Schappes, Morris U. "Faulkner as Poet." *Poetry: A Magazine of Verse,* 43 (October, 1933), 48-52.

Schwartz, Delmore. "The Fiction of William Faulkner," *The Southern Review,* 7 (Summer, 1941), 145-160.

Scott, Arthur L. "The Faulknerian Sentence," *Prairie Schooner,* 27 (Spring, 1953), 91-98.

Sherwood, John C. "The Traditional Element in Faulkner," *Faulkner Studies,* 3 (Summer-Autumn, 1954), 17-23.

Simon, Jean, "William Faulkner," *Le Roman américain au xxᵉ siècle.* Paris: Boivin, 1950. Pages 119-131.

Slatoff, Walter J. "The Edge of Order: The Pattern of Faulkner's Rhetoric," *Twentieth Century Literature,* 3 (October, 1957), 107-127. WF III

Smith, Henry Nash. "William Faulkner and Reality," *Faulkner Studies,* 2 (Summer, 1953), 17-19.

Smith, Thelma M., and Ward L. Miner. "Faulkner," *Transatlantic Migration.* Durham: Duke University Press, 1955. Pages 122-145.

Snell, George. "The Fury of William Faulkner," *Western Review,* 11 (Autumn, 1946), 29-40. Reprinted in *The Shapers of American Fiction.* New York: E. P. Dutton, 1947. Pages 87-104.

Sosa, Lopez Emilio. "El problema del mal en William Faulkner," *Sur,* No. 247 (July-August, 1957), 55-63.

Soulac, Anne-Marie. "William Faulkner," *Romanciers américains contemporains.* Paris: Didiers Cahiers des langues modernes, No. 1, 1946. Pages 239-249.

Spiller, R. E. "The Uses of Memory: Eliot, Faulkner," *The Cycle of American Literature.* New York: Macmillan, 1955. Pages 291-300.

Stavrou, C. N. "Ambiguity in Faulkner's Affirmation," *The Personalist,* 40 (Spring, 1959), 169-177.

Stewart, Randall. *American Literature and Christian Doctrine,* Baton Rouge: Louisiana State University Press, 1958. Pages 136-142.

———. "Hawthorne and Faulkner," *College English,* 17 (February, 1956), 258-262.

Swallow, Alan. "A General Introduction to 'Faulkner Studies,'" *Faulkner Studies,* 1 (Spring, 1952), 1-3.

Swiggart, Peter. "Time in Faulkner's Novels," *Modern Fiction Studies,* 1 (May, 1955), 25-29.

Taylor, W. F. "A Wider Range," *The Story of American Letters.* Chicago: Henry Regnery, 1956. Pages 471-481.

Thompson, Alan R. "The Cult of Cruelty," *The Bookman,* 74 (January-February, 1932), 477-487.

Tritschler, Donald. "The Unity of Faulkner's Shaping Vision," *Modern Fiction Studies,* 5 (Winter, 1959-1960), 337-343.

Vickery, Olga W. "Faulkner and the Contours of Time," *Georgia Review,* 12 (Summer, 1958), 192-201.

————. "Gavin Stevens: From Rhetoric to Dialectic," *Faulkner Studies,* 2 (Spring, 1953), 1-4.

Vittorini, Elio. "Faulkner come Picasso?" *La Stampa* (8 Dicembre, 1950). Reprinted in *William Faulkner: Venti anni di critica,* Frederick J. Hoffman and Olga W. Vickery (eds). Parma: Guanda, 1957. Pages 162-164.

Wagenknecht, Edward. "Erskine Caldwell and William Faulkner," *Cavalcade of the American Novel.* New York: Henry Holt, 1952. Pages 417-425.

Waggoner, Hyatt H. "William Faulkner: The Definition of Man," *Books at Brown,* 18 (March, 1958), 116-122.

————. "William Faulkner's Passion Week of the Heart," *The Tragic Vision and the Christian Faith,* Nathan A. Scott Jr. (ed). New York: Association Press, 1957. Pages 306-323.

Warren, Robert Penn. "Cowley's Faulkner," *The New Republic,* 115 (August 12, 1946), 176-180; continued (August 26, 1946), 234-237. WF III

————. "William Faulkner," *Selected Essays.* New York: Random House, 1958. Pages 59-79.

Watkins, Floyd C. "The Gentle Reader and Mr. Faulkner's Morals," *Georgia Review,* 13 (Spring, 1959), 68-75.

West, Ray B. Jr. "Hemingway and Faulkner," *The Short Story in America, 1900-1950.* Chicago: Henry Regnery, 1952. Pages 85-106.

Wheeler, Otis B. "Faulkner's Wilderness," *American Literature,* 31 (May, 1959), 127-136.

White, William. "One Man's Meat: Societies and Journals Devoted to a Single Author," *The American Book Collector,* 8 (November, 1957), 22-24.

Whittemore, Reed. "Notes on Mr. Faulkner," *Furioso,* 2 (Summer, 1947), 18-25.

William, Cecil B. "William Faulkner and the Nobel Prize Awards," *Faulkner Studies,* 1 (Summer, 1952), 17-19.

Woodworth, Stanley D. "La Critique faulknérienne en France: Essai de synthèse," *La Revue des Lettres Modernes,* 4 (2ᵉ Trim., 1957), 178-190.

———. "Problèmes de traduction des romans américains contemporains," *La Revue des Lettres Modernes,* 5 (Hiver, 1958-1959), 345-364.

Wykes, Alan. "The Perceptive Few and the Lost Generation," *A Concise Survey of American Literature.* London: Arthur Baker, 1955. Pages 165-174.

Young, T. D., and Floyd C. Watkins. "Faulkner's Snopeses," *The Mississippi Quarterly,* 11 (Fall, 1958), 196-200.

Zink, Karl E. "Faulkner's Garden: Woman and the Immemorial Earth," *Modern Fiction Studies,* 2 (Autumn, 1956), 139-149.

———. "Flux and the Frozen Moment: The Imagery of Stasis in Faulkner's Prose," *PMLA,* 71 (June, 1956), 285-301.

———. "William Faulkner: Form as Experience," *South Atlantic Quarterly,* 53 (July, 1954), 384-403.

# VI

## STUDIES OF INDIVIDUAL WORKS

### A.

*ABSALOM, ABSALOM!*

Arnavon, Cyrille. " 'Absalon, Absalon!' et l'Histoire," *La Revue des Lettres Modernes,* 5 (Hiver, 1958-1959), 250-270.

Barjon, Louis. "Retour aux enfers de Faulkner: 'Absalon, Absalon!' " *Études,* 279 (November, 1953), 225-236.

Brooks, Cleanth. " 'Absalom, Absalom!' The Definition of Innocence," *The Sewanee Review,* 59 (Autumn, 1951), 543-558.

Campbell, Harry M. "Faulkner's 'Absalom, Absalom!' " *Explicator,* 7 (December, 1948), item 24.

Coanda, Richard. " 'Absalom, Absalom!' The Edge of Infinity." *Renascence,* 11 (Autumn, 1958), 3-9.

Coindreau, Maurice E. " 'Absalon, Absalon!' " *La Nouvelle Revue Française,* 48 (January, 1937), 123-126.

Cowley, Malcolm. "Poe in Mississippi," *The New Republic,* 89 (November 4, 1936), 22.

Greene, Graham. "The Furies in Mississippi," *The London Mercury,* 35 (March, 1937), 517-518.

Hoffman, A. C. "Faulkner's 'Absalom, Absalom!' " *Explicator,* 10 (November, 1951), item 12.

———. "Point of View in 'Absalom, Absalom!' " *University of Kansas City Review,* 19 (Summer, 1953), 233-239.

Korn, Karl. "Moira und Schuld," *Die Neue Rundschau,* 49 (December, 1938), 603-607.

Lind, Ilse Dusoir. "The Design and Meaning of 'Absalom, Absalom!' " *PMLA,* 70 (December, 1955), 887-912.

McClennen, Joshua. " 'Absalom, Absalom!' and the Meaning of History," *Papers of the Michigan Academy of Science, Arts, and Letters,* 42 (1956), 357-369.

Moussy, Marcel. " 'Absalon, Absalon!' " *Les Lettres Nouvelles,* 1 (October, 1953), 1030-1035.

Poirier, William R. " 'Strange Gods' in Jefferson, Mississippi: Analysis of 'Absalom, Absalom!' " *William Faulkner: Two Decades of Criticism,* Frederick J. Hoffman and Olga W. Vickery (eds). East Lansing: Michigan State University Press, 1951. Pages 217-243.

Pouillon, Jean. "A propos de 'Absalon, Absalon!' " *Les Temps Modernes,* 9 (October, 1953), 742-752.

Rousseaux, André. "L'Enfer de Faulkner," *Litterature du vingtième siècle,* V. Paris: Albin Michel, 1955. Pages 115-133.

Scott, Arthur L. "The Myriad Perspectives of 'Absalom, Absalom!' " *American Quarterly,* 6 (Fall, 1954), 210-220.

Sewall, Richard B. " 'Absalom, Absalom!' " *The Vision of Tragedy.* New Haven: Yale University Press, 1959. Pages 133-147.

Sullivan, Walter. "The Tragic Design of 'Absalom, Absalom!' " *South Atlantic Quarterly,* 50 (October, 1951), 552-566.

Thomas, Douglas M. "Memory-Narrative in 'Absalom, Absalom!' " *Faulkner Studies,* 2 (Summer, 1953), 19-22.

Troy, William. "The Poetry of Doom," *The Nation,* 143 (October 31, 1936), 524-525.

Whan, Edgar W. " 'Absalom, Absalom!' as Gothic Myth," *Perspective,* 3 (Autumn, 1950), 192-201.

Zoellner, Robert H. "Faulkner's Prose Style in 'Absalom, Absalom!' " *American Literature,* 30 (January, 1959), 486-502.


*AS I LAY DYING*

Backman, Melvin " 'Tandis que j'agonise,' " *La Revue des Lettres Modernes,* 5 (Hiver, 1958-1959), 309-330.

Blotner, Joseph L. " 'As I Lay Dying': Christian Lore and Irony," *Twentieth Century Literature,* 3 (April, 1957), 14-19.

Campbell, Harry M. "Experiment and Achievement: 'As I Lay Dying' and 'The Sound and the Fury,' " *The Sewanee Review,* 51 (Spring, 1943), 305-320.

Collins, Carvel. "The Pairing of 'The Sound and the Fury' and 'As I Lay Dying,' " *The Princeton University Library Chronicle,* 18 (Spring, 1957), 114-123.

Friedman, Melvin J. "Le Monologue Intérieur dans 'As I Lay Dying,' " *La Revue des Lettres Modernes,* 5 (Hiver, 1958-1959), 331-344.

Garrett, George P. Jr. "Some Revisions in 'As I Lay Dying,' " *Modern Language Notes,* 73 (June, 1958), 414-417.

Goellner, Jack. "A Closer Look at 'As I Lay Dying,' " *Perspective,* 7 (Spring, 1954), 42-54.

Handy, William J. " 'As I Lay Dying': Faulkner's Inner Reporter," *The Kenyon Review,* 21 (Summer, 1959), 437-451.

King, Roma Jr. "The Janus Symbol in 'As I Lay Dying,' " *University of Kansas City Review,* 21 (Summer, 1955), 287-290.

Larbaud, Valery. "Un roman de William Faulkner. 'Tandis que j'agonise,' " *Ce Vice impuni, la lecture . . . domaine anglais.* Paris: Gallimard, 1936. Pages 218-222.

Le Breton, Maurice. "Le Thème de la vie et de la mort dans 'As I Lay Dying," *Le Revue des Lettres Modernes,* 5 (Hiver, 1958-1959), 292-308.

Randall, Julia. "Some Notes on 'As I Lay Dying,' " *Hopkins Review,* 4 (Summer, 1951), 47-51.

Reaver, J. Russell. "This Vessel of Clay: A Thematic Comparison of Faulkner's 'As I Lay Dying' and Latorre's 'The Old Woman of Peralillo,' " *Florida State University Studies,* No. 14 (1954), 131-140.

Sawyer, Kenneth B. "Hero in 'As I Lay Dying,' " *Faulkner Studies,* 3 (Summer-Autumn, 1954), 30-33.

Stonesifer, Richard J. "In Defense of Dewey Dell," *The Educational Leader,* 22 (July, 1958), 27-33.

Vickery, Olga W. " 'As I Lay Dying,' " *Perspective,* 3 (Autumn, 1950), 179-191.

Wasiolek, Edward. " 'As I Lay Dying': Distortion in the Slow Eddy of Current Opinion," *Critique,* 3 (Spring-Fall, 1959), 15-23.

*A FABLE*

Baker, Carlos. "Cry Enough!" *The Nation,* 179 (August 7, 1954), 115-118.

Barth, J. Robert. "A Rereading of Faulkner's Fable," *America,* 92 (October 9, 1954), 44-46.

Braem, Helmut W. "Das scandalon William Faulkner: Die metaphysische Kampfstatt und ein sadistischer Jehova," *Deutsche Rundschau,* 84 (October, 1958), 944-950.

Carter, Thomas H. "Dramatization of an Engima," *Western Review,* 19 (Winter, 1955), 147-158.

Collins, Carvel. "War and Peace and Mr. Faulkner," *New York Times Book Review* (August 1, 1954), 1, 13.

Connolly, Thomas E. "Faulkner's 'A Fable' in the Classroom," *College English,* 21 (December, 1959), 165-171.

Cowley, Malcolm. "Faulkner's Powerful New Novel," *New York Herald Tribune* (Books) (August 1, 1954), 1, 8.

Einsiedel, Wolfgang von. "Revolte des Menschensohnes: Zu William Faulkners 'Eine Legende,' " *Merkur,* 10 (March, 1956), 282-290.

Fiedler, Leslie A. "Stone Grotesques," *The New Republic,* 131 (August 23, 1954), 18-19.

Flint, R. W. "What Price Glory?" *The Hudson Review,* 7 (Winter, 1955), 602-606.

Hafley, James. "Faulkner's 'Fable': Dream and Transfiguration," *Accent,* 16 (Winter, 1956), 3-14.

Hartt, Julian N. "Some Reflections on Faulkner's Fable," *Religion in Life,* 24 (Fall, 1955), 601-607.

Highet, Gilbert. "Sound and Fury," *Harper's Magazine,* 209 (September, 1954), 98-104.

King, Roma A. Jr. "Everyman's Warfare: A Study of Faulkner's 'Fable,' " *Modern Fiction Studies,* 2 (Autumn, 1956), 132-138.

Kohler, Dayton. " 'A Fable': The Novel as Myth," *College English,* 16 (May, 1955), 471-478.

Lytle, Andrew. "The Son of Man: He Will Prevail," *The Sewanee Review,* 63 (Winter, 1955), 114-137.

Miner, Ward L. "Faulkner and Christ's Crucifixion," *Neuphilologische Mitteilungen,* 57 (1956), 260-269.

Mohrt, Michel. " 'A Fable,' 'Nouveau Testament' de Faulkner," *Le Nouveau roman américain.* Paris: Gallimard, 1955. Pages 119-123.

Podhoretz, Norman. "William Faulkner and the Problem of War," *Commentary,* 18 (September, 1954), 227-232.

Pritchett, V. S. "Time Frozen," *Partisan Review,* 21 (September-October, 1954), 557-561.

Rice, Philip Blair. "Faulkner's Crucifixion," *Kenyon Review,* 16 (Autumn, 1954), 661-670. WF III

Rousseaux, André. "Parabole de Faulkner," *Le Figaro Littéraire,* 13 (June 14, 1958), 2.

Sandeen, Ernest. "William Faulkner: His Legend and His Fable," *Review of Politics,* 18 (January, 1956), 47-68.

Schwartz, Delmore. "William Faulkner's 'A Fable,'" *Perspectives U.S.A.,* No. 10 (Winter, 1955), 126-136.

Stavrou, C.N. "William Faulkner's Apologia: Some Notes on 'A Fable,'" *Colorado Quarterly,* 3 (Spring, 1955), 432-439.

Straumann, Heinrich. "Eine amerikanische Seinsdeutung, Faulkners Roman 'A Fable,'" *Anglia,* 73 (Heft 4, 1956), 484-515. WF III

Tafur, José Luis. "'Una Fábula' de Faulkner," *Estudios Americanos* (Seville), 12 (August-September, 1956), 153-159.

Taylor, Walter F. "William Faulkner: The Faulkner Fable," *American Scholar,* 26 (Autumn, 1957), 471-477.

Vallette, Jacques. "Un Apologue à la gloire de l'homme," *Mercure de France,* 325 (October, 1955), 330-334.

Wagner, Geoffrey. "Faulkner's Contemporary Passion Play," *The Twentieth Century,* 156 (December, 1954), 527-538.

## GO DOWN, MOSES

Cowley, Malcolm. "Go Down to Faulkner's Land," *The New Republic,* 106 (June 29, 1942), 900.

Gregory, Horace. "New Tales by William Faulkner," *New York Times Book Review* (May 10, 1942), 4.

Litz, Walton. "Genealogy as Symbol in 'Go Down, Moses,'" *Faulkner Studies,* 1 (Winter, 1952), 49-53.

Mizener, Arthur. "The Thin, Intelligent Face of American Fiction," *Kenyon Review,* 17 (Autumn, 1955), 507-519.

Rugoff, Milton. "The Magic of William Faulkner," *New York Herald Tribune* (Books) (May 17, 1942), 2.

Taylor, Walter F. Jr. "Let My People Go: The White Man's Heritage in 'Go Down, Moses,'" *South Atlantic Quarterly,* 58 (Winter, 1959), 20-32.

Trilling, Lionel. "The McCaslins of Mississippi," *The Nation,* 154 (May 30, 1942), 632-633.

## THE HAMLET

Benét, Stephen Vincent. "Flem Snopes and his Kin," *Saturday Review of Literature,* 21 (April 6, 1940), 7.

Cowley, Malcolm. "Faulkner by Daylight," *The New Republic,* 102 (April 15, 1940), 510.

Greet, T.Y. "The Theme and Structure of Faulkner's 'The Hamlet,'" *PMLA,* 72 (September, 1957), 775-790. WF III

Hawkins, Desmond. " 'The Hamlet,' " *The New Statesman and Nation*, 20 (September 28, 1940), 312-314.

Hopkins, Viola. "William Faulkner's 'The Hamlet': A Study in Meaning and Form," *Accent*, 15 (Spring, 1955), 125-144.

Kronenberger, Louis. "The World of William Faulkner," *The Nation*, 150 (April 13, 1940), 481-482.

Leaver, Florence. "The Structure of 'The Hamlet,' " *Twentieth Century Literature*, 1 (July, 1955), 77-84.

Lisca, Peter. " 'The Hamlet': Genesis and Revisions," *Faulkner Studies*, 3 (Spring, 1954), 5-13.

Stonesifer, Richard J. "Faulkner's 'The Hamlet' in the Classroom," *College English*, 20 (November, 1958), 71-77.

Warren, Robert Penn. "The Snopes World," *Kenyon Review*, 3 (Spring, 1941), 253-257.

Watkins, Floyd C. and Thomas Daniel Young. "Revisions of Style in Faulkner's 'The Hamlet,' " *Modern Fiction Studies*, 5 (Winter, 1959-1960), 327-336.

## INTRUDER IN THE DUST

Allen, Walter. "Mr. Faulkner's Humanity," *The New Statesman and Nation*, 38 (October 15, 1949), 428-429.

Breit, Harvey. "Faulkner after Eight Years," *New York Times Book Review* (September 26, 1948), 4.

Bunker, Robert. "Faulkner: A Case for Regionalism," *New Mexico Quarterly*, 19 (Spring, 1949), 108-115.

Cowley, Malcolm. "William Faulkner's Nation," *The New Republic*, 119 (October 18, 1948), 21-22.

Elias, Robert H. "Gavin Stevens: Intruder?" *Faulkner Studies*, 3 (Spring, 1954), 1-4.

Geismar, Maxwell. "Ex-Aristocrat's Emotional Education," *Saturday Review of Literature*, 31 (September 25, 1948), 8-9.

Glicksberg, Charles I. " 'Intruder in the Dust,' " *Arizona Quarterly*, 5 (Spring, 1949), 85-88.

Gloster, Hugh M. "Southern Justice," *Phylon*, 10 (First Quarter, 1949), 93-95.

Hardwick, Elizabeth. "Faulkner and the South Today," *Partisan Review*, 15 (October, 1948), 1130-1135. Reprinted in *William Faulkner: Two Decades of Criticism*, Frederick J. Hoffman and Olga W. Vickery (eds). East Lansing: Michigan State University Press, 1951. Pages 244-250.

Lytle, Andrew. "Regeneration for the Man," *The Sewanee Review*, 57

(Winter, 1949), 120-127. Reprinted in *William Faulkner: Two Decades of Criticism*, Frederick J. Hoffman and Olga W. Vickery (eds). East Lansing: Michigan State University Press, 1951. Pages 251-259.

Milano, Paolo. "Faulkner in Crisis," *The Nation*, 167 (October 30, 1948), 496-497.

Seyppel, Joachim. "Faulkner's Dichtung—'Der Weg in die Sackgasse,' " *Neuphilologische Zeitschrift*, 4 (No. 6, 1952), 369-372.

Welty, Eudora. "In Yoknapatawpha," *The Hudson Review*, 1 (Winter, 1949), 596-598.

Wilson, Edmund. "William Faulkner's Reply to the Civil Rights Program," *The New Yorker*, 24 (October 23, 1948), 106, 109-112. Reprinted in *Classics and Commercials*. New York: Farrar, Straus, 1950. Pages 460-470.


## KNIGHT'S GAMBIT

Algren, Nelson. "Faulkner's Thrillers," *New York Times Book Review* (November 6, 1949), 4.

Jones, Howard Mumford. "Loyalty and Tiresias of Yoknapatawpha," *Saturday Review of Literature*, 32 (November 5, 1949), 17.

Justo, Luis. "La Antropologia de Faulkner—a proposito de 'Gambito de Caballo,' " *Sur*, No. 206 (December, 1951), 126-130.

Pouillon, Jean. " 'Le Gambit du cavalier,' " *Les Temps Modernes*, 7 (February, 1952), 1490-1496.

Visentin, Giovanni. "Considerazioni su un ladro di cavilli," *La Fiera Litteraria*, 6 (June 10, 1951), 1.


## LIGHT IN AUGUST

Abel, Darrel. "Frozen Movement in 'Light in August,' " *Boston University Studies in English*, 3 (Spring, 1957), 32-44.

Adams, J. Donald. "Mr. Faulkner's Astonishing Novel," *New York Times Book Review* (October 9, 1932), 6, 24.

Applewhite, Davis. "The South of 'Light in August,' " *The Mississippi Quarterly*, 11 (Fall, 1958), 167-172.

Arland, Marcel " 'Lumière d'août,' " *La Nouvelle Revue Française*, 45 (October, 1935), 584-586.

Benson, Carl. "Thematic Design in 'Light in August,' " *South Atlantic Quarterly*, 53 (October, 1954), 540-555.

Bernberg, Raymond E. " 'Light in August': A Psychological View," *The Mississippi Quarterly*, 11 (Fall, 1958), 173-176.

Breuil, Roger. "William Faulkner: 'Lumière d'août,' " *Esprit,* 1 (January, 1936), 612-614.

Brooks, Cleanth. "Notes on Faulkner's 'Light in August,' " *The Harvard Advocate,* 135 (November, 1951), 10-11, 27.

Cestre, C. "William Faulkner: 'Light in August,' " *Revue Anglo-américaine,* 10 (June, 1933), 466-467.

Chase, Richard. "The Stone and the Crucifixion: Faulkner's 'Light in August,' " *Kenyon Review,* 10 (Autumn, 1948), 539-551. Reprinted in *William Faulkner: Two Decades of Criticism,* Frederick J. Hoffman and Olga W. Vickery (eds). East Lansing: Michigan State University Press, 1951. Pages 205-217.

Coindreau, Maurice E. "Le Puritanisme de William Faulkner," *Cahiers du Sud,* 12 (April, 1935), 259-267.

Cottrell, Beekman W. "Christian Symbols in 'Light in August,' " *Modern Fiction Studies,* 2 (Winter, 1956-1957), 207-213.

Frazier, David L. "Lucas Burch and the Polarity of 'Light in August,' " *Modern Language Notes,* 73 (June, 1958), 417-419.

Gavin, Jerome. " 'Light in August': The Act of Involvement," *The Harvard Advocate,* 135 (November, 1951), 14-15, 34-37.

Greer, Scott. "Joe Christmas and the 'Social Self,' " *The Mississippi Quarterly,* 11 (Fall, 1958), 160-166.

Hirshleifer, Phyllis. "As Whirlwinds in the South: 'Light in August,' " *Perspective,* 2 (Summer, 1949), 225-238.

Holman, C. Hugh. "The Unity of Faulkner's 'Light in August,' " *PMLA,* 73 (March, 1958), 155-166.

Kazin, Alfred. "The Stillness of 'Light in August,' " *Partisan Review,* 24 (Fall, 1957), 519-538. Reprinted in *Twelve Original Essays on Great American Novels,* Charles Shapiro (ed). Detroit: Wayne State University Press, 1958. Pages 257-283. WF III

Lamont, William H.F. "The Chronology of 'Light in August,' " *Modern Fiction Studies,* 3 (Winter, 1957-1958), 360-361.

Leavis, F.R. "Dostoevsky or Dickens?" *Scrutiny,* 2 (June, 1933), 91-93.

Lind, Ilse Dusoir. "The Calvinistic Burden of 'Light in August,' " *The New England Quarterly,* 30 (September, 1957), 307-329.

Linn, James W., and Houghton W. Taylor. "Counterpoint: 'Light in August,' " *A Foreword to Fiction.* New York: Appleton-Century, 1935. Pages 144-157.

Longley, John L. "Joe Christmas: the Hero in the Modern World," *Virginia Quarterly Review,* 33 (Spring, 1957), 233-249. WF III

McCamy, Edward. "Byron Bunch," *Shenandoah,* 3 (Spring, 1952), 8-12.

McElderry, B. R. Jr. "The Narrative Structure of 'Light in August,' "

*College English,* 19 (February, 1958), 200-207. Reprinted in *The Mississippi Quarterly,* 11 (Fall, 1958), 177-187.

Morra, Umberto. "William Faulkner: 'Luce d'Agosto,' " *Letteratura,* 3 (July, 1939), 173-174.

O'Connor, William Van. "Protestantism in Yoknapatawpha County," *Hopkins Review,* 5 (Spring, 1952), 26-42. Reprinted in *Southern Renascence: The Literature of the Modern South,* Louis D. Rubin Jr. and Robert D. Jacobs (eds). Baltimore: Johns Hopkins University Press, 1953. Pages 153-169.

Pearson, Norman Holmes. "Lena Grove," *Shenandoah,* 3 (Spring, 1952), 3-7.

Smith, Hallett. "Summary of a Symposium on 'Light in August,' " *The Mississippi Quarterly,* 11 (Fall, 1958), 188-190.

Stone Geoffrey. " 'Light in August,' " *The Bookman,* 75 (November, 1932), 736-738.

## THE MANSION

Cowley, Malcolm. "Flem Snopes Gets his Come-Uppance," *New York Times Book Review* (November 15, 1959), 1, 18.

Hicks, Granville. "The Last of the Snopeses," *Saturday Review,* 42 (November 14, 1959), 20-21.

Howe, Irving. "Faulkner: End of a Road," *The New Republic,* 141 (December 7, 1959), 17-21.

Lemay, Harding. "Faulkner and his Snopes Family Reach the End of their Trilogy," *New York Herald Tribune* (Books) (November 15, 1959), 1, 14.

O'Connor, William Van. "The Old Master, the Sole Proprietor," *The Virginia Quarterly Review,* 36 (Winter, 1960), 147-151.

West, Anthony. "A Dying Fall," *The New Yorker,* 35 (December 5, 1959), 236-243.

## MOSQUITOES

Aiken, Conrad. " 'Mosquitoes,' " *New York Post* (June 11, 1927), 7. Reprinted in his *A Reviewer's ABC: Collected Criticism from 1916 to the Present.* New York: Meridian, 1958. Pages 197-200.

Gwynn, Frederick L. "Faulkner's Prufrock—and Other Observations," *Journal of English and Germanic Philology,* 52 (January, 1953), 63-70.

Vickery, Olga W. "Faulkner's 'Mosquitoes,' " *University of Kansas City Review,* 24 (Spring, 1958), 219-224.

## PYLON

Blanzat, Jean. "Pylône,' " *Le Monde Français,* 4 (October, 1946), 316-321.

Connolly, Cyril. " 'Pylon,' " *The New Statesman and Nation,* 9 (April 13, 1935), 525.

Cowley, Malcolm. "Voodoo Dance," *The New Republic,* 82 (April 10, 1935), 284-285.

Fauchery, Pierre. "La Mythologie faulknérienne dans 'Pylon,' " *Espace,* (June, 1945), 106-112.

Jarlot, Gérard. " 'Pylône,' " *Fontaine,* 10 (November, 1946), 653-657.

Le Breton, Maurice. "William Faulkner: 'Pylon,' " *Revue Anglo-américaine,* 12 (October, 1935), 81-82.

Madge, Charles. "Time and Space in America," *The London Mercury,* 32 (May, 1935), 83.

Marvin, John R. " 'Pylon': The Definition of Sacrifice," *Faulkner Studies,* 1 (Summer, 1952), 20-23.

Monteiro, George. "Bankruptcy in Time: A Reading of William Faulkner's 'Pylon,' " *Twentieth Century Literature,* 4 (April-July, 1958), 9-20.

Pouillon, Jean. "William Faulkner: un témoin," *Les Temps Modernes,* 2 (October, 1946), 172-178.

Redman, Ben Ray. "Flights of Fancy," *Saturday Review of Literature,* 11 (March 30, 1935), 577, 581.

Stallings, Lawrence. "Gentleman from Mississippi," *The American Mercury,* 34 (April, 1935), 499-501.

Torchiana, Donald T. "Faulkner's 'Pylon' and the Structure of Modernity," *Modern Fiction Studies,* 3 (Winter, 1957-1958), 291-308.

———. "The Reporter in Faulkner's 'Pylon,' " *The History of Ideas News Letter,* 4 (Spring, 1958), 33-39.

Troy, William. "And Tomorrow," *The Nation,* 140 (April 3, 1935), 393.

Van Doren, Mark. " 'Pylon,' " *New York Herald Tribune* (Books) (March 24, 1935), 3.

Veruly, A. "Vliegerromans," *Critisch Bulletin,* (1935) 313-317.

Vickery, John B. "William Faulkner and Sir Philip Sidney?" *Modern Language Notes,* 70 (May, 1955), 349-350.

## REQUIEM FOR A NUN

Baker, James R. "Ideas and Queries," *Faulkner Studies,* 1 (Spring, 1952), 4-7.

Castelli, F. "Tragedia e distruzione dell 'uomo nell' opera di William Faulkner," *La Civilta Cattolica,* 104 (March 7, 1953), 530-543.

Cowley, Malcolm. "In Which Mr. Faulkner Translates Past into Present," *New York Herald Tribune* (Books) (September 30, 1951), 1, 14.

English, H. M., Jr. " 'Requiem for a Nun,' " *Furioso,* 7 (Winter, 1952), 60-63.

Guérard, Albert Jr. " 'Requiem for a Nun': An Examination," *The Harvard Advocate,* 135 (November, 1951), 19, 41-42.

Heilman, Robert B. "Schools for Girls," *The Sewanee Review,* 60 (Spring, 1952), 304-309.

Howe, Irving. "Faulkner: An Experiment in Drama," *The Nation,* 173 (September 29, 1951), 263-264.

Lemarchand, Jacques. " 'Requiem pour une Nonne,' " *La Nouvelle Revue Française,* 4 (November, 1956), 896-900.

McLaughlin, Richard. "Requiem for Temple Drake," *Theatre Arts,* 35 (October, 1951), 50, 77.

Poster, Herbert. "Faulkner's Folly," *The American Mercury,* 73 (December, 1951), 106-112.

Savelli, Giovanni. "Paràbola di Faulkner," *Litterature Moderne,* 4 (May-June, 1953), 337-342.

West, Ray B. Jr. "William Faulkner: Artist and Moralist," *Western Review,* 16 (Winter, 1952), 162-167.


## *SANCTUARY*

Bergel, Lienhard. "Faulkner's 'Sanctuary,' " *Explicator,* 6 (December, 1947), item 20.

Brown, James. "Shaping the World of 'Sanctuary,' " *University of Kansas City Review,* 25 (Winter, 1958), 137-142.

Campbell, Harry M. "Faulkner's 'Sanctuary,' " *Explicator,* 4 (June, 1946), item 61.

Canby, Henry Seidel. "The School of Cruelty," *Saturday Review of Literature,* 7 (March 21, 1931), 673-674. Reprinted in *Seven Years' Harvest.* New York: Farrar and Rinehart, 1936. Pages 77-83.

Cantwell, Robert. "Faulkner's 'Popeye,' " *The Nation,* 186 (February 15, 1958), 140-141, 148.

Chamberlain, John. "Dostoyefsky's Shadow in the Deep South," *New York Times Book Review* (February 15, 1931), 9.

Collins, Carvel. "A Note on 'Sanctuary,' " *The Harvard Advocate,* 135 (November, 1951), 16.

————. "Nathaniel West's 'The Day of the Locust' and 'Sanctuary,' " *Faulkner Studies,* 2 (Summer, 1953), 23-24.

Fadiman, Clifton, "The World of William Faulkner," *The Nation,* 132 (April 15, 1931), 422-423.

Flynn, Robert. "The Dialectic of 'Sanctuary,' " *Modern Fiction Studies,* 2 (Autumn, 1956), 109-113.

Frazier, David L. "Gothicism in 'Sanctuary': The Black Pall and the Crap Table," *Modern Fiction Studies,* 2 (Autumn, 1956), 114-124.

Howell, Elmo. "The Quality of Evil in Faulkner's 'Sanctuary,' " *Tennessee Studies in Literature,* 4 (1959), 99-107.

Junior, Junius. *Pseudo-Realists.* New York: The Outsider Press, 1931.

Kubie, Lawrence S. "William Faulkner's 'Sanctuary': An Analysis," *Saturday Review of Literature,* 11 (October 20, 1934), 218, 224-226.

Lisca, Peter. "Some New Light on Faulkner's 'Sanctuary,' " *Faulkner Studies,* 2 (Spring, 1953), 5-9.

Malraux, André. "Préface à 'Sanctuaire' de William Faulkner," *La Nouvelle Revue Française,* 41 (November, 1933), 744-747. Translated and reprinted in *Yale French Studies,* No. 10 (Fall, 1952), 92-94.

Marichalar, Antonio. "William Faulkner," *Revista de Occidente,* 42 (October, 1933), 78-86.

Massey, Linton. "Notes on the Unrevised Galleys of Faulkner's 'Sanctuary,' " *Studies in Bibliography,* 8 (1956), 195-208.

Monteiro, George. "Initiation and the Moral Sense in Faulkner's 'Sanctuary,' " *Modern Language Notes,* 73 (November, 1958), 500-504.

O'Connor, William Van. "A Short View of Faulkner's 'Sanctuary,' " *Faulkner Studies,* 1 (Fall, 1952), 33-39.

Pilkington, James Penn. "Faulkner's 'Sanctuary,' " *Explicator,* 4 (June, 1946), item 61.

Saint Jean, Robert de. " 'Sanctuaire,' " *La Revue Hebdomadaire,* 43 (April 21, 1934), 487-491.

Thompson, Alan R. " 'Sanctuary,' " *The Bookman,* 73 (April, 1931), 188-189.

Wasiolek, Edward. "Dostoevsky and 'Sanctuary,' " *Modern Language Notes,* 74 (February, 1959), 114-117.

## *SARTORIS*

Carpenter, Richard C. "Faulkner's 'Sartoris,' " *Explicator,* 14 (April, 1956), item 41.

Howell, Elmo. "Faulkner's 'Sartoris,' " *Explicator,* 17 (February, 1959), item 33.

Sartre, Jean-Paul. " 'Sartoris,' par William Faulkner," *La Nouvelle Revue Française,* 50 (February, 1938), 323-328. Translated and reprinted in *Literary and Philosophical Essays.* London: Rider, 1955. Pages 73-78.

Thorp, Willard. "Four Times and Out?" *Scrutiny,* 1 (September, 1932), 172-173.

Vickery, Olga W. "The Making of a Myth: 'Sartoris,' " *Western Review,* 22 (Spring, 1958), 209-219.


*SOLDIERS' PAY*

Pritchett, V. S. "Books in General," *The New Statesman and Nation,* 41 (June 2, 1951), 624, 626.

Vickery, Olga W. "Faulkner's First Novel," *Western Humanities Review,* 11 (Summer, 1957), 251-256.


*THE SOUND AND THE FURY*

Adams, Robert M. "Poetry in the Novel: or, Faulkner Esemplastic," *Virginia Quarterly Review,* 29 (Summer, 1953), 419-434.

Backus, Joseph M. "Names of Characters in Faulkner's 'The Sound and the Fury,' " *Names,* 6 (December, 1958), 226-233.

Bowling, Lawrence E. "Faulkner and the Theme of Innocence," *Kenyon Review,* 20 (Summer, 1958), 466-487.

————. "Faulkner: Technique of 'The Sound and the Fury,' " *Kenyon Review,* 10 (Autumn, 1948), 552-566. Reprinted in *William Faulkner: Two Decades of Criticism,* Frederick J. Hoffman and Olga W. Vickery (eds). East Lansing: Michigan State University Press, 1951. Pages 165-179.

Brooks, Cleanth. "Primitivism in 'The Sound and the Fury,' " *English Institute Essays* 1952, Alan S. Downer, ed. New York: Columbia University Press, 1954. Pages 5-28.

Campbell, Harry M. "Experiment and Achievement: 'As I Lay Dying' and 'The Sound and the Fury,' " *The Sewanee Review,* 51 (Spring, 1943), 305-320.

Collins, Carvel. "A Conscious Literary Use of Freud?" *Literature and Psychology,* 3 (June, 1953), 2-3.

————. "Faulkner's 'The Sound and the Fury,' " *Explicator,* 17 (December, 1958), item 19.

————. "The Interior Monologues of 'The Sound and the Fury,' " *English Institute Essays 1952,* Alan S. Downer (ed). New York: Columbia University Press, 1954. Pages 29-56. Reprinted as Massachusetts Institute of Technology Publications in the Humanities, No. 6 (1954).

————. "The Pairing of 'The Sound and the Fury' and 'As I Lay Dying,' " *The Princeton University Library Chronicle,* 18 (Spring, 1957), 114-123.

Duesberg, Jacques. " 'Le bruit et le tumulte' de William Faulkner," *Revue Générale,* 72 (December 15, 1939) 834-841

Edel, Leon. *The Psychological Novel,* 1900-1950. New York: Lippincott, 1955. Pages 147-154.

England, Martha Winburn. "Teaching 'The Sound and the Fury,' " *College English,* 18 (January, 1957), 221-224.

Gwynn, Frederick L. "Faulkner's Raskolnikov," *Modern Fiction Studies,* 4 (Summer, 1958), 169-172.

Howell, Elmo. "A Note on Faulkner's Negro Characters," *The Mississippi Quarterly,* 11 (Fall, 1958), 201-203.

Humphrey, Robert. "Form and Function of Stream of Consciousness in William Faulkner's 'The Sound and the Fury,' " *University of Kansas City Review,* 19 (Autumn, 1952), 34-40.

Labor, Earle. "Faulkner's 'The Sound and the Fury,' " *Explicator,* 17 (January, 1959), item 29.

Lee, Edwy B. "A Note on the Ordonnance of 'The Sound and the Fury,' " *Faulkner Studies,* 3 (Summer-Autumn, 1954), 37-39.

Lowrey, Perrin. "Concepts of Time in 'The Sound and the Fury,' " *English Institute Essays 1952,* Alan /S. Downer (ed). New York: Columbia University Press, 1954. Pages 57-82.

Mueller, W. R. "The Theme of Suffering: William Faulkner's 'The Sound and the Fury,' " *The Prophetic Voice in Modern Fiction.* New York: Association Press, 1959. Pages 110-135.

O'Connor, William Van. " 'The Sound and the Fury' and the Impressionistic Novel," *Northern Review,* 6 (June-July, 1953), 17-22.

Powell, Sumner C. "William Faulkner Celebrates Easter, 1928," *Perspective,* 2 (Summer, 1949), 195-218.

Ryan, Marjorie. "The Shakespearian Symbolism in 'The Sound and the Fury,' " *Faulkner Studies,* 2 (Autumn, 1953), 40-44.

Sartre, Jean-Paul. "A Propos de 'Le Bruit et la Fureur': La Temporalité chez Faulkner," *La Nouvelle Revue Française,* 52 (June, 1939), 1057-1061; continued, 53 (July, 1939), 147-151. Translated by Martine Darmon and reprinted in *William Faulkner: Two Decades of Criticism,* Frederick J. Hoffman and Olga W. Vickery (eds). East Lansing: Michigan State University Press. Pages 180-188. WF III.

Scott, Evelyn. *On William Faulkner's "The Sound and the Fury."* New York: Jonathan Cape and Harrison Smith, 1929.

Stewart, George R., and Joseph M. Backus. "Each in Its Ordered Place: Structure and Narrative in 'Benjy's Section' of 'The Sound and the Fury,' " *American Literature,* 29 (January, 1958), 440-456.

Swiggart, Peter. "Moral and Temporal Order in 'The Sound and the Fury,' " *The Sewanee Review,* 61 (Spring, 1953), 221-237.

Thompson, Lawrance. "Mirror Analogues in 'The Sound and the Fury,' "
  *English Institute Essays 1952,* Alan S. Downer (ed). New York: Co-
  lumbia University Press, 1954. Pages 83-106. WF III
Tilley, Winthrop. "The Idiot Boy in Mississippi: Faulkner's 'The Sound
  and the Fury,' " *American Journal of Mental Deficiency,* 59 (Jan-
  uary, 1955), 374-377.
Vickery, Olga W. " 'The Sound and the Fury': A Study in Perspective,"
  *PMLA,* 69 (December, 1954), 1017-1037.
Whicher, Stephen E. "The Compsons' Nancies—A Note on 'The Sound
  and the Fury' and 'That Evening Sun,' " *American Literature,* 26
  (May 1954), 253-255.
Wilder, Amos N. "Faulkner and Vestigial Moralities," *Theology and Modern Literature.* Cambridge: Harvard University Press, 1958. Pages
  113-131.


## THE TOWN

Kazin, Alfred. "Mr. Faulkner's Friends, The Snopeses," *New York Times
  Book Review* (May 5, 1957), 1, 24.
Lombardo, Agostino. " 'The Town' di William Faulkner," *Criterio,* 2 (Feb-
  ruary-March, 1958), 132-139.
Longley, John L. "Galahad Gavin and a Garland of Snopeses," *Virginia
  Quarterly Review,* 33 (Autumn, 1957), 623-628.
Lytle, Andrew. " 'The Town': Helen's Last Stand," *The Sewanee Review,*
  65 (Summer, 1957), 475-484.
Marcus, Steven. "Faulkner's Town: Mythology as History," *Partisan Re-
  view,* 24 (Summer, 1957), 432-441. WF III.
Meriwether, James B. "Snopes Revisited," *Saturday Review,* 40 (April 27,
  1957), 12-13.
Rugoff, Milton. "Faulkner's Old Spell in a New Novel of Yoknapatawpha,"
  *New York Herald Tribune* (Books) (May 5, 1957), 1.
Rubin, Louis D. Jr. "Snopeslore: Or, Faulkner Clears the Deck," *Western
  Review,* 22 (Autumn, 1957), 73-76.
Scott, Nathan A. Jr. "The Vision of William Faulkner," *The Christian Cen-
  tury,* 74 (September 18, 1957), 1104-1106.


## THE UNVANQUISHED

Birney, Earle. "The Two William Faulkners," *The Canadian Forum,* 18
  (June, 1938), 84-85.
Boyle, Kay. "Tattered Banners," *The New Republic,* 94 (March 9, 1938),
  136-137.

De Voto, Bernard. "Faulkner's South," *Saturday Review of Literature,* 17 (February 19, 1938), 5.

Kazin, Alfred. "In the Shadow of the South's Last Stand," *New York Herald Tribune* (Books) (February 20, 1938), 5.

Knoll, Robert E. " 'The Unvanquished' for a Start," *College English,* 19 (May, 1958), 338-343.

Kronenberger, Louis. "Faulkner's Dismal Swamp," *The Nation,* 146 (February 19, 1938), 212, 214.

Neville, Helen. "The Sound and the Fury," *Partisan Review,* 5 (June, 1938), 53-55.


## THE WILD PALMS

Coindreau, Maurice E. "Préface aux 'Palmiers Sauvages,' " *Les Temps Modernes,* 7, (January, 1952), 1187-1196.

Cowley, Malcolm. "Sanctuary," *The New Republic,* 97 (January 25, 1939), 349.

Fadiman, Clifton. "Mississippi Frankenstein," *The New Yorker,* 14 (January 21, 1939), 60-62.

Galharn, Carl. "Faulkner's Faith: Roots from 'The Wild Palms,' " *Twentieth Century Literature,* 1 (October, 1955), 139-160.

Howe, Irving. "William Faulkner and the Quest for Freedom," *Tomorrow,* 9 (December, 1949), 54-56.

Kazin, Alfred. "A Study in Conscience," *New York Herald Tribune* (Books) (January 22, 1939), 2.

Marceau, Félicien. "Étrange Amérique," *La Table Ronde,* No. 54 (June, 1952), 152-156.

Maxwell, Allen. " 'The Wild Palms,' " *Southwest Review,* 24 (April, 1939), 357-360.

Mohrt, Michel. "Les Prisonniers du temps," *La Table Ronde,* No. 59 (November, 1952), 160-165.

Moses, W. R. "The Unity of 'The Wild Palms,' " *Modern Fiction Studies,* 2 (Autumn, 1956), 125-131.

————. "Water, Water Everywhere: 'Old Man' and 'A Farewell to Arms,' " *Modern Fiction Studies,* 5 (Summer, 1959), 172-174.

Redman, Ben Ray. "Faulkner's Double Novel," *Saturday Review of Literature,* 19, (January 21, 1939), 5.

Reed, John Q. "Theme and Symbol in Faulkner's 'Old Man,' " *The Educational Leader,* 21 (January, 1958), 25-31.

Richardson, H. Edward. "The 'Hemingwaves' in Faulkner's 'Wild Palms,' " *Modern Fiction Studies,* 4 (Winter, 1958-1959), 357-360.

Stonesifer, Richard J. "Faulkner's 'Old Man' in the Classroom," *College English,* 17 (February, 1956), 254-257.


## BARN BURNING

Howell, Elmo. "Colonel Sartoris Snopes and Faulkner's Aristocrats," *The Carolina Quarterly,* 11 (Summer, 1959), 13-19.


## THE BEAR: See also *Go Down, Moses*

Blum, Irving D. "The Parallel Philosophy of Emerson's 'Nature' and Faulkner's 'The Bear.'" *Emerson Society Quarterly,* No. 13 (4th Quarter, 1958), 22-25.

Butor, Michel. "Les Relations de parenté dans 'l'Ours' de William Faulkner," *Les Lettres Nouvelles,* 4 (May, 1956), 734-745.

Chapman, Arnold. "Pampas and Big Woods: Heroic Initiation in Güiraldes and Faulkner," *Comparative Literature,* 11 (Winter, 1959), 61-77.

Collins, Carvel. "Are These Mandalas?" *Literature and Psychology,* 3 (November, 1953), 3-6.

————. "A Note on the Conclusion of 'The Bear,'" *Faulkner Studies,* 2 (Winter, 1954), 58-60.

Foster, Ruel E. "A Further Note on the Conclusion of 'The Bear.'" *Faulkner Studies,* 3 (Spring, 1954), 4-5.

Hettich, Blaise, "A Bedroom Scene in Faulkner," *Renascence,* 8 (Spring, 1956), 121-126.

LaBudde, Kenneth. "Cultural Primitivism in William Faulkner's 'The Bear,'" *American Quarterly,* 2 (Winter, 1950), 322-328.

Lewis, R. W. B. "The Hero in the New World: William Faulkner's 'The Bear,'" *Kenyon Review,* 13 (Autumn, 1951), 641-660. Reprinted in *Interpretations of American Literature,* Charles Feidelson Jr. and Paul Brodtkorb Jr. (eds). New York: Oxford, 1959. Pages 332-348.

————. "William Faulkner: The Hero in the New World," *The Picaresque Saint.* New York: Lippincott, 1959. Pages 179-219.

Lydenberg, John. "Nature Myth in Faulkner's 'The Bear,'" *American Literature,* 24 (March, 1952), 62-72.

Moses, W. R. "Where History Crosses Myth: Another Reading of 'The Bear,'" *Accent,* 13 (Winter, 1953), 21-33.

O'Connor, William Van. "The Wilderness Theme in Faulkner's 'The Bear,'" *Accent,* 13 (Winter, 1953), 12-20. WF III

Stanzel, Franz von. "Die Zeitgestaltung in William Faulkner's 'The Bear,'" *Die Neueren Sprachen,* Heft 3 (1953), 114-121.

*DRY SEPTEMBER*

Bache, William B. "Moral Awareness in 'Dry September,'" *Faulkner Studies,* 3 (Winter, 1954), 53-57.


*THE HOUND*

Jones, Leonidas M. "Faulkner's 'The Hound,'" *Explicator,* 15 (March, 1957), item 37.


*OLD MAN*: See *The Wild Palms*


*A ROSE FOR EMILY*

Brooks, Cleanth, and Robert Penn Warren. *Understanding Fiction.* New York: F. S. Crofts, 1943. Pages 409-414.

Going, William T. "Faulkner's 'A Rose for Emily,'" *Explicator,* 16 (February, 1958), item 27.

Johnson, C. W. M. "Faulkner's 'A Rose for Emily,'" *Explicator,* 6 (May, 1948), item 45.

Stewart, James T. "Miss Havisham and Miss Grierson," *Furman Studies,* 6 (Fall, 1958), 21-23.

Watkins, Floyd C. "The Structure of 'A Rose for Emily,'" *Modern Language Notes,* 69 (November, 1954), 508-510.

West, Ray B. Jr. "Faulkner's 'A Rose for Emily,'" *Explicator,* 7 (October, 1948), item 8.

———. "Atmosphere and Theme in Faulkner's 'A Rose for Emily,'" *Perspective,* 2 (Summer, 1949), 239-245. Reprinted in *William Faulkner: Two Decades of Criticism,* Frederick J. Hoffman and Olga W. Vickery (eds). East Lansing: Michigan State University Press, 1951. Pages 259-267.

West, Ray B. Jr., and R. W. Stallman. "Theme through Atmosphere," *The Art of Modern Fiction.* New York: Rinehart, 1949. Pages 270-275.


*SPOTTED HORSES*: See also *The Hamlet*

Gordon, Caroline. "Notes on Faulkner and Flaubert," *The Hudson Review,* 1 (Summer, 1948), 222-231. Revised and reprinted in *The House of Fiction,* Caroline Gordon and Allen Tate (eds). New York: Scribner's, 1950. Pages 531-534.

## THAT EVENING SUN

Frey, Leonard H. "Irony and Point of View in 'That Evening Sun,' " *Faulkner Studies,* 2 (Autumn, 1953), 33-40.

Harrington, Evans B. "Technical Aspects of William Faulkner's 'That Evening Sun,' " *Faulkner Studies,* 1 (Winter, 1952), 54-59.

Pearson, Norman Holmes. "Faulkner's Three 'Evening Suns,' " *Yale University Library Gazette,* 29 (October, 1954), 61-70.

Whicher, Stephen E. "The Compsons' Nancies—A Note on 'The Sound and the Fury' and 'That Evening Sun,' " *American Literature,* 26 (May, 1954), 253-255.